Simon Wilde has been cricket correspondent of the *Sunday Times* since 1998, reporting on more than 300 Test matches. He is the author of thirteen books, three of which have been shortlisted for the William Hill Sports Book of the Year award. His biographies of Ian Botham and Kevin Pietersen, and David Gower's autobiography *An Endangered Species*, on which he collaborated, were also published by Simon & Schuster, as was his history of the England cricket team, *England: The Biography*. He has reported on England Test matches from 58 different grounds around the world and been on almost 50 international tours. Follow him on @swildecricket.

Praise for *The Tour*

'A fine and comprehensive history ... plenty of fun tales' *The Times*

'No sport has tours like cricket tours ... which is why Simon Wilde's comprehensive history of the English cricket team abroad is so packed with interest ... Riveting' *Daily Mail*

'This entertaining account is as much social history as sports reporting, as he engagingly dissects the various political, economic, social and practical aspects of sending England teams around the world, as well as delving into how England teams can be successful overseas' *Country Life*

Also by Simon Wilde

England – The Biography: The Story of English Cricket 1877–2018

Ian Botham: The Power and the Glory

On Pietersen

The Tour

THE STORY OF THE ENGLAND CRICKET TEAM OVERSEAS

Simon Wilde

**SIMON &
SCHUSTER**

London · New York · Sydney · Toronto · New Delhi

First published in Great Britain by Simon & Schuster UK Ltd, 2023

This edition published in Great Britain by Simon & Schuster UK Ltd, 2024

1 3 5 7 9 10 8 6 4 2

Simon & Schuster UK Ltd
1st Floor
222 Gray's Inn Road
London WC1X 8HB

Simon & Schuster: Celebrating 100 Years of Publishing in 2024

www.simonandschuster.co.uk
www.simonandschuster.com.au
www.simonandschuster.co.in

Simon & Schuster Australia, Sydney
Simon & Schuster India, New Delhi

Images © Getty Images

A CIP catalogue record for this book
is available from the British Library.

Paperback ISBN: 978-1-4711-9850-2
eBook ISBN: 978-1-4711-9849-6

Typeset in Bembo by M Rules
Printed and Bound in the UK using 100%
Renewable Electricity at CPI Group (UK) Ltd

To Gayle, Freddie, Lily and Eve,
who know about the ups and downs of touring

CONTENTS

NOTE ON THE TEXT

Several cities and countries mentioned in the text have changed names during the past century and a half. As a general rule, I have used the name that applied at the time in question, or the one by which the place was, or is, more customarily known. Among those cities to which this relates are Bombay (now Mumbai), Calcutta (Kolkata), Bangalore (Bengaluru), Madras (Chennai), Poona (Pune), all in India; Dacca (Dhaka) and Chattogram (Chittagong) in Bangladesh, itself previously East Pakistan; and Port Elizabeth (now Gqeberha) in South Africa. The countries include British Guiana (now Guyana), British Honduras (Belize), Ceylon (Sri Lanka) and Rhodesia (Zimbabwe).

PREFACE

England's Test tour of Pakistan in late 2022 was a stunning success. Through skill and audacity, a team playing under a devil-may-care captain in Ben Stokes – leading the side for the first time overseas – won all three matches in a country where previously English teams had been victorious only twice in 24 Tests. They became the first visitors to achieve a whitewash in Pakistan.

What made the result all the more impressive was the number of challenges they overcame. Tours routinely pose problems to the travelling side, but this one encapsulated many of the difficulties which make touring so demanding – tactically, technically and mentally. Of all destinations, Pakistan has been the most troublesome for English sides through on-field disputes, bouts of food poisoning, clashes of culture and security concerns, and this was the first time England had played Tests there since 2005, so there was little for the players to fall back on in terms of relevant experience, except for a few T20 matches.

In the weeks before, Pakistan was engulfed in a political crisis when an attempt was made on the life of the former cricket captain and recently deposed prime minister Imran Khan during a rally in Wazirabad, as a consequence of which there was a chance the tour might not take place at all, or that the first Test would be moved from Rawalpindi due to its proximity to the capital Islamabad. In the end the schedule remained unchanged. The England players were subjected to presidential levels of protection, largely locked down in hotels when not at the cricket and at all times shadowed by armed guards.

Despite taking all precautions, including employing a full-time chef, around half the playing group succumbed to a viral infection in the 48 hours before the opening Test; only on the morning of the game was it confirmed that England could muster an XI. With Ben Foakes too unwell to take part, Ollie Pope was deployed as a makeshift wicketkeeper and the uncapped Will Jacks drafted into the side around half an hour before the start. Even so, England kept faith with their plan to attack and struck a record 506 runs on the first day.

Touring teams often fail to adapt to alien conditions, but in this instance England showed versatility in selection and strategy in an environment where weather and pitches tend to deaden traditional English bowling strengths. Nearly 50 per cent of all previous Test matches had been drawn. With most Tests in Pakistan taking place in winter because the summer months are too hot, daylight hours can be short; in Rawalpindi the sun set at around 5 p.m. To compensate, Stokes demanded an extraordinarily aggressive approach to batting – plus a daring attitude to setting targets – as a means of creating time for the bowling attack to take 20 wickets; the bowlers, in turn, excelled in ways historically foreign to them. In a reversal of the norm, England's seamers made better use of reverse swing than their Pakistani counterparts to help seal a win in Rawalpindi with barely ten minutes of viable daylight left. Mark Wood's raw pace won the match in Multan, while the wrist spin of Rehan Ahmed, making his debut as England's youngest Test cricketer, proved the difference in Karachi.

Afterwards, head coach Brendon McCullum said that, considering everything that was thrown at his players, the performance was 'pretty close to perfect'.

This is something that could not often be said of England touring teams of the past 150 years. The story of the England cricket team overseas is generally one of struggle, setbacks and spats, punctuated by the occasional glorious highs of the sort seen in Pakistan – all the more precious for their rarity. But results are only part of a rich and vivid history: cricketers lucky enough to go on major international tours are guaranteed some of the greatest adventures of their lives.

CHAPTER 1

The Fragile Machine
Why touring is so tough

A major international cricket tour is a phenomenon with few parallels in team sport. England's national football and rugby sides do not spend long on the road together: they nowadays travel only for a matter of days to fulfil a foreign fixture, or for a few weeks for rare tournaments such as the Euros or World Cups, or a Lions tour – typically staged every few years. Domestic teams tend to operate to a pattern of home and away fixtures which might involve sending them on the road for a few nights. Cycling teams spend three or four weeks at the Tour de France or Giro d'Italia. Yachtsmen spend three months navigating the globe in races held every few years. Perhaps the closest comparison is North American baseball leagues, which involve more than 150 matches a year across states, but at least players are moving around familiar territories; the cultural dislocation is nothing like as great. As the most northerly based major Test cricketing nation, England are in a position to tour more frequently than others in their sport, and every winter are in action in faraway places for typically five to six months. And these missions are distinct from the matches they might play at home between May and September – when other teams visit them.

Modern tours are shorter, more streamlined beasts than the early pioneering expeditions conceived amid the grandeur and ambition of the Victorian era – what is now accepted as England's first Test tour to Australia in 1876–77 spanned more than eight months, three of which were spent at sea – but even today when England tour Australia or the subcontinent these are still vast undertakings for which planning begins months in advance. Moreover, air travel may have drastically speeded up the process, and allowed players to come and go more easily, but that has simply created scope for more frequent trips. In addition to an established roster of Test series, there are also one-day internationals and Twenty20s (T20s) to be played, as well as an increasing number of ICC global tournaments.

In the winter of 2006–07, England sent teams to play a Champions Trophy in India and a World Cup in the West Indies, between which they fulfilled a full Ashes tour of Australia. With only 20 days at home between assignments, they were on the road for 179 days, the longest England have been on duty in any one winter since the days of boat travel. Andrew Flintoff, Kevin Pietersen and Andrew Strauss were among seven players who took part in everything. In six winters since then, England teams have topped 150 days and in 2021–22 the programme was arguably even more arduous, with time in the Gulf States, Australia and the Caribbean totalling 162 days away out of 178, admittedly with a substantially changing cast list (in part because results were so poor that some players and coaches were sacked after the Ashes), but with the added complication of Covid-19 protocols needing to be observed and quarantine to be undertaken.

For 2022–23, England were scheduled for the first time to fulfil five separate assignments – three white-ball tours (one of which spanned Pakistan and Australia) and two red-ball ones; it was something only possible because they were by now operating quite distinct groups of players specialising in one format or another, under separate head coaches.* Anyone involved in all three white-ball tours faced about 110 days on the road, substantially more than the Test-only players, for whom this represented a relatively light winter at around 70 days away from home. Some players, of course, would be involved in elements of both. Winters are no longer made up of one grand tour of a single region, but mental resilience and physical stamina remain fundamental aspects of touring.

The tour of Pakistan and Australia was, at 72 days, by a distance the longest tour England had undertaken involving just limited-overs matches. A typical 'white-ball only' trip would usually span anything up to five weeks, often much less. This one was twice as long and, interestingly, paid rich dividends as a result, as it allowed the players under a relatively new short-form captain, Jos Buttler, to gel in advance of the main event, a T20 World Cup. On the night England won the trophy by beating Pakistan in Melbourne in front of 80,000 spectators, Buttler spoke about the value of the time spent beforehand playing seven T20s in Pakistan – the opportunity it presented to get to know each other, to build relationships and trust, and to formulate tactics. Modern touring teams are often 'time poor', but this one arrived in Australia well drilled, full of confidence and primed to win.

Globally, bilateral international cricket is facing an existential threat from the domestic T20 leagues that have sprung up in all the major cricketing territories, with the one-day international format the one most affected, but if any country is likely to continue regularly exchanging tours it is England, whose home season clashes least with these other competitions.† For reasons

---

* Before 2022–23, there had been only one winter in which England teams fulfilled as many as four separate tours: in 2009–10 they competed in a Champions Trophy in South Africa and a World T20 in West Indies, as well as making bilateral tours of South Africa and Bangladesh.

† The number of T20s played by England in a calendar year overtook ODIs for the first time in 2020, and remained ahead in 2021 and 2022.

of history and culture as much as cricket and finance, a tour by England remains a powerful draw everywhere.

One of the other main differences between old-style touring and the game today is that in the past tours took the cricketers to the towns and the countryside, and provided them with the opportunity to expand personal horizons; it was an experience in the broadest sense of the word. A modern tour largely takes them only to the stadiums of the big cities and their satellite hotels, and seems to present an ever narrower view of the world.

When Andy Flower took over as head coach in 2009 and the team crashed to an embarrassing Test defeat in Jamaica in his first match in charge, he subsequently laid out an ambitious plan for them to become the first England team to reach no. 1 in the world rankings, presenting the players with a daunting outline of the series they would need to win to get there. 'It's going to take two years and six times around the world,' he said. Remarkably they hit their targets, though at a price. After another two years, they had been around the world as many times again, and in a highly dysfunctional state sank to a 5–0 whitewash in Australia. Two leading players, Jonathan Trott and Graeme Swann, quit the tour before it was over, Trott through what might best be termed burn-out and Swann because his bowling arm was ruined through over-work. Afterwards another player, Kevin Pietersen, was sacked and Flower himself never worked with the team again. Everyone had been living in each other's company too long.

Time on the road is one thing. Another is that there are fundamental differences in the way the game is played from place to place, providing an array of challenges that only the best can master. This variety is what gives cricket much of its interest and charm, but for visiting players the adjustments required are considerable. Home sides inherently understand their own conditions better and every touring team has to find ways to narrow the knowledge gap as best they can.

In England, pitches tend to be grassier and the ball moves more through the air and off the pitch. Go abroad and you typically encounter fast, bouncy surfaces in Australia, the West Indies and on South Africa's Highveld, where the carry of the ball is accentuated by 1,500 metres of altitude; on the subcontinent, they are drier and sometimes break up so much that when the ball lands it produces explosions of dust – spin bowling then becomes king. Within the space of a few weeks an England batsman might go from fending balls off his face in one country to dealing with others elsewhere that barely threaten to reach his thigh. These are almost different sports, and neither is necessarily familiar to cricketers who learned the game in England. The ferocity of the sunlight alone can take time to get used to. Back in the interwar years, Herbert Sutcliffe, one of England's greatest and most versatile batsmen, reckoned it took him six weeks in Australia to get used to the light and the speed of the pitches, which he considered four yards faster than the uncovered ones he played on at home. In northern India and Pakistan, though, the sun can set early and the light be milky at best.

In Adelaide, the wind off the interior can generate temperatures of 45 degrees, leaving players reporting burnt eyeballs and bowlers vomiting on the boundary edge. James Southerton, a member of the very first England team to play Tests abroad, described this wind as 'almost hot enough to set your clothes on fire'. Adelaide's flies are a constant infuriation to visitors. In Brisbane, bowlers can experience scalding sensations in the chest after sending down only a few overs. Bob Wyatt, the England vice-captain, described conditions there during the famous Bodyline series of 1932–33 as almost unbearable. 'It was a terrible day for a fast bowler; the humidity was so great that the air actually felt soggy, but [Harold] Larwood and [Gubby] Allen accepted the challenge. I can't imagine that there has ever been better bowling on any cricket field than there was from these two that morning.'

That England won the match, and with it the Ashes, was also due to the heroism of Eddie Paynter who, suffering from acute tonsillitis, rose from his hospital sickbed to fight off aching muscles and blurred vision to play an innings of 83. The heat in Melbourne can be scarcely less taxing, as Douglas Jardine noted in writing about the same tour: 'Anyone who has fielded out for a day in Melbourne, with "a northerly" blowing, will readily subscribe to the belief that this most unpleasant wind does in fact hail from thousands of miles of desert . . . it is like the blast from a furnace door which is opened in one's face.' Towards the end of an exhausting day in the field, Jardine delegated all-rounder Wally Hammond or Hedley Verity, his left-arm spinner, to bear much of the burden in the final hour in order to spare his pace men further hardship – and this was in an era when a day of Test cricket in Australia spanned five hours rather than the six or more it does now. In more recent times, any young fast bowler who is not fit enough for such a harsh environment can expect short shrift from their elders, who will tell them: 'Don't expect me to bowl your overs at five o'clock.'

Joe Root on his first tour of Australia as captain ended the series with gastroenteritis and dehydration after experiencing sunstroke in temperatures of 44 degrees in Sydney; when the last ball was bowled he was so debilitated that he was asleep on the physio's bed in the dressing room. Ranjitsinhji, the Indian batting genius who made his career in England, once scored 175 in a Test in Sydney while suffering from a similar condition to Paynter. Len Hutton, like Jardine one of the few England Test captains to win there, once said of Australia: 'The grounds are hard, the ball is hard, the men are hard.' Such conditions have finished off the careers of many who are ageing or just past their best.

It was noticeable that when Jos Buttler's side won the T20 World Cup, the team's coaching staff had a strong Australian contingent: head coach Matthew Mott, batting consultant Mike Hussey and fast bowling coach David Saker were all Australians and understood local conditions intimately. It also helped that some of the most influential players in the squad, such as Alex Hales and Adil Rashid, had experience of Australia's domestic T20 competition, the Big Bash (although Sam Curran, named player of the tournament, was new to the country). This was one occasion when an England team were not blindsided by Australian pitches and grounds, which may explain why they won five of their six matches, losing only a rain-affected game to Ireland.

The West Indies is not much easier. England have won there only once since 1967–68. Probably one of the greatest innings ever played for England in an overseas Test was Len Hutton's nine-hour double-century in searing heat in Jamaica in the 1950s. In Sri Lanka and southern India, the humidity is such that frequent changes of shirts, gloves and pads are basic requirements; it is not unusual for batsmen playing long innings in Colombo or Chennai to get through 12 sets of gloves. An innings fit to be mentioned alongside Hutton's was Tony Greig's century in Calcutta while running a high temperature; it did much to set up an historic series win. Since that tour in 1976–77, England have won only two multi-match series in India. During a group match in Peshawar, Pakistan at the 1996 World Cup, Warwickshire all-rounder Neil Smith was violently sick while opening the batting, having already spent several hours in the field. The heat was simply too much. England cricket manager Keith Fletcher, who in his day had been a highly accomplished batsman in subcontinental conditions, once said of Sri Lanka, 'It's very nearly too hot here for Europeans to play cricket.' Sand blowing off the Sind desert once created such a storm that it brought an early end to an England Test match in Karachi. Dust storms have also cut short games in South Africa's interior.

Many overseas venues are situated by the sea, bringing water tables and breezes into play. Bowl at the WACA in Perth, where the heat and light can be fierce, and every afternoon the 'Fremantle Doctor' blows down the ground. Bowl in Port Elizabeth, and if the wind is coming off the ocean it is known as a 'bowling wind' and if it comes off the land, carrying with it waves of heat, it is a 'batting wind'. Many a bowler's spirit has been broken by gales off the Cook Strait buffeting the Basin Reserve in Wellington. Some of the strongest crosswinds anywhere are those at the Sir

Vivian Richards Stadium in Antigua and Kensington Oval, Barbados. You need to have experienced these conditions to develop the skills to harness them.

Most venues in Australia and India, too, are larger than those in England. Bigger playing areas make a hot day in the field even more taxing, and while some crowds are adulatory many are unwelcoming. The Melbourne Cricket Ground is an unforgiving amphitheatre, and when England are touring 80,000 will turn up on Boxing Day for the ritual bashing of the Poms. The sense of the stadium as a colosseum is heightened in the minds of visiting players by the dressing-rooms being situated beneath ground, from where it is a 50-metre walk to the playing area. You feel the heat and hear the noise long before you reach the field of play. At the 'Bull Ring' in Johannesburg, the players walk through a covered tunnel to protect them from projectiles thrown from a crowd with a history of hostility towards touring teams; not even the tunnel, though, can shield them from verbal abuse. The most vociferous and hostile Australians tend to drift away early or don't turn up at all if their side is losing; they do not care for cricket so much as their team winning. They are not often disappointed.

As hard as it is for England to win on the subcontinent or in the Caribbean, Australia remains a challenge apart, not least because of the prestige attached to going there and returning victorious. John Woodcock, cricket correspondent of *The Times* for more than 30 years, once wrote that 'the protracted physical and mental effort of taking part in a Test match against Australia before large crowds and generally in great heat has no parallel in the world of sport.'

In England, players have their home comforts. They know the hotels they stay in. They know the drive to the ground. They see familiar faces everywhere. The crowds are behind them. There is also more scope to play first-class county cricket by way of preparation, admittedly usually in the build-up to the first Test match of the summer rather than once the Tests are underway. It is a fact of life that the modern player has to hone his technique more in the nets than in domestic matches, but however he prepares there are generally more opportunities at home. Tours starve reserve players in particular of game time.

In respect of winning, touring has always been tough, but it has got tougher. Until the late 1970s, England's overseas record was creditable – they won slightly more matches than they lost – but once the game started to become more broadly professional their win/loss record deteriorated, and between 1 May 1979 and 1 September 2023 stood at minus 43.* In earlier times, England might have expected to win, or at least hold their own, on most tours outside Australia even if they could not send their strongest side, but there were simply no international tours of that nature any longer.

Busier schedules meant less scope for proper acclimatisation and less chance to recover from a bad start. In fact, in July 2018 the International Cricket Council agreed to changes in the conduct of tours designed to reduce the impact of 'home advantage' and develop a culture of greater respect. 'Touring teams should be treated as guests, with a standard of accommodation, travel and catering equal to that for the home team, and the opportunity to mix socially. They should be able to prepare for international matches under conditions similar to those expected during the series, including the same standard and variety of net bowlers and training pitches.' But cricketers have never been under any illusions about the value of local knowledge and the comfort that familiar surroundings grant one side over another. When Len Hutton gave his first press conference on arriving in Australia as captain, he concluded

---

* Before 1 May 1979, England's record away from home was: played 282, won 99, lost 89, drawn 94. Between 1 May 1979 and 1 September 2023, they played 238, won 59, lost 102, drew 77. During this second period, Australia and South Africa were narrowly in credit in terms of wins and losses away from home, but every other major Test team was in deficit by at least 18 – counting the United Arab Emirates, which Pakistan used as a temporary home for 35 Tests between 2002 and 2018, not towards Pakistan's record, but as an away venue for their opponents.

with the words: 'I think the chances are even, but of course Australia will be playing at home in conditions to which they are used, and there's a great deal in that, you know.'

The growth of T20 leagues has played its part in touring becoming technically more challenging. Admittedly, it has made the big stadiums in India and Australia more familiar to the top players, but it has also done more than anything to unpick some of the traditional skills needed to be a successful Test cricketer, such as a solid defensive technique and the ability to build a long innings. The sheer ubiquity of the format, too, has bred a tolerance of mixed results – the 'win-some, lose-some' mentality – and a culture lacking the intense scrutiny on individual performances that comes when national prestige is on the line. For many, touring with a national team has simply come to seem too much like hard work.

Of course, some England players prospered overseas. Alastair Cook scored hundreds against eight different opponents away from home, Ian Bell against seven, and Ken Barrington, Colin Cowdrey, Kevin Pietersen and Graham Thorpe six. Those few bowlers of genuine pace that England have produced have thrived on the harder, bouncier surfaces of Australia, South Africa and the West Indies: Harold Larwood, John Snow and Frank Tyson enjoyed many of their finest moments on tour, as has Mark Wood, who before the Ashes in 2023 averaged 24.6 with the ball overseas compared to 40.7 at home. But most England players have found adjusting their games from bowler-friendly conditions at home to flat pitches elsewhere simply too difficult. Overall, in home Tests, England's batsmen average 31.7 and their bowlers 28.6 (in credit by +3.1), while overseas the batsmen average 28.9 and the bowlers 31.8 (a deficit of 2.9). That would translate into a weighty difference across the course of a full Test match.*

---

* The difference is even more marked in overseas ODIs: batsmen average 27.3 and bowlers 33.2 (a deficit of 5.9). At home, the figures are respectively 32.1 and 31.7 (a credit of +0.4).

Efforts have been made to address these problems. In May 2018, Andrew Strauss, England's director of cricket and a former captain who led the team to their only Ashes win in Australia since 1986–87, commissioned an investigation into England's difficulties away from home. The research was led by Nathan Leamon, a former Cambridge mathematician and schoolteacher, who had been recruited in 2009 as England's first full-time analyst. One of the main conclusions was that efforts should be made to break the pattern of selecting the same XIs home and away; in other words, a team that might be well tailored to winning a Test in Manchester or Birmingham might be feebly equipped to do so in Mumbai or Barbados, and the temptation to take on tour players who had performed well at home should in some cases be resisted. In future, it was proposed, selection should be more bespoke and more of a squad system should operate than previously. In the last press conference Strauss gave before stepping down several months later owing to his wife's terminal illness, the focus of a lot of his comments was on how England might win more games of cricket away from home. Developing a world-class system for identifying the best players was one ambition.

An early example of this new thinking came when Dawid Malan, who had performed well in Australia and New Zealand the previous winter, was dropped three Tests into a home season. Ed Smith, the national selector, publicly stated that 'it may be that his [Malan's] game is better suited to overseas conditions.' But the highest profile cases were Stuart Broad and James Anderson, the greatest wicket-takers in England's history and two champions in home conditions, who would be left out of a number of overseas Tests before being dropped altogether for the tour of the West Indies in 2022. It was not so much that Broad and Anderson were poor players overseas, rather that away from home there was a greater need for variety, and to avoid seam attacks entirely made up of right-arm medium-fast bowlers – which was a central weakness of the 2017–18 tour (ironically, the sought-after variation was lost once Mark Wood broke down during the first Test in Antigua). The Malan decision caused debate but the treatment of Broad and Anderson developed into a major controversy, with both players publicly expressing their dismay. The situation was further complicated by the pandemic in 2020–21, forcing teams into bio-secure bubbles and leaving England no choice but to rotate large numbers of players for the sake of their mental health.

Who to select was only one element of the puzzle. Another was how best to nurture cricketers with the relevant skills to win in foreign climes. This required altogether more radical action. 'The big solution would be county cricket played on much flatter pitches, with more spin bowling and more fast bowling,' Smith told me in June 2020. 'Then you produce cricketers that naturally bowl 90mph and rip it. I don't see that coming soon.'

There were some successes. During the winters of 2018–19 and 2020–21, England's results overseas did improve. They won 3–0 in Sri Lanka deploying what for England was a radical bowling attack containing three spinners, 3–1 in South Africa and 2–0 in Sri Lanka again. When they then took the first Test of a series in India in Chennai, they had won six straight matches away from home, the best sequence in their history. Admittedly the last three games were largely determined by huge hundreds from one player, Joe Root.

India responded with a string of underprepared surfaces which brought their spinners more into the game and England were then soundly beaten three times, totalling no more than 205 in any of their six innings.* When England were then put away 4–0 in Australia in 2021–22 in a series lasting only 20 days, Root reprised the concerns already articulated by Strauss and Smith, bemoaning the lack of relevant experience provided

---

* England's two-day loss under lights in Ahmedabad, where they were dismissed for 112 and 81, was their swiftest loss in any overseas Test.

by the English domestic game. 'Look at some of the young batters – when have they had the opportunity to go out with 450
to 500 on the board and deal with scoreboard pressure? The
only time they're exposed to it is in this environment. When
have they had to go out to save a Test match against a turning
ball in spinning conditions? They've never been exposed to it.
Yet we're expected to go to the subcontinent and win games
against the best spinners in the world, to come here [Australia]
and deal with pace and bounce when we might face one guy
who bowls over 90mph a season.'

Putting together a coherent plan to address these problems
was made harder by the inevitable turnover in management personnel. Strauss stepping down as full-time director of cricket in
2018 was one thing, changes to the coaching structure in 2019
and 2022 were others. From spring 2021 there was also the temporary discontinuation of the role of national selector. However,
Strauss returned as director in an interim capacity in February
2022 and, in explaining the omissions of Broad and Anderson
from the West Indies tour, he reaffirmed that a bespoke selection
policy remained in place: 'When you are looking at selecting
teams you need to make a distinction between England teams
at home and away. They are different things.'*

For all that, touring has always had – and still retains – an aura
of romance and adventure for players and public alike. For those
at home following events via newspapers, TV or radio or social
media, an England win overseas can brighten a dark and cold
winter's night or morning – all the more for its rarity value. And
of course the camera shots of turquoise seas and blood-orange
sunsets only serve to give these expeditions an exotic dimension
regardless of the result.

Geoffrey Howard, tour manager on Len Hutton's tour of

---

* Anderson's absence was more contentious than Broad's: he made significant contributions to three of England's ten overseas wins between 2018 and 2021 (in Cape
Town, Galle and Chennai), whereas Broad took a total of only 13 wickets in the six
victories he was involved in.

Australia in 1954–55, was deeply conscious of the impact the
team's misfortunes in the first Test would have when news
reached home of wicketkeeper Godfrey Evans being too ill to
play, Denis Compton injuring himself in the field and being
unable to bat, and England being heavily outplayed. In a letter
to his family, he wrote: 'Why do these things have to happen
to touring cricket teams? You will all be so horribly fed up
and disappointed – I could weep for you all – all of England.'
Miles Kington, writing in *Punch* in the 1980s, defined spring
as the time when, 'somewhere very hot and very far away,
England will be batting to avoid an innings defeat in the
final Test'.

For those at home, how and when they learned the latest
news from these faraway places depended on the time difference and their willingness to stay up late, or rise early. Many in
the UK would not have gone to sleep the night England won
by 3 runs in Melbourne in the Boxing Day Test of 1982, or
the night they completed a huge win over Australia in Sydney
in 2011. Many fewer might have listened as New Zealand's
last man Danny Morrison hung on for almost three hours to
deny England in Auckland in 1997, a game that finished at
4 a.m. UK time. Waking early on 5 December 2006 would
have been particularly traumatic as news filtered through of
England's shock defeat at the hands of Shane Warne in a match
they dominated for much of the early stages. At least cricket in
the Caribbean takes place at a time of day in England when it
is acceptable to have a stiff drink at hand. This was probably
very necessary when Mike Atherton's team collapsed to 40
for eight in Trinidad in 1994 (at around 9.30 p.m. GMT), or
Strauss's side were routed for 51 in Jamaica in 2009 (at about
7.30 p.m. GMT).

A fundamental aspect of any major cricket tour is its suscep-
tibility to being destabilised. Sending away a relatively small
group of players – a typical tour party might be made up of 16

men – does not allow much margin for error, and because they go on so long, in profoundly disadvantageous conditions, tours are inherently fragile enterprises. Things are liable to occur that jeopardise the mission: a couple of injuries, a couple more players out of form, and quite quickly the situation becomes critical in a way it would not be were England at home, where more resources are readily at hand. Yes, additional players can be flown out, but they would be relatively unprepared and not acclimatised. Any newcomer must play catch-up. Noting how England's strength was eroded by injuries when they were beaten in Australia in 1936–37 despite taking a 2–0 lead, Neville Cardus calculated that to compensate for the likely physical deterioration, 'to win a rubber in Australia, an England team needs a technical superiority of say 30 per cent.'

Cricket tours can, of course, be highly successful, but one of the reasons why they more often spiral into failure, and sometimes chaos, is because of this inherent fragility. It is also why tours are often so dramatic, and take on a soap-opera quality. If there is a narrative thread to this story, this is it.

Not only cricketing issues complicate things. Real life also has a habit of intruding. A wife or child back home might become unwell or be struggling to cope; parents have died, leading to emergency dashes home (the player generally rejoining the tour later). For reasons such as these, and others besides, a touring cricketer himself is in an emotionally vulnerable state when away from home and deprived of the usual support of family and friends. He might suffer homesickness, drink more than usual or stay out later than is wise.

There have been countless scrapes – adventures and misadventures, some trivial, others serious. A captain has appeared in court in South Africa, and a wicketkeeper once jailed in New Zealand. One England cricketer of the 1920s, a former Test captain, ended up in a coroner's court in Melbourne during a Test match following a late-night car crash in which the driver was killed. Ken Barrington, the team's assistant manager and in his day one of England's bravest and most successful touring batsmen, died of a heart attack aged 50 on the second evening of a Test in Barbados in 1981. As a player, Barrington suffered acutely from nervous tension and was forced into retirement after suffering a heart attack while playing in a double-wicket tournament in Melbourne; he approached his managerial responsibilities with the same intensity. The Barbados Test resumed after a minute's silence, during which several England players were visibly distraught; Robin Jackman bowled the first ball of the day with tears in his eyes. England lost.

There have been times when the places England have visited have not been the most stable politically. Disorder at grounds is much less common than it once was, though still not unknown. In the days before some territories achieved political independence from Britain – and all England's opponents were colonies at one time or another – the relationship with the Mother Country was sometimes riven with tension, and it could take only a small incident in the ground for trouble to explode. Extraordinarily, England once played a Test match in British Guiana only two months after a British-orchestrated military coup; that there was a riot at the match should have surprised no one. There have been several instances of pitch invasions and missiles being thrown at English players at grounds around Australia; sometimes, serious trouble has only narrowly been avoided. On England's first day in India in 1984, Prime Minister Indira Gandhi was assassinated, throwing the country into tumult and forcing the team to decamp to Sri Lanka until things calmed down.

On that occasion, as so often, the tour went on. Precisely because it is so often held up as a symbol of good relations between the respective countries, an England tour is not lightly abandoned or cancelled. When the ECB pulled the plug on a short visit to Pakistan for two T20s in 2021, for what would have been their first games there since 2005 and as repayment for Pakistan touring England during the early months of the pandemic, it caused an outcry and swiftly led to the departure of Ian Watmore as board chairman.

A touring party is therefore a fragile piece of machinery, and every care needs to be taken to make sure it can withstand any stresses that come its way. One reason why England tours of Australia are so tough is because their hosts are well aware of this potential area of weakness, and the Australian team, the local press and the local population will take every opportunity to throw their guests off balance. 'Playing in Australia, everyone's just looking, [asking] where can we break this team apart?' said Matt Prior, who toured there twice with England in the 2010s.

Alex Bannister, *Daily Mail* cricket correspondent, writing in the 1950s, said that every England tour of Australia between 1924–25 and 1950–51 had seen claims of bad behaviour directed at England players: it went with the territory of touring there. In 2006–07, on the morning of the team's arrival, the local drugs-testers turned up at the England team's hotel in Sydney, banged on the doors of the players and woke them from their beds. The next day, there were photographers camped outside the restaurant where six of the players were having lunch. 'I'd been there four years previously, so I knew what Australia was like,' Steve Harmison recalled. 'I had first-hand experience – and it was telling me we've got three more months of this.' The allegation that Jonny Bairstow 'head-butted' an Australian player, Cameron Bancroft, in a Perth bar in the early days of a tour was a classic instance of a 'get-up' designed to destabilise a tour; the story, propagated by local media and the Australian team themselves, did not emerge until the first Test was underway more than three weeks later – at the point of maximum embarrassment for the England team.

Players chosen for a tour must not only have cricketing skills but also be good team men. They will be living together

in alien environments for weeks on end, under acute pressure to perform on the pitch. If they are to individually and
collectively achieve their goals, they must be conditioned to
help one another. 'Cricket is a unique sport in how much
time you spend together travelling the country and abroad,'
Ben Stokes, England's latest Test captain, said. 'You have
to be tight as a group on the field but also off it.' Brendon
McCullum, appointed England's Test coach to work alongside
Stokes, reinforced this idea by stripping back the size of the
support staff.

A touring team is most analogous to a small military unit.
Everyone is required to live a highly regimented lifestyle.
They wear uniforms on the pitch – whites for day-time Tests,
coloured clothing for white-ball games – as well as suits or
blazers (or 'number ones') when attending the official functions
that were once a regular feature of tours (although in recent
years they have largely disappeared). A tour runs by the diary
and the clock, with no leeway afforded latecomers, as Graeme
Swann found to his cost when he missed the bus to the ground
on his first England tour; he was not chosen again for eight
years. Another young player, finding himself one morning after
a night on the tiles in a part of rural Australia devoid of taxis
and telephones, had in his desperation not to miss the coach to
resort to bicycling frantically after it, much to the hilarity of
teammates looking out of the back window.

Ahead of travel days, bags must be packed at an appointed
time. Transport leaves for matches, training sessions and airports
at specified times. Pecking orders are drawn up for who gets
first use of nets. No wonder many of the early tour managers – and sometimes captains and vice-captains – were former
military officers, chosen for their familiarity with organisation
and discipline.

Geoffrey Howard managed England Test tours of India and
Australia in the 1950s having served in the war, and considered
a six-month cricket tour as very like six months of soldiering.

'You have these short periods of action and, just like in war, people have to deal with all the time in between. Some go and have a few beers, others fall to philosophising.' Old touring cricketers will be among the most punctual people you will meet.

There is a rigid command structure. Today, power resides in the head coach rather than a manager, and beneath him the captain, although in reality their spheres of influence are slightly different: a head coach will be responsible for things off the field, the captain for those that take place on the pitch. But in matters of broad policy such as discipline, a director of England cricket, who might not necessarily be on the tour at all times, would be the final arbiter. Underneath the captain come his vice-captain and senior players, experienced tourists whose views will be sought on issues on or off the pitch. A touring team will only be successful if people stick together, and some captains and coaches have happily encouraged their players to view the outside world as an enemy, in the belief that a siege mentality can be a good thing. It can equally be damaging on a long, tiring tour on which things are not going well.

However it comes about, a sense of loyalty to one another and the team must come before self and everything outside the team 'bubble'. Creating this environment is one of a captain's primary functions. 'You cannot consider yourself a seasoned captain until you have done a winter abroad,' wrote Michael Vaughan, one of England's most successful captains. 'It is so much easier when you are playing at home because you can jump in your car and get away from everyone, whereas on tour there is an enormous caravan moving around and you have to keep people happy.'* Doug Insole, who led Essex in the 1950s and was Peter May's deputy

---

* Arthur Gilligan, who led a team in Australia in the 1920s and was a member of the British Fascists, a minor anti-communist organisation, went further than most on this point when he wrote in an article for *The Bulletin*, a publication of the British Fascists: 'On cricket tours, it is essential to work solely on the lines of fascism.' England lost the series 4–1.

on a tour of South Africa, said a captain needs to be 'a public relations officer, agricultural consultant, psychiatrist, accountant, nursemaid and diplomat', as well as a player, selector and tactician.

Since the earliest days of touring, players' contracts have contained clauses about good behaviour, with the scope for fines to be imposed or good conduct bonuses withheld in the case of egregious breaches. More recently, England teams under Joe Root and Eoin Morgan, respectively Test and white-ball captain, devised their own code of conduct under which unity and respect for teammates were central themes and a sense of belonging to the team was regarded as more important than appeals to a shared nationality (a number of the players, including Morgan, were either born overseas or came from families with overseas origins). All this could make for an artificial and claustrophobic existence, but the intention was to condition the players to work with collective purpose. Woe betide anyone with a reputation as a bad tourist.

Of course, there have been instances of managements becoming too regimented in their approach, as happened with Andy Flower towards the end of his time as head coach. Flower was born and raised in southern Africa, and played for Zimbabwe for 11 years before settling in England where his coaching career reached fruition, and he later admitted that his background coloured the way he handled his players. 'My past certainly influenced me as a coach,' he said. 'Growing up in a colonial hierarchy system, you do what you're told, there's not much quarter given and that's not necessarily the healthiest way to operate ... I look back at some of the decisions I made [as England coach] with regret. If I had my time again I'd definitely try to work with the person as much as I'd work with the player and understand the place he was coming from.' Flower's family life also suffered, and ultimately the job cost him his marriage. 'At the height of our touring, I was away from home for 250 nights a year and perhaps didn't give my family – not perhaps, certainly – the priority that I should have.'

But a more disciplinarian style is perhaps better than the alternative. When a laissez-faire attitude takes hold, players are granted too much freedom and order breaks down, as appeared to happen on a number of tours in the early 1980s, when several high-profile players admitted to using recreational drugs. Such cases are relatively rare; perhaps the sheer ubiquity of touring life trains most cricketers to conform. (International rugby tours, for example, are less common but arguably have a more checkered history.)

Over the years, various means of developing esprit de corps have been employed, some more successful than others. For many years, an England team was expected to leave together at the start of a tour and return home as one group at the end, thereby giving a sense of shape and purpose to the overall mission. This principle could be followed to an insensitive degree. Ahead of a tour of Australia in the 1960s, Ken Barrington – the same man who would later die on tour in the West Indies – went to Lord's to ask if he could fly out a few days later than the rest of the team because his father-in-law was seriously ill. The request was denied and no sooner had the team landed in Perth than Barrington received a telegram telling him his father-in-law was dead.

For many years, players on tour were made to share rooms, with younger or newer members usually billeted with seniors to help them assimilate. If a player was injured and could take no further part in a tour, he would be removed immediately to preserve the unity among those who remained. This notion of togetherness was further enforced by rules preventing outsiders – specifically families – from accompanying the tour except for short, strictly defined periods. When wives and children joined the players for Christmas in Australia in 1974–75, John Woodcock wrote: 'Lord Hawke [a former Yorkshire and England captain famed for his autocratic nature] might have taken the same view as I do about having families on tour. It is no more the place for them than a trench on the Somme.

Cricket tours are for men.' When in the 1990s Darren Gough protested to Tim Lamb, chief executive of the Test and County Cricket Board (the precursor to the ECB), about a blanket ban on partners during a winter in Zimbabwe and New Zealand spanning more than 100 days away, Lamb replied: 'What would you do if you were in the army?'

Players who asked to be sent home early would get short shrift. Towards the end of the 1974–75 tour, which lasted 147 days, Brian Luckhurst put in just such a request once it became clear he was not going to feature in the Tests in New Zealand, but it was refused. He was chosen for the two ODIs that followed the Tests, scoring 0 and 1, and never played for England again.* Modern England tours are more welcoming towards families and in any case see Test and one-day specialists come and go at different times, so they are by nature less cohesive, more fluid entities, but there remains a sense that a player who leaves a tour early – or asks to leave early, as Luckhurst did – is committing an act of betrayal, however compelling the reason.

It was once the game started to become more professionalised that what had been quite a common habit of players making themselves unavailable for less glamorous tours became increasingly frowned upon. When Mike Brearley, a man with a distinguished captaincy record, said in 1980 at the age of 38 that he no longer wanted to tour but remained available for home Tests, the selectors initially refused to pick him for any matches (although later, in extremis, they recalled him as captain midway through a home series against Australia).

---

* Some did find ways to get home from tours early. Somerset batsman Herbie Hewett was supposedly called home on important business from South Africa in the 1890s, but the tour had been caught up in the chaos caused by the Jameson Raid, the playing schedule was suspended for nine days, and when the team crossed the Transvaal frontier they were searched by armed commandos. There was alarm when Hewett's cylindrical toothbrush was briefly suspected of being a revolver. He never toured again and never played Test cricket. In the 1950s, Dusty Rhodes, the Derbyshire bowler, decided within a few weeks of arriving that he had seen enough of India; he complained of a rumbling appendix and was flown home. He too never played Test cricket, though he did umpire in it – in England.

Subsequent to that, several leading England players – Ian Botham, Graham Gooch and David Gower among them – took winters off without facing sanctions, but their decisions were not viewed with favour. Even when it was agreed with the board that Andrew Strauss, as captain, should miss a short tour of Bangladesh in 2010 to conserve his energies for an Ashes and World Cup coming up the following winter, it sparked the ire of several former captains who had never enjoyed such privileges themselves.

Powerful bonds form on tour between players who effectively become each other's surrogate families. They spend more time with each other than they do with their wives, girlfriends and children and become accustomed to leaning on one another for support at times of greatest pressure. Spirits within a touring party can fluctuate wildly from one week to the next, depending on how the team is faring on the field and how individuals are coping on a personal level. It is everyone's job to keep things on an even keel. Inevitably, they occasionally need to let off steam. The saying 'What goes on tour, stays on tour' reflects both a desire to keep indiscretions secret and the need to maintain unity. Touring not only demands compliance, but at times also demands silence.

CHAPTER 2

Staying Sane
Another bloody tour

One thing needs to be understood: the way someone deals with touring is not a fixed thing. His attitude to the travel, the endless hotels, the chameleon-like cricket and the different chemistry between one group of players and another, shifts as the winters pass. Some might tour only once or twice, but those who have lengthier international careers must come to terms with this strange, itinerant life if they are to survive.

Broadly speaking, a player's enthusiasm for touring is inversely proportional to how many tours he has done. The more he does of it, generally the less it appeals. Even if there are technical challenges on the pitch, most players love their early tours. 'Can you believe it?' they say. 'We're being paid to play cricket in these exotic places. The sights are amazing. The stadiums are amazing. The sun shines. What's not to like?' Briefly, it seems like the best thing you'll ever do. But the more tours a player does, the more his senses dull, the more likely he is to chafe at the regimentation, the more likely he is to be weighed down by the accumulated memories of games lost and humiliations endured in the places to which he is returning. Self-preservation kicks in. The longer he tours, the older he gets, the more likely he is to be leaving at home a young family. Personal priorities mutate while the pressure to perform, and to justify a place in the side, grows.

Such an analysis may jar with onlookers. To the outsider, England cricket tours possess an aura, an indisputable glamour. Whatever is happening on the pitch, the life itself appears wonderful. TV pictures, radio commentary and newspaper columns or photographs convey an idyllic existence: golden sunshine and golden sunsets, swimming pools and sightseeing, cricket grounds with picture-postcard backdrops. 'How profoundly lucky are these guys?' they think. 'They are being paid very good money to travel the world in style, playing a sport they love.' And it is true: selection for a major England Test tour remains the fulfilment of many a dream. And yes, there will be wine-tasting trips to the Barossa Valley, safari drives in South Africa, and white-water rafting or fishing expeditions in New Zealand. They will be given access to some of the best golf courses in the world – many times. One England cricketer, Derek Pringle, admitted that on his first full England tour to Australia, as a young unmarried man, his cricket went backwards but he advanced his sexual experience 'exponentially'. Yes, there is fun to be had, for sure.

The idea that a touring cricketer's life is tough will be sniffed at by many. But touring has changed: in the old days, the rhythm of a tour was more sedate and there was time for days of leisure, and the scope for adventure, and appetite for it, were much greater. There were simple pleasures in touring too; often, food in places such as Australia and South Africa was far better and more plentiful than in Britain. But now an England tour is more streamlined, more functional. With three formats of international cricket to be packed in, downtime has been stripped to a minimum. The sunsets may be great, but the best chance a cricketer has of seeing one may be from the playing arena during a floodlit match, or from a coach window on the way back to the hotel.

Nor were the stories of old always quite what they seemed: tour books by Neville Cardus and Alan Ross are still cherished today for the quality of their prose, but neither man committed themselves to daily reporting from the frontline. They came and went on a tour as they saw fit. Their version of touring was neither that of the players nor of most other reporters, and in the end both exhausted the patience of their newspaper offices with their dilettantism. Cardus even declined the *Manchester Guardian*'s suggestion that he cover the Ashes tour of 1932–33, not wanting to be away from his mistress for six months.

However gilded the life, the cricketers themselves are never free from the tyranny of the 'numbers'. They know their tour will be judged by how many runs they score and wickets they take. And now, more than ever, what happens on the pitch is important. Vast sums of broadcast revenue depend on the England teams, and therefore the players, being successful. Performance is ultimately what cricketers get judged on, and this brings a pressure that means that the gilded days off, such as they are, are never quite as free and easy as they appear. That said, Ben Stokes and Brendon McCullum, as the new captain and coach of the Test team in 2022, seemed refreshingly intent on bringing back the enjoyment element to representing England – and it brought with it a significant uptick in results.

It is probably no coincidence that the weariness, even cynicism, with the touring cycle started to manifest itself in the post-war period when England began touring almost every winter. Tony Lock, who went on five Test tours of the 1950s and 1960s, once said: 'We all get homesick sooner or later; we get hangovers; we get on each other's nerves; we develop private grievances.' Bob Willis spent 11 winters out of 14 away with England between 1970 and 1984, and admitted during the last of them 'how lonely touring life can become'. Graeme Fowler, who opened the batting for England in the 1980s and later suffered from mental health issues, admitted in his diary to misgivings as the team assembled in London ahead of a four-month tour of India and

Australia. 'It is a long time away from home, and I'm not really looking forward to it,' he wrote. 'I'd like to spend the winter at home with Stephanie [his wife]. This is my third tour, so I'm feeling a bit blasé about it. The first one is a novelty; the second, you know the ropes; and the third is "another bloody tour".'

One month into the trip, he noted his emotional fragility: 'On tour everything is heightened, and if you build up your hopes and then the outcome is not favourable it can often leave you depressed and distraught.' And, a week after that: 'I try to keep my feelings repressed, which is the way to cope through tours anyway. I never allow myself to look forward to anything, because that means you can never be disappointed . . . Eat, sleep, drink, watch and play, and no more. It's a strange existence, strange to have to catch your emotions, bottle them and throw away the bottle, but it helps you to cope . . . When I was a kid I would never have thought that an England cricketer could cry for any reason. This one can.'

During the second Test match, Fowler noted how moods differed from player to player. Paul Allott had picked up an injury that meant his tour was over and he was about to be sent home, Fowler himself was unwell, while Tim Robinson had just scored a century in the Test. 'Touring is a peculiar life,' he wrote. 'One of us is totally depressed. One is ill. One is totally elated. And a few [others] bored rigid. [It's] such a funny way to live.'

Phil Edmonds was a member of the same tour, having spent two earlier winters on England duty, and shared similar views about the Three Tour Rule. 'You talk to some of the experienced pros, they will tell you that the third tour is the dangerous one. The first tour is new and exciting, and you are learning . . . The second is new to the extent that it is a different place, but by the end of it, you are beginning to wonder. And by the third, about halfway through, you think – shit! What am I doing here in this place for four months when I could be home with the wife and kids?' Simon Barnes, Edmonds' biographer, who covered several England tours for *The Times* rightly observed that the exaggerated chumminess among players was a symptom of homesickness, and a coping mechanism.

Mike Atherton experienced ten winters touring with the full England sides between 1990 and 2001 before accompanying many more tours as a broadcaster and journalist. In January 2020, in an article marking England's 500th Test match overseas, he wrote of the importance of not allowing cricket to consume your every moment: 'International cricket, above all, is a mental challenge, exacerbated on tour by the lack of home time: it is a long, arduous game that gives you a lot of opportunity to think about what could go wrong. You need – or at least I needed – time away; I needed things to occupy my mind so that I didn't think about cricket 24 hours a day. Maintaining some kind of balance helped me to sustain an international career over a lengthy period of time.'

Andrew Strauss toured with England sides for nine straight winters between 2003 and 2012 and, speaking to me for this book, conceded he found it only got harder.

> The first few tours you go on, there's something incredibly alluring about visiting new countries, staying in great hotels and being treated as VIPs. You feel like you're doing something important. There's the challenge of playing in other parts of the world. Early days, it is an incredible thing to go on an England tour. But that does wear off. The more you are involved, the more you go from tour to tour. Even just walking out the door to get on that plane in the first place is an incredibly tough mental hurdle. I used to find myself getting really irritable in the days up to a tour, and for my wife Ruth and the kids there was that separation thing that took place every time you left. You don't exactly start off on the best foot, and then it [often] goes downhill from there.

For Steve Harmison touring was difficult from the outset. He had a traumatic experience as an England Under-19 cricketer when he was sent on a tour of Pakistan; he had barely been abroad in his life and was thrust into a place and culture he didn't know existed, and struggled to comprehend. Unable to cope in the middle of the night, he knocked on the door of the team captain Andrew Flintoff – with whom he would later share many full England tours – and begged to be sent home. Nine days into the tour, he left. Whether he would have been permitted the same licence on a Test tour is debatable. Subsequently, as a young father, Harmison found time away almost intolerable but nonetheless toured with England for seven straight winters, even though his returns tended to decline year on year. After some notable early successes in Sydney and Dhaka in 2003, and Jamaica and Trinidad in 2004, he took only one four-wicket haul in his last 23 overseas Tests before being dropped in the Caribbean in 2009 after the West Indies' last-wicket pair held out for a draw in Antigua.

'The only thing that kept me going [on tour] – that kept me from anxiety and depression – was playing cricket,' he told me.

> If I got sick or injured, I'd feel I would have to come home. Ask Strauss [Harmison's captain in the West Indies in 2009]. The minute I was left out I became a nightmare. I became a nightmare to myself, and a nightmare and a liability to my teammates. I knew I was going to self-destruct. Playing helped occupy my mind and got me through. The minute playing was taken away I became a difficult person. I just flipped and had a rant at Strauss. I didn't really feel as though our relationship recovered from that. It can get to you. It's something I did regret, but that unfortunately comes with touring.

In Bangladesh in 2003, even taking wickets in the first Test in Dhaka was not enough to keep Harmison happy; he was according to one teammate 'utterly miserable throughout ... complaining about the heat, the humidity, everything', and went home before the second Test with a back strain.

Harmison admitted he found the subcontinent particularly difficult, as wandering through the streets in cricket-mad countries was simply not practical. 'Rarely did you leave the hotel,' he said.

The hotels were often magnificent, but it became difficult on the mental side. You spend 14 hours a day in a place in which you wish you weren't. I'd got three young kids at home. I tried to find things to help me sleep, alcohol and things like that. The mental anxiety and underlying darkness just mounted up. You become isolated [from other members of the team] when you're not playing. I was diagnosed with a type of clinical depression in 2000, but if I'd said [publicly] I had a mental problem that probably would have cost me my career.

There are always anxieties with professional sport, but I was a young dad – my second child was born during my first Test tour and I didn't see her for three months – so my priorities on tour were a bit different [from those of other players]. Things at home were a worry. The minute you get back to the hotel, your mind starts to wander to what the kids are doing. When time drags, it becomes a mental challenge. That for me was what touring life was.

He added: 'I don't think anybody could say everything about touring life has been fantastic, that they have not sometimes found it hard.'

As another father of young children, Ashley Giles, an England player between 1997 and 2006, endured similar problems. His toughest winter was his fourth one away in Bangladesh, Sri Lanka and the West Indies in 2003–04, the only time England have fulfilled three Test series in the same winter.* He played

---

* England were scheduled to play three Test series in the winter of 2019-20 but, after touring New Zealand and South Africa, the final leg in Sri Lanka was abandoned during the final warm-up match because of the coronavirus pandemic.

with mixed results in eight of the nine Tests, missing only the last in Antigua through illness. Like Strauss a former director of England cricket as well as a former Test player, Giles agreed to be interviewed for this book. 'Turn on your telly at home, and you see the team walking out on the field in, say, Cape Town and it looks great,' he said.

> What a life that is. But the viewer just sees the six or seven hours the players are on the pitch. You don't see the bits in between that can be dark and lonely, particularly if you're having struggles with your game or with the family. It can be tough. You almost have to operate as a split personality to keep sane. You can be this father and husband – I had two young children when I was touring – but as soon you enter the touring environment you become driven, selfish, focused. Your meals are made for you, your bed is made, your clothes washed. You're in this bubble that is in some parts of the world revered.
>
> I've been in bad places a couple of times. I remember being in a hotel room in Bangladesh thinking, *I just don't want to be doing this*. I was really struggling with my game. It took my wife to talk me down. They are the dark moments when the lights go out and your mates are somewhere else. I went on to Sri Lanka and did all right, but the underlying thing, the mental side of it [was still problematic]. I was never diagnosed but must have been suffering from something. In the West Indies, it was a great tour, but I came away feeling shit. That's just not normal.

Alastair Cook retired from the international arena in 2018 having played more Tests and scored more Test runs for England overseas than any other player, yet he never appeared to have serious issues with being away. In only two out of 13 winters did he fail to score a Test hundred, one of which was as captain in Australia when the team lost 5–0. He did accept however that touring in all its aspects was a test of mental fortitude.

In the subcontinent, it is about dealing with the heat, the constant probing of quality spinners and avoiding the cabin fever which comes when you spend most of your time at the hotel, ground or airport.

In Australia, it is an acceptance that the challenge will be relentless – on and off the pitch. The media and fans will be at you from the moment you land and won't let up until you fly home or have beaten their own side. The relentlessness on the pitch derives from the fact that whereas in England you can lose six wickets in a session and hope that your bowlers can claw your way back into it, that seldom applies Down Under ... In Australia, if you are not at it for the duration, the game slips away slowly but inexorably. Against the backdrop of an oppressive heat and home crowd, it then starts to feel like a very long tour.

The psychologically corrosive effects of life on the road were articulated well in *The Test*, a novel by Nathan Leamon, who accompanied the England team on many tours in the years following his recruitment as analyst in 2009. Leamon's job was to interpret every aspect of performance in numbers – 'Numbers' became his nickname – but he was clearly also fascinated by, and conscious of, the harder-to-quantify elements in a cricketer's existence. The book actually began life as a coaching manual, but he turned it into a novel as, he admitted, 'I wanted to put the reader into the England dressing-room without me breaching confidences.'

The protagonist was James McCall, who reflected on his long international career thus:

I am coming towards the end of my twenty-fifth consecutive summer. I haven't spent a winter in England since I was 20. Just summers at home and summers away, for nearly 13 years ... Touring brings a weariness that permeates your bones and stays there, as you trudge down an endless trail of

airports, hotels and training grounds, year after year ... The
road becomes home. Home becomes a foreign town.

When Bob Woolmer, a former England cricketer, died in a hotel
in Jamaica while coaching Pakistan at the 2007 World Cup, Peter
Roebuck wrote, 'To a greater and lesser degree all sportsmen
die in hotels.' Roebuck, himself a county cricketer of note with
Somerset, never played or toured with a full England team, but
subsequently spent many years reporting on international cricket
before his own death occurred in 2011 at a hotel in Cape Town –
in contentious circumstances – while reporting on a South
Africa–Australia Test match. Roebuck's words were poignant
given his own fate, but they also touched on a fundamental truth
about the nature of professional sporting existence – that it is both
solitary and largely stripped bare of human warmth. Ultimately,
cricket like all team sports is played at an individual level, and
when on that personal level things go badly life can be intolerable
and lonely – never more so than on tour.

Most cricketers have managed to cope with touring life,
even if at times only with great difficulty, but for some it simply
proves too much. There might have been an expectation that,
however bad things felt, they would stick with the tour for the
sake of the team, but in some cases this simply became impossible. Whatever the consequences, they had to leave.

A paper published in December 2020 into mental illness
in cricket, co-authored by Dr Nick Peirce, the England and
Wales Cricket Board's chief medical officer, highlighted the
mental demands of touring at elite level. The paper reviewed
previous studies which indicated that current and retired
English cricketers were more likely than members of the general public to experience anxiety and depressive symptoms.
'Touring', it noted,

is an important characteristic of the elite game resulting in
prolonged time away from home and consequent dislocation

from many individuals' normal support mechanisms. Players may develop pathological defence mechanisms when faced with stress outside of traditional social supports and environment. A recent narrative review focused on mental health emergencies in elite athletes and suggested an 'emergency action plan' is essential for sport stakeholders to implement . . . [and] suggests management strategies, with emphasis on early intervention.

It went on: 'Environment and timings of training and matches, especially early on during a tour, should be arranged and optimised to improve sleep in order to minimise impact on well-being and mental health as well as on physical performance.' The paper recommended the 'creation of a psychologically aware and welcoming environment'. It may not have been coincidence that around this time – late 2020 – England's selectors and management started to develop a rest-and-rotation policy, although this was popularly attributed to the impact of the pandemic rather than more deep-seated concerns about how cricketers coped with major tours.

The issue had been brought to the fore by a number of cases of England players leaving tours – or coming very close to leaving them – in a highly distressed mental state.

Marcus Trescothick had been involved in eight Test tours in the space of five winters, and rarely missed an England match home or away in six years, when in the space of 12 months he nearly walked out of a tour of Pakistan and then did leave tours of India and Australia within two weeks of each of them starting – an unprecedented sequence of events for an England cricketer. From age-group cricket onwards, Trescothick had routinely suffered from what he termed 'early-tour blues' every time he went abroad – sleeping badly and feeling agitated and homesick for the first week, before settling into the cricket and putting those feelings to one side. He learned to cope partly with the help of sleeping pills.

In many respects, these were classic symptoms, probably felt by many touring cricketers, but by the time of the Pakistan tour in late 2005 Trescothick was going away for the first time since the birth of his first child, Ellie, six months earlier. Then during the tour itself, his father-in-law fell from a ladder at home, hit his head on a rockery and was placed in intensive care. His wife Hayley asked him to come home, but he was talked into completing the tour by his captain Michael Vaughan. 'Looking back, I almost cannot believe that I managed to persuade myself that my captain's needs were greater than my wife's, that the England cricket team was more important than my family,' Trescothick wrote later. 'Staying on tour was completely and utterly the wrong thing to do. I have carried the guilt with me ever since.' But Trescothick was only doing what many touring cricketers have done, putting the team's mission before everything else – because it was what was required.

In Trescothick's view, this episode almost certainly contributed to the anxiety attacks that so swiftly cut short his tours to India and Australia. The situation in India was complicated by him suffering from a virus which meant he was confined to his room for a few days, which only further allowed him to brood on his separation from home. The virus would also provide him with a ready-made means of disguising the true nature of his mental health problems. By this time, he said, Hayley was also suffering from post-natal depression.

In his first public interview after returning to England, Trescothick put down his sudden departure midway through the final warm-up match to 'a bug', and even England's head coach Duncan Fletcher was not apprised of the full facts until several months later. Eventually it was publicly acknowledged that he had been suffering from a 'stress-related illness' but the details, such as Trescothick spending several months on anti-depressants, remained private. This medication provided him with enough stability to believe he could get through an Australia tour, but no sooner had he arrived than he began to suffer from what he described as 'separation anxiety', and once again returned home during the warm-up phase.*

A cognitive behavioural therapist who worked with Trescothick explained his breakdown thus: 'You've had six years of constant playing, training and travelling with England . . . and the exhaustion you are suffering from has led to you being physically depressed.' He contemplated a comeback the following year, but Peter Moores, who had taken over from Fletcher, made it clear that Trescothick could not make himself available for the World T20 in South Africa and then not the matches in Sri Lanka that followed. 'Surely he could have helped me just to try and have a go at doing the Twenty20 without nudging me further about what might happen afterwards,' Trescothick wrote in his autobiography. But, as ever, the unwritten rule that players could not pick and choose which parts of a tour they went on over-rode everything. He never played for England again.†

Several years later, Jonathan Trott, who was for a period a highly successful no. 3 Test batsman, developed similar difficulties. His situation was not simply to do with touring – he had developed problems dealing with short-pitched bowling – but he too had suffered from homesickness and found going away on youth and age-group tours challenging. 'Homesickness was a recurring problem,' he conceded. It followed a pattern too: he would start a tour well but his returns with the bat would tail off as the weeks went by, something that was also a feature of Trescothick's tours.

With Trott, there were signs of trouble during the home season of 2013 and Kevin Pietersen, a teammate, had suggested

---

* After the opening warm-up match in Canberra, Trescothick told Steve Harmison that he had not seen the ball from Shaun Tait that dismissed him. 'He meant he literally couldn't see the ball, like his brain wouldn't focus on it,' Harmison recalled. 'I knew then he wasn't going to last.'

† Trescothick rarely played overseas again in any form of cricket, although after retiring as a player he joined the ECB's coaching staff, initially as a consultant and later in a full-time capacity, and worked on several England tours. 'It felt different because the stresses, strains and intensity of playing were not there,' he said.

to Andy Flower that Trott be allowed to have his wife Abi with him from the start of the following winter's tour of Australia, even though partners were barred from coming out until the third Test. Flower insisted there could be no exceptions. Trott then broke down during the first Test in Brisbane and was sent home on the instruction of the medical staff, who diagnosed a 'work-related stress condition'. Flower later apologised to Pietersen for not acting on his advice. 'His [Trott's] departure put the jitters up the side,' Flower conceded. 'He had been our rock for so long. To see him in that state was a shock to the guys.'

One of those particularly affected by Trott's withdrawal was left-arm spinner Monty Panesar, who had been going through his own difficulties, including alcohol problems. His behaviour became increasingly unpredictable on the remainder of the tour and he spent a lot of time alone in his room, but through force of circumstance England had to pick him in Melbourne (for what transpired to be his last Test) after the team's other frontline spinner, Graeme Swann, suddenly retired three matches into the series. Swann's action in abandoning the tour was widely condemned; Bob Willis, then a pundit with Sky TV, described him as 'creeping into the lifeboat on the *Titanic* with the women and children'. Swann insisted that a long-standing elbow problem simply made it impossible for him to bowl as he once had. Alastair Cook, his captain, regretted how it looked: 'Given my time again, [I] would have asked him to . . . remain on tour for appearance's sake . . . He accepted he would be portrayed as a bottler, a bloke who abandoned ship. His decision, in the middle of a series, was far from ideal.'

Flower was probably thinking of Trott when he said that if he could have had his time again he would have tried to 'work with the person as much as the player'. Trott made a brief, unsuccessful comeback on a tour of the West Indies but knew after two matches that it was not working. He contacted the director of cricket Andrew Strauss and the psychologist Steve Peters, and was told to 'see the job through', which he did, playing the final

Test and failing to score in both innings. 'I felt I had to [stay] after leaving the Ashes tour,' he said.

One of Steve Harmison's hardest moments came when he experienced what might best be described as a panic attack ahead of a Test series in South Africa in 2004–05. 'That was my "Marcus Trescothick moment", my "Jonathan Trott moment",' he reflected. 'I was hyper-ventilating at practice. I was really struggling. The anxiety was too much. I didn't think I could make the first Test match.'

Fortunately there were people he could turn to for help. Kirk Russell, the team's physiotherapist, had known Harmison since England Under-19s and took him to see a breathing specialist. Harmison eventually played not just the first Test but the entire series.

> I felt he [Russell] was not only on my side but cared. Rob Key [an England teammate] saw that I was struggling and spent more time with me than a good friend should. The people you toured with, the 'club', that was always very important. If your team had a good spirit, time flew. But in 2006–07 in Australia, things weren't going well, factions developed and everybody was looking over their shoulder. Then touring is not great. You can only win abroad if you've got a good team spirit.

Trescothick may have initially bottled up his problems, but ultimately by articulating them as thoroughly as he did in 2008 in his autobiography, *Coming Back to Me*, he made it easier for others to speak more openly. Not everyone felt able to do that, of course, as evidenced by Trott's breakdown in the early weeks of the 2013–14 Australia tour. 'Test cricket is 90 per cent mental, 10 per cent skill,' said Stuart Broad, who witnessed Trott's tears in the dressing room at the Gabba. 'Some people don't want to show weakness. People fight their own battles behind closed doors sometimes.'

Many players had reason to be grateful for Trescothick breaking a taboo, however. 'Trescothick's book was brilliant at opening up people who had been too worried to talk about these things,' said Jos Buttler in 2020, who had his own challenges trying to play all three formats all year round. 'Now, people are less afraid to say something, whether it's to a close confidant or a coach. It's about being strong enough to say, "Look, I'm not okay at the moment, I'm struggling" ... Mental health awareness has become a much more open conversation.' Two years later, Buttler elaborated: 'Time is a tough one in terms of cricket. Cricket is a long game. There's a lot of time you're actually not involved. And the game allows your thoughts to run away with you ... And that time can be really tough to deal with.'

Strauss knew from his own experiences how mentally exposed touring cricketers felt. 'When you're on a tour, you are much more mentally and emotionally vulnerable,' he told me.

When you have that perfect storm of a long tour, a long stint between seeing your family, the team's not playing well and you're not doing well [personally], it's very tough ... The truth is it's very hard to win away from home, so the odds are that you are not going to do that well. That's what tends to happen, especially the big long tours to Australia and India, and South Africa to a certain degree. Those are all very tough tours. The truth is I can't remember one easy tour away from home, ever. The ones we won, we had to dig pretty damn deep, and we lost a lot, especially on the subcontinent.

On a personal level, Strauss's hardest tour came in New Zealand in 2008, midway through his eight years as a Test cricketer. He was returning to the England side after being omitted for a series in Sri Lanka, and had gone to New Zealand early to play domestic cricket for Northern Districts.

If you play poorly [for England] for a certain period of time, then it gets very stressful. Your place in the team is on the line. For the only time, I couldn't sleep properly. If you get caught in that negative spiral it's very hard to get out of it, and hotel rooms are a bleak place to be. I always felt the best way to embrace a tour was to get out of the hotel and see things and meet people, but increasingly that felt like a harder thing to do, with camera phones and security and the like.

Being out of form on tour can cause acute distress: sleepless nights in a lonely hotel room thousands of miles from home allow the worst fears to flourish, sending the victim on what Strauss called 'a mental ghost train'.

Another England player, Matthew Hoggard, went through an even more difficult time on the same New Zealand tour. Whereas Strauss revived his Test career with a century in his final innings of the series in Napier, and within a year would be appointed captain, Hoggard's career was effectively ended by a personal crisis during the first Test. It was an episode which highlighted the extent to which players will sacrifice themselves and their families in order to do what they see as the right thing by a touring team – just as Trescothick had done in Pakistan. It was a tour which began in unhappy circumstances for Hoggard, with his wife Sarah, he said, suffering post-natal depression. She was due to fly out and join him, but when she got to the airport with their young son, she suddenly wanted to go home, and only through the persuasion of her parents did she board the plane.

Learning of this while the first Test was going on in Hamilton, Hoggard was distraught. At one point, as he walked back to his bowling mark, he said to his captain Michael Vaughan, 'Vaughany, I think I'm going cuckoo, I'm doing a "Tres" [Trescothick].' Hoggard later elaborated: 'I felt like I wanted to sit down and cry. To admit that to your captain maybe wasn't the best career move.' He did not bowl well in a match England lost and was dropped for the next two Tests, both of which England won with a new-look seam attack.

Hoggard's state of mind was certainly a factor in the decision to drop him, and head coach Peter Moores told him he need not do 12th man duties if he did not want to, but Hoggard felt that would not have looked good. 'My wife said, "Now that you've been dropped can we go home?" She was begging me. And I said, "No, because it would look like I'm running away." I put cricket above my family and that was a massive mistake. I don't know if the management would have let me go but I should have gone. Not doing that put a massive strain on the [marital] relationship.' Hoggard and his wife had what he described as a horrendous falling-out: 'Sarah said that I'd done things on this tour that she never thought I would do. I'd failed to back her up when she needed me most.'

After retiring as a player in 2007, Ashley Giles took up coaching and management. He spent two years back on the road coaching England's white-ball teams, splitting the job with Andy Flower, who continued to manage the Test side, in a move designed to lighten the workloads of the coaching staff. Later he succeeded Strauss as England's director of cricket, a role that afforded him fresh insights into how the modern generation of players coped with life on the road. He concludes they were under even greater stress than players of his day. 'Nowadays it [the pressure] has ramped up to another level,' he told me in in 2020.

We were still able to have some downtime. Players nowadays spend a lot of time isolated in their rooms. It's a strange existence. It hurts when I know my job is to manage this group of people. We drive performance, but to think some of our guys are going through that [strain] regularly, that's a concern. I have the greatest respect for them because I know it's tough. People ask do I miss playing for England. I'm realistic. I wouldn't want to be on the road for 300 days a year. I just don't think I'd be able to cope.

As many past touring players have explained, the best chance of staying upbeat was to stay in the team. When Steven Finn was dropped in Australia in 2010–11 despite being the leading wicket-taker in the series, he struggled to cope. 'I just remember locking myself in the toilet and thinking, *What the fuck's happened?*' He was taking wickets but leaking runs, so England replaced him, and he tried so hard to get his bowling right that when he spoke to the team doctor he found himself bursting into tears. 'If you're consumed by the game of cricket when you're away on a tour of that length you'll drive yourself bonkers ... Psychological trauma is the toughest thing about Test cricket.' Finn took 125 wickets in Tests, but his England career was over by the age of 27.*

The relentless nature of the sport, whether home or away, took its toll on even the most resilient personalities. Ben Stokes is one of the toughest and most durable competitors England have ever possessed, but even he briefly dropped out of international cricket in 2021 after eight years as a Test player, citing mental health along with a chronic finger injury as the cause. This was at a time when England teams had been spending a lot of time in bio-secure bubbles because of the pandemic, and Stokes had also recently lost his father Ged to brain cancer.

When he eventually announced a comeback several months later, Stokes wrote in a ghosted newspaper column: 'I probably didn't realise just how much of an issue the finger was causing me until I got it sorted ... But I had also been struggling with bubble life and events off the field. I don't want anyone to feel the way I did, because I wasn't in a good place and I'm not afraid

---

* A few months after the Finn incident, one of England's short-format specialists Michael Yardy withdrew from a World Cup on the subcontinent directly before a quarter-final tie against Sri Lanka, citing depression. 'Leaving at this stage of the World Cup campaign was a very difficult decision,' he said, 'but I felt it was the only sensible option and I wanted to be honest about the reason behind that decision.' Yardy had not been on many international tours, but it was telling that his breaking point came when he was away from home and deprived of what Dr Nick Peirce termed 'normal support mechanisms'.

to admit it. I was in a real dark place and having some difficult thoughts.' He later elaborated on this in an Amazon Prime documentary made about by him by the Oscar-winning director Sam Mendes, admitting that his anxiety had gone through the roof and that on one occasion he had suffered a 'massive panic attack' in his hotel room.

At the end of the 2021 season the ECB's chief executive, Tom Harrison, acknowledged that the demands on players were a matter of concern, whether in a pandemic or not.

> We have to understand that when it comes to matters of mental health, not just in this case [Covid-19] but to do with schedules and on-going commitments that we ask players to fulfil, administrators have to keep listening and make sure we're taking action against putting too much pressure on players ... When you pull a hamstring or a calf muscle, everyone understands you're going to be sitting on the sidelines for a while; but we're only just starting to understand the situation with respect to mental health. Players at this [international] level of the game need to be as mentally fit as they are physically fit ... The topic of touring, and touring within the context of a pandemic, it does build up and wear on your mental health and well-being, and your ability to perform.

Strauss's view was that the heaviest burden is borne by the captain, who is afforded less time off than other players and is inevitably more isolated due to his seniority.

> Touring as captain is tough. In the natural rhythm of a tour, the [other] players are fully 'on' over the course of a Test match. Then they have a couple of days off [and their] intensity goes right down. For a captain, that's usually when the management is peaking, planning for the next Test. As captain, you are always at that high level – and without the support network you'd normally have at home of your family

and your mates to help you get out of the bubble. As captain in particular, at the end of a tour you feel exhausted.

Like the fictional James McCall, I know something about our summers and their winters, and how roots atrophy through too much time on the road. As a newspaper correspondent for 25 years, I've gone round the world countless times reporting on England Test tours and World Cup campaigns. Until the pandemic prevented journalists covering the tour of Sri Lanka and India in the winter of 2020–21 – probably the first England tour to be unaccompanied by reporters for more than 70 years – I'd missed only two England Tests since 1998. I have covered 39 of their last 42 Test series away from home, and typically spent between three and five months every winter watching them play anywhere from Peshawar to Pietermaritzburg, from Queenstown, New Zealand to Queen's Park Oval, Trinidad.

For me, the early tours were, as Strauss suggested, unimaginably exciting, as was the notion of winter never coming. Flying for the first time into Cape Town over the cloud-draped Table Mountain, or Sydney with its labyrinth of bays, was breathtaking. You did indeed feel as though you were involved in something important, even if denizens of the press were mere observers of the drama, ranking far below participants, and spared the tyranny of being measured every day by runs and wickets in the way players were. You generally stayed in good hotels, and ate and drank at someone else's expense.

But the timing was not great. I was sent on my first full England tour a year after the birth of my first child, and within five years I was father to a son of six and daughters aged four and three. One Saturday afternoon, while I was sat on the boundary at the Bagh-e-Jinnah ground in Lahore watching an England warm-up match, my wife Gayle rang and, plainly upset, shouted down the phone that she could not cope with handling three young children on her own. Sometime later, when I explained the nature of the conversation to a colleague from another

Sunday newspaper, he said: 'Doesn't she know not to phone you on a Saturday? It's your working day.'

My wife wasn't the only one wondering if she could handle such a life. Around this same period, I was about to head out of the door for another tour when my son Freddie demonstrated that he was now old enough to grasp that me leaving with a large suitcase meant I was not coming home for a long time. Stretching his small body across the width of our hallway, legs and arms jammed against the two walls, he successfully blocked my exit while screaming, 'Don't go! *No!*' Of course, I had to go. To add to my annual misgivings, my youngest daughter was born in late November, which meant I was often away for her birthday, often in a time-zone that made phone calls home at suitable hours well-nigh impossible.

Whether they are players or journalists, hardened cricket tourists and their families somehow *do* learn to cope, the children possibly faster than the adults. Everyone manages in different ways. Wayne Larkins used his entire tour fee in daily phone calls home to his wife. Even so, as a parent on tour, the heaviest part of your travel luggage is guilt. I endorse Graeme Fowler's theory of repressed feelings. But things cannot have been too bad: my son now works in cricket as the data analyst for the England white-ball teams, and goes away in the winters himself.

I've observed at close quarters highly dysfunctional touring teams, and highly functional ones. Unsurprisingly, the happiest tours are the winning ones; the players are more willing to talk, and relations with the press are more amicable than when the criticism is flying. As a camp-follower, you want them to win, but eventually you cover enough tours to realise that your mood cannot be dictated by how well or how badly the team performs. As Fowler said, if you built up your hopes and the outcome was unfavourable, it would leave you downcast. As a journalist, you need to develop an outlook as independent of the team as it is from your family at home. It's the only way to cope.

Many of the graphic stories recounted in this chapter belong to recent times but, as we will see, earlier generations of touring cricketers appeared to feel the pain of dislocation from home no less acutely. John Lever for example, who was regarded by teammates as an ideal tourist, and regarded himself as someone who liked to enjoy life, later admitted that he was taken aback by the length of his first tour to India and Australia in 1976–77. He suffered badly from homesickness. These generations were also subjected to brutal fixture schedules and arduous travel conditions. Society in the past may have demanded a more stoical response to hardship and separation, and perhaps those who endured two world wars were conditioned to articulate that pain less readily than people do now, but the anguish of being on the other side of the world on Christmas Day, or learning by letter or telegram of the birth of a son or daughter, or the death of a parent, was no less real. There is no reason to think that today's generation is less resilient. More likely, touring has become even more mentally taxing: in line with all top-level sport, it involves greater intensity and intrusion, and fewer opportunities to get out and about. The decision to give every player a hotel room of their own (rather than share, as was the case for many years) and thereby grant them more privacy may have inadvertently heightened feelings of isolation for some. It is a pressure-cooker life.

England cricket tours have evolved over 150 years from on-the-hoof pieces of entrepreneurism to sleek, micro-managed business trips; what was once a small group of adventurers is now an audaciously conceived circus of players, coaches, medics, broadcasters, reporters and supporters. But something fundamental has stayed the same: they were, and still are, about people thrust into strange environments striving for ways to cope.

CHAPTER 3

Why Tours Are Arranged

Gate receipts and TV deals

Money is, and has always been, the thing that makes tours tick. They are fundamentally financial enterprises. These days they may have to jostle for space in the calendar with World Cups, World T20s and the rapacious Indian Premier League, among other domestic leagues, but England tours are economically highly profitable, as are most of those undertaken by teams coming to England. That England's off-season happens to be the time when most of their opponents enjoy high summer only places them in even greater demand as potential visitors.

Nowadays, tours generate money primarily through media deals which take in TV and radio broadcasting rights and digital clips and streaming, but for more than a hundred years international cricket was nourished chiefly by gate receipts. The stark necessity of getting people to come and watch inside the ground gave tours their original shape; matches had to be taken across the length and breadth of countries in search of fresh audiences. To an extent this pattern still exists, even if in some, though not all, countries attendances for Tests have sharply declined. The enthusiasm for watching in person an ODI or T20 remains strong and there remains purpose in choosing the venues that best maximise numbers.

For English cricket, broadcast revenue overtook gate receipts as a chief source of income around the mid-1990s, and for India, now the dominant cricket market in the world, around the same time.* Gate receipts remain significant in bigger cities such as London, where ticket prices are higher and a sell-out crowd at Lord's or the Oval can generate over £1 million per day, but these are relatively small sums in the grand scheme. The overall value of a major Test match in England is put at around £40–45 million. Today, 75 per cent of the game's revenues are generated by media rights.

The rise of satellite TV also facilitated an explosion in the value of broadcast deals for World Cups and other one-day tournaments. When the World Cup was staged in South Asia in 1996, the host nations marketed every aspect of it aggressively and successfully, but the biggest deal was the television one worth $14 million, closely followed by a title sponsorship of $12 million. The UK rights fetched $7.5 million, compared to $1 million for the tournament held four years earlier in Australia and New Zealand. By the time multi-year media rights were being sold across periods taking in the 50-over World Cups in India in 2011 and 2023, the ICC was securing deals that could be measured in billions of dollars.

Bilateral tours operate today on a reciprocal basis, with the financial risk lying with the hosts. When a team go on tour, their national board pays the wages of its players and coaching staff, and the cost of the international flights to and from their destination, but from the moment of arrival transport, hotels, meal allowances and other reasonable out-of-pocket expenses are taken care of by the hosts. In turn, the hosts keep all TV revenues (accruing from both domestic broadcast deals and selling on coverage to broadcasters in overseas territories), plus

---

* England's tour of India in 1992–93 was the first there to be shown on satellite TV, the Indian board receiving $600,000.

net gate receipts and any commercial spin-offs. The venues keep the lion's share of local commercial income, such as sponsorship, corporate hospitality, merchandise and perimeter advertising. So a touring team make nothing out of a tour, but they tour on the understanding (enshrined in contracts) that the favour will be repaid when their opponents visit them. The number of matches is subject to negotiation, but whatever is agreed would usually be returned in kind, not always in the same format; England prefer staging Tests, many other countries favour ODIs and might forgo a Test for more white-ball games.

This long-standing system has been questioned by some who feel it is unfairly weighted towards England and India especially, and to a lesser extent Australia, whose markets are richer. Other countries enjoy less commercial leverage within their own domestic economies, and for some Test cricket – unless it is played against the 'big three' – is fast becoming too costly to stage. They argue that the cricket family is small and fragile, and should share resources; this has become an increasingly popular argument of late, without cutting through to the 'big three'. Another flaw is that national boards will sometimes shoehorn series into their schedules which they and their players are contractually obliged to play but care little about, save for the revenue generated.

Even so, an England tour to any country carries with it the promise of significant overseas broadcast rights to the home board and a significant boost to the local economy through the team bringing along the biggest group of travelling supporters in world cricket. When Cricket West Indies announced dates for England's tours in early 2022 to play five T20s and three Tests, the estimated economic value of each T20 was put at $4 million and each Test at $20–25 million, meaning the whole tour was worth nearly $100 million to the region. Such are the stakes that the local territories are required to submit bids to the West Indies board, knowing that they should still turn an overall profit thanks to the influx of British supporters. As a result, recent England matches in the Caribbean have tended to gravitate towards the most popular tourist destinations of Barbados and Antigua.*

Broadly speaking, England have throughout their history as an international team alternated incoming and outgoing Test tours with every country they played. There have been occasional instances of this pattern being broken, sometimes simply due to scheduling difficulties, but over the course of almost 150 years the number of home and away series England have played against each side has been roughly the same: England have hosted 146 Test series and undertaken 138 Test series overseas.

The biggest imbalances involved West Indies and Pakistan. Since 1960, England have hosted West Indies 17 times for Tests while touring the Caribbean on only 12 occasions, largely because the Caribbean is one of the most logistically challenging and expensive places to tour and the West Indies cricket board has never been wealthy. During some of this period (roughly the early 1970s through to the late 1990s), there was a system of hosts paying touring teams a fee, but England were in the case of West Indies happy to pay a fee to the West Indies, but not take one themselves when they went to the Caribbean.† England were content to host them more often because they recognised that the West Indies economy was not as big as their own, and because for much of this time West Indies were the strongest team in the world as well as being among the most attractive, and they themselves benefited financially from visits

---

* Trinidad and Guyana may be less popular destinations with English teams and their supporters, partly because of their equatorial locations and the humidity, increased risk of rain – and malaria. The Providence Stadium, Georgetown is 6.8 degrees north of the Equator and Port of Spain, Trinidad 10.4 degrees north. The venues closest to the Equator where England played internationals are: Nairobi, Kenya (1.3 degrees south; two matches, 2000); nine grounds in Sri Lanka (situated between 6.1 degrees and 7.9 degrees north; 52 matches, 1982–2021); Berbice, Guyana (6.2 degrees north; one match, 1981); Georgetown, Guyana (6.8 degrees north; Bourda and Providence stadiums, 17 matches, 1930–2010); and Kochi, India (9.9 degrees north, two matches, 2006–13).

† The ECB also chose not to take a large part of its fee when England toured Zimbabwe in 1996–97.

by West Indies. Even so, every England tour of the Caribbean between 1973–74 and 1989–90 lost money for the West Indies cricket board.

In the case of Pakistan, the issue was more complex. For many years, England teams toured the subcontinent with reluctance: they simply found the heat, the alien food, the shortage of good hotels and the long internal journeys too taxing. In the 30 years following the Second World War, they toured India only three times, and then later – when hotels among other things were much improved – they did not go there once in eight winters between 1993 and 2001. As well as their prejudices, they took with them tinned food and, in one instance, their own microwave ovens. It did not help that some of their most influential players were dead set against going. Ian Botham fell ill in Pakistan on his first visit in 1977–78 and only went back with reluctance in 1983–84, when injury cut short his stay. He returned home, made some disparaging remarks about the place, and never went back as a player.

In respect of Pakistan, there were additional factors at play, including the sterile nature of the pitches and what English cricketers judged a questionable standard of umpiring. After the acrimony of the 1987–88 tour, which culminated in a stand-off between the England captain Mike Gatting and Shakoor Rana which cost a day's play in Faisalabad, England did not play Tests there again until 2000–01, by which time one neutral umpire was officiating in every Test. More recently, security issues led to Pakistan using the United Arab Emirates as a temporary home – England played Tests there in 2011–12 and 2015–16 – before a phased transition began towards matches once more being played within Pakistan's borders. During this time, England hosted Pakistan for Tests in 2016, 2018 and 2020, but their own next visit to Pakistan for Tests did not come until 2022–23. This is one of only two cases of either England or their opponents touring the other more than twice in a row without return, the other being England hosting Sri Lanka for one-off

Tests in 1984, 1988 and 1991 without themselves paying a visit to the island – chiefly a consequence of the Sri Lankan civil war which meant incoming international tours were suspended for several years.* Overall, England have played only ten 'away' Test series against Pakistan while staging 16 against them at home.

Until the early years of this century, national boards were essentially at liberty to agree between themselves who they were – or were not – going to play. England's schedule was the product of various subtly shifting alliances, some definitely stronger than others. Their relationship with Australia stood on a level above all the rest: the teams had exchanged regular tours since the late 1800s and they had long since settled into a rarely disturbed pattern of playing home and away within a four-year cycle.

After both world wars, Australia pushed hard for England to swiftly restore the cycle and fulfil tours abeyed as a result of conflict – too swiftly in fact for the visitors to do themselves justice. Of the 1920–21 tour, Sidney Rogerson, biographer of one of the England players, Wilfred Rhodes, wrote: 'The decision, albeit taken under strong pressure from Australia, who had asked for a visit the year before, was unwise. It underrated the degree of mental and physical prostration that afflicted the home country after four and a half years of total war. It ignored the effect that the loss by death or disablement of so many of her proven and promising players would have on the selection of an English team.'

Considering England eventually had seven other major opponents with whom they were interested in exchanging regular tours, this Anglo-Australian arrangement placed a constant strain on fitting everything in. England tended to get round this by favouring whichever opponents were most fashionable and

---

* England played what are now regarded as Test matches on five tours of South Africa between 1888–89 and 1905–06 before South Africa first made a Test tour of England, but four of these tours were only retrospectively viewed as holding Test status.

promised greatest financial reward. So, for example, between August 1979 and August 2000 they played 55 Tests against West Indies but only 27 against India, then between August 2000 and August 2021, 34 against West Indies but 47 against India.

Potential commercial value determined not only whom England might play, but also over how many matches. An Ashes series against Australia has with only a few exceptions spanned at least five matches for the past 125 years. England have also played five-match series against South Africa, West Indies and India, depending on when circumstances suggested this might be financially advantageous. But they have never signed up to any tour of New Zealand, Pakistan or Sri Lanka for anything more than three Tests, and they have never played more than two Tests in a series against Zimbabwe or Bangladesh, home or away.*

After an inaugural visit to New Zealand in 1929–30, England's next nine Test tours of New Zealand were tagged onto the end of visits to Australia, before they began making regular stand-alone tours there from the late 1970s. The very fact England ventured to New Zealand for Test matches at all greatly upset the Australians, who jealously guarded their relationship with the Mother Country. 'The Australian cricket authorities were extremely upset by the MCC's decision that its side should return home by way of New Zealand, playing [Test] cricket on the way in that Dominion,' Douglas Jardine, the England captain, wrote of the first time this happened. 'I could not see any possible grounds for objection which the Australian authorities could have on this score ... On more than one occasion I was left with the unpleasant impression that by visiting New Zealand we were in some way flouting or slighting Australia.'

---

* England played four Tests on their first full tour of New Zealand in 1929–30 but the fourth match was added at short notice after the third one in Auckland was ruined by rain.

Sure enough, when next England visited in 1936–37, they went on to New Zealand for a few games but did not play Tests. They did not resume playing Test cricket in New Zealand until after the war. In the mid-1950s the Australians were complaining again, proposing an additional fixture against New South Wales after the final Test in Sydney was badly hit by rain. When it was pointed out that England had fixtures to fulfil in New Zealand, they were told: 'Oh, it doesn't matter about New Zealand.'

Tim Lamb was closely involved in tour negotiations between 1988 and 2003 in his roles as cricket secretary of the Test and County Cricket Board and later chief executive of the TCCB and its successor body the England and Wales Cricket Board. 'There was disappointment on the part of the less rich nations that we were in a better position because our economy was bigger, and we kept a lot more revenue than they would have done, but we argued our cost base was also bigger in terms of upkeep of facilities, salaries etc.,' he told me.

> We got away with not playing Pakistan for a long time, and a lot of concern was expressed not only by the Pakistan board but other observers that we were tending to play against those countries from whom we made greatest amount of revenue, and playing five matches against them and a lesser number against others. When I started, the financial arrangements were different for virtually every country. There was no consistency, and allowances were made depending on the economy of the countries we were playing against. There was not a standard formula.

By the 1990s, deals were often negotiated and sealed through face-to-face meetings between one national board chief executive and another on the fringes of the ICC's twice-yearly meetings. There were no contracts or legally binding documents; agreements were taken on trust or through an exchange of letters. Neither were there penalties for anyone pulling out. Lamb found this out almost to England's cost when an agreement he had struck with Ali Bacher, head of the South African cricket board, threatened to unravel under Bacher's successor Gerald Majola.

Lamb and Bacher had agreed that five Tests would be played in South Africa in 1999–2000 and five in England in 2003, and the ECB had concluded a lucrative TV deal on that basis. However, while Lamb was in New Zealand during an England tour early in 2002, Majola's board informed ECB it was only willing to play three Tests in England. 'This was potentially disastrous,' Lamb recalled.

At one o'clock in the morning, I drafted a letter which my PA in London faxed to the South African board. They remained equivocal. So, with the approval of [ECB chairman] Ian MacLaurin I got on a plane from New Zealand to Johannesburg, went to see Gerald face to face, told him how serious it would be for English cricket if they didn't stick with five Tests, returned to the airport and flew back again. I don't know what difference my going in person made, but it emphasised how important it was to us, and we got our five Test matches. Legally, there'd not have been much we could have done if South Africa had stuck to their guns.

Ironically, commercially South Africa Test series have proved a hard sell, and since 2008 England have only played them over three or four matches.

The informality of the process was phased out with the introduction in May 2001 of a Future Tours Programme, under which each Test team committed to playing each other home and away within a ten-year period. Under a binding agreement signed off two years later, penalties were attached for the non-fulfilment of tours – except in the case of *force majeure* – involving forfeited points towards a new rolling Test championship (in which the no. 1 team would be crowned each April) and fines of $2 million, or the net budgetable profit of any tour, whichever was the greater. This was subsequently reinforced by the threat of a year's suspension.

Lamb supported the move towards an FTP, but it caused the ECB many difficulties in the early years over the ethics of England maintaining sporting ties with Zimbabwe and thereby seemingly endorsing President Robert Mugabe's regime.* As a consequence of these new, stricter terms of engagement, England were obliged to fulfil a four-match one-day series in Zimbabwe in 2004. The ICC subsequently acknowledged that some international fixtures were simply too politically sensitive to be viable outside major white-ball tournaments (the prime example being India and Pakistan playing one another), and England successfully pleaded not to meet Zimbabwe in bilateral series thereafter, a stance that long outlasted Mugabe's removal in 2017.

The FTP underwent various modifications and, by the time of the 2019–21 World Test Championship, culminating in a first-ever championship final, each team was required to play six of the eight others home and away in a two-year period. England thus began to play a more even number of series against their leading Test opponents, even if they retained the freedom to play more matches against some teams such as Australia.† Under the FTP spanning 2023–27, England have arranged four five-match series against Australia and India, while proposing to play only 23 Tests in nine series against other sides (before a one-off Test against Zimbabwe in 2025 was added later).

---

* At the World Cup in 2003, the England players, largely on their own initiative but ultimately backed by their board, refused to play a group match against Zimbabwe in Harare, citing security concerns. The legitimacy of these concerns was rejected by ICC and $3.5 million was withheld from the ECB's share of distributed funds arising out of the tournament.
† Between May 2001 and December 2022, England played the following number of Test series against each opponent: Australia 12, India 12, New Zealand 11, West Indies 11, Sri Lanka 10, Pakistan 10, South Africa 9, Bangladesh 5, Ireland 1 and Zimbabwe 1.

Lengths of England's Overseas Test Series

The lengths of England Test series vary according to the strength and status of the opposition. England have generally played more matches against Australia, South Africa, West Indies and India, though these things are relative: they have not played five Tests in South Africa since 2004–05 or more than three Tests in the West Indies since 2008–09. They have never signed up to a series of more than three Tests against anyone else, although a fourth match was arranged on the 1929–30 tour of New Zealand when rain badly affected an earlier game in the series.

Destination	First Test tour	Scheduled matches in a series*				
		1–2	3	4	5	6
Australia	1876–77	6**	2	2	29	3**
South Africa	1888–89	3**	1	3	13	
West Indies	1929–30		3	5+	9+	
India	1933–34	2	4	2	7	1
New Zealand	1929–30	10	11++			
Pakistan/UAE	1961–62		11			
Sri Lanka	1981–82	4	4			
Bangladesh	2003–04	3				
Zimbabwe	1996–97	1				

*Number of matches in the original schedule
**Only one Test was played in Australia in 1878–79 because a second match, in Sydney, was cancelled following a riot during a state match at the SCG. Only two Tests were played in South Africa in 1898–99 because the hosts were unable to raise a team for a planned match in Port Elizabeth. Six Tests were scheduled in 1970–71, but when one match in Melbourne was completely lost to rain a replacement fixture was added (in effect a seventh Test).
+In the West Indies, two series scheduled for five matches actually saw only four played owing to the loss of the fixture in Guyana (to political considerations in 1980–81 and to rain in 1989–90); another two series, also scheduled for five matches, saw an extra, sixth game put on after the early abandonments of a Test in Jamaica in 1997–98 owing to a poor pitch, and a Test in Antigua in 2008–09 because of a dangerous outfield.
++A fourth match was arranged in 1929–30 when rain badly affected an earlier Test in the series.

During the days when gate receipts were the principal source of income, tours were a financially precarious business. Whole days of play – whole matches – could be lost to bad weather, and when that happened not only ticket sales were lost but also all the money that might be earned from catering, and the like. Those charged with managing tours lived in a constant state of anxiety and this led them to pack the itinerary with fixtures, on the basis that the more matches they arranged, the greater the scope for profit – or the avoidance of losses. There was a fine art to constructing a good fixture list: a touring side needed to play in the places where the local population had a desire to see them play and the money to pay for it.

Only once broadcasters in the 1990s began to pay significant sums up front to screen ever more Tests and ODIs did the pressure on cramming in 'side' matches ease. Broadcasters had no interest in these games, which became simply warm-ups for the main events; if they happened to generate additional funds, that was a bonus.* Their decline was precipitous: on the tour of Australia in 1990–91, England played 15 non-international fixtures (in addition to five Tests and eight ODIs), but by the time they toured there in 2017–18 the number of games additional to five Tests, five ODIs and two T20s had shrunk to four.

Under the old system, simply for a tour to take place required money to be advanced to cover costs until such time as the match revenue started coming in. This might come from a variety of sources. The pioneering first tour by an English team to North America in 1859–60 was chiefly organised by W. P.

---

* The notion that the revenue from broadcasting contracts was rock-solid was tested by the coronavirus pandemic in 2020–21. In order not to lose this income, national boards had to find ways to continue staging internationals in a safe environment. Initially, the only way this could be done to the satisfaction of governments was to play matches behind closed doors within a carefully constructed bio-secure bubble to protect players, coaches, match officials and other key personnel. It was an expensive course of action, but it enabled the ECB and other boards to fulfil their contractual obligations with media rights holders. Had a pandemic in the pre-broadcast era led to spectators being barred from entering venues, financially everything would have been lost; no tour would have been viable.

Pickering, a former Surrey player who had settled in Montreal; the tour was able to go ahead because he secured financial guarantees for certain matches to be played, for example £500 from a Mr Waller for two fixtures in New York. The first tour of Australia in 1861–62 was underwritten by Spiers and Pond, a catering firm with interests in Melbourne and the city's surrounding goldfields. James Lillywhite's tour of Australia in 1876–77, which involved what are regarded as the first Test matches, was financed by Arthur Hobgen and Charles Stride of Chichester, Lillywhite's home town. Lillywhite later took on the management of four subsequent tours of Australia in partnership with two Nottinghamshire players, Alfred Shaw and Arthur Shrewsbury, a rare case of participating players being closely involved in the financing of a tour.*

Drawing on Shaw's expertise as manager, Lord Sheffield subsequently sponsored an entire seven-month tour of Australia on his own (and might have turned a profit had he not paid W. G. Grace, the world's most famous cricketer, £3,000 to captain the team). When Pelham Warner's team toured South Africa in 1905–06, they did not play matches in Rhodesia precisely because Rhodesia could not raise the necessary financial guarantee. It was a promise from the Australian board of a minimum £10,000 that enabled the 1907–08 tour of Australia to proceed.

The Marylebone Cricket Club, having taken over the regular organisation of major England tours in the early 1900s, created a Foreign Tours fund to cover the costs of trips until such time as it received the 50 per cent share of gate receipts that became the standard cut for such ventures. At a farewell dinner to the team that set out for Australia in 1924–25, Lord Harris, the MCC's treasurer and presiding force, stated that the club had

---

* Shrewsbury took a full part as a player in all four tours, but Lillywhite and Shaw were more selective: Lillywhite appeared only in minor matches, while Shaw played a full part in the first tour, then appeared only in minor matches during the second and third. He stayed in Nottingham for the final tour to manage affairs from home.

put up £16,000 to ensure the tour went ahead, 'and took the risks of the gates failing to recoup them [the funds]'.

By this stage, the risks attached to an Australian tour were actually not that high, such was the draw of Anglo-Australian contests and so great were the attendances at the Tests, which were played to a finish and could last many days; tours to other places generally drew much smaller crowds and were financially less certain enterprises. Early English tours of South Africa were supported by local shipping and railway magnates such as Donald Currie and James Logan, before the fledgling South African Cricket Association acted as guarantor, but even they expected some sort of return. With gold-mining on the Rand temporarily stalled at the time of the second English tour of South Africa in 1891–92, Currie declined to subsidise the team's travel and, finding themselves indebted before the first gate money came in, Walter Read, the captain, and Edwin Ash, a Cape Colony businessman, turned to Logan for financial assistance. Logan advanced in the region of £750–£1,000 for a 'small turn of 7–8 per cent interest', but the tour lost money and, as it reached its end, Logan, unable to recover his money, turned to Cape Town's Supreme Court. Read and Ash were arrested and only released in the nick of time to join the ship home. A court case in June 1893 duly found against them.

The funds raised by SACA were modest, and the association would telegraph MCC asking that the English touring party contain enough amateurs to keep down the costs of funding the English professionals. When England first toured New Zealand to play Test matches, MCC agreed the 14-man party would contain six professionals, paid for by the club, and also met a request that Duleepsinhji, Ranjitsinhji's nephew and one of the best batsmen in county cricket, as well as Frank Woolley would be included as their presence was sure to add to the gate.

Early Test tours of the West Indies operated on similar lines. A. C. O'Dowd of British Guiana was a key backer of the two tours before the Second World War, but every effort was made to keep costs down. Bob Wyatt, England's amateur captain in 1934–35, typically received around £100–£125 in tour expenses, but on this occasion was initially told there would be no expenses at all; eventually he managed to negotiate himself £25. Unsurprisingly, the less generous the expenses, the lower the quality of the amateur players prepared to sign up. Many amateurs ended up significantly out of pocket on the tours they did go on.

Bhupinder Singh, the Maharajah of Patiala, financed an English tour of India in 1926–27 that spanned six months and paved the way for India's elevation to Test status shortly afterwards. As so often, the support came at a price for the English cricketers, who were worked ferociously hard on and off the field. They fulfilled 34 mainly two-day fixtures and were required to attend numerous social functions, while travelling between venues by bus, boat and ill-ventilated trains. With exhaustion taking hold, reinforcements were summoned as a matter of necessity. The idea that a blank day on tour cost the organisers money also informed the planning of England's first Test tour of India seven years later when again they got through 34 matches. The only time they were beaten came after a night journey from Calcutta.

When England toured India and Pakistan in 1961–62 for eight Tests, the most undertaken in one winter to that point, MCC were actually guaranteed £6,000 per Test, plus £1,500 for all but one of the three-day 'side' games, but this may have been a satisfactory arrangement for the host boards as the Tests drew attendances that totalled 1.2 million. When the D'Oliveira Affair led to the cancellation of a series in South Africa and a replacement tour was sought, potential hosts were asked to put up £20,000 as guarantee. India baulked at the sum, but not Pakistan, and as a result Colin Cowdrey led a team there for three Tests. When the final Test in Karachi was abandoned on the third morning owing to rioting, tour manager Les Ames was handed a cheque for £10,000 as the remainder of the guarantee.

Before MCC took over, a total of 20 English tours of significance took place between 1859–60 and 1901–02. Almost all had Australia or South Africa as their principal destination and between them they did an enormous amount of invaluable exploratory work, establishing connections with local cricket clubs in major cities and towns, finding out which places could support worthwhile fixtures and which ones could not. This reconnaissance was often undertaken in extremely taxing conditions, at a time when ocean voyages were brutally hard and railway routes were still being established. Some journeys taken by horse-drawn carriage could be measured in days rather than hours. Only on the ninth tour of Australia in 1886–87 was it possible to travel between Melbourne and Adelaide by train rather than boat, cutting a journey that used to take 50 hours to around 28 hours.

These tours established that North America was not financially worthwhile; the sort of profits seen on the 1859–60 tour – which led to the players taking away £90 per man against an initial promise of £50 – were not repeated on later visits, partly because of the disruption caused by the American Civil War of the 1860s. Nobody went there again in the hope of making serious money after Lillywhite, Shaw and Shrewsbury only just covered their costs in 1881–82, having originally hoped to clear £1,200.

Similarly, five teams, having reached the south-eastern coast of Australia, sailed across the Tasman Sea to New Zealand, but rarely came back richer. They found some cricket grounds lacking proper enclosure, so it was difficult to charge admission, while other places simply lacked sufficient enthusiasm for the game (or for their visitors). After Lillywhite's team turned up at Greymouth and took just £32 on the first day, James Southerton ruefully reflected: 'A nice sum to come 14,000 miles for.' So, by the end of this period, it was clear that Australia was the prized destination, both as a cricketing challenge and a financial opportunity. Nowhere else came close on either front.

Generally these early tours made profits, sometimes very

good ones, and generally the players were well rewarded through fixed tour fees agreed in advance plus bonuses and occasional spin-offs such as selling cricket kit they took with them. The sheer frequency of the visits – on average, once every three years to Australia – was evidence of their success. It was not uncommon for cricketers to turn down an invitation to tour – after all, a trip to Australia meant seven months away from home and one to South Africa at least four months – but plenty went back for more. William Caffyn of Surrey went on each of the three tours between 1859–60 and 1863–64. Johnny Briggs, the Lancashire all-rounder, made seven Test tours in the space of 14 years and George Ulyett of Yorkshire six in 13 years. Briggs noted that on his final trip in 1897–98, the Melbourne Cricket Club were more generous than their Sydney counterparts and co-organisers, Melbourne paying the Englishmen's travel expenses as well as giving each man a £25 gratuity.

Good organisation was an absolute requirement if things were to run smoothly: reliable men were needed to collect gate money (not all *were* reliable: 'The amount taken never comes up to the assumed number of people in the ground,' Southerton grumbled), as well as a capable ground agent to arrange fixtures, liaise with the locals and deal with problems as they arose. W. P. Pickering conducted the 1859–60 party through their travels, paying all expenses along the way. In 1873–74 W. G. Grace was initially stuck with a chancer called William Biddle, a vice-president of the Melbourne club. The son of a London fishmonger, Biddle headed to Victoria in the 1850s too late to catch the gold rush, and later failed as a victualler. His attempts to put together a fixture list for Grace's team were shambolic.

Jack Conway, sometimes described as the father of Australian cricket, worked closely with Lillywhite on his first tour, then with the Australians on a hugely profitable tour of England in 1878, and two of the tours Lillywhite arranged with Shaw and Shrewsbury. 'If you bring a strong eleven', wrote Conway ahead of the 1881–82 tour, 'there is a cartload of money waiting for you.' Conway drove such a hard financial bargain on behalf of the 1884–85 side that some of the Australians refused to play against them in protest at their own, inferior terms. In an attempt to take the heat out of the situation, Lillywhite removed Conway from his post midway through the tour. Major Ben Wardill of the Melbourne club and Philip Sheridan of the Sydney Cricket Ground Trust escorted Andrew Stoddart and his players throughout England's tour of 1894–95, which generated the biggest profits in more than 30 years.

Even with the involvement of a ground agent, an itinerary could remain fluid: the 1861–62 team were making preparations to return home when they were offered £100 per man (the equivalent of £13,000 today) to stay on in Australia an extra four weeks and play additional matches. Eager for home, they declined. Lillywhite's team were kept waiting until they landed in Adelaide to discover their programme, and even then found that Joseph Bennett, the original ground agent before Conway got more involved, had only three fixtures finalised. Admittedly, matters were confused by plans for a rival tour under E. M. Grace, W. G.'s elder brother, which eventually fell through. Arrangements remained haphazard, and the tour involved only 68 days of cricket in a stay in Australia and New Zealand of almost six months. Similarly, it was only when Pelham Warner and his team arrived in South Africa in 1905–06 that they discovered what their fixture list looked like. It was, frankly, a mess, and remained as such.

Once a tour was confirmed, local committees would contact the main organisers – in the case of Australia, usually the authorities in Melbourne and Sydney – and make a financial offer to stage a fixture. Once the bid was accepted and a deposit placed, the committee would set about recouping its investment through ticket sales and selling 'pitches' inside the ground to local caterers, victuallers and the like. On the very first tour of Australia, Bathurst, a gold rush town over the Blue Mountains west of Sydney, paid £500 to host the English team. They sought to raise this sum through local pledges, publicans purchasing booths at the ground and match tickets which went on sale at a local hotel; even though the third and final day of the game was obliterated by rain, the honorary treasurer of the match committee announced a surplus of £100–£160, which was passed to charity.

Tamworth in northern New South Wales was less fortunate when it hosted Ivo Bligh's team in 1882–83. In order to fence off the playing area and charge admission, it was decided to relocate the match to the local racecourse, where a rudimentary matting pitch was put down, but no sooner had the players gone onto the field than it started to rain and did not let up for two days. The match was abandoned without a ball bowled. How much was recovered of the £200 Tamworth paid to stage the fixture is not known, but the organisers may have been saved by a large crowd having gathered inside the ground by the time of the appointed start.

When Euroa hosted the English team of 1950–51 for a two-day fixture against a Victoria Country Districts which was spoiled by rain, English journalist Bruce Harris noted:

> It is terribly hard on these small communities when an unreliable climate like that of Australia wrecks all the hopes, cricketing, social and financial, which had been cherished for months ... Quite often the committeemen give a hand with the ground preparations, their wives look after the catering and waiting, there are sub-committees running receptions and dances. Two days' rain, the whole things goes phut and the local cricketers have to make up the loss somehow.

Small up-country towns could muster quite large crowds because people would come considerable distances – by train, carriage or even on foot – to catch a glimpse of 'very England'. Candelo in southern New South Wales had a population of only 200, but its ambitious offer of £300 to play host to an English team in the 1880s was fully justified when on the day seemingly everyone from 15 miles around descended on the ground. It was not necessary to search far for an explanation. There was, according to the historian Richard Cashman, 'a great dearth of leisure facilities in the early days of the colonies and, at the same time, there was a great thirst for leisure because of the harshness of existence and the rigours of work'. Not every story ended in success. When Gawler, north of Adelaide, staged the opening fixture proper of the 1894–95 tour, a combined attendance of 1,500 across two days generated insufficient revenue to cover costs. The venue never staged another match of importance.

This system also rarely gave proper consideration to the demands made of the visiting players, who would be sent up-country to play hopelessly weak opposition, at a cricket ground barely fit for purpose, in a town with inadequate facilities and connected by questionable means of transport. W. G. Grace recounted how on his first tour of Australia, 'for the sake of a few pounds', his team were obliged to play at Kadina in the Yorke Peninsula rather than Adelaide; Kadina, in a rich copper mining district, was 100 miles from Adelaide by coach, of which 70 miles were over bush track, and the ground on which the match was played was 'covered with small stones'.

What quickly became clear was the enormous economic benefit of staging matches over holiday periods such as Christmas and New Year, when the public had time to attend sporting events and the social functions that attached to them. The very first match played by an English team in Australia began on New Year's Day 1862 and proved such an attraction that it enabled tour sponsors Spiers and Pond to cover the entire costs of the tour through one fixture alone. When an English tour came to town, it became common to declare a local public holiday on the day of the game and for extra transport to be laid on, with discounted fares to help boost attendances.

During England's first Test tour of India in 1933–34, Delhi's government shut down during the Viceroy's XI match, and the Governor of Bombay declared a public holiday to coincide with the opening day of the first Test, a game which attracted an estimated overall attendance of 100,000. Public holidays coinciding with the visit of English teams were also routinely granted around the West Indian territories. The investiture of Grantley Adams as Barbados's first premier in 1954 took place early in the day in order to prevent a clash with the island's match against MCC. In Trinidad, oil employees were given two half-day holidays during a Test match on the island.

The biggest early lesson was that, for all the adventuring further afield, the real financial riches lay in the big cities. On Lillywhite's tour, it was calculated that the three matches in Sydney generated profits of £3,000 and the three in Melbourne £2,500, against an overall profit for a tour encompassing 23 fixtures of £4,000. This gradually led to a winnowing of the more logistically taxing up-country trips: during the 1884–85 tour, the English team played 22 matches outside the major centres of Melbourne, Sydney and Adelaide, but by the end of the century this number had more than halved.

Getting rid of these games completely took far longer. It was also established that an English tour could sustain two Tests each in Melbourne and Sydney and one in Adelaide, and this remained the pattern until the late 1920s. The standard of cricket was also higher in the big cities: only in Melbourne, Sydney and Adelaide, and then Brisbane from the mid-1890s, could strong enough local sides be assembled to challenge the touring team on the equal terms of 11 versus 11; elsewhere the opposition would typically consist of anything from 15 to 22 players. A similar pattern featured on tours of South Africa, with Cape Town, Johannesburg and to a lesser extent Port Elizabeth the strongholds.

Half a century of exploration had established that English cricket tours of Australia – and to a lesser extent South Africa – were economically viable, provided they incorporated visits to certain key centres, were carefully planned and well run. By no means could these requirements be taken for granted. The time was ripe for things to be put on a more professional basis.

CHAPTER 4

How MCC Ran Tours

The exploitation of players

MCC took over the running of major tours because there was a growing demand for a centralised body to liaise with the authorities overseas and agree a schedule and the terms under which it would function, as well as coordinate selection. A number of episodes had brought matters to a head, among them the farcical situation of two English teams touring Australia at the same time in the winter of 1887–88, to the detriment of all concerned, and Archie MacLaren hastily assembling a team to go there in 1901–02 when MCC was already starting to explore the possibility of sending a team for the first time.

In 1898 a board of control had been set up to govern home Tests, and MCC was strongly represented on it, so it was inevitable that the management of tours would be similarly consolidated.* The Australians in particular wanted clarity about plans for incoming tours and who they should best deal with, while English players and administrators felt they were

---

* The creation of an Australian Board of Control for International Cricket in May 1905 served a similar purpose in Australia of transferring power from players to a central group of administrators.

not getting as much financially out of tours of Australia as the Australians were getting out of tours of England. Lord Hawke, the presiding force at Yorkshire, responded to MacLaren's initiative by refusing to release George Hirst and Wilfred Rhodes, two of England's best bowlers, for his tour, Hawke explaining that he 'did not see why our players should go out merely to put money into the hands of the Melbourne club'.

Much of the groundwork for subsequent tours came to be laid by a string of long-serving MCC secretaries, who would – with varying degrees of competence and enthusiasm – inform players of selection, brief captains before departure and stay in touch with captains and managers by cable, airmail letter or whatever means were available.* 'The success of a tour depends, to a very large extent, upon the preliminary arrangements at headquarters,' wrote Frederick Toone, who managed three tours of Australia, in 1930.

Whether the Tests were at home or abroad, there was a self-serving element to the MCC takeover; it was essentially an upper-class coup to run the game for and on behalf of its own. Eventually, the club fell irreconcilably out of step with the times, but clung on to power for an extraordinarily long period.

E. M. Wellings, in his book on the 1950–51 tour of Australia, put forward a cogent argument for ending MCC's authority.

At present they, a private club, are solely responsible for sending teams abroad. It is the MCC that those teams represent. They take the title England only when playing Test matches. But abroad those teams are always regarded as representing England. We think of the MCC playing Victoria. The Australians do not. To them the match is Victoria v England. It is billed as such, and those are the two titles which appear

---

* Five secretaries of the club spanned the period during which MCC managed England tours: Francis Lacey (in post 1898–1926), William Findlay (1926–36), Rowan Rait Kerr (1936–52), Ronnie Aird (1952–62) and Billy Griffith (1962–74).

on the scoreboard. It is time the counties, who provide the players, took over the control of tours ... it is fantastic that these events [England–Australia Tests] are so haphazardly run on our side.

He added: 'If we are to compete we must ... eliminate nineteenth-century ideas and prejudices.'

Yet it took until 1968 for MCC's grip to be formally broken (although to an extent the club influenced affairs beyond that point for some time). That it took the wider English game so long was testimony to the control exercised by what Len Hutton, the first professional since the 1880s to captain England, called the 'inner circle': steered by such *éminences grises* as Lord Harris, Pelham Warner and Gubby Allen – directing policy but with one aim above all others, to perpetuate and protect the club's influence.

One reason Bodyline created such a bitter legacy was because it took this 'inner circle' so long to disentangle itself from responsibility for what had happened. Some 20 years after the event, Hutton found 'the spectre of Bodyline still haunted the corridors of power.' (Hutton's own background could hardly have been further removed from those privileged members of the inner circle: brought up in an austere Moravian community in Fulneck village, near Pudsey, he left school at 15 to join his father at a local building firm while continuing his apprenticeship as a Yorkshire cricketer.)

Wellings's views were widely shared by the popular press in the post-war years. Frank Rostron delivered a stinging rebuke to MCC in the *Daily Express* in October 1955, calling for the institution to reform itself if it was to be truly representative of North as well as South, and fill the role of a national governing body.

How much MCC materially improved matters beyond the early organisation and underwriting phase is a moot point; the day-to-day running of tours was often sketchy at best. MCC inherited an extremely advantageous blueprint as to how to arrange a tour of Australia and, to a lesser extent, South Africa. The places to go and the places to avoid were already mapped out. This was evident from MCC sticking to tried and trusted venues on the first three Test tours of Australia it ran. The only new territory explored was Perth, the first port of call in 1907–08: the team played a three-day match there before sailing on to the customary starting point of Adelaide; even then, several members of the touring party did not even leave the boat for that game.

In his published account of the first of these tours in 1903–04, Pelham Warner, the captain, who had personally championed the idea of MCC taking control of major tours, recounted the praise his team received for playing a match in Brisbane, then still an emerging cricketing location, but English teams had actually been going there for more than 20 years. Andrew Stoddart's two touring sides both played first-class matches there in the 1890s. Warner complained that matches against 'odds' – opposition sides made up of more than 11 players, as a means of balancing up the respective strengths of the two teams – were 'a weariness of the flesh' and doubted whether they did much good locally; 'nothing is more tiring, or more detrimental to success against strong antagonists, than match after match against inferior fifteens and eighteens.' (See table on pages 253–55.)

But these games remained a common feature on MCC-managed England Test tours until the Second World War, even when Warner might have had influence in the matter during spells as tour selector and tour manager and been in a position to halt the practice. As late as 1970–71, another captain, Ray Illingworth, was complaining about them as 'utterly meaningless', while appreciating that spectators had often travelled 100 miles or more and were entitled 'to their only glimpse of the touring side in action and the only chance they get in a year or more to see first-class cricketers play'.

The structure of MCC tours was often chaotic and some-times bizarre: on the 1903–04 tour there was only a one-day gap between the fourth and fifth Tests, and part of that time was spent travelling overnight between Sydney and Melbourne, while the tour of South Africa in 1905–06 (also captained by Warner) saw the last four Tests played within the space of 28 days following a two-month gap since the first match of the series. Towards the end of Hutton's tour of the West Indies, the team were required to play a five-day match against Trinidad ahead of a six-day Test match on the island, with only a one-day gap between. When Charles Palmer belatedly asked the local authorities if the island game could be kept to four days, he was told it was too late as tickets for day five had already been sold. With the pitches in perfect conditions for batting (another means by which revenues could be protected), there was next to no chance of games finishing early.

By the time responsibility passed to the newly created Test and County Cricket Board in the late 1960s, international cricket was in crisis. Attendances were falling and players scandalously underpaid. It would take another ten years for the consequences of such maladministration by the MCC and other national governing bodies to play out, but the warning signs were long there. From the start of MCC's involvement, there were no obvious signs of greater efficiency: the big tours of Australia continued to be plagued by difficulties in getting the best players to agree to travel and schedules continued to chop and change. The number of fixtures on an Australia tour crept up, and when a New Zealand leg was tacked onto the end still nothing was done to cut back on the less important, financially marginal fixtures. MCC feebly justified the bloated tour programmes it agreed with host boards by arguing that it had a duty to spread the game's gospel, almost out of fealty to the British imperial mission, but the approach of maxim-ising the number of 'earning' days on tour – however thin the returns – directly hindered England's chances of winning

Test matches and placed intolerable strains on the players on and off the field.

MCC's tight control of the purse strings was one of the most significant aspects of the club's takeover and certainly not to the financial benefit of the players. Ahead of the very first tour of Australia run by MCC, professionals such as Len Braund, George Hirst, Wilfred Rhodes and Johnny Tyldesley expressed dissatisfaction with the tour fees that were being offered, but were advised that there was nothing they could do and they should accept; eventually, with reluctance, they agreed. Tour fees for professional players stagnated and expenses for professionals and amateurs alike were closely monitored, neither of which made touring more attractive. It was almost a condition of touring life that the players lived frugally simply to keep within their modest daily allowances and return home with some of their tour fee intact.

Even so, MCC failed to make a profit on the 1903–04 or 1911–12 tours, despite its cabled request in advance of the first of these tours for 50 per cent of the gate receipts being met (thereby mirroring the arrangement for Australian teams coming to England). Warner's book on the 1903-04 tour, based on articles he wrote for *The Sportsman* and the *Westminster Gazette*, reads in parts like a business report to his MCC masters. Once it became clear it would finish in the red, he tried to make light of it: 'As regards the loss sustained, that was scarcely germane, and they [the tour party] did not grieve because the financial result had not been profitable.'

He wrote a similar account of the 1911–12 tour, for which he was also appointed captain, although he missed the Tests through illness and spent most of his time as observer. This time he concluded: 'Under the terms at present offered by the Australians it is quite impossible for an English team to make ends meet. In future we must ask for half the gross gate.' Warner estimated the loss to rain of a Saturday gate during a match against New South Wales in Sydney at £600, roughly equivalent to the overall loss on the tour.* MCC were indeed granted half the gross gate on the next tour after the First World War, and with interest especially high after a break for war the estimated costs of £16,000 had been covered by the time of the third of the five Tests.

Plenty of managers and captains on later tours would fret over gate takings in the same way, and constantly worry about running costs and returning a surplus to the counties. In 1950–51, MCC agreed with the Australian board a new ruse to reduce the number of non-remunerative days by deploying Sundays – at that time a strictly non-playing day in Australia, as it was in England – as travel days. 'We had three or four journeys on Sundays, the one day in the week where we could pull ourselves together and do some personal organising,' bemoaned Bruce Harris of the *Evening Standard*.

When rain washed out the Saturday of the opening Test in Brisbane it was to the grief of Jack Nash, joint tour manager and effectively treasurer, because Saturdays were always the best chance of a full house. More bad tidings came down the line: the Saturday of the final Test in Melbourne was also lost. This tour also saw many more internal flights than previously, which spared the players many exhausting journeys, but one of the upshots was that more nights were spent in hotels and fewer on trains – at greater cost – and the customary fixture list was simply shoe-horned into a shorter time frame. The consequence was that MCC made £3,842 on the tour compared to £17,505 on the previous visit to Australia in 1946–47, and a few months later the club conveyed the gloomy news to the first-class counties that they would be receiving nothing by way

---

* Even outside Tests, matches in Sydney and Melbourne between 1897–98 and 1954–55 could generate attendances in excess of 50,000 and highly lucrative gates. The fixture against an Australian XI, viewed as almost another Test, drew 109,501 in 1932–33 and 91,923 in 1946–47, both at Melbourne. Then came the decline: by 1965–66 no match outside the Tests drew 40,000; by 1974–75 none mustered 30,000; and in 1982–83 the best gate just crept over 15,000.

of distribution. By way of further justification, MCC referenced losses and charges totalling £3,592 from recent tours of the West Indies and South Africa.

The impression of an organisation out of its depth was reinforced by Geoffrey Howard, manager of the 1954–55 tour of Australia, reaching Perth, the first port of call, to discover that Ronnie Aird, the MCC secretary, had failed to advance any money, so that until the early shares of gate receipts came in, there was no means of funding the team's running costs. Aird actually spent much of the winter travelling in New Zealand and Australia, watching some of the cricket, so he was illplaced to address some of Howard's concerns. (It became a convention that MCC presidents and secretaries would pay a visit on major England tours, 'to meet people, form relationships, discuss cricketing developments and so forth', but this was more usually in the days of air travel and would be confined to one city.)

Howard set up a personal account and negotiated an overdraft, which at one point rose to £20,000. 'I don't think MCC knew till I got back that they hadn't made any provision,' he recalled. 'How much easier I would have found it,' he went on, 'if MCC had provided me with the two things I didn't have – help and money.' Frank Tyson was a playing member of that side and on two subsequent tours in the 1950s: 'Touring teams economised and were expected to return a profit to headquarters,' he noted; 'nor did teams always stay at the best hotels – their cost was a factor to be considered.'

Such was the importance of an accurate oversight of the money that some tours had two managerial figures, one to look after the cricketing side of things and liaise with the local cricket authorities, the other to handle the books – as happened when Jack Nash acted as treasurer in 1950–51. Brigadier Mike Green, who worked alongside Nash on that tour, recalled that for many years a manager carried with him a heavy wooden box in which was kept all the paperwork. Managers were also expected to act as backstops to the captain, sweeping up letters and writing stereotyped replies for him to sign.

Things were not always that well thought through. Alec Bedser's appointment as assistant manager in Australia in 1962–63 was intended as a means of having on hand an experienced former Test cricketer to coach and guide the players, and as such was something of an innovation, but his position was undermined by the extraordinary choice of Bernard Fitzalan-Howard, the Duke of Norfolk, as overall manager. The duke was a member of the MCC committee and had offered his service once it transpired that Billy Griffith, the club secretary, would be unable to act as manager as intended, because he needed to remain at Lord's to oversee the changes necessitated by the long-overdue abolition of amateur status.

The duke, described by one travelling reporter as a 'portly, florid aristocrat', knew nothing about anything as vulgar as keeping accounts, with the result that Bedser had to take over, getting up at 6 a.m. to deal with paperwork before attending to his cricket duties. 'Books had to be kept and gate receipts checked,' Bedser wrote. 'I had a wry smile at the end of the tour when I read [in the newspapers] the inevitable criticism that I should have devoted more time to the actual cricket and less to other chores.' Fred Trueman, England's premier fast bowler, whose background was somewhat earthier than his lordship's, said of the duke, 'he had no track record or qualifications suited to the job.' He was not even able to stay for the whole tour, returning home for a month and Griffith flying out briefly in his stead.

Purely as an ambassador, however, the duke was a great success. He was certainly an improvement on Tom Pearce, who had combined a long career working in the wine trade with playing for and captaining Essex, and the previous winter had been in charge of a tour of India, Pakistan and Ceylon. 'He was hopeless,' remembered John Murray, one of the players. 'Six and a half months in India with no decent hotels. He couldn't organise.' Another member of the team, Bob Barber, recalled: 'He was incompetent and wasn't fit to be a manager.'

That there should have been a loss on the first post-war South Africa tour in 1948–49 was a surprise; George Mann's team attracted what were unprecedented crowds for South African cricket and receipts topped £90,000. It highlighted the flaws in the way England's overseas assignments were financially arranged. In his tour report, Green recommended that things should be changed so that MCC took 50 per cent of the outer gate and paid all expenses out of that (a system that had enabled the Australians to make a good profit from touring England in 1948, and which Green believed would have turned MCC a good profit in South Africa). 'I fear some of the professionals started talking about what they were paid when compared with players visiting England, and that it did not seem fair that they were not given more, or a percentage of the profits,' he wrote. 'Certain sections of the press found this a good subject for comment, and started a campaign for more pay for the English players.' As a result, shortly before the final Test match, the South African Cricket Association came up with an extra £75 per man.

Fundamentally, though, nothing changed. When the team went to the Caribbean under Len Hutton five years later, the West Indies board paid all the expenses and took all the profits, but also called all the shots – and the players paid the price. 'The West Indies Board of Control virtually exercises control of the MCC cricketer from first to last,' Alex Bannister wrote in *Cricket Cauldron*: '[It] pays the wages and expenses of the visiting players, makes all travel and hotel arrangements, takes whatever profit the tour brings in or stands any loss. And, doing all these things, they largely dictate the terms.'

Bannister pointed out that the custom of the hosts being responsible for financial matters was a hangover from the time when countries like South Africa and West Indies had to persuade MCC to send out missionary teams, which MCC was prepared to do as long as the club did not incur a loss. But the possibility of a loss had become much more remote. 'Surely, then,' Bannister concluded, 'the MCC should take a firmer line in the tour itinerary and arrangements?'

In an editorial in *Wisden* in 1955, Norman Preston picked up on the problems of the West Indies tour and the broader issue of inequitable revenues. He produced figures which showed that Test profits from tours to England in the nine seasons since the war had amount to £746,500, of which English cricket received £465,900 and the visitors £280,600 (their share varying depending to how much money was generated; Australia received almost half, other countries around a quarter). 'While the British public contribute freely to the coffers of visiting teams', Preston wrote, 'MCC have received scant reward from many of their overseas tours; and when our men are subject to the treatment they received in the West Indies, where there is no profit for the visitors, one begins to wonder whether some of these tours are worthwhile from an English cricket point of view.'

It was telling that the players were now bold enough to speak out about the meagreness of their rewards. Trevor Bailey had just completed the West Indies tour as Hutton's vice-captain when he published *Playing to Win*. In it he provided a blunt assessment of the way MCC handled major tours, including, in the words of his biographer Jack Bailey, 'pertinent, though often critical, observations which drew attention to organisational deficiencies in tour arrangements generally and MCC's part in them particularly ... [and] the treatment of the professional cricketers taking part in tours, and the financial arrangements and the disadvantages he felt English cricket was placed under by them'.

Trevor Bailey's opinions were all the more powerful for him being an amateur, and therefore having less to directly gain from speaking as he did – though he was not beyond arguing the amateur cause either. He had been instrumental in successfully lobbying for an increase in the amateur allowance in Australia in 1950–51. Soon after the book appeared, Hutton was unavailable through ill health to lead England at home to Pakistan, and Bailey might have been seen as the natural choice to act as stand-in, but he was overlooked in favour of David Sheppard, a clear indication of how badly his comments had been received in the corridors of power.

The following winter in Australia, not only was he no longer vice-captain, but he was also not even a member of the tour selection group, despite his seniority. Like many players of his and other generations, Bailey was to fall foul of the inner circle, and in particular Gubby Allen, who since first captaining England in the 1930s had been one of the most influential voices inside the MCC committee room. As chairman of selectors from 1955 to 1961 Allen was in a position to make sure Bailey was never promoted to the national captaincy and – as we shall see – would, as president and treasurer of the club, assume an even stronger influence over MCC affairs while maintaining a close involvement in, and not always benign influence upon, the selection of England teams well into the 1970s – beyond the point at which MCC formally relinquished control of tours.*

The players were not deterred, however. In Australia, Hutton as captain, in a speech at an Australian board dinner, made a spiky reference to the stark contrast between the board's substantial profits and the players' modest earnings.

Perhaps in an effort to head off further dissent, MCC announced while Peter May's party were on their way to Australia in 1958–59 that it was seeking to shorten future tours, not that it specified which matches should be sacrificed for this

---

* The players were not the only ones to grumble over the terms of their tour fees. Geoffrey Howard was deducted his salary as Lancashire secretary for the time he was away managing the tour of India in 1951–52, meaning that after tax he made £50. 'Honour? Glory? Doubtful. Six months away from home – certain!' he wrote in a letter to his family.

to happen. In a rare admission, MCC accepted that those who played for England came under considerable strain and were separated from their families for long periods, and that, in the interests of player welfare and the maintenance of standards in county and international cricket, 'the duration of the longer MCC tours must be curtailed.' Over the next few years, tours did become slightly shorter, but the reduction was essentially down to plane travel replacing boats, with the England team making their long-haul journeys exclusively by air from 1963 onwards. The number of matches did not come down in the way suggested; indeed, on the 1962–63 and 1965–66 tours of Australia and New Zealand, the number of fixtures actually went up to 32, a figure exceeded on only two earlier England tours.*

With more Tests played by more teams after the Second World War, with more of a nationalistic mindset, international cricket became increasingly defensive. Trevor Bailey, nicknamed 'Barnacle' for his tenacious occupation of the crease, was far from alone in his results-first mentality. Hutton and May received frequent requests, bordering on demands, from the MCC hierarchy for their England teams to play in an enterprising manner, but remained resolutely pragmatic in outlook. After all, what had Gubby Allen and Freddie Brown ever won when they were England captains? They might have been well received as leaders in Australia, but both lost, as did Allen in the West Indies. Perhaps the players might have played brighter cricket had they been better rewarded, but as administrators Allen and Brown, and their ilk, showed no interest in improving the lot of the players under them. On the contrary, they pointedly treated the ranks of professionals like serfs, and if anyone such as Bailey had the temerity to complain, retribution was swift and merciless.

---

* The 1884–85 side played 34 matches in Egypt and Australia and the 1933–34 side 34 matches in India.

Unsurprisingly, the trenchant approach to play had a deleterious effect on attendances. The average daily gates for the Ashes series in England in 1968 and in Australia in 1970–71 were the lowest in more than 50 years, and in England in 1972 they fell lower still to just 12,819.

As a result, offering a visiting team 50 per cent of receipts became less viable, hence the switch to guaranteed sums, which in the case of the 1972 Australians amounted to just £12,000. Many of these terms were hardly advantageous, and when England received £30,000 for touring Australia in 1979–80 for three Tests and what turned out to be nine ODIs, Geoff Boycott, who had been touring with England for 15 years, claimed it must be relatively 'the smallest bonanza ever to come out of a series in Australia'. This was the start of the long slide towards touring teams being given nothing.

The switch to the TCCB taking over the running of the professional game from MCC in the late 1960s did nothing to stop the casual exploitation of players. For a start, many of the newly created posts at TCCB were filled by MCC men. The manner in which a decision was taken in 1970–71 to summarily abandon a rain-delayed Test in Melbourne and instead play a limited-overs match – the first ever one-day international – typified the servility to which players were condemned. Allen, along with Cyril Hawker, the MCC president, and tour manager David Clark, agreed in a meeting with Sir Donald Bradman, the Australian board chairman, to not only the one day match being added to the schedule, but also an extra Test match.

The England players, already unhappy at their parsimonious meal allowances, were neither consulted nor offered any additional financial reward. Only after a heated meeting in the hotel room of the captain Ray Illingworth was their assent secured. In reality they had little choice: tour contracts were framed by length of mission rather than number of engagements. Fortunately, a hurried sponsorship deal with Rothmans meant the teams received an additional £560 each. The England players also got £50 per man for the extra Test, a small reward considering it generated receipts of £70,000.*

Jim Swanton, who had been covering tours of Australia for the *Daily Telegraph* for 25 years and was an arch apologist for the MCC's hegemony, ran into one of the players at the Windsor Hotel in Melbourne and was told it was disgraceful that the team had not been consulted and that the sooner things were managed by professionals the better. 'To Swanton, this exchange was symptomatic of a truculent spirit that had developed among some of the senior players which he'd never experienced before,' wrote Mark Peel in his history of post-war MCC tours.

It was hardly unexpected therefore that in 1977 six high-profile England cricketers were among those to join Kerry Packer's breakaway World Series Cricket.† Packer's intervention – driven by a desire to have cricket to show on the Channel Nine TV station he owned – did two big things in respect of the conduct of international cricket. One was that he forced national boards to pay their top players more: the fees to professionals had hovered around the £800 mark for several post-war tours of Australia before rising to about £3,500 in 1974–75; then in the mid-1980s, when Packer gave players an alternative source of income, these fees jumped to the region of £10,000 for a major tour.

The other was that he demonstrated how successfully one-day cricket could be marketed if innings were limited to 50 overs per side and played as floodlit matches in the evening when the public could best come and watch. ODIs became

---

* These were not the only cases of additional international fixtures being suddenly inserted into England tour programmes. In Australia in 1978–79, an extra ODI was added at three days' notice once the series stood at 1–1. In 1989–90, a scheduled Test against West Indies in Guyana was abandoned after three days and an ODI staged on what would have been the fifth day. 'Any resemblance between international cricket and the desultory fare served up to a sparse, confused crowd at Bourda was purely coincidental,' Alan Lee wrote in *The Times*.
† Dennis Amiss, Tony Greig, Alan Knott, John Snow and Derek Underwood joined as players and Mike Denness as a team manager.

an established feature of future England tours, especially in Australia where these innovations were most readily accepted. Whereas in almost nine years to May 1979 England played only 11 ODIs on all tours combined, over the next nine years they would play 81, including 17 day–night matches in Australia.

The popularity of ODIs offset the decline in Test match attendances, but also changed the nature of touring. From now on, a much larger proportion of the schedule was given over to international cricket in its various guises. In the first winter after the national bodies made their peace with Packer, England and West Indies toured Australia concurrently, and in addition to three Tests each they took part in a triangular ODI tournament which, had the best-of-three final between England and West Indies gone to a final match, would have involved 15 matches (which was as many as were required to stage the entire 1975 or 1979 World Cups).

England's schedule was hurriedly put together, and it left them with one or two days at most to prepare for each Test; as a consequence they refused to play the Test series – in any case much shorter than the usual five or six matches – for the Ashes. England's subsequent tours of Australia in 1982–83 and 1986–87 allowed for more conventional Test preparation but still saw them involved in similar three-way one-day events, which again proved a big hit with crowds (in 1982–83, the 17 ODIs were watched by 451,098, including a world record 84,153 for an England–Australia match in Melbourne)

To accommodate the one-day games, the number of side matches against states, provinces and minor teams was cut back; the 1982–83 tour was the first to Australia not to feature any matches outside the main cities. This was a profound shift in emphasis.

Bob Willis and Mike Gatting, respectively captains of these two Ashes tours of the 1980s, were alarmed by the frantic tempo of the itineraries. 'We were down for ten one-day games in the space of 25 days . . . the first four crammed into a six-day period in three different cities,' Willis noted in his diary. When it came to Gatting's tour, a second one-day competition was included, the Perth Challenge, which coincided with yachting's America's Cup off Fremantle, meaning England played 19 internationals in all, a record not beaten until 2002–03. 'Physiotherapist Laurie Brown is fast becoming a key figure in our party,' Gatting wrote in his diary towards the end of four and a half months in Australia. 'Most of the players are now having problems with throwing. We are almost reaching the stage where getting out of bed to face another day's play is becoming an unthinkable act.'*

The next winter was little better. A World Cup in India and Pakistan was followed by Test and one-day series in Pakistan, before a short break ahead of Tests and one-dayers in Australia and New Zealand. 'We will be touring 22 out of 26 weeks,' Gatting said at a press conference ahead of the team's late-September departure. 'That is a hell of a long time. These tours have got to get shorter or we will fall by the wayside. Professionals cannot be asked to keep going for 12 months every year. This will be a big disadvantage for us. It has been a long year for us all and we really need time to wind down and relax . . . our mental condition could be a problem.'

The injection of television revenue a decade later did nothing to reduce the schedule but did boost the size of the match and tour fees paid to the players, while also enabling the ECB to put the leading performers on annual retainers, or central contracts, from 2000 onwards. Quite quickly, the players' earnings could be measured in the hundreds of thousands of pounds; playing

---

* Despite the dramatic increase in the number of lucrative internationals in the 1980s, financial concerns still loomed large. Peter Lush, manager in 1986–87, had to prepare for the team to make a swift get-away should they fail to reach the finals of the triangular series. 'The Australian board would cut off the tour expenses for the side which failed to reach the finals as soon as the qualifying rounds were over,' Gatting wrote. In the event, England reached and won the finals. Even more quaintly, Bob Willis described how he and A. C. Smith, as captain and manager in New Zealand in 1983–84, 'met the man from the local bank, sorting out the end-of-tour finances, a necessary chore'.

regularly for England had never been so worthwhile. Within a few years, however, the economics of international cricket were altered even more dramatically than they had been by Kerry Packer's arrival with the creation of the vastly wealthy Indian Premier League, and other domestic T20 leagues that sprang up in its wake.

Suddenly, bilateral international cricket in general faced an existential threat, but particularly England, whose season over-lapped with an IPL competition slated for each April and May. Initially, the ECB refused to release its players for the Indian tournament while exploring other means of enriching them. This led chief executive David Collier and chairman Giles Clarke into an ill-starred alliance with a Texan businessman, Allen Stanford, who put up $1 million per man to the winning side in a one-off T20 in Antigua in November 2008 between his own All Stars XI (essentially a West Indies side) and an England team captained by Kevin Pietersen en route to a more conventional tour of India. No England side before or since has played for such a purse, but they were heavily beaten and came away with nothing. A few months later Stanford was arrested on fraud charges and jailed for life. It was a disastrous misadventure for English cricket, the most shameful aspect of which was that the side took the field under the banner of the national team.*

England's Washouts

The loss of a whole day's play to bad weather could have a particularly big impact on a tour's finances in the period before broadcasting revenue became the dominant income stream. In all, 66 whole days have been lost to bad weather during England's 522 overseas Tests (including two that were entirely washed out).

---

* The match itself was not ranked as an official international as England's opponents were not affiliated to a governing body.

This constitutes a ratio of one day lost for every 7.9 Tests played, compared to 106 days lost in 548 home Tests (including two entirely washed out), or one day for every 5.2 Tests – confirmation perhaps that the weather is generally better on tour. With improved drainage and pitch coverings, washouts have become less common in recent times; England have experienced only two in 126 Tests abroad since October 2002: at Centurion in 2004–05 and Dunedin in 2012–13.

Host country	Tests	Washouts	Centres where washouts occurred and number of days lost
Australia	186*	20	Melbourne 9, Sydney 9, Adelaide 1, Brisbane 1
New Zealand	53	18	Christchurch 6, Auckland 5, Wellington 4, Dunedin 3
South Africa	85	14	Centurion 7, Durban 6, Johannesburg 1
West Indies	75*	10	Guyana 6, Jamaica 3, Antigua 1
India	64	3	Delhi 2, Bangalore 1
Zimbabwe	2	1	Harare 1
Pakistan	27	0	
Sri Lanka	18	0	
Bangladesh	6	0	
United Arab Emirates (all v Pakistan)	6	0	

*Includes one entire five-day Test match washed out (v Australia, Melbourne 1970–71 and v West Indies, Guyana 1989–90).

England were involved in 14 ODIs overseas between 1978 and 2019 that were completely washed out: four in the West Indies, three each in Australia (all at Melbourne) and South Africa, two in Sri Lanka and one each in India and Zimbabwe. They had one overseas T20 match washed out against Australia in Melbourne in 2022.

CHAPTER 5

Picking the Right Man

The selection of the captain

Selecting the right tour party is a high-stakes game. Pick an England team for a home game and the selectors can draw on any number of players spread across 18 first-class counties. They can change tack several times in a summer; they can call up replacements within hours. And if they want to indulge a whim, they will get the chance at some point. Pick a player for a major overseas tour, however, and any error has the capacity to live large; every day that player remains on tour is another reminder of the selectors' erroneous judgment and the player's shortcomings. It may not be the player's fault: he just may not be the right type of player for the conditions the team find themselves in. Whatever the reason, a precious slot in the squad has been wasted.

Pick the wrong captain and the consequences can be even more catastrophic, as history suggests there is little scope for changing leader midway through a tour however badly things are going. The last England captain to drop himself, or be dropped, during an overseas Test series was Mike Denness in Australia almost 50 years ago. More recently, the England selectors repented at leisure their decision to appoint Andrew Flintoff as Test captain for Australia in 2006–07, a series for which the first-choice leader

Michael Vaughan was unfit, but as the side's principal all–rounder Flintoff had to play and therefore, realistically, had to remain captain even when things unravelled. Beforehand the selectors were split over whether to go with Flintoff or Andrew Strauss, but Duncan Fletcher narrowly favoured Flintoff and as he, as head coach, was the one who would have to work closely with whoever was chosen he was granted the final call. In the event, Flintoff was overwhelmed by the job and privately broke down in tears after three of the five Tests. He later admitted he was never the same player again. England lost the last two Tests in seven days and sank to a 5–0 loss, their first such defeat in Australia for 86 years.

Until the post was put on a more permanent footing, identifying a suitable captain was virtually the first job of tour selectors. There were two main areas to be considered in determining who might fit this role, and to an extent there still are. One involved cricketing credentials, which would cover a candidate's abilities as a player – the extent to which they were worth a place in the best XI in their own right – and as an on–field leader; could they manage men and did they possess a sufficiently strong grasp of tactics?

The second area was diplomacy. Whether the players liked it or not, an England touring team were viewed as ambassadors, and as such the captain was an important figurehead. When he spoke in public, as he was often required to do, he spoke as a representative of his team and his country. There have been many occasions when an England captain's conduct overseas, or the conduct of the players under him, became a matter of national or even international debate. In arguing the need for good-conduct bonuses to form part of professional contracts, Gubby Allen in the 1930s stated that 'he regarded the behaviour of individuals on tour as more important than their actual playing ability.' 'Most of them [the players] realised what was expected of them,' one tour manager of the 1950s wrote, 'and that they were not only cricketers who had to produce their best for their side, but that they were unofficial ambassadors.' When a dispute between England captain Mike Gatting and Pakistan umpire Shakoor Rana brought the Faisalabad Test of 1987 to a stand-still, British High Commissioner Nicholas Barrington was among those drafted in to try to broker a deal.

The modern practice of national flags being displayed on the outfield, and national anthems being sung, before the start of international matches is a potent reminder of this concept.

Asked about the ambassadorial dimension of life as a touring cricketer, Ashley Giles, as England's director of cricket in 2019–22, told me in 2020: 'I wouldn't sit them [the players] down before each tour and tell them, but I'd certainly hope they'd feel it was part of their responsibilities – ambassadors of ECB and England. We're trying to instil a bit of that [notion] again, what it means to wear the Three Lions.' Whether cricketers welcomed it or not, or were even cognisant of the point, any international cricket tour bestowed on the host country an imprimatur simply by taking place, especially when the tour was being made by an English team to one of Britain's former colonies. This was why South Africa during the apartheid era was so eager to arrange rebel sports tours such as the two undertaken by unofficial English sides in the 1980s: it gave their abhorrent political system a legitimacy it lacked. This too was why England playing cricket in Zimbabwe during President Robert Mugabe's reign became such a sensitive issue – and why England ultimately refused to go there. Photographs of the team shaking hands with Mugabe on the 1996–97 tour, before his worst excesses manifested themselves, came back to haunt them.

In announcing on the eve of the Test series in Pakistan in 2022 that he would be donating his match fees to the victims of recent floods in the country, Ben Stokes seemed to be showing that he had some notion of these wider responsibilities as an England captain.

The relative importance to the England captaincy of these two areas – cricketing credentials and diplomacy – has shifted over the years. From the time MCC first got involved in tour management, and then for many years after, diplomacy was probably a weightier consideration than cricketing ability; in the modern era, cricketing credentials have come first by a distance, but diplomacy remains a small but vital ingredient in the job. Jim Swanton alluded to this when he wrote, 'The jobs of England captain at home and abroad are quite different, and the qualities required are by no means identical.'

By emphasising the quasi-ambassadorial aspects of the captaincy, the MCC hierarchy gave themselves greater discretion as to who was best suited to lead the team abroad, and in the club's eyes that generally meant those like themselves educated at public school or Oxbridge, or with close ties to the MCC itself. But even today there is a largely unspoken understanding that a touring captain has responsibilities beyond cricket and must be made of 'the right stuff'. In the words of one former MCC tour manager, all touring players – not just captains – 'must be men of good character, high principle, easy of address and in every personal sense worthy of representing their country, in all circumstances'.

To ensure these criteria were met, the deliberations of the selection panel were often overseen by several MCC officers or grandees, and the selectors' recommended party went before the MCC committee for final approval. A similar process was adopted once power transferred to the TCCB, who created an overseas tours committee chaired for many years by Doug Insole, a former amateur with experience of England tours as player, selector and manager. Even today the choice of captain requires the approval of the ECB board and specifically the chairman.*

---

* One of the most delicate situations a captain found himself in ahead of an England tour came in the winter of 1980–81 when Ian Botham was involved in an incident outside a pub three weeks before the team was due to depart for the West Indies. Botham and a friend, Joe Neenan, the Scunthorpe United goalkeeper, were charged with assault occasioning actual bodily harm. Neenan pleaded guilty at a magistrates' court and was fined £100; Botham denied the charge and chose to go to trial, with his solicitor successfully arguing for a delay until such time as Botham was not away playing cricket. Given the proximity of the incident to the start of the tour and Botham's denial of the charge, it was hard for the TCCB to do anything other than keep faith with their captain. The trial eventually took place in September 1981, when Botham was found not guilty. Frank Keating, in his account of the tour, described it as 'an unprecedented shadow to fall on an England touring leader'.

When Len Hutton was appointed England captain, one of the most hotly debated issues was whether he would be socially equipped to handle an overseas tour. As it happened, his first tour was to the West Indies at a time when the region was in a highly charged political state. As Hutton and Douglas Jardine among others discovered, the style of cricket an English team adopted could also have consequences for how the team were received. As a ground-breaker, Hutton was acutely conscious of not being an MCC member, in part because so many of those who had led tours abroad before him had been. In the end, he was only confirmed as captain after the fourth of the five home Tests against Australia the previous summer, so he was kept waiting several weeks longer than would normally have been the case.

Since the late 1990s and the advent of central contracts, the national captaincy has been bestowed on a more permanent footing, so that rather than being appointed on a season-by-season, tour-by-tour basis, an England captain is given charge of the team until such time as he retires, resigns or is sacked. This has generally been a beneficial arrangement, offering reassurance to the captain, continuity to the team and the scope for more coherent long-term planning, even if sometimes the faith shown in a captain in these circumstances can appear near-blind.

Shortly after Joe Root had failed in 2019 for the second time as captain to win a series against Australia, Ashley Giles publicly gave Root his backing two years out from the next Ashes tour. 'We have talked about him leading and winning in Australia,' Giles said in a radio interview. 'We've not said, "Maybe if you get there." We plan for him to be captain.' Ten days later, Giles confessed: 'I'm not quite sure what anyone is expecting me to say. "We'll see how we go"? That's not a great vote of confidence ... He's our captain and he takes us forward.'

Even central contracts, though, did not always preclude a turbulent transition in the captaincy. When Kevin Pietersen fell out with head coach Peter Moores during a tour of India, leading to both men being sacked from their positions, Andrew Strauss was appointed as Pietersen's replacement only two weeks before the team departed for the Caribbean. The tour party itself had been named eight days earlier.

It was because there was more to the selection of a tour captain than simply cricketing ability that for many years the process often aroused lively debate. In those days, very few of those appointed to lead a tour were given a clear run by press or public. The first MCC-led Test tour to Australia in 1903–04 generated fierce argument in the popular papers about the relative merits of Pelham Warner and Archie MacLaren – Warner being described by one supporter as 'the most abused man of the day' – and it set a pattern that would be routinely followed, with the cricketing skills and social background of the candidates being standard features of discussion. Warner's case was in some ways typical: he was deemed to have the diplomatic skills necessary to three times be chosen to lead MCC tours abroad but was never asked to captain Test matches at home, when more candidates were available and plain cricketing ability was sufficient to determine the matter. Warner's side won the Test series 3-2 in 1903–04 but R. E. Foster, who was effectively his deputy, wrote in his diary during the tour how very bad his captaincy had been all through.

The burden of the off-field responsibilities – from managing players to attending functions to speechmaking – weighed heavily on many touring captains. In the case of Guy Jackson of Derbyshire, it even led to him pulling out of a tour of South Africa in 1927–28 just 11 days before departure with what today would be termed a 'stress-related illness'. With the 1927 season drawing to a close, Jackson asked Bob Wyatt to take a walk with him along the seafront at Folkestone, where they were taking part in a festival match, and Jackson confessed to his anxiety at being appointed captain. 'Jackson seemed ill at ease, and as soon as the forthcoming tour cropped up he said to Wyatt in some distress: "I'm not at all happy about this trip,'" Wyatt's biographer Gerald Pawle wrote. "'I'm worried about all the speech-making and I'm wondering if I can possibly face it.'"

Wyatt himself, in his autobiography, published in 1951, instanced Jackson's case as one 'where a captain who was due to take the side on tour had a nervous breakdown at the prospect before the tour began and couldn't go'. In Jackson's absence, the captaincy passed to Ronnie Stanyforth, who had been a late addition to the tour party as second wicketkeeper; he had never played county cricket – though he would soon do so for Yorkshire – but had represented MCC and services teams, and as an army captain could be relied on to fulfil all aspects of his duties on tour.* Jackson never did play Test cricket.

Percy Chapman, the captain chosen for England's next tour, to Australia in 1928–29, proved a better fit. 'The captain of a team going to Australia has an important role to fulfil. He must be a sportsman at heart, a good player, and a jolly good sort off the field as well as on the field. In Percy Chapman we found another Arthur Gilligan; and so he turned out to be when tested in the fire of the Australian barrackers,' wrote Maurice Tate, the team's senior bowler. Frank Mann, who uniquely both captained England in Tests overseas and produced a son George who did likewise, advised his son before leaving for South Africa that he should eat each evening in the team hotel so that he was readily available to his players. 'It should be the time and place ... where he could always be found.'

The diplomatic dimension to the job was more firmly imprinted on the consciousness of English cricket once Jardine's Bodyline tactics of 1932–33 prompted cries of foul play from the Australians, a highly charged exchange of telegrams between the two boards and governmental pressure to find ways to

---

* At the team's first official function at Government House in Cape Town, Stanyforth was praised as a public speaker 'of the very highest order' by General Smuts, a former prime minister and one of the founders of the Union of South Africa.

defuse the row. Viscount Hailsham, Secretary of State for War, who took over the MCC presidency soon after the series ended, chaired a committee of investigation and led attempts to persuade the Australians to set their differences aside and tour England in 1934. Hailsham also met Jardine ahead of the following winter's tour of India to convey to him the need for the mission to be a political success at a time when Indian demands for independence were pressing. The cricket was turbulent and not without controversy, but Jardine just about met his brief.

To further smooth things over, a year in advance of England's next Ashes tour in 1936–37, MCC sent a team to play six matches in Australia en route to a non-Test tour of New Zealand. Errol Holmes, who had followed the same path as Jardine from Oxford to Surrey, and had succeeded to the county captaincy in 1934, was chosen to lead this goodwill trip and would have been regarded as a safe pair of hands (Jack Hobbs later said of him that he 'would not tolerate anything shady or underhand'). Holmes recalled being sent for by William Findlay, the MCC secretary, to receive instructions. 'We were to make active efforts to induce Australia to bury the hatchet by being cheerful and pleasant and by playing the game in the proper spirit ... Each member of the team had been carefully selected, not only for his cricketing abilities but, equally, for his ambassadorial potentialities.'

Holmes had already gained some experience of leadership as vice-captain to Wyatt on a Test tour of West Indies the previous winter. '[I] learnt something of the social aspect of a touring team and just a little about the necessary and arduous duty of speech-making,' he wrote. 'I had seen, too, how things can go wrong on even the best conducted tours, and that difficult situations can arise which call for quick decisions on the part of the captain, and that, in such circumstances, firmness is necessary plus a genuine attempt to be fair, at all times.'

In cricketing terms, Nigel Howard was among the weakest of England tour captains, appointed to lead in newly partitioned

India and Pakistan in 1951–52 largely because of his amateur status at a time when the pool of amateur talent was shallow. This was also a tour on which few senior players wanted to go. Howard had the advantage of his father Rupert being Lancashire secretary at the time he first played for the club and was made captain (Rupert had managed the tour of Australia in 1936–37). He led Lancashire to the championship title in 1950 but was greatly assisted by Cyril Washbrook, his senior professional and an established England player, and many in the county felt he should have stepped down to allow Washbrook to take over.

The powers-that-be were well aware of the fragility of Howard junior's position, Donald Carr, his vice-captain in India, stating that Howard had been advised before the tour 'not to stand down under any circumstances'. But Howard, who at 26 was the youngest man to be appointed captain of an England Test tour since the 1880s, spent much of the time in fear of illness and the local culture, leading his manager to conclude, 'He'd had things too easy in his life.' Howard resisted a proposal from one of his players to leave himself out of the second Test against India, but ultimately succumbed to pleurisy and missed the final match of the series, which was drawn 1–1. Howard did not bowl, had a highest score in the series of 23, and never played Test cricket again.*

When Hutton was appointed to lead the next England Test tour, to West Indies two winters later, MCC assuaged their concerns that he might not altogether be capable of upholding the good name of English cricket abroad – even though he was unquestionably among the greatest batsmen the country had ever possessed – by sending Charles Palmer, an amateur cricketer of moderate ability, as player-manager to work

---

* Eight men have led England Test tours before the age of 27: Ivo Bligh (Australia 1882–83), Nigel Howard (India 1951–52), Peter May (South Africa 1956–57), Ted Dexter (India and Pakistan 1961–62), Ian Botham (West Indies 1980–81), Mike Atherton (West Indies 1993–94 and Australia 1994–95), Alastair Cook (Bangladesh 2009–10) and Joe Root (Australia 2017–18).

alongside him. It was a bizarre arrangement, which cast Palmer as Hutton's superior off the field but junior to him on it, but it satisfied MCC that it had in place an acceptable back-up should Hutton somehow fall short.

In the event, Hutton's relentless focus on victory on a tour scarred by riots and umpiring disputes, and Palmer's inability to handle the crises that unfolded, meant the trip was remembered as the second most acrimonious after Bodyline.* Denis Compton, one of the senior players, described Palmer as 'a kind, efficient, delightful man but no disciplinarian. He seemed to leave most of the difficult decisions to Hutton, which Len accepted without complaint but never relished.'

Hutton was not only up to the job but far more capable than many of his predecessors, but the strain took a heavy toll. The political, diplomatic and disciplinary problems that beset the tour meant that Hutton's reappointment for the following winter in Australia was by no means guaranteed. Some within MCC circles favoured a switch to David Sheppard, an amateur of the right pedigree but as a cricketer far less certain to command a place in the team. In the end, the MCC committee decided in May 1954 against giving 'special instructions' concerning the captaincy, which effectively left the door open to Hutton's retention. In the event he was chosen unanimously.

For Australia, Hutton recruited the services of Bill Edrich, a close contemporary, whom he recognised as better suited to handling the off-field demands of touring. 'I became a sort of aide-de-camp, adviser, secretary and front man,' Edrich recalled. 'My form had hardly warranted selection, but it became obvious after we sailed from Tilbury that Hutton was to make the fullest

---

* The MCC explained Palmer's appointment as player-manager by saying that the West Indies board would not pay for a sixteenth player on the tour, but Palmer as an amateur ought not to have cost much and England had never previously sent more than 15 players on a West Indies tour; neither did they do so on the next tour there in 1959–60. Palmer played the second Test in Barbados having batted only twice on the tour, scored 22 and 0, and did not play for England again.

use of my extrovert nature to compensate for his more retiring personality. He was never an extrovert, preferring to have a couple of sherries at a reception and then slip quietly away. My job was to fly the flag when he made his exit.'

There was further official agonising over the best choice of captain for Australia in 1962–63. Chaos reigned for several weeks after Walter Robins, who had taken over from Gubby Allen as chairman of selectors, effectively sacked Ted Dexter two matches into a home series against Pakistan after Dexter inadvertently failed to applaud the Pakistan batsmen as they left the field at Lord's on a Friday evening. 'As soon as I was inside the pavilion he [Robins] gave me a resounding bollocking for being "unsportsmanlike",' Dexter recalled.

Not only was Colin Cowdrey appointed to lead the next Test, but Robins also gave serious consideration to recalling David Sheppard to the captaincy, even though Sheppard had not played first-class cricket since 1960 or Test cricket since 1957 owing to his involvement with the church. In the end, Dexter got the job, thereby becoming at 27 the youngest Englishman to captain a tour of Australia since Ivo Bligh.* Dexter did not enjoy the process he was put through. 'I'd found the tension created by Robins' selection process mentally and emotionally gruelling,' he reflected. This was par for the course for the MCC hierarchy, which spared little thought for the feelings of the players, professional or amateur.

Hutton may have broken the mould as the first professional captain of modern times, and amateur status may have finally been scrapped in November 1962, but MCC were nevertheless nervous when the prospect loomed of Brian Close, a hard-headed northern 'pro' in the style of Hutton, leading the side in

---

* Despite his lack of recent cricket, Sheppard nonetheless went on the tour, to wide-spread incredulity among players past and present. Trevor Bailey, whose own Test career had ended in 1958–59, later suggested that Sheppard only agreed to go to further his clerical career: 'It must help in the ecclesiastical profession to be a bishop who is known to the general public.' In 1975 Sheppard became Bishop of Liverpool.

West Indies in 1967–68. Close had a successful home summer as England captain in 1967, but even before he landed himself in hot water with time-wasting tactics as Yorkshire captain in a Championship match, he heard on good authority that the cricketing establishment was looking for ways to remove him.

Sure enough, when it came to a vote in a meeting with the Test selectors, MCC representatives stymied Close's appointment – as was their procedural right. '[They] believed there would be a most unfavourable public reaction [to Close] ... in the West Indies,' MCC minutes noted. Many among the local white elite in the Caribbean had taken umbrage at Hutton as a professional being sent as captain in 1953–54, and there was little appetite for another of his ilk, among either what was left of the old planter class in the West Indies, or the reactionaries at Lord's. The Tonbridge and Oxford-educated Colin Cowdrey eventually took Close's place, led the team to victory and was later effusively praised by MCC for the way he handled things.

The off-field dimension to the job carried considerable weight well into the 1970s. Denness, who succeeded Cowdrey as Kent captain and was appointed to the England job for the winter of 1973–74, might have later led a disastrous tour of Australia, but diplomatically his stewardship was viewed as a success. 'Denness suffers by comparison with his predecessor Ray Illingworth as a "player's captain",' Christopher Martin-Jenkins, then BBC radio's cricket correspondent, wrote. 'He is neither so astute a tactician nor so gifted a mixer with his own men. Yet as an ambassador Denness was almost faultless. Winning on the field is the first consideration, but, despite the cynics, presenting the right public image is very important too.'

Two years later, Martin-Jenkins praised the way Tony Greig approached the wider responsibilities of the role in India: 'His handling not only of the crowds but also of the media was masterly ... His handling of the umpires was equally tactful and diplomatic.' As late as 1980, Geoff Boycott, an arch northerner, was grumbling about the advantages of social privilege when it came to Mike Brearley's position as captain. 'There's more than a touch of who you are rather than how well you can perform,' he wrote. 'England seem to have a fixation with so-called leadership qualities – and it has usually meant background.'

Brearley, who led England through three winters, may have been educated at Cambridge and captained Middlesex for many years before playing Test cricket, but he was acutely aware of the potential pitfalls of touring captains being required to hold frequent press conferences – occasions laden with opportunities to misspeak. 'Exposure does involve risk, especially to captains, whose responsibility it is to act as spokesmen for the team and themselves,' he wrote. 'The danger lies as much in their misjudgments as in misrepresentation or unfair comment. One *faux pas* may haunt a captain who, as cricketer, did not embark upon his profession with public speaking in mind, nor did he have any training in the process.' Modern England captains *are* given media training, but Alastair Cook, who officially held the post between 2013 and 2016, nevertheless shared Brearley's concerns: 'I realised pretty soon that I needed to be briefed and to have read what was being written about me, my team and sometimes even stuff that had nothing to do with cricket. This didn't mean that I allowed what was written to influence me, but it did mean I wouldn't be blindsided by any questions.'

A further complicating factor in the selection of captains was that for many years first-choice candidates were not always available. Amateurs could not necessarily find time to spend several months away from home, and occasionally some professionals opted for winters off too. Generally, the less high-profile or attractive the tour, the harder it was to recruit the best players. It was not uncommon for a tour of South Africa to be captained by someone without experience of Test cricket; this also happened, less often, in respect of other destinations, including the subcontinent.

Given the potential difficulties, the process of identifying and naming a captain often took place several months in advance of a tour and well in advance of confirmation of the rest of the squad. This contributed to the absurd situation of Percy Chapman being named captain for South Africa in 1930–31 at a stage of the summer when two Tests of a home series against Australia had yet to be played; he was then sacked as captain ahead of the final Test, partly because his freewheeling approach to batting seemed unsuited to a timeless Test and partly because of rumours surrounding his drinking. The selectors turned to the more dependable Bob Wyatt instead. Chapman nevertheless took the team to South Africa, with Wyatt playing under him.

As late as the 1960s and 1970s, players in line to lead winter tours declared themselves unavailable for various reasons. This happened with Colin Cowdrey ahead of the India and Pakistan tour in 1961–62 (when he wanted a rest from Test cricket) and the tour of India in 1963–64 (when he was suffering from an arm injury). It also happened with Ted Dexter ahead of South Africa in 1964–65, when he chose instead to stand in the General Election on 15 October, the day the team was due to depart; in the event, he failed to win his seat and was added to the tour three weeks later as vice-captain.

Mike Smith of Warwickshire, a captain with a relaxed style perfect for long tours even if technically he was not quite good enough to handle the faster bowling found in Test cricket, proved an able stand-in in 1963–64 and 1964–65, and might have done so again on two subsequent occasions. Smith was offered the captaincy for West Indies following Brian Close's sacking but declined, at which point Cowdrey stepped in. Cowdrey subsequently said he felt 'like a schoolboy who ran third in an egg-and-spoon race and had been awarded the prize because the first two had been disqualified'. Smith was also invited to lead England on a four-month tour of India and Pakistan in 1972–73 – by which time he was 39 years old – after Ray Illingworth, who had led England in their previous 25 Tests and was himself 40, chose to spend the winter at home. Tony

Lewis, who had not played for England before but had recently led Glamorgan to the championship, took the team instead.*

Illingworth was the last incumbent England Test captain to unilaterally declare themselves unavailable for a particular tour – as distinct to ruling themselves out from ever touring again, as Mike Brearley did in 1980.†

In most cases, though, anyone in a position to lead an England tour would readily take the opportunity and regard it as one of the highest honours in the game. A few, perhaps, having captained England overseas several times before, were persuaded to do so again more out of a sense of obligation to a team short of alternatives than because they still had the appetite, or they were likely to benefit personally. Wally Hammond taking a team to Australia directly after the Second World War at the age of 43, Mike Atherton being persuaded to remain in charge for one more tour to the West Indies in 1997–98, and possibly even Joe Root leading a side in the Caribbean shortly after a heavy defeat in Australia might all fall into this category. All three lost. All three left the captaincy.

Given the store MCC placed on finding the right men, the club's record of picking good captains was poor – certainly if the sole measure was cricketing ability. Considering how important the captaincy of a major tour was, it is remarkable how often they got things wrong in this respect. The chosen men were often not physically fit enough or technically good

---

* Lewis provided the thirteenth and most recent instance of a previously uncapped player being appointed captain of an England Test tour. The only other cases since 1945 were George Mann (South Africa 1948–49) and Nigel Howard (India 1951–52).
† By mutual agreement with board officials and coaches, Graham Gooch as captain in 1992–93 returned home after the India leg of the tour and missed a Test and ODIs in Sri Lanka, and Andrew Strauss was rested from a Test and ODI tour of Bangladesh in 2009–10, the captaincy temporarily passing to Alastair Cook, his eventual long-term successor. Eoin Morgan, as white-ball captain, took a personal decision to miss an ODI series in Bangladesh in 2016–17 on security grounds following a recent terrorist attack in Dhaka. Given the circumstances, the players were offered the choice not to tour if they wished, and Morgan and Alex Hales duly took that option. Because he was captain, Morgan's decision was not well received among some high-ranking ECB officials.

enough, and for this reason several played in only part of the series they were appointed to lead. For instance, Henry Leveson Gower played only three of the five Tests in South Africa in 1909–10, Ronnie Stanyforth only four out of five in South Africa in 1927–28 and Gubby Allen three out of four in West Indies in 1947–48. Allen was 45 years old and hardly fully fit at any stage of the tour, and should never have agreed to go in any capacity other than manager. But he sat on the MCC committee, as did Leveson Gower in 1909, and allowed himself to be persuaded. He remains the oldest man ever to lead an England tour.*

The tour was a spectacular failure: for the first time an England team abroad failed to win a match of meaningful description, and Allen, ambitiously designated captain-manager, soon lost the confidence of senior players and needed the help of Billy Griffith, a future MCC secretary, to keep things functioning off the field. It was a tour covered by few journalists and no account was published by any of the participants, so the full extent of the dysfunction remains hidden.

Of those Test tours organised by MCC, the first 11 to Australia, the first six to South Africa and the first three to West Indies did not see one captain average more than 40 with the bat and in only one instance – Johnny Douglas in South Africa in 1913–14 – did a captain score a century. It was an astonishing record of mediocrity, but in keeping with much that MCC did.

Another important decision that lay most closely with the captain was the appointment of a deputy. The role of vice-captain dated back to the earliest Test tour when James Southerton, the

---

* Allen was 45 years 145 days when the team departed for the West Indies on 23 December 1947. W. G. Grace (1891–92) and Walter Hammond (1946–47) were both 43 years old, and Freddie Brown (1950–51), Graham Gooch (1992–93) and Alfred Shaw (1881–82) all 39, when they led England abroad. Norman Gifford was 44 when he captained England in a one-day tournament in Sharjah in 1984–85.

oldest member of the party, acted as first lieutenant to James Lillywhite. As Lillywhite played every match, Southerton was not required to deputise on the field, but a vice-captain's role also included shouldering some of the burden that fell on the captain, from speech-making to arranging and running practice sessions.*

Once MCC took control of tours, the vice-captaincy – like the captaincy – was habitually given to an amateur, at least until Denis Compton was appointed deputy to Freddie Brown in Australia in 1950–51. That was a ground-breaking moment in the sense that it put the job in the hands of a professional for the first time in the twentieth century, but Compton was an odd choice when the more sober and diligent Len Hutton was also in the team. It was not altogether surprising that Compton struggled tactically when he stood in for Brown in state games, and also let himself down with his off-field behaviour.

The vice-captain's duties continued to be wide-ranging until at least the 1960s, when former England professionals such as Alec Bedser, Les Ames and Ken Barrington were appointed assistant managers or managers with the brief to supervise cricketing matters – forerunners to Micky Stewart's appointment as full-time cricket manager in 1986. Even as late as 1978–79 Bob Willis noted in his diary after being told that he was to be Mike Brearley's vice-captain in Australia: 'Between games, one of my most important tasks will be to organise the net practices ... [also] always to be available to listen to the grouses and the problems of other players.' Willis's appointment was actually a bone of contention, with John Murray resigning as a selector in part because of the preferment of Willis as vice-captain over Geoff Boycott.

Generally, a vice-captain would also be part of the on-tour

---

* E. F. S. Tylecote in 1882–83 was the first to deputise as captain in any sort of match on an England Test tour, Ivo Bligh being forced to miss the first six matches in Australia because he injured a hand during the outward voyage.

selection committee, which would typically also include the captain and senior managers or coaches. There was always the chance, though, that a vice-captain would need to step up and lead the team in a Test match, and he needed to be appointed with that possibility in mind. Johnny Douglas led England in all five Tests in Australia in 1911–12 after Pelham Warner, the appointed captain, fell ill after the first state match.

The vice-captaincy might also be considered preparation for future elevation. Although he captained England 27 times, including on tours of West Indies and Pakistan, Colin Cowdrey served as vice-captain on four tours of Australia under four different players without ever leading a side there himself.* By the last time, as deputy to Ray Illingworth, Cowdrey was 37 years old and plainly disgruntled at being passed over again. In hindsight, Illingworth felt Cowdrey should not have toured. 'It took him three weeks to accept the offer of being vice-captain – he shouldn't have been my deputy if it took that long. He showed no interest – sometimes he didn't even turn up at practice.'

Just as MCC's record in appointing tour captains was checkered, so too was its choice of tour managers. In the days before full-time, officially designated coaches, a manager's brief could include a range of responsibilities from discipline to organising net practice to making speeches at functions to spare the captain always having to. He would deal with the hotels. He would liaise with the local cricket authorities and government officials about which receptions the players might or might not attend.

---

* Cowdrey first captained England overseas in two Tests in the West Indies in 1959–60 after Peter May fell ill. He is one of 20 players to lead England overseas having not been appointed official captain for the tour; these players captained 40 overseas Tests, exactly one in 13 of England's 520 Tests away from home. The others were Johnny Douglas, Freddie Fane (both five matches), Geoff Boycott (four), Andrew Flintoff, Allan Lamb, Archie MacLaren (three), David Gower, Alec Stewart (both two) and Monty Bowden, Donald Carr, Kenneth Cranston, John Edrich, Timothy O'Brien, Walter Read, Greville Stevens, Marcus Trescothick, Jack White, Bob Wyatt and Norman Yardley (all one). Stewart stepped in as replacement for Graham Gooch in Madras in 1992–93 with about an hour's notice after Gooch went down overnight with suspected food poisoning.

He would also be responsible for sorting out for the team tickets to theatres, cinemas and golf courses and the like.

Those with a background in the services might have been considered good at instilling discipline, but less good at arranging cricket training. Sometimes they fell short in both. E. M. Wellings felt that Mike Green in Australia 'certainly did not act as the strong, tactful disciplinarian, which a team on tour needs'. He also held him partly responsible for some desultory early practice sessions in Perth which failed to set the right tone for later in the tour.

Players have recounted the extent to which both Freddie Brown and Tom Pearce as managers drank more than was appropriate, either for their own well-being or the image of an England team on tour. MCC were also inclined to use tour managers as they did chairmen of selectors, as a means of pressuring captains into adopting a more entertaining approach on the field. Billy Griffith and David Clark, respectively managers in Australia in 1965–66 and 1970–71, both pushed for brighter cricket, but their efforts did not end well. 'In six major tours overseas to Australia and New Zealand, South Africa and the West Indies, I never once felt entirely satisfied with the choice of manager,' Denis Compton wrote. 'Disciplinarians were marvellous at imposing rules but often lacked tact, sensitivity and a ready ear for the tourists with a personal problem. Similarly, those who sympathised with the pain in your knee would probably neglect a problem of much greater importance.'

Organisers of England Tours 1876–77 to 2022–23

The number of England tours has grown exponentially since authority passed from the MCC to the Test and County Cricket Board, and subsequently to the England and Wales Cricket Board. The last winter when England did not tour was 1988–89 (when a scheduled tour of India was cancelled) and before that 1975–76, which was originally slated for a tour of South Africa before the anti-apartheid boycott was imposed.

Period	Tour organisers	Winters with tours	Winters without tours	Total tours
1876–77 to 1901–02	Privately arranged	14	12	16
1903–04 to 1968–69	Marylebone Cricket Club (MCC)	35	19*	36
1970–71 to 1996–97	Test & County Cricket Board (TCCB)	24+	3	29+
1996–97 to 2022–23	England & Wales Cricket Board (ECB)	27+	0	65+
		99	**34**	**145**

*Excluding winters covered by war: 1914–15 to 1919–20 and 1939–40 to 1945–46.
+The switch from the TCCB to ECB was made on 1 January 1997 during a tour of Zimbabwe and New Zealand; the 1996–97 winter is therefore counted in both these periods.

CHAPTER 6

Picking the Tour Party

Finding the right balance

Once confirmed, a captain would typically play a role in picking the rest of the tour party. Captains in modern times in particular have generally, though not always, been given the players they want – whether at home or abroad – on the basis that they are the ones who lead them on the field and against whose names the wins and losses stand. That a captain must have faith in the players under his command is perhaps even more important on tour, when they spend so much time together, than it would be for home matches.* This of course was why it was so important that the identity of the captain be established before other elements of a tour were put in place.

However, although their wishes continued to count for a lot, most England captains since 2003 have forgone their traditional voting rights in selection in favour of a consultative role,

---

* Some captains have been suspected of using their powers to take long-time friends on tour. Ian Botham's team to the West Indies in 1981 included Roland Butcher, who had been on the Lord's ground staff with him, and Graham Stevenson, with whom he had played club cricket in Melbourne. David Gower was closely involved in the selection of Chris Cowdrey, under whose captaincy he had played for England Young Cricketers, for India in 1984–85.

a move designed to protect their relationship with the players under them.* Only once a squad was chosen, and the team was on tour, would a captain then become formally involved with narrowing down a squad to a starting XI. That said, there have been a few instances where a tour captain was appointed so late that the party had already been selected, as happened with Ronnie Stanyforth (South Africa 1927–28) and Andrew Strauss (West Indies 2008–09).

In the days when tour parties were selected by a large group including high-ranking MCC officials, it was by no means certain that a captain would get what he wanted. The greater the number of voices, the more scope there was for muddled thinking and unsatisfactory compromises. The squad chosen for Australia in 1950–51 was a classic case in point. The selection panel consisted of 11 members and yet the party chosen was riddled with flaws. Those picking it displayed little knowledge of the relative merits of the various candidates. Indeed, until two months before departure they mistakenly thought Norman Yardley would be in a position to take on the captaincy; it transpired he was not, which led to a frantic search for a replacement and resulted in the appointment of Freddie Brown at the age of 39. The party of 17 was also chronically short of experienced middle-order batsmen and slip fielders. 'They [the young batsmen] had to be flung straight into the battle, untrained youths under real fire for the first time,' E. M. Wellings wrote. Alec Bedser, who led the bowling attack, recalled many years later: 'We picked the worst squad that had ever been selected.' Neville Cardus described it as 'the weakest conglomeration of cricketers which has ever represented this country at cricket against Australia ... Grave if not grievous risks were taken by the selection committee at Lord's when

---

* This practice ended when Ben Stokes was appointed Test captain in April 2022 and took a formal, voting role in selection on an ad hoc panel chaired by Rob Key, the new director of cricket. The post of national selector had been discontinued the previous year.

only three seasoned Test match batsmen were chosen, one of them [Denis Compton] not certain to survive the physical strain of an arduous tour.'

In terms of selection, things were little better by the time Hutton led his first Test tour to the Caribbean in 1953–54. Rather than too many opening batsmen, as had been the case in 1950–51, now there were too few of them, leaving Hutton himself to open with Willie Watson and Trevor Bailey, neither of whom had gone in first in Tests before.

Mike Green, who managed two Test tours in the immediate post-war period, criticised the bloated selection panels. These consisted of 'mostly ex-England captains and players, each with formed and definite ideas. Many of their ideas are, quite frankly, obsolete.' Green wanted the selection panel chosen for home seasons to operate all year round. But it would be a long time before that happened – or before the English game was given a national governing body worth the name.

The timings of selection meetings and the announcement of touring parties were governed by the date of departure: when teams to Australia travelled by boat, this typically meant the selectors picking the squads with several weeks of the English season still remaining – hardly an ideal situation. This contributed to the practice of the party being chosen in several stages – again, hardly satisfactory.

Until the amateur–professional divide was formally scrapped, the Gentlemen–Players fixture at Lord's in July was often treated as a tour trial, and once that had taken place selection discussions began in earnest. Freddie Brown's century in the 1950 match certainly helped secure his selection as captain for Australia. After leading a losing tour of Australia in 1936–37, Gubby Allen expressed his disquiet at such practices in his report to Lord's. 'The team should not, in my opinion, be chosen in four lots,' he wrote. 'No doubt it is desirable to announce the names of six or seven outstanding players during the month of July but ... the remaining selections should be made en bloc, say four or five weeks before the date of sailing. This would prevent hasty decisions and probably produce a more balanced side.'

Allen was right to complain: the squad he led could have done with an experienced player of spin such as the left-handed Eddie Paynter, who had done well in Australia in the past, and an experienced opening batsman, although on this issue Allen himself was largely responsible for the absence of Herbert Sutcliffe, admittedly 41 years of age but still one of the best batsmen in the country.* Many years later Allen publicly expressed regret that he had not taken Compton, who would blossom into one of England's most brilliant if mercurial batting talents, but Compton was only 18 at the time and uncapped in Tests, and Allen's argument that he had considered Compton too inexperienced was probably accurate. Whether Compton was seriously considered is a moot point. Allen never apologised to Sutcliffe for his omission, which probably owed much to Sutcliffe's support for Bodyline and his intolerance of Allen's pusillanimity on the issue.

Nothing changed, of course. Selection for the West Indies tour of 1953–54 spanned five meetings across several months, the last of them held – extraordinarily – on the second evening of the deciding Test against Australia at the Oval, a match England were striving to win to secure the Ashes for the first time in 19 years. What was enormously taxing to Hutton, the captain, was done chiefly to suit the travel arrangements of the 79-year-old Pelham Warner, who was in London at the time.

When Allen became chairman of selectors in 1955, he was in a position to modernise the process, but effected only limited change; for the 1958–59 tour of Australia and New Zealand

---

* No one fought English cricket's class war more energetically or more damagingly to England's cause than Allen. He and the socially upwardly mobile Sutcliffe had long not seen eye to eye.

departing on 21 September, his panel named their entire party in one go, but did it so early, on 27 July, that Ted Dexter, one of three young players chosen for a Test against New Zealand at Old Trafford as a sort of trial, was unable to bat until the following day because of adverse weather. As a consequence, Dexter was left out – although he was subsequently summoned as an emergency replacement.

In later years, it became traditional to name a winter tour party around the time of the final Test of the summer, then to do so after the final of the county knockout tournament, the Gillette Cup or NatWest Trophy, at Lord's in early September. There was a time when a good performance in that final was reckoned a potential route to clinching one of the last remaining tour places. More recently, some squad announcements have been left as late as possible: in 2016, a Test team for Bangladesh and India was not named until two weeks before departure in order to assess how various players fared in the penultimate round of county championship matches. In 2021, owing to delays in securing guarantees about how quarantining in Australia would operate for players and their families, the squad was not named until 10 October, the latest-ever date for an Ashes tour.

Another reason why tour squads used to be named early was because the authorities were unsure how many players were willing to accept invitations. When Yorkshire blocked their great all-rounders George Hirst and Wilfred Rhodes from touring Australia in 1901–02, concerns were first raised in late July, which was a huge blow to Archie MacLaren's hopes of taking a strong team but at least left him time to find alternatives. As Warner once noted, 'The ideal team upon paper is not so easily transferred to a liner.'

Some amateurs needed winters at home in order to earn the money that enabled them to play cricket in the summer, and before the advent of central contracts some counties were reluctant to see their star players sent off repeatedly on exhausting winter assignments. All these were reasons why MCC might have been reluctant to arrange major Test tours every winter (only once prior to the 1960s did England Test teams tour in four successive winters). The solution was to send second- or third-string sides to the less powerful, less attractive destinations, and this was a standard ploy in the case of tours of the subcontinent. Of England's first five Test tours to India up to and including 1972–73, there were never more than five players in the original squad who had been on England's previous major tour, and that was in 1961–62 after a two-year gap since the previous tour. Even when a player was sounded out about his availability well in advance, it did not always stop him changing his mind and pulling out. Bob Taylor did this in respect of the 1972–73 tour of the subcontinent, as did Geoff Boycott over the Australia and New Zealand tour two winters later.

Once Test tours became settled as annual events, the demands on the top players grew ever greater. Ian Botham, English cricket's biggest star of the 1980s, opted to miss a tour of India in 1984–85 having toured for the previous seven winters, and then during a tour of Australia two years later signed a deal to play three seasons for Queensland, saying that he no longer wished to tour with England again. In fact, he made himself available for West Indies in 1989–90 but was not chosen, and then did go to New Zealand and Australia for a tour that took in the 1992 World Cup (the TCCB allowed him special dispensation to join the team late because he was involved in a Christmas pantomime).

When David Gower sat out the winter of 1987–88, having toured with England for the previous nine years, Mike Gatting, the captain, suggested that players in such a situation should be recompensed anyway by the TCCB because the need for rest was a direct consequence of the player's workloads – effectively anticipating the need for the sort of central contracts that were introduced more than ten years later. Even central contracts did not prevent some players wanting winters off: Alec Stewart and Darren Gough sought to miss the tour of India but not the one to New Zealand in 2001–02, but were told at a highly charged meeting with head coach Duncan Fletcher that they could opt out of one format for a winter but not select which places they played (effectively preventing the sort of cherry-picking of destinations that earlier generations had got away with). In the end, Gough agreed to play ODIs but not Tests in India and New Zealand, while Stewart sat out the whole winter.

A fundamental task of any panel of selectors was deciding how large a tour party was required. Since the mid-1960s, England have typically taken 16 or 17 players on most major Test tours, with 17 most commonly used for the longer Australian expeditions. This allowed reserve players to cover most of the principal areas: spare opening batsman, spare middle-order batsman, second wicketkeeper, back-up spinner and two back-up fast bowlers, although obviously precise allocation of resources depended on the destination; there would be more emphasis on pace bowling stocks for Australia and South Africa, and more on spin when going to the subcontinent. Taking more players than is strictly necessary is not going to help team dynamics, and there are usually persuasive financial and logistical reasons why keeping a tour party as streamlined as possible is advantageous. Finding the right balance to cover every eventuality could be difficult, especially when injuries or illnesses might throw the best plans into disarray. This was a constant obsession for those in charge.

In three instances, England actually named Test parties of 18 men. For Australia in 1954–55, there were doubts about Compton's fitness following a recurrence of a long-standing knee problem and Vic Wilson was a late addition to the party before departure; Compton stayed at home for treatment before joining the team two weeks after their arrival. Geoffrey Howard, the manager, conceded that with so many in the party it was difficult to keep everyone match-ready. For the 2012–13 tour of India, England took a larger squad because an attempt was being made to reintegrate Kevin Pietersen after a falling-out with teammates and it was uncertain how this might go; Pietersen had been dropped for the final Test of the home summer, not selected for a World T20 in Sri Lanka, and the renewal of his central contract was put on hold. For Australia in 2021–22, a party of 17 was named, but Ben Stokes was subsequently declared fit and added to the group two weeks later.

The restriction on numbers is one of the defining features of any tour. The most players England have ever deployed in one overseas Test series is 18, but they have drawn on more players than that 33 times at home (or almost one in four of all home series).* Douglas Jardine felt that this compactness was a virtue, allowing a group of players to gel in a way that was less easy to achieve at home, though his was an era when touring involved more 'side' fixtures than they do now, and perhaps more opportunities to forge a collective spirit. 'I am inclined to think that a side representing England in Australia is likely to be more formidable than an XI chosen for one match only from our scattered counties at home,' Jardine wrote in his account of the 1932–33 tour, *In Quest for the Ashes*. 'Frequently men chosen for a Test match at home have never before played together.'

Modern captains and coaches have tended to share this view, seeing a tour as a good chance to impose a new culture on a group of players. Michael Vaughan and Duncan Fletcher used Vaughan's first tour as captain to Bangladesh and Sri Lanka in 2003–04 to push the squad to new levels of fitness, action which soon bore fruit, and when England under Joe Root sought to rebuild their Test team in 2021–22 they began the

---

* England used 18 players in five Tests in Australia in 2013–14; 16 of the 17 players who began the tour featured in the series, plus Tim Bresnan and Scott Borthwick, who were called up later. Steven Finn was with the team throughout the Test series but was never selected.

process on a tour of West Indies with a radically different set of players from those who had just lost heavily in Australia. That however worked less well: England lost and Root subsequently resigned.

Early England tours were staffed by remarkably few players, especially considering that replacements could not be readily summoned. No party sent to Australia before 1900 containing more than 13 players. This was essentially a means of keeping down costs and, when the players were in charge of their own affairs, maximising profit-sharing, but it placed an enormous burden on the frontline bowlers in particular. But provided everyone was fit, the concept of players sitting around as non-participants appeared a novel one. Lord Harris, who captained a team largely made up of amateurs in 1878–79, regretted bringing as many as 13 players: 'I made a great mistake ... They are all so keen to play that it would have saved me a lot of bother had I [only] brought 11.'

Things started to change as a consequence of the misfortunes of Andrew Stoddart's second mission to Australia in 1897–98, when Hirst sustained a back injury in the third Test and was not the same for the rest of the series. So tough did England find things in the field that William Storer, the wicketkeeper, took off his pads and bowled in four of the five matches. Across the next six tours of Australia the size of tour parties was raised from 13 to 17, a transformative difference, and this was probably one of the areas in which MCC's management of tours proved a benefit.

There was still some scepticism at the growth in numbers, Warner referencing the abuse MCC received for selecting seven bowlers (in a squad of 14) for the 1903–04 tour. Gradually, the concept of providing injury cover for every department came to be accepted as the basic minimum; as a consequence of that, it became accepted that those players who started as reserves might actually force their way into the team through their performances in matches outside the Tests – and that competition for places on tour was actually a good thing.* A switch of wicketkeeper from Herbert Strudwick to Tiger Smith after the first Test of 1911–12, and a decision to rest Herbert Sutcliffe from the final match of the 1928–29 series and bring in Maurice Leyland, who scored 137 and 53 not out, were notable for their novelty, and success.

The number of players taken to South Africa remained relatively small until after the Second World War owing to the need to keep down costs. It took some creativity to find space for even a fifteenth player on the 1927–28 tour, when Ian Peebles, a young uncapped leg-spinner, was added late on as secretary to the captain (originally Guy Jackson, but in the event Ronnie Stanyforth). Peebles ended up playing in four of the five Tests; he is one of only four teenagers to play Test cricket for England overseas.

For many years, a defining feature of a tour was that it saw a group of players leave home together as one body of men and return several months later still as one.† But that notion has been eroded since the late 1990s as tour parties have fragmented, red-ball and white-ball specialists coming and going at different times. More recently still it was challenged by the Covid-19 pandemic and the need for players to be given breaks from living in bio-secure bubbles. For the mental well-being of those involved, a three-month tour of Sri Lanka and India in 2020–21 was broken into blocks – three pairs of two Tests, and

---

* It is notable that the three major tours since the Second World War for which England originally selected fewer than 16 players saw them send for reinforcements: in the West Indies in 1947–48 and 1959–60 and in India in 1963–64. The smallest party England have deployed in modern times for any Test tour was 14 for Zimbabwe in 1996–97. The original plan was to take 15 players, but Dominic Cork was a late withdrawal and was not replaced before departure. Halfway through the tour, Craig White was summoned as a replacement. Cork joined the squad in time for the second leg of the winter in New Zealand, when there were 16 players.

† When at the end of the 1909–10 tour of South Africa some of the amateur members of the team went on to Rhodesia while the professionals returned home, on the basis that they had not been paid to remain any longer, the captain Henry Leveson-Gower wrote: 'I was sorry not to have been one of the party on the homeward voyage, for we had had a very pleasant trip out together, and it would have been nice to finish the tour by travelling back with them.'

white-ball matches – with most multi-format players missing at least one block in order to have some time at home. In total, the Test squad consisted of 16 players plus seven reserves, as quarantine measures meant it was not possible to fly in injury or illness replacements in the usual way. 'We are being pragmatic,' Ed Smith, the then national selector, said.

> If you keep people in a bubble unchanged for three months and expect them to play every game in every format, they will not be able to play to their best ... The concept of a tour needs to be modernised. We're not travelling by boat, we don't go away for five months at a time, we need to be more nimble, and if we need to break a tour up so we can get people in and out, for their good and for England's good, we'll do it ... It's a policy we really believe in and we've had incredible support from the players. They know we're doing it for the right reasons.

The intentions may have been worthy but the chopping and changing was not helpful towards results, and the policy was gratefully abandoned once the pandemic subsided.

Size of England Test Tour Parties

The number of players chosen in an original tour party, not taking account of those who joined after departure as additions or replacements; tours of four or more Test matches only.

Players	Australia	South Africa	West Indies	Subcontinent	N Zealand
12 or 13	1881–82 to 1897–98	1913–14			
14	1901–02 to 1907–08	1905–06, 1909–10 and 1922–23	1929–30 and 1934–35		1929–30

Players	Australia	South Africa	West Indies	Subcontinent	N Zealand
15		1927–28 to 1938–39	1947–48 and 1959–60	1963–64	
16 or 17	All tours since 1911–12 *except 1954–55 and 2021–22*	All tours since 1948–49	1953–54 and all tours since 1967–68	1951–52, 1961–62 and all tours since 1972–73 *except 2012–13**	
18	1954–55 2021–22*			2012–13	

*England took 16 players plus seven reserves to play six Tests in Sri Lanka and India in 2020–21 owing to logistical difficulties created by the Covid-19 pandemic. For the 2021–22 tour of Australia, also during the pandemic, they picked 18 players in the main squad plus a back-up group of 15 Lions players to train with them and play internal matches in the early weeks of the tour.

In 2006–07, England took a squad of 16 to Australia, but also arranged for 14 academy players to be based in Perth as reserves, a consequence of the previous tour of Australia being hit by several early injuries. Having standbys close at hand subsequently became common practice.

Touring life was generally hardest for those players who did not play much. This was always liable to happen to those cast from the outset as spare wicketkeepers or spinners, so selectors needed to be mindful of picking those who were good, clubbable tourists, and would not complain if they spent most of their time carrying drinks and helping out in the nets, while staying ready to play should the need arise. A captain might want real scrappers to take onto the field, but the reserves needed to be supportive, biddable and uncomplaining.

If a player was having a tough tour, it would often manifest itself in his daily behaviour. A young Ian Botham, on his first full tour, behaved highly erratically, 'driven crazy by the boredom of not being in the team'. As the number of side matches on tours diminished, so too did the opportunities for fringe players to get a game, something Geoff Boycott noted on England's first post-Packer tour to Australia in 1979–80: 'The tour simply involved too much travelling and not enough cricket ... Our reserve players got very little cricket in the middle and it was quite soul-destroying for them.' On the next visit there three years later, Bob Willis, the captain, made a similar observation: 'Those who consistently fail to make the Test team can often eventually become bored, irritable and homesick ... A tour can be lonely and depressing if things go wrong.' He added: 'For a player who cannot get in the side ... the whole experience can become one of abject misery.'

Vic Marks was one of the marginal players on the Test leg of that tour – as was always likely, as he was among three off-spinners in the squad – and admitted to finding the experience testing: 'I can understand how cricketers are more likely to become depressed on tour. Sometimes there seems no escape from a vicious circle. Too many failures and you are out of contention; then there is too much time on your hands ... Guilt creeps in since there is a wife and young child back at home battling away in your absence ... All too easily the bar becomes a haven.'

When Chris Broad spent three weeks on the sidelines at the 1987 World Cup on the subcontinent, he convinced himself he would be recalled for the final against Australia, a team against whom he had scored a lot of runs, and when it was confirmed he would not be playing he could not hold back his tears of disappointment. One of the curiosities of international team sports is that you can be among the best 16 or 17 players in the country and still endure long periods not playing. In those circumstances a cricket tour can feel like a prison, especially when your captain tells you in advance that you are unlikely to feature in the Tests and then hardly speaks to you again. This was the fate of Surrey fast bowler Peter Loader in Australia and New Zealand under Len Hutton, who as the tour neared its end asked him when they happened to stand next to each other in the urinals: 'Did you have a good tour, lad?'

With side matches against local teams removed from tour itineraries altogether during the 2020–22 pandemic, Matt Parkinson went through an entire three months in Sri Lanka and India without playing a match other than an early intra-squad warm-up, while Moeen Ali, who spent the first two weeks of the same tour in isolation after testing positive for Covid-19 and was later sent home to spare him more time in the bio-secure bubble, played only one of the six Tests. He later cited this experience as a contributory factor in his retirement from Test cricket ahead of England's next major tour to Australia. 'I was thinking about the Ashes and how I would love to have gone back and done well there,' he said. 'But it's such a long trip if I'm not "in it" and I think it'd be very difficult. And if I felt like I did against India when I was out there, then I would probably retire after one match. So it's done.'*

Some resorted to gallows humour: on one tour, Jack Birkenshaw took to writing on immigration forms that asked his occupation, 'net bowler'. Among wicketkeepers, Bob Taylor spent two tours of Australia understudying Alan Knott, and Steven Davies spent three successive winters as reserve to Matt Prior. At least on the first of his tours, Taylor's captain Ray Illingworth saw to it that he won a first Test cap when the team moved on to New Zealand, while on the second, not quite as satisfyingly, he developed a healthy suntan ('He now knows the swimming-pools of Australia almost an intimately as the streets of his native Stoke-on-Trent,' Christopher Martin-Jenkins wrote). Davies never did play a Test match, home or away. Harder than going on tour as a designated reserve was to set off in the expectation of playing, only to be overtaken by a rival, as happened to David Bairstow when Paul Downton was

---

* Nine months later, in May 2022, it emerged that Moeen was prepared to reconsider his retirement decision, but after several months of reflection he opted against making a return. He came out of retirement to play the home Ashes series of 2023.

preferred to him as keeper in the Caribbean in 1980–81. 'Not once did he show it [his hurt] or let up his irrepressible cheer,' Frank Keating wrote.

Not everyone earmarked for making up the numbers did so. David Allen, the Gloucestershire off-spinner, was told by manager Walter Robins during the early days of his first England tour to the West Indies that he would not be playing much. 'I'll have a lot of speeches to make,' Robins informed him, 'so I'd like you to look after my briefcase.' As it turned out, Allen played all five Tests and was spared secretarial duties – and would go on to make 25 Test appearances overseas, more than any specialist English spinner to that point except Wilfred Rhodes.

Conversely, players with reputations for being difficult people or rather too lively tourists could find themselves overlooked, and pairs of known troublemakers could expect to be kept apart. Bill Edrich's unquenchable thirst for late-night revelry eventually caught up with him and he was left out of the Australia tour in 1950–51, to the incredulity of the Australians, who according to Neville Cardus viewed Edrich's omission as 'yet another instance of "old school tie" officiousness and stupidity'. Edrich said that he was asked by Rowan Rait Kerr, the MCC secretary, to withdraw his name from tour selection – presumably to spare everyone the embarrassment of publicly explaining the reasons for his exclusion – but he declined. It must have been some consolation to him that he was so highly regarded by the captain of the next tour of Australia, Len Hutton, that he was given a quasi-official role in the team.

Fred Trueman was passed over for two major tours after receiving a critical report from Hutton in the Caribbean in 1953–54. Trueman overdid the short ball and struggled to keep his colourful language in check, but some offences ascribed to him were probably committed by others who got off scot-free. Johnny Wardle's invitation to tour Australia in 1958–59 was withdrawn following a public falling-out with Yorkshire after the county announced they would be releasing him at the end of the season, because as was later explained 'his general behaviour on the field and in the dressing rooms left much to be desired'. When Wardle responded with critical articles in the *Daily Mail* which broke his county contract, Yorkshire sacked him with immediate effect, prompting MCC to pull him off the tour, referencing in a statement the grave disservice he had done to the game with his comments.

Wardle had made four Test tours prior to this and never been regarded as an easy companion, Godfrey Evans noting 'not many people on tour have got on well with Johnny.' MCC perhaps had little choice but to follow Yorkshire's lead, but there was no excuse for the decision not to replace Wardle with another spinner. Peter May, the captain, said he was happy with just two spinners – Jim Laker and Tony Lock – but it was the responsibility of Gubby Allen as chairman of selectors to ensure there was sufficient back-up; sure enough, after the tour began a spare spinner, John Mortimore, had to be summoned.

The jeopardy was all the greater because Laker's own place on the tour hung by the finest of threads following a falling-out with May, his county captain at Surrey; it was only after mediation resulted in a peace being brokered that Laker withdrew an earlier statement that he would be unavailable.* Laker had been left out of an earlier tour of Australia because Len Hutton had doubts about his stomach for the fight when batsmen got after him.

Allen was also the focal point of the most extraordinary and self-destructive of all vetoes in respect of an England tour selection when he intervened to prevent John Snow going to Australia in 1974–75. Snow was England's premier fast bowler, had been pivotal in the Ashes being won Down Under four

---

* Laker would also not have endeared himself to the inner circle when he told Allen before the tour that he was thinking of turning amateur because he understood that he could earn more that way; while he would be paid £800 as a professional, he understood that Trevor Bailey as an amateur was to receive £1,000 in expenses and broken-time payments.

years earlier, and still held a psychological advantage over the Australian batsmen. Snow's crime was to have bowled an over of under-arm deliveries at Geoff Boycott during a Test trial at Worcester the previous summer in protest at the futility of the exercise.

Dennis Amiss, who was at the non-striker's end, recalled:

Snowy said, 'What am I doing here bowling to these two seasoned players on a flat wicket? I can't get the ball above knee height, what sort of trial is this?' Gubby was not happy, the selectors were not happy. They'd wanted the trial and wanted Snow to test us. Snow was not picked for any of the home Tests against India and Pakistan. Tony Greig, Alan Knott, Keith Fletcher, Derek Underwood and I had dinner with Mike Denness [the captain] and urged him to push for Snow's inclusion [for Australia]. It was no good. Mike told us Gubby came into the meeting and said under no circumstances does John Snow go to Australia.

This was a flagrant breach of the principle of a captain getting the players he wanted.

Generally, the driving forces behind such exclusions were captains or head coaches rather than full-time selectors or administrators. Phil Edmonds was left out of several winter tours because he was considered difficult, first by Mike Brearley and then Bob Willis. The breaking point with Brearley was Edmonds's slothful approach to 12th man duties which led to the two men squaring up in the dressing room at the WACA.

David Gower's omission from a tour of the subcontinent in 1992–93 came largely at the instigation of Graham Gooch, whose patience with Gower had been tested by events in Australia two years earlier where, in Gooch's eyes, Gower did not approach his obligations as a senior player with sufficient seriousness; their relationship was complicated by Gower's recent sacking as England captain for a second time. 'I'm not sure that Graham was ever entirely happy with David on tour once he became captain himself,' wrote Jack Russell, another member of the team. Bizarrely, at a press conference to unveil the touring party, Ted Dexter, who chaired selection, refused to discuss why players had been left out. Gooch later admitted that he got things wrong with Gower, but taking ex-captains on tour was generally one of the riskier selection gambles. Such dynamics were probably lost on those MCC members who as a result of Gower's omission forced a largely symbolic confidence vote in the Test selectors among the club's constituents (which they lost). Alec Stewart, in conjunction with head coach David Lloyd, left out Phil Tufnell and Andrew Caddick from a tour of Australia in 1998–99, but Lloyd later expressed regret that Caddick was not picked more often during his reign.

One of the most dramatic omissions was that of Ben Stokes who, within hours of being named vice-captain of an Ashes tour in September 2017, was suspended by the ECB following the emergence of camera-phone footage of him fighting in a Bristol street hours after playing in a one-day international. Stokes was arrested but not initially charged. However, extracts of the footage shown on *The Sun*'s website were ugly enough for the board to suspend him from playing pending the outcome of its own internal investigation, which itself largely depended on a police inquiry. Stokes missed the Australia leg of the tour before joining the team for some matches in New Zealand. Several months later he was cleared of affray at Bristol Crown Court.

Tour selectors also needed to be cognisant of blending experience and youth. A tour party needs to contain mature players who understand the particular demands of life on the road and local conditions, but must also have space for juniors who bring energy and enthusiasm, and hopefully will learn enough to be of value the next time England tour the same place. Striking the right balance is one of the hardest things to achieve, especially as age is not necessarily the only indicator of when a player might approach their sell-by date. Sometimes it is miles on the clock. There were high hopes that the teams sent to Australia in 1958–59 and 2013–14 would do well; as it turned out, too many members of these teams had been together too long and they were emotionally spent. On the other hand, a lot of the players who won in India under Tony Greig in 1976–77 said that they had gained invaluable experience touring the subcontinent four years earlier. Convincing both older and younger players that they were equally important to the overall mission was also an important task for any management. Mike Gatting and Micky Stewart, as captain and cricket manager of the Australia tour of 1986–87, worked hard with both groups around the time of departure to gain their confidence.

Inevitably, some young players were chosen too soon, to their detriment. The team that went to Australia in 1950–51 was, as mentioned, badly put together, and one of the major criticisms was that it was too inexperienced for such a major assignment. Among the many absurdities was John Warr being preferred as seamer to Les Jackson, who was the far better bowler and was at 29 six years Warr's senior (Warr returned bowling figures of one for 281 in the series).* Another member of the party who struggled was Brian Close, who was only a teenager and remains the youngest England cricketer ever to play a Test match in Australia. Like Fred Trueman in West Indies three winters later, he was generally reckoned to have toured too soon. Close in fact never played another Test match overseas.

Not all fears that someone was being prematurely chosen were realised. When Pelham Warner pushed for the inclusion on an Australia tour of J. W. Hearne at the age of 20, Hearne's county Middlesex lobbied MCC not to pick him, only to relent two weeks before the team departed. In the event, Hearne scored a century in his second Test.

---

* Their backgrounds probably hinted at the real reason why one went and the other did not: Warr was a Middlesex amateur, while Jackson came from Derbyshire mining stock.

In terms of average age, England's most youthful tour party was that to Sri Lanka in 2007–08 under Peter Moores, whose first winter it was as head coach. The Test series was lost, but the tour laid some of the ground for the team to go on to reach no. 1 in the world under Andrew Strauss and Andy Flower.

Whether it is actually better to start a Test career overseas rather than at home is a moot point. Mark Ramprakash made a difficult start to his England career at home against a strong West Indies pace attack and never completely established himself in the side despite playing more than 50 Tests, but his batting found greatest expression overseas. 'Playing home Test matches were very nerve-racking experiences,' he told me, 'and going on tour perhaps helped me deal with that side of things better. Being part of a squad, there was more continuity [to selection], and that was important. I enjoyed playing in the heat and sunlight. By and large I coped with being away and I enjoyed trying to adapt to the different conditions. Perhaps I felt there was less of a spotlight on me.' Harry Brook had played only once at home before touring Pakistan in 2022 and scoring heavily, and he felt that helped him settle into Test cricket.

Nathan Leamon, England's long-serving analyst, said that the data actually suggested it used to be harder debuting on tour. 'Yes, there can be less scrutiny, less pressure, and fewer text messages from family and friends etc.,' he said, 'but the figures are reasonably clear that it was harder. People who debuted away from home had shorter Test careers on average. But recently that effect seems to have disappeared.' Nevertheless, the desire to avoid blooding new players overseas remains strong. Chris Silverwood, the then head coach, said six months out from the Ashes tour in 2021–22 that it was the management's aim 'to get to the point where we're not debuting anybody in Australia'. In fact, they had to give one player a debut when Sam Billings was called up as an emergency wicketkeeper for the final Test, but by then the series was already lost and the team heading for an overwhelming defeat.

Leamon also said there was evidence to suggest that players got better the more they toured.

I did a bit of [research] work on winning in Australia and India, and it was interesting that visiting players tended to improve in India in terms of people on their second tours outperforming their first tours, people on their third tours outperforming their first ... and that wasn't the case in Australia. That's not something I can explain but it seemed reasonably clear from the figures, even when you adjust for the fact that people who get three tours tend to be better players. They improve their own performances.

As English cricket became more professionally run, so the number of full-time support staff accompanying the players on tour grew – from Bernard Thomas, the first permanent physiotherapist (who toured with England for many years from 1968–69 onwards), to strength and conditioning coaches (starting in 1996–97), masseurs or masseuses (2004–05) and analysts (2008–09), among others.* It required not only greater funding for such roles to be properly filled but also a willingness among the administrators and players to recognise that they were genuinely worthwhile additions. As long as the amateur class held the reins of power, poor choices of backroom staff were likely if not probable, often because it was difficult to find good-quality people who could afford to be away for several months at a time without proper remuneration. This

---

* Gradually the number of specialist coaches and medics, plus analysts, media officers and security men travelling with England teams increased to the point where by the tour of Australia in 2013–14 they actually outnumbered the players. There have been several tours in recent years on which the backroom staff numbered more than 20. Bernard Thomas's value on tour was demonstrated in a wider sense when his quick actions saved the life of Ewen Chatfield after the New Zealand no. 11 was struck over the temple by a delivery from Peter Lever during a Test at Eden Park, Auckland in 1974–75; Thomas prevented Chatfield from swallowing his tongue. In a similar incident in Adelaide four years later, John Emburey, one of the England players, helped free the breathing of Australia batsman Rick Darling after he was struck in the chest by a ball from Bob Willis and swallowed his tongue.

is how English cricket got into the absurd situation of appointing the Duke of Norfolk tour manager.

England's cricketers have learned of their selection in all manner of ways, from letters, telegrams, phone calls and texts from chairmen of selectors and captains, to less direct methods such as radio announcements, calls from journalists, and public address systems at cricket grounds where they were playing. For every happy story of a player being chosen, there are others of someone's unexpected omission, and there have been notorious instances of players not even receiving the courtesy of a message telling them that they had been overlooked. In the early days, an amateur might receive a letter of polite enquiry about his availability, whereas a professional might be sent something more along the lines of a command. When the MCC secretary wrote to a young Jack Hobbs inviting him to join the team for Australia in 1907–08, Francis Lacey stated bluntly: 'I have been instructed to invite you to accompany the team. The terms of engagement are embodied in the [enclosed] agreement. If you accept the invitation, please sign and return the agreement.' First-time selection was an especially satisfying moment, and Hobbs understandably accepted his with alacrity, but four other professionals rejected the financial terms on offer for that tour, which Hobbs – with typical modesty – thought might have improved his chances of being included in the party.

Colin Cowdrey at the age of 21 learned of his first tour selection in 1954 – a shock not only to him but also most of the country – via a stranger's car radio while standing in the car park at Blackheath, where his county Kent had been playing a championship match. Moments earlier, Cowdrey had walked through a stonily silent Surrey dressing room on his way out of the pavilion unaware that news had already filtered through of the unexpected exclusions of Jim Laker and Tony Lock. That same day Frank Tyson heard of his inclusion after the end of Northamptonshire's match against Middlesex while sipping an end-of-play drink. He too was listening to the radio announcement, which listed the players alphabetically after the name of Hutton as captain: Keith Andrew, a county teammate came first, but Tyson had a long wait for his own name, which was greeted with cheers and back-slaps from colleagues. Tyson and Andrew then went back onto the field at Wantage Road to pose for photographs for the local paper, before returning to the dressing room where the phone rang and rang with calls from well-wishers.

At New Road, Worcester in 1982 there were contrasting experiences for three Middlesex players when over the tannoy the uncapped Norman Cowans learned of his selection for Australia and Phil Edmonds and Mike Gatting heard of their rejections. '[It] was surprising news to all three,' teammate Simon Hughes noted. Matthew Hoggard learned of his selection for a West Indies tour in 2004 when his mother-in-law saw the news on BBC's teletext service.

Official confirmation would come in the post from Lord's via a special invitation on embossed card. The sort of contract sent to Jack Hobbs continued for many years to be sent out to touring players outlining what they could and could not do, or say; good behaviour was always an integral part of any player–board contract and was for many years enforced by threat of withholding tour bonuses.

However the news arrived, for most of those chosen selection was cause for great satisfaction and pride. It was reward for hard work and in many cases the fulfilment of a dream. Quite soon, though, a sense of anticipation jostled with anxiety as to what lay ahead.

CHAPTER 7

Final Days, Final Minutes

How teams prepare before departure

Once a touring party was chosen, thoughts turned to planning and preparation. What might the players do on an individual level and what might the team do collectively, to be ready come the day of departure? Of course, there might be cricket to be played for the remainder of the English season, for a matter of days or weeks depending on the timing of the squad announcement. The time available also depended on the summer season of the place England were touring. Australian tours were typically the first to start and West Indies the last: England teams heading to Australia would usually depart in September in the days of boat travel and October once they began going by plane; those heading to the Caribbean would leave in late December or early January. There was therefore always more urgency – as well as anxiety, given the status of the mission – about getting ready for an Australian tour than other places.

'Departure day seemed to arrive so fast,' one England captain noted in his diary of an Australian tour. 'A month ago we were still playing county cricket, and the few brief weeks since the season ended have been cluttered with engagements of every kind. There has been no time for a real holiday; every day was accounted for.' When England made a full tour of Australia in 2013–14 hard on the heels of hosting a home Ashes series followed by white-ball matches, many of the players were emotionally and physically spent even before boarding the plane. 'We had guys who didn't want to be there,' recalled one of them, Ian Bell.

For the next tour Down Under four years later, Moeen Ali found it hard to properly turn his thoughts to the challenge that lay ahead after a personally successful home season which did not end until 29 September. 'I went there [Australia] on the back of being in some of my best form for England,' he reflected. 'I was confident, but I probably didn't do as much planning as I should have and could have.' Understandably, after a long English summer, the players need to get out of each other's way for a while and re-connect with their families, but that can compromise preparations.

Jack Russell toured West Indies and Australia in successive winters, and his assessment of the contrasting state of the players' mindsets when they set off was striking. Ahead of West Indies, the team had had time for training sessions at the national sports centre at Lilleshall, which improved their overall fitness; in Russell's view they were 'the best-prepared England party ever', and once they got to the Caribbean they took the West Indies team by surprise with their intent. The following winter, there was simply no time to properly get ready for Australia during a short turnaround period once the English season was over. 'We just weren't fit enough,' he said. 'We just didn't have time to train properly . . . we caught up when we got there [but] we got the balance wrong, having only five days off on the whole tour.'*

For many years, touring players would continue turning out for their counties right up to the end of the season, or until such

---

* There have been six calendar years in which England were involved first in a Test tour of the West Indies running into April and later one in Australia, and generally their results were poor: 1954 (drew, won); 1974 (drew, lost); 1986 (lost, won); 1990 (lost, lost); 1994 (lost, lost); 1998 (lost, lost). Russell's comments related to 1990.

time as they were due to depart. In 1907, Jack Hobbs played nine three-day matches after receiving his invitation to go to Australia, the last of them nine days before the team's boat left Tilbury. In 1946, when the team sailed on 31 August, the earliest date any England tour has started, Alec Bedser took part in a championship match at the Oval that finished only the previous day. Denis Compton and Bill Edrich would have been in the same position had not Middlesex beaten Essex with a day to spare at Lord's.

For many years, there was a practice of touring parties shortly before departure putting out a team – generally under the banner of an MCC Australian XI or an MCC South African XI – at Scarborough or Folkestone against a strong invitation side, in what amounted to an early bonding session. In terms of such games being first-class fixtures, this first happened shortly before the First World War and continued ahead of most major tours until shortly after the Second, when ahead of a South Africa tour Compton entertained the crowds at Scarborough with two quick-fire centuries.* In 1924, 13 of the 17 members of Arthur Gilligan's party for Australia took part in a match between Yorkshire and the Rest of England at the Oval – Gilligan captaining the Rest to an innings victory over the strongest county in the country – and were entertained to a lunch by MCC on the second day. Two days later the players assembled at Victoria Station and were on their way.

Douglas Jardine's team for Australia in 1932–33 actually played two matches prior to departure, the first at Scarborough, the second at Folkestone, although Jardine himself did not feature in either. However, most of the team's front-line bowlers took part and Harold Larwood, bowling at great pace, and Bill Voce used the Folkestone game to try out their Bodyline tactics,

---

* Some of the earliest touring teams played informal, non-first-class 'send-off' fixtures ahead of departure. James Lillywhite's side of 1876–77, for instance, took on a local XVIII at Priory Park, Chichester in a game spanning the three days before they sailed from Southampton.

as they had already done for Nottinghamshire. This time, they were bowling at Frank Woolley and Bryan Valentine; Woolley, one of the finest batsmen of his generation but now 45 years of age, asked curtly, 'Are you trying to hurt me, Harold?'

This method of attack had been agreed early the previous month in the grill room of the Piccadilly Hotel in London, where Jardine had discussed the merits of a leg-stump line of attack against Don Bradman with Larwood and Voce in the company of their county captain Arthur Carr. This must rank as one of the earliest instances of detailed strategy being devised in advance of a tour. Over a few drinks and a meal, Jardine made clear his plan. 'Jardine asked me if I thought I could bowl on the leg stump,' Larwood recalled, 'making the ball come up into the body all the time so that Bradman had to play his shots to leg. "Yes, I think that can be done," I said. "It's better to rely on speed and accuracy than anything else when bowling to Bradman."'

Jardine's preparations went further. Subsequent to the dinner, he paid visits to Frank Foster's flat in Belgravia to discuss field-placings for leg theory bowling, Foster having used this tactic to great effect in Australia in 1911–12. Jardine also studied the charts of Australian batsmen compiled by Bill Ferguson, the long-serving scorer who had pioneered the method of plotting where each batsman scored his runs.

The idea that it might be advantageous to prepare players physically and mentally was slow to take hold, but if there was a good time to do this it was prior to a tour, when there was the chance to work with a relatively small, clearly defined group of players, rather than attempt to institute a more rigorous approach across many first-class counties. Len Hutton brought a practical dimension to his appointment as captain when he wrote to each of his players before they left for West Indies in 1953–54, asking them to make sure they were fit for what lay ahead. Two members of the squad were league footballers so this was less of an issue for them, but several Lancashire and

Yorkshire bowlers worked in the indoor nets, while Hutton himself went running.

Walter Robins, as manager, arranged for his players to attend a demonstration of circuit training from a senior athletics coach at Lord's before the West Indies tour of 1959–60. On Ted Dexter's tour of Australia, the team trained on board ship and arrived much fitter than other post-war teams. 'There was no loafing in bed as on previous tours,' one said. Colin Cowdrey, generally not the most enthusiastic trainer, was one and a half stones lighter than on previous visits.

As captain of the West Indies tour of 1967–68, and with the team not departing until late December, Cowdrey himself arranged for the players to attend a two-day camp at Crystal Palace, where they held net sessions and talked strategy; his prime motive was to unite the team following the dramatic removal of Brian Close. He made sure newsreel cameramen were in attendance to bear witness to the gathering and also arranged for Ted Heath, the Leader of the Opposition, to entertain the team at the Carlton Club. Cowdrey left his players with one request, 'For now I merely ask you to get plenty of exercise and keep fit.' Tom Graveney, who had first toured with England in 1951–52, praised the initiative: 'Even before we got into the aeroplane, the attitude of the MCC party was better than I had experienced before.'

Incoming captains and head coaches generally have licence to create new regimes, even if they do not always know how long they will remain in post. Cowdrey spoke to his players about a long-term plan that also took in a tour of Australia in 1970–71, for which he was eventually passed over as leader, but it was better to think that way; English cricket was for decades crippled by short-termism. When Graham Gooch took over as captain in the late 1980s, he immediately set about improving the players' fitness. He aimed to hold a week-long training camp at Lilleshall ahead of the tour of India scheduled for the winter of 1988–89 which was eventually cancelled, but when he was reappointed for the following winter's tour of West Indies he revived the plan, to good effect. He also used a one-day tournament in India, the Nehru Cup, to build team spirit and, in his words, 'see which of the guys coped best with the pressure'. He also got the squad to talk cricket for long periods, 'how we could revive our international standing and how to prepare for tours in the future'.

They also discussed strategy, and arrived at a plan for their fast bowlers to operate to a line 1ft outside off stump to frustrate the West Indian fondness for playing the ball through the leg side. Three of the four fast bowlers he intended to use in the Caribbean all played in the Nehru Cup. The camp at Lilleshall involved intensive physical and technical work and, importantly, the fitness tests fired the competitive instincts of the players, meaning they took them seriously. There was also a three-day session in Leeds run by Gooch's former Test opening partner Geoff Boycott, an accomplished player of fast bowling, in which the batsmen worked on dealing with the short ball by facing deliveries from 18 yards rather than 22. Little wonder Jack Russell thought them the best-prepared England party up to that point.

Lilleshall became the standard venue for pre-tour camps, and when Keith Fletcher was appointed cricket manager he and Gooch gathered the players there over a six-week period ahead of a tour of the subcontinent in 1992–93. They trained with Indian cricket balls and put down special mats on which the ball turned and bounced more. How useful these sessions proved was debatable, with one ball hitting Mike Atherton on the head and drawing blood. Fletcher also flew to Johannesburg to cast his eye over the Indian players during a Test against South Africa. When David Lloyd became head coach in 1996, he took the players on a week-long camp to a sports complex in Portugal, where they focused purely on fitness and were put through their paces by physiotherapist Wayne Morton and Dean Riddle, a recent Lloyd appointee as strength and conditioning coach.

Once Loughborough University became the site of a national performance centre in the early 2000s, the national teams had a permanent base from which to operate in the build-up to tours. Duncan Fletcher held a two-day gathering there ahead of the 2006–07 winter which he described as the most detailed pre-tour gathering he was involved in as England coach; it included a presentation 'to ensure the players were aware of how difficult a winter it was going to be'. Outdoor nets could be held inside large marquees heated up to replicate overseas climates, and fitness sessions held in state-of-the-art gyms and swimming pools. With the acclimatisation period at the start of tours getting shorter, the need to hit the ground running became ever greater. Small groups of players would also prepare at fast bowling camps in South Africa or spin camps in India. Loughborough remained the standard starting point for the next 20 years.

For England's 2010–11 tour of Australia, Andrew Strauss and Andy Flower felt they needed to implement new levels of thoroughness. Strauss had been a member of the team whitewashed 5–0 in Australia four years earlier and was well aware how quickly things could unravel on tour; of his eight previous Test series away from home, as player or captain, only two had been won. Flower's instinct was to look for every marginal gain he could find. One of his earliest acts after being appointed head coach the previous year was to appoint Nathan Leamon to provide analytical data that might underpin tactics. No England tour had ever been subjected to such advance planning. The idea was to get ahead of the game, and stay ahead, in the knowledge that once a tour began time had a habit of shrinking.

Strauss, the coaches and various other members of the support staff were as usual involved in the initial preparations, but what was different this time was that the players were introduced into the process early the previous summer. 'We brought the players in much earlier than on most tours,' Strauss recalled.

That's not easy because often their head space is elsewhere. You're speaking to them while they're in the middle of another match, or just before another match, so it's not a tactic you can use all the time. All through the summer we were taking them out for dinner and talking through the Ashes, really just to try and get them to buy into our approach – [that] as soon as we landed we were all systems go. A lot of tours you tend to ease your way in and then suddenly you're into the first warm-up game, and if you're not fully switched on you can find yourself playing poorly, and that sets the tone. Once a tour starts to go wrong, it's too late. So you have to start the tour well, which means you've got to have done a lot of preparation and then be 100 per cent on it from ball one.

Leamon was working on plans from April onwards, which was necessary if selection for the home internationals and training during the domestic season was to be tailored accordingly. 'I built a model of playing Test matches in Australia, and simulated the Ashes ahead of that summer,' he told me.

It showed that if both teams performed to their past levels of performance we had an 8 per cent chance of winning at that point. There were conversations with Andy Flower and Andrew Strauss about what we had to do to increase those numbers. By the time we got to the start of the Ashes in Australia, we were up at about 35 per cent, so we were up at about evens given that they [England] held the Ashes [and only needed a draw to retain them].

Leamon summarised three main mental and technical areas that the players were encouraged to work on.

One was [batsmen] leaving really well. As you go wider of the stumps in England, batting averages go up – averages on the stumps are about 20, then by the time you are 1ft wide of off stump they are 40-odd, but in Australia they actually fall because you've got more pace and carry in the pitches, particularly in places like Perth, so leaving well is the crucial skill. Another thing was the importance of accuracy. We really focused on line-and-length stats and just being able to 'bowl dry' for long periods when the ball stopped moving. Thirdly, there were a number of different things to try to take away home advantage. There was, for example, an explicitly stated policy of relishing being in Australia and relishing the contest. All the interviews with the players, they said, 'Australia is a great country, we're really excited about being here, and it is a great challenge for us.' There was a policy of not getting in your bunker, not rounding up the wagons.

Strauss and Flower also broke new ground by arranging a five-day boot camp in a Bavarian forest in late September, departing within hours of the tour party being announced. The Australians had organised a boot camp ahead of the previous Ashes series Down Under and that had been deemed a success, and England had taken their players to the battlefields of Flanders in the build-up to the home Ashes of 2009, but they had never done anything like this leading into an overseas tour. 'The genesis of the trip was our Ashes planning, and asking ourselves, what do we need to win in Australia?' Strauss added. 'Australia is a harsh environment in which to tour on all sorts of different levels, and we just thought we needed to be more resilient. We're good when we're on top but when things aren't going our way we tend to implode. So, how could we become more resilient? That took our line of thinking towards a boot camp.'

The players were shocked at the harshness of the experience. The weather was cold and the surroundings bleak, and the camp was run by Special Forces personnel who deprived them of sleep, made them run up hills and, in the most stressful task, carry bricks for three or four hours without being permitted to put them down. In one boxing drill, James Anderson sustained a cracked rib – not part of the script. On the final day, the squad visited the memorial site to the Dachau concentration camp. But it achieved its aim of creating a sense of togetherness among a group of players about to embark on a tour that would ruthlessly expose any vulnerability. 'Shared hardship brings people together,' Flower said. 'It allows people to respect the effort that their team member has put in right there next to them, and it gave everyone an understanding of the hard work that would go into winning an Ashes Test series.'

Strauss said that the most important moment for him was when the players were sitting around a campfire one evening and Mark Bawden, the team psychologist, began asking everyone what motivated them. '[We were] absolutely exhausted,' Strauss recalled.

> People were just talking about their life experience. Players were saying, 'My biggest concern is that I just don't think I'm good enough. I play for my family. I'm so worried about letting them down.' What you're effectively doing is baring your soul. 'I'm willing to let you hear this because you are my teammates and I know you'll protect me. You're not going to use this against me.' . . . That was the one moment that made it all worthwhile for me.

The problem was that such bonding missions were not easily repeated. There was not always the time to arrange them, and you cannot surprise people with it again, which was half the benefit of the Bavaria trip in the first place. In fact, the team management – with Flower still head coach but Alastair Cook now captain – did revisit the boot camp ahead of the next tour of Australia in 2013–14, this time with the Special Air Service near Stafford, but it was held straight after fitness testing at Loughborough and much nearer to the start of the tour, and had a far less positive impact. Many of the players were the same, but at different stages of their careers, and did not need challenging in the same way.

This time the cricketers were to be trained in surveillance techniques, in an operation that would culminate in a fire fight. Alastair Cook described it as shambolic: 'The food was awful. We were briefed for hours, sitting uncomfortably in parked cars, before undertaking a farcical set of exercises ... Half of the team got lost before the final fire fight.' David Saker, the bowling coach, simply left and went home. Strauss reflected later: 'One of the most dangerous things you ever do in sport is fall in love with your wins. You win doing it one way and therefore you think you can repeat that. Sport isn't like that. Nothing is ever the same.'

Leamon found planning did not always run as smoothly as it did ahead of that Australia tour, and cited India in 2012–13 as an example. 'We ended up playing a different series to the one we were expecting,' he said. 'A lot of preparation that we'd done, we'd looked at teams who had succeeded out there before – there weren't many – and South Africa had won there with their seamers taking all the wickets, and when the Australians had won over there Glenn McGrath and Jason Gillespie were extraordinary. So we were thinking we'd end up relying on our seamers.' England won the series, but not in the way they had planned – their spinners took 40 wickets, their seamers 16.

For the Ashes tour of 2021–22, head coach Chris Silverwood and Mo Bobat, the head of talent identification and later performance manager, began planning two years in advance, around the time they took up their posts in autumn 2019. Speaking nine months out from the tour, Joe Root, the captain, said: 'You need to make sure work goes in a couple of years ahead of being out in Australia ... since the last Ashes [in 2017–18] we've been looking very closely at what we need to do to build a team that's going to win in those conditions.' But for all the detailed planning, the tour ended in abject failure.

Were captains and coaches guilty of over-thinking and

over-preparing? Brendon McCullum and Ben Stokes, who took over from Silverwood and Root a few months later, certainly seemed to think so. As batsman and captain with New Zealand, McCullum had developed a relaxed, free-wheeling style designed to liberate his players from the pressures of top-level international sport, and he brought the same thinking to his appointment as England's Test coach (the coaching roles were split, with Matthew Mott, an Australian, taking charge of the white-ball teams).

With England's cricketers having endured a tough period during which they had won only once in 17 Tests, McCullum preached a philosophy of fearlessness and enjoyment, which chimed with the outlook of Stokes, who encouraged his players to see themselves as entertainers. They scrapped some of the warm-up routines and generally encouraged a more bespoke approach to preparation, and it was announced that when they toured New Zealand early in 2023 the team would head out a week earlier than originally planned to spend a week in Queenstown, which billed itself as the country's adventure capital, purely to spend time bonding over games of golf and other non-cricket related activities – the first time an England pre-tour camp had actually taken place at the destination itself. During the home summer, the England Test team responded by playing in a wonderfully liberated manner, confirming a suspicion that the modern game had probably become over-managed and over-professionalised. Finally, it seemed, those in charge had remembered that cricket was a game to be enjoyed, not endured.

The final hours were generally the most painful. The sands of time that had been running down since the team was selected were reaching the bottom of the glass and with this came conflicting emotions. Feelings of regret and guilt as tearful goodbyes were made to wives, girlfriends, children and families mingled with anticipation and apprehension at what lay ahead. How many cricketers' young families have sat at home in distress, harbouring irrational fears that a boat could sink or a plane might crash, and they may never see their father again? Reputations of captains, players and teams were about to be made or broken. While the younger players new to touring perhaps saw only possibilities, the older ones were more apprehensive about what might go wrong. Not a ball had been bowled, nor bat swung. Everything was still possible. But the precariousness of the assignment was evident in the depth and feeling of the messages of support that accompanied departure.

The final days were exhausting, and too much for some. A daughter of Wilfred Rhodes, one of England's greatest cricketers who made seven Test tours, recalled the work that faced her mother Sarah washing and ironing his whites ahead of a tour of Australia in 1920–21. In the weeks beforehand, Rhodes briefly returned to his home near Kirkheaton in Yorkshire after a county match with only enough time to pick up fresh kit before heading to the Scarborough festival for ten days, then he was back again for one night before taking a train south to play for the Rest against Middlesex at the Oval, a match finishing three days before the boat sailed for Australia.

'There were no such modern luxuries as washing machines or spin dryers,' Rhodes's biographer wrote in 1960. 'It had all to be done on a washboard with the aid of a dolly or peg tub, exhausting, back-aching work in the steam-laden atmosphere of the kitchen or wash-house.' Her final batch of washing done, Sarah Rhodes went to London to deliver to her husband his shirts and flannels before he left on his seven-month tour, so tired she slept 'the sleep of exhaustion stretched full length on the seat of her railway carriage'. Once he was away, she would fret that there would not be enough money to survive, even though Rhodes was fastidious about living within his means and always left enough in the bank before going away.

In later years, MCC provided shirts and flannels, along with the traditional tour jackets, sweaters and caps. There was an MCC overseas cap adorned with a George and Dragon, a subtle appropriation of a national cause by a private club. All these things would be sent to the players' homes, or the players would collect them from outfitters such as Simpson's in Piccadilly. Collecting new bats and boots, and purchasing the dinner jackets needed to dine as a first-class passenger aboard ship or attend the many civic functions that awaited them on the tour itself, became one of the rituals of a touring cricketer. For many old-time tourists, the real countdown began once they received through the post their ticket for the voyage, along with a passenger list and MCC luggage labels to attach to the cricket kit that would spend weeks stowed in the ship's baggage-rooms.

By the 1980s, a modicum of effort was made to review the health and fitness of the players prior to departure. They would be summoned to Edgbaston to be given the once-over by Bernard Thomas, the physiotherapist, and handed pieces of paper on which were written instructions such as 'get fit' and 'see your dentist' (Vic Marks said he combined the two by playing squash with his). In later years, more formal medicals were conducted on the meeting days at Loughborough.

Stories of chaotic departures were legion. Denis Compton was disorganised at the best of times, but getting him to Australia in 1954–55 proved particularly difficult. Having stayed behind for treatment on his knee, he had his car and all his kit stolen on the eve of departure, and then his flight had to be rearranged because he missed his inoculations appointment. When he finally arrived in Adelaide following a tortuous journey which involved a crash-landing in Karachi and going without proper sleep for six nights, he found that he had left behind the keys to his two suitcases.

The England management were left stumped when Dominic Cork pulled out of a tour of Zimbabwe in 1996–97 only 72 hours prior to departure citing personal problems following the recent breakdown of his marriage, a situation complicated by him having a two-year-old son. 'I have some personal matters that need to be resolved,' he explained in a statement. David Lloyd, the coach, said that Cork had the full support of the team, but later expressed disappointment at Cork's failure to join up with the tour until it had moved onto New Zealand six weeks later. George Duckworth dared not tell his wife he was touring Australia as assistant manager and simply left a note on the table: 'I'm going to Australia. I'll be back in April.'

Generally speaking, the longer the tour, the more tortuous the parting, and the greater the jamboree beforehand. With teams almost always assembling in London to then catch a train to the docks at Tilbury or Southampton, or head to Heathrow or Gatwick airports, there was often a farewell lunch or dinner organised on the eve of the journey.*

The very first English team to venture to Australia under the captaincy of Heathfield Stephenson in 1861–62 spent their last night at the Bridge House hotel near London Bridge as guests of the Surrey club that was heavily involved in arranging the tour. The team's health was drunk and the players saluted with a song, the chorus of which went:

> *Success to the Eleven of England!*
> *The toast is three times and one more.*
> *May they all meet success o'er the briny,*
> *And safely return to our shore!*

It might have been the first drinking song associated with an England tour, but would not be the last.† The next morning, the players – all bar George Wells, who had taken an earlier

---

* In the days when teams travelled by boat, the most common ports of departure were Southampton, which was the standard starting point for voyages to South Africa, and Tilbury, often used for sailings to India and Australia. Bristol, and on one occasion Liverpool, were used to take teams to the Caribbean.

† Maurice Turnbull and Maurice Allom in their account of the New Zealand tour of 1929–30 quoted four verses of their MCC drinking song, the first verse of which went: '*Drunk last night, / Drunk the night before, / We're going to get drunk tonight / As we've never been drunk before. / When we're out, / We're always on the spree / For we're all members of the MCC.*'

boat – lined up outside their hotel in the Haymarket to be photographed, an image that would become common with departing England teams whether the players were stood at the doors of trains, on the decks of ships or the steps of planes. Not many followed the example of Stephenson's men of being photographed in their cricket gear. Whatever the mode of transport, every tour began and ended with a journey – and the moment of departure was perhaps every mission's most poignant moment.

The eve of departure dinner also became an opportunity for the game's rulers – whether from MCC, the TCCB or ECB – to instil into the cricketers any last words of encouragement or guidance. A young Colin Cowdrey recalled a function held in the Tavern at Lord's before Len Hutton's team headed for Australia at which Lord Cobham, the MCC president-designate, 'addressed us as though we were just off to Agincourt instead of Adelaide'. Cobham urged the players not to disgrace English cricket's image even if it meant losing – a not unfamiliar refrain from an MCC officer but one perhaps inspired in this instance by Trevor Bailey's recent book which had caused such consternation around the corridors of power. 'I want you all to go out there not thinking that you're playing cricket *against* Australia but that you're playing *with* them,' he said. His words cut little ice with the players, one of whom, Frank Tyson, wrote, 'Some of us in the touring party held other opinions about polite behaviour taking precedence over victory!' The farewell dinner to the first post-war team to head to Australia was attended by Prime Minister Clement Attlee.

When teams travelled by sea, they were usually seen onto their boat-trains at Waterloo or St Pancras by crowds of well-wishers, families and friends, cricket administrators and press men. 'From end to end the platform was black with people, and it was with difficulty we reached the special saloon and carriages reserved for us; the crush being so great that the porters and the police had to fight a passage for us,' Pelham

Warner wrote of the scene at St Pancras in September 1911. 'Eventually, however, all scrambled aboard, the guard blew his whistle, and amidst tremendous cheering, waving of hats, and shouts of "Bring back the Ashes!" we started on our long tour.' Among the throng were a large number of cricketers past and present, including Lord Harris, who himself had led a team to Australia more than 30 years earlier and who in the station waiting room invited Warner's group to drink a 'stirrup cup', and 'in a charming speech full of good feeling and love of the game' proposed their health.

A Mrs Stevens and her sister who idolised the glamorous Percy Chapman, headed to Victoria Station in the hope of catching a glimpse of the England captain as the 1928–29 team boarded the train for the overland journey to Toulon, where they were to meet the boat. Describing it as 'quite the most exciting event of our lives', she said they got there early to ensure they were in front of a crowd that was estimated at 2,000.

'What excitement as the players arrived!' she exclaimed.

Mrs Chapman, the captain's mother, was there with a large tray of small bunches of white heather tied with ribbon that she pinned to each player's coat as he arrived, and Chapman was given an enormous horseshoe bound with the MCC colours and decorated with white heather, and as he at last boarded the train with the rest, he stood at the open window and someone called to him to put his head through the horse-shoe, which he did. I will never forget the picture he made . . . It was a wonderful day.

The distribution of sprigs of white heather as a good luck charm was something of a tradition. Arthur Gilligan's mother did it when her son's team set off in 1924–25, and Chapman's mother did it again when he and his players left for South Africa in 1930–31. Geoffrey Howard received a slightly more mixed message on the platform at St Pancras when as manager he left for the subcontinent in September 1951, Rowan Rait Kerr, the MCC secretary, saying to him simply: 'Well, good luck, old boy. Rather you than me. I can't stand educated Indians.'

With Hutton's team holding the Ashes when they departed for Australia, there was more than the usual interest as they boarded the train to Tilbury docks under the many eyes of photographers and TV cameras. Margaret Hughes, a member of the press corps, found herself getting in their way as she too rushed to secure a seat. 'I jumped into a carriage doorway and stood at the window to wave to my family, only to hear a dozen raucous voices shouting at me to get out of the way,' she wrote in her account of the tour, *The Long Hop*. 'I was blocking the photographer's view of the England captain, who was about to lean out of the window and wave for the official send-off picture. Hutton, seeing my embarrassment, smiled gently, patted my shoulder and in his soft Yorkshire brogue murmured: "Ay, it's me they want. Better get it over."' Then, as the train meandered through the London suburbs, the passengers could see from their carriage windows messages scrawled or painted on the fences or walls of terraced houses, such as 'Bring back the Ashes' and 'Good luck Len'.

Family and friends would often accompany the players onto their ship. When Andrew Stoddart's first team boarded RMS *Ophir* on their way to Australia, Johnny Briggs and Tom Richardson had to comfort their weeping wives, before Stoddart responded to a champagne toast from the ship's captain in the smoking room. Ivo Bligh, the man who had captained the mission in 1882–83 to recover the mythical Ashes and had now come to see off Stoddart and his players, then led a chorus of 'For He's a Jolly Good Fellow' before the 'All Visitors Ashore' message sounded and the cricketers were left alone.

Stoddart's second team was similarly treated to a reception on board ship at which Mr C. E. Green, a director of the Orient Line, wished them every success, before the English captain made a speech of reply, 'assisted by shy glances at the marginal notes on his shirt cuff'. In later years, the cricketers would check into their cabins before taking their families to lunch in the air-conditioned comfort of the first-class lounge and say their farewells. They would often find telegrams awaiting them when they boarded ship and spend their last minutes writing letters.

Tyson poignantly described – in a colourful account published almost 50 years later but based on contemporary diaries – how as the *Orsova* prepared to leave Tilbury the families now on the quayside would throw streamers, creating 'a multitude of rainbow-hued umbilical cords'. Then: 'The shore crew retract the last gangway. The *Orsova*'s siren sounds three deep baritone blasts, as the tugs on the river side of the ship take the strain, slowly manoeuvring the huge liner into mid-stream. The gap between ship and wharf widens until the boat and land are connected by nothing but paper streamers, slowly slipping through the fingers of those leaving and those staying behind.' A last message of support could be glimpsed on the side of a shed where a wharf-man had chalked: 'Bring back the Ashes.'

The practice of former England touring captains seeing off the party went back a long way. Lord Harris, the first amateur captain to lead a Test tour of Australia, sent Bligh, the second, on his way with a writing desk to use on board ship. Warner's 1911–12 team was bidden farewell by not only Harris but also Stoddart and Lord Hawke, and Warner himself saw off Johnny Douglas and his players when they headed to Australia in 1920–21, even taking the train out to Tilbury with them. Having listened to Lord Cobham's appeal for Hutton's side to play the game like gentlemen, Colin Cowdrey received a rather different message from Douglas Jardine, a former tour- ing captain of notoriety, when Jardine, by now spare of frame and stooped but immaculate in a pin-stripe suit, turned up at Tilbury and advised the first-time tourist, 'When you get to Ceylon, Cowdrey, have a hit and get your eye in. Then when you reach Australia, just remember one thing. Hate the bas- tards!' On this same occasion, Len Hutton took aside Cowdrey's father and reassured him he would look after his boy. Even in modern times, Mike Brearley, who had led England on their previous Ashes tour, turned up to wish Bob Willis and his team well before they flew to Australia in 1982–83, as did Peter May, the chairman of selectors and another captain of yore.

The departure for South Africa in 1930–31 was the first to be marked by a talking film on the platform at Waterloo, and over the years that followed it became common for captains to broadcast farewell speeches on board ship. Jardine and Freddie Brown both did so ahead of their Australia tours, and this practice gradually morphed into the more formal captain's press conferences given at docksides and airports. Conscious that they needed to be more open with the press, MCC even arranged a party for cricket correspondents ahead of departure for Australia in 1962–63.

By the 1970s, Lord's had become the default venue for tying up all the last-minute arrangements, what Cowdrey described as 'an elaborate prelude of conferences, net practices and photo-calls for the press'. The players would collect all the accoutrements of touring, including playing kit, tour brochures containing the tour's itinerary, travel schedule and hotel accommodation. Sometimes players were presented with more personnel mementoes such as cufflinks or watches. Photographs would be taken and interviews given by captains to TV, radio and newspaper reporters. Frank Keating of the *Guardian* described one such gathering at Lord's ahead of the West Indies tour of 1980–81: 'Sponsors' Girl Fridays, all look-alike with tight little bottoms and too much make-up, were doling out T-shirts inscribed with their company's crests, organising autographs and benefit brochures and generally looking very pleased at being on Christian name terms with the centres of attraction. Their bustle, pointless as it seemed to an outsider, added to the air of fizz and expectation.'

Reputations ready to be made, ready to be broken: Keating looked around the 16 members of that tour group with a tender eye. 'Somebody from this placid party will get back home on Maundy Thursday shell-shocked, perhaps beyond recovery. Somebody always does. Another one or two might write their name large in the legends with mention after mention in dispatches. The intrigue is to live with them now and wonder who and how it will be.' One of the 16, Geoff Boycott, who had toured with England since 1964–65 and was now aged 40, wrote in his diary that England were facing probable defeat, but that this sober reality would be forgotten come April. 'There will be no logic then, no reminders that West Indies are the best, no allowances made at all. People will look at the figures and use them to bury somebody's Test career.'

CHAPTER 8

The Outward Journey

The perils of travel

In modern times, at least when a pandemic was not complicating things, England's cricketers have been shepherded past every inconvenience on their international travels. They report to an airport hotel the night before departure where as a group they check in themselves and their luggage away from the hubbub of a busy terminal. On the day of travel itself, they are fast-tracked to an executive lounge before boarding. They are allocated seats at the front ends of planes.

On landing, protocols vary according to which countries they are in, but the principles are the same. In Australia or New Zealand, they typically collect their own bags and clear customs themselves, before being met landside by local ground agents and sped away – with a police escort if necessary – to their hotel, while an operations manager stays behind to corral their cricket kit into a separate vehicle. On the subcontinent, they are usually met airside and taken through their own passport control in a private room to minimise the time spent in public areas. On reaching their hotel, they will be taken to a team room – an area designated for meetings and get-togethers, and the storing of kit for the duration of their stay – to sign papers and collect keys.

They head for their rooms, and within the hour there will be a knock on the door and a porter will present them with their bags. Hitches can happen, but it is usually a frictionless process.

It needs to be like this because air travel, whether for business or recreation, has been a mass population activity for 50 years, and a major England cricket tour requires the regular navigation of crowded international and domestic airports. With tour schedules ever more closely packed, there is little margin for error: bags and people cannot be late, or mislaid. Hence England's appointment in 1999 of a full-time operations manager in Phil Neale, whose business for more than 20 years was to ensure the smooth logistical running of tours, a more hands-on version of the role performed by the old-style manager.

International travel is routinely gruelling, and if cricketers were not handled like special delivery parcels they would find touring life even more mentally debilitating than it is anyway. Once in the country they are visiting, they are sped between hotels and cricket grounds in coaches flanked by police outriders whose job it is to clear the highways. They experience culture through the prism of designer sunglasses and tinted windows. Official functions in which they might press the flesh of the locals have largely been wiped from the itinerary.

In some respects, the twenty-first-century international cricketer might be considered lucky. Tours may be conducted at a frantic pace, and there may be more of them, but they are shorter than they once were thanks to air travel, which became standard for England teams in the 1960s and has over the succeeding years got not only faster and safer but also considerably more comfortable; they escaped economy-class seating in the late 1990s. When an England team first flew all the way to Australia in 1965–66, they were still required to stop over in Colombo long enough to play two one-day matches against local opposition. On their next Ashes tour, they had a night's stopover in Singapore, and on the one after that in 1974–75, Mike Denness's ill-fated team was forced by engine trouble to spend eight hours in Beirut; a journey from London to Adelaide that can now be done in 21 hours took them 33 hours. Nowadays there is no need to refuel; it is even possible to take non-stop commercial flights direct from London to Australia's east coast.

What can now be achieved in a day, only a couple of generations ago would have taken a few weeks, and before that longer still. The first of all English teams to venture abroad headed to North America in part because such a journey was relatively short and practical. The voyage from Liverpool to Quebec still took two weeks in what was described as a 'new-fangled sail-and-steam ship with unreliable engines', and the crossing was so rough, and the *Nova Scotian* rolled so alarmingly, that it put off many English cricketers from ever attempting such a venture again.

The first team to Australia under Heathfield Stephenson took 65 days to sail from Liverpool to Melbourne and the second under George Parr, who had taken the first pioneering side to North America, 61 days; both journeys were taken on Brunel's *SS Great Britain*. Thanks to the opening of the Suez Canal in 1869, the journey had come down to 52 days by the time W. G. Grace led a side to Australia in 1873–74 – before the Canal, travellers were required to make a strenuous overland trip through Egypt – and what is now recognised as the first Test match tour three years later under James Lillywhite saw the west coast of Australia reached 46 days after the English cricketers left Southampton. By the early 1900s, the journey was taking less than six weeks, but there were subsequently only small improvements on this time until after the Second World War, when thanks to advancements in ocean liner technology it could be done in less than four.

The first English team to go to South Africa took 24 days to get to Cape Town, but thereafter voyages there typically took anything between 15 and 18 days, making a South Africa tour for some a much more attractive option than a winter in

Australia. Similarly, the voyage from Avonmouth, Bristol or Liverpool to Barbados, the traditional starting point for many of the early West Indies tours, took around two weeks. There was, of course, the prospect of additional voyages between the different Caribbean territories, notably from British Guiana to Jamaica which in itself took almost two weeks, but even so West Indies tours have always been among the shortest. The early big tours to the subcontinent required voyages of between two and three weeks to get from Tilbury to Bombay, again with the advantage of going through the Suez Canal.

The first England team to leave home by plane was Len Hutton's side to the West Indies in 1953–54. It was a move initiated more by the Bermuda Cricket Association than the MCC, Bermuda offering to pay the difference between the touring party's sea and air fares if they would stop over en route to Jamaica, on that occasion the first port of call in the Caribbean.* The costs were underwritten by a local businessman, Stanford Joel, son of Solly Joel, the diamond magnate. Bermuda had little cricketing pedigree, but there was an eagerness to secure the social cachet a visit from quasi-ambassadorial figures from the UK would bestow.

This was another instance of how finance and politics, rather than strict cricketing necessity, could influence tour schedules. It proved an unsatisfactory detour, not least because the ten-day stay meant the players spent an indifferent Christmas there before flying to Kingston. The first hitch came when the plane developed engine trouble and was forced to land at Gander, Newfoundland, where the tour party – dressed in light

---

* Before this, there had been a few cases of individual players being flown out to bolster tour parties, including Hutton to the Caribbean in 1947–48. Cyril Washbrook only agreed to go on the 1950–51 tour of Australia if he was permitted to set off later than the main group, travelling by plane whereas they had gone by boat, and also return home earlier by plane, because of business commitments. With reluctance, MCC agreed, but Washbrook, a professional, who turned 35 during the 1950–51 tour, was never chosen for another Test tour. Brian Statham and Roy Tattersall also flew out to join the same tour as reinforcements.

suits – encountered severe frost and snow lying a foot deep, and spent nine hours waiting for the plane to be fixed. The three matches staged in Bermuda, all played on matting pitches, at a ground at Somerset 12 miles from Hamilton, the capital, all proved damp squibs, although there was the sensation of the England captain being dismissed to the first ball of the first match. Much to the players' frustration, at the end of the tour the team returned home by banana boat.

The MCC had for many years an ingrained caution when it came to air travel, and the players' contracts included clauses forbidding them from travelling by plane without special dispensation from the club's top brass. But from the earliest times, many players wanted to fly, though a few found the experience nerve-wracking and preferred to travel by sea, even if it took longer. The post-war period saw a slow but steady expansion in international civilian air travel. The transition from propellers to jet engines, complete by the late 1950s, accelerated the process, as did an array of new planes such as the ill-fated de Havilland Comet (which serviced the London–Johannesburg route but whose reputation was broken by several early crashes), the Vickers VC-10 and the Boeing 707.

The challenge for the cricket authorities was that many tour destinations required long-haul journeys, which were the most testing for passengers. The new jets were expensive, and economically airlines were keen to develop straight-through services, but there were doubts as to whether passengers would put up with the exhaustion; many passengers also experienced airsickness. An analysis of the London–Sydney route in the early 1950s operated jointly by BOAC and Qantas showed that the outbound journey took 87 hours, with two nights on the plane and two nights on the ground; the actual flying time was almost 48 hours. 'It is apparent that both passenger comfort and fatigue requirements of the present day necessitate night stops, and that there are limits to the extent of flying that the average passenger will undertake without a rest ... Does a passenger want an express service which will take him to his destination in the shortest possible time, but in a fatigued condition?' It was also the case that ocean liners were getting faster: the journey to Australia in 1954–55 was accomplished in 23 days, the fastest yet.

Even so, it was surprising that it took so long after the Second World War for England teams to give up sea travel altogether, which they did from the India tour of 1963–64 onwards, given that players were permitted a certain amount of freedom about whether they sailed or flew home. Some players chose to fly back from Auckland at the end of the seven-month tour of Australia and New Zealand in 1946–47, as they did after the corresponding tour four years later (when the team took plenty of lengthy internal flights around Australia itself). Some also flew back from Jamaica after the West Indies tour of 1947–48. So air travel was hardly an unfamiliar experience. Yet for many years MCC's preferred practice was to send touring teams out by boat.

The Munich air crash of February 1958 which killed 23 Manchester United players and officials, and reporters, undoubtedly shook confidence in transporting large numbers of sportsmen in the same plane, and there were a few instances of the cricketers travelling in two planes to hedge the risk. Denis Compton's crash-landing in Karachi on the way to Australia in 1954–55 may not have done much for confidence either. The team that left for Australia in September 1958 took a curious route which involved sailing to Bombay, then flying 1,200 miles to Colombo, before sailing on to Fremantle, a journey no shorter than that taken by the team four years earlier when they travelled solely by the *Orsova*.*

A storm-lashed crossing from Bristol to Barbados at the start

---

* The absurdity of this journey was highlighted by Willie Watson being given permission to fly ahead from Colombo to Perth to receive treatment on a knee he injured on board ship.

of the 1959–60 tour left a deep impression on many of those condemned to live aboard the SS *Camito,* an unladen banana boat. 'It pitched and rolled for most of the ten-day voyage and some of the team never left their cabins,' wrote Ted Dexter, who fared better than some only because his doctor had given him seasickness tablets. 'Sea transport on the way out to a tour was preferred because it allowed players to acclimatise gradually, to adapt to changes in temperature, humidity and light that they would find on the cricket field,' he added.

That experience prompted Walter Robins, the manager, to demand an end to sailing to the Caribbean, which duly happened. But the next Australia tour under Dexter in 1962–63 still involved a substantial outward leg by sea: the team flew to the Crown colony of Aden, where they stayed two nights before sailing on the P&O liner *Canberra* to Colombo, where they stopped to play a one-day match, before moving on to Fremantle. The journey was easily the fastest transit to Australia yet, taking 13 days. It would be the last time any major England touring team travelled by boat. By then, Dexter had already led a team that flew to and from the subcontinent – arriving in Bombay and leaving via separate planes from Colombo – and when M. J. K. Smith's teams flew both ways without mishap to India in 1963–64 and, in two planes, to South Africa in 1964–65, the die was cast. There was simply no logical case for any longer travelling by sea.*

Even air travel did not quickly put an end to stopovers. When in 1983–84 an England team for the first time flew from

---

* In all, the main body of England Test touring teams sailed outward and homewards on 39 occasions between 1876–77 and 1956–57, of which 21 were to Australia and New Zealand, 13 to South Africa, three to the West Indies and two to the subcontinent. In addition there were four pioneering tours to North America in 1859–60, Australia in 1861–62 and 1873–74 and Australia and New Zealand in 1863–64 in the days before Test cricket started, when teams also sailed both ways. There were a further seven Test tours (five to Australia and New Zealand and two to the West Indies) for which they travelled by boat and plane. By May 2023, England had made 100 international tours purely by air.

London to New Zealand (as opposed to going on there from
Australia or, as happened on one occasion, from Pakistan), it
was arranged for them to spend two nights in Fiji on the way –
what Bob Willis, the captain, described as 'our acclimatising
and flag-waving stop-over'.* The team landed at 4.10 a.m., but
nonetheless local cricket association officials were there to welcome the players, who were then treated to champagne and a
three-piece band at their hotel. Some of the cricketers later flew
to a neighbouring island for lunch. Making do without proper
practice facilities, they played – and won – matches against local
teams on matting pitches in Laukota and Suva.

Flying may be quick but is rarely stress-free. A press conference given by Nasser Hussain and Duncan Fletcher in an
airport hotel at Heathrow on the eve of departure for India in
2001 was interrupted by news that a plane had crashed into
buildings in New York, an incident that came only weeks
after the 11 September attacks on the city. Already two players, Andrew Caddick and Robert Croft, had declined to join
the tour, citing security concerns, based in part on Foreign
Office advice that Westerners travelling in India should keep
a low profile. Afterwards, players and media stood around the
hotel lobby anxiously watching TV footage of the aftermath
of the crash. It was a tense morning, but the players boarded
their flight the next day as planned, and the tour proceeded
without problem. A lot of people were nervous about flying,
but most recognised that the benefits outweighed the infini-
tesimal danger.

The benefits were naturally greatest in respect of getting to
Australia, a distance of 9,000 miles. Flying drastically reduced
travel times and for a period at least created more downtime for
England's cricketers at the end of their domestic season. In the

---

* Willis's team flew via Los Angeles and Honolulu and lost an entire day crossing the
international dateline. The first England team to cross the dateline was the 1881–82
party that played matches in the United States before moving onto Australia via
Honolulu; the loss of a day 'utterly confused most players'.

post-war period, the departure date for an Ashes tour moved back from 31 August in the winter of 1946–47 to 24 October by 1978–79, a saving of more than seven weeks.

Travelling by boat, the MCC flag flying proudly from the mast, might have had its small pleasures but it was gruelling in its sheer tedium, the days stretching out like the horizon in their relentless sameness – assuming the oceans were calm, which they not always were. There were often very rough seas to navigate, and in the early years voyages could be brutally hard and dangerous. Seasickness was a constant problem for many and a matter of mortal dread for a few. For the most part, the challenge was the mental one of finding ways to cope with the confinement and boredom of shipboard life. This was particularly difficult for active sportsmen, who also had to find ways of staying in good physical condition when food and drink was plentiful and the means to train was not.

Depending on the route, the stopovers to take on fuel, supplies and passengers created welcome diversions, an opportunity to go ashore to shop or dine, experience a different culture and re-discover land legs. These visits generated excitement chiefly for their novelty, plus the vital opportunity to visit post offices to send and collect mail, and were often chaotic, dozens of passengers seeking to disembark together and make the most of the short time available and make it back to the ship by the appointed hour. Even as the boat dropped anchor, it would be assailed by a flotilla of small boats filled with hawkers looking to tempt passengers with their wares.

At Naples in 1920, these boats carried, according to Rockley Wilson, 'coral beads, mandolins, fruit and vegetables, including some truly gigantic marrows'. He also noted with satisfaction: 'Many cases of Vermouth were also taken on board.' On that same stop, Percy Fender and Frederick Toone, the tour manager, went to Pompeii, got caught in heavy traffic and had to take a tender to catch up with the departing ship; fortunately, the captain spotted the MCC hatband on Toone's trilby and took them aboard.

For the English cricketers, these ports of call were also occasions when they were sometimes expected to bring out bat and ball and take on local teams, usually made up of Europeans. The quality of play was often undistinguished, but this was not the point of the exercise; the games were as much public shows as competitive contests. After weeks of idleness, it was a chance for the players to reaffirm the purpose of their mission. There were times, though, when these quasi-circus acts led to mishaps, with the cricketers picking up injuries which kept them out of more important fixtures later on the tour.

In terms of the potential for seasickness, the Bay of Biscay was a particular source of horror. Most sea routes required navigating the Bay, and for many its reputation preceded it. Cricketers who went once, and suffered, would vow never to make the journey again. Among those most badly affected were Ranjitsinhji, Jack Hobbs and Gilbert Jessop, who estimated he was ill for 30 days in a row on one journey (and would surely have toured more but for his dread of the voyages). Arthur Shrewsbury noted, in one of his letters home during the 1886–87 tour, how seven of the 11 players on the boat were unwell and would be absent from dinner, with William Gunn the worst affected. 'Gunn talked of leaving the ship at Naples, as he said he could not stand the journey, but of course now that he is all right he don't [sic] think anything of the kind,' Shrewsbury wrote. 'It was like a transformation scene, seeing him being led about one day and the following day dancing, romping and singing about the deck, having forgotten all about being ill.' Pelham Warner described how on an outward voyage to South Africa, 'the waves swept right over the boat, bulwarks were stove in, and the windows of the smoking-room and cabins shattered.' It therefore became common for some to take the overland route by train and meet the ship at one of its Mediterranean stops. On the earliest Test tours, it was not unusual for many of the team to join the boat as far down as Suez. Half of the 1903–04 tour party took the overland route, and in 1928–29 all 17 players plus manager boarded the ship at Toulon.

The experiences for first-time travellers could be profound. In his memoirs W. G. Grace recalled the aftermath of a terrific storm in the Mediterranean on his maiden voyage to Australia: 'The brilliant rays of the sun fell on the foam which was flying before the wind and produced one of the most lovely sights I ever remember in the form of hundreds of miniature rainbows.' Brian Close making the same journey many years later was rapt by the beauty of the sunsets: 'The colour of the sky is most wonderful. It changes from a lovely shade of blue to yellow, then to orange and finally to a deep red ... If there are any clouds round they reflect the sun to you long after the sun has gone down.' James Southerton on the run between Aden and Ceylon wrote of the night-time beauty of the sea, 'which has been highly changed with phosphorescent light, giving to the ship the appearance of sailing through a sea of splendid green-coloured liquid fire and smoke'.

Some of the harshest journeys involved Atlantic crossings to North America and the Caribbean, when ships slammed into anvils of waters and passengers regretted ever agreeing to ascend the gangplank. George Parr's team that sailed from Liverpool to Quebec endured such a torrid voyage that it took four days longer than expected and several of the men were badly afflicted with seasickness. Of the ninth day of sailing, Fred Lillywhite wrote: 'This day will be long remembered by all the cricket-ers ... The waves were mountains high, and one passenger who had crossed the Atlantic 60 times, said he had never experienced it so rough ... we had no concert this evening, being totally unable to sit, stand, walk, or do anything but to bring one's self to an anchor on deck, and stand the drenching.' In compensa-tion they sighted porpoises, the northern lights and icebergs.

The sailing to the West Indies in 1934–35 was so rough that it left the players barely fit for cricket when their opening match against Barbados began two days after arrival in Bridgetown. Similarly, the first post-war team to go there had such a difficult passage on a banana boat out of Liverpool that they arrived three days late. Unsurprisingly, perhaps, both of these sides had the worse of a drawn match with the island side. Ken Barrington was once sick for a week on the way out to the West Indies.

Of course, the seas were not always roiling. Alan Ross, cricket correspondent of the *Observer*, wrote of one passage to Australia: 'For three weeks, all but a few hours and two slight monsoon squalls, we have lived in sunshine and under clear skies.' To everyone's relief, the Bay of Biscay was calm, although in any case by the 1950s ships were equipped with stabilising fins which could cut the roll from 20 degrees to four.

Calm seas may have been welcome, but they also allowed time to hang heavy. One way to pass the days was to log the ship's progress. When E. M. Grace kept a diary of the two-month voyage to Australia in 1863–64, he began each entry with a note of the miles covered every 24 hours from noon to noon; 200 miles represented good going. By Alan Ross's time, this had risen to around 500 miles, a telling illustration of how much more efficient ocean-going vessels had become. So fundamental was this metric to everyone's existence on board ship that it was standard practice to hold a sweepstake to see who could most accurately guess the distance covered.

Interaction with fellow passengers – and between cricketers obliged to share cabins for weeks on end – could be a fraught business. Bobby Peel's pranks of cutting through the ropes of a teammate's hammock, or locking him in the boiler room, were jokes that probably wore thin. 'A long voyage is always a test of human nature,' reflected Bishop Welldon, who shared the outward voyage with Warner's team in 1903–04 and wrote a foreword to Warner's account of the tour. 'If two persons cannot agree perhaps they quarrel; but if they quarrel they cannot as on land keep out of each other's way; they must rub shoulders every day on the quarter-deck ... We were a mixed party but we got on well together; we called each other names at least occasionally, but we thought each other jolly good fellows ... We tried to fight against the cliqueism which is nowhere so great a curse as on board ship.'

Neville Cardus complained that 'the snobbishness on an ocean-going liner is appalling' and denounced the social climbers vying for the recognition of the ship's captain, but by his later tours Cardus himself was a menace aboard ship to those who had listened to his stories before and didn't want to hear them again. The breakdown in Douglas Jardine's relationship with Warner on the Bodyline tour of 1932–33, on which Warner was manager, was reckoned to have started from their time aboard ship, and the disintegration of morale among the 1958–59 team also had its seeds in the outward voyage.

Travelling by boat only served to preserve the class system that cricket clung to for far too long. When the team sailed on the *Durban Castle* for the first South Africa tour after the Second World War, the whole team went first-class but George Mann, the captain, Brigadier Mike Green, the manager, and the three other amateurs in the team sat on a separate table in the dining room (Mann thereby hardly adhering to the advice of his father to make sure that every evening he was accessible to all his players). M. J. K. Smith, whose touring career just caught the end of the sailing days, said that a long voyage simply gave fellow cricketers time to get fed up with one another. Ted Dexter was accused of not mixing enough with his players on the way to Australia in 1962–63. It was amazing the ritual lasted as long as it did, but for that the cricketers had MCC to thank.

The languid tempo of life and debilitating heat made concerted mental activity hard. Despite his intentions to begin earlier, Alan Ross did not begin his journal of the 1954–55 tour until the boat was past Colombo and into the third week of its voyage because, as he put it, 'the sun liquefies the conscience as it does the body.' He added: 'Cutting cleanly through the middle seas of the world in this stately hotel, life has seemed to have no future, no past. Once the painful ties [with home] have been broken, the separation achieved, only the blueness remains real.' Also: 'Shipboard life has a romantic antique ritual of its own which pleases, interests and bores in turn.' The quiet-living Jim McConnon, preferred to Jim Laker as off-spinner on his first Test tour, was feeling homesick by the time the boat reached Aden.

Ross wrote several tour books, and a number of times touched on the role alcohol played in getting passengers through the longest journeys. Of the one to Australia he wrote, 'There is, of course, consistently too much drinking and eating, and too little sleep'; and when he sailed to South Africa, he noted: 'All bar records for the line have been broken. One felt oneself gingerly all over every morning and assessed the damage. Only after dark did the ship come properly to life.' He said some passengers took up drinking positions 'so formally stabilised that one had to look twice to realise they were not part of the furniture'.

Victorian travellers were no better. George Ulyett, the no-nonsense Yorkshire all-rounder, proved adept at smuggling gallons of whisky on board. 'We have plenty of good singing among our own fellows each night after dinner and so by that means the nights pass pretty quickly on,' Arthur Shrewsbury observed, before adding, less cheerily, 'Aboard ship life is not very pleasant, you have a great deal too much idle time in your hands.' Victorian seafarers also had rats for company.

Eating, like drinking, was a fundamental part of the daily routine and, as Ross suggested, everyone ate too much. One of the highlights of the early tours was the quality and quantity of the food available to passengers travelling first-class, as the cricketers then did, although James Lillywhite worried that his players 'have led an idle life on board and partaken freely of the good things that life affords'.

In Britain's post-Second World War austerity, the food available was a revelation. The cricketers' eyes widened in astonishment when white bread was laid out on the dining tables as they began their outward journey. The young Brian Close, having been given leave of absence by the army, could not conceal his excitement at the meals. 'It's nothing to have four eggs or more for breakfast,' he wrote home to a friend, 'two or three steaks for lunch and then at dinner we usually go "right through" the menu.'

Frank Tyson, noting that food, fuel and clothes were still being rationed at home when the 1954–55 tour began, wrote: 'The first lunch I ate on board was the most food I had seen in my life.' For working-class members of touring parties especially, such feasts were bound to make a strong impact, as did the accompanying tablecloths, napkins, crystal glasses and silver cutlery. Tyson described a four-week voyage to Australia as manna from heaven: 'several of us quickly acquired the reputations of being good trenchermen.' With another seven weeks in Australia before the first Test, Tyson put on 21lb before his serious work started. This was to prove crucial to his subsequent success in Australia's extreme conditions.

Other activities included race meetings, musical concerts, fancy-dress and cocktail parties and film evenings; on Sundays church services were held on deck if the weather allowed and they were generally well attended. The sunsets never lost their attraction. Cardus observed one inter-war touring party aboard the *Orion*: '[Hedley] Verity read *Seven Pillars of Wisdom* from beginning to end. [Walter] Hammond won at all games, from chess to deck quoits. Maurice Leyland smoked his pipe, and [George] Duckworth danced each evening with a nice understanding of what, socially, he was doing. [Bob] Wyatt took many photographs and developed them himself.'

For some, there was wooing to be done. Archie MacLaren was among the first English cricketers, though far from the last, to meet his future wife – Maud Power, an Australian socialite – on an outward voyage. Frank Foster and Johnny Douglas tried out their charms on the way to Australia before the First World

War. The younger members of the 1935–36 team that made a non-Test tour of Australia and New Zealand 'wasted little time in getting to know the best-looking girls aboard', according to Errol Holmes; John Human married one of them. Brian Close in his correspondence mentioned striking up a friendship with an 'extremely pretty' New Zealand girl.

Frank Tyson, whose mother Violet had warned him to steer clear of Australian women, thinking them 'fast', wrote in his diary: 'I have become very attached to a good-looking Sydney girl called Margaret, whom I met on our second day out of Tilbury. Our parting on the last evening on board was very emotional ... It strikes me that I am looking forward, perhaps more eagerly than normal, to seeing her again in Sydney.'* On that same tour, Bill Edrich, who would be married five times, formed a close attachment to a girl on the boat out and kept in touch with her throughout the tour. Manager Geoffrey Howard recalled: 'I was in his [Edrich's] cabin one day, having a few drinks, and there was a photograph of his wife. And he suddenly said, "I hate my wife," and threw it out of the porthole.'

The cricketers strove to ready themselves as best they could for the challenges ahead. Often as important as good food on board ship was rest, particularly for those fast bowlers who had got through immense workloads at home the previous summer. Many put themselves through training regimes as best they could. On the later tours, the ships offered swimming pools. Close calculated that by completing seven circuits of the deck house he could run one mile. Some players bridled

---

* Tyson did indeed see her again when he descended on her home on Christmas Day 1954 with Northants teammate Keith Andrew. Her parents were not best pleased: 'I had the distinct impression that Keith and I were not the most welcome of guests. We opted to take our leave early.' Heart-wrenchingly, Tyson also spent his last evening in Australia with her too; what he described as 'one of the worst nights of my inexperienced existence'. Their romance subsequently petered out, but another girl Tyson met on the same tour, Ursula Miels, came to England the following summer and they were married in Melbourne in 1957. After retiring as a player, Tyson, like Harold Larwood before him, emigrated to Australia.

when Gordon Pirie, a former British Olympic medal-winning runner, who happened to be on the same voyage to Australia, was commandeered to run fitness sessions.

Rudimentary cricket nets could be constructed on deck, with mats nailed to the boards, and teams also took with them slip-catching cradles. There was scope too for captains to discuss tactics with their players on an individual basis and in a relatively informal manner, as Jardine was said to have done with certain players aboard ship on the Bodyline tour. Hutton took the opportunity to get together some of the younger members of his Australian tour party and advised them that they would not be expected to play a major part in the Tests. This may have been designed to provoke a response; certainly it galvanised Tyson, who trained all the harder aboard the *Orsova*. Johnny Wardle took to the deck to practise bowling for three hours a day.

Mishaps inevitably occurred. Ivo Bligh so badly damaged his right arm in a game of tug-of-war that he missed the first month of matches in Australia. George Vernon slipped on a companionway and could not play for three weeks. Sam Staples developed such serious back trouble that shortly after arrival in Australia the decision was taken to send him home.

Voyages to South Africa, completed with a run down the Skeleton Coast and into Cape Town, tended to be not only among the shortest but also the least eventful beyond Biscay, usually with only brief stops at one of the Portuguese or Spanish islands. Madeira was the most regular port of call, giving passengers the opportunity to make the 300ft ascent of Terreiro da Luta by train, take in the spectacular view over Funchal, and then descend by toboggan. Pelham Warner's team of 1905–06 thoroughly enjoyed their few hours on shore at Madeira, 'where lovely hothouse flowers were growing out of doors and large baskets of roses were being offered for a shilling each'. But when the cricketers stopped there in the late 1940s, they found the hotels still closed from the war.

Peter May's 1956–57 side stopped at Las Palmas for around

12 hours; Alan Ross, making the journey a few weeks later in time to report on the Tests, described the island's 'mauve peaks swathed in turbans of cloud, the dark capes of Grand Canary struggling up out of the dawn'. His stay was shorter than that of the players, giving him the chance only to take a trap through the seedy port district to the Moorish Santa Catalina hotel, the official residence of the early governors which housed a statue to which Columbus prayed before setting out to discover America. Ross also noted how busy the shipping lanes were as a result of the re-routing of traffic due to the Suez Crisis.

Boats taking teams to Australia and India headed past the Rock of Gibraltar – where some of Gubby Allen's side of 1936–37 stopped to make the ascent – and on through the Mediterranean, picking up supplies at Marseilles, Toulon or Naples, where there might be time to visit Pompeii or cast their eyes up to the peak of Vesuvius. A contingent of Yorkshire players led by Len Hutton and including Bill Bowes, now covering tours as a reporter, used this stop to go to Caserta to lay white roses on the grave of Hedley Verity, who died in service of the Green Howards during the Second World War, and take photographs to give to Verity's widow Kathleen. Hutton and Bowes had both shared England tours with Verity.

The ship carrying the 1911–12 team had to take care to avoid mines laid off Taranto in Italy's war with Turkey. W. G. Grace's side of 1891–92 played a match on the Naval Ground at Malta. Several of the 1884–85 side went on a tour of the Pyramids and Cairo, and to return to the ship Alfred Shaw and George Ulyett sought the help of two locals: 'The Arabs rowed half the distance and then refused to go further without extra payment. Ulyett grabbed one oarsman by the collar and threw him into the sea, then proceeded to row to the ship, while the man swam alongside to the accompaniment of some decorated Yorkshire lingo.'

Two years later, another party of English cricketers was obliged to quarantine at Port Said, their boat having come from

Naples where a cholera outbreak had been reported. 'We have not the slightest illness on board, and it is very strange to me to see the yellow flag flying at the mast head, to denote that no one is allowed to board us,' Shrewsbury wrote, adding: 'They [the local tradesmen] are not allowed to handle the coin that is sent down to them in a basket before it has been pitched into a tin with water in it, as a kind of disinfectant.' A contingent of Douglas Jardine's 1932–33 side also paid a visit to the Pyramids to satisfy the curiosity of George Duckworth.

Port Said was a place to buy the best Turkish and Egyptian cigarettes, and take in the world from street cafés. Brian Close and Denis Compton managed to swing an invite to a morning cocktail party where they met some 'extremely nice girls'. 'They escorted Denis and I round the town,' Close wrote, 'and then we went back to the ship for lunch, in time for the ship to leave. They were rather sorry they couldn't come on board, in fact we were.'

Hutton's team at Port Said recorded messages to send to the British troops in the Canal Zone, thereby meeting their ambassadorial obligations, and then as the *Orsova* went through the Suez Canal they were cheered and saluted with pipes and drums by the soldiers. At Suez itself, through the latest collection of mail, Tom Hayward in 1903 learned from home of his mother's death. James Southerton recorded that many in James Lillywhite's party thought Suez 'the most filthy, wretched, and disgusting place they had ever been in'.

The passage through the Red Sea could see some of the most brutal heat of any voyage. If the breeze died altogether, as it often did, passengers were left searching futilely for respite from the sun's furnace; night-time, when sleeping on deck was allowed, was little better. Shrewsbury in the 1880s cited a chief steward recounting that he had made the crossing 17 times but never experienced temperatures like it: 'In our cabin the heat registered 96 degrees, in the daytime it was more and in the sun it would be about 160 degrees ... For two days and nights it has been a continual Turkish bath, perspiration coming out of every pore in your body and under-clothing being always wet through. There have been two deaths, a child yesterday and an old woman of over eighty this morning, both of which have been duly confined to the deep.'

Cardus wrote of the Red Sea passage: 'There is scarcely a soul on board who is capable of any form of sleep, either on deck or below the deck, in cabin or under the starry heavens; the Red Sea is at its hottest, its stickiest, its cruellest ... the *Orion* makes not a wisp of a breeze as she goes her patient course ... "She's a lovely ship," said [Walter] Hammond, "but I wish she had wings!"'

As the last practical stop before making land in Australia, Ceylon was a regular calling place. It was the chance for a lengthy break, sometimes with overnight stays. Even a day in Colombo might be enough to cram in a civic reception and a visit to the sprawling seafront Galle Face Hotel where light-weight shirts, suits or sunhats might be measured and made before the return to the ship. On one occasion, several coach-loads of passengers, among them the reporter Bruce Harris, made an 11-hour round trip to the hill town of Kandy before returning at 9 p.m. for a press party at the Galle Face before rejoining the ship at midnight.

Ceylon was also the most regular venue for a game of outward-bound cricket, with the Englishmen's thoughts now turning towards the more serious contests ahead. Crowds of several thousand were guaranteed.* These games did not always go as smoothly as the visitors would have liked. Arms and faces were often left blistered and red from the sun. In 1950–51, Len Hutton, England's best batsman, was twice hit on the same

---

* The first match played in Ceylon by an England Test touring team, by Ivo Bligh's side against XVIII Europeans in 1882, took place on Galle Face Green on the seafront, and play on the second and final day began at 8 a.m. to allow the players to return to the boat for a 3 p.m. departure. This is probably the earliest start made to a match by any England team.

finger already damaged during the home Tests against West Indies, and as a consequence he missed the first three matches in Australia.

As this match itself was coming to an end, a bamboo-framed stand with a coconut-matting roof caught fire. The source of the blaze was unclear, but there were suspicions that it was started by spectators. As a result, on the next tour the English players were given a police escort to the ground and some sections of the crowd were kept behind wire; even so, those around the pavilion slapped the players on the back if they got the chance and at the end of the game pelted the dressing-rooms with stones. 'One could sense that violence was only just around the corner,' Frank Tyson wrote. Bob Appleyard was accidentally injured by one spectator.

Tyson, like many others, found Colombo's humidity draining. 'We thought we were playing in an open-air sauna bath,' he wrote. 'I became so dehydrated before the match ended that I cramped, even while I was running up to the wicket.' Reflecting on this drawn match, Margaret Hughes suggested that Ceylon were capable of winning such a fixture and that the English team ought to fly straight to Colombo, spend a week there, and play two two-day games. This never happened as a prelude to an Australia tour, but eight years later Ted Dexter's team were bowled out for 127, the lowest score by a visiting England team in Ceylon since the nineteenth century.

The run from Ceylon to Australia witnessed the most serious accident involving any touring England team when one evening in 1882, with Ivo Bligh and his players some 350 miles into the voyage, their boat *Peshawur* collided with the *Glenroy*, an iron ship bound from Mauritius to Madras. 'All in a moment there loomed out of the darkness a large ship right upon us coming at an angle,' Bligh wrote in his diary. 'The whole crowd [on the quarter-deck] went helter-skelter across the deck falling over each other and everything else, all possessed with but one idea in that sudden death was both upon them and those dear to them . . . a fearful crash told us that the vessel was into us ... The utmost alarm prevailed for some time as the very general idea shared also by the officers was that we must sink in a few minutes.'

Amid the panic, two of the cricketers prepared to abandon ship, one with, in Bligh's words, 'a young lady's arms round his neck'. Dick Barlow was among those who inwardly said his goodbyes to his loved ones back home. The *Glenroy* – whose captain would ultimately be found culpable for the accident – ground along the side of the *Peshawur*, taking three of the *Peshawur*'s lifeboats with it, but fortunately the large hole it left in the *Peshawur*'s side was above the waterline. However, the *Glenroy* began shipping water, so the *Peshawur* with difficulty had to tow her back to Ceylon, where both boats were repaired.

The detour added ten days to the team's journey.* Among those injured was Fred Morley, the Nottinghamshire bowler, who was standing alongside Barlow and Walter Read on deck when the collision happened. He had several ribs broken, but this was not discovered until the team reached Melbourne, where one day Barlow found him in his bedroom 'crying like a child' and saying: 'I don't know what is the matter with me, but there is something seriously wrong somewhere.' Morley played some matches in Australia, and again briefly when he returned home, but was a less effective bowler than usual, the accident having in Barlow's words 'laid the seeds of a fatal illness'. Morley soon died of lung trouble.

The two weeks from Colombo to the western coast of Australia, across the Equator and into the north-east trade winds, was perhaps mentally the most taxing. Britain had long since been bidden farewell to, but there was still a long way to go, and there was almost no sight of land throughout this leg. Dropping supplies at the isolated Cocos Islands only reinforced the notion of the vast emptiness of the Indian Ocean. 'In a

---

* During this hiatus back in Ceylon, Bligh arranged for his team to play a match against a local garrison XVIII, the Royal Dublin Fusiliers.

towering sea two little boats came bravely to take a barrel from the *Orion* containing the quarterly supply of rations for the handful of men who work on the islands,' Cardus wrote. 'The last we saw of the little boats was their plungings and swayings as they returned to the island, with the man waving farewell in return; there was not a person on board the *Orion* who did not feel the emotion of the scene. "It makes a lump come into your throat," said William Voce of Nottinghamshire.'*

The length of a voyage varied according to wind and sea and this made planning the first days of a tour difficult. James Lillywhite's team reached Australia a week earlier than expected, and with the fixture list in any case still in a makeshift state this resulted in a ten-day wait before their opening game with a South Australia XXII in Adelaide. Bligh's team's first match began a day late because of their accident off Colombo; the delay might have been longer but under pressure from the local welcoming committee they reluctantly agreed to start play after lunch on the very day of their arrival.

When Walter Hammond's team arrived in Western Australia well ahead of schedule, organisers added two minor matches at Northam, an agricultural town 60 miles north of Perth, and Fremantle, both of which had not previously staged fixtures on England Test tours (nor would they do so again). Early England teams generally first saw Australian land at Fremantle or Albury, where they could climb Mount Clarence, before sailing on for up to four days to Adelaide through what could be rough seas beneath albatross skies in the Great Australian Bight.

---

* Cardus apparently remembered this eerie encounter when less than two years later he described in the *Manchester Guardian* Len Hutton setting a new world Test record score of 364 at the Oval: 'As the ground became resonant with the cheering the thought occurred to me that it was being heard far and wide, all over the Empire, not only all over the country. People walking down Collins Street in Melbourne would hear it, and it would roar and echo in Kandy, Calcutta, Allahabad, Penang: they would hear it in the Cocos Islands and join in, and on liners going patiently their ways over the seven seas they would hear it too, and drink Hutton's health.'

Cricket in Western Australia was not considered strong enough to warrant regular fixtures until the 1920s. After the First World War the 1,650-mile journey from Perth to Adelaide was taken by train across the Nullarbor Plain, but still required three nights in sleeping cars. Only after the Second World War was the journey east from Perth possible by plane. Fremantle marked the end of an interminable journey, but otherwise had little to recommend it beyond its cobalt blue skies. Neville Cardus called it 'a door of bleak utility', Frank Tyson 'a shabby ghost town'.

Unfortunately for Johnny Douglas's side, the first to visit Australia after the First World War, they and about 180 fellow travellers were obliged to spend a week in army huts at Woodman Point, a few miles south of Fremantle, serving quarantine after the discovery of a typhoid case during the stop at Colombo. The cricketers killed time by bathing, fishing, playing football or cards, and dancing to music played on a gramophone brought ashore by one of the other passengers. Coconut-matting was laid down, but it was too rudimentary for serious cricket practice. Percy Fender, making his first tour, thought the week did no harm: 'We had to get up early, and there was nothing to keep us up late. There was plenty of good plain food and nothing but tea or milk to drink. We were in the open air all day long and slept with hut doors wide open, and a week of this, after five weeks on board, undoubtedly did us a tremendous lot of good.' A scheduled three-day match in Perth was reduced to a one-day affair.

Whether arriving by boat or plane, English cricketers quickly had their chance to exchange pleasantries. As Percy Chapman left the boat in Perth in 1928, he was greeted by a dock worker who shouted, 'Good luck, Chapman! Have you brought the Ashes with you?' 'Yes', the England captain replied. 'I'll show them to you on the way back.' Four years later, Douglas Jardine's team were greeted by a marine band playing 'See the Conquering Hero Comes', a piece of music that had also been used to welcome the very first team to Australia in 1861–62.

Jardine soon made plain to Australian journalists that he would not be assisting them with any early indications as to his team selections, and the cool feelings were reciprocated. 'As soon as we landed in Australia and during our visit to the various states, two things were made extremely clear to us,' Jardine wrote. 'The first was that our chances of winning the rubber were hardly worth considering ... [and] we had, it appeared, one important function to perform – we were to supply opportunities for the cream of Australian cricketers to make and break records.' Many English teams since have experienced this same patronising attitude.

Jardine also adopted a measured tone when he led an England team to India, the land of his birth. In a broadcast speech delivered amid some chaos on the quayside in Bombay, he spoke with great diplomacy at a delicate time in Britain's relationship with India and in English cricket's relationship with other countries following the Bodyline furore. 'May I express the hope and belief that both on and off the field this team, which the Marylebone Cricket Club has sent to India, will be deservedly popular,' he said, 'for we represent the goodwill which the premier club bears to all lovers of cricket throughout this great Indian Empire.'

Hammond's team to Australia was met on board ship by reporters and photographers wanting to know everything about him and his players. Denis Compton was asked about his hobbies. Not knowing what to say, he blurted out something about bowls, which led to a flurry of invitations to play bowls throughout the tour. Eventually he accepted one. 'It took my hosts less than the time it takes to drink a pint of beer to expose my ignorance of bowls,' Compton recounted. '"No, sir," said the club official, "woods have a natural bias, you don't have to use wrist-spin."' Australian newspapermen were equally keen to meet Freddie Brown's team, and Len Hutton's. Both captains sought to disarm their hosts with charm offensives, Hutton in particular navigating a potentially awkward press conference on deck with charm and skill, adroitly playing down the potency of his fast bowlers, and his team's chances of success.

Eventually, the weary cricketers would be driven to the centre of their first city, and their first hotel. When George Parr's team arrived in Melbourne in 1863–64 after travelling for more than 60 days, and were transported by open carriage to Marshall's hotel, the first thing they did on entering their rooms, separately and then together, was to cheer out loud that they had made it there in one piece.

Matches Played on the Outward Journey of England Tours

None of these matches was first-class.

Country	Period	P	W	L	D
United States	1881–82	5	2	0	3
Ceylon*	1882–83 to 1965–66	17	4	0	13
Egypt	1884–85	1	0	0	1
Malta	1891–92	1	0	0	1
Bermuda	1953–54	3	1	0	2
Fiji	1983–84	2	2	0	0
Total		**29**	**9**	**0**	**20**

*Not counting a match in 1907–08 which involved only five members of the touring team, or a match in 1958–59 that was abandoned without a ball bowled.

CHAPTER 9

Board and Lodging

The need for unity

In November 1903, the English team led by Pelham Warner arrived at Largs Bay after almost six weeks at sea. A launch, sporting the South Australian colours and carrying Australian cricket officials, came out to meet the *Orontes* and convey the team to port, where a short journey by train took them to their hotel, also decorated in banners. In the days when international cricket tours were a novelty, and involved such lengthy journeys, the welcomes were often lavish, and large crowds would gather for a glimpse of the visitors from 'home'. Later that day, Warner and his players went to the Adelaide Oval to practise for an hour, and then in the evening were hosted at the town hall by the local mayor among an audience of 2,000, the stage decked with the Union Jack, the colours of MCC and the South Australian Cricket Association.

Warner's team were successful. By winning 3–2, they not only regained the Ashes but ended a sequence of four losing series to Australia. Warner was not a top-rank batsman, but the tour cemented his reputation as leader and ambassador and he was subsequently invited to take charge of two further major Test tours, to South Africa in 1905–06 and Australia again in

1911–12, when illness prevented him taking part in the Tests but not from influencing England's tactics.* One of the principal reasons for the success of Warner's first team was the sense of togetherness fostered by the captain – even if some such as R. E. Foster had their doubts about his leadership qualities on the field.

In the speech he made at the town hall that evening, Warner spoke about a winning team relying not so much on individual brilliance as 'combination', adding: 'As a side, I feel confident we shall work well together ... on a long tour like this it is most necessary to have not only good cricketers but good fellows, and the professionals you will find not only great on the field of play but a credit to themselves and their profession off it.' A crucial factor in bringing the players together was the decision to house them all, amateurs and professionals alike, at the same hotels. In his account of the tour, Warner highlighted the importance of this step: 'This was quite a departure from precedent, and I am glad to say that it was a tremendous success. It keeps the team much better together, and promotes a much keener mutual understanding and a feeling that you are all one side, working together to a common end.' That there was an unbridgeable divide between the two classes of cricketer was, however, plain from Warner's own patronising allusion to the professionals being a credit 'to themselves and their profession' on and off the field.

The separate housing of amateurs and professionals was a running sore during the tour led by W. G. Grace in the 1870s and

---

* Warner was the first man to be appointed England captain of three official Test tours. Lord Hawke was chosen to captain a tour of Australia from which he returned early because of the death of his father, and also led two tours of South Africa that were later regarded as of Test status. Arthur Gilligan captained a tour of Australia in 1924–25 and another to India in 1926–27 that effectively cemented India's future Test status, and but for ill health would have captained the first Test tour of New Zealand in 1929–30; he withdrew a month before departure and his place was taken by his brother Harold. The second man to be named captain of three bona fide Test tours was Peter May in the 1950s.

contributed to several subsequent tours there largely consisting of professionals or amateurs, rather than both. The amateurs in Grace's party were also invited to social events from which the professionals were excluded and it did Grace, the professional in amateur clothing, no 'credit' that he did not take steps to stop this happening. But from the outset it was the split accommodation that grated most.

James Southerton, one of the professionals, described in one of his dispatches how on first arriving in the country, 'We were driven off at a rattling pace to Melbourne . . . the gentlemen portion of the Twelve stopping at the Port Philip Hotel; whilst the professionals, much to their disgust, were driven to the Old White Hart at the top of the town; consequently the Twelve were separated immediately they arrived, causing no little indignation, and some nasty remarks not only from the players themselves, but also from a large number of the population of Melbourne itself, who were disgusted with arrangements which made a distinction between the men who had come 12,000 miles to play the national game together.' Southerton pointedly added: 'As all were paid for coming out, all ought to be considered professionals, and treated as equals, but the promoters of the trip apparently thought otherwise.'

Even by the 1890s, amateurs and professionals lodging or dining together was the exception rather than the rule. They stayed separately on Andrew Stoddart's first tour of Australia and generally did so on his second, although at the start he appeared to make a last-minute decision that they should share the same hotel in Adelaide, possibly in an attempt to discourage Australian critics – always ready to denounce the iniquities of the English class system – revisiting the divisions between English amateurs and professionals that had surfaced during the Test series in England the previous year, when professionals took strike action in protest at the payments to leading amateurs, Stoddart included.

When Lord Hawke's team toured South Africa in 1895–96, amateurs and professionals generally stayed in different hotels: at Pietermaritzburg, for instance, Hawke was put up at Government House and the other amateurs with the 7th Hussars, while the professionals were left to sort out their own accommodation as best they could. Frank Milligan, in South Africa three winters later, travelled with his servants.

Despite its positive effect on esprit de corps, Warner's blueprint was not always followed on later tours. In many places outside the cities, large and good hotels were in short supply, and it was common for local well-to-do families to put up the amateur (and therefore to them more socially acceptable) members of a touring party. The incentives to perpetuate this system were obvious to those higher up the social scale, and one of the chief beneficiaries was the captain. In 1909–10 – so after Warner's first tour – Henry Leveson Gower as captain stayed with the Archbishop of Cape Town at his home at Bishop's Court overlooking Table Mountain.

Good accommodation was not always available even to amateurs. On the first tour of South Africa following the First World War, conditions left Arthur Carr underwhelmed: 'I was glad when the trip was over. The constant travelling and moving from one bad hotel to another – and it seems to me that most of the hotels were bad – was very trying and tiring . . . When we arrived at one of the bad hotels we found that they had arranged for my wife, myself and [Percy] Fender to share a room and were quite astonished when we said that this arrangement would not suit us.'

While the amateurs were in a position to eat, drink and socialise all evening, the professionals were often confined to modest lodgings where the hours of drinking and eating would be more limited. Persuading amateurs to buy into a collaborative approach was not always easy. When Warner jointly managed the Australia tour of 1932–33, Gubby Allen, one of the senior amateurs, hardly endeared himself to his colleagues by being so frequently absent. He had family and friends in Sydney, where he was born, and sought to stay there as often as he could. When Jardine insisted Allen join the team for their two weeks in Tasmania over Christmas, Allen was furious; it was in this context, rather than any reservations he may have had about Jardine's tactics, that Allen made his celebrated remark about Jardine in a letter home: 'Sometimes I feel I should like to kill him.'

The way touring teams are accommodated is fundamental to their comfort and contentment, and therefore to their prospects of success, and this should always be one of the top priorities of any tour organiser. The first overseas hotel any English touring team stayed in, the St Lawrence Hall, Montreal, which took into its embrace George Parr and his weary troupe in 1859–60, might have served as the ideal – provided no gym work or strength and conditioning was necessary, or any cricket played. Guests were woken from their slumbers in comfortable beds and spacious rooms by the ringing of a large gong, before heading down to a large breakfast. Lunch at noon consisted of cold meats, poultry, vegetables and pickles, and dinner at four of soup, fish, more poultry, joints, pies and Indian corn. Fred Lillywhite noted contentedly: 'Tea immediately follows; and from nine till eleven o'clock, supper may be had.'

Things moved onto a slightly more professional system in the inter-war years, at least in Australia. Frederick Toone, who managed three tours of Australia in the 1920s, outlined his thought in an article on tour management.

The selection of the hotels at which the team will stay are made on the other side but they have to be ratified by the MCC. The carrying out of these arrangements, of course, devolves upon the manager, who makes it his first duty to see that the comfort of the players is properly provided for. This, indeed, is the constant consideration of the manager and it necessarily involves some degree of tact and not a little patience. No trouble must be spared; no little detail overlooked. The health of the players, too, must be a special managerial care.*

By 'the other side', Toone meant the tour organisers and ground agents in the host country on whose skills the smooth running of a tour really depended. But things went backwards after the Second World War, with MCC's administrators less thorough, less caring and generally less well prepared. When tour managers returned home and advised that it would be beneficial if somebody was dispatched in advance to check accommodation, nothing was done. With tour parties heavily populated by professionals, the amateur class at headquarters probably considered it beneath them to fuss over their comfort.

Until the advent of internal air travel, England teams were obliged to spend many nights on trains moving between cities large distances apart. Philip Trevor, manager of the 1907–08 tour of Australia, said that one of the few demands he made of the local authorities was that his players should not spend the night before Test matches on trains – 'all that I asked was that my men should have a complete night in bed at the place where the match was to begin' – and that his requests were invariably met, if necessary with the hours of play on the last day of the preceding game adjusted. This was very necessary because many journeys were gruelling: Jack Hobbs once described how on a 27-hour train journey from Brisbane to Sydney the carriages were 'like furnaces'. Toone estimated that the 1928–29 team spent between 20 and 30 nights travelling

---

* Toone would probably have supervised further England tours had he not died suddenly in 1930 aged 61; he had some difficult relationships with players such as Wilfred Rhodes, whom he dealt with in his capacity as Yorkshire secretary for 27 years, but few other managers of his era matched his energy or thoroughness. He was knighted in recognition of his work in promoting good relations between the Commonwealth and 'the Mother Country'.

on trains, although he did not specify whether that included the night before any Test.

India tours, with their up-country venues and shortage of Western-style hotels, posed particular challenges, with the class system fastidiously observed whether the Englishmen liked it or not. On the first Test tour there in the 1930s, Jardine and a fellow amateur, Charles Marriott, stayed with the Commissioner in Karachi while the professionals were put up by local merchants, and in Delhi the captain stayed at the Vice-Regal Lodge while others were dispatched to a hotel. Hopper Levett, the wicketkeeper, recalled how train journeys – mercifully first-class – could last several days, and when the team arrived each man would be assigned a bearer. 'Then we would be taken to our hosts' home, have breakfast and immediately there would be cricket – after four days on the train.'

When they next returned in the 1950s, the manager and amateurs were put up by a maharajah in the state guest house in Bahawalpur, in newly created Pakistan, while the professionals were housed in a tent in the prime minister's garden. At other times they stayed with local merchants or families, occasionally at hotels. Geoffrey Howard, the manager, described a hotel in Ahmedabad as 'very crude', and recounted monkeys stealing breakfast the moment someone's back was turned. 'It [accommodation] was hit or miss as far as we were concerned,' he said. 'We took what we were given. Now they [modern players] would reject it out of hand.' With the team often spread far and wide, end-of-day debriefs on the cricket were nigh-on impossible.

When the team travelled by overnight train across the Sind desert from Lahore to Bahawalpur, about 60 miles south of Multan, only Howard and the three amateurs were put into an air-conditioned coach. One of them, Donald Carr, the vice-captain, recalled: 'We had quite a decent sleep, had a wash and put our blazers on. Then I said to Geoffrey, "Shall I let the troops [professionals] out?" I went along to their carriage and, when I opened the door, they all came out, coated in red sand

and gasping. I can still see Allan Watkins at the front of them, his face all red, and I couldn't help myself. I just burst out laughing.' Watkins exclaimed: 'It's all right for you fucking amateurs!'

Whose decision it was to segregate the players like this is unclear, but it was surely Howard's responsibility to get the arrangement changed. For the Test against India at the Brabourne Stadium in Bombay, the home of the Cricket Club of India, the English players actually stayed on the ground in dormitories, as some visiting teams do to this day (though the venue no longer stages Tests). 'You could fall out of bed and walk straight down to the dressing-rooms,' Tom Graveney recalled. Howard was less enamoured with people wandering through his room at all hours, especially as he had to use it as an office.

Toone's claim that MCC vetted selected hotels was not always carried through. Only when Len Hutton's team arrived in Kingston, Jamaica did they discover that the rooms they were sharing were small and, once full of baggage, terribly cramped. Charles Palmer, the manager, made his feelings known but the West Indies board, no doubt mindful of cost, said nothing could be done. More spacious accommodation was provided when the team returned to the island later on the tour. Trevor Bailey thought Palmer a poor appointment given that he had never been to the Caribbean before, but conceded, 'We were slightly arrogant and distinctly intolerant of the accommodation provided.'

By the post-war period, fresh efforts were being made to create a sense of togetherness among the playing group, and there were regular meetings of a Saturday Night Club. This was a dinner which everyone was required to attend, and at which fines would be administered for breaches of arcane club rules such as only drinking with the left hand on a Saturday or not wearing a touring tie at breakfast on Mondays. These sorts of occasions were practical in an era when families rarely joined tours and Sundays were usually rest days (prior to the 1970s, cricket was not played on a Sunday anywhere England visited except the subcontinent). By the early 1960s, the club had been disbanded, sacrificed on the altar of discipline, but was quickly revived by Ted Dexter in Australia and also featured on Tony Lewis's tour of the subcontinent in 1972–73.

Quite who instigated the Saturday Night Club is unclear, but it appears to have had its origins in the '46 Club' evenings that operated on the first post-war tour of Australia and involved a similar system of rules and fines. One such evening took place on a train from Melbourne to Sydney; the strait-laced, teetotal Paul Gibb noted that he had seldom seen so many people 'tight' at once. Alex Bannister, in his account of the 1953–54 tour of West Indies, said the club had for a number of years been 'the custom of all MCC touring teams'. When there was a riot on a Saturday afternoon of a Georgetown Test, and the players were trapped in the ground for several hours, the club held its get-together in the Bourda dressing room and the evening included a heartfelt toast to the day they would return home. There were also some tours during the inter-war years which featured 'club' meetings.

These nights worked well as bonding exercises, but they could not paper over the differences between amateurs and professionals, who naturally and increasingly resented the conventions by which amateurs could be paid by their counties for assistant secretaryships which demanded little work and enabled them time off to play without breaching their status. 'The segregation of a touring side into amateur and professional is only a nominal distinction nowadays, but since most amateurs earn money from cricket it is silly to emphasise even a distinction in name only, when team spirit is at stake,' wrote Frank Tyson, shortly after touring Australia with an ageing and divided team in 1958–59. 'It does little to improve the morale of a touring team when it is known that the amateurs may even receive more money in expenses than the professional earns in salary, when tax has been deducted.' As will be discussed in Chapter 20, there were many things wrong with the dynamics of this tour party; Bill Edrich, who reported on it as a journalist, described the atmosphere as 'halfway between uneasy and poisonous'.

Worse was to come. When England went to Australia in 1962–63, amateur status was formally abolished during the early weeks of the tour, but the men appointed to run the team could hardly have been more 'old school'. Ted Dexter and Colin Cowdrey, the captain and vice-captain, were both educated at private school and Oxbridge, while another senior batsman, David Sheppard, not only shared their background but since being ordained into the church had only sporadically played first-class cricket – and would never do so again once the tour was over. He was the last of the part-timers.

The manager was the patrician Duke of Norfolk, who was president of Dexter's county club Sussex and shared Dexter's passion for horses. Part of the reason for Norfolk's appointment was that it was thought he might work well with Dexter, who had a reputation as difficult to manage. Dexter was regarded by many of his players as distant and detached, as well as tactically wayward. To compound matters, Dexter's wife Susan took the opportunity to join the tour and do some modelling work. All this raised hackles.

Fred Trueman, who was nearing the end of a lustrous Test career, spikily told an Australian journalist he was a bit confused, 'not knowing whether we were supposed to be playing under Jockey Club rules, for Dexter Enterprises, or engaged on a missionary hunt'. Ray Illingworth rejected Cowdrey's attempts to use him as a hired help and spoke out about poorly organised nets and selection – among other things. The upshot was that Trueman and Illingworth both received critical tour reports by Dexter and the Duke, Dexter docking both men £50 from their good-conduct bonus for not contributing more to team spirit. Trueman was incensed at the fine, calling it a 'filthy insult' and vowing to never play for England again. Unsurprisingly, public sentiment in England and Australia favoured the player, and numerous donations towards Trueman's sanction were forthcoming. Trueman did play for England again but never went on another major tour.

Illingworth never forgot his treatment. 'None of the professionals were ever invited to dinner ... not that we would want to have gone anyway, but all the amateurs dined with the Duke of Norfolk and that created divisions. The team were provided with four cars and only the amateurs used them. I never felt at ease in the set-up.' Being asked to open the batting in the final innings of the series because Cowdrey did not fancy it was the final straw. 'It was one of the reasons I didn't perform for England until I became captain,' he added. 'I was not bothered about playing for England because of this type of thing.' Illingworth did not tour with England again until he led them to glory in Australia in 1970–71.

Touring varied greatly depending on the country being visited, but each destination presented its own challenges. There may have been a wider choice of entertainment available in Australia, New Zealand or South Africa, where the local culture had more in common with home and there were the easy attractions of barbecues, beaches and beer, but the players were then more likely to go off individually and meet friends, which could give the tour a more fragmented feel. On the subcontinent, there was less to do and exploring was complicated by the god-like status accorded cricketers, so the players became more reliant on each other for company and the team more closely knit as a result. In recent years, most if not quite all the places England visited possessed high-quality hotels, so the discomfort was less acute than it used to be, but equally that reduced the scope for the players to be brought together through shared hardships.

Tales of the grimmest experiences of lodging up-country were passed down from one generation to the next in the manner of war veterans recounting old battles, their sufferings almost a badge of honour. Sahiwal, where touring parties were usually put up at the Montgomery biscuit factory, would feature high on any list of horror stories. The Test tour to Pakistan under Mike Gatting involved five nights in Sahiwal – then a town with only one phone-line – in the lead-up to the notorious match in Faisalabad where Gatting had his spat with umpire Shakoor Rana, and probably played its part in shortening fuses. The players were housed three or four to a room and slept on camp beds, to the accompaniment of rats scratching along the walls. With no nets to protect them from mosquitos, Jack Russell, the team's reserve keeper, went to bed wearing socks, tracksuit and wicketkeeper's inner gloves.

Conditions were arguably even worse when on a wholly inadequate budget an MCC under-25 team toured Pakistan in 1966–67, Dennis Amiss describing the accommodation in Sahiwal as 'basic in the extreme' and adding: 'On arrival at our hotel we found goats in the bedrooms. What's more there was only one shower, which had to be shared by the entire team during our week-long stay.' But what was a difficult and stressful tour – the team had to negotiate stifling heat, illness and a ludicrous schedule that meant they played 26 days of cricket in isolated locations across West and East Pakistan in less than five weeks – brought the players close. 'It could have been a thoroughly miserable experience,' Amiss wrote. 'In fact the reverse was true, and we quickly became a cohesive and tight-knit group.'*

Expectations with regard to Pakistan hotels were low and pleasant surprises few and far between. Pat 'Percy' Pocock managed to contrive one for Colin Milburn when he was sent to the airport to collect Milburn, who had been summoned as emergency cover for the final Test in Karachi and spent two days travelling from Australia, where he had been playing Sheffield Shield cricket. Pocock deliberately took him to a fleapit

---

* Three full England international tours paid visits to Sahiwal – in 1968–69, 1977–78 (for a one-day international) and 1987–88. An England under-19 team led by Andrew Flintoff also played there in 1996–97.

boarding house pretending it was the team hotel and delighted in watching Milburn's jaw hit the floor. The team's real hotel must have seemed like a palace by comparison.

Dennis Amiss later went on two senior tours to Asia, the first in 1972–73 spanning three Tests in Pakistan and five in India. England drew the series in Pakistan and lost 2–1 in India, but the tour was deemed a qualified success under Tony Lewis's leadership and several of the players on that tour, including Amiss, credited their experiences then with laying the ground for the decisive victory that followed under Tony Greig in India in 1976–77. 'It seemed to me they enjoyed the tour both for the experience it provided and the companionship it afforded,' John Woodcock wrote of Lewis's team. 'Companionship can be a great thing on tour and there is more opportunity for it in India and Pakistan, where there are fewer diversions, than in Australia ... [There are] corporate advantages of constantly living together.'* Christopher Martin-Jenkins similarly credited the team spirit under Greig as partly the result of 'travelling together in a strange land'.

Greig's team stayed on several occasions in the less modernised towns at circuit houses, small colonies of cottages designed for use by itinerant civil servants and government ministers. It may have been at one of these places that Ken Barrington, the tour manager, with a local reception to attend, reached into his wardrobe for his England blazer only to find that one of the shoulders had been shredded by a rat. The players would typically eat together at long tables inside a tent in the garden. Martin-Jenkins painted a semi-idyllic scene of one such circuit house at Nagpur: 'They [the team] were well fed beneath a colourful tent of red, blue and yellow stripes and housed in simple, relatively spartan bungalows dotted about a compound full of lawns, flowers and trees.'

---

* When the players arrived at Sainji's Hotel in Hyderabad, Pakistan they found the hotel manager's body being carried out on a board. According to one account, 'he had been stabbed to death and the cook had been arrested.'

But some of the players had less fond memories of Nagpur's circuit houses when England returned there in 1981–82. '[They were] bungalows with no more than a hot-water geyser and a bucket for washing,' David Gower recalled. 'There was a field kitchen which produced some grey chicken, but we declined that and lived off fried eggs and chips, saving the oranges for anti-rat missiles.' John Emburey viewed it as one of lowest points of his touring career. 'I got to this villa I was sharing with Jack Richards and we found a padlock on the door. It felt like it hadn't been used for a decade and when we finally got inside the rats were scampering everywhere.' Freezing cold at night, the players slept in socks and tracksuits. A month later, the team were in Jullundur for a one-day international. 'The England party stayed in one of those hotels of naked light bulbs and doleful fried eggs staring up from a Formica table every breakfast,' Scyld Berry, a journalist covering the tour, wrote. 'It was the best hotel in town.'

As late as 2005–06, when England for the first time played a Test match in Multan in Pakistan, one of the players sent a sorrowful text message: 'Multan. Oh my god. What a s**t-hole.' There was one serviceable hotel in the city. When England returned for another Test in late 2022, things had improved considerably, although the teams came and went by chartered plane as domestic flights only irregularly stopped there.

The quality of the food was a major factor in determining the happiness of a touring party, or even determining whether certain players were prepared to tour at all. Until relatively recent times, senior cricketers often opted out of tours of Asia – indeed, between 1987 and 2000 England in only one winter sent a team to play Tests in any part of Asia – and the scope for illness was one of the major factors. A popular remedy for killing off stomach upsets was alcohol; members of the 1951–52 tour of India were advised to drink whisky, and because certain states had introduced prohibition following political independence in 1947 the team transported with them numerous cases of Murree beer.

Once tours of Asia became more common, past experience tended to inform how future expeditions were managed. Crates of Spam would be shipped out with teams heading for Pakistan, and David Gower's team in India took with them hundreds of tins of Argentinian corned beef. Banana sandwiches were another lunchtime favourite. When Keith Fletcher managed the 1992–93 tour of the subcontinent, a place he toured three times as a Test player, corned beef sandwiches were again used as emergency back-up fodder. Jack Russell, remembering the traumas of Sahiwal and in any case a faddy eater, took to eating steak and chips every night of the four weeks he spent in India at the Nehru Cup in 1989–90. For all the precautions, there were still several high-profile cases of players falling ill.

Pakistan's poor hotels also tainted the country in the eyes of English players and media, along with its lifeless turf pitches, and did much to inspire the sort of comment Ian Botham made in a BBC radio interview after returning from there in the 1980s: 'Pakistan is the sort of place every man should send his mother-in-law to, for a month, all expenses paid.'

Wherever the tour, it was important the players ate healthily, and this could be as hard to do in places where there was plenty of nutritional food as in those where it was hard to find. In Australia and South Africa, food was generally plentiful and good, but only in modern times have cricketers been properly educated about what constitutes a sound diet. Maintaining a healthy lifestyle was often compromised by the readiness of hosts to lavish free food and drinks on their guests, and with the cricketers on daily allowances such offers were gratefully received.

On the very first tour of Australia, William Caffyn recounted how 'scarcely a day passed without our being entertained to champagne breakfasts, luncheons and dinners.' For many years, the players sought to sustain themselves through long days in the heat by drinking beer or champagne during lunch breaks, thinking this was the best fortification available. During one visit to Brisbane, the Englishmen were one evening invited by a local supplier to eat as many oysters as they could manage, and a young Percy Chapman put away more than 17 dozen in one sitting; fortunately there followed a rest day before the match with Queensland resumed, allowing Chapman time to recover.

Colin Cowdrey said that the practice of staying with local families in South Africa on Peter May's tour had a deleterious effect on fitness because hosts insisted on feeding the players lavishly, and this directly contributed to England losing the fourth and fifth Tests and surrendering a 2–0 lead. 'If we were not actually killed by kindness we were certainly reduced to something well short of the fitness a Test team must maintain,' Cowdrey wrote. 'In the end this was quite noticeable in the cricket we played. Our standards dropped alarmingly.'

Only once the players stayed together in a better standard of hotel, with a good standard of international cuisine readily available, was it even realistic to attempt to manage the players' diets on a collective basis. The need for the players to replenish their energy levels during the course of five-day Tests, especially in places where the heat and humidity was high, was only properly understood with advances in sport science.

When England won the Ashes in Australia under Andrew Strauss, it was calculated that the players were losing 1kg of weight for every hour spent in the field in temperatures of 90–100 degrees, and so they were made to consume 1.5 litres of drinks designed by a nutritionist to replace the salts and carbohydrates lost. When the players returned to the changing room they would be given appropriate food or shake-drinks, which were easier to digest than a normal meal. 'This needs to be done immediately, as the quicker they get food and fluid on board the quicker they recover,' Huw Bevan, the team's strength and conditioning coach, said. The players would also be weighed at the start and end of the day to ensure they were maintaining body weight.

Such practices are now standard, and players are constantly encouraged to eat during the lunch and tea intervals to compensate for what they have been putting in on the field, with fast bowlers and all-rounders typically burning off the most energy. 'We compare it to a car petrol tank: if they don't replenish that petrol, you will eventually run out of energy and you risk picking up injury or illness because they are under-fuelled. So we try to get them to eat something in the middle of play if they can,' said Emma Gardner, who first worked as the team's nutritionist in South Africa in 2019–20.

Established England international players typically spend around 270–290 nights away from home during the course of a year and need guidance about what to eat. 'It shocked me when I started,' said Gardner, who worked with Great Britain's Olympic squad before moving into cricket.

> There's food everywhere and it's constant. There are tea breaks, snack tables, a post-match meal, and food at the hotel. For some of them [the players], there's always the opportunity there, and that can be a positive and a negative ... A lot of my work with these guys involves understanding cuisine when we travel because that's very different to a lot of sports. We spend huge amounts of time away where you have to get used to eating quite a different diet.

It emerged on England's 2013–14 tour of Australia that they had taken with them a recipe guide to be given to local hotels that ran to more than 50 pages, but Gardner said that had now been greatly reduced. 'When we tour, we give our hosts some indication of dietary requirements, such as halal, but we ask them to tell us what they produce and we will tweak it if needed.' The catering guideline now consists of three pages. To Pakistan in 2022–23, when the team were largely confined to their hotels in the evenings, they took with them their own chef, Omar Meziane, who had previously worked with the England football team.

*

One of the commonest ways of touring teams nurturing team spirit was by making players share rooms. There would have been a cost-saving element to this practice too, but it survived into the 1990s largely because it was considered a good means of bringing together players who might not know each other and of preventing newer, less experienced tourists falling prey to homesickness or loneliness. It was also one of those things that had been done as long as anyone could remember, so it continued because no one was bold enough to change it. Only the captain and vice-captain, along with the manager, were given their own rooms. Everyone else had to share, and who they got for a 'roomie' was down to the manager, who would shuffle the pairings from one venue to the next for the sake of variety but also to prevent cliques developing. Room-sharing served as an education in tolerance and diluted grievances that might otherwise build up during a long tour among those not playing well or unable to get into the team.

How successful room-sharing really was is open to question. When Tony Lock and Fred Trueman, two young players on their first England tour, were put together in the West Indies, it probably only served to marinade their grievances towards senior players, especially when they felt they were wrongly blamed over an incident in which two players were rude towards some hotel guests who subsequently lodged a complaint. Mike Gatting confessed in his captain's diary of the 1986–87 tour of Australia that he had been on tours in the past – and by that point he was making his seventh England tour – where younger players had not been well integrated: 'Some "new boys" had appeared a little overawed and had been left on one side, not sure how they should approach more senior and experienced players,' he wrote.

Touring, with its love of social committees, silly fines and fancy-dress parties, tended to infantilise grown men, and room-sharing was one of the most brutal manifestations of that process. It chafed with some older players, who preferred their own company and found compromises irksome. 'At 35 years of age I am too old for the dormitory ethic,' Phil Edmonds said. 'I like the occasional bit of privacy, so I am deemed not to be a team man ... I have never been enamoured of the schoolboy ethic of mucking in.' Mike Brearley gave more thought to the best management of players than most England captains, but even he did not break the shibboleth of room-sharing, though he understood that cricket produced diverse characters; 'some of these,' he wrote, 'are eccentrics, loners, people who don't easily fit in'. Accommodating them on tour, literally, was not easy.

Brearley himself needed time away from the group, even as captain, and on one tour of Australia found refuge at the house of a friend in Sydney, Jack Lee, who introduced him to friends from the arts, people with different lifestyles from those of a touring cricketer. 'This world was a godsend to me, a stimulating escape,' Brearley recalled. Cricket is unusual as a sport in demanding both a collegiate atmosphere and individualism; what Brearley called a 'tension between narcissism and "groupishness".' England cricket tours generally came down on the side of groupishness and 'enforced sociability'.

Room-sharing was a lottery. On a tour of the Indian subcontinent, Graeme Fowler was early on put with Richard Ellison, who snored and talked in his sleep; 'clad in vest, pyjamas and under all the blankets he often gets up at about 4 a.m. to get a drink because he is hot,' Fowler observed. Later, Fowler roomed with Pat Pocock, who at 38 was the oldest member of the party and could not have been more considerate.* He would sort out Fowler's laundry, turn down his bed and fill in the breakfast card. When Fowler subsequently shared with Allan Lamb, it was the first time in three tours they had done so, the management having kept them apart because 'we are too high-spirited for each other and would be a nuisance'. Edmonds was a particularly tricky room-mate as he could manage on four hours sleep

---

* Pocock on his first Test tour to the West Indies in 1967–68 played alongside Colin Cowdrey and on his last tour to India in 1984–85 played with Cowdrey's son Chris.

and spent the rest of the night avidly reading books and news-papers or listening to the BBC World Service. On this same tour, he and Jonathan Agnew used a tea cosy to half-cover the light bulb so that Edmonds could read while Agnew slept. For the following winter's tour of the West Indies, Edmonds asked for a single room but was refused.

There was also the incontrovertibly delicate issue of players seeking to bring back female company to their room and asking room-mates to make themselves scarce by wandering the hotel corridors or sitting in the lobby. It was a facet of touring as old as the tour itself. 'Ever since I have been in the game, tours have involved a certain amount of drinking and a certain amount of female hangers-on,' Bob Willis wrote in his diary of his last tour as an England player in 1983–84.

Robin Smith, who was among the last generation to share rooms, was so easy-going that he was routinely put with the eccentrics. He shared with Wayne Larkins, who was a chain-smoker, because his own father had smoked heavily, and with Chris Lewis, who liked to go to bed at 8 p.m. and get up at 1 a.m. to head off to a nightclub. 'He didn't drink so it didn't affect his performance,' Smith remembered. 'He just got his eight hours' sleep in a different way to the rest of us.' Smith also happily shared with Jack Russell, who had taken up painting to fill time on his first tour, when he was reserve keeper, and would set up his easel in the room. Russell's clutter did not stop at painting apparatus; he liked to recycle teabags, and also did not trust hotels to wash his underwear, so he would do it himself and leaving it drying all over the bathroom. Russell was once summoned to Australia as injury cover only to find himself put in the same room as Steve Rhodes, the player with whom he was effectively competing for the wicketkeeping spot. It was an arrangement satisfactory to neither.

Room-mates discovered wicketkeepers were a breed unto themselves. Dennis Amiss shared with Alan Knott, arguably England's greatest keeper, on several tours.

His fastidious routine would begin at around 10 p.m. on the night before a game with the careful unfolding and laying out of his back warmer, together with the vest and cricket shirt that he would be wearing . . . These would then be given pride of place in the hotel airing cupboard . . . the whole process, which was conducted in an almost ceremonial manner, lasted until midnight. At 7 a.m. he would be up for a ritual of stretching and ablutions that lasted for at least an hour. As a result we were often late for the team bus, much to the irritation of the management.

A captain was usually granted the privilege of his own room, although in one instance this merely left him vulnerable to mischief that might not otherwise have occurred. Towards the end of a tour of Zimbabwe and New Zealand, a one-day series presented the players with some opportunities for fishing. Among the keenest anglers were Mike Atherton, the captain, and fast bowler Alan Mullally, who grew up in Australia and had been fishing all his life. 'He [Atherton] is making all these flies and catches nothing,' Mullally recalled. 'I go fishing and land this mako shark. It had to be 90–100kg. I stick it in the ute [truck]. David Lloyd, who was coach, says, "You know what you've got to do with it? But you will get dropped." I say, "Yeah. You're a selector, help me out." He says, "No . . . but you have to do it."' So Mullally took the bloodied, stinking fish back to the hotel, put it over his shoulder and asked at the reception desk for the key to Atherton's room.

'Ironically, he was in the room next to me. I get his key, go in and throw it on the bed. I wrote a note, stuck it on the pectoral fin. It said, "Athers, this is a fish." I go back to my room, he comes back and all I hear is "F***ing hell, Mullally!"' The next day, Mullally was dropped, and did not feature in the last three ODIs of the series, having played in the first two.

As it transpired, that was the last winter of room-sharing. The practice was finally ended by Lord MacLaurin, who had just been appointed chairman of the newly created ECB, the successor body to the TCCB. MacLaurin had visited the team in Zimbabwe and been shocked to find the tour management staying in a different – and superior – hotel to the players. He was told this was long-standing practice. MacLaurin was then driven to the players' hotel and was horrified by what he found: 'Two players apiece to each pokey room in which, at best, the air-conditioning worked to a regime of its own ... small wonder that it was proving to be such an unhappy tour. If I'd believed that the old distinction between gentlemen and players was a thing of the past, the Zimbabwe experience quickly disabused me.' He not only ended room-sharing but also saw to it that the players stayed in better hotels.

Since then, England's touring players have tended to live in physical comfort in five-star hotels with state-of-the-art gyms and swimming pools, and multiple restaurant options. Technology also served to better connect them with families and friends at home through Skype, FaceTime, WhatsApp and numerous forms of social media. There were many obvious advantages to them having greater independence, but single rooms also left players potentially more isolated and vulnerable if things got difficult. One former England player likened a single room to a prison cell. Modern touring life became both more frantic – with busier schedules, more high-profile matches and less leisure time – and more fragmented, with red-ball and white-ball specialists joining and leaving tours with such regularity that proper relationships could be hard to establish, let alone maintain.

It was noticeable that after the switch to single rooms there were a number of high-profile cases of players suffering from stress-related illnesses. The England management tacitly acknowledged there was a problem when in 2019 Mark Saxby, who originally joined the team as massage therapist, was appointed to a broader role overseeing mental health and well-being. Players now have a wellness app on their phones to record their general sense of well-being. This issue became even more acute during the Covid-19 pandemic, when players were required to serve periods of isolation in which they could be confined to their rooms for many days. 'Mark has been unbelievable,' Dawid Malan said. 'He has been the glue, [someone] we all speak to and get things off our chest, and he listens so well, especially on long tours.' Speed of travel and ease of communication suggest touring should be easier, but in many ways it is not.

Ian Bell, who went on 19 separate Test tours between 2001–02 and 2015–16, agreed that the solitariness of the single room was an ordeal for some and that the subcontinent could be a particular challenge. 'Sometimes with security being so high, you don't get to go out as much as you would do in Australia or New Zealand,' he told me.

> Cricket is such a big thing over there. You go back to your room and every single sports channel can be cricket. You feel like you can be a bit cricket 24/7 ... [Once] you'd have a room-mate to keep you going, whereas now everyone is in single rooms. If things aren't going well, you've got to be careful you don't just shut yourself away. Then tours can be very long. There is a part of touring which is looking after each other and making sure people are getting out of their rooms when things are tough.

A persuasive case could be made for touring players being given the choice as to whether they would rather share rooms, if not for a whole trip then for part of it, perhaps especially during the early days before the internationals get underway. There might be something to be said for a more flexible management style on this issue, rather than a one-size-fits-all approach.

CHAPTER 10

The Political Dimension
How England tours perpetuated white supremacy

For many years, an incoming England tour provided a link between the hosts and the Mother Country, even if it was a home that many of those living in the colonies or dominions had never actually seen. To the majority of the local population, it was important that the cricket was played in a friendly spirit, as an affirmation that the bonds between countries – between the heart of the Empire and its far-flung territories – remained strong. For others, Britain's historic subjugation of these peoples, and their economic exploitation of them, had not – and could not – be forgotten, and cricket became an instrument with which a country with aspirations to political independence could turn the tables on their masters. This was an argument encapsulated in the epigram of Learie Constantine, the pioneering West Indian cricketer, and promoted by C. L. R. James, 'They are no better than we.' Cricket became an agent of decolonisation for several countries exchanging regular fixtures with England, which meant England tours took on a dimension beyond sport, and English touring cricketers sometimes became the unwitting focal point for political and economic grievance, a target for anti-British sentiment in a way they would never have been at home.

This process was the reverse of what many of those who organised the early tours espoused, which was that the game was playing its part in binding the colonies and dominions to Britain through 'crown and cricket'. England tours may have been driven principally by economics, but they were also a public relations arm of Empire.

With Britain having long since divested itself of its former overseas territories, such issues are not commonly a feature of modern tours, but some relationships remain sufficiently delicate that it does not take much to reopen old wounds. An England tour still has a political and symbolic power, and simply by taking place can be interpreted as hosts and guests exchanging mutual seals of approval. Equally, by suspending tours, the opposite message is conveyed: de-legitimisation. Hence the termination of sporting contacts with South Africa during the apartheid era and the ECB stopping sending teams to Zimbabwe while President Robert Mugabe and the ZANU-PF party remained in power there, both steps taken with the encouragement of the British government.

When the ECB at short notice cancelled a visit to play two T20s in Pakistan in October 2021, for what would have been England's first matches there for 16 years, and had been advertised as some sort of repayment for Pakistan touring England at the height of the pandemic, it caused an outcry. It was a crass decision and left the board facing accusations of old-fashioned colonialism and arrogance.

Those who sent English teams abroad were naturally keen that relations between the nations remained cordial. If future tours, and future profits, were to be protected, a stable environment was desirable. The alternative – a gradual erosion of ties with Britain – was both unpalatable and potentially costly. Barely a tour went by without someone, whether it was a manager, captain or administrator at Lord's, declaiming the virtues of tours. 'Equality and fraternity between England and her Colonies are now established with a completeness that is at once the astonishment and the envy of the other nations of the world,' Alfred Shaw, the Nottinghamshire professional and organiser of several tours in the 1880s, wrote in his reminiscences in 1902.

The MCC's inner circle naturally championed cricket's civilising mission. The rising frequency of English cricket tours to various parts of the Empire coincided with a surge in British imperialism, and cricket was recruited to the cause. 'This sporting imperialism wasn't just an adjunct of economics; cricket, by emphasising and enhancing the common cultural inheritance of the British Empire, gave additional depth and substance to imperialism,' wrote Richard Bentley with reference to a spate of early English non-Test tours of the West Indies coinciding with a decline in the sugar trade. Several prominent English administrators and captains of early Test tours had political and business interests overseas, including Lord Harris, Lord Hawke, Pelham Warner, Henry Leveson Gower and Stanley Jackson.*

The long-term problem for English cricket, and for the players who were sent on tour and had to deal with the fallout, was that from the outset it was fatefully aligned to one side of a social and racial argument that would eventually be lost. The principal countries with which England played cricket all ultimately secured their political independence while the white communities who had once held sway in some of them surrendered much of their influence.

The early England tours of South Africa, for instance, served only to bolster the practice of the South African authorities selecting whites-only teams, a practice that survived into the late 1980s before the collapse of apartheid brought it to an overdue end. Similar selection policies, if not quite as extreme, were pursued around the Caribbean territories until the 1960s; again, English administrators could be criticised for their collusion

---

* Jackson, who played 20 Tests between 1893 and 1905, later served as Governor of Bengal from 1927 to 1932, during which time he survived an assassination attempt by a young Indian nationalist.

with the local white elites. Nor was visiting post-independence India an always comfortable experience, and eventually an England tour there was cancelled in its entirety when India's Prime Minister Rajiv Gandhi took exception to the close connections of some of the selected English players to the South African system. 'Cricket has been used as a tool through history to perpetuate white supremacy,' Ebony Rainford-Brent, the first black cricketer to represent the England women's team, said in 2021. And in no respect was this more the case than with England tours.

Australia, England's closest cricketing rival and the country they exchanged most regular tours with, had its own colour bar. The White Australia policy was a term used to summarise a series of legislative acts dating from federation in 1901 which were designed to ban entry to non-white immigrants. It was only after the Second World War that the policy began to be dismantled, and the process took until 1973 to complete. Even before this shameful period, Ranjitsinhji, as an Indian and the first non-white cricketer to play for England, faced paying a far from insignificant entry fee of £100 after being chosen as a member of Andrew Stoddart's team for Australia in 1897–98 – until the authorities, no doubt mindful of Ranji's potential impact on gate receipts, wisely chose to waive it. This minor act of generosity did not prevent Ranji from being less than enamoured with his experiences. Some of his criticisms of Australians, made in print during a series of articles he wrote on the tour, were not well received and J. T. Hearne one day noted in his diary that Ranji was 'harsh on Australians generally'.

Ranji might have travelled to South Africa with Lord Hawke in 1895–96 but it was clear that his presence would have caused difficulties both to a society and a fledgling cricket system already shaped towards racial segregation and exploitation. Similarly, Ranji's nephew Duleepsinhji was not selected for a South Africa tour in 1930–31 despite having been a notable success for England in Test cricket.

Any embarrassment English cricket might have felt collaborating with South Africa and Australia was probably diluted
by its own treatment of ethnic minorities, and the fact that
before 1980 only five non-white cricketers represented them
in Tests.* In 1909 England, along with Australia and South
Africa, founded the Imperial Cricket Conference (later the
International Cricket Council), and drove its decision-making
for many years, yet it took the ICC almost 100 years to introduce a mandatory anti-racism code. Even then, it only happened
after there had been a significant shift in cricketing power away
from the three traditional white strongholds towards the Asian
subcontinent.

Such a complex political and racial backdrop put a lot of
strain on England's touring cricketers, who through no choice
of their own were cast as representatives of Britain and by
extension upholders of Britain's policies towards its overseas
territories. Whether they liked it or not, this was their lot. This
was particularly the case in the era before air travel made it
easier for high-profile British representatives to travel abroad
on a regular basis. For example, it was not until 1954 that a
reigning British monarch – Elizabeth II – visited Australia;
before that there had been only a handful of visits by members
of the wider Royal Family.† It was understandable therefore
that a party of touring English cricketers might be expected to
serve as quasi-ambassadors. Gubby Allen was required to make
a radio broadcast to the whole of Australia shortly after his
team arrived in the country in 1936, and a common theme in
his many speeches on the tour was the role the team might play

---

* The five were Ranjitsinhji, Duleepsinhji and the Nawab of Pataudi, all Oxbridge-
educated members of the Indian princely class; Raman Subba Row, an Anglo-Indian,
who similarly attended Cambridge University; and Basil D'Oliveira, categorised as a
Cape Coloured, who relocated to England to pursue a career denied him at the highest
level in his native South Africa.

† Queen Elizabeth subsequently visited Australia many times, and attended the
Centenary Test in Melbourne in March 1977, the only occasion on which the British
monarch has been present at an England Test match overseas.

in cementing the bonds between the countries. The cricketers routinely met local dignitaries, and when a match of national or international importance took place high-ranking local officials would regularly turn out; this was the case with Australian state governors and even Australian governors-general; so too South Africa's governors-general. When England toured West Indies in 1934–35, each of the four Tests was attended by the local governors; Claude Hollis, governor of Trinidad, even made a radio broadcast the night before the game in Port of Spain.

When George V died in 1936, an English team was making a non-Test match tour of New Zealand; unable to secure guidance from a higher authority, their captain Errol Holmes unilaterally decided that a scheduled match in Palmerston North should be postponed until later in the tour, and the following day the entire tour party attended a proclamation ceremony in the market square presided over by the local mayor. When George VI died in 1952, England were playing a Test match in Madras. They were contacted by Rowan Rait Kerr, the MCC secretary, and told to wear black armbands as a mark of respect. Flags were lowered to half-mast. They were also advised not to play the next day, which is what duly happened, before the game resumed a day later. Somewhat generously, England's defeat – their first in a Test in India – was put down by their hosts to them being upset at news of their monarch's passing. When Britain's ill-fated military adventure over Suez began in October 1956, Peter May's side were in South Africa, and there were initial suggestions that the tour might have to be abandoned – rather as though the English cricketers were diplomats being summoned home in a crisis. In the event, the tour continued. As late as 1981, the England players touring West Indies were described by one travelling journalist as 'our 16 trainee ambassadors'.

One of the biggest problems with this notion of international cricketers as diplomatic envoys was that for many years England touring teams hardly gave the impression that they represented a racially diverse society. Aside from the few exceptions already noted, they were until the 1980s exclusively groups of white men. This was not the kind of picture of Britain designed to endear itself to the black and Asian communities in southern Africa, West Indies and the subcontinent. It particularly jarred in the period after the Second World War when the racial make-up of British society was changing rapidly but the skin colours of those playing county cricket, let alone taking the field for England, remained steadfastly pale. With such little common ground, it was no wonder that flashpoints sometimes occurred. In recent times, the national teams, especially those involved in ODI and T20 cricket, have been much more multi-cultural, and it was a source of great pride for Eoin Morgan, the Dublin-born captain, that this was the case. He said his World Cup winning team of 2019 'derived strength from diversity and represented the best of our country'.

Tour itineraries have generally been tailored to the economic and social strengths of the host country, with games taken to the places most likely to draw good crowds and provide visitors with the best impressions. These broad principles still apply, with big fixtures often allocated to venues which might attract the greatest home and travelling support. England teams tend to take with them large contingents of fans, and it has become standard practice to lure them to the best tourist destinations such as Perth and Sydney, Barbados and Antigua, Cape Town and Galle.

In the days before mass tourism, however, tours often went to centres of high economic activity, such as mining centres. The early English teams to Australia typically took in the towns and settlements that had exploded into life through the goldrush. Bathurst, soon connected to Sydney by a remarkably engineered railway line across the Blue Mountains, was among the earliest regions to discover gold, and Heathfield Stephenson's team was just the first of many to go there; eight of the first 12 English tours played at the Sports Ground in Bathurst. Later visitors included Jack Hobbs, Harold Larwood and Geoff Boycott.

Three touring sides of the 1880s also played matches at Wade Park, Orange, close to what was reckoned to be the original site of gold in Australia at Ophir.* Ballarat and Bendigo, the main centres of gold-digging in Victoria, also became regular ports of call. Australia was proud of its discoveries and would routinely take visiting cricketers to mining sites. When William Scotton top-scored in a match at Gympie on the 1884–85 tour he was presented with 250 shares in gold. On a visit two years later to Ballarat – known as 'the Golden City' – Alfred Shaw purchased £500 of shares in the 'yellow stuff'.

Andrew Stoddart's first team visited mines at both Ballarat and Bakers Creek, reputedly the richest in New South Wales. It was a tradition that died hard. Herbert Sutcliffe was presented with two gold nuggets by miners from Kalgoorlie, Western Australia in the 1920s, and as late as the 1980s Bill Athey earned himself a nugget after scoring a century there in a one-day match.† Less glamorously, Newcastle, a coastal centre north of Sydney built on coal mining, was also a regular stop-off, featuring on 25 England Test tours from James Lillywhite's time through to the 1990s. Brian Close wrote of it as 'a dirty little town, with old, rusty derelict barges and ships rotting on the sides of the river and dirty buildings all over the place – a typical mining town'.

Until modern times, there was little recognition of the indigenous culture or communities in Australia or New Zealand, though three members of Len Hutton's team visited an Aboriginal settlement at Woorabinda, Queensland shortly

---

* The Orient liner which carried the 1894–95 and 1907–08 teams to Australia was called the *Ophir*.
† Sadly, such practices died out. When Mark Butcher was man of the match at Lilac Hill, Perth in 1998 his prize was a trouser press.

after the first Test in Brisbane and returned with souvenirs.* The
2013–14 tourists went to Uluru, and it is now common practice
for there to be a Welcome to Country ceremony before Test
matches in Australia to acknowledge the cultural significance
of the area to Aboriginal clans. The man- of-the-match medal
in the Boxing Day Test at Melbourne has also recently been
named the Mullagh Medal in recognition of the indigenous
Australian cricketer Johnny Mullagh. Before the Test at Mount
Maunganui in 2019, Maori elders blessed both the New Zealand
and England teams.

South Africa was in a state of political and social turbulence,
but also great expansion, at the time of the early English tours,
due to the discovery of diamonds and gold. This triggered
enormous economic activity but also contributed to a war
between the British and the Boers, culminating in Britain's
victory in 1902 and the creation of the Union of South Africa
in 1910. Kimberley, the centre of diamond mining from the
1870s, and Johannesburg, which was built on the discovery of
gold on the Witwatersrand in 1886, were permanent fixtures
on the cricket schedules from the outset; both featured on every
international tour made by England to South Africa up to and
including 2015–16.† There was nothing pretty about these
places: Kimberley in the 1930s was compared to 'a vast prison
camp with barbed wire and armed guards', and Johannesburg's
grey mine dumps a quarter of a century later to Dante's Inferno.
English cricketers were taken on mine visits here just as they
were in Australia.‡

---

* The Test ground in Brisbane, the 'Gabba', is in the surburb of Woolloongabba, an
Aboriginal term with various meanings, one of which is 'fighting place'.
† Curiously, although Kimberley featured regularly on tour itineraries, it had by the
end of 2022 staged only one official England international, an ODI against Zimbabwe
on 30 January 2000, whereas England teams had played 29 Tests and nine white-ball
internationals in Johannesburg. England played their second international fixture in
Kimberley in February 2023, beating South Africa in an ODI by 59 runs.
‡ Bill Edrich remembered Aubrey Smith telling him that on the 1888–89 tour an
unnamed English player had been caught attempting to smuggle a large diamond out
of a mine, and Smith had to talk the locals out of charging him.

Other venues to host tour matches were places of strategic importance such as railway towns or military forts. It was noticeable that once the Boer War was over, a number of subsequent England tours visited places that had been of significance during the conflict: Potchefstroom and Middleburg had both housed British concentration camps; Roberts Heights was a British military base; and Ladysmith – like Kimberley – had been under siege. Pelham Warner's team went there barely three years after the conflict ended. They were entertained on board a ship at Simon's Town where the British were in the process of developing a major naval station, and viewed many battlefields and war memorials during the long train journey from Cape Town to Kimberley. 'We were passing through a land full of tragedy and sorrow, but, above all, of heroism,' Warner wrote. At Kimberley itself, Warner and his team were given a tour of the sights of the siege by the mayor and stayed in a hotel owned by De Beers that was still equipped with a Maxim gun on the balcony. England teams were still playing fixtures at the ground in Randjesfontein, owned by the Oppenheimer family which chaired De Beers, in the 2000s.

Mining was central to the British Empire's interests in southern Africa and central to MCC's early support for those interests. Lord Harris, the presiding force within MCC for forty years, was also chairman of Consolidated Gold Fields which mined for gold in the Transvaal, while Abe Bailey, who effectively ran South Africa cricket, also worked for the company. By supporting South Africa's place in international cricket, they safeguarded their own commercial interests, and it was an arrangement from which MCC never sought to extract itself. As historians Richard Parry and Andre Odendaal observed, 'The ideological, political and economic partnership between Lord Harris and MCC shared a mantra of "mines, empire and cricket" with the South African establishment ... The MCC stuck rigorously to its strategic policy of accommodating and conciliating the South African regime between 1906 and 1968.'

From the outset, this regime was savagely racist, built on the exploitation of cheap black African labour, and the violent suppression of any kind of protest at intolerable working conditions.

When Johnny Douglas's team toured in 1913–14, they arrived to find industrial disputes crippling the country, and while they were there martial law was declared. This meant getting permits to move around and observing a 9 p.m. curfew, hardly an agreeable end to so many days spent playing cricket. 'Anybody in the street after that hour was arrested by the military patrols, and night after night we heard the tramp of those outside our windows,' Jack Hobbs recalled.

In fact, the team were not impartial bystanders in the crisis, enrolling as special constables in Johannesburg to combat a transport strike called in support of white miners, which authors Bruce Murray and Christopher Merrett described as 'a remarkable political act by a sports team'. Lionel Tennyson, one of the younger, more privileged members of the team, said: 'We were regarded as ambassadors from the old country.' However, it has also been suggested that the cricketers were chiefly enrolled as a means of allowing them to move about in the evening during the curfew. A two-day fixture at a mines ground at Vogelfontein, east of Johannesburg, was played without spectators owing to a ban on public gatherings, an eerie experience. Scarcely less remarkable, when Frank Mann's team toured in 1922–23, their itinerary included a two-day match in Benoni, another mining centre on the Witwatersrand, which had seen a workers' uprising violently crushed by the state only a few months earlier.

English teams hardly had a free hand in choosing where they played. They were guided more by the local cricket authorities and ground agents, and knowledge gleaned from previous visits, but there was little to suggest they objected to the places they played at, or the people and policies they were expected to work with. Their instinct was to deal with local cricket clubs established and run by white British residents, clubs that typically served to reinforce the notion of the superiority of the colonisers. 'It is one of the tragedies of South African cricket that the English tourists showed so little interest in and concern for cricket played by other communities,' Parry and Odendaal stated.

The role of the whites-only sports club was central to the psyche of the colonists and to the operation of cricket tours. 'Sport, and more especially cricket, thus defined British imperial space in far-flung corners of the world, not only metaphorically but also physically, in circumstances that were generally perceived as hostile,' Murray and Merrett wrote. 'Psychological security required familiarity and the stamp of Britain upon exotic landscapes.' Whites-only cantonments were a fundamental part of colonial existence and whites-only sports clubs were an intrinsic part of such a life. English tours naturally gravitated towards them.

Nowhere illustrated this better, or with more lasting impact, than the Western Province Cricket Club based at the idyllic Newlands ground in Cape Town, the city in which every England tour started until the 1960s. One of the WPCC's members, Major Robert Warton, organised the first English tour in 1888–89, and the club was to play a central role in shaping South African cricket, with all its gross imperfections, while maintaining close ties to the British cricket and political establishments. 'Not for nothing did the club ... become known as "the MCC of the Cape Colony",' Odendaal wrote.

The non-white communities in the Cape were passionate about cricket. The early English teams were well aware of this, and when Walter Read's team finished a Test match at Newlands in 1891–92 they held an impromptu game against a Malay XI including Krom Hendricks, whose bowling they praised in the highest terms. But Hendricks' prospects as a cricketer were to be blocked by the WPCC and the Western Province Cricket Union, the regional organisation. Malays continued to impress English cricketers as net bowlers over the next few years, but both the club and the union became increasingly obstructive to non-white communities, who were only allowed to watch games at Newlands in specified, less privileged sections of the ground long before rigid apartheid became normalised. Not until the 1970s did a black cricketer again play at Newlands.

Yet England teams continued to play there as a matter of course, and in 1964, when an England Test match formed the highlight of WPCC's centenary celebrations, the guest of honour was Dr H. F. Verwoerd, the architect of apartheid. To the disquiet of some of the players, Verwoerd even visited the England dressing room. 'The Newlands-based cricket establishment were ... directly responsible for racial segregation becoming official policy in South African cricket,' Odendaal added.* The English cricket establishment did nothing to hinder this process, although by the 1950s and 1960s many English cricketers would have welcomed the idea of playing non-white sides in front of integrated crowds. The English amateur class who organised the majority of the early tours, on the other hand, would have had a natural bias towards playing fixtures against clubs whose facilities replicated those at home, such as separate dressing-rooms for amateurs and professionals.

Those organising the early tours of South Africa unashamedly used them to promote the British cause, and English cricketers were recruited to drive home the message. Monty Bowden, vice-captain of Warton's inaugural expedition, stayed on in South Africa after the tour ended and joined the Pioneer Column which colonised Rhodesia, while Charles Coventry, another member of that side, took part in the Jameson Raid, a failed attempt to overthrow the Boer government of Transvaal. Lord Hawke, who led the third English team to the Cape in 1895–96, visited some of the British nationals imprisoned for their parts in the Raid.

---

* In 2002 the Western Province Cricket Union, by then the multi-racial governing body in the post-apartheid era, bought Newlands from the WPCC.

The Wanderers club in Johannesburg was scarcely less politically charged than Newlands; it was formed in 1889 as a focus for sporting and leisure activities for the Randlords and Abe Bailey, another whose fingerprints were on the Raid, was the club captain. Bailey's role in the Raid did not prevent him from managing a South Africa cricket tour of England in 1904 or being a prime mover in the creation of the ICC and the triangular Test tournament of 1912.*

MCC's complaisance towards South Africa's politicians did not waver even with the rise in the late 1920s of hard-right Afrikaner parties, who were then no friends of the British. When a request was made for Walter Hammond's team to play a match in Pretoria to coincide with the centenary celebrations of the Boers' Great Trek into the African interior, it was agreed to without a murmur. The players were met by the local mayor in full traditional costume, as well as the governor and deputy prime minister, and Hammond, Les Ames and Hedley Verity rode out to meet a reenactment of the Trek. During the match, both teams lined up in salute.

Ten years later, George Mann's team were also co-opted by a government that ought to have been repugnant to British representatives. D. F. Malan's nationalist party, which had recently won South Africa's elections and would stay in power until the 1990s, was built on the Broederband, which mirrored German National Socialism, would formalise apartheid, and had as its dream a republic free of British and Jewish influence.† When Mann's side played in Bloemfontein, a town with a nationalist majority, the MCC flag flying over the cricket pavilion briefly went missing in what was taken to be an act of hostility towards the British. The Test series itself was deliberately arranged to

---

* The English cricket authorities also agreed to undertake a five-month non-Test tour of South Africa in 1924–25 which was sponsored by Solly Joel, a mining and railway magnate and another of the ringleaders of the Jameson Raid.

† In 1939, the South African parliament had narrowly voted in favour of backing the war on the side of the Empire, though the Afrikaner parties had supported Germany.

start on 16 December 1948, the centenary of the Voortrekkers' victory over the Zulus.

On the next tour in 1956–57, the players were advised by the MCC president to not discuss race or colour. As it happened, while they were there, the nationalists further tightened their grip on the country, most controversially when security forces arrested 140 people, including Nelson Mandela, on charges of treason. The first hearings at the Drill Hall in Johannesburg, which triggered mass protests suppressed by batons and guns, took place directly before England arrived in the city for a Test match starting on Christmas Eve. Alan Ross wrote that parliamentary democracy was at stake but conceded, 'It is far easier, in this easy country, to remember a Christmas Day, with old, good friends, the swimming and tennis and cocktail parties and laden, decorated tree.'

English cricket did very little to distance itself from the iniquities of apartheid. In fact, when the MCC hierarchy was weighing the relative merits of candidates who might lead the team to Australia in 1962–63, the matter of David Sheppard's known opposition to apartheid South Africa surfaced as a potential determining factor.* 'On the eve of the selection it was brought to life again in the guise of a red herring,' E. M. Wellings wrote. 'What, it was suddenly asked, would be his [Sheppard's] reaction if questioned on tour about the White Australian policy? Would his answer be embarrassing to MCC?' In the event, Sheppard was not chosen as captain, and Ted Dexter was.

The first time an England touring team played matches outside white areas of South Africa was on the first post-apartheid tour of 1995–96, more than 100 years after the first English tour, when they played games in the Soweto and Alexandria townships. This initiative might have been better received had the tour not been marred by a breakdown in the relationship

---

* Sheppard had been one of four England cricketers to write a letter to *The Times* in July 1958, signed by 20 figures across sport, protesting at South Africa's exclusion of non-white athletes from the team it was sending to the Commonwealth Games. The others were M. J. K. Smith, Maurice Tremlett and Alan Wharton.

between Devon Malcolm, the only black member of the England touring party, and tour manager and chairman of selectors Ray Illingworth.

The England cricketers also found themselves in a difficult position when the 1964–65 tour of South Africa began in Rhodesia at a time when Rhodesia was locked in a bitter argument with the British government over how it might achieve political independence (several months later, Rhodesia's white minority government unilaterally declared its independence, to widespread international condemnation). During a four-day match in Salisbury, UDI was the dominant topic of conversation. 'We were well briefed before we left to lay off talking politics in Africa, but gee, nobody talks anything but politics to us,' said John Murray, England's reserve wicketkeeper.

Charles Fortune, South Africa's radio voice of cricket, whose sympathies lay with apartheid, in his account of the tour praised the local white population's courtesy towards the touring party 'at a time when the new Labour Government in England was subjecting Rhodesians to a barrage of wordy intimidations', but conceded: 'Several [players] mentioned feeling some relief on being away from the strong political tensions that had worried them in Bulawayo and Salisbury.' When the next tour of South Africa – scheduled for 1968–69 but ultimately abandoned – was being planned, the Rhodesia leg was dropped on British government advice because of Rhodesia's UDI. A full England cricket team did not play there again until 1996–97, by which time Rhodesia had become Zimbabwe, was officially independent, and had moved to black majority rule.

In the West Indies the most influential clubs around the various territories belonged to the white minority communities. Again, these were the clubs with which England touring teams instinctively dealt, and it was on their grounds that Test matches were played as part of what historian Gordon Lewis called an 'entrenched system of racialist prejudice'. The pavilions and clubhouses of these 'boss' clubs, as they were known, made welcome sanctuaries for players who at times found the wider world inhospitable. The description of Guiana by Ken Farnes, who toured in 1934–35, as 'the worst place in the world' was shared by many. When Hutton's team toured in the 1950s, the MCC's associations with these clubs were probably a contributory factor in the hostility displayed by the rest of the population towards the visiting players.

In Barbados, social hierarchies were more heavily based on colour than other territories. There were two dominant white clubs, Wanderers and Pickwick, and it was at Pickwick's ground, Kensington Oval, that England played against the island side and Tests against West Indies. The Oval was on the Kensington plantation and leased for a nominal sum. Control later passed to the Barbados Cricket Association. Matches there would draw large multi-racial crowds, but blacks were generally blocked from taking part in amateur competitions. They could work on the ground staff or operate the scoreboard, as a young Everton Weekes and Garry Sobers did, but not play for Pickwick. Their route into the game was through mainly black or coloured clubs such as Spartan and Empire, and was much tougher; this was how Frank Worrell and Clyde Walcott – the other two members of the great 'Three Ws' triumvirate – emerged, although their progress was smoothed by attending respectable secondary schools. By the time of Peter May's tour of the Caribbean, Alan Ross noted that 'strict segregation [in Barbados] scarcely exists any more'.

In Trinidad, clubs were also structured along race and class lines, even if selection for the island team was in the main conducted on merit, a policy which tended to draw talent from other islands and helped them enjoy more success against touring sides.* The dominant force was the Queen's Park club,

---

* Trinidad were the first territorial side to record a victory against the visitors on an England Test tour; their win in 1929–30 was not emulated until Barbados did so in 1959–60. They were not beaten at home in any representative fixture for almost a quarter of a century before Hutton's side did so in 1953–54 to complete a unique set of four wins against the four major territories.

whose ground had the best facilities and staged the Test matches on the island, and this too had an almost entirely white, affluent membership in the early years. It unashamedly modelled itself on MCC. The Shannon club, which boasted the Constantines, was more powerful on the field but inevitably less influential off it.

In Jamaica, the Kingston club, the oldest in the West Indies, was based at Sabina Park and served the white planter elite's mercantile allies, while the coloured professional class used the Melbourne club. Lucas CC was another champion black club. A ground near Spanish Town, which staged minor England tour matches in 1954 and 1998, was on a sugar plantation. Needless to say, Tests were played at Sabina Park, but Melbourne Park was sometimes used for England's matches against island sides, not always without local hostility towards the British manifesting itself. When Hutton, as England captain, sought to bring into Melbourne Park two guests, he was refused by the gateman. 'That the captain of England should be subjected to such a humiliation was a disgrace,' Alex Bannister wrote. The leading club in British Guiana was Georgetown CC, another watering hole for whites.

The close ties between MCC and British foreign policy were further in evidence when at the end of Peter May's tour the team went from Trinidad after the final Test to Honduras – a westward journey of 1,850 miles, so a significant detour from the path home – to play two one-day matches at Newtown Barracks, even though cricket in Honduras was undeveloped and received few visiting sides. Honduras was the only British possession in Central America and had recently seen the rise of the People's United Party led by George Cadle Price, an independence activist who would ultimately lead the country to autonomy in 1981, so this fleeting visit, which drew crowds of 4,000, may be seen as an attempt to keep local sentiment sweet. It is the only instance of a full England tour taking in matches in Central America.

The difference between West Indies and South Africa cricket was that in the Caribbean black players were chosen for the West Indies team, even if not in the numbers that they should have been, and even if the Test captaincy remained almost exclusively in the hands of whites until 1960.

England's early Test tours of the West Indies in 1929–30 and 1934–35 took place against a backdrop of mounting unrest among the working class over low wages, high unemployment and mistreatment at the hands of their employers and government. In 1933 C. L. R. James published *The Case for West Indian Self-Government*, and over the next few years there were a number of labour rebellions across Trinidad, Barbados, Jamaica and British Guiana, which were the territories the English cricketers visited.

In 1935, while Bob Wyatt's team were playing the final Test of their tour in Jamaica, former oilfield workers in Trinidad who had lost their jobs after striking over low pay staged a hunger march on Port of Spain. Although the march was halted short of its destination, it was the precursor to more widespread industrial action against British rule; two years later, the British even sent a navy ship and troops to Trinidad to quell the unrest. 'Sullen resentment and dissatisfaction were ... swelling steadily among the working people and the unemployed in all the British colonies in the Caribbean area,' Richard Hart wrote. 'By the middle years of the decade [1930s] the situation was like a cauldron of liquid slowly coming to the boil.'

The Second World War and India's independence in August 1947 accelerated the move towards a West Indies Federation and self-government, and it was a relief to the Englishmen when the 1947–48 tour passed off smoothly. The trouble came instead on Hutton's tour six years later. The situation was delicate even before the team arrived, but was made immeasurably worse by poor umpiring, the churlish response of the touring players to perceived injustices, and the win-at-all-costs mentality of their captain.

However, the background was exceptional: only two months before the tour, the British government instigated a *coup d'état* against the democratically elected government of British Guiana out of fear (almost entirely unfounded) that the People's Progressive Party, led by Cheddi Jagan, which had won a landslide election victory six months earlier, had Marxist links. Under orders from Prime Minister Winston Churchill, the Governor Alfred Savage dismissed Jagan's government and Guiana was kept under military occupation for the next seven years.

Perhaps it was unsurprising, then, that the Georgetown Test, at which Savage was formally introduced to the teams, witnessed the worst crowd trouble of the tour, when a bottle-throwing riot broke out when local player Clifford McWatt was run out with West Indies well behind in the game. 'I doubt whether the real reason ... will be unearthed, or whether anyone can prove either that it was spontaneous mob reaction to an unpopular umpiring decision or an organised political anti-British demonstration,' Bannister wrote in his account, although later in the same book he added: 'I know of a letter sent from a British Guiana official to a prominent West Indies Board of Control member saying that political influences were feared to be at the back of the demonstration.'

When the Test ended in an England victory, Bannister estimated 'some two or three score of English residents and other friends and well-wishers of the players hurried out to form an avenue of protection for the cricketers to walk through as they left the field.'

While this match was going on, a stand was burned down at the Queen's Park Oval, Trinidad venue for the next Test. C. L. R. James said that such explosions of temper were caused by popular suspicions that what he called 'anti-nationalists' could be found in any number of positions of authority; he listed cricket selectors and umpires along with politicians, policemen and newspaper editors.* James directly pointed the finger at Hutton's team too. 'There is evidence to show that the team had given the impression that it was not merely playing cricket,' he wrote, 'but was out to establish the prestige of Britain and, by that, of the local whites.'

The visit to Bermuda at the start of this tour was not without its embarrassment either, as Hutton's men found themselves playing against teams largely made up of black players while their social engagements were with whites – all this on an island which still had a colour bar. Whatever James might have thought, around the Caribbean islands themselves Hutton's players chafed at being urged by European residents to beat West Indies in order to, in Trevor Bailey's words, 'uphold the so-called racial supremacy'. The failure of Gubby Allen's team to win a single match of note in 1947–48 had sharpened those demands, one expat complaining: 'After the last tour every Britisher here had a right to expect this time a team who would fight every inch of the way for the old country.' 'We wanted to win,' said Charles Palmer, the manager, 'but not for them.'

Cricket and cricketers had become pawns on the political chessboard. Alex Bannister wrote in the *Daily Mail* at the time that the players were all 'shocked at the intensity of anti-British feeling here' and, reflecting on the tour many years later, strongly felt that the Foreign Office let down Hutton and his team.† Palmer also believed they were 'not adequately briefed'

---

* This view was perhaps widely held, and might have explained the storm of criticism that erupted when Hutton was perceived to have snubbed Alex Bustamante, Jamaica's chief minister, by failing to acknowledge him as he returned to the pavilion during his match-winning double-century in the final Test in Kingston. Hutton, exhausted after many hours at the crease, said he simply did not see him. The matter was quickly smoothed over among the parties concerned, but the local press were reluctant to let the matter drop.

† The fallout was still being felt when England next toured the Caribbean in 1959–60. 'The constant on-and-off-the-field complaints about that [1953–54] tour – and also about MCC's tour of South Africa in 1956–57 – became one of our most constant burdens when receiving hospitality,' wrote Alan Ross, who covered the later tour for the *Observer*. 'The truth was that several veteran members of those teams, Test-tour weary, affected a distant superciliousness of manner that often wounded and offended.'

by government or MCC about various political issues. David Wodehouse, in his authoritative book on the tour, summed up the situation thus: 'On the 1953–54 tour, the imperial mindset and the amateur ethos were dancing one of their last duets.'

On the subcontinent, the British administrative strongholds of Bombay, Calcutta, Madras and the vice-regal seat of Delhi, as well as Lahore and Karachi in what would become Pakistan after partition, featured heavily on an MCC tour of 1926–27 under Arthur Gilligan, which laid the ground for India's elevation to Test status and the inaugural Test tour led by Douglas Jardine in 1933–34. These centres had whites-only gymkhanas as in Bombay or similar elite clubs such as the Roshanara in Delhi and the Calcutta Cricket Club, which dated back to the eighteenth century and admitted only a handful of Indian members prior to the 1960s.

Most of the other matches took place on private grounds belonging to princely rulers with whose help the British maintained power, or privileged schools such as Mayo College, famed as India's Eton, and Rajkumar College at Rajkot, where Ranjitsinhji was educated. To their credit, Gilligan's team objected to the social and racial discrimination they encountered and, when the professionals in the team were excluded from certain invitations in Calcutta, Gilligan told his hosts that everyone from his team would be invited to attend, or the team as a whole would stay away. Lord Willingdon, governor of Bombay and then Madras, and later Viceroy of India from 1931 to 1936, and himself a former Cambridge and Sussex cricketer, was also against whites-only entry policies; he fostered mixed-race teams and helped establish the Board of Control for Cricket in India in 1928.

Somewhat surprisingly, Jardine's tour also included a three-day fixture at a newly built ground at Amritsar, where 14 years earlier several hundred Sikhs had been massacred close to the Golden Temple after General Dyer, a British officer, ordered his men to fire on a peaceful crowd, an act of barbarity that galvanised the independence movement and ultimately came to be seen as a decisive event in the end of British rule.* The visit seemed to be as much diplomatic as sporting, with the team's stay heavily laden with functions, and members of the Sikh, Hindu and Muslim communities given the opportunity to fraternise with the cricketers.

Two weeks later, Jardine led out his players in less perilous social waters with a match against the Viceroy's XI at the Feroz Shah Kotla in Delhi. Among the many in attendance was the Viceroy himself, Lord Willingdon, as well as several ruling princes, and the match was followed by a great ball at the Gymkhana club. Commenting on this occasion, Indian historian Ramachandra Guha noted: 'Cricket was once more the means by which the permanence of British rule would be assured.'†

Crowds attending matches at the main centres were multiracial but heavily tilted towards the social elite. The allocation of seating at Eden Gardens, Calcutta when Gilligan's team played there was typical: distinct blocks were given over to each of the European and Indian clubs, while the areas provided for the general public amounted to less than half the overall seats.

For England's first Test match on Indian soil, at the Bombay Gymkhana in 1933, which was watched by an estimated 100,000 over four days, the public were given an even smaller share as gymkhanas, clubs, colleges and schools took priority, leaving them with just 400ft of frontage onto the playing area. Only by special dispensation were the India team allowed to use the

---

* Three subsequent England Test tours took in matches in Amritsar, the last of them in 1972–73.

† Some English cricket administrators such as Lord Harris, a former Test captain who served as Governor of Bombay in the 1890s, encouraged the development of Indian cricket along communal lines, but this came to be seen as an obstacle to greater integration. The 1926–27 tour, which Harris helped arrange, contained 13 matches against teams of Hindus, Muslims, Parsees and Europeans, but such fixtures had all but disappeared by the time of Jardine's tour. A domestic tournament along communal lines continued on and off until 1946.

pavilion. When England next toured India for Tests in 1951–52, a few years after independence, the Test in Bombay was staged at the Brabourne Stadium, a ground which Willingdon's successor, Lord Brabourne, helped create. Home to the Cricket Club of India, it was another bastion of privilege, an exclusive club with many attractions besides cricket, such as tennis and dancing, but it granted only one-third of the frontage to the ordinary spectator.

Such venues tended to inspire local players to raise their games against the English. C. K. Nayudu, Indian cricket's first popular hero who, in Guha's words, 'transcended the barriers of caste, class, gender and religion', struck dazzling centuries against Gilligan's and Jardine's teams at the gymkhana grounds in Bombay and Lahore respectively. 'Every sixer hit by CK against the visitors' slow bowlers was as good as a nail in the coffin of the British Empire,' one onlooker recalled. 'We madly cheered each shot past the boundary not only as a cricket performance but also as an assertion of our resolve to throw the British out of India.' The night England won the Test series under Jardine, the India team pointedly absented themselves from a post-match dinner at the all-white Madras Cricket Club.

Following independence, there was a marked shift in the culture of cricket watching on the subcontinent. Naturally, the racial make-up of the crowds changed. The local spectators, no longer penned in relatively small sections, became rowdier and the mood more febrile. The first Test staged at the Brabourne Stadium, against West Indies in 1948–49, witnessed a cacophony of firecrackers and bugle-blowing, leading to complaints from both sets of players. But more radical was the marginalisation or replacement of the old venues closely associated with the Raj. In their place came government-funded new stadia designed to accommodate large numbers of spectators, concrete behemoths deliberately stripped of the baroque charm of the old British clubs.

To English minds, perhaps the most painful wrench was a new venue in Bombay, the Wankhede Stadium, which supplanted the spacious grandeur of the Brabourne in the mid-1970s. A similar process occurred in the newly created Pakistan. The leafy Bagh-e-Jinnah ground in Lahore gave way to a purpose-built stadium, while in Karachi a new National Stadium replaced the gymkhana. The English cricketers who first played at the National Stadium during a non-Test tour in 1955–56 were amazed at both its 50,000-seat capacity and the speed of its construction, inside five months.

Crowd disturbances became a common feature of Tests in India and Pakistan in the 1960s, and although England tours were affected, some of the worst trouble occurred at matches involving other visiting teams. 'Touring conditions in places such as India, Pakistan and the West Indies are not what they were before the war,' stated Crawford White, a Fleet Street cricket correspondent for almost 30 years. 'However much MCC might feel that racialism, nationalism and politics are "not cricket", the hard fact is that they are at the core of these new problems.'

Politics and commerce would continue to shape tours – and where England played. In 2021, they were allocated two Tests at a venue in Ahmedabad recently rebuilt to the largest capacity for any cricket stadium worldwide. On the morning of the first game, it was renamed after Narendra Modi, India's Prime Minister, with the two ends given the names of two of his biggest business backers, Adani and Reliance.

In the end, English cricket's past caught up with it. The association with an abhorrent regime in South Africa proved particularly painful. The MCC's' usual advice to players going to South Africa was to avoid discussing politics, but this stance became increasingly difficult as the situation in South Africa deteriorated and demands grew from the non-white bloc for coordinated action. Even after the proposed 1968–69 tour was cancelled after South Africa raised objections to the presence in the England squad of Basil D'Oliveira, a non-white player, the English game still pushed ahead with plans for an incoming tour by South Africa in 1970 (until it was scrapped on the instruction of the British government).*

The TCCB, the MCC's successor body as overseers of the England team, were just as incapable of spotting trouble on the horizon. When Robin Jackman was summoned as a replacement bowler for the 1980–81 tour of West Indies, it ought to have been obvious that the many winters Jackman had spent playing and coaching in South Africa and Rhodesia might be a problem to a country as rigidly anti-apartheid as Guyana, which was where Jackman flew first ahead of the second Test. After all, only four years before this Guyana had refused entry to some members of a Young England team because they had previously played in South Africa. Sure enough, Guyana's president Forbes Burnham refused to accept Jackman. As a consequence the Test was cancelled, although the tour itself was salvaged after the other Caribbean territories decided not to follow suit, Barbados possibly reflecting on the £1 million British cricket tourists were estimated to be ready to spend during two weeks on the island.

The close links between English cricket and South Africa remained a topic of bitter contention with non-white countries until the end of apartheid, all the more so after a group of English players, among them high-profile personalities Graham Gooch and Geoff Boycott, played a series of unsanctioned matches in the republic only the year after the Jackman Affair. England's next tour of the Caribbean was conducted amid barely disguised hostility from some host territories, even though Guyana was left off the schedule. On arrival in Trinidad for the second Test, Boycott, now working as a commentator, was arrested at the airport along with Matthew Engel of the *Guardian* and confined to room-arrest in a hotel for 24 hours. '[We were] told we would

---

* Had the 1968–69 tour gone ahead, it would have meant England had spent more winters since the Second World War playing Test matches in South Africa (four) than in all parts of Asia (three).

be deported – ostensibly for not having a work permit, in reality as surrogates for the England party who elements in Trinidadian politics did not want in their country for reasons tangentially connected to South African apartheid,' Engel recalled in 2017. Gooch, who was still playing, went through some fierce wrangling with the Antigua government, and only took part in the final Test on the island with great reluctance. England's tour of India in 1988–89 was scrapped altogether because of objections to the links of Gooch and others to South Africa.

Some tours encountered socio-political problems, others met with crises which came with little warning and placed the safety of the cricketers at risk. These more often occurred at the start of tours, which suggested that perhaps with better intelligence some of the difficulties might have been anticipated, but there was also no accounting for dumb bad luck. A political crisis in the host country could push a tour to the brink of abandonment, but it took a lot to stop an England tour; the instinct at administrative level was always to carry on if possible. In this, the feelings of players often came second to diplomatic and financial considerations. For many years, teams were at the mercy of the imperfect judgment of cricket administrators, acting on the less than flawless guidance of the Foreign Office or High Commissions. More recently, the ECB has assigned teams with full-time security officers, and things have run more smoothly as a consequence.

Certainly during some of the early crises, the cricketers felt coerced and under-valued. The tour of Pakistan in 1968–69, hastily arranged to fill the void create by the cancelled trip to South Africa, was ill-advised from the start. Pakistan was politically in turmoil and Field Marshal Ayub Khan, who had seized power in 1958, was fast losing his grip on East Pakistan, which within two years would break away to become Bangladesh. Seventeen days after the early abandonment of the tour, Ayub Khan himself would be gone.

James Lillywhite's pioneering team at Chichester ahead of departure for Australia in September 1876, for what is now accepted as the first ever Test match tour. The twelve players are joined by one of their financial backers, Arthur Hobgen (centre, back row). Lillywhite is in the middle of the seated row.

R. E. 'Tip' Foster, the scorer of England's first Test match double-century overseas. His 287 at Sydney in 1903 remains the highest innings for them in Australia.

Pelham Warner (right) was appointed captain for Australia in 1911–12 but was too ill to play the Tests. Douglas (centre) was the preferred stand-in ahead of Frank Foster (left). Despite the switch, England won 4–1.

The tour led by Ivo Bligh (middle of the seated row) in 1882–83 gave substance to the Ashes legend.

Jack Hobbs scored 2,493 runs and nine centuries in Tests in Australia, both still England records.

Percy Chapman (left of centre) holding a lucky horseshoe as his team departs for Australia, September 1928.

Douglas Jardine (left, in hat) finishes introducing his players to the ship's captain before they leave Tilbury on the *Orontes*, September 1932.

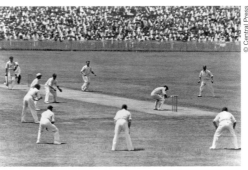

Harold Larwood bowling to a classic Bodyline field at Brisbane in 1933.

Jardine relaxing on deck – as much as he ever relaxed – during the month-long outward voyage.

Denis Compton (left) and Godfrey Evans (right), seen here at Pinewood Studios, were two of England's greatest post-war cricketers and two of their most energetic tourists.

Peter May (right) and Colin Cowdrey leave the field after Australia won in Adelaide to reclaim the Ashes, February 1959.

The four Yorkshire players Willie Watson,
Fred Trueman, Johnny Wardle and Len Hutton on
the first England tour to start by plane, to the
West Indies 1953–54.

Ray Illingworth is chaired off
the field in Sydney 1971 upon
regaining the Ashes for England
after a 12-year wait.

Big holiday crowds were a common sight
during England Tests in Australia: here 77,000
watch on in Melbourne on Boxing Day, 1974.

Geoff Boycott batting on the India tour
of 1981–82 before he returned home
early in controversial circumstances.

The England players around the hotel pool, Trinidad 1968. Colin Cowdrey,
the captain, and tour manager Les Ames are sitting in the centre.

John Snow is manhandled by
a spectator during a fractious
conclusion to the 1970–71
tour of Australia.

Tony Greig (left) walks out with Australia's captain Greg Chappell ahead of the dramatic Centenary Test match, Melbourne 1977.

Mike Brearley takes a brilliant slip catch to dismiss Kerry O'Keefe off Derek Underwood's bowling during the same game.

David Gower and Ian Botham take time out during one of England's most brutal tours, to the Caribbean in 1986.

Botham, batting here in Delhi in 1981, was the first England cricketer to do the 2,000 runs–100 wickets double in away Tests.

England's players line up on the outfield at Bridgetown, Barbados, following the death of assistant manager Ken Barrington, March 1981.

When the England players arrived from Ceylon, almost immediately a Test in Dacca was foisted on them, even though avoiding East Pakistan had been a precondition of them coming in the first place. On them reaching Dacca it was clear that the city was in the hands of rioters; the Tests still went ahead without police or army protection and, remarkably, stayed free of trouble. That did little to assuage the players. 'Our preferences counted for nothing,' Keith Fletcher recalled. 'We went, virtually on the insistence of our Foreign Office, who apparently feared recriminations against the English population of Dacca if we pulled out.' 'The MCC party were let down over Dacca,' said Tom Graveney, the vice-captain, 'and nothing that was said at the time or has been said since alters the situation.' The tour ended early when a riot broke out on the third morning of the final Test in Karachi.

The first Test of England's 1977–78 tour of Pakistan in Lahore also became the focus of political demonstrations. For two days play was halted early: first, a heavy-handed police response to a pitch invasion prompted by Mudassar Nazar reaching a century triggered even greater disorder among spectators, and then Begum Nusrat Bhutto, who was lobbying for the release of her jailed husband and former Prime Minister Zulfiqar Ali Bhutto, turned up at the ground with several hundred supporters. In response, anti-Begum supporters set fire to the ladies' stand, leading to ugly fighting and the use by police of tear gas.

The greatest political crisis to engulf an England touring team occurred at the start of the 1984–85 tour of India under David Gower. Having arrived in Delhi from the UK overnight, they woke to news that India's Prime Minister Indira Gandhi had been assassinated. The city was in chaos – the players could see fires burning from their hotel and there were reports of the road to the airport being blocked – and when 12 days of national mourning were announced the tour was left in limbo. The players held a fractious meeting with the management. 'Tony Brown [the tour manager] was a bit harsh in putting down some people's legitimate fears,' Graeme Fowler wrote in his diary. 'The mood among the players is fragile.'

Eventually, they were relocated to Sri Lanka to train and play until the mourning period ended. Then, on the eve of the first Test in Bombay, Percy Norris, the Deputy High Commissioner who had entertained the players the previous evening, was shot dead on the way to his office. Everyone was understandably horrified and shaken. 'When the news sunk in, we also began to wonder where that left us,' Fowler recorded. 'I suppose we shall ride out this storm and every other one until one of us gets shot. Then it will be too late.'*

Once Tony Brown had consulted Lord's and the Foreign Office the Test match went ahead. 'No one seems too concerned with what the players think, although I'm sure that a vote would see a large majority for calling it all off now,' Fowler added on the eve of the game. 'Believe it or not, we practised. I was not at my best mentally.' As England won the toss, Fowler ended up facing the first ball of the match. 'I would be a liar if I said that the thought of being shot at didn't cross my mind,' he said. But he survived unscathed, and England completed their tour without further drama, other than that – remarkably – they won a series they were expected to lose.

When England next made a Test tour of India in 1992–93, things were far from peaceful. A prolonged period of rioting and inter-communal violence across Ahmedabad and Bombay left hundreds dead and threw the proposed fixture list into doubt. A one-day international scheduled for Ahmedabad was cancelled several days out over security concerns, with a replacement game played in Gwalior later on the tour, but the Test match in Bombay went ahead several weeks later without problem.

The value of bespoke security advice was clear when another

---

* Indira Gandhi was not the only local Prime Minister to be assassinated during an England tour; Liaquat Ali of Pakistan was killed in Rawalpindi in October 1951 while the England team were just over the border in India, travelling from Indore to Amritsar. The Pakistan leg of the tour went ahead as planned three weeks later.

tour of India in 2008–09 was halted during the one-day series by terrorist attacks on Mumbai. Guided by Reg Dickason, their head of security, the team flew back to the UK for several days, while the siege of the Taj Hotel reached its bloody conclusion, before heading to a holding camp in Abu Dhabi. Each player was told they did not need to rejoin the tour if they did not want to, but all eventually did so and two scheduled Tests were completed safely at different venues from those originally chosen. Both were played under heavily armed guard.

Since then, England teams have made more than a dozen visits to Asia for Test tours and white-ball tournaments without political turmoil or security crises disrupting their schedule.

England Matches Affected By Crowd Trouble

Crowd trouble has largely been eradicated by stricter policing, limits on alcohol consumption and harsher penalties for spectators entering the playing area. Improvements in facilities have also helped; overcrowding was a key element in some of the worst cases, which often happened on Saturdays when crowds were largest. A notorious incident occurred on one of the earliest tours when Lord Harris's side played New South Wales at the SCG; a run-out triggered such a serious riot – thought to be linked to betting and drinking, and dissatisfaction at the umpiring – that, as a pitch invasion ensued, the English players left the field using stumps as protection and 'Monkey' Hornby reportedly threw a man through a committee-room window. Harris refused to play a Test match scheduled for Sydney later on the tour.

The Saturday of the Adelaide Test during the Bodyline series of 1932–33, when 50,000 were packed into stands not designed for so many, witnessed a febrile atmosphere when two Australian players took blows to the body from England's bowlers; play was not stopped but mounted police were sent for.

Australia, Sydney, 1903–04 (first Test, fourth day): with Australia trailing by 292 on first innings, the run-out of Clem Hill, the fifth second-innings wicket to fall with England still leading, created a hostile reaction from the crowd towards Melbourne umpire Bob Crockett. Pelham Warner, the England captain, went towards the grandstand to address the spectators but could not be heard over the continued booing. 'The game was delayed for a long time,' *The Times* reported. There was further trouble at the same ground during the final Test of the series when on the Saturday light rain kept the players off the field for 80 minutes; bottles and rubbish were thrown onto the cycle track around the field and a small number of spectators among a crowd of 35,000 attempted to rush the playing area but withdrew at the appearance of the police. No playing time was lost

West Indies, Georgetown 1953–54 (third Test, fourth day): play stopped for ten minutes after a section of the crowd threw bottles and invaded the playing area in response to local batsman Cliff McWatt being given run out by Badge Menzies, brought in to officiate after Len Hutton rejected the original choice of umpires. Hutton's refusal to leave the field and the English fielders persuading Menzies to stay defused the situation.

West Indies, Port of Spain 1959–60 (second Test, day three): Charran Singh's run-out with West Indies in grave trouble, possibly combined with overcrowding in the stands, led to bottle-throwing and several thousand spectators coming onto the field, leaving the players marooned in mid-pitch until they were able to leave flanked by police. Fighting broke out and mounted police entered the arena; there were 30 hospital casualties. The 75 minutes that were lost were made up the next day

West Indies, Kingston 1967–68 (second Test, day four): Basil Butcher's wicket to a low leg-side catch led to bottles being thrown and the players leaving the field. The arrival of an armed riot squad only made things worse, with tear gas spreading across the ground and into the dressing-rooms. The 75 minutes of lost play were made up on an unscheduled sixth day.

Pakistan, Karachi 1968–69 (third Test, day three): Pakistan was experiencing severe political turmoil and all three Tests were played against a backdrop of rioting and unrest; this final Test was abandoned on the third morning after a mob, in the words of John Woodcock, 'broke into the stadium, tore up the stumps, savaged the pitch and wrecked the officials' enclosure'. Pitch invasions cost 30 to 45 minutes on each of the first two days.

Australia, Melbourne, 1970–71 (fifth Test, first day): there was an invasion of 1,000 out of a crowd of 42,000 when Ian Chappell reached his century, resulting in a seven-minute delay. Melbourne CC secretary Ian Johnson said that the club would consider fitting barbed wire to the perimeter to prevent a repeat. 'Today's episode was disgraceful,' he said.

Australia, Sydney 1970–71 (seventh Test, second day): Ray Illingworth led his England team off the field on the Saturday evening after beer cans were thrown at John Snow. Snow had just bowled a short ball that struck Terry Jenner in the face, leading to an altercation between Illingworth and umpire Lou Rowan over a warning given to Snow for intimidatory bowling. The players returned to the field after seven minutes when Illingworth was warned by the umpires that the match would be awarded to Australia unless they went back out. Eleven spectators were arrested.

Pakistan, Karachi 1972–73 (third Test, days one and three): several interruptions led to the loss of about 100 minutes. A number of these were due to pitch invasions, the most serious occurring when Majid Khan reached his fifty; police used batons to clear spectators and a stand was set alight, and as a result play ended 40 minutes early on the first day.

Pakistan, Lahore 1977–78 (first Test, second and third days): the first disturbance was linked to Mudassar Nazar's century, with a pitch invasion leading to running fights and police taking refuge in the dressing room; 25 minutes was lost. The second was more serious and had a political motivation, with Begum Nusrat Bhutto, wife of the jailed former Prime Minister Zulfiqar Ali Bhutto, turning up with several hundred supporters. There was a fire in the ladies' stand, tear gas was used and 55 minutes of play were lost.

Australia, Perth 1982–83 (first Test, second day): fighting between fans on the terraces on the Saturday afternoon resulted in a delay of 15 minutes, and 25 arrests. Terry Alderman, the Australian bowler, dislocated his shoulder tackling a spectator who had run onto the field and hit him on the head.

CHAPTER 11

The Build-Up

Acclimatisation and the early warm-up matches

The period between the start of a tour and the first international match has long been considered vitally important to the success of the enterprise, but how a touring party should best use this time has been the subject of constant debate. There seemed to be no perfect answer. How long does it take for everyone to acclimatise? How many warm-up games are enough to get people in form and ready for battle? England teams have gone into the first Test of an overseas tour having played anything from one first-class match up to nine, and in recent years have even played none at all, but however long or short the build-up the schedules were often criticised as unsatisfactory. The fundamental problem was that what each player needed varied. Some trained avidly, while others regarded warm-up matches as a waste of time and could not find motivation from anything other than the internationals themselves.

What every player might have felt during this phase was a sense of anticipation – a mix of trepidation, even fear perhaps, and excitement – at the proximity of a career-defining event. For many there would be anxiety over their place in the side and an eagerness to impress the captain, manager or coach. A young

Brian Close ahead of his first tour was advised by Norman Yardley, a former England captain, to make sure he started well because the captain – in this case Freddie Brown – had limited time to decide on his best team.

This argument still holds. Given any sort of build-up, at some point the management will put out what it thinks is the best XI in an effort to establish strengths, iron out weaknesses and accustom everyone to their roles. Later in the tour, side games might see frontline players rested and reserves given more opportunities, so these become less important contests, but the opening fixtures can feel like they count for a lot. A touring party in the early weeks operates at a feverish tempo that cannot be maintained over many weeks or months, but at the start it is important that everyone is charged with a sense of purpose.

For many years these early games, like others outside the Tests later in the tour, were important in their own right. They drew large crowds and generated valuable gate receipts, and both sides were keen to win, or at least not lose. Local sides put out their best teams and were eager to make their mark because a stand-out performance against a touring side could lead to an international call-up. For the English players, a game against New South Wales or Victoria, traditionally the two most powerful Australian state sides, or Barbados, Transvaal or Bombay, were definitely contests to be won in their own right.

Nor was it unusual for itineraries to include fixtures against select XIs – what were extra Test matches in all but name. An Australian XI provided opposition before the first Test on all but one England tour between 1928–29 and 1965–66. The exception was Freddie Brown's trip in 1950–51 when the fixture was played directly before the second Test. On that occasion the Australian XI's top six was made up entirely of players who featured in the Tests, and not surprisingly they racked up 526 for nine declared.

Don Bradman turned out for the Australian XI ahead of every home series he played against England, and when he did so in the 1932–33 fixture (which drew a total gate of more than 100,000) the English pace trio of Harold Larwood, Bill Voce and Bill Bowes gave their Bodyline tactics the fullest outing yet. Bob Wyatt, the acting captain, noted portentously that Bradman 'was decidedly uncomfortable when he played this type of bowling from Larwood'. It was a South African XI, two weeks before the first Test of 1956–57, that inflicted on an English team their first ever defeat on a turf pitch in South Africa; the match-winner was Hugh Tayfield, who would go on to take 37 wickets in the five Tests.

The notion that matches in the early weeks should be treated merely as glorified net sessions, and that the hosts might hide their best players from the visitors, only came later during a less generous era of competition in which hospitality lost almost all its meaning. Touring teams would be deliberately provided with local opposition shorn of extreme pace or spin, depending on what they might be about to face in the Tests, or pitches totally unlike those they would encounter in those Tests.

That Alastair Cook's side found themselves playing against second-rate opponents on seamer-friendly surfaces in three warm-up matches in India in 2012–13 probably played its part in England going without warm-ups altogether when they next toured there in 2016–17. Australia even sought to use geography to their advantage ahead of the traditional first Test in Brisbane by providing England with a final warm-up fixture not at the Gabba itself, as they did for many years, but more than 2,200 miles away in Perth, with a two-hour time difference, or in the cooler, more temperate climate of Hobart, as the starkest contrast to the sweltering heat and humidity of Brisbane.*

Time being money, teams were put to work as soon as possible. The arrival of Arthur Shrewsbury's team of 1886–87 was

---

* Tasmania, sometimes allotted the period over Christmas, could be a dangerously relaxed environment; a lengthy stay there in 1965–66 was reckoned to be a contributory factor in England going soft and surrendering a 1–0 lead when they returned to the mainland.

delayed by more than a day by headwinds, but because their first match was scheduled to start on a Saturday, with the expectation of a lucrative gate, the original itinerary was kept to. Thus, a group of players whose boat had anchored off Adelaide at 5 p.m. on the Friday, headed for the nets first thing the next morning before commencing play at 12 noon. Thanks to a century from Shrewsbury himself they performed creditably enough.

Arthur Jones's side of 1907–08 began their opening fixture against Western Australia less than 48 hours after arrival, as did Bob Wyatt's team in the Caribbean in 1934–35, both times in order to meet Saturday starts. At the first net session at the Kensington Oval, Errol Holmes observed to Wyatt that the pitch looked so good that 'all we need to do is to play forward – we'll never get out'. In fact, they were all out for 170 and had to scrap for a draw. 'The atmosphere is probably "rarer" and it is possible that the ball travels a little faster and further through the air than in England,' Holmes noted by way of explanation.

Whatever the destination, there was the strong likelihood that the cricketers would have to adjust their eyes to what one observer described as the 'arc-light glare of the sun'. Inevitably, there needed to be a period of adjustment. 'It is always difficult to play well in the first match of the tour, no matter how much practice and how many nets you have to build up to it,' Geoff Boycott wrote. 'Players are rusty … bowlers struggle to get loose and batsmen need to re-sharpen their timing.' When it came to long-haul travel by plane, it took several years for it to be realised that everyone needed an interval of several days to overcome jet lag.

Before air travel and ODIs redrew the organisational map, the preliminary weeks of tours were lengthier, more structured and more determined by geography. From 1907–08 to 1965–66, the build-up to Australia Test series typically spanned anything from six to nine weeks and would take in five, six or seven first-class matches. Once Perth became the standard first port of call, the team would work an eastern passage round the crescent to Brisbane, stopping en route to play state sides in Adelaide, Melbourne and Sydney, plus other stop-offs in the bush along the way. Even after planes replaced boats, through to the mid-1990s, this phase typically lasted around five weeks and involved three or four first-class matches.

Remarkably, the build-up during South Africa tours became even more bloated, presumably at the instigation of the South African Cricket Association's accountants. The first MCC-led mission there in 1905–06 had a lead-in of five weeks, and this period grew in size with each successive visit so that by 1956–57 the team had been in the country for 67 days and played nine first-class fixtures before the Test series opened on Christmas Eve – the most protracted warm-up to a five-Test series in England's touring history.*

For tours of the West Indies, teams started in Barbados before heading westward via Trinidad and British Guiana to Jamaica, with Antigua and Grenada added as additional stop-offs in the 1950s, though for practical and financial reasons the pattern was different: each territorial visit usually involved one or two matches against the local island side followed by the Test match.

Inevitably, as cricket spread to new regions, local facilities did not always meet with the approval of international sportsmen impatient to sharpen their skills. To a degree, this had always been a problem, but that did not lessen the frustration when difficulties arose. When for the first time England paid a visit to St Vincent in the early weeks of Ian Botham's tour of 1980–81, they were met with hopelessly inadequate – if not downright dangerous – practice facilities and unhelpfully rainy weather. Boycott resorted to having a net with a car tyre propped on

---

* The longest periods spent by England in opposing countries ahead of Test series are: 67 days in South Africa 1956–57 (nine first-class matches); 64 days in Australia 1924–25 (seven); 64 days in India 1933–34 (seven); 58 days in Australia 1946–47 (seven); and 55 days in South Africa 1948–49 (eight). In the first six of the nine matches played on the 1956–57 tour, England came across just one Test player; one newspaper correspondent described them as practically useless as Test preparation. England won five of these games by an innings.

planks for a wicket, with cows, goats and pigs for fielders. 'Our mental state was badly affected by the lack of organisation we met time and time again,' he said. Frank Keating reported that when an organiser was asked if there were any further practice facilities, he replied: 'All the spare nets have gone fishing.'

This proved to be just the start of English frustrations on St Vincent. Five years later, England returned to Arnos Vale to open their tour and were well beaten by a Windward Islands team that were among the weaker territorial sides; they were bowled out for 186 and 94. It was a particularly embarrassing defeat for the captain, David Gower, who chose to miss the game and was photographed enjoying an outing on a yacht while the match was going on. Things did not get any better. In Antigua, there were no nets and the practice ground had cows walking over the pitch. All three warm-up games were played on pitches totally unrepresentative of what the players came up against in the Tests.

On the 1990 tour, the Windward Islands were again involved in England's warm-up phase, with a match on St Lucia, and this time they beat Graham Gooch's side by one wicket after forcing the visitors to follow on. Such early defeats were rare, but when they happened they could cause shock waves and threaten morale. Nine of the first 13 England Test tours of Australia in the twentieth century saw the side unbeaten in the lead-up to the first Test, an impressive record, and the first side to lose two first-class matches before the opening Test was Ted Dexter's in 1962–63. One of the most eye-catching defeats was inflicted on Mike Atherton's team in Zimbabwe in 1996–97, when they were beaten by Mashonaland by seven wickets with the assistance of James Kirtley, a young English seamer who would later play Test cricket for England, as their overseas recruit.

What the performances of touring teams during this warm-up phase signified was notoriously hard to tell. Sometimes there was no mistaking the signs: when Johnny Douglas's side of 1920–21 was beaten by New South Wales, a state which provided three-quarters of the Australia Test XI, it was hard to see why the outcome of the Tests themselves should be any different – and they weren't. Douglas Jardine's team beating South Australia, Victoria and NSW by an innings proved an equally reliable barometer. But some touring teams would start brightly and then fade; others might struggle to put together a decent game only for everything to click by the time of the first Test. Either way, it was only to be expected that journalists would not hesitate to rush to judgment – and often repent at leisure.

Arthur Jones's side went unbeaten in six first-class matches at the start of the 1907–08 tour, only to go on and lose the Test series to Australia 4–1. Gubby Allen's team lost to New South Wales, were outplayed by an Australian XI and trailed Victoria on first innings, but went on to win the first and second Tests (before capitulating in the remaining games of the series). Peter May's team were beaten soundly by a powerful Barbados side directly before the first Test of 1959–60 but proceeded to win the series and not lose another match on the tour. When Mike Denness's side of 1974–75 went into the first Test unbeaten, it proved bitterly misleading, prompting Christopher Martin-Jenkins to reflect: 'The events of the first month of a long cricket tour appear large and important at the time [and] relatively insignificant in retrospect. Rarely, indeed, can any cricket team have so flattered to deceive as this MCC party.'

When Queensland won England's opening first-class match of their 1986–87 tour, Martin Johnson in the *Independent* wrote off the team's chances in no uncertain terms. He should perhaps have known better, as only two years earlier Gower's side in India had lost by an innings to an India Under-25 XI and still gone on to win the Test series. Sure enough, Gatting's team went on to win with something to spare. Gatting said that once he and his players saw what Johnson had written it had provoked a 'We'll show 'em' response. And they did.

For individual players, their early form – or lack of it – could be no less confusing. Denis Compton started the 1950–51 tour with hundreds against Western Australia and Victoria and 92 against New South Wales, but in the Tests themselves he was an extraordinary failure for such a great player: he managed just 53 runs in eight innings. He was troubled by a football-related knee injury, and missed the second Test as a result, but the fact that he scored 829 runs at 92 in other first-class matches in Australia suggested he was not channeling his energies into the games that mattered. Similarly, Peter May began in South Africa in 1956–57 with four centuries in his first four first-class innings, the last of them a double, and added a fifth hundred in his last match before the opening Test as England completed a largely serene build-up. But come the Tests, May's form deserted him. He managed only one fifty and averaged 15 for the series.*

Mark Butcher had a very different experience at the start of his first tour of Australia in 1998–99. He was hit on the head in the opening fixture as he attempted to come to terms with Australia's bouncier surfaces, and was then involved in a training ground collision with Peter Such. By the time of the opening Test at the Gabba he was simply grateful to be in the side, as he had a top score of 5 in three warm-up games and was sporting a blackened left eye and a scar above his right eye where ten stitches had been. 'I'd managed more stitches than runs,' he recalled ruefully. He began his first innings in the Test late on the second day with England under the pump, Australia having made 485. 'I decided to borrow a bat off Alec [Stewart],' he said. 'I was trying anything to find the middle of the bat. I also decided to be ultra-aggressive. Nothing else had worked. I drilled one back past Glenn McGrath early on and that was that, I was away. Admittedly, I nicked a few through slip and had a bit of luck, but it was happy days again.' Butcher ended

---

* May's loss of form may have baffled many, but those superstitious members of the tour party were unsurprised. After the fourth of his hundreds against Rhodesia, the England captain was publicly presented with a live duck by the mayor of Salisbury. May duly got a duck in his next match against Transvaal to begin his slump in form. 'The bird brought Peter nothing but bad luck,' Denis Compton recalled.

with 116, England kept the deficit to 110 and thanks to a late thunderstorm escaped with a draw.

Butcher, who played in ten overseas Test series, was one of those who struggled to find value in tour warm-ups. 'At home you were left to your own devices in terms of preparation. You'd do the things you needed to do,' he explained to me:

> When you were on tour, you were guided by timetables of net sessions and what the pecking order was. There wasn't a lot of flexibility. I probably wasn't selfish enough to put my foot down and make sure I had enough time to get prepared in the way that I would have done at home.
>
> Some people really liked warm-up games. I could not stand them. You spent hours in the field when all you wanted to do was hit balls. You couldn't even practise the particular thing you wanted to work on. You were concerned about staying in. Geoff Boycott would say time in the middle is worth more than any amount of time in the nets, but I always felt it was more important to groove everything and not worry about scoring runs, which can cloud the thing you're trying to fix or perfect. There's nothing on warm-ups except your first-class record. For me, they were a chore. What was always missing was a bit of adrenalin.

On the first of his tours, to the West Indies, he was not even chosen for the two warm up games, which meant he went into the first Test at Jamaica – as a replacement 30 minutes before the start after Jack Russell fell ill – hopelessly under-prepared. 'There were no net facilities and there wasn't really a way of getting yourself ready,' he added. 'When I walked out to face my one and only ball of the Sabina Park Test [abandoned after 10.1 overs due to an unfit pitch], I had literally not faced a bowler the entire time I'd been on the tour.'

Like Butcher, David Gower found it difficult to motivate himself for warm-up matches and by Australia in 1986–87, his ninth straight winter of England touring, his captain Mike Gatting decided to let him miss a match against South Australia even though he was in need of runs. 'Leaving him out was more a protective move to shield him from himself,' Gatting said. 'He gets tired and, to a certain extent, irritable when questioned about his form every time he fails to make at least fifty.' Gower played the next game against Western Australia and was out for 0 in both innings, but when it came to the Tests he instinctively found form and averaged 57.71 for the series.

In the end, modern tours became more streamlined for a variety of reasons. The more the international fixtures went from strength to strength in terms of TV rights valuations, the more precipitous was the decline in gate-receipts from every other type of match. This, in turn, freed up the growing number of coaches who were accompanying teams on tour, and the players themselves, to ask what it was they wanted to gain from the warm-up phase. From there, it was a small step to conclude that bespoke training sessions – where time allowed – might well serve better.

At around the time this process was gaining momentum, England appointed as head coach Duncan Fletcher, whose second winter in charge took in tours of Pakistan and Sri Lanka. For these, he used tailored practice sessions to hone his players' skills against spin bowling, a long-standing English weakness. 'The beauty of playing under Fletcher that winter was the specific way we practised,' Ashley Giles recalled. 'The old-fashioned way was to have a few throw-downs, have a hit against the fast bowlers, and crack on. But on this tour, we made it difficult, facing balls that were chucked into the rough.'

In large part thanks to the improvements they made, England unexpectedly won both Test series. Fletcher also began the regular practice of using tour warm-ups to allow more than 11 players to take part by rotating them in and out of games; he did this not only with one-day games, as had briefly happened when David Lloyd was coach, but also with matches scheduled for three and four days. This stripped the games of first-class status but created the opportunity for more players to get time in the middle.* Critics argued that the games became little more than glorified middle practice, and lacked intensity, but many players favoured the move.

This practice became even more common under subsequent head coaches, who would also swap a scheduled four-day game, designated as first-class, for two two-dayers which officially had no standing. Chris Silverwood, who took over from Trevor Bayliss in 2019, briefly put an end to such shenanigans before the Covid-19 pandemic struck – which temporarily ended warm-ups against local sides altogether on bio-security grounds, intra-squad matches taking their place.† Overall, since the late 1990s only a handful of tours (three to Australia, one to South Africa) have involved even as many as three first-class matches ahead of the first Test.

One of these tours was the Andrew Strauss/Andy Flower-led mission to Australia in 2010–11, when they strove to invest greater intensity in the games against Western Australia, South Australia and Australia A by treating them as a mini-series to be won in its own right. Rain thwarted them against South Australia, but the other matches were won handsomely. As the last of these games took place in Tasmania – the old

---

* The first time this happened was in the winter of 2003–04 in respect of two three-day matches in Bangladesh (in Dhaka and Savar) and one match in the West Indies (in Kingston, Jamaica).

† Something else that altered the dynamics of tours was the staging of ODIs (or T20s) ahead of the Tests. This first happened in Australia in 1979–80, when an ODI tri-series between England, Australia and West Indies was interspersed with Australia playing Tests against England and West Indies. It became common for England tours of the West Indies to include ODIs and Tests during each territorial visit. From 2000–01 onwards, tours were generally broken up into blocks of games according to format and sometimes white-ball matches would be played before Tests. This happened on all five England tours of New Zealand between 2001–02 and 2019–20. This pattern helped England win some Test series they might otherwise have lost, such as the one in Sri Lanka in 2018–19. 'Playing the one-day series first meant our batsmen were confident against their spinners. We made a conscious decision to take them down and worked out quite a lot of their mystery,' said Paul Farbrace, England's then assistant coach.

Hobart–Brisbane trick again being played by the Australian organisers – England sent the fast bowlers earmarked to play in the first Test ahead to Queensland to train and acclimatise. England went on the win the Test series, and their highly focused preparation was held as partly responsible, although it was never quite replicated on later tours.

Nathan Leamon explained:

The number of warm-up matches is important, and playing two or three definitely helps, but the quality is the key thing. That '10 –11 tour was the last time I can remember the warm-up matches being decent preparation – they had the right level of opposition, on similar surfaces [to those used for the Tests]. So many times these days you play against players who are barely first-class or on surfaces that, say, in India might be green-tops [and therefore irrelevant to the Tests]. It's getting harder to adjust to conditions through warm-up games. It was a nice part of the planning [in 2010–11] that we took six seamers with the express intention of flying the bowling attack to Brisbane ahead of our last warm-up.

ECB performance director Mo Bobat said that intra-squad matches were going to replace conventional tour warm-ups regardless of the pandemic, due to a general dissatisfaction with the quality of the opposition on offer. 'Warm-up games in recent years across [various] countries haven't been as competitive as we wanted them to be,' he said ahead of the Ashes tour of 2021–22. 'We certainly found on the last Ashes trip [in 2017–18] that was the case, and it didn't serve the purpose we wanted. Also, with games among ourselves we've been able to be flexible and to dial up the intensity when we wanted to. It's about having an element of control.'

An additional challenge for modern teams was to make sure that, having travelled out by plane and with less time available to them than their predecessors before the internationals began, the players were able to bond and achieve a common sense of purpose. Flower did not allow wives or girlfriends to join their partners during this period for this very reason, to give space to what Alastair Cook described as 'boys' nights out, playing golf [and] enjoying the privileges of being international cricketers abroad'. New captains or coaches might use the early weeks of a tour to set the tone and make it clear to the group how they intended to approach things, which usually meant instilling a new culture of hard work and discipline, and thereby creating a sense of togetherness. Gatting and Micky Stewart did this in Australia in 1986–87, as did Graham Gooch and Stewart in the West Indies in 1989–90 and Michael Vaughan and Fletcher in Bangladesh in 2003–04, all with good effect.

Not everyone bought into the sense of earnestness that could pervade these formative days. The longer the period that lay ahead before the serious business began, the more some players thought it allowed them scope to enjoy themselves, because later on there would be next to no chance for fun and frolics. The 1982–83 tour of Australia was five days old, and the first Test match still 24 days away, when Bob Willis had a word with his players about over-doing the socialising. 'It is all too easy to get carried away in the bar at night, especially before the Test series begins,' he noted.

Four years later, Ian Botham had as his room-mate first-time tourist Phillip DeFreitas. 'We had a great time for the first few weeks,' DeFreitas recalled. Robin Smith, another senior player, took under his wing Matthew Maynard on his first tour to the West Indies in 1993–94, and during an early match in Antigua stayed out later than they should have done. Their high jinks back at the hotel landed them in trouble with Mike Atherton, the captain, and after Smith missed the team bus the next morning he was instructed to apologise to the team in the dressing room.

Gradually, the realisation dawned on team managements that the longer the build-up the more scope there was for trouble.

This accelerated the move towards tours becoming more like no-frills business trips.

The sheer amount of travel and cricket that used to be crammed into this period was certainly not conducive to ensuring the players arrived at the first Test in the best physical or mental state.

The three weeks leading up to what is now regarded as England's first ever Test match, in Melbourne in March 1877, were extraordinarily draining for James Lillywhite's 12-man party. To avoid further days at sea, they occasionally took overland routes, once spending three days journeying by train, coach and omnibus between Newcastle and Melbourne, and it was for this reason that they took an ill-fated decision to cover the 200 miles from Greymouth to Christchurch by stagecoach across the mountains rather than round the coast by steamer (all except Ted Pooley, who went with the luggage by boat).

Amid heavy rain they had to perilously traverse a swollen gorge near Otira, dragging horses and two coaches across the rapids, and only narrowly escaping with their lives. 'What each one thought he was afraid to admit afterwards, but that there were serious misgivings as to our safety is beyond doubt,' James Southerton wrote in a dispatch ten days later from Dunedin. 'There we were in the bed of the river, with the elements as bad as anyone can possibly imagine, on either side of us a mountain 3,000ft high, the river rising rapidly, no one knowing which way to move in the utter darkness, and not a soul to hear us, shout as loud as we could.'*

The strongly built Yorkshireman George Ulyett would recall more than 20 years later: 'I could swim, and I had to swim, too, at one stage ... or I should not have been here now.' The journey took three days, and within a few hours of arrival the

---

* John Gibb (1831–1909), a Scottish-born artist who settled in Christchurch the previous year, accompanied the cricketers on the journey and produced an oil painting of the crossing of the Otira gorge.

players were taking the field at Hagley Park. 'We were so stiff, cold, and sore with being wet and cramped up in the coach that we could scarcely bowl or run,' Ulyett added. Fortified by a case of champagne that evening, they rallied to win the game.*

It took seven days to sail from Invercargill on the southern tip of New Zealand to Melbourne, by which stage, in Alfred Shaw's words, 'not one of us was fit to play cricket ... I was simply spun out of myself. Others of our bowlers were also completely knocked up.' Conditions aboard ship were so bad that some slept on deck. They also arrived without Pooley, their wicketkeeper, who had been arrested following a fracas – in which some of his teammates including Ulyett were also involved – arising out of the non-payment of a bet during their time in Christchurch. Pooley was acquitted at trial but too late to take part in the two Tests, which meant only 11 players were available to face the combined strength of Australia.

The first Test began at the Paddock in Yarra Park – on the site of what is now the MCG – just 24 hours after they reached Melbourne. 'People at home do not know or do not think that it is quite a different thing to play a match at home, fit and well, and to play one out here after the very rough travelling by land and sea,' Southerton wrote on the day the match was lost on the fourth day.

Several generations of touring cricketers later, journeys that ought to have been straightforward were still wearying to the marrow. South Africa in 1956–57 not only featured the longest build-up of any England Test tour but also such penny-pinching that Peter May's players, having completed their opening

---

* Some of the early journeys around southern Africa between railheads could be similarly treacherous. Aubrey Smith's side needed reviving with brandy after completing a harrowing crossing of the swollen Sundays River on the way to Oudtshoorn in two-man carts. Three years later, en route from Johannesburg to Pietermaritzburg, and with the party travelling in two groups, the professionals were caught in heavy rains and waylaid overnight near a spruit, with little food or water; the amateurs fared even worse, taking so long to get there that they missed the next fixture. George Hearne, a professional, captained the side against a Pietermaritzburg XVIII.

first-class fixture in Cape Town, were sent to Port Elizabeth not by plane but on a train journey that took 30 hours. Later on the tour, they made the same journey by coach over two days. Following complaints from May and tour manager Freddie Brown, plans for the team to spend three days going from Salisbury to Johannesburg by train were scrapped; instead they flew and were there in three hours.

Some of the most arduous experiences came on the subcontinent. The side Ted Dexter led around Pakistan and India in 1961–62 was effectively an A team of the untried and untested, and they were made to travel in their captain's words 'thousands of miles . . . in ancient, lumbering trains and buses rattling over rutted and potholed roads, staying in accommodation that Mowgli might have recognised'. Nor did the schedule for the early weeks of the 1976–77 tour of India seem to have the best interests of the visitors at heart, as four three-day games in four different cities were packed in before the first Test. 'After the brief settling-in period in Bombay the team had been either travelling or playing every day [before the first Test], wrote Christopher Martin-Jenkins. 'There was no time to take stock, to relax.'

The corresponding phase of the next full Test tour of India five years later was every bit as hectic, again with only a few precious days free of cricket or travel. What added to the claustrophobia was the passion for the game among the local population, something particularly evident during a train journey from Bombay to Poona. 'Whenever the train did stop, a sea of faces submerged the carriage; windows were forced open from outside, garlands and autograph books foisted through,' Scyld Berry wrote in *Cricket Wallah*. 'Some players wished the multitude were not quite so ardent. To avoid pandemonium in Poona, the England party got off the train at the station before.' Perhaps the ultimate test came on the 1992–93 tour, when because of a strike among Air India staff the team often had to travel internally by train or coach.

Especially arduous were the up-country fixtures, particularly but not exclusively in Australia, when the relative comforts of the big cities were swapped for protracted and difficult journeys, and erratic standards of accommodation and catering. The hope was that the players would act as proselytisers while also enjoying the experience, but those who arranged these games were not often required to endure the endless hours of discomfort in horse-drawn coaches, railway carriages, buses or planes – each exhausting expedition all too soon followed by another.

Monty Noble, the former Australia captain, wrote in his account of Arthur Gilligan's tour of 1924–25 that what he termed these 'picnic matches' were designed 'partly with a view to keeping up practice and partly to enable the players to see something of the country'. And see some of the country they did – lots of it. John Woodcock recalled of the post-war period that these flag-flying expeditions up in the bush typically brought to town 'graziers and shearers and jackaroos', and Alec Bedser, who made three tours of Australia in that period, said he loved them. These people were, he said, 'the true Australians'. Certainly, if the visitors played badly, they would let them know about it.

Phillip Sheridan, manager of the Sydney Cricket Ground, who was closely involved in the organisation of a number of early England tours, claimed rather loftily ahead of the 1907–08 tour that up-country games also served the morally beneficial purpose of keeping the travelling players out of mischief in the big cities. 'How are your dozen or so young men, exposed to the temptation offered by the hospitality, say, of Melbourne, to resist those temptations if time hangs heavily on their hands? What harm could it do them, instead of resting a fortnight in the city, to make a few days' trip up to Bendigo or Ballarat, and play in a friendly match there? Surely no great strain is placed upon them, and the advantages of averting the work that Satan finds for idle hands [are] obvious.'

No doubt he was right. After all, had not William Caffyn said of the first Australia tour, 'We once more had high jinks at Sydney'? Their lungs filled with cleaner air and their minds with purer thoughts, the English cricketers often enjoyed the opportunity for some sport once out in the country. They shot kangaroos in the 1880s and were still doing it in the 1960s. They fished in the rivers and streams of New Zealand, South Africa and Tasmania, hunted for caimans in Guyana, and for tarantulas and vampire bats in Trinidad. On the early tours of India, they shot lions, tigers and panthers. And, of course, they played endless rounds of golf.

These country trips may have improved their souls – while putting money in the pockets of organisers – but they did not necessarily do much for their cricketing skills. The standard of opposition was routinely poor, sometimes desperately so, and the quality of pitches could be terrible. W. G. Grace's team that toured Australia in 1873–74, the third English team to visit, played a match at Stawell, a gold-mining town 12 hours by rough bush track from Ballarat, on a ground in a deplorable state. 'Here and there were small patches of grass, but the greater part was utterly devoid of any herbage,' Grace recounted. 'We were not surprised to hear that the field had only been ploughed up three months before, and that the grass had been sown in view of our visit. The wicket was execrable, but there was no help for it – we had travelled 70 miles through bush and dust to play the match, and there was no option but to play. Of course, the cricket was shockingly poor, and the match a ludicrous farce.' Perhaps because of their knowledge of conditions, the local XXII won, a fact which no doubt coloured Grace's withering verdict.

Up-country pitches and players may have improved slightly over the years, but such fixtures loomed too large for too long. The teams which fulfilled major Test tours through the 1960s and 1970s played anything from three to five fixtures in the Australian interior before the first Test, and they were generally far more of a hindrance than a help to preparations.*

What signed the death warrant of these matches as much as anything was the increased chance of injury. Two weeks into the 1936–37 tour, Bob Wyatt broke his left forearm during a one-day match on a treacherous pitch in the Clare Valley; the bone was then set unsatisfactorily, and when Wyatt got to Sydney a specialist re-broke the arm over the back of a chair and re-set it properly. As a result, Wyatt was unfit for ten weeks and was only available for the last two Tests.

E. M. Wellings denounced the playing of four matches against Country XIs ahead of the first Test on the 1970–71 tour on the grounds that several injuries occurred during 'one-day games of no consequence', adding that 'an international side should consistently meet worthy opposition, and not be asked to frolic with up-country teams of club standard.' By 1978–79, Geoff Boycott suggested that, '[though] it is a very important PR exercise to take cricket into the districts and there is no doubt it is very popular . . . perhaps the district teams could also travel to meet the tourists'. That, of course, never happened.

No less wearying than the travel was the round of social functions that until recently were a common feature of touring. Every new town or city wanted to celebrate their guests, and vied to outdo one another in the lavishness of their hospitality. Invitations poured in not only from local communities, but also from British residents and High Commissions. The cricketers appreciated the free food and drink, and the offers of complimentary tickets to cinemas, theatres and dances, but it could come at the price of crushingly dull conversation.

These functions could be foisted on them with little warning directly after a day's play, and if they demurred there could be

---

* The nearest that modern English cricketers in Australia came to experiencing this kind of festival fixture was when the four tours between 1990–91 and 2002–03 opened at Lilac Hill, on the outer suburbs of Perth, against a WACA President's XI or later an ACB Chairman's team.

consequences. Gubby Allen estimated he made more than 50 speeches at official functions in Australia and New Zealand when he was captain, and in his tour report observed: 'I am convinced that a captain of an MCC touring team in Australia has little chance of doing himself full justice as a cricketer on the field as things stand as present. The cricketing performances of Gilligan, Chapman, Jardine and Holmes, the last four MCC captains in Australia, confirm this view.' Allen's own form tailed away badly.

The first team to go to India after the war was invited to endless tea parties and musical evenings. It was one of the chief functions of a tour manager to stop these requests getting out of hand, but it was important not to offend hosts, and certain social obligations had to be met. Someone, usually the captain or manager, was required to speak on such occasions, and the same few sentences of thanks, polished as smooth as pebbles, would be wheeled out with just the place names changed as the venue required. Captains would happily pass on this task to a vice-captain if they could. The passing of this tradition was not mourned. Modern touring captains might find themselves required to speak at such functions once or twice, if at all.

Attendance at these events was often a source of friction. Frank Tyson reported that it was not unusual for the players to attend six functions in each state capital on the 1954–55 tour, before the management sought to impose a one-per-city rule. Margaret Hughes could not disguise her incredulity at such mindless repetition. 'They have to be officially welcomed in each city with the usual speeches and much the same people as they go along; they go on official visits; appear in public places; always answering the same questions; always talking cricket, cricket, cricket; playing it for five hours a day and then on to it again at night.'

The formality of dress codes was another wearisome feature: black tie was a standard part of a touring cricketer's wardrobe well into the 1960s and a chore to wear in hot climates. In

Asia, large formal gatherings with lengthy speeches were the norm, but at least there was sometimes access to alcohol which might otherwise be hard to find. Of the India tour of 1933–34, Hubert Preston wrote: 'The heat, travelling and constant social functions, always very pleasant, could be held responsible for anyone failing to do himself justice.'

Even if dinner jackets were no longer a part of a touring cricketer's wardrobe, functions on the evenings of Test matches remained a feature into the 1980s and beyond, much to the dissatisfaction of many. 'The last thing you want in the middle of a Test match', Derek Underwood said of his last England tour to India in 1981–82, 'is to go to a cocktail party at the British High Commission, having been playing all day in a cauldron'.

A considered assessment of the many different ways in which England teams have prepared for the first Test matches of an overseas tour would conclude that rarely has the right balance been struck. For many years, this build-up period was intolerably protracted, with too many matches and too much travel. In modern times, proper preparation has been sacrificed on the altar of a packed year-round international programme that simply does not allow space for practice matches – or sightseeing. Over-baked or under-cooked, the cricketers just had to make to the best of it.

Against the Odds

One of the features of England tours was the many matches against 'odds' – teams of more than 11 players as a means of levelling up contests involving weaker opposition. These sides might be made up of anything from 12 to 24 players, depending on estimations of their strength, and were usually based in rural districts where playing standards were lower; the main cities, with their access to more good cricketers, were generally where touring sides were most likely to play XIs (and of course where they played full internationals on level terms).

The chief intention of an odds team was to bolster the batting; when they were in the field, they might sometimes use only 13 players, or even 11 (although any number of people could bowl). Odds matches were most common in Australia and South Africa, although English teams also played against odds in New Zealand, Ceylon and North America; they did not feature at all on early Test tours of Asia, and hardly at all in West Indies. The size of the odds teams declined as standards rose, and by the 1930s odds matches had all but died out.

Playing against large teams on rudimentary pitches and out-fields was not easy, and defeats for the touring side were rare but not unknown. Heathfield Stephenson's team of 1861–62 lost to a Victoria-New South Wales XXII, James Lillywhite's side were beaten by two individual XVs from those two states, and the first English team to South Africa in 1888–89 – barely of good club standard itself – lost several games against odds. Lord Hawke's team in 1898–99 was beaten by a combined Colleges XXII in Cape Town, but successfully lobbied for the result to be scrubbed from the record on the grounds that it was a replacement for a can-celled match.

Overwhelmingly, though, the boot was on the other foot. W. G. Grace's 1873–74 XI dismissed a Kadina XXII for 13 and in the 1880s a Moss Vale XXII were all out for 14, with Bobby Peel taking 18 for seven, and a Lithgow XXII for 18 and 27, Johnny Briggs returning match figures of 27 for 20. In South Africa, Briggs once took 28 wickets against a XXII and George Lohmann 26 wickets against an XVIII. Briggs also took 24 wickets against a Bowral XXIV in 1891–92 in the only fixture an English touring side played against as many as 24 players (15, 18 and 22 were the most common configurations). As the place that raised Don Bradman, a batsman commonly reck-oned to be worth several men, Bowral would later have its revenge on English cricket.

Size of opposing teams on major England tours 1859–60 to 1936–37

(including the four pioneering tours of 1859–60 to 1873–74 and all Test tours between 1876–77 and 1936–37)

Period	11 players	12–15 players	16–18 players	20–24 players	Total odds matches	Odds matches as % of total
1859–60 to 1873–74	8	2	4	42	48	85.7
1876–77 to 1891–92	69	25	69	107	201	74.5
1894–95 to 1901–02	45	22	26	10	58	56.3
1903–04 to 1913–14	93	18	11	2	31	25.0
1920–21 to 1936–37	243	24	2	0	26	9.7
Total	**458**	**91**	**112**	**161**	**364**	**44.3**

CHAPTER 12

The Shock of the First Test

Barbed wire and glassy pitches

The first Test of a series tends to be the moment when ambitions and dreams bump up against reality. However much a touring party may have prepared, and however much good cricket they have played in the weeks beforehand, nothing can really serve as preparation for the heightened intensity of the occasion – the quality of the opposition, the size of the crowd, the depth of the scrutiny. The jeopardy is greater for the visitors than their hosts. They largely showed their hand with the announcement of their squad before leaving home. The way they deployed their resources in the warm-up matches gave further clues as to their thinking. The hosts, by contrast, are able to draw on a larger pool of players and potentially have many more tricks up their sleeve. They could hide a particular fast bowler or mystery spinner. The hosts have also had a strong element of control over the terms under which the opening Test was conducted, such as the choice of ground and type of pitch. Against that, a touring captain can name his XI at the very last moment without administrative inconvenience.

It is the scope for the unexpected in these final days and hours that can lead to agitation and anxiety among the visitors. Are they good enough? Are they ready? Will their plans survive first contact with the enemy? The eve of the first Test, the first day of the match itself – these are days like no others on a tour. Individually and collectively, morale is tested. 'For everyone the nerves are always worse on the first day of a new series, especially abroad,' one England captain wrote. 'There is no pretending that the first Test match of an Australian tour is not a nerve-wracking affair,' Douglas Jardine stated: 'perhaps even more for the old hands than for the new.'

Traditionally, some days out from the first Test, the opposing captains would meet – in modern times in the company of a match referee – and review any playing conditions that might diverge from the Laws of Cricket. In years gone by, these might have related to such things as pitch covering, new balls and the number of bouncers per over, this last point being an opportunity to smell the fear of the other side. Whoever wanted more freedom over the bowling of bouncers probably fancied he had the livelier attack. These days, such matters are enshrined in standard ICC playing regulations.

England's history is littered with traumatic experiences in opening Tests of overseas series, particularly against fast bowlers and spinners whose methods came as an unwelcome surprise. Jeff Thomson's explosive pace sent shock waves through an unsuspecting England camp on the 1974–75 Ashes tour in what was a classic example of this type of home-town heist; Thomson not only took nine wickets but knocked out two frontline batsmen, Dennis Amiss and John Edrich, from the next Test with broken bones.

Patrick Patterson's impact on the 1985–86 series in the Caribbean was scarcely less chilling; in a three-day rout on a corrugated surface, he claimed seven wickets and instilled fear in the hearts of the visitors. A rejuvenated Mitchell Johnson also hit unexpected heights at the start of 2013–14 Ashes with nine wickets and a controlled ferocity largely missing from his earlier appearances against England. Perhaps the most spectacular opening passage of play to a major series was England slumping to 2 for 4 against Allan Donald and Shaun Pollock on a damp, green pitch at the Wanderers – statistically the worst start any side has made to any series – before recovering to 122 all out. No less embarrassing was England being bowled out in the first session of a two-match series in New Zealand for 58 in a day–night Test in Auckland, where the pink ball moved around handsomely for Trent Boult and Tim Southee. Match over and, as it transpired, series won.

English cricket's historic frailties against unorthodox spin meant that slow bowlers also enjoyed eye-catching early gains against batsmen who had not yet deciphered their methods. South Africa's pioneering googly bowlers had a big impact on the opening Tests of England's 1905–06 and 1909–10 tours. Reggie Schwarz possessed a superb googly and made the ball jump and turn in a baffling way, while in the first Test of the 1909–10 series Bert Vogler and Aubrey Faulkner shared all 20 wickets.

Bhagwat Chandrasekhar and Shane Warne, two of the greatest leg-spinners of all time, returned their career-best figures in the first Tests of home series against England. Asian tours saw England sides come badly unstuck when they first came up against Anil Kumble, Muttiah Muralitharan and Saeed Ajmal, all spinners with unconventional methods. With time and greater exposure, England might sometimes come to terms with the challenge. Laxman Sivaramakrishnan was an Indian leg-spinner who took 12 wickets in the first Test of the 1984–85 series but only 11 more in the next four games as David Gower's England side successfully neutralised his threat. Often, though, the damage proved too great to overcome.

The problems were sometimes as much in the mind as anything. After England were all out for 228 in the first innings of the 1979–80 series in Australia, having at one stage been 90 for six, Mike Brearley felt they had played Dennis Lillee and Jeff Thomson too much on their reputations, as the pair were reunited against England for the first time since their destructive pomp four years earlier. Geoff Boycott agreed: 'The pre-match publicity would have had us believe that the pair were so fast they were unplayable, and I think many of us expected far worse than we actually received ... we made a mess of our first innings because we feared and anticipated the worst.'

Overall, the evidence brooks little argument. Since the Second World War, England have won the opening Test of a series only twice in 21 attempts in Australia, twice in 15 attempts in West Indies and eight times in 31 series away to India, Pakistan and Sri Lanka combined. They have fared best in South Africa and New Zealand, a country whose conditions most closely resemble their own and whose cricket was relatively weak until the 1970s; New Zealand are certainly no pushovers any longer, and England have won a first Test there only once in their last five visits. With the greater levels of professionalism and levelling up in standards that followed the Packer revolution, England have proved particularly slow starters away from home since 1979, their loss ratio being 50 per cent in first Tests in that time.* They failed to start with a win during any series in nine successive winters from 1992–93 and 2000–01, and lost the first Test 15 times in 26 away series between 2005–06 and 2019–20.

There was a long tradition of England players gathering for dinner the night before a Test, and this was considered especially important at the start of an overseas series. There were periods when this ritual fell into abeyance, but it has been returned to time and again as one of the best means of reinforcing the concept of collective purpose. Mike Gatting as captain in Australia resurrected the pre-match dinner to good effect. 'I insisted we should start the series by having one at least,' he wrote. 'I felt that in Australia where there are so many other attractions it

---

* These figures discount one-off Tests, of which England have played nine overseas, and four since 1979–80. There is a list of these games on page 277.

would be easy for the team to become fragmented. The dinner was the chance to bring everybody back together again . . . The response was excellent.'

The evening would typically involve a review of the opposition and a reprise of tactics, plus reminders to everyone about such routine housekeeping matters as what time the transport would leave for the ground and what kit was required; it was as close to a business meeting as most touring teams experienced. Geoff Boycott, who toured with England from 1964–65 to 1981–82, reflected in one of his diaries: 'I have sat through these dinners dozens of times, and much of what is said is repetitive, a resumé of what we have discussed at previous dinners brought up to date in the light of new experiences . . . [but] that does not matter. It is important to remind ourselves of some of the basic philosophies of Test cricket, and in any case there are always newcomers who may not have played in Test matches or not faced this particular opposition.'

With a touch of black humour, he additionally noted: 'The food is good – often the best we have on tour – which usually brings on some comment about condemned men and hearty meals.' Michael Vaughan as a member of the rank and file in Australia in 2002–03 found some of the conversation on the eve of battle hard to stomach. 'I do not think we especially helped ourselves with our team meeting,' he reflected. 'There was a bit too much building up the Australians into supermen.'

Among the least pleasant duties for the captain was informing those who were not playing of their omission from the XI. 'Everyone builds towards this moment early in a tour,' Bob Willis reflected, 'and to have it confirmed suddenly that you will not be part of the Test team can't be easy.'

Pre-series nerves could afflict tour selectors every bit as much as players. Carefully thought-through plans could be consigned to the bin, and logic cast to the wind, for no other reason than it felt reassuring to make a bold eleventh-hour switch – the comfort of action over inaction. Normally selection on tour was in the hands of a small group of senior figures: the coach, captain and vice-captain, and perhaps one or two of the more experienced players. In the days when managers rather than head coaches were present, a manager might oversee a selection meeting but have little or no input. If a chairman of selectors, or selector, happened to be on the tour, they would also be involved. The Schofield Report of 2007 even recommended that a selector always be present overseas to provide an additional voice, but this was not fully followed through with.

Whatever the configuration of personnel, mistakes happen. When Arthur Jones fell ill during the early weeks of a tour of Australia, his replacement Frederick Fane and his advisers sought to shore up the batting by picking the back-up keeper, the bespectacled Dick Young, ahead of the man he was understudying, Joseph Humphries; Young was a better batsman but less experienced with the gloves. The move backfired: Young made costly errors behind the stumps and failed in both innings as an opening batsman. 'The side suffered considerably through the blunder in playing Young,' *Cricket* reported. The person who would have opened the batting had not Young played was the young Jack Hobbs, who proved to be one of England's greatest batsmen; Hobbs debuted in the second Test instead, but by then England were 1–0 down. Not dissimilarly, on Freddie Brown's tour the selectors convinced themselves to select reserve keeper Arthur McIntyre as a batsman in the first Test in large part because McIntyre had scored a century during a stop-over match in Ceylon; Gilbert Parkhouse, a specialist batsman, was left out instead. McIntyre scored eight runs in a low-scoring game which England lost by 70 runs.

Mike Brearley was a captain famed for his astute judgment, but he once went into the first Test of a series at the WACA preferring Geoff Miller, who in six years as a professional cricketer had never scored a first-class century, to Graham

Gooch, who would eventually retire as England's all-time leading run-scorer. Boycott described the decision as a 'blunder', and 'a surprise and a disappointment to me as well as to him [Gooch]'.

Gooch himself as captain started a series in India on a bare, dry surface in Kolkata with a bowling attack consisting of four seamers and Ian Salisbury, who had originally joined the tour only as a net bowler, but was selected ahead of the squad's two frontline spinners, Phil Tufnell and John Emburey. India chose three spinners who took 17 wickets between them in an eight-wicket win. Twenty years later, England began another series in India under Alastair Cook by backing seam rather than spin and sank to a heavy defeat in Ahmedabad; unlike on Gooch's tour in 1992–93, they recovered after deploying two spinners in later games to take the series 2–1.

On Joe Root's first tour of Australia as captain, his attack for the first Test was made up of four right-arm fast-medium seamers and a finger spinner, with predictable results, and the following winter in the Caribbean he and his fellow selectors opted for a short-built left-arm medium-pacer in Sam Curran over the taller, faster and more experienced Stuart Broad on a pitch at Bridgetown, Barbados with a reputation for helping bowlers of precisely Broad's type. England lost by 381 runs.* Root in conjunction with head coach Chris Silverwood made another controversial decision at the start of his second Ashes tour in charge when on a green surface at the Gabba they left out Broad and James Anderson, the side's two most senior bowlers. Again, England were heavily beaten.

Misreading pitches at the start of a series was a common fault. Perhaps the most infamous error of all occurred when

---

* The Bridgetown Test highlighted the occasional problems over selection protocols on tour. Ed Smith, in his first winter as national selector, was in Barbados and was thought to be the prime mover behind Curran's inclusion in the XI. Smith was later told to not involve himself with on-the-ground selection on tour; two years later his post was discontinued and selection placed in the hands of the head coach.

Len Hutton chose to go into a Test at Brisbane with an all-pace attack, which he publicly revealed two days out from the game. He then chose to bowl first in favourable batting conditions; England dropped a dozen catches and Australia racked up more than 600. Hutton spent the rest day of the game hidden away, ruing his folly. England lost by an innings and 154 runs.

There is nothing quite like the first morning of a big Test series. It always was an occasion invested with excitement and anticipation, but also a degree of pomp, and this has only grown since television companies took a more central role in international cricket's affairs. They want the hour leading up to the start to whet the appetite of viewers, and the playing of national anthems, the toss and team announcements have become essential rituals in that process.

Kerry Packer's Channel Nine was the first to demand on-pitch access to the captains before the start of play, and England captains who toured Australia in the early years of Nine's coverage found the practice disconcerting – as they did the general enthusiasm for interviewing players and umpires. After losing the toss ahead of the first Test of the 1986–87 Ashes, Mike Gatting noted:

[The toss] is a very public occasion over here, unlike at home where it is conducted privately by the two captains with, perhaps, the groundsman hovering a few yards away awaiting instructions. In Australia, Channel Nine television cameras are everywhere. There is one to greet AB [Allan Border] and myself in the middle, along with former England captain Tony Greig complete with microphone to intrude on the moment and carry out interviews. The toss winner is always the first to be interviewed about his intention and hopes, and I was left in the background to reflect on what it all meant.

When a TV camera caught Gatting looking downcast, his players teased him on his return to the dressing room, but he and they had the last laugh as England, put in, negotiated the first day for the loss of only two wickets. More recent Ashes series have used for the toss specially minted silver coins, delivered in silk-lined boxes. Whereas once captains would conduct the toss while still in their 'civilian' clothes, more recently captains have worn their playing whites and, with a nod to the formality of the occasion, team blazers.

On the back of television's hunger for content, other ceremonies sprang up. Local dignitaries and sponsors wanted their moment in the spotlight, and since the mid-1990s England teams have increasingly been required to stand during the playing of national anthems ahead of Test matches and at global one-day tournaments. Some series have also begun with flag-raising ceremonies.

Before the first Test of the 2002–03 Ashes starting on 7 November, the Australians inserted a remembrance ceremony to commemorate not only the war dead but also victims of recent bomb blasts in Bali which killed more than 200 people, including 88 Australians and 23 Britons. Steve Waugh, the Australia captain, recited an ode and the players of both sides wore poppies. The England players were both distracted and disturbed by this. 'I found the unusual ritual of playing the national anthems before the game a bit of a strange experience,' Michael Vaughan wrote. 'It involved us going out onto the field 15 minutes early, and for some reason it was a bit deflating and unsettling afterwards and I did not feel at my mental peak from the start.' With England in the field following Nasser Hussain's surprising decision to bowl first – a clanger to rival Hutton's – Vaughan, fielding at point, was sufficiently disorientated to let the second ball of the day through his legs.

The clamour among spectators to be inside the ground in time for the start is never as great as for an opening Test. In the

Caribbean, with opportunities for spectators to watch the game for free by scaling trees outside the ground or perch on top of adjacent buildings ('private contraptions complete with sofas, deckchairs and awnings, constructed on the corrugated-iron roofs of shanties,' Alan Ross observed), the eagerness to secure an early spot could be acute. When Port of Spain staged the first game of England's tour under Colin Cowdrey, the anticipation among the Trinidadian public was palpable.

'An hour before the start on the first day, the Queen's Park Oval was an unforgettable sight,' Henry Blofeld wrote. 'The gates had been open since seven o'clock and still there were long chattering queues outside. Inside, the excitement and suspense were extreme. Already more than 20,000 people were in position, talking, gesticulating, and waiting ... The crescendo of the expectant chatter from the ring gave it all a gladiatorial atmosphere.'

So long were the queues at the Gabba turnstiles one year that some press men, needing to get their tickets punched, struggled to get into the ground on time. In desperation they climbed over a fence.

The first ball of a series was particularly rich with significance. Leaving the dressing room to begin an innings, Jack Fingleton of Australia could feel the intense scrutiny of thousands of eyes on him: 'It drilled into your back as you walked out of the gate to take the first ball of a Test against England.' The simple fact that a much-anticipated contest had finally arrived was reason enough to pause for thought. Writing of the start of Hutton's series in Australia, Ross wrote: 'When [Alec] Bedser prepared to bowl the first ball of the series to [Les] Favell, one was conscious of how many miles had been travelled, how many weeks spent in preparation, for just this. The shirt-sleeved, chattering crowd lying out on the warm green slopes or under the fig trees suddenly quietened.' In these situations, the players themselves often blocked from their minds the hubbub of a big crowd, so rapt were they in concentration, only to notice the drop in decibels when the throng suddenly fell silent in anticipation of the first ball.

When Phillip DeFreitas started the 1994–95 Ashes with a wide long hop which Michael Slater rifled to the backward point boundary, it immediately deflated England supporters, who had seen their team well beaten the three previous times by Australia. There was a widespread feeling of 'Here we go again', and events proved their fears fully justified. Twelve years later, Steve Harmison made an even more portentous opening when he flung his first ball wide of the cut surface and first bounce into the hands of his astonished captain Andrew Flintoff at second slip.

Harmison later confessed that it had hit him the night before the game that he was not ready – he had played too little cricket, and was not fit enough. 'There was a part of me which said, "I'll do it, I'll just turn up", but in the back of my mind I knew I was under-prepared, big time. We are normally under-cooked as bowlers on tour anyway, but I was even more so. This was all sitting, nagging, at the back of my mind.' He was also deeply conscious that the first ball had to be good: 'This can't be just any other ball. I've got to bowl that million-dollar fast ball that everybody wants, that everybody has been pumping me up for.'

Scarcely less dramatic was Rory Burns' dismissal to the first ball of the 2021–22 Ashes, bowled behind his legs by Mitchell Starc as he sashayed over to off stump as much out of nerves as anything. Whereas Harmison's delivery prompted gasps of incredulity, this wicket triggered unrestrained joy among Australians. It was the first time since Ernie McCormick of Australia bowled at Stan Worthington on the same ground 85 years earlier that a wicket had fallen to the first ball of an Anglo-Australian series. 'McCormick's first ball, which he bowled like a hurricane, pitched short, and rose high at Worthington's left shoulder,' Neville Cardus wrote. 'Worthington hooked impulsively, foozled his stroke, skied it, and [Bert] Oldfield, after starting late, ran forward in a panic, and held the catch. Poor Worthington stood dazed a moment, then departed head down.'*

Given the circumstances described, it is perhaps little wonder that the first days of the Ashes series in 1994–95, 2002–03 and 2006–07 rank statistically among England's worst in the field: Australia reached stumps on the respective tallies of 329 for four, 364 for two and 346 for three.†

For many years, the venue for the first Test of an overseas series was determined by practicalities rather than any strategy on the part of the hosts. Itineraries were arranged with travel considerations uppermost. Because teams touring Australia would start in Adelaide, and later Perth, and work their way eastwards, playing local sides as they went, it made sense to play the first Test at the end of that journey and then work back round the 'crescent' – and back across Australia's time zones. For many years that meant starting in Sydney, which hosted England in the first Test on every tour between 1894–95 and 1924–25, and later in Brisbane once Queensland cricket had grown in strength and the city could support a big match. Similarly, England started their early West Indies Test tours in Barbados before heading across the regional territories of the Caribbean to the westernmost point of Jamaica.

Two principal factors broke down these stately patterns. One

---

* Apart from Burns and Worthington, the only other England batsman to have been out to the first ball of an overseas Test series was Herbert Sutcliffe in New Zealand in 1932–33. James Anderson provided the only instance of an England bowler taking a wicket with the first ball of an away series when he dismissed Dean Elgar of South Africa at Centurion in 2019–20.

† Since 1 January 1970, England's own best batting efforts on day one of an overseas series have been: 506 for four v Pakistan, Rawalpindi, 2022–23 (a world record for any side on the opening day of a Test); 374 for three v Bangladesh, Dhaka 2009–10; and 341 for five v West Indies, Antigua 2014–15. They were dismissed for 58 v New Zealand, Auckland 2017–18 (with New Zealand in reply 175 for three by the close); 122 v South Africa, Johannesburg 1999–2000 and 131 v West Indies, Trinidad 1973–74. England dismissed New Zealand for 65 in Christchurch 1970–71, Australia for 116 at Brisbane 1978–79 and Sri Lanka for 135 at Galle 2020–21.

was that once air travel became the norm it became much easier to move around without being governed by shipping routes and railway timetables. The other was that as the sport widened its appeal, more hosting centres became available. Up to 1970, England played 235 Test matches in the six regions they had visited to that point – Australia, South Africa, New Zealand, West Indies, India and Pakistan – in just 24 cities; since then, they have played 259 Tests away to those same six opponents in 45 cities, so almost twice as many.* Once the options became greater, local cricket boards had more of a choice about where to allocate the games, and from there it was a small step to starting a series at a ground that best played to their own strengths and might expose weaknesses in the visitors.

It is also worth noting that it was only after it became standard practice to cover pitches from rain – rather than leave them open to the elements during hours of play, as was common overseas until the mid-1950s and into the 1970s in England – that host boards could properly exploit the distinct characteristics of individual venues. If a thunderstorm could strike at any time and change the nature of the playing surface – to the advantage of either side depending on who was batting and bowling at the time – then the idea that certain venues might give the home team a particular advantage had less meaning.

England won several overseas Test matches in places such as Melbourne, Sydney, Brisbane and Bridgetown with the help of heavy rain followed by a hot sun turning the pitch into a 'glue-pot' or 'sticky dog' on which the ball would grip and turn sharply (though they lost plenty of times on such wickedly unplayable surfaces as well). 'Sticky dogs' were generally even harder to bat on overseas, where thunderstorms could be heavier and the drying sun hotter. Melbourne acquired the reputation as the trickiest place to bat on such occasions. One of England's

---

* The tally of 45 includes three venues in the United Arab Emirates used as a proxy home for Pakistan in two series in 2011–12 and 2015–16.

greatest wins came in just such circumstances at the MCG in 1928–29 when they chased down 332 in the fourth innings thanks to a century from Herbert Sutcliffe.

The ground that has most often staged the first Test of an England tour is the Gabba in Brisbane. The inaugural Test in the city, the opening game in the 1928–29 series which featured Don Bradman's debut for Australia in a crushing win for England by 675 runs, was played at the Exhibition Ground, originally designed for agricultural shows, but it was soon permanently displaced by the Gabba. The Gabba, with pitches made from Merri Creek soil from Victoria, had staged tour matches since the 1890s, and by the 1930s had established itself as Brisbane's premier cricket ground largely because it could better control public entry, and therefore charge for it.

It certainly did not secure its pre-eminent position through charm: the Gabba was a forbidding place, the tone set by Queensland Cricket Association president Jack Hutcheon, who ran the place with the iron rod of a prison governor, with barbed wire keeping the general public – and journalists – from mixing with members and players into the 1950s. The imperious Charles Fry, a former England captain turned reporter, was incensed both by the denial of access to the pavilion and the squalor of the press box. Bill Bowes during his days as a newspaper reporter called it the worst-appointed ground in Australia with its rickety wooden stands under red corrugated roofs. The dressing rooms were only 15 yards from the press box, but requests for information had to be phoned through via a press liaison officer. Margaret Hughes wrote: 'The press box is the dirtiest I have been in – in fact the whole of the members' section was scattered with rubbish, empty bottles and old scrap ... [I] should not have been surprised to see all sorts of animals making their way up the steps of the press box.'

In brutal heat, the Gabba staged the fourth Test of the Bodyline series of 1932–33, before its place in the schedule was moved to the opening match when the Australian summer was cooler, though there was greater risk of encountering rain. Only twice since 1936–37 – in the unconventional three-match series of 1979–80 and in 1982–83, when the WACA was given the first Test – has the Gabba surrendered its front spot.

The Gabba's reputation for producing fast, bouncy pitches made it a natural place for Australia to start a home series, giving them a chance to exploit any early technical deficiencies among the visitors. Even when it was used as the venue for the second match in 1982–83, England's batsmen struggled with the additional bounce and lost 19 of their 20 wickets to catches. From 1989 until 2020 Australia put together an unbeaten run at the Gabba against all-comers spanning 31 Tests (24 wins, seven draws), including six wins and two draws against England. During this period Craig McDermott, Glenn McGrath and Mitchell Johnson enjoyed great success against England, just as Jeff Thomson and Geoff Lawson had done in the 1970s and 1980s.* By the turn of the century, the grassy hill, fig trees and greyhound track that ran around the boundary edge had long gone, and so had the last semblances of foliage; the rural feel was bulldozed aside as one of Australia's smallest, quaintest Test venues was transformed into a characterless cathedral of concrete, with enormously enhanced capacity.

Inevitably, as Australia's formidable record there grew, the Gabba acquired an ever more intimidating aura for visiting players. It was one the Australians themselves, who liked to dub it the 'Gabbatoir', did nothing to dispel. The sense of foreboding among England teams was in place by the time they made the journey to the ground. Andrew Flintoff's side felt this acutely, their tour coming on the back of the epic 2005 series in England. At the end of the first day – the one that began with Harmison's wide – Ashley Giles admitted: 'We were all pretty

---

* England's three wins at the Gabba all came under the leadership of Middlesex players: Gubby Allen in 1936–37, Mike Brearley in 1978–9 (against an Australia team depleted by mass defections to Kerry Packer) and Mike Gatting in 1986–87.

tense. The bus was quiet this morning. We have all been there before – the first day of an Ashes series – but you can't prepare that well for it . . . This has probably been the most hyped series in Ashes history.'

Ian Bell, who was making his first Ashes tour, told me that he believed England made a mistake with their choice of transport:

> We were on a big coach with blacked-out windows. It felt like we were trying hard to isolate ourselves from what was going on around us. The time we won the Ashes there [four years later in 2010–11], they scrapped the big coaches and used small Combis, so you were nearly down at ground level. The windows were open. It felt like you were more accessible, rather than stuck away where people can't get to you. All the KFCs had turned green-and-gold, there were flags everywhere and you were getting banter. It was such a better way of doing it. When you go to Australia you have to embrace everything that comes with it.'

England emerged from the 2010–11 game in credit after scoring a staggering 517 for one to secure a draw, but they found on subsequent visits to Brisbane that little had really changed, the sense of hostility plain in the words of Michael Clarke, the Australia captain, to James Anderson during the rout of 2013–14: 'Get ready for a broken fucking arm.' Speaking in 2021 of this same match, which was his first Test in Australia, Joe Root said: 'I knew it was going to be brutal, I knew it was going to be hostile . . . it almost felt like genuine hatred towards me as an individual. Absolutely it intimidated me. If I'd been asked about this five years ago, I'd have said no it didn't. But it did.'

Sabina Park in Kingston, Jamaica – an island culture apart, alienated as it was from the eastern Caribbean by geography – was for a long time another fortress, West Indies going unbeaten there for 35 years and losing only twice in 30 Tests against all sides between 1958 and 1994. It staged the first Test of every

England tour between 1986 and 2009, and although England won two of these six games they also suffered two of their most traumatic defeats. The ground was unconventional and unwelcoming: hemmed in by private residences, with space at a premium; the straight boundaries were unusually short, and it was often said that a fast bowler could start his run-up by pushing off from the sightscreen. There was officially room for only 10,000, although often more than that would be in attendance, many entering illegally and squatting on the galvanised roofs of the stands until they were cleared, or fell off and broke a leg, as happened in the case of one spectator at the 1960 Test.

Eventually, infiltration was made harder by liberal use of barbed wire.

The compact nature of the stands meant Sabina Park had the noisy, feverish atmosphere of a bullring; Alan Ross described Kingston as a 'steaming, hideous, shanty suburb of a capital' and the cricket ground as 'a steeply enclosed cockpit of a ground'. Henry Blofeld called it 'the smallest Test ground in the world' and a 'jumble of a ground', adding: 'Kingston does not have a happy atmosphere ... it is a poverty-stricken majority who by their attitude to their fellows and their reaction to life give the place its feel. In Kingston there is enough for them to be afraid of.'

The clay-like soil originally produced pitches of marble that were considered among the fastest and truest in the world. Alex Bannister wrote of the pitch in 1954: 'Shorn of grass, it shone like the polished floor of a house-proud wife.' There was moisture beneath the surface, though, and it became dented, enabling Trevor Bailey to take a match-winning seven for 34. Colin Cowdrey played two heroic innings in the 1960 Test, in which Easton McMorris spat blood after being hit over the heart by Brian Statham and players on both sides wore makeshift padded vests for protection.

Eight years later, the pitch started well and deteriorated into a mosaic of cracks as West Indies collected an assortment of bruises but fewer than 150 runs. More than one disastrous relaying of the surface dramatically changed its nature: the pitches lost some of their pace and acquired unpredictable bounce. David Gower in 1980–81 was unconcerned; his verdict was that Sabina Park could be frightening for 15 to 20 minutes, 'but I revelled, once in'.

But the unreliable bounce was certainly a contributory factor on the next tour in Mike Gatting's nose being broken by Malcolm Marshall in an ODI and then, a few days later in the first Test match, England being blown away in both innings inside 45 overs, all 20 wickets falling to four fast bowlers of high quality: Marshall, Joel Garner, Michael Holding and the fearsome Patrick Patterson. John Woodcock wrote that, with the exception of a Test at Old Trafford in 1976, 'I have never felt it more likely that we should see someone killed.' Desmond Haynes, fielding at bat-pad, said: 'I saw some very scared faces . . . when Patterson ran in, the fear in the English batsmen's eyes was a frightening sight in itself.'

Another hasty relaying of the surface ahead of the first Test of England's 1997–98 tour, in search of the pace that would maintain West Indies' customary advantage, proved a disaster. After 56 minutes of play, during which England lost three wickets for 17 and their physiotherapist was summoned onto the field six times, the umpires judged the pitch too dangerous to continue.

England enjoyed a measure of revenge with their wins in 1989–90 (which ended a winless run of 29 matches against West Indies home and away) and 2003–04 (when Steve Harmison took seven for 12 as West Indies capitulated to 47 all out), but they were themselves again on the receiving end on their next visit in 2008–09 when they were bowled out for 51.

Down the years, the pitches at Bridgetown's Kensington Oval, which staged the opening Test on four of England's first five tours, were more dependable in pace and bounce than Sabina Park, but after a long run of drawn Tests in the 1960s and 1970s more grass was left on the surface and it played into the hands of the many fast bowlers available to West Indies, who with a long run of victories extended their unbeaten sequence on the ground to 48 years. It was in 1980–81 that Holding bowled his great first over at Geoff Boycott. After West Indies and England played out a sterile, high-scoring draw in 2008–09, a decision was taken to again revert to livelier surfaces when possible, and it served a new crop of fast bowlers well, never more so than when England were skittled for 77 in 2018–19.

South Africa enjoyed one of the most clear-cut home advantages when games were played on the Highveld, so far above sea level that the ball tended to travel fast and far. Four of England's six Test series since South Africa's readmission to international cricket in the 1990s have involved opening matches at Supersport Park in Centurion, which is at an altitude of 1,450 metres, or the Wanderers in Johannesburg, where the altitude is 1,750 metres. Despite playing some of their warm-up matches at altitude as well, England did not win any of these games.

Writing about England's 1964–65 tour, Charles Fortune noted the touring team's failure to prepare for these very particular conditions during an early match at the Wanderers: 'MCC touring teams rarely give much attention to fielding during practice days. Yet this should be something for immediate attention with any cricket team coming to the Transvaal. In an atmosphere with barometric pressure under 25in every projectile, golf ball, cricket ball and javelin alike, tends to travel further through the air than at sea level. Catches come more quickly to fieldsmen in the slips and go over the head of the man in the deep.'

There was less of a pattern to which grounds hosted the start of England's tours of Asia, although the Gaddafi Stadium, Lahore generally staged the series opener in Pakistan before the move to the United Arab Emirates for security reasons. The most obvious case of an Asian country using a particular venue to create as big a culture shock to visitors as possible was Sri Lanka's deployment of Galle; the pitches there turned extravagantly and in Muttiah Muralitharan and Rangana Herath the hosts possessed spinners skilled enough to capitalise.

Between 2000 and 2017, Sri Lanka won 14 out of 22 first Tests played at Galle, and this included for England two defeats and a draw secured only with their last pair at the crease. It was greatly to England's credit, and showed how much they had improved against spin, that they won in Galle in Herath's last match in 2018 and again in 2021. Thanks in part to them winning the toss and Joe Root scoring an outstanding double-century, England backed up the second of those wins a few weeks later with a 227-run victory in the first Test against India at Chennai. Generally, wherever the match was played, England teams found starting in Asia difficult because the lower, slower bounce and the amount the ball spun were so different from home. Their combined record in first Tests in India, Pakistan and Sri Lanka was significantly worse than in later games in the series, suggesting a failure to acclimatise was part of the problem.

The broad pattern was that how England fared in a first Test set the tone for the rest of the series. Of the 50 defeats England suffered in first Tests away from home, they went on to lose the series 36 times and win only eight. In 31 series since 1979, the figures were even starker: 25 series losses and five wins. Three of those wins were on the subcontinent, confirming the idea that although it is difficult to start there, it is perhaps easier to adjust to spinning pitches over the course of several games than those with pace and bounce – provided the turn is slow and the surfaces are not deliberately underprepared in the way they were in India in 2020–21 in response to England taking an early lead in more conventional conditions.

Starting well is imperative, and any early chances that present themselves have to be taken. When England toured the Caribbean under Ian Botham, they were fortunate to start with a Test at Port of Spain, Trinidad because it was a ground with the slowest, most spin-friendly pitches in the region, and was therefore the venue least helpful to the West Indies pace attack.* It represented England's best chance of avoiding defeat. Yet despite operating with four fast bowlers and no front-line spinner, West Indies won the game by an innings inside four days. 'Never mind, lads, there are still four Tests to go, we can still pull it back if we keep our heads up,' Botham told his men afterwards. It was a common cry, but one too often uttered in vain.

How England Have Fared in First Tests

England have since 1979 lost almost half of the 64 first Test matches they have played in overseas series, a much higher loss ratio than in the second, third and fourth matches. They lost slightly more than half their fifth Tests, but substantially fewer series went to five Tests (23 in all), so the sample size was smaller. Across all overseas Tests since the first in 1876–77, England have lost more than half their first Tests in Australia, where until the Second World War Test matches were typically played to a finish.

England batsmen have scored 105 centuries in the opening Tests of overseas series (excluding one-off matches). The first to do so was William Barnes at Adelaide in 1884–85, and the highest innings was R. E. Foster's 287 at Sydney in 1903–04. Twenty-three were scored in Australia, and of these only seven were in matches since the Second World War – by Tony Greig, Derek Randall, Ian Botham, Mark Butcher, Andrew Strauss, Alastair Cook and Jonathan Trott. Across all opening matches, Cook has scored seven centuries, Ken Barrington six, and Joe Root and Strauss four each. There have

---

* Before it was squeezed off the roster, Port of Spain staged more England Tests than any other territory in the region, but it rarely enjoyed a fixed position in the schedule partly owing to the need to avoid a clash with the Trinidad Carnival, held on the two days preceding Ash Wednesday. The only time an England team have been in Trinidad throughout carnival was in 1947–48, when the Test started on Ash Wednesday. It hardly proved ideal preparation. 'In this colossal funfair I understand that our cricketers had an exceedingly good time,' Walter Hammond wrote. England, with only 11 fit players, had the worst of the game but got away with a draw.

been 16 cases of England bowlers taking ten wickets in the first Test of a multi-match overseas Test series; no bowler has done so more than once.

The table below covers all overseas Tests but not one-off matches, of which there have been nine: four in Australia (in 1878–79, 1887–88, 1976–77 and 1987–88), two in Sri Lanka (1981–82 and 1992–93), and one each in South Africa (1891–92), New Zealand (1946–47) and India (1979–80). Of these, four were won, three lost and two drawn.*

By country

Country	Span	P	W	L	D	Win %
Bangladesh	2003–2016	3	3	0	0	100.0
*South Africa	1889–2020	19	10	6	3	52.6
New Zealand	1930–2023	20	9	4	7	45.0
Sri Lanka	1982–2021	6	2	3	1	33.3
Australia	1877–2021	38	11	20	7	28.9
India	1933–2021	15	4	6	5	26.7
Pakistan/UAE	1961–2022	11	2	4	5	18.2
West Indies	1930–2022	17	3	7	7	17.6
Zimbabwe	1996	1	0	0	1	0.0
Total		**130**	**44**	**50**	**36**	**33.8**

* South Africa figures include three series in 1888–89, 1895–96 and 1898–99 which were only subsequently recognised as Tests; England won the first Test in each instance.

* After Ivo Bligh's team completed a scheduled three-match series in 1882–83, an extra game was played; although it is regarded as distinct from the original fixtures it is counted as a fourth match, rather than a one-off contest.

By venue

(Excluding one-off Tests; five matches or more)

Venue	Span	P	W	L	D	Win %
Gabba, Brisbane (Aus)	1936–2021	20	3	12	5	15.0
Sydney (Aus)	1887–1932	10	6	4	0	60.0
Christchurch (NZ)	1930–2002	9	5	4	0	55.6
*Old Wanderers, Joburg (SA)	1899–1938	7	2	4	1	28.6
Kingston, Jamaica (WI)	1954–2009	7	2	4	1	28.6
Lahore (Pak)	1961–2000	6	1	1	4	16.7
Bridgetown, Barbados (WI)	1930–2019	5	1	1	3	20.0
Galle (SL)	2001–2021	5	2	2	1	40.0

*All the matches at the Old Wanderers were played on matting, not turf.

CHAPTER 13

The Role of Crowds

Players under fire, umpires under pressure

The first Test can be an assault on the senses of the visiting players beyond whatever occurs on the pitch. These opening games often attract the biggest crowds of the tour so far, and the locals have not simply turned up to see a good contest. They want their team to win, and for the price of admission they want their say on the matter. Many see themselves as active participants. When they came from far and wide, as they often did in the early days, they felt entitled to make their opinions heard – what Thomas Horan, the former Australian Test cricketer, described as 'bronzed men from country parts'.

Some of the biggest turnouts for overseas series came on the back of recent defeats for the home side at the hands of England. The largest recorded gate for any Ashes series came in Australia in 1936–37 after England had won 4–1 on both their previous visits, including the inflammatory Bodyline series; almost 950,000 watched the five Tests that saw England go 2–0 up only to eventually be beaten 3–2. Similarly, there were big rises in attendances in Australia in 1958–59, 1974–75 and 2006–07, ranging from 10 per cent to almost 50 per cent on England's previous tours; on all these occasions England arrived as holders of the Ashes and left heavily beaten.

Brisbane was originally one of the smaller Australian venues – its attendance during the bumper 1936–37 series was only around 75,000 – but once it was redeveloped its gates for first Ashes Tests rose from 51,000 in 1998–99 to 164,000 in 2006–07, since when it has always remained above 120,000. However large or small the crowd, and whichever side of the 'barbed wire divide' they sat, the Gabba's patrons were not averse to dishing out abuse to opposing players. When Simon Jones agonisingly ruptured his knee chasing a ball to the boundary after his foot caught in the sandy sub-surface of the outfield, and was stretchered from the field, he was greeted with a shout from the stands of, 'Get up, you weak Pommie bastard.' Subsequent English teams have not yet forgotten this.

The rise of one-day cricket, and in particular evening matches under lights, brought with it more partisan and loutish behaviour, at least until ground authorities tightened up their act with firmer stewarding and heavier penalties for anti-social conduct. When in the late 1970s England first played a significant number of ODIs in Australia as well as Tests, Mike Brearley, the captain, went on local radio mid-way through the tour to say he considered it dangerous to place a fielder within 15 yards of the boundary for fear of him being hit by a missile.

Crowds at Tests in the Caribbean were never more populous or passionate than during the Sixties, Seventies and Eighties when West Indies cricket was at its height and the region's territories were savouring political independence. This was an era when cricket meant so much to West Indians that fans would occupy every available vantage point inside and outside of grounds, and spectators took an active part in proceedings, playing drums and blowing on conch shells and bugles, and listening avidly to radio commentary of the game. So many members of the crowd would hold transistors to their ears, and so close were the crowd to the field of play, that the players and umpires could hear what the commentators were saying as they stood in the middle – at least until umpires, perhaps nervous for their reputations, asked for the sound to be turned down.

The grounds then were compact and the dressing-rooms cramped, and at some venues it was necessary to walk out and over a road to find some nets. The cricketers would fight their way through crowds at the start and end of the day just to get into the pavilion. 'You felt you were part of something that mattered to people,' Mike Atherton wrote.

Every ground, too, had its local character, such as King Dyal at the Kensington Oval and Gravy at the Recreation Ground in Antigua, who would parade and emote with unbridled confidence on proceedings, and generally provide entertainment to all and sundry. C. L. R. James said, 'West Indians crowding to Tests bring with them the whole past history and future hopes of the islands.' This was surely the case in the lead-in to the first Test in Jamaica in 1953–54, as *Wisden* noted: 'A certain amount of tension was created before a ball had been bowled. This quickly became heightened through crowds, whose intense noise, coupled with almost ceaseless torrid heat, provided a background in which tempers too easily became frayed.'

Queen's Park Oval, Trinidad could hold up to 30,000, more than any other venue in the Caribbean, and the atmosphere could be incendiary. Colin Cowdrey discovered as much when he claimed a catch off Rohan Kanhai there in the opening Test of the 1967–68 series; so too did Tony Greig with his opportunistic running out of Alvin Kallicharran as the batsman strayed out of his ground at the non-striker's end at the conclusion of the second evening of the 1973–74 series, prompting angry crowd scenes (England withdrew their appeal overnight and Kallicharran was allowed to continue batting).

Seven years later, when Ian Botham's team sank to their embarrassing defeat in four days, the Trinidadians showed the England players no mercy by directing obscene chants at them during the post-match ceremony. 'The actual terms of the abuse did not concern me over-much,' Geoff Boycott wrote. 'What worried me as a professional was that they should be so dismissive, so scornful of our ability – and so soon.' Some of the most serious rioting at England Test matches has occurred on grounds in the West Indies (see list on pages 229–232).

Indian crowds were usually not overtly hostile, but there were still many instances of England fielders being pelted from the terraces with items ranging from fruit to more dangerous objects such as bricks and metal bolts fired from crossbows (as happened at Kanpur in the final Test of the 1963–64 series). Nor was it unknown for mirrors to be used to deflect sunlight into the eyes of visiting batsmen. Until relatively recently, pitch invaders would take their chances against *lathi*-wielding policemen. The sheer size of the crowds, the persistent noise they made and their blind passion could be intimidating to those who had not experienced it before. Ted Dexter's tour of 1961–62 saw around 1.2 million spectators watching the five Tests in India and three in Pakistan, and in the pre-television era warm-up matches against local Indian sides could draw daily gates of 20,000 or 30,000. Some determined fans would phone a players' hotel room, or make their way to their hotel door, in order to meet them, seek an autograph or demand match tickets.

Describing the closing passage of play on the first day of the opening Test of the 1976–77 series in Delhi, Christopher Martin-Jenkins wrote of the behaviour of the 30,000 crowd: 'All day the game has been played in a hubbub of noise which frequently developed into a crescendo as ball hit pad or a shot was struck in the air anywhere near a fielder, and now, as the shadows lengthened, the spectators, knowing that another wicket would mean the exposure of the England tail, bayed for blood.'

Different captains dealt with Indian crowds in different ways. Douglas Jardine ordered one of his bowlers to wait until unruly comments from the crowd ceased, but Tony Greig used his natural talent as a communicator to win over the throng, before each Test match parading his team in their colourful touring blazers in front of the stands. 'There was usually a double purpose behind his performances,' Martin-Jenkins noted. 'Greig is a natural entertainer and he enjoys making crowds laugh; but he also knew that England's chances could only be enhanced by having the crowd, if not exactly on his side, at least not hostile.'

However charming the offensive, though, nothing was going to quench the enthusiasm of the massed ranks if their side was winning. As Keith Fletcher's side sank to defeat in the first Test in Bombay in 1981–82, firecrackers were repeatedly thrown onto the field as 50,000 celebrated India's impending triumph. 'These firecrackers made the stadium an artillery range,' Scyld Berry wrote. 'The end of the match might have been the climax to the *1812 Overture*.'

Alan Knott, who spent seven winters touring with England between 1967–68 and 1976–77, taught himself to embrace the pressure that came with playing big matches in hostile environments. 'I've heard stories of Olympic teams being made to train while the noise of the crowd in the stadium is played to them at full blast,' he said. 'I used to do something similar but without the sound effects. I'd dream I was in the cricket stadium in Calcutta or Melbourne in front of 100,000 people. Then I'd wake up and feel that I was actually there. I could smell the atmosphere. It was *real*. I recreated it just by dozing off in a chair. There can't be any better way of preparing yourself mentally for what's to come. All those things affect you – sights, sounds, smells.'

John Edrich, a contemporary of Knott's, who went on one of the most hostile of all England tours in 1974–75, felt the tone was set by the confrontational approach of Ian Chappell and his players.

The attitude of the entire Australian side was very aggressive ... The younger players were all subject to abuse and many of them were intimidated by it. The Australian team's

behaviour encouraged the crowd to turn hostile. Every time
Lillee or Thomson came in to bowl, there'd be loud chants
of 'Kill, kill, kill!' I'd never experienced anything quite like
it. The nearest was in the West Indies when we won in 1968.
There were riots in Jamaica and some very fast bowling
coming our way.

Like Knott, Jack Russell took steps to block out opposing players and fans by wearing sunglasses, something that stood him
in good stead during a famous rearguard action with Mike
Atherton at the Wanderers.

Public hostility towards England players on tour has probably been around as long a touring itself. In his account of
the 1907–08 tour he managed, Philip Trevor wrote of the
Australian crowds: 'There is a more or less continuous flow of
uncomplimentary remarks, which not only goes unchecked by
official authority, but which also meets with no practical protest
from the law-abiding majority.' Four years later, Jack Hearne,
playing his first Test match at the age of 20, was meted out some
rough treatment by the Sydney crowd, prompting Jack Hobbs
to complain: 'I defy any seasoned player to do himself justice
while under fire of this kind.' Hearne did well enough in fact,
scoring 76 and 43.*

Douglas Jardine attributed the Australian enthusiasm for
barracking visiting players – for it was never directed at their
own – to an English team serving as 'a symbol which gives them
[Australian spectators] an opportunity of demonstrating their
loyalty . . . one is sometimes left with the unpleasant feeling that
demonstrations of hostility are not always solely directed against
the players.' A similar kind of dynamic appeared to be at work

---

* Not all Australian hecklers were crude or unkind. The most celebrated Australian
barracker was 'Yabba' (Stephen Gascoigne, 1878–1942), who had a genuine knowledge
of the game and a ready wit, and for many years was a regular on the Hill at Sydney.
When Hobbs made his last appearance there, he went over and shook his hand. A statue
to 'Yabba' was erected at the SCG in 2008.

around the same time in South Africa. When Percy Chapman's team were beaten at the Old Wanderers ground in Johannesburg in front of a holiday crowd they found it hard to take. The local *Star* newspaper acknowledged the highly charged atmosphere, noting that of 'the overpowering impulse which comes from the crowded stands ... some [spectators] are highly critical, the majority are decidedly unsympathetic'. The England captain was one of the principal targets for abuse.

Mike Brearley was singled out for the ire of Australian crowds on his second tour there as captain, having perhaps committed the unforgivable crime of winning his first. 'I was seen by the man in the Sydney street as the embodiment of all that's bad in the British,' he reflected a few years later. 'I talked too much, too glibly, and with the wrong accent. And when they had a go at me on the field I ignored them, like the stuck-up Pom that they knew I was ... On the whole, crowds have become more unkind, opinionated and noisy. They have made the captain's job just a little more fraught.'

John Lever, who went to Australia under Brearley, said that the local people the players encountered outside the grounds were friendly. 'The Aussies we met in the grounds were the ugly ones. Coming to the cricket changed their focus. They would say, "I've seen better-looking heads on a crab," or they would throw cans of warm piss at you.' John Edwards, the Australian team manager, issued a statement expressing his shame at the Melbourne crowd's behaviour towards the England captain.

Nothing changed. Several years later, Gladstone Small, England's Barbados-born fast bowler, was targeted by a section of the MCG's notoriously boorish Bay 13, which 'amused itself (and many others) by making monkey noises and throwing bananas'.

The first time England took the field in Australia on the 2006–07 tour, for what was supposed to be a relatively gentle opening fixture at Canberra, two players whose families originated from outside the UK, Kevin Pietersen and Monty

Panesar, were subjected to abuse by the crowd and eight spectators were ejected from the ground.

As Edrich suggested, there was something of a symbiotic relationship between the opposition team and their fans; indeed, Australia's head coach Darren Lehmann made a direct appeal to the Australian people to give Stuart Broad a hard time when he toured there shortly after an incident in a Test match at Trent Bridge in which Broad did not walk after being caught at slip but given not out by the umpire (Australia had used up all their reviews under the Decision Review System). Lehmann's call on a Sydney radio station for the Australian public to force Broad home in tears resulted in him being fined and issuing an apology, but it did not stop the fans following through as best they could on the instruction. Most players managed to contain themselves well in the face of vile and concerted abuse, but a few did snap and respond in kind, and if they were unlucky and their words were caught on microphone they faced likely censure as a consequence.*

The partisan nature of crowds also served to create an unspoken pressure on umpires to favour the home team, especially in the era when match officials were drawn from the home nation and many of those on the terraces and in the stands felt it was an umpire's duty to not do visiting teams a favour. Even if they were not actually overtly biased towards the home team, umpires might have subconsciously felt inclined not to inflame the feelings of the locals, or to have feared the consequences of doing so, particularly in front of a full house when the match was delicately balanced. In fact, many early England teams took with them on tour one of their own approved umpires, precisely in order to guarantee what they

---

* This happened to Ben Stokes at the Wanderers in 2019–20 after he verbally responded to a fan's abuse as he left the field after being dismissed for 2 late on the first day of a Test. Stokes received one demerit point and a fine of 15 per cent of his match fee under the ICC Code of Conduct for an 'audible obscenity'.

regarded as independent adjudication. This practice effectively stopped by the mid-1930s.

The stakes were rarely higher than in an opening Test, with both teams striving to land the first blow, and these games featured some of the hottest disputes. When England toured Australia for the first time under the auspices of MCC in 1903–04, their captain Pelham Warner came close to taking his team from the field in the first Test at Sydney when protests erupted from the members' pavilion at Clem Hill being adjudged run out by umpire Bob Crockett, one of the best umpires in the country, as Australia battled to recover from a large first-innings deficit.

Warner sat down on the outfield with his opposite number Monty Noble until the tumult subsided, before opting to play on even though the catcalls resumed. 'People in England can have no conception of the yelling and hissing that went on that afternoon right up to the drawing of stumps; even such hardened Test match players as [George] Hirst and [Wilfred] Rhodes were quite upset,' Warner wrote. 'There was absolutely no excuse for this demonstration, which was as disgraceful as it was unwarranted.' When the teams left the field, Crockett was jeered again by some, though applauded by others, and left the ground under the care of two detectives. England went on to win the match and the series, with Crockett officiating in all five matches.

Don Bradman's infamous reprieve by umpire George Borwick, who turned down England appeals for a catch in the gully after Bradman had stood his ground (a practice not then as common as it later became), took place before lunch on the first day of the first post-war Ashes series, at a moment when Bradman was uncertain whether he still had a future as a Test player. In the event, Bradman, who had batted scratchily for 28 at that point, went on to make 187 in an innings that shaped the match and series, and shattered his relationship with Wally Hammond, the England captain.

As a consequence of umpire Perry Burke giving out a local Jamaica player John Holt lbw for 94 on his Test debut in the opening match of Len Hutton's tour of West Indies, Burke's family were assaulted. And in the first session of the 1970–71 Ashes, Keith Stackpole was given not out by umpire Lou Rowan following a direct-hit throw by Geoff Boycott; Stackpole, then on 18, survived to score 207. Still photographs confirmed Stackpole was short of his ground.*

Even before a ball had been bowled in the series in India in 1981–82, the England team management sent a letter to the Indian board saying that up to that point they had not been 'terribly pleased' with the standard of umpiring in the warm-up matches. When England then lost a number of first-innings wickets to questionable umpiring decisions, the manager and captain Raman Subba Row and Keith Fletcher called an unofficial press conference with the British press to put their feelings on the record before the match was over, to avoid – so they said – the accusation of sour grapes were the match to be lost (which it was).

After the game, Subba Row issued an official statement saying that bad umpiring would jeopardise existing good relations between the teams. The Indian board rejected the initial accusation for want of specific examples, but in fact the umpiring for the rest of the series proved less contentious, suggesting that England's early protests bore fruit. Scyld Berry, reporting on the tour, supported the notion that Indian umpires were biddable, asserting that 'a visiting side has to be half as good again to win in India ... [owing] to the effect of vast crowds and strange conditions which naturally work to India's advantage ... England's players were convinced that the umpiring formed another, vital element.'

---

* Rowan stood in five of the six Tests in that series and did not give one lbw appeal in England's favour; neither did either of the other umpires used, Tom Brooks and Mel O'Connell.

The most notorious of all umpiring rows involving England –
the spat between Mike Gatting and umpire Shakoor Rana in
Faisalabad – had its origins in the previous match, the first
Test of the series in Lahore, where Shakil Khan gave a string
of debatable decisions during a Pakistan innings victory. Chris
Broad's refusal to walk on the third evening of the game – until
he was ushered away by his batting partner Graham Gooch –
was initially supported by Gatting, the cricket manager Micky
Stewart and tour manager Peter Lush, who put out a statement
saying: 'Today's incident involving Chris Broad was a culmination of the frustrations that have built up over the first three
days of the match.' England were particularly aggrieved that
they had not been informed of the umpires for the match until
they read of them in the newspapers 48 hours beforehand.
English fuses were dangerously short before the team ever got
to Faisalabad.

Even when third-country 'neutral' umpires started to be
used in the late 1990s, it was not unknown for match officials
to pander to local wishes. Duncan Fletcher, in his first match
as England head coach, felt this was the case when umpires
David Orchard and Srini Venkataraghavan, and match referee
Barry Jarman, allowed a Test match at the Wanderers to start
on time. 'The pitch was so wet and the light so bad that it was
embarrassing,' Fletcher wrote. 'Winning the toss in any match
usually brings with it a considerable advantage but here it was
tantamount to winning the match . . . The match referee should
have done something about it. But he did not.'

Allan Donald, who with Shaun Pollock reduced England to 2
for 4 inside three overs, concurred: 'We shouldn't have started in
bad light. The pitch was damp, because the groundsman wanted
to make sure that cracks wouldn't develop.' Nasser Hussain,
England's captain, who batted number three, said: 'As I took
my guard, I could feel water just below the surface, almost bub-
bling up. The soil was really dark and very moist and I thought,
"We're in a bit of trouble here".'

England's Test Attendances in Australia 1884–85 to 2021–22

Of the ten highest average daily attendances in Ashes series in Australia, only two saw England victorious – in 1954–55 and 2010–11. The table lists series of five or more matches. Comprehensive data is unavailable for tours to other countries.

Season	Tests (days played)	Total attendance	Daily average (excluding whole-day washouts)
1884–85	5 (19)	94,134	4,954
1894–95	5 (22)+	276,342	13,159
1897–98	5 (22)	331,623	15,074
1901–02	5 (21)	309,590	14,742
1903–04	5 (23)+	313,522	14,251
1907–08	5 (27)+	281,713	10,835
1911–12	5 (24)++	342,125	15,551
1920–21	5 (24)	478,020	19,917
1924–25	5 (31)	692,242	22,330
1928–29	5 (33)	857,600	25,988
1932–33	5 (26)	761,163	29,276
1936–37	5 (26)	948,498	36,481
1946–47	5 (27)+	846,942	32,575
1950–51	5 (21)++	612,147	32,218
1954–55	5 (23)+++	703,397	35,170
1958–59	5 (27)	765,737	28,361
1962–63	5 (24)	736,274	30,678
1965–66	5 (22)++	573,847	28,692
1970–71	7 (35)+++++	616,196	20,540
1974–75	6 (29)+	777,333	27,762
1978–79	6 (29)	370,574	12,778
1982–83	5 (25)	556,601	22,264
1986–87	5 (23)	333,466	14,499
1990–91	5 (22)	394,255	17,921

Season	Tests (days played)	Total attendance	Daily average (excluding whole-day washouts)
1994–95	5 (25)	478,126	19,125
1998–99	5 (21)+	545,820	27,291
2002–03	5 (21)	568,774	27,085
2006–07	5 (22)	819,627	37,258
2010–11	5 (23)	764,463	33,238
2013–14	5 (21)	753,868	35,899
2017–18	5 (25)	866,732	34,670
2021–22	5 (20)	488,071	24,404

Figures up to 1982–83 are drawn from Richard Cashman's *Australian Cricket Crowds: The Attendance Cycle, Daily Figures 1877–1984* and since then from *Wisden*.
Tests in Australia were played to a finish between 1884–85 and 1936–37; then generally over six days between 1946–47 and 1958–59, and generally over five days thereafter.

+ including one day washed out
++ including two washouts
+++ including three washouts
 +++++ including five washouts

CHAPTER 14

Players as Reporters
How the early tours were chronicled

From the earliest days of touring, cricketers committed their thoughts and feelings to paper. They wrote diaries and letters home to wives and children, sweethearts, parents, brothers and sisters that were never intended to be publicly viewed. They kept scrapbooks and took photographs. Some such as Maurice Turnbull, Charles Palmer, Trevor Bailey and Dermot Reeve used moving film, Palmer shooting 30,000ft of cine film on tours of South Africa and West Indies shortly after the war and Reeve taking a camcorder to India in the early 1990s, with which he generated images that formed the basis of *Spinwash '93*, a documentary of an eventful, ill-starred tour of the subcontinent screened on Sky Sports TV in 2021.

They wrote letters and accounts to newspapers and periodicals that *were* intended to be read, even while a tour was going on, or shortly after it finished. These articles were sometimes collated into books, and later in life some touring cricketers wrote books of reminiscences in which they would expand further on their adventures overseas. Some divulged the true state of a tour's progress and the relationships at the heart of the team, others expertly covered up what really went on, or no more than hinted at where the fault lines in losing campaigns actually lay. These accounts could cause their authors difficulties but, to varying degrees, such processes helped alleviate the emotional burden and mental strain. Apart from anything else, writing was one way to fill the long hours on tour.

In more recent times, Graeme Swann kept a video diary of the Ashes tour of 2010–11 which was posted on YouTube and the ECB website and proved a huge success, in part because it told the story of an historic winning campaign. One of the seven episodes had more than half a million views. Players now routinely post images on Twitter, Instagram and other forms of social media.

For many years, the players' version of events stood largely unchallenged. Not until after the Second World War were major England tours accompanied by significant numbers of British newspaper correspondents, and later still by teams of radio and television broadcasters. Only three reporters from the UK plus Jack Hobbs, recently retired from international cricket, who put his name to ghostwritten columns in *The Star*, accompanied the Bodyline tour of 1932–33, about which millions of words came to be written, and despite the intense interest generated by that series only six went with the following Australia tour four years later.

Until the number of reporters began to rise after the war, the players and tour managers were among the very few in a position to provide informed eye witness accounts of what had happened to audiences back home, and without their personal testimony those audiences would have had only a limited understanding of events. English newspapers carried reports and scorecards, but the costs of sending such information by cable were such that there was usually little room for anything but the spare details. As with everything else, if exceptions were to be made, and money was invested, it was in respect of Test matches in Australia; tours elsewhere were usually treated to a skeleton service.

As the practicalities and economics of sending specialist correspondents on tour gradually became more favourable, alternative voices emerged. These newspaper reporters accompanying the team, even travelling out with them by boat or plane, were able to file more regular reports than the players themselves could ever have done, and in the end came to do so virtually every day of a tour. They, too, would write their own tour books, containing more considered assessments of what had occurred than were possible when the writer was subjected to the tyranny of daily deadlines. Some of these correspondents, moreover, were former cricketers themselves, even old teammates and friends of those in the England team, and their opinions could not be lightly dismissed. Then, in increasing numbers, came commentators and summarisers working for radio and television, many of them not only former England cricketers but also England captains, whose criticisms could be acutely felt by those battling for success on the field.

Suddenly there was a multiplicity of voices, and in more recent times with the advent of social media the number of people with an opinion and a means of expressing it expanded beyond all reckoning. Where once the cricketers appeared to have a monopoly on the truth of what had happened on the field of play, there were now many versions of the truth, and many of these versions were articulated by people not within a thousand miles of the action, and whose qualifications for holding any view worth listening to were flimsy at best. To fail on the field of play, either as an individual or as a team, could now be the trigger for a torrent of adverse comment. In the hothouse atmosphere of a tour, this can be harder to come to terms with than it would be during a home season, when there are opportunities to escape the goldfish bowl existence.

The players, of course, continued to tell their stories, through ghosted newspaper columns, daily press conferences and radio and television interviews before, during and after matches, but their testimony was diluted by the sheer volume of opinion and the banality of much of what they themselves chose to say (partly out of fear of breaching various codes of conduct if they were too outspoken). In terms of the public debate, the players ceded ground, leaving them to look inwards to themselves, their teammates and their backroom staff for validation of their views. When efforts were made under the captaincies of Joe Root and Eoin Morgan to better address the issue of mental well-being, one of the suggested coping mechanisms was for the players to log their innermost thoughts by keeping diaries. It was not difficult in this environment for a team to see the world through a prism of 'them' and 'us' – hardly a healthy state of affairs.

Fred Lillywhite was the first chronicler of an England tour. Son of William Lillywhite, the 'Nonpareil' round-arm bowler, Fred – who reached no great heights as a player himself – accompanied George Parr's groundbreaking tour of North America as scorer and keeper of records and on his return published a vivid and entertaining account of the team's travels (which he carefully estimated covered 7,364 miles) to play five local sides and three exhibition games, entitled *The English Cricketers' Trip to Canada and the United States in 1859*. It proved to be the forerunner of many tour books.*

Fred's older brother John was one of the 11 players Parr took with him, and he scored one of the few half-centuries made on a tour played on the most rudimentary of pitches. 'To have left no record ... of so novel an occurrence as this memorable expedition would, the writer feels, have been a subject of universal regret,' Fred wrote in his preface to a work that, interestingly, contained some criticism of a group of players who appeared to grow weary of his fussing over the transportation of the printing press and scoring tent he took with him. He suggested they might occasionally put aside their aversion to acting as his porters.

---

* There have been in excess of 100 tour books written by participating England players, managers and coaches, as well as travelling former players and journalists.

Several years after this, MCC withdrew its support for an annual guide Fred produced on the grounds that he had 'exceeded the fair limits of criticism upon cricketers', a gripe that has been made of reporters ever since. Fred never accompanied another tour and died in 1866, aged just 37, 12 years before his cousin James Lillywhite, another member of this mighty cricketing dynasty, captained England in their first Test match in Melbourne.

Fred may have gone but John and James Lillywhite produced their own annual guides, as did John Wisden with the famous almanack that outlasted all its contemporary rivals, but it was the amateur class rather than the professionals who were the more regular diarists on the early tours.

E. M. Grace wrote a lengthy and colourful diary of Parr's second tour to Australia and New Zealand. Shortly after boarding the SS *Great Britain*, Grace could not hide his disappointment at finding in first class 'seven or eight rather plain young ladies', though he added there was a Miss Jordan whom he termed 'middling'. Upon arriving in Australia, he concluded there were two Miss Gordons who looked prettier on shore and, were he to make the voyage again, 'I should get sweet on the eldest.'

James Southerton filed reports for the *Sporting Times* on W. G. Grace's tour of 1873–74 and four years later, as second-in-command on James Lillywhite's inaugural Test tour, wrote a series of discursive pieces for *The Sportsman* under bylines such as One of the Twelve and One of Them. (Another player, possibly Lillywhite himself, wrote more formal match reports as Our Special Correspondent for *The Sportsman*). Southerton also kept a detailed diary of the tour that ran to five volumes. His pioneering work would be built upon by his son Sydney half a century later when he accompanied Percy Chapman's team to Australia.

Vernon Royle kept a rather humdrum diary of England's second Test tour under Lord Harris in 1878–79, Ivo Bligh a more candid and interesting one when as captain he led a team in the first quest for the mythical Ashes four winters later. Bligh also wrote reports for *James Lillywhite's Cricketer's Annual*. The Nottinghamshire professional duo of Alfred Shaw and Arthur Shrewsbury, as principal organisers, wrote an account of their first venture to Australia in 1884–85. As with the tour Fred Lillywhite accompanied, these were such ambitious enterprises that they deserved chronicling.

A pattern emerged of those in positions of authority taking principal ownership of reporting events, with others following what Southerton, and Shaw and Shrewsbury, started. Pelham Warner set new standards with his comprehensive accounts of three of the earliest MCC tours, for all of which he was appointed captain: to Australia in 1903–04, South Africa in 1905–06 and Australia again in 1911–12, when even though he was too unwell to play in (or in some instances even attend) any of the Test matches, he assembled detailed descriptions of play through interviews with players from both sides and reports in Australian newspapers and journals.

Even tour managers got in on the act: Philip Trevor, who had served in the Boer War and written for *The Sportsman*, sent dispatches to both the London *Daily Telegraph* and the *Sydney Morning Herald* while stewarding the 1907–08 Ashes series, pieces later compiled in book form for the only considered account produced of that tour by a member of either camp (Jack Crawford, the young English all-rounder, also filed pieces for the *Daily Mirror*). The justification for Freddie Brown and Alec Bedser immediately writing books respectively about the unsuccessful Ashes assignments of 1958–59 and 1962–63 was similarly based on their managerial roles, but at least both had previously toured Australia as players, in Brown's case as captain. Trevor's credentials primarily lay with his journalism.

There was also a practical element at play: those amateur-ranked players who filled senior management positions generally needed to find ways of supplementing their incomes if they were to tour, and writing was deemed an acceptable way of doing so. Charles Fry, who never toured Australia as a player, might have done so had he been able to secure the necessary journalistic deals. Some of Warner's books were based on letters and articles he filed to publications such as the *Westminster Gazette*, and Ranjitsinhji's book on the 1897–98 tour, *With Stoddart's Team in Australia*, was drawn from articles first sent to the Australian *Review of Reviews*.

Rockley Wilson and Percy Fender, two amateur members of the 1920–21 team in Australia, were both sending back reports to British newspapers, and Fender subsequently re-worked his pieces into an admired book, *Defending the Ashes*. Maurice Allom and Maurice Turnbull, of Surrey and Glamorgan respectively, co-authored two entertaining journals covering tours of New Zealand and South Africa in the inter-war period. Douglas Jardine's motivation for writing his account of the Bodyline series would have had less to do with financial reward than a desire to get across his version of much-disputed events to a domestic audience short of first-hand testimony.

Professionals kept diaries too. Hard-worked bowlers J. T. Hearne and Tom Richardson privately chronicled the same tour as Ranjitsinhji, and Bert Relf regularly had pen in hand on the 1903–04 tour, one of his entries noting the receipt of a poignant cable from home: 'I have another daughter.' Paul Gibb kept a diary of increasing sadness during the 1946–47 tour of Australia on which he was rarely called on to play after the first Test; he filled his hours going to the cinema, eating ice-cream and playing an astonishing amount of golf.

Professionals were also recruited to assist local and national newspapers. Albert Knight, the Leicestershire batsman, sent regular letters back from Warner's first Australia tour to the *Sheffield Daily Telegraph*, David Denton provided the *Yorkshire Post* with pieces from South Africa in 1905–06 and a book on Warner's second Australian mission appeared under Jack Hobbs's name. As with Jardine, Harold Larwood's account of Bodyline was in demand. Bill Bowes, the Yorkshire fast bowler who dismissed Don Bradman for a duck in the Melbourne Test, kept a diary of that tour which might have provided future generations with valuable insights – except that it was lost on the team's train journey home across North America.

Perhaps most controversially, umpire Jim Phillips, who accompanied several England teams overseas to stand in matches alongside local officials, also turned his hand to journalism on Andrew Stoddart's first tour as captain in the mid-1890s. Diaries were more often written by first- or second-time tourists on whom the sights and sounds of new lands made an especially strong impression; some of these inevitably petered out, as the relentless sameness of touring life defied further description or contemplation.

One of the most common themes to these accounts was the arduous nature of the travel, particularly the many internal journeys, which were every bit as hard if not harder than the original transcontinental ones. This was perhaps one aspect of touring that outsiders never fully appreciated, and which the players were always keen to emphasise in their accounts. On the early tours of Australia, the sea voyage between Adelaide and Melbourne, or Melbourne and Sydney, could be as harrowing as anything experienced between Britain and Australia. Sailing between Sydney and Melbourne, George Parr's team was involved in a direct collision with another boat, which sank, leaving Parr himself paralysed with alarm and George Tarrant so panicked that he jumped into a lifeboat intended to rescue those abandoning the other vessel.

When W. G. Grace's team made this same journey ten years later, he recounted in his memoirs that it laid everyone low for two days. 'The constant attacks of seasickness to which they [sea voyages] subjected the members of our team seriously affected our cricketing form,' he wrote. He gratefully noted that on his return in 1891–92 railway extensions 'enabled us to dispense with the tedious coach drives through the bush and the uncomfortable coasting voyages'.

Perhaps the journey which induced most dread was sailing the Bass Strait from Melbourne to Tasmania. Describing this voyage on the 1894–95 tour, Jack Brown wrote in a letter home with feeling how 'the ship rolled awfully', while Pelham Warner noted in his account of the 1911–12 tour: 'Once outside Port Philip, the *Loongana* began to jump, and the majority of the MCC [players] were not seen again until we entered the Tamar River early next morning.' But the *Loongana*, he noted, was a far superior vessel to the *Burrumbeet*, which, Warner added, 'members of the MCC 1903–04 team remember to this day with feelings of terror'.

Not that railway journeys were without their tribulations: in the 1880s, it was not unknown for English cricketers in Australia to spend 20 to 30 hours on the same train, and on one occasion one of the carriages caught fire, delaying the team's arrival into Melbourne. Warner, like Fred Lillywhite, kept a tally of miles travelled, calculating that on his tour of South Africa the team covered more than 5,300 miles by rail and spent 22 nights on trains of varying comfort, although both figures were eclipsed on Percy Chapman's tour in 1930–31 when the team travelled in excess of 10,000 miles and slept 25 nights in railway carriages. Warner's team had one rail journey halted for several hours by a swarm of locusts. Dick Spooner reckoned he travelled 22,000 miles on a tour of the subcontinent in 1951–52.

When George Ulyett, the great Yorkshire all-rounder, returned home from the 1876–77 tour, at eight and a half months the longest ever undertaken by an England team, and spoke to the *Sheffield Daily Telegraph*, he ascribed many of the defeats 'to the immense toil they underwent in getting from place to place'. The paper added: 'George has about had his fill of Australia.' He would not be the last to say that.

With Len Braund also sending back letters for publication and Bernard Bosanquet writing for the *St James*, the 1903–04 tour of Australia saw the player-as-reporter phenomenon reach new heights, and with it greater risks than ever of a misjudged sentence or phrase causing offence. 'A peculiarity of the present English cricketing combination on tour in Australia is the number of its members who are also acting as press correspondents,' the *Daily Chronicle* stated.

> Fully half of the team appears to be 'supplementing their incomes' in this fashion. The combination of player and critic in one person is apt to generate indiscretions and unpleasantness, and Australian teams, before starting their English tours, are probably well advised in signing an engagement not to contribute to any newspaper. It is an open secret that one prominent English cricketer has made himself impossible for another tour in Australia on account of certain criticisms during his last one in his capacity of press correspondent.

This last comment was probably a reference to Ranjitsinhji, who did not return to Australia again after 1897–98, when his comments in print about the bowling action of Australia's Ernie Jones and his criticisms of the barracking of crowds did not go down well with local audiences. W. A. Bettesworth, writing in *Cricket* before the 1903–04 tour, expressed the hope that Warner 'will not allow the fascinations of journalism and book-writing to interfere either with his cricket or his duties as captain'. Bettesworth may have been disappointed in that respect, but as England won the series, beating Australia for the first time in eight years, Warner probably got away with it.

MCC would have been reluctant to introduce a ban on players engaging in journalistic work, because it threatened to exclude impoverished amateurs from touring. Sure enough, trouble resurfaced on the 1920–21 Ashes tour, when Wilson and Fender cabled their criticism of the Sydney crowd during the final Test for barracking Jack Hobbs for his laboured movements in the field, the onlookers unaware that Hobbs was suffering from a torn thigh muscle.

Wilson's comments in the *Daily Express* and Fender's in the *Daily News* were quickly relayed back to Australia, and when he went out to bat Wilson (who earlier in the tour had publicly drawn attention to 'disgusting barracking' during a minor match at Bendigo) was subjected to booing and calls of 'liar' for the duration of his short innings. Then, as he returned to the pavilion, he was subjected to further verbal abuse, and only the intervention of teammate Harry Makepeace, a professional footballer as well as cricketer, and former Australia captain Monty Noble prevented what the *Sydney Morning Herald* suggested might have developed into 'an affray with serious consequences'.

Hobbs, who owing to his injury was batting down the order and was next man in, and therefore closely witnessed the incident, stated: 'Wilson was naturally amazed that the pavilion people [members] should have done such a thing ... Several people made as though they would attack him, but fortunately nothing happened.' The crowd accorded Hobbs a generous welcome while still giving Fender a torrid time when he went out to bat. While condemning the barrackers, Philip Trevor, now working purely in a journalistic capacity, correctly read the runes when he wrote in the *Daily Telegraph* two days after the event: 'Only a very little while ago Lord Hawke made some wise and pertinent remarks, pointing out the undesirability of a cricketer criticising in the public press the game in which he was taking part, and the comrades and the opponents who were also taking part in it. There is not the least doubt that the cricket world is solidly with Lord Hawke in his contention.'

This episode led to MCC introducing a rule preventing England players from writing about or commenting on matches in which they were playing, without prior permission, and tour contracts contained clauses to this effect into the 1970s. This led to the remarkably rigid situation of generally the only people providing information to the press being the manager and captain. Initially at least, these strictures were intended as a weapon to be wielded only if the authorities saw fit. Broadly speaking, MCC allowed those of acceptable social hue, or who toed the club line, to write or give comments to the press, while those who were viewed as potential troublemakers were warned off, or retrospectively punished if their printed words caused offence.

In reality, few spoke – or wrote – at all. On the Bodyline tour, every player on the tour agreed to refrain from giving interviews or writing articles, a vow that was kept except in one respect when, after the incendiary third Test during which the Adelaide crowd and the Australian press gave vocal expression to their hostility to England's tactics, and in response to claims of disunity in the camp, the English players issued a jointly agreed public statement. At Jardine's instigation and without their captain present, they gathered to discuss whether they remained supportive of their leader and his tactics, and they wholeheartedly did.

'The members of the MCC England team have no desire to enter into public controversy, for they deplore the introduction of any personal feeling into the records of a great game,' they said. 'In view, however, of certain published statements to the effect that there is, or has been, dissension or disloyalty in their team, they desire to deny this definitely and absolutely, while assuring the public of England and Australia that they are, and always have been, utterly loyal to their captain, under whose leadership they hope to achieve an honourable victory.'*

If that statement was deemed a justifiable venture into public comment, Larwood was treated differently after the tour when some newspaper articles as well as a book, entitled *Bodyline?* and published under his name six weeks after his return to England,

---

* The unified approach of the English players towards media work was not mirrored by the Australians. Don Bradman missed the first Test after he signed a deal to write for the Sydney *Sun* in contravention of an Australian board ruling against players working as journalists, but throughout the series the Australian players were permitted to broadcast on the radio descriptions of the matches at close of play. 'I fail to see what useful purpose can be served by such performances,' Jardine wrote.

contained a trenchant defence of his bowling methods. Jardine's account of the tour, *In Quest of the Ashes*, could have been used against him but it did not prove necessary; he made it clear well in advance of England's next series against Australia that he would be unavailable. Larwood might have played another Ashes series, but it was the view of *Wisden*'s editor and others in positions of influence that his public statements 'put him beyond the pale of being selected for England'. He never played for England again.

Perhaps Pelham Warner had to tread the finest line: as a journalist of authority in retirement, he was obliged to abide by the stricture that those involved in England selection – as he was at various times between 1926 and 1938 – could not comment on those Test matches, something he just about managed. Some thought that his journalism ought to have precluded him from co-managing the Bodyline tour, a view that gained credence when the Australians threw back at him his earlier criticisms of leg-theory.

Whatever the MCC guidelines stated, it was obvious that nothing was going to stop players and press interacting on long tours; off-the-record information was regularly passed on. Indeed, when the issue of remuneration came up on the first post-war South Africa tour, manager Mike Green was well aware of the role of the players in the story's propagation: 'I knew some of the professionals in the team who had started this campaign [for England players to receive an additional cut of gate receipts], and I was annoyed to think that some of the most senior were responsible. I felt the juniors could hardly be blamed if a senior professional had given the press his views.'

When in 1954 Trevor Bailey published his book *Playing to Win*, in which among other things he criticised MCC's management of tours, his cardinal sin was commenting directly on events on a recent West Indies tour on which he had been vice-captain – in breach of the contractual clause which prevented players from addressing on-field issues that happened during the previous 12 months. Bailey compounded matters by publicising his book in a series of articles in *The People*. He argued unconvincingly that the first article had been altered from his original without agreement, but he accepted that he had failed, as promised, to send a copy of the book's manuscript to Lord's prior to publication.

MCC secretary Ronnie Aird told Bailey that had he done so, 'I am quite sure that the MCC committee would have asked you to delete several paragraphs.' Bailey argued that as an amateur he was not bound by the 12-month rule in the way professionals were, but MCC rejected that claim while Aird took swift action to draw up 'a special form of agreement' for amateurs to ensure no loophole existed. Bailey would have been a candidate to succeed Hutton as England captain, but this episode gave the mandarins at Lord's all the excuse they needed to remove him from the line of succession. Bailey's educational and sporting background, Dulwich and Cambridge via scholarships, had never quite satisfied them, and neither had his win-at-all-costs approach to cricket, or acquisitiveness in life in general.

Others continued to fall foul of the rules: assistant manager George Duckworth was admonished for giving an interview on Hutton's Australia tour in which he expressed the opinion that Fred Trueman ought to have been selected, another reminder that only captain and manager were permitted to speak to the press.

As time went by, senior England players became increasingly willing to challenge, or at least resist, MCC writ. Ted Dexter, another amateur, secured with the help of one of the earliest players' agents, Bagenal Harvey, what Dexter termed a financially 'useful' deal to write for *The Observer* while captaining England in Australia. He wrote some pieces for the paper before departure without hearing of any objections but then, on the final day of the second Test match, he received a message from Lord's informing him that his pieces were breaking the terms of his contract. The Duke of Norfolk, the tour manager, replied on Dexter's behalf: 'Don't bother us, we're trying to win a Test.' It was the last that was heard of the matter.

Clifford Makin, *The Observer*'s sports editor at the time,

revealed in 1979 that the deal had actually been given the bless-
ing of Billy Griffith, the MCC secretary. If that was the case,
Dexter was lucky. A few years later, Barry Knight, the Essex
all-rounder, was not selected for a tour of Pakistan because he
had put his name to newspaper articles without permission.

The power of the cricket administrators to gag England
players continued to be challenged into the 1980s. The *Sun*
successfully contested the right of the TCCB to prevent players from writing newspaper columns when they signed up Ian
Botham, the England captain, for a West Indies tour, although
this outcome might not have been in the best interests of a player
who was the most magnetic personality in the English sporting
firmament. Botham's newspaper deal merely provoked rival
publications into chasing news stories about him all the harder.
The rules as to what players could and could not say remained
strict. Bob Willis was fined for simply expressing the opinion
on radio that Botham was too young to have been given the
captaincy. Vic Marks, a Somerset colleague of Botham's, was
allowed to write diaries for *The Cricketer* magazine of three
England tours he went on between 1982 and 1985, but was
required to have his words vetted by the TCCB.

As late as the 1986–87 tour of Australia, the management
imposed draconian restrictions on the players speaking in
public in the days leading up to departure: Ian Botham, for
instance, was prevented from appearing on an eve-of-tour television sports programme. 'We wanted to go there as a team
and not a collection of individuals,' Mike Gatting, the captain,
said by way of explanation. Gatting and Botham were not best
pleased when another member of the party, Phil Edmonds, then
appeared on *Wogan* without seeking permission. Edmonds cir-
cumvented the rules by getting his wife Frances to answer some
of Terry Wogan's questions on his behalf, an absurd if neat way
of keeping on the right side of officialdom.

This hardline approach contributed to Martin Johnson,
cricket correspondent of a new daily newspaper, *The Independent*,

making his famous jibe when Gatting's team started the tour poorly about there being only three things wrong with them: 'They can't bat, they can't bowl, and they can't field.' Johnson said that those words might never have been typed without the follow-up in the next paragraph: 'They can't talk either – at least to their tabloid ghosts.'

Broadly speaking, since then players' newspaper columns have been vetted by media officers before publication, with a general catch-all clause in their contracts about bringing the game into disrepute leaving them liable for any remarks that might be deemed unacceptable. From 1997 England teams were assigned a full-time media manager, which was partly a response to the decline of the old-school tour managers who had previously taken care of the needs of the press, and partly a consequence of team sponsors pushing for the players to appear in the national press and on TV branding their products. The manager would try to help players navigate their way through what they could and could not say.

Occasionally a player would fall foul of the disrepute charge with ill-advised social media posts, a number of which related to the decisions of selectors in leaving them out of tours.

Nothing has been more incendiary than Kevin Pietersen's text messages to opposition South Africa players in a home series in 2012 which temporarily cost Pietersen his place in the side, including for a T20 World Cup in Sri Lanka, and a fake Twitter account followed at around the same time by several other England players mocking Pietersen. Pietersen's subsequent autobiography, published in 2014 following his sacking from the team, and laced with criticisms of teammates and coaches, not only finished his international career for good but also made the ECB doubly determined to tightly control what was said in print.

More generally, there has been a shift away from players articulating their thoughts in newspapers in favour of television, and specifically through Sky Sports TV as the principal financial stakeholder in the England teams (apart from the ECB). In recent years, Sky has routinely been rewarded for its investment with ready access to players before and after play, and sometimes even during matches. These conversations tend to focus on an analysis of play – in the case of Test matches, about the day just gone and what lies ahead – but occasionally stray into other territory. Sometimes a player has used a broadcaster to give an interview on a sensitive issue in the belief that they can better control the line of questioning, and edit their answers before going to air. Marcus Trescothick did this (with mixed results) to talk about his early return from India in 2006, and Stuart Broad also gave an interview to Sky to express his frustration at being left out of a Test at Southampton in 2020 – even while the match was going on.

The broadcaster–player relationship has never been as close as it is now. Injured England players frequently make guest appearances on Sky or BBC, to provide punditry as well an update on their state of fitness. A contract to work for a broadcaster is often part of the modern player's retirement plan. There has also been a recent trend towards coaches and administrators giving exclusive interviews to the ECB's own website; Brendon McCullum first spoke after his appointment as England's new Test coach in this way.

CHAPTER 15

The Rise of the Press and TV

The relationship with the media and ex-players

The limitations on what members of touring parties could say only strengthened the case for newspapers, and later radio and eventually television companies, committing to the expense of sending out their own men and women. The commercial case for doing so also grew with the explosion of interest in England–Australia contests during the inter-war years, while crucially staffing overseas tours became more viable once the means of transmitting information became faster and more reliable, and of sending someone there got quicker. Once this happened, the demands grew for someone from the team, principally the captain, to speak directly to the press on behalf of his players. Thus a tradition which began in Victorian and Edwardian times with captains addressing crowds from the balcony of a pavilion at the end of a Test match – and which survived through the inter-war years and into the 1950s – evolved into something far bigger and less easy to control.*

---

* One of the earliest instances of a player's comments at the ground being broadcast live during a Test match occurred at Sydney during the 1928–29 series, when a shilling fund to mark Jack Hobbs's forty-sixth birthday led to a ceremony in front of the pavilion during a rain break. Monty Noble, the former Australia captain, presented Hobbs with a wallet containing 46 sovereigns, and after Noble had spoken Hobbs gave a short reply.

The rise of the international telegraph system in the second half of the nineteenth century had a transformative effect. W. G. Grace's first tour of Australia in 1873–74 saw scores being sent back by telegraph for the first time, and when the team returned home they were surprised to discover how people had been following their efforts 'with the keenest possible interest'. Costs, however, were prohibitive. When the Ashes were at stake, though, the expense was reckoned to be worth it, and Andrew Stoddart's two tours of Australia in the 1890s were groundbreaking in terms of communicating news from the Tests across continents.

The first of these series was also the first to see a report appear in an English evening newspaper, the *Pall Mall Gazette*, the same day – some five hours after play had ended. Scoreboards would even be posted outside the offices of Fleet Street newspapers giving the latest scores. But the international system was fragile. It was not uncommon for there to be interruptions to the service, with newspapers explaining 'report delayed in transmission' or 'cable communication with Europe went down'. For many years, publications such as *The Times* and the *Manchester Guardian* carried match reports from Australia, South Africa or the West Indies under the bylines of a Reuters correspondent or labelled a Press Association Foreign Special, with occasional supplementary pieces from a correspondent at home. When West Indies beat England 2–1 in 1934–35, *The Times* ran a short verdict from 'Our Cricket Correspondent' in which he gave credit to the home team for their victory but concluded: 'Is there not too much of this so-called Test match cricket?'*

---

* *The Times* cricket correspondent at the time was Beau Vincent, who held the position from 1930 until 1951. His tenure came to an end shortly after he took an early boat back from Sydney during Freddie Brown's tour, feeling disenchanted and homesick. *The Times* recruited Raymond Robertson-Glasgow, a former Oxford University and Somerset bowler, who was in Australia for *The Observer*, to fill the breach. Vincent may have had a point in questioning the growth of Test cricket. The 1930s saw England play 72 Tests, more than in any previous decade, but things would only get worse: in the 2010s, England played 126 Tests.

Those few journalists who did travel with England teams before the Second World War were often – though not always – treated by the players as members of the family. Martin Cobbett, who was the first travelling reporter to cover a Test tour of Australia, for *The Sportsman*, was liked by the England captain Ivo Bligh and invited to play in one match in Tasmania, and acted as umpire in two others.* The *Sheffield Daily Telegraph* sent James Stainton to cover Pelham Warner's tour of 1903–04, on which the northern trio of George Hirst, Wilfred Rhodes and Johnny Tyldesley were central figures.

When Sydney Southerton, son of James Southerton, covered Percy Chapman's tour in 1928–29 for Reuters and the Press Association, he not only set new standards for overseas reporting in terms of the vividness of his accounts, but he also won the trust of the players. 'He never let us down once, and was universally popular with the members of the England team and the Australians,' Chapman wrote. 'He was made a member of the team and came into our dressing room. We knew he would use his discretion in his reports.' Even in the 1950s, when Brian Statham and Roy Tattersall arrived as reinforcements on Freddie Brown's tour, John Woodcock, a young member of the travelling press, was entrusted to collect them from the airport. When, four years later, Woodcock suffered a burst ulcer in Hobart, Len Hutton still welcomed him into the dressing room in Adelaide to convalesce, even though Hutton was intently focused on the singular mission of regaining the Ashes. From his privileged vantage point, Woodcock watched England take an unbeatable 3–1 lead in the series. It was the kind of access that would be unimaginable to later generations of reporters.

The significant time difference between Britain and Australia

---

* Crawford White and Jim Swanton provided another instance of reporters playing for a touring team when they turned out in a one-day match against South Trinidad at Pointe-à-Pierre during a spate of injuries on the 1947–48 tour of West Indies.

worked well for the London evening newspapers, who were among the first to regularly staff overseas tours; they provided two of the three reporters who accompanied the Bodyline tour – Jack Ingham, who wrote for the London *Star* as well as its sister paper, the daily *News Chronicle*, and Bruce Harris of the *Evening Standard*. The third reporter was Gilbert Mant for Reuters. This was the first of what would be five Ashes tours for Harris, while E. M. Wellings of the London *Evening News* would cover six between 1946–47 and 1965–66.

The English contingent were therefore heavily outnumbered by their Australian counterparts, who largely controlled what became a heated debate: on the first day of the series Hugh Buggy in the Melbourne *Herald* coined the loaded phrase 'Bodyline', which Jardine protested falsely suggested the bowler's intention was to physically harm the batsman, while during the third Test an Adelaide newspaper secured a leak from an Australian player (now generally accepted to be Bradman) about a dressing-room exchange between Australia's captain Bill Woodfull and England's tour manager Pelham Warner, which decisively shifted Australian opinion against England's tactics.*

The number of travelling correspondents leapt up after the Second World War, especially when it came to the Ashes. For instance, there was a sufficiently large number on the first post-war tour under Wally Hammond for the English pressmen to form a Cricket Writers' Club, largely to play their own matches. Hutton's tour of the West Indies was covered by eight English correspondents, more than for any tour outside Australia up to that point. Large regional papers such as the *Yorkshire Post* and the *Manchester Evening News* were also willing to send to Australia on a regular basis.

---

* Woodfull reportedly told Warner, who had come to enquire after his well-being after Woodfull was struck in the chest by Larwood's bowling: 'I don't want to see you, Mr Warner. There are two teams out there. One is trying to play cricket and the other is not.'

Freddie Brown's team of 1950–51 was accompanied by 22 travelling press-men from the UK – thus outnumbering the team for the first time – and four years later the pack touched a fresh high of 24 as England sought to successfully defend the Ashes in Australia for the first time since 1928–29 – 24, that is, if one counts Neville Cardus, of whom tour manager Geoffrey Howard wrote in a letter home: 'Neville Cardus on the Tests should be *good*! I don't think he saw a ball bowled in any of them – perhaps just a little at Sydney but that is all.' With Hutton at the helm, two Yorkshire evening papers as well as the *Yorkshire Post* covered the tour. By this time, technology was largely equal to the mighty task of connecting more than 50 journalists in one press box, each with cables and telegrams to be sent, and some with multiple 'takes' to file, to offices in Australia, the UK and around the world.

Margaret Hughes, who became on this trip the first woman to report on an Ashes tour, having persuaded Sir Frank Packer – father of Kerry – to let her travel out to cover the series for the Sydney *Daily Telegraph*, and subsequently wrote a wide-ranging diary of the trip, *The Long Hop*, reflected on the scene in one press box: 'Most of the press use typewriters for their reports and these are going hell for leather most of the time. Then at the back of the box there is a miniature post office of teleprinters and radio receivers ... It is in fact a complete word factory, with boys leaping up and down the gangways at the call of, "cable", "telegram", "boy", and at the close of the innings there is supreme chaos.'*

The larger cities in most countries England visited generally

---

* In its obituary of Hughes, *Wisden* in 2006 quotes her as saying that she was treated as a 'freak' by her male colleagues in Australia in 1954–55 and states that it was thought no other woman reported on an Ashes tour for a daily newspaper until Chloe Saltau of *The Age* in 2005. Frances Edmonds, whose husband Phil was a member of the England team at the time, accompanied tours of West Indies in 1985–86 and Australia in 1986–87 and wrote books about them both, proudly highlighting her position as an 'inside observer' unencumbered by the 'Test and County Cricket Board's "censorship" restrictions which usually apply to players who write books'.

offered good communications with the UK, even if it sometimes required reporters to spend anxious hours at cable or
telex offices, but more rural venues remained challenging into
the 1980s in places such as the Caribbean and the subcontinent.
For this reason, if there was a suspicion of a big news story
in the offing, reporters might hesitate before heading off the
beaten track.*

By the early 1970s, Sunday newspapers such as the *Sunday
Times* which had long possessed dedicated cricket correspondents were following the earlier example of *The Observer*
and sending them regularly on tour. The *Observer* had used
Raymond Robertson-Glasgow and then Alan Ross, among
others, on major England tours since 1950–51. Robin Marlar
first covered overseas matches for the *Sunday Times* in the subcontinent in 1972–73, and two winters later caused a sensation
when he called for England captain Mike Denness to be sent
home from Australia because his performances and those of his
team were not up to scratch.

This explosion in on-the-ground reporters changed the
dynamics of touring for the team, in particular the captain and manager. If they did not satisfactorily engage with
reporters, especially local ones, they could find life difficult,
as Hammond discovered after he failed to go out of his
way to help them when he arrived in Perth in 1946. When
England next visited, Freddie Brown and Mike Green were
determined to make a better showing and arranged an intro-
ductory get-together between players and press, which was
widely praised. They also appointed a liaison officer from each
group of journalists – Reg Hayter for the English and Tom

---

* When the Robin Jackman Affair triggered the cancellation of a Test in Guyana in
1980–81, England were playing an ODI at Albion, 80 miles from Georgetown; the
players flew there by helicopter, but the press left by bus at 5.30 a.m. and crossed the
Berbice River by ferry. The following winter, when news broke of Geoff Boycott's
peremptory return home from India, most of the travelling pressmen were attending
the team's match in Jamshedpur with poor lines of communication. In both instances,
those journalists who stayed in the city were at an advantage.

Goodman with the Australians – to receive and distribute news bulletins, and coordinate press conferences, a role that survived until the arrival of a formal England press officer in the late 1990s.

But the honeymoon proved short-lived. When the team arrived in Sydney for the first time for a state match, Brown was accosted by two local reporters up against deadline as he came off a plane and was about to be greeted by Prime Minister Robert Menzies. When he brushed them aside and said he would talk later, the afternoon papers ran, according to Green, 'large headlines saying that Brown was becoming a second Jardine, unapproachable and unwilling to help'. Moreover, with England struggling in the build-up to the first Test, there was no shortage of criticism directed their way, which, in Bruce Harris's words, led to 'a regrettable aloofness between Brown and most of the journalists'. Harris added that on the tours led by Jardine and Gubby Allen it had been possible to get off-the-record information, but 'Brown was not accustomed to giving it, and his long period of silence towards the press was only ended when he called a conference after the end of the series.' This suggests Brown did not speak to the press at all for the duration of the five Tests, which if true was an extraordinary state of affairs.

For Green, this was the second time he had filled a managerial role on an England tour, and he found the experience in South Africa two years earlier a happier one, partly because fewer journalists covered the matches 'and they were not the type who wanted sensation and scandal'. In an autobiography published in 1956 which focused heavily on his two tours in charge, Green reflected: 'The press provides one of the biggest problems the manager has to deal with, and each tour becomes more complicated as the number of correspondents following the team increases ... often the news given was mistimed and inaccurate. This meant a great deal of impatience on our part to let the stories and remarks be forgotten without comment or

correction.' He went on: 'The damaging effect of destructive
and damning articles on the team as a whole, and on the individual players, cannot be over-estimated ... The captain and
manager should aim to have the press on "their side" throughout a tour, and to do this it is necessary to help the writers in
all ways possible.'* That strategy might still be reckoned to be
in operation today, with mixed success.

Four years later the managerial role fell to Geoffrey Howard,
the Lancashire secretary, and his task of handling the press
was made easier by Hutton's team winning, and Hutton using
Jim Kilburn of the *Yorkshire Post*, a close friend, as an informal liaison officer. Hutton had also by this stage grasped the
need to give the press something if he was to keep them on
side. Howard's private thoughts of the press pack were hardly
complimentary. Of the popular press's view of the *Daily
Telegraph*'s Jim Swanton he wrote in his diary: 'They all hate
him, of course, but then they all hate each other.' He later
admitted this was an exaggeration. On another occasion he
chided Swanton: 'Your business is to criticise decisions. I have
to make them.'

Hutton was of a similar view. Following the heavy defeat in
Brisbane, Hutton was asked by one of his players if he had read
the *Telegraph*'s verdict – Swanton was nearby in the hotel lobby
with a copy of the paper under his arm at the time – at which
Hutton went over, took the copy from Swanton and pointedly
opened it and perused his share prices before handing it back
and declaring: 'Yes, I've seen the *Daily Telegraph*.'

Possibly the tour on which 'quote-backs' – or local newspapers reporting what the travelling British journalists had filed to

---

* Green briefly fell out with Charles Bray of the *Daily Herald* when, on the boat to
Australia, Bray discovered that Green had instructed the chief wireless officer on
the *Stratheden* to let him know, before sending, any messages reporters had for their
newspaper offices about the precarious state of Denis Compton's knee. '[I] received a
lecture on the illegality of myself or the ship's captain censoring press cables,' Green
recalled, but he persuaded Bray that he merely wanted to discuss any messages with
the author before they were sent.

their desks back home – caused most difficulty was Hutton's the previous winter to the West Indies, when several English correspondents had their copy syndicated in island papers, sometimes prompting hostile reactions. 'They rake up all the mud they can find and throw it about with carelessness,' declared the Jamaica *Gleaner*. But the English camp took exception to what they saw as the *Gleaner*'s selective and partial coverage of some of the more contentious incidents.

Before the English contingent expanded, the main inquisitors were local reporters eager for a word with their gilded guests. On one occasion in up-country Victoria, W. G. Grace had just fallen into his bed after an exhausting 19-hour journey when he was woken by a bang on the door. 'It was a reporter from one of the papers but, as may be imagined, I did not think that midnight was the right hour for a man who had been travelling all day in the rain to encounter an interviewer ... I did not receive the intruder with any kindly feeling, and turned him away with very little "copy".'

Over the years, well-meaning inquiries gave way to less friendly, more calculating behaviour. Green identified a distinct pattern among some Australian correspondents.

The usual method is to give a visiting side a good welcome ... [but] as the first Test approaches, the press barrage becomes intense. The visitors are reported on as being out of form, or it is suggested a number disagree with the captain, and will not obey the manager. There is discord, go on the allegations, and the team spirit is poor, with disciplinary action being taken against certain members. This form of press attack reaches its climax just as the team for the first Test is selected. Often a visiting player is 'pushed' by the press if the reporters think he is on the borderline of being selected, and it would be to the home team's benefit if he were included.

There was another, subtler problem. Some journalists who covered these tours were working for newspapers with the space to indulge their literary skills at length, and on expense accounts that enabled them to give full expression to their tastes for the high life. With time on their hands between Tests (such was the leisurely nature of touring at that time), they were able to create a romanticised version of touring life that, once established, was hard to gainsay. They might have had deadlines to meet, but their lives were far less stressful than those of the cricketers they were writing about. They might have had matches to report on, but they also had the opportunity – unlike the players – to provide a travelogue of countries that most of their readers had never visited and probably knew little about. It was an entertaining but fundamentally misleading impression of what touring was like, at least as the cricketers experienced it.

No one took up the opportunity more readily than Alan Ross, who went out of his way not to be shackled by England's fixture list and to explore the places he was visiting; little surprise, then, that he wrote perhaps the most vivid body of tour books. During the 1959–60 tour of the Caribbean, Ross took the opportunity of a few quiet days at the start of the Jamaica leg – quiet for Ross if not for the cricketers, who had matches against a Colts XI and the full Jamaica team to fulfil – to stay with his friend Ian Fleming at his house, Goldeneye, near the port of Oracabessa. Fleming had been going there for several years to write his James Bond novels. 'My days there,' Ross recounted, 'resolved themselves into a delicious pattern of early morning bathe and breakfast of pawpaw and eggs, of work sessions and pre-lunch swim over the reef with Perelli-mask and spear, of pink gins and shrimps, grilled silk fish and strawberries, of siesta and swimming and work and dinner and early bed. While Ian slave-drove [James] Bond on the typewriter, Ann [Fleming's wife] painted fish in the great windowless room that looks out over the blue reef . . .'

Both Ross and Henry Blofeld, on the next tour of the West Indies, took time out from stops in Georgetown to take boat trips up the Demerara River and along the Kamuni Creek to visit an Amerindian settlement and Anglican mission at Santa – 'wild South America', as Blofeld called it. Needless to say, most of the players savoured little of this sort of thing, lacking either the time or the curiosity, but in popular imagination the two lives – those of travelling cricketers and travelling journalists filing reports – became conflated.*

As the numbers of reporters rose, so the responsibility for handling them shifted somewhat uneasily away from the captain and onto the manager. Some journalists such as Harris felt that what the team needed was a full-time press liaison officer, but remarkably this would not happen for another 40 years. Some managers proved better than others at dealing with the press. Frederick Toone, who oversaw three tours of Australia, was described as an invaluable helper, and Mike Green and Geoffrey Howard were also conscientious in this aspect of their role.

Astonishingly, given his own checkered experiences as captain, Freddie Brown as manager in Australia in 1958–59 took upon himself the task of handling the media. This was done partly with the encouragement of Peter May, the captain, who attributed his own poor returns in South Africa two winters earlier to the strain of always being required to answer reporters' questions, and with around 50 journalists expected to attend the first Test in Brisbane May feared being inundated with requests for interviews. However, Brown was ill-suited to the task, as became clear on the

---

* In the end, Alan Ross became a victim of changing times; his days as a touring correspondent ended in the West Indies in 1967–68 amid rumours that he went off the beaten track once too often for the liking of his editor. He continued reporting on England home Tests until August 1970. The tour-book-as-travelogue went the same way, pushed out of fashion once satellite television started to show England games overseas and transmit shots of exotic locations into people's sitting-rooms – which only further fed the myth of cricket tour as glamour-shoot.

outward voyage when he instructed the players not to talk
to the press at all.

Walter Robins sought to improve relations when he managed
the following winter's tour of the West Indies, but his attempts
to curry favour with journalists only antagonised the players.
'He had very little to do with the players and everything to do
with the press,' David Allen complained. Robins' demand that
Colin Cowdrey – who during the series tour took over as captain when May fell ill – should declare on the final morning of
the final Test to make a game of it particularly incensed them.
Needless to say, his suggestion was rejected.

The Duke of Norfolk as manager in Australia in 1962–63
went to some trouble to win over the press, but demanded
blind loyalty in return, which was never going to work with
some. When Wellings and Denys Rowbotham of the *Guardian*
criticised the captain Ted Dexter for appearing to be more
interested in playing golf than cricket, and for leaving the South
Australia match to go racing with the Duke and other members
of the team, the Duke put out a statement to the effect that the
team's critics were harming Anglo-Australian relations and as
a consequence would be denied press privileges. Rowbotham
responded in print with a tart observation that the Duke seemed
to be putting himself forward as 'a press censor', while the wasp-
ish Wellings claimed that the team's fibre had been sapped 'by
the presence of a sycophantic following of English writers who
think none should criticise the Duke's followers'.

Such incidents highlighted not only the inherent fragility of
relations between the team and a large group of reporters, but
also the tensions running through the press pack themselves.
There were class divisions among them just as there were among
the players, and Scyld Berry remembers that these still existed
when he started covering tours for *The Observer* in the late
1970s. Tom Graveney's recollection that many of the broadsheet writers were not happy when Len Hutton was appointed
as the first modern professional captain reflected where many

of these writers stood politically, and the *Daily Telegraph*'s Jim Swanton would have been counted among them. Swanton took grave exception to Wellings's comments about sycophancy towards the Duke, even threatening legal action before thinking better of it.*

The broadsheet correspondents were certainly treated with deference. John Woodcock, *The Times* correspondent, recalled that the order of precedence at social events involved dignitaries first being introduced to the tour manager, then *The Times*, then the *Daily Telegraph*, and only after that the England captain.

By the 1970s, the notion that a large group of sportsmen could be contractually barred from speaking to the media unless they had managerial clearance, or that the captain and manager could be the mouthpiece of the team for an entire tour, was coming under severe strain. Such totalitarian control was out of step with society at large. When Geoff Boycott gave a TV interview on the balcony of the Headingley pavilion after scoring his hundredth first-class hundred in a Test against Australia it broke new ground, and such immediate media interactions became increasingly common over the years that followed, the whole process given impetus by Kerry Packer's intervention in the way cricket was presented. Even before Packer, England had in the South African-born Tony Greig a captain far readier than any of his predecessors to engage with the media, as Christopher Martin-Jenkins noted on Greig's one overseas Test tour as captain, to India, Sri Lanka and Australia in 1976–77.

---

* Broadsheet correspondents also tended to produce fewer tours books than their colleagues from the evening or popular papers. Bruce Harris produced books on each of his five tours of Australia between 1932–33 and 1954–55 and Wellings covered six Ashes tours from 1946–47 to 1965–66 and wrote books about four of them, rarely holding back in his criticisms of MCC. Swanton wrote seven tour books, though some were collections of his newspaper articles, and a one-volume summary of his eight tours of Australia from 1946–47 to 1974–75. Christopher Martin-Jenkins produced accounts of six winter tours, most of them during his time as BBC radio's cricket correspondent.

'Greig is well aware of his responsibilities as a major figure in the game and he is always happy to make himself available for interviews with those whose typewriters and microphones enlarge his reputation in the public eye,' Martin-Jenkins wrote. 'If Greig is a shrewd enough businessman to know that public self-promotion is a kind of free advertisement for his various off-the-field interests he is also a godsend to journalists. Incidents on the field which in the days of old might have been interpreted by guesswork from the press box can now be verified or explained by direct reference to the captain.'

Greig's tenure as England captain was cut short by his recruitment by Packer, with whom he became a groundbreaking performer with microphone in hand. Mike Brearley, who replaced Greig as captain, also showed himself more willing and able to engage articulately with the media than many who had gone before him.

The rest day, which was a standard feature of Test cricket until it was phased out under pressure from TV companies such as Packer's in the 1980s and 1990s, became another opportunity for a captain to give his thoughts to press, television and radio. Initially, the rest-day press conference was driven less by reporters and more by the team management wanting its views to be known about something that had occurred on the field. Donald Carr, on the first of his three assignments as manager, called one amid an umpiring crisis on the South Africa tour of 1964–65 with the aim of quashing any impression that England were nursing a grievance at Eddie Barlow being granted an umpiring reprieve on the way to him scoring a century (though in actuality they were).

Greig similarly called one in Bangalore to discuss the umpiring and some scurrilous articles relating to allegations that earlier in the series the England players had been guilty of ball-tampering. Gradually, rest-day briefings became a fixture, but helpful though they were in providing copy to newspapermen, they were a minefield for captains, who could easily come to regret some casually chosen words. When on the rest day of a Test in Trinidad, Ian Botham confidently anticipated a draw and said, 'if we lose, a few heads will roll', he soon came to wish he had not been so firm in his opinions. England lost.*

It was a common assumption, not without foundation, that media men were prepared to turn a blind eye to certain excesses among touring players in order to protect friendships and contacts. When Greig had an epileptic attack at the airport on the way home from the West Indies in 1974, reporters agreed not to refer to the incident, or over subsequent years his condition, an indication of the deference still shown towards England captains by pressmen at that time.

Don Mosey, who made several tours for BBC radio in the late 1970s and early 1980s, defended this approach, referencing in a memoir several years later the covering-up of an England player's misdemeanours on a tour of the West Indies. 'There was ... a potential front-page story for every national paper involving one England player. If the story had broken, the player would almost certainly have been recalled from the tour ... That action by cricket correspondents might well be regarded as reprehensible by the news editors of their own papers.' Mosey argued it was the only way to operate.

On tour, the cricket correspondent travels and is usually accommodated with the team. For three or four months he lives, eats, drinks, talks and socialises with the players. If conversations over a beer were not regarded as strictly off-the-record unless otherwise mutually understood, any kind of social contact would be impossible ... with a good manager and a good captain there is no need for a dog-eat-dog

---

* The last Test match England played overseas with a rest day was the Melbourne Test of 1994–95; with the game starting on 24 December, Christmas Day was taken off. That instance apart, Tests in Australia had generally gone without rest days for some years before that. All five of England's Tests in the West Indies in 1993–94 had rest days.

attitude among the media. There are regular conferences and briefings; personal relationships with individual players are not discouraged . . . providing everybody observes the rules.

This was not necessarily quite how the players themselves saw things. Boycott in one of his tour books made reference to the Janus-faced press: 'They smile and then they stab – and they think the next time they come along for a comment you are going to forget the wounding things they write and obligingly talk to them.'

Things began to change once Ian Botham came on the scene and the tabloids began fiercely competing for stories about him. The mood altered in part because of the way Botham objected to his treatment, notably once in Pakistan, on his first England tour, and also on the way home from the West Indies when he was captain. On both occasions he physically manhandled English journalists to whose judgments he took exception.

In Pakistan, following a High Commission function in Islamabad, a scuffle ensued in a car park after Botham shared a taxi ride back to the hotel with Steve Whiting, the cricket correspondent of the *Sun*. Whiting described it as more of a wrestling match than a fight. After returning to his room, Whiting was visited by another England player who asked if he intended to write about the incident and Whiting said no. 'I remember the kerfuffle the incident caused,' Pat Gibson, of the *Daily Express*, recalled to me. 'I told one or two of the players that there wasn't much future in players hitting press men.'

The case in the West Indies occurred at an airport in Bermuda on the way home, Botham taking issue with Henry Blofeld's observation that he 'captains the side like a great big baby'. According to Blofeld, Botham, urged on by two team-mates, came over, tried to punch him and missed, with Blofeld falling to the floor in the process. What was perhaps most significant about this story was that the cricket correspondents present agreed not to write about it. Details of what happened only came to be published when other journalists came to hear about it later. The *Sunday People* ran the story on its front page nine days after the team arrived home.

Botham was also incensed by criticism of him in *The Times* by Simon Barnes during a later West Indies tour, in part because Barnes was at the time working on a book with Phil Edmonds, a member of the England team; as a consequence, Botham was furious with both writer and cricketer, whom he suspected of leaking information. On one occasion during the Tests, as Botham trudged off the field with another low score to his name, he made a noose sign towards the press box in resentment at the treatment he expected the correspondents were about to hand out. But in truth the spats were fleeting; some of Botham's firmest friends were journalists.

Bob Willis was much more wary. He was no Greig or Brearley when it came to handling the media; indeed, at the start of one tour he vetoed players consorting with pressmen in hotel bars, at least until it became clear how unrealistic such a move was and he softened his stance. In his published captain's diaries of two winter tours he several times alluded to the uneasiness of player–press relations, and he personally gained such a reputation for dourness that once, in an attempt to improve his image, he turned up to a press conference with a cigar ('and a smile') in a conscious attempt to look more cheerful.

Another time, after refusing to disclose his XI ahead of a Test in Auckland, his patience snapped at a reporter's repeated demands for information, telling him to next time bring his typewriter 'so that I could write his story while he waited'. On the same tour the *Daily Express* ran a story about a window being broken in a hotel room shared by Botham and Allan Lamb. 'We are by no means the first sporting side overseas to suffer this apparent obsession with putting the blame for defeat on anything, so long as it is more sinister or sensational than simple poor form or limited ability,' Willis wrote sorrowfully. When he became an assistant manager 18 months after finishing playing Test cricket, he was no friendlier, being an influential voice in the press being excluded from official functions on tour. But, oh, how he turned: in a subsequent career as a TV pundit, Willis became an inveterate and sharp-tongued Jeremiah.

The requirements of travelling newspapermen and radiomen were changing. A daily interview with one of the touring players came to be seen as a standard requirement, perhaps the turning point being the Botham-led tour of the Caribbean, which was so heavily freighted with news events, and so blighted by wet weather, that 'talking heads' were in more demand than usual. A pattern was being set. Mosey may have articulated the case for keeping confidences between players and pressmen, but his employers at the BBC did not agree. They were sufficiently dissatisfied with Mosey's reporting of the tour that the following winter a producer, Peter Baxter, was sent to accompany him to the subcontinent. Baxter conducted the interviews with all players except Geoff Boycott, a famously difficult character whom Mosey knew well through their shared northern background. When in early 1984 England spent seven weeks in New Zealand, Mosey calculated that he conducted 68 player interviews.

This trend, eventually reinforced by the advent of a 24-hour news cycle and internet reporting, led to the role of tabloid correspondents in particular fundamentally changing; where once they relied on well-formed and strongly held opinions, now a daily slab of quotes from an England touring player underpinned their dispatches. Peter Smith's loyalty to Botham effectively resulted in him leaving the *Daily Mail* in 1988 after nine years as a highly respected correspondent, as a generation of long-serving reporters found the climate changing in favour of newsy off-field stories which had previously rarely been in their domain. A number of stories generated by specialist news reporters had emerged during the 1980s involving high-profile England cricketers, among which was Ian Botham's admission in 1986 of recreational drug-taking, which suggested more was going on behind the scenes than many camp followers were letting on. To an extent, broadsheet newspaper reporting also became more quotes-based and 'newsy'.

Both journalists and players were coming under ever greater pressures: journalists were asked to provide more than just a report on the play, because many cricket fans had already followed the game live on television or radio, while the players found themselves under scrutiny from a wider array of media outlets. Channel Nine, though some in the England camp thought its commentary bordered on the hysterical, gave cricket far greater exposure in Australia than the BBC, the rights holders for England's home matches, did in the UK; early on in a tour a visiting England captain could expect to be asked to appear on Nine's breakfast show before 8 a.m. – a strange experience in the 1980s.

In particular, the tabloids were on the hunt for off-field scandals about Botham and his allies and deployed specialist news reporters in search of the prize. 'This led to some outrageous scenes in the West Indies when newsmen and photographers hid in bushes outside the team hotel,' one player recalled. The unmarked exclusion zone around the team was being eroded by the media's desire to bring the action ever closer to the outside world. The new proximity was illustrated by an incident that occurred during England's first overseas Test series to be shown live on TV, when Jack Russell went over and shouted into a camera as he walked out to bat in Barbados following a disputed dismissal of Rob Bailey. Russell could not contain himself. Similarly, two winters later during a Test in Wellington, when an intrusive cameraman repeatedly tried to film from close quarters the England players carrying off David Lawrence after the Gloucestershire fast bowler sustained a fractured kneecap, cricket manager Micky Stewart pushed him out of the way and forcibly tried to remove him from the scene.

This changing landscape, plus poor results, led to an overhaul of England's management structure: Stewart was brought in as cricket manager (a job title that soon morphed into that of head coach) while Peter Lush, a man with long experience of newspapers, marketing and public relations, was appointed manager of a string of tours between 1986–87 and 1990–91; gradually, both helped lighten the load on the captain. Lush brought a more disciplined approach to media affairs, which was reinforced by the TCCB creating in 1989 a new role of public relations manager, first filled by Peter Smith, whose time at the *Daily Mail* and before that at the *News of the World* left him well placed to understand the media's evolving requirements. Communication between players and press improved, as did mutual understanding. There were still missteps, such as when Mike Atherton responded to an abstruse question by a local Pakistani journalist (following a match in Rawalpindi at the 1996 World Cup) by muttering in an audible aside: 'Will somebody remove this buffoon?' He apologised the following day.

This process was taken a step further when in 1997 the England team was given its first full-time media officer, who travelled with the team home and away. In November 1991, Tetley Bitter became the first sponsors of the England team, initially paying £3 million over three years before renewing the deal; in return they expected to see players interviewed and photographed in newspapers and on television wearing their branded kit. By the turn of the century, a healthier interaction between players and the media had become a necessity, not a choice. Daily press conferences with a chosen player of the day enabled team management to regain some measure of control of the news agenda, and restrain what it saw as the mischief-making of the popular press. It came at a heavy price, though, as by and large players instead churned out well-honed comments of unutterable dullness.

The team's relations with the English media may have gradually moved onto a more business-like footing, but the commercial necessity to promote every event as the next big thing meant that the opposition – regardless of who they were – became demonised. More than ever, sport became a 'war' and a 'battle'. Rival camps became polarised, and the participants were expected to play along in the phoney war. This was particularly the case when it came to England v Australia.

'One of the first things that hit me upon arriving in Australia was the coverage in their newspapers, which I had been warned about – though I was still taken aback,' Michael Vaughan wrote in his autobiography in respect of his first Test tour Down Under. 'In the build-up to the first Test there was a double-page spread in the paper, with [Glenn] McGrath going through our whole team and openly saying what our weaknesses were.'

Things were no different four years later. 'You'd go out for dinner and there'd be people chirping away, and you'd get back to the hotel almost more drained than when you went out,' Paul Collingwood said. 'Open the newspapers and there would be pictures of boarding passes for the England players . . . Go home, Poms. It was pretty brutal.' He even found himself being sledged by the public address announcer in Melbourne, who during the one-day leg of the 2006–07 tour took the mickey by calling him 'Paul Collingwood MBE', a reference to Collingwood's award for playing one Test in the winning 2005 Ashes series.

The jingoism was certainly not confined to Australia. The English media enjoyed the patriot games too. The media in general played their part, unwittingly or not, in heightening the sense of theatre that attached to big sporting contests, and to work properly it needed two sets of camp followers playing their part. When it was unclear whether English reporters would be allowed to enter Australia to cover the Ashes series in 2021 22 owing to Covid restrictions, England's Stuart Broad lamented the possibility. 'It does make a difference . . . English writers and press to ask different questions, to give a different balance to articles written, is healthy for an Ashes series. A press conference purely with Australian journalists is only coming out one way, isn't it?'

*

The criticism was usually hardest to bear when it came from those working in the media who were themselves former England players, and often former captains. This was increasingly the case when it came to radio and television pundits, although they might also put their names to newspaper columns. With these media, the judgment was both immediate and inescapable. Since England's overseas Tests began to be covered live by satellite broadcasters in 1990, primarily Sky Television but also BT Sports, ex-England captains have been a staple of the commentary box, and radio coverage has also called on recently retired members of the team. These ex-cricketers knew the game and the challenges, so their words were likely to be listened to in the dressing room. When things were not going well on the field, the verdicts handed down could be painful to hear when they came from old friends and acquaintances, and once trusted allies. Of course, experts on the ground such as these might also dispense technical advice, encouragement and solace to players when it was needed, so to an extent the relationship was double-edged. The dilemma was: should their comments be heeded, or ignored?

Geoff Boycott and Michael Vaughan were among those captains turned pundits whose verdicts caused most distress. Boycott's criticism in his newspaper columns incensed England coach Duncan Fletcher in the early 2000s, and Vaughan's disparaging remarks about Alastair Cook's one-day credentials led to Cook refusing to talk to him for a while. When Vaughan advocated dropping Stuart Broad or James Anderson from the Test side after the first Test match at home to Pakistan in 2018, to 'ruffle' the dressing room by showing that no one had a divine right to a place in the team, Broad was unsparing: 'It's a complete shot in the dark because he doesn't know what the changing room is like ... The players don't talk to him about cricket or what's going on ... But it's personal columns, it's radio shows that need "likes" and air-time.'

By the 1920s, players who had themselves played Test cricket but had either retired or dropped out of the team were becoming common sights in press boxes and behind the microphones of the new radio coverage. Perhaps the first non-participating player of note to cover a major England tour was Percy Fender in Australia in 1928–29. He wrote articles for English and Australian publications and later an account in book form, *The Turn of the Wheel*. Fender had written contemporaneous reports of an Ashes tour while a member of the side eight years earlier, upsetting the authorities in England and Australia in the process, but he now returned as an observer – although he remained an active county cricketer and would return to the England side for one Test the following summer.

Jack Hobbs, retired from Tests but still playing for Surrey, accompanied the 1932–33 tour, when England were led by Douglas Jardine, his county captain, and put his name to columns ghosted by Jack Ingham. Charles Fry, one of the giants of English cricket during the late Victorian and Edwardian eras, and Jardine both reported on the 1936–37 tour of Australia and Harold Larwood, Jardine's spearhead on the 1932–33 tour, returned there to give his thoughts on Freddie Brown's tour for the *Sunday Express*. Bill Bowes, another member of Jardine's team, reported on several post-war tours for the *Yorkshire Post* and established a significant reputation as a critic. Arthur Gilligan, Ian Peebles and Bill Edrich all travelled overseas with England sides in a journalistic capacity having previously done so as players, Gilligan as one of the early radio summarisers, featuring mainly on Australian networks at a time when little live commentary from Australia was heard back in England.

Former captains could be in high demand if they had recently dropped out of the side or had led past tours to the country England were visiting. Len Hutton was reportedly offered £10,000 to cover the Australia tour of 1954–55 in the event he should not go as either captain or player; of course, he went in both capacities – and was financially worse off as a result, at least in the short term, though reputation-wise he came back much richer. Brian Close was recruited as a columnist by the *Daily Mail* for a tour of West Indies in 1967–68 which only a few months earlier he had been expected to lead. In the same vein, David Gower worked as a TV commentator on an England tour of India in 1992–93 for which he might well have been chosen; those members of the public outraged at his omission from the touring party had to make do with listening to him instead. Denis Compton and Ted Dexter both had long careers as newspaper columnists after they stopped playing.

The first overseas Tests to be covered by BBC radio reporters – for the benefit of listeners back home – were in South Africa in 1938–39. Jim Swanton provided short spells of commentary towards the end of the day, and after the war his evening summaries became an established feature of England Tests at home and abroad. After the war, Rex Alston also covered several tours for the corporation and produced similar 'eye-witness accounts' as they were known to UK listeners, while also working on live commentary for local networks.* Before becoming a national newspaper correspondent, John Woodcock accompanied Freddie Brown's team to Australia, where one of his principal roles was to shoot cine film which was then flown back to the BBC; some of this footage ended up in the film *Elusive Victory*.

Regular ball-by-ball radio commentary of home Tests in England was provided by the BBC from 1957, but it was a long time before overseas matches received the same treatment. The poor quality of communications from some countries was one factor, another was that there was no dedicated channel for such time-consuming sports coverage, so there was a long battle to

---

* Commentating on a Test in Trinidad in 1959–60 which erupted in a riot, Alston had no sooner denounced the insurrectionists on air in his Cambridge-educated tones than he found his vantage point – a wooden commentary box on stilts in one of the stands – set alight; he had forgotten that local spectators liked to listen to the game on transistors, and they were quick to make known their feelings about his interpretation of events.

secure airtime. There was also a feeling that there was little appetite among listeners to stay up through the night, as would have been generally the case (only West Indies being behind GMT rather than in front of it).

Things changed after Brian Johnston went to Australia in 1958–59, originally in a freelance capacity during long service leave from the BBC; he was a few years later appointed the corporation's first official cricket correspondent. This established a pattern of someone being sent by the corporation on most major tours to file regular bulletins and occasionally provide live commentary at times of high drama. Johnston commentated live on the closing stages of the final Test in Guyana in 1967–68 when last man Jeff Jones blocked out the last over to secure England a series win, and Christopher Martin-Jenkins, who succeeded Johnston, commentated on the thrilling climax to the final Test in Trinidad on the following West Indies tour, when Tony Greig's off-breaks bowled England to a series-levelling win by 26 runs.*

The turning point came with a decision to broadcast every ball of the final day of the Centenary Test in Melbourne in 1977, which began with England on 191 for two in pursuit of 463. Derek Randall's brilliant innings of 174 kept them on course, but eventually they fell short by 45 runs. After that, all-night coverage of England Tests in Australia became the norm, and for the 1982–83 tour the BBC sent its own commentary team, including former players Trevor Bailey, Mike Denness, Tony Lewis and Fred Trueman. Part of Bob Willis's team talk at the start of that series was 'reminding them [the players] of the millions at home who would be tuning into the game on their

---

* Concerns over the quality of communication meant that the BBC did not send anyone to India and Pakistan in 1972–73 and instead relied on Crawford White, a long-serving Fleet Street correspondent with experience of radio work; White was principally there to report for the *Daily Express*. White provided the BBC with bulletins when he could get through, though problems prevented him filing from Delhi on England's Test victory on Christmas Day.

radios. We did not want to let them down.' Comprehensive coverage from other countries soon followed, lines of communication permitting.

Well before live TV coverage back to the UK of England's away games became the norm, local newsreel men were a common sight from the 1950s onwards, while terrestrial organisations such as BBC and ITN would send news teams to provide regular bulletins.* Both BBC and ITN did this for the Caribbean tour of 1985–86. Sometimes the BBC would put together a highlights programme of 30 minutes taken from local television: among other occasions, this was done from the losing campaigns to Australia in 1974–75 and West Indies in 1980–81, and selected matches at the World Cup on the subcontinent in 1987–88 when England fell agonisingly short of winning the final against Australia, a game that pivoted on Mike Gatting's miscued reverse sweep off Allan Border's part-time spin.

With TV coverage still relatively unsophisticated, certainly outside Australia and England, such news-team footage was hungrily latched upon by the players; Geoff Boycott made a point of paying a visit to the BBC crew in their hotel in Barbados to play back and study Michael Holding's great over to him there in 1980–81. TV coverage in India was so poor in the early 1980s, when it relied essentially on two fixed cameras, that most people preferred to follow the game by radio, but unfortunately for Keith Fletcher, a moment of petulance when he flicked his bat into the stumps, dislodging the bails, after being given out caught behind sweeping in a Test in Bangalore, was caught by a BBC crew and showed his actions clearly enough. The footage became a piece of evidence in the case for removing Fletcher as captain after the tour ended; a letter of apology to the Indian board could not save him.

As a news-setting tool, television built on work already begun

---

* The first Test match to be televised within Australia was the opening game of the 1958–59 series in Brisbane.

by specialist photographers, who for many years were prevented from accompanying England teams abroad by logistical issues surrounding the speedy filing of images. By the 1970s these were starting to be resolved. Patrick Eagar, son of Desmond, the Hampshire secretary who served as assistant manager on England's 1958–59 tour, went to Australia in the mid-1970s to cover the Perth, Melbourne and Sydney Tests. Working for the *Sunday Times* and *The Cricketer* rather than a daily newspaper afforded him a little more time to get his pictures back to London, which he did by means of an elaborate and imperfect system of taking prints into a local post office, from where they would be sent on to the UK. 'It was not disconnected with the idea of telex, but it was more technical,' Eagar explained to me.*

Eagar also recruited air crews and holidaymakers returning home to take with them rolls of film for posting on once they were back home. The *Daily Mirror* sent Eric Piper, a news man, for the third and fourth Tests of the same Ashes series. Adrian Murrell joined the next major England tour to India two years later. He, like Eagar, had challenges getting his pictures home, and in Pakistan in 1977–78 he resorted to each night after play in the Hyderabad Test taking a bus to Karachi airport – a journey of around 100 miles – to try to find a friendly face willing to carry his packages, an extraordinary commitment. By the West Indies tour of 1980–81, Graham Morris, with a background in news, made the first of what would prove to be almost 40 successive England Test tours. Morris invested in a portable wire machine, which cost him a small fortune and was cumbersome to transport, but enabled him to file fast, accurate pictures.

It paid its way almost immediately when, late on the first day

---

* Problems with transmission also limited the scope for cartoonists to accompany overseas tours. Arthur Mailey produced several books of sketches and caricatures relating to seven Ashes series in Australia and England between 1920–21 and 1932–33, in the first four of which he took part as a player for Australia. When a dispute over image rights prevented photographers working at England's Tests in India in 2012–13, Alan Tyers in the UK filled the breach for the *Daily Telegraph* with a series of cartoons.

of a Test match in Faisalabad, with the light fading, Morris – alerted to the rising tension on the pitch through listening in on the stump microphones that radio broadcasters had begun experimenting with – caught the inflammatory argument between Mike Gatting and umpire Shakoor Rana. It only began to dawn on him that he might be the one person to have an image of the moment when a couple of local international agency guys knocked on his hotel room door that evening. 'It really was the only picture [of that incident] that existed,' Morris said. 'Ten years later, I was interviewed on radio with Gatting, and he said that but for your photo I might have kept my job [as captain].'

Other instances of photographic images causing problems to players included the incident of David Gower and John Morris in a Tiger Moth buzzing the ground at Carrara in Queensland where their teammates were involved in a game. 'I think they wanted you to see that they were not great fans of authority,' Graham Morris said. 'If they didn't, they wouldn't have gone back, put flying gear on and sat in the planes to have their photos taken.'

Local photographers had of course served their own markets long before the 1970s, and occasionally they too produced images that influenced public opinion.* This was very much the case with the shots of Bill Woodfull and Bert Oldfield taking blows to the body during the Bodyline series – in that instance by Herbert Fishwick, an English émigré who worked for the *Sydney Mail* and *Sydney Morning Herald*. There was also the case of Denis Compton being photographed with a black eye after a night out in Melbourne after England's defeat in the second Test over Christmas 1950, a picture carried by *The Truth* on the front page alongside what Mike Green called a 'scurrilous and disgusting article'.

---

* Charles Nettleton (1826–1902), an English-born photographer who settled in Melbourne in 1854, boarded the *Great Britain* to photograph the first English cricketers arriving in Australia in December 1861, and also produced some images of their famous opening fixture at the Paddock in Yarra Park, Melbourne (on the site of the current MCG).

Green's autobiography makes clear that he refused permission for any photographs to be taken inside the hotel – 'I warned Compton and confirmed my action with [team captain Freddie] Brown' – but a photograph was nevertheless taken of Compton 'wearing pyjamas, in bed, unshaven, hair untidy, and the largest black eye imaginable'. The length of time it took Compton, Green and Brown to produce a statement explaining the injury understandably aroused suspicion, and the version of events they came up with, that Compton had cut his eye on a water spout while sitting at a table of a friend's house, was one that Compton stuck to for many years, 'although the smile playing at the side of his lips suggested there was more to it'.

Unhelpfully, Green in his book suggested an alternative version: that it was as a result of 'ragging with [Godfrey] Evans'. *The Truth*'s version was that Compton 'unwittingly knocked against a lamp post in the wee sma' hours' after visiting Claridges' nightclub with some teammates including Evans and Reg Simpson, before an unnamed lady 'escorted England's gay cavalier of the cricket field back home for a little happy supper'.

Wally Hammond, writing in the 1940s, alluded to Australia, 'with its batteries of press cameras . . . [and] hawk-like reporters'. When Frank Tyson was struck on the head by a Ray Lindwall bouncer in Sydney and rushed to hospital for X-rays, the tour manager Geoffrey Howard was furious that photographers pursued them 'right into the hospital'.

All in all, the changes in the way England tours are now covered – whether through television and radio, newspaper and internet reporting, or social media – compared to even a couple of generations ago constitute a barely conceivable transformation. It is true that in some instances a significant time difference involved in playing overseas means that live domestic TV and radio audiences are often relatively small, but very little now escapes scrutiny, on or off the pitch. Life as an international cricketer is lived in a goldfish bowl on tour as it is at home.

CHAPTER 16

Births, Marriages and Deaths

Wrong place, wrong time

England's tour of Australia in 2021–22 witnessed an unusual display of player power. With the pandemic still raging and Australian states in varying degrees of lockdown until vaccination rates improved, planning for the tour was mired in uncertainty for months, but one thing became increasingly clear: many of the England players were not prepared for their families to be denied entry to the country to join them for some part of a two-month tour, which for some members of the team would follow hard on the heels of a T20 World Cup in the United Arab Emirates, with no time at home between.

If they were to sign up to the tour, they wanted their 14-day hard quarantine softened, and for their partners and children to be with them without having to go through extended periods of quarantine themselves. The attitude of the players was shaped not simply by the prospects of what might lie ahead in Australia, but by what they had already been through in the previous 18 months in bio-secure bubbles home and abroad. Early in 2021, England had played in Sri Lanka and India for three months, and players had been rotated in and out to spare them too much artificial and unhealthy living. It happened, too, that a lot of the

A captain's rest-day press conference was for many years a staple of overseas tours. Here David Gower speaks to reporters in Bombay in 1984.

Facing the West Indies fast bowlers on their own patch could be a brutal business, as Phil Edmonds shows.

Graham Gooch breaking a finger in Trinidad proved a pivotal moment in the 1990 series, when England lost after taking an early lead.

A fancy dress party was a regular feature of Christmases on tour.
This one dates from Australia 1982–83.

Pakistan umpires Shakoor Rana and
Khizer Hayat, England captain Mike Gatting
and tour manager Peter Lush discuss the
impasse at Faisalabad in 1987.

Mike Atherton and Jack Russell take
a breather during their long battle to save
the Johannesburg Test in 1995.

Politicians often used England tours to burnish their own standing. Here Zimbabwe president Robert Mugabe meets the England team in Harare in 1996, a few years before he became persona non grata with British governments.

Graham Thorpe and Nasser Hussain leave the field after England's remarkable moonlit victory at Karachi in 2000.

© Clive Mason

© Clive Mason

Marcus Trescothick eventually found touring as a player intolerable; here he celebrates a hundred at the Wanderers in 2005.

Gareth Batty, Ashley Giles, Matthew Hoggard, James Anderson, Geraint Jones and Paul Collingwood enjoy England's series win in South Africa in 2004–05.

A terrorist attack on the Taj hotel, Mumbai in November 2008 brought a temporary halt to England's tour of India.

Kevin Pietersen and captain Paul Collingwood with the T20 World Cup trophy in Barbados in May 2010.

Alastair Cook (left) batting with Andrew Strauss during England's triumphant series in Australia 2010–11. Cook has scored more runs and centuries in overseas Tests than any other England batsman.

Strauss's team celebrate retaining the Ashes in Melbourne in 2010 with their 'sprinkler dance'.

Joe Root has led England in more overseas Tests, and scored more overseas runs as captain, than anyone else.

Stuart Broad and James Anderson have been two of England's most durable Test match bowlers; here they walk off together having kept out the final twelve balls to secure a draw at Sydney in January 2022.

England's travelling fans, as ever, make their presence felt during the T20 World Cup final at Melbourne, November 2022.

Jos Buttler with the T20 World Cup after England's taut victory over Pakistan at the MCG.

© Aamir Qureshi/AFP

Ben Stokes led England to a remarkable tactical success
in the Test series in Pakistan in 2022.

© Matthew Lewis

Rehan Ahmed, England's youngest Test cricketer, enjoys one of seven
wickets during his debut at Karachi in December 2022.

players under consideration for the Ashes tour were fathers to young families. It was believed that up to ten first-choice players were ready to say no unless their demands were met.

Jos Buttler indicated shortly in advance of his wife Louise giving birth to their second child in August that he and his family were close to breaking point. Asked if he might withdraw from the Ashes tour, he said: 'You have to be open to that ... I've sacrificed a lot for cricket and my wife and family have sacrificed a lot ... It would be incredibly disappointing if some players feel like they can't do it, but we're in a world where that is a possibility. If that means missing cricket, I'll miss cricket.' He added: 'If this was the first time we were potentially going away in this manner you might find it more manageable, but having spent a long time in Covid environments already, it makes it tough.'

His views appeared to be representative of many. Some former England captains of recent vintage weighed in, saying such enforced separation was unacceptable, and insisted the tour should be called off if the players' families could not travel to Australia. 'Quite simply, if they can't, they should call the Ashes off,' Michael Vaughan wrote. Kevin Pietersen said: 'Families are the most important part of a player's make-up.'

Largely as a result of the players' views, the Australian government accommodated their wishes. Hard quarantine was reduced, and families were allowed to join them during the two weeks the team spent at a resort hotel on the Gold Coast upon arrival, or later over the Christmas period. 'We're very grateful to get the opportunity to go there under the conditions we've got,' Joe Root, the England captain, said on the eve of departure. 'It is a long tour and a long time that guys have spent away from home ... We need to provide an environment which allows players to play Test cricket at the level expected of an Ashes series, and having that support around us with our families is a big part [of that].'

The power the players exercised on this issue would have

astonished earlier generations. For most of the twentieth century there were battles between touring England cricketers
and administrators on the issue of partners and families joining tours, and they were battles the players generally lost. The
players did not then possess the leverage they had acquired in
the modern era, when many could walk away from the international arena and play T20 franchise cricket for large sums
of money if they wished. Wives were routinely discouraged
from joining their partners on tour, and if they did come it was
at the players' expense. Even then, couples were barred from
spending more than 21 nights together. As ever, in the heyday
of the class system, captains and amateurs were granted more
leeway than professionals, which only further fuelled the sense
of resentment.

Over the years, no issue in relation to England tours caused
more upset and aggravation than this. Nothing made touring
tougher than enforced separation from loved ones, and nothing
better showed up the antediluvian attitudes of the mandarins at
Lord's. Neither did the lack of sympathy end with the miserliness of the access granted families; the players also found it hard
to negotiate time off for the birth of children, or sometimes
even the deaths of close relatives. Real-life events did not stop
happening when tours were going on, but it was clear that those
running English cricket would prefer it if they did.

Graeme Swann once said, 'Touring before you've got kids
is the best thing you'll ever do. You spend time with some of
your best mates, [in] five-star hotels, playing cricket for your
country. It's amazing.' But the unstated flipside to this was that
once you had a young family, touring was less fun and far more
complicated.

To its credit, the ECB has more recently gone to much
greater lengths to keep players connected with families. The
board started to subsidise the cost of families joining tours,
while paternity leave and compassionate leave was no longer an
unreasonable demand but an inalienable right. Indeed, so many

partners and children came on tour that the board employed dedicated family liaison managers to make sure their needs were met. There were sometimes some hard discussions about when they could come out – there were bitter exchanges concerning Australia in 2006–07, with Duncan Fletcher eventually agreeing to them coming once the warm-ups were over, having originally argued that they should wait until after the second Test – but generally the arrangements were arrived at amicably enough. Technology, too, made it easier for the families apart to stay in touch via Skype, FaceTime or Zoom calls available at a couple of clicks of a button. There was now no need for players to spend a small fortune in phone charges to keep in daily contact with home.

The way in which permission for wives to join tours was granted or withheld had rarely been equitable or fair. It was a practice introduced and perpetuated by MCC, whose officers could scarcely have made it clearer how little regard they had for women (whom the club did not even admit to membership until 1998), and even after it formally relinquished its grip on touring affairs it still took more than 30 years for the most pernicious attitudes to be swept away. As ever, MCC's authority was largely wielded as a means of maintaining amateur privilege: an amateur cricketer had a far better chance of being accompanied on tour by his wife than any professional, provided a couple could afford the time and any associated costs.

It was probably not necessary to impose an outright ban; it was enough simply for MCC to make plain its displeasure at the idea of wives accompanying their husbands, and without financial assistance it was effectively something that was out of the reach of the majority. Once teams travelled by plane it became easier for wives to join tours for a short period, and it was at this point that the 21-day limit was brought in. If a partner was to stay longer, she had to take separate accommodation. That a touring player might actually perform better on the field if he had his wife or girlfriend with him never seemed to occur to anyone in a position of authority.

The very first English tour of Australia saw one of the 12 players, George Wells of Sussex, take with him his wife, although the circumstances were slightly unusual as he planned to settle in Melbourne at the end of the trip; in the event they gave up within a few months after he struggled to make an impact on the tour itself or at the club he joined, Richmond CC. When W. G. Grace led an English team to Australia he was joined by Agnes, his wife of two weeks, on what was dubbed a 'honeymoon tour'. He was also accompanied by his brother Fred and best man Arthur Bush, who were members of the team.

Pelham Warner similarly took his fiancée Agnes Blyth with him on his first Test tour of Australia, having first secured the agreement of MCC, which was supervising its first England Test tour. This appeared to set something of a precedent. Johnny Douglas in 1920–21 travelled to Australia with not only his wife but also several members of his family, prompting the team's baggage-manager Bill Ferguson – who had been used by Douglas as something of a valet on the South Africa tour shortly before the war – to complain that he was being commandeered as a nursemaid. Several senior members of the team felt Douglas was as a result distracted from his cricket. These circumstances probably contributed to a brief discussion as to whether Douglas should not drop himself for the third Test after starting the series poorly.

Noticeably, such privileges were not often extended to those who were not captains. S. F. Barnes, a professional who knew his own worth, insisted that he would only go on the 1920–21 tour if his wife was allowed to go with him, but the request was turned down, so he stayed at home.

On a tour of South Africa two years later, several players took with them their wives at their own expense, including Frank Mann, the captain, whose wife was described as a tactful chief of staff off the field – an indication, perhaps, that a captain's wife might have been expected to play a role in helping to ensure that, in social terms, a tour functioned smoothly. Arthur Carr, Arthur Gilligan and the Kent professional Frank Woolley all took their wives with them, and in Woolley's case his family as well – an interesting development given that Woolley was one of those players who had expressed concerns about how Douglas had performed in Australia with his family around him. Admittedly, a South Africa tour was a lower-key affair. Mann noticed that the players' partners were more inclined to complain about selection than their husbands.

When Gilligan then led a tour of Australia in 1924–25, Jack Hobbs, the most eminent professional in English cricket, was eventually allowed to bring his wife, at his own expense, after initially declining to go because he had received a more attractive offer to join a private non-Test tour of South Africa funded by Solly Joel. Desperate to secure Hobbs's services, MCC set aside their usual hardline resistance and Hobbs agreed to tour after all. He thrived too, as he was always likely to, scoring 573 runs in the five Tests.

Such a case was very much the exception: however long a tour, most requests for players to bring out their wives were dismissed out of hand. Reg Simpson had been married for only a couple of weeks when he headed off on his first England Test tour to South Africa in 1948–49, which ran from 7 October until 1 April. Simpson said he was racked with guilt at leaving his wife behind and his form suffered as a consequence; after failing twice in the first Test he did not play again in the series.

The increasing regularity of tours in the post-war years, combined with the relative ease with which wives and girlfriends could join their partners thanks to air travel, served to sharpen the debate and harden the players' reluctance to being browbeaten into submission. The first team to fly out by air, under Len Hutton to the Caribbean, saw a number of wives come out: Denis Compton's wife arrived after the third Test and Hutton's wife and Godfrey Evans's wife flew into Jamaica for the last 11 days of the tour.

Alex Bannister detected the shifting attitudes and that a crisis was in the offing:

> Normally the MCC, like other cricketing bodies, frown in disapproval of wives accompanying the team. This is a human problem which MCC should tackle, with the accent on the heart rather than the head. More than one married player . . . told me he would not agree to go on another tour, if invited, without his wife, and as the celebrities of cricket nowadays are globetrotters theirs is not an unreasonable case. These are the men who bring in the gate-money.

He went on: 'I suggest it would not be asking too much of the authorities to pay the passage money of as many wives as are able and want to accompany their husbands on tour.' Bannister conceded that it might not be practicable for partners to travel with the players to every venue, but even if they were based in one city, 'much heartburning and loneliness would be saved.' In an echo of Reg Simpson's experience in South Africa, Bannister reckoned that the form of some cricketers was affected by long separations, and cited Compton as an example of someone who was far happier once his wife arrived.

The resistance to change was resolute. One problem was that, with a small group of privileged wives joining most England tours from 1953–54 onwards, tour managers – not usually chosen for their liberal attitudes – were habitually reporting back to Lord's that those players joined by their partners effectively cut themselves off from the tour, in their eyes to the detriment of collective spirit.

In fact, when it came to England's attempt under Hutton in 1954–55 to win in Australia for the first time for 22 years, the players were refused permission to bring out their wives until the final stages, even if they bore the cost themselves. Margaret

Hughes thought this was a bad idea for the same reasons as Bannister. 'If wives want to join their husbands at their own expense I think they should be allowed to do so, because winter tours have now become so frequent that cricketers – Test match cricketers – must see less of their homes than they would if they were serving in one of Her Majesty's Forces.'

She suggested wives would not need to attend the official functions to which the players were subjected on a regular basis, although in fact their presence would surely have made the experience more tolerable for everyone. As Reg Simpson had been, Keith Andrew was only just married when he embarked on this, his first Test tour, and as he was called on for just one Test – standing in for the ill Godfrey Evans, he dropped a difficult but as it proved extremely expensive catch – he must have found the tour similarly arduous. Geoffrey Howard was among the more sensitive and caring managers, and had a young family of his own back home, but he still had no time for spouses on tour. When Hutton, Evans and Trevor Bailey were joined by their wives for the final leg in Sydney, with the Ashes already won, Howard noted in his diary: 'From the moment they arrived, their husbands have virtually left the party and I strongly disapprove! . . . It is not right in principle and I shall say so.'

It was a measure of MCC's male-orientated view of the world that while it forcibly kept married couples apart it nevertheless granted permission to Alec Bedser's twin brother Eric, himself a professional at Surrey but never chosen for an England Test tour in his own right, to accompany the teams to Australia and South Africa for which his brother was chosen. Alec, who never married, saw no equivalence when he later served as chairman of selectors for 13 years and manager of two tours of Australia – he remained throughout a staunch opponent of wives coming out on tour.

One of the consequences of more journalists accompanying tours was that they had more opinions about more things. They may have been willing to turn a blind eye to the occasional indiscretions of the players, but many of them seemed to share the same view as the MCC when it came to partners on tour – perhaps in part because they too usually did not have their wives with them – and they were prepared to say so. Peter May, for instance, was heavily criticised for taking with him his new fiancée when he led England in Australia, and for spending so much time with her when she was there. Mind you, some of May's players agreed. 'There's no doubt the whole business was a distraction,' said Tom Graveney. Nonetheless May was joined by Virginia, now his wife, in the Caribbean the following winter, when everyone agreed her presence was a benefit when he fell ill. Within a couple of years May had retired, and the scrutiny on his private life was accepted to have played its part.

Ted Dexter and Raman Subba Row were also joined by their partners for part of the West Indies tour. Susan Dexter's flight was paid for her by her father, and Dexter reflected that 'few professional cricketers could have afforded it.' When Dexter had a poor game, his wife's presence was blamed, and when she joined the tour of Australia that Dexter captained three years later she was again labelled an unhelpful distraction. On that tour, Colin Cowdrey and David Sheppard also had their wives with them for part of the time. M. J. K. Smith, as captain in Australia in 1965–66, was joined by his wife and family for a significant period, much to the indignation of E. M. Wellings when he wrote his tour review in *Wisden*. All these players – May, Dexter, Subba Row, Cowdrey, Sheppard, Smith – were members of cricket's patrician class. Had a run-of-the-mill professional been able to afford to do the same, and had the temerity to suggest such an arrangement to Lord's, it would, Frank Keating suggested, 'have caused mass suicide (by apoplexy) of the committee in the Long Room'.

Journalists criticised wives for being on tour, but wives complained at being left at home.

Fred Trueman's first wife Enid took the opportunity while

being interviewed for a valedictory BBC film of Trueman's Test career in May 1964 to articulate her frustration and unhappiness at the life of a touring widow. 'When you're married to a famous person, everyone expects it to be absolutely out of this world and marvellous,' she said. 'You can also be a very lonely person in the world on your own while your husband's thousands of miles away ... and you won't miss me half as much as I miss you because you've all the social contacts, the cocktail parties, the organised dinners. I have none of those things, I just have the telephone and the reporters and the menace.' She could have been speaking for any number of England players' wives down the years, but emotionally she was at the end of the road. Within weeks, Fred and Enid separated.

As Enid Trueman suggested, there were times when the task of keeping home in the absence of the cricketer-husband was broken by the husband turning national hero. Then, friends and the press would descend on the house in droves. Frank Tyson's exploits in Australia, which turned a 1–0 deficit into a 2–1 lead, resulted in Violet Tyson suddenly opening her door to all and sundry. 'The house hasn't been empty all day,' she informed the *Daily Telegraph.*

Tom Cartwright's reservations about touring South Africa in 1968–69 were not confined to his well-known opposition to the country's politics, which he reviled, but also to a deep reluctance to be away from his young family. Keith Fletcher decided he and his wife would solve the problem of him being away for five months in 1970–71 by her spending most of the winter in Australia while he was there, but it cost him almost his entire tour fee for her to do so.

Dennis Amiss found it difficult touring India and Pakistan for four months in 1972–73 without his wife Jill and one-year-old child, but it was neither affordable nor practical for them to accompany him. 'They [wives] were regarded with huge suspicion by administrators who seemed to believe that their presence would undermine the authority of the management and "esprit de corps" among the players,' Amiss wrote in his autobiography. 'Throughout my Test career the 21-day limit was a source of considerable tension between players and administrators. It also put marriages and relationships under unnecessary stresses and strains ... There is little doubt in my mind that a ruling, supposedly designed to promote team spirit, was utterly counter-productive.'

The tensions Amiss alluded to led to some concessions. For the 1974–75 tour of Australia, six players availed themselves of an opportunity to bring out not only their wives for three weeks but also children over the Christmas period – still at their own expense – a development that led to some strong words from old-time players who still viewed touring as an extension of war. Newspapers dubbed the three weeks of access as a 'love ration', but the players were no longer in the mood for seeing the light-hearted side of the situation. Two players would not have gone on the tour had their wives not been able to come at all. Inevitably, the presence of wives and children was blamed on England's heavy defeat, though in fact the likes of Mike Denness, Alan Knott and Peter Lever did well in the fifth and sixth Tests when their families were with them. '[This] is an emotive issue which is bound to be raised again when MCC next go on tour, and it is time that the unfortunate wives, who have come under attack from almost every journalist and a number of old players commenting on the tour, were reprieved,' Christopher Martin-Jenkins wrote. In fact, when England next went away – to India and Australia in 1976-77 – no wives went with them.

The resentment generated by this issue made it all the easier for players to walk into the arms of Kerry Packer when he offered them an opportunity to join his breakaway World Series Cricket. More astute than the administrators of the establishment game, Packer grasped that players needed to feel emotionally content if they were to perform at full capacity, and he moved swiftly to arrange accommodation for wives and children. In the legal battle fought out in the High Court in London between Packer and cricket authorities, Alan Knott, the England wicketkeeper, who had toured regularly for ten years, cited the issue of families as a major factor in his defection. 'I have played my best cricket when I have been with my wife. Players must be happy and contented. If wives are accepted, things will be very much better.' But still the penny did not drop. When the warring parties made peace and Packer's players returned to their national sides, Knott was still refused permission to place his family in a flat in Sydney while England toured Australia in 1979–80 – so he refused to tour.

With pay levels rising in the post-Packer years, more players could afford to bring out their wives or girlfriends on tour when they wished, and the 21-day rule caused ever greater irritation. Of course, not every player wanted their partners with them: some performed better on the field when they were around, but others found it placed unwanted pressure on them when they might have preferred to focus on their cricket and get enough rest for the next day's game. 'Touring is an unnatural existence and not all wives can be expected to adapt and understand the pressures,' Bob Willis wrote, though clearly his wife Julie did not fall into this category as she stayed in Australia for three months when he led the side there in 1982–83 – a throwback to the old days of captain's privileges.

Having retired as a player, Willis was assistant manager in the West Indies in 1985–86 when wives were banned for the first six weeks in order to allow the players to bond; given that England lost the Test series 5–0 this plan hardly worked for the best. Neither was any financial assistance forthcoming from the TCCB. 'It is difficult to conceive of any company or organisation which would expect such frequent and lengthy absences from its male employees without making some token contribution to a consort's travel,' Frances Edmonds, wife of Phil Edmonds, wrote. 'If a player feels he is prepared to pay give-or-take £1,500 to see his wife for a fortnight, then no one, not even the most egregious members of the TCCB and the press corps, should have the temerity to comment on it.' When she and other wives did join the tour, she felt they 'tended to create a more cohesive and convivial collective'. Graham Gooch was sufficiently disenchanted that he opted out of the following winter's trip to Australia to spend time at home with his wife Brenda and their two young twins.

In return for their attendance at a benefit dinner in London, Robin Smith paid for the wives and partners of several players to join the team over the Christmas period in South Africa in 1995–96. They appreciated the gesture but Ray Illingworth, the tour manager and head of selection, was less pleased, as it increased the size of the travelling group under his command to 64 over the Christmas period. Smith and Illingworth were coming at the issue from diametrically opposed positions. Smith said: 'My argument was that it would reduce stress and make players happy – and therefore improve performances in the middle.' For Illingworth it went a long way towards explaining why England's performances tailed away towards the back end of the Test series. 'It is impossible for a cricketer to be as focused on the tour with his wife there, as much as when she is at home,' he wrote. 'It cannot help the cricketing side of the tour in any way.'

The experiences of that tour contributed to partners being banned altogether from the following winter's 14-week tour of Zimbabwe and New Zealand, a decision taken by a new head coach in David Lloyd and the same captain who had been in charge in South Africa in Mike Atherton, which only further drove a wedge between players and administrators. This was the tour from which Dominic Cork withdrew owing to his domestic circumstances.

Around this time, Darren Gough, England's leading fast bowler, had a heated phone call with board chief executive Tim Lamb. 'I asked him what other sportsmen go away for such a long period of time and are denied their conjugal rights by their employers,' Gough wrote. 'Lamb's answer was typical. "What would you do if you were in the army?" "I'm not in the fucking army, Tim! I'm in the England cricket team. I should be allowed to bring out my wife for ten days in the middle of a three-and-a-half-month tour."' Lamb's riposte to this, according to Gough, was: 'Isn't your marriage strong enough for you to go away this winter without your family?' At which point, Gough lost it. Gough's marriage broke up a few years later.

Andrew Strauss said that even when he first toured with England in 2003–04 there remained a remnant of the old-school attitude of partners distracting the players from their cricket. 'It was disrespectful to the women and did not take into account the positive aspect of having your family around you when you are a long way from home and in a stressful working environment . . . You cannot overestimate the power of having your family around.' He said that, more broadly, family members generally understood that for a period your work came first. 'There are sacrifices. Where it becomes hard is when those sacrifices are non-stop. My feeling is that your wife finds it hard to talk to you about this because if they raise it, then it becomes an issue and you think they are saying: "I don't want you to do this."'

By the time Strauss became England captain and Andy Flower was head coach, the issue of families coming on tour had been more or less resolved to everyone's reasonable satisfaction following discussions in which everyone was involved. It was recognised by all parties that there were periods when the players needed to be left alone to prepare – typically this might be in the lead-up to a major Test series – but also understood and accepted that a touring cricketer and his family would be happier if they were able to spend some time together during a long tour – and that families ought, if possible, to be with the players in their moments of triumph, as happened when England won the T20 World Cup in Melbourne in 2022. The truth was that different relationships operated in different ways, and the scope for partners to come out on tour might depend on whether a couple had children, and if so if they were of school age. It was an important step forward when the cricket authorities were finally prepared to subsidise family travel.

Lengthy separations from wives and girlfriends were one thing, but until quite recently many cricketing fathers also missed the births of their children because they were away on England duty overseas. It was just considered the luck of the draw as to whether the birth happened when they were away or not, and little thought was given to accommodating anyone's wishes to be at home. In the days of boat travel, a quick dash home to be at a birth was simply not practical; air travel made it theoretically possible, but in practice a touring cricketer was still expected to cut himself off emotionally from everything to do with family for the duration of any trip. Times changed and societies expected different things of fathers, but neither was the desire to see a new-born child invented in the 1990s. Many an England cricketer has complained of missing much of the first year of their child's life, and such separations helped finish off their careers as touring cricketers.

All many could do was wait for news. Bert Relf's diary from an Edwardian tour of Australia recorded, as poignantly as anyone has, of the addition of a new member to his family. 'I have another daughter,' he wrote. Lines of communication were of course much better by the 1980s, but even so, when Bob Willis's daughter Katie was born while he was captaining England in New Zealand he missed the phone call from his wife Julie because he was in a management meeting about an injury replacement, and the news had to be passed on to him by the manager A. C. Smith. To spare them worry, some fathers were kept from the full picture; when Geoff Cope's child was born while he was in Pakistan, his wife did not relay to him the details of the complications surrounding the birth until he got home. A rare act of clemency occurred towards the end of the 1959–60 tour of West

Indies when Colin Cowdrey and Fred Trueman were allowed to leave early, missing the four-day detour to Honduras, Cowdrey to get home to see his week-old son Jeremy, and Trueman because the birth of his daughter Karen was imminent.*

In time, of course, there was pushback from players. Graham Gooch withdrew altogether from the tour of Australia in 1986–87 because his wife Brenda gave birth to their twins Sally and Megan – they already had a four-year-old daughter Hannah – and the following winter he chose only to play in the World Cup in India and Pakistan, and the Tests that followed in Pakistan, but not the subsequent tour of Australia and New Zealand. 'Our three children put me under pressure,' he said. 'Yet I am enjoying being a father.' Such cherry-picking rarely met with approval; either administrators or journalists with a column to write tended to look askance at anyone not prepared to put country first.

At a time when it was almost unheard of for sportsmen to miss matches for the birth of a child, Robin Smith negotiated an agreement that he could fly home from an Australia tour for the birth of his son Harrison, which was due to take place during a four-week gap between the first and second Tests, only for members of the management – ironically including Gooch himself as captain – to change their minds because Smith was struggling for form and it was thought he should remain on tour and make runs in some one-day matches instead. Smith delayed telling his wife Kath of the change until the last minute: 'It was heartbreaking when I finally told her,' he recalled. 'The first time I saw my son was a photograph in one of the [British] tabloids.' His original decision won little support from the older generation of players, Geoff Boycott calling him a 'big baby'.

As captain in Australia in 2002–03, Nasser Hussain took the radical step of going out three weeks early with his wife Karen

---

* One of the earliest cases of an England player flying home was Jim Laker from the West Indies in 1953–54, through a combination of circumstances. He had sustained an eye injury and his wife was expecting a child. The rest of the team went home more slowly by boat.

so that she could have their second child Joel there rather than at home. 'I couldn't play cricket while a child I had never seen was back at home in England,' Hussain wrote. 'I'd seen it happen to Ashley Giles and I knew how much it hurt him ... It was a huge thing for her [Karen] to decide she was going to have our baby in another country without her family around her.' The ECB agreed to pay virtually all the costs.

But one of Hussain's players, Steve Harmison, was less fortunate. His daughter Abbie was born at home in the early weeks of the same tour, and it would be three months before he would see her in person. Initially all he had was a picture of her that had been scanned and emailed. 'I printed it off and stared into her eyes,' Harmison said. He had originally hoped to go home after the final Test, when some one-day internationals were being played, but that plan was scuppered by a mounting injury list. The team then flew straight on to South Africa for the World Cup. Harmison was a young player on his first tour and conscious of the financial rewards on offer; he was not really in a position to pick and choose. The tour as a whole lasted 140 days.

Soon after that, things changed permanently for the better. Andrew Strauss was allowed to fly home from Pakistan in 2005–06 – missing the final Test in the process – to attend the birth of his son Sam before flying back within 24 hours. Phil Neale, who as cricket operations manager accompanied England teams overseas for 20 years, said Strauss's return marked a distinct shift in priorities. 'Him [Strauss] coming home from Pakistan for the birth of his first child was the first time I'd really been conscious of family taking precedence over England,' Neale said.

It has since become commonplace for players to fly back from a tour to attend the birth of children, and if they miss Test matches or other big games then so be it. Kevin Pietersen flew home from a World T20 in the Caribbean and James Anderson from Australia, only to be back with the team within a few days. Such arrangements were hardly satisfactory, even if they were better than the alternative. Alastair Cook, as captain, briefly left the build-up phase of a Test series in Bangladesh to be at the birth of his second child Isobel. 'Alice gave birth at 10.30 p.m. and then at 6.30 p.m. the next evening I was getting in a car to go to the airport and not coming home for ten weeks,' he recalled. 'I did not feel great.' Neither were such flits home an exact science. Dawid Malan had been hoping to be at the birth of his daughter after the Ashes tour of 2021–22, but the baby was born prematurely and arrived while the final Test in Hobart was going on. He was pulled to one side in the dressing room to be told the news.

Absence from loved ones is one thing, but being overseas at a time of a family bereavement is an altogether more distressing experience. For some, this happened only shortly after they had embarked on a five- or six-month tour, as was the case with Tom Hayward when he was informed of his mother's death when his boat reached Suez, and Maurice Turnbull, a member of Percy Chapman's team heading for South Africa, who received a cable just after the boat had left Madeira informing him his father had died.

Colin Cowdrey similarly found a telegram waiting for him when he arrived at the Palace Hotel in Perth, telling him that his father had died. Cowdrey was only 21. According to Cowdrey's own account, towards the end of the players' dinner at the hotel that evening, Len Hutton came over to Cowdrey, put his hand on his shoulder and, with tears in his eyes, tried but failed to articulate his sorrow. 'I knew then that it had taken him [Hutton] a long time to work out how to react,' Cowdrey wrote. 'He never mentioned my father again, but from that moment he made certain that I was occupied every minute of the day.' After Geoffrey Howard, the tour manager, spoke to Lord's by phone, it was established that Cowdrey's mother insisted that her son should continue with the tour.* In spite of his youth, Cowdrey responded to this personal crisis with remarkable resilience, playing an innings of 102 in the third Test at Melbourne when England were in serious difficulties.† England went on to win the game.

George Lohmann, while playing a Test match in Sydney, learned by letter of the death of his mother from heart disease almost six weeks earlier. He had taken 8 wickets for 35 runs in the first innings – which to this day remain the best figures for England in a Test in Australia – but understandably he was much less effective in the remainder of the game. Lohmann and his Surrey teammate Walter Read both wore crepe bands around their arms as a sign of mourning, probably the first gesture of this kind by England cricketers during a Test match. Andrew Stoddart was leading his second tour of Australia when on the eve of the series he learnt of his mother's death. With Ranjtisinhji, the team's star batsman, also unwell, the Sydney ground trustees as a consequence took the unprecedented step of postponing the start of the game by 24 hours. This allowed Ranjitsinhji time to recover, but Stoddart was still not in a fit state to play, so the captaincy passed to Archie MacLaren. All the England players wore black armbands on the first day. Stoddart also sat out the second Test and managed only 81 runs in the two games he played in a series England lost 4–1.

Gubby Allen had the unenviable task of informing Ken

---

* Possibly without his mother's instruction, Cowdrey's first tour would have been over before it had effectively begun. There have been others less fortunate in this regard. Douglas Robinson, the Gloucestershire amateur, was chosen as a wicketkeeper for South Africa in 1913–14 but fell ill on arrival and never played a match. Ricardo Ellcock broke down after bowling six balls in the nets at the start of the West Indies tour of 1989–90 with what was later diagnosed as a stress fracture of the back. His tour was over and he, like Robinson, never toured again – and never played for England.
† In later years, when the team travelled by plane, Cowdrey three times left tours early owing to personal circumstances: from the West Indies in 1959–60 owing to the recent birth of his first son; from Pakistan in 1968–69 because of the death of his father-in-law; while in 1974–75 he missed the New Zealand leg of the Australasia tour because his wife was unwell.

Farnes, one of his players in Australia, that Farnes's mother had been killed at home in a car crash. Farnes was naturally devastated, but a few weeks later was still able to play a full part in the last two Tests of the series, and take 11 wickets for his side.

With air travel it became easier for players to return home for a few days on compassionate grounds. Pat Pocock and Geoff Cope both left tours of India in such circumstances in the 1970s. But it took far longer than it should have done for the administrators at Lord's to stop instinctively finding reasons to block every request of this sort. There was no set policy because no committee ever sat down and thought to establish one, and as a result responses varied from case to case, depending on who was in charge.

Brian Statham was given permission to leave a West Indies tour early when his young son was taken ill, but Ken Barrington was not so fortunate when his father-in-law fell gravely ill shortly before Barrington was due to depart for Australia in 1965. Barrington expressly travelled to Lord's to ask for permission to fly out later and join up with the team in Perth – which would only have meant missing the stopover in Colombo – only to be told (presumably by Billy Griffith, the MCC secretary) that his request was denied. 'No, they said,' Barrington recalled, 'because nobody could put a time on how long your father-in-law would live.' Sure enough, having gone with the team from the outset, Barrington received on arrival in Perth a telegram informing him that his father-in-law had died. To his immense credit, Barrington, who was one of the most prolific batsmen England ever had overseas, managed to put his distress to one side to score heavily, recording hundreds in each of the last two Tests.

There was an expectation, which was really based on nothing more than decades of cold-hearted precedent, that a tour must always go on, and those selected must always put themselves second to the needs of the collective. Geoff Boycott's mother died of cancer four weeks before the start of an Australia tour;

he had always lived with her and was devastated both by her gradual, inexorable decline and her passing. To make matters worse, he was summoned by the Yorkshire committee two days after her death and told they were stripping him of the captaincy. The tour was a difficult one for him emotionally and psychologically, and during a conversation with the manager Doug Insole in which he virtually broke down he said that he was not in the right frame of mind to play in the second Test. He was eventually talked round.

David Gower's mother died a week before he left for a tour of West Indies as captain. 'It was a terrible shock, and perhaps had I been in a calmer state of mind I would have delayed my departure,' he reflected later. 'My overriding emotion was to not sit around moping, and I thought getting on with my cricket would be the best thing to do. But once I actually got to the West Indies I realised how emotionally drained I was.' Gower opted out of the first game of the tour against Windward Islands and was widely criticised for doing so when the team lost.

To an extent, the cricketers' families were complicit in this process. When Alec Stewart's mother Sheila was taken into hospital and underwent surgery for a brain tumour, the news was kept from him until after the conclusion of a Test match in Cape Town. He then spoke to her in intensive care by phone and, after much debate among the family, was persuaded, chiefly by his father Micky, himself a former England cricketer, that there was nothing to be gained by him going home, so he stayed on to play in a one-day series. His mother eventually got the all-clear some six months later. Ben Stokes played a Boxing Day Test match at Centurion despite his father Ged, who had travelled to South Africa to watch the series, being taken ill in the days leading up to the game. Stokes missed training on Christmas Eve to spend the day by his father's bedside, but his father's condition improved enough for Stokes to play in the game. Ged died the following year at his home in New Zealand.

*

Some tourists left home single men, but did not always return that way. There was in fact something of a tradition of England cricketers finding future wives on overseas trips, though these cases would have been heavily outnumbered by the marriages that fell apart under the strain of long periods of enforced separation.

The extent to which cricket tours became opportunities for womanising and infidelity was not a topic that cricketers' memoirs tended to dwell on, at least until more recent times (and even then only elliptically). There were occasional clues. On the very first English cricketing expedition overseas, Fred Lillywhite's eye was caught by the ladies of Philadelphia: 'If any additional incentive had been required to induce the English Eleven to exhibit their skill to the greatest advantage, it was afforded by the presence of so large and beautiful an assemblage of the fair sex ... one of the most delightful pictures that the eye of man could rest upon.'

On James Lillywhite's tour, the team's plans for an early morning departure from Greymouth for their next destination were delayed, 'owing to one of our lot fancying some other person's bed better than his own', as James Southerton put it. It took the rest of the party more than an hour driving round to various places where it was thought most likely he would be found. 'He was at length unearthed, looking as fresh as – a salt fish.' On the first of his four tours of Australia, Andrew Stoddart met a young woman who was already married, and embarked on a relationship with her that eventually resulted in them marrying nearly 20 years later.

'On tours cricketers come in for a great deal of hero worship, some of it from members of the fair sex,' stated Arthur Carr, who toured South Africa in the 1920s, in *Cricket with the Lid Off*, published in 1935. 'After a long day you are far more anxious to have a drink and a bath than stand signing your name in books and exchanging commonplace remarks with even pretty young women.' Carr may have been protesting too much. Hopper

Levett, a wicketkeeper on Douglas Jardine's tour of India, referenced many years after the event some of the perks laid on by the Maharajah of Patiala. 'Dancing girls? Oh yes, they were at our behest if required. That was part of the set-up in India, part of the hospitality.'

Wally Hammond, described by his biographer David Foot as 'a philanderer on the grand scale', was well known for his enthusiastic pursuit of women home and abroad. Hammond once described the southern Cape as 'a glorious place when you come creaming in on a surf board beside a South African girl', and it would be a South African girl, a beauty queen called Sybil Ness-Harvey, whom he encountered at a reception in Durban on the 1938–39 tour, who accelerated the end of his first marriage. When photographs of them together found their way back to the English newspapers, Hammond's wife Dorothy headed out to South Africa in a tragic and futile bid to salvage the relationship. Within months of the divorce being granted after the war, Wally and Sybil were themselves married.

It was unnecessary to have a degree in anthropology to discern where the interests of groups of young cricketers might lie when not actually involved in sport. Sometimes steps were taken to protect the decency of young females when the cricketers arrived in town. When one post-war English troupe reached the dairy and agricultural town of Lismore in New South Wales, and a dance was organised by the local cricket association, 'all the girls who wanted to come had to pass a "test" by going in front of a board composed of men from the local cricket council.' The reminiscences of some of the players suggested that the vetting process – whatever it was – may not have been entirely successful. Margaret Hughes had it drawn to her attention by Keith Miller, the most glamorous of Australia's sporting icons of the 1950s, how 'all the beautiful young girls of Melbourne' would sit in front of the players' dressing-rooms at the MCG to catch their eye.

Correspondents of many years' standing were little better

than the players when it came to disclosing everything that went on. Those who did were liable to make themselves unpopular. When Doug Insole said of Charles Bray and Frank Rostron that they were prepared to write about off-the-field stories, or the social side of touring, it was not meant as a compliment. Ian Wooldridge, the *Daily Mail* columnist, alluded long after the event to Godfrey Evans notching a certain kind of century on a boat trip to Australia in 1946–47. Michael Davie, covering an Australian tour for the *Observer*, referred to 'the same knots of awed local girls in the hotel lobbies choosing their favourites'.

It took someone with a different perspective to tell things as they were. 'It is pointless to pretend that three- and four-month tours are not going to involve a fair amount of hanky-panky,' Frances Edmonds noted in her account of a West Indies tour. 'There are quite a few ships, or even British Airways 747s, that pass in the night. The regular press corps turns a very blind eye to what goes on.' She added: 'Homesick and homeless people are understandably liable to misbehave.'

Single men, of course, could do what they liked, and a cricketer from this same era, Derek Pringle, in an autobiographical work published almost 40 years later, alluded to some of what that entailed. Bob Platt recounted long after Fred Trueman's first tour had taken place how Trueman, no doubt still nursing a grievance at being docked bonus money, grumbled about what else had gone on during the tour. 'He used to say, "Some players on that tour were shagging . . . and all I did was fucking swear."'

When Allan Lamb published a post-retirement autobiography, he agreed to his wife Lindsay contributing a chapter which addressed the impact Lamb's behaviour on tour had had on their relationship. His first Test tour was to Australia in 1982–83 and she joined him for some of the time. 'It took just one tour to convince me that the wives were better off joining part of the tour rather than staying at home – and not just to shorten the time of separation,' she wrote. 'I am not stupid. I know that cricketers are no different from other young men on the loose.'

The following winter in New Zealand generated tabloid headlines of womanising and the use of recreational drugs. 'It would be dishonest to say that things didn't change after that tour of New Zealand,' she went on. 'I was shattered when all sorts of rumours started to come out, [and] it was the sex stories that tore me apart ... I was not so much bothered whether it was true or not, I just couldn't take it being all over the front pages.' It took a few years to stabilise the relationship, but the marriage survived. 'If you don't keep your husband's bed warm at night,' Lindsay Lamb concluded, 'then someone else might.'

The most significant liaison involving an English cricketer overseas must have been Ivo Bligh's courtship of Florence Morphy, governess to the children of William Clarke, head of one of the leading families in Victoria, which gave material substance to the Ashes legend when Lady Janet Clarke, the family matriarch, in alliance with Florence, presented Bligh with an urn supposedly containing the ashes of English cricket during Bligh's tour of Australia in 1882–83. Bligh returned to Australia two years later to marry Florence, having in the meantime secured the approval of his father, the Earl of Darnley.

In the 1890s, Archie MacLaren, one of England's best batsmen of the era, met on his first voyage to Australia his future wife, Kathleen Maud Power, the daughter of Robert Power, a director of the Dalgety pastoral empire and founder member of the Victoria Racing Club. By the time of his next tour, the wedding was in train. MacLaren left England two weeks earlier than the rest of the team to spend time with his future in-laws, and the wedding itself took place in a Catholic church in South Yarra two weeks after the completion of the Test series. It was attended by 12 members of the tour party and was a chaotic event, with onlookers forcing entry. One newspaper reported that 'the church was crammed to suffocation with highly excited spectators.'

In similar fashion, Percy Chapman married Beet, sister of Tom Lowry, the New Zealand cricketer, at the end of the

Ashes tour of 1924–25. They had first met at Cambridge and become engaged at the Lowry family home in Okawa, North Island during a non-Test tour of Australia and New Zealand. As a couple in England, they would feature prominently on the society pages of newspapers. Eddie Dawson moved more swiftly still. He met a girl during an early match against Natal on the 1927–28 tour of South Africa and was engaged to her by the time he returned to Durban for the final Test match.

Johnny Human, another of those who went to India with Douglas Jardine, was subsequently a member of the side sent to Australia in 1935–36 on a bridge-building exercise following Bodyline. He was still in his early twenties. During the outward voyage, he spotted an attractive young woman diving elegantly into one of the ship's swimming pools and was immediately smitten. Errol Holmes, the team's captain, warned Human he was too young to be leaving his heart behind in Australia. 'That is just what he did *not* do!' Holmes recalled later. 'Instead, he eventually married the girl, who was as sweet and charming as she was pretty.' Molly Walder was the daughter of the then Lord Mayor of Sydney, and Human ended up settling in the city. 'He was our only "casualty",' Holmes noted.

When George Mann's team arrived by train in Durban in 1948–49, the local liaison in charge of transport, an English army officer, met the players on the platform and announced that he had arranged for a hand-picked group of drivers to take them to their hotel. There on the steps outside the station were ten 'attractive, smart and charming girls'. The drivers joined the players for coffee at the hotel.

One of them, Valerie Platt, who came from a wealthy South African family, became romantically involved with Denis Compton, whose first marriage to Doris, a dancer, following a wartime romance, had quickly cooled. Valerie eventually became the second Mrs Compton and they had two sons, Patrick and Richard, but this marriage too did not last, partly because Valerie favoured living in South Africa and Denis could not give up England, even though he regarded South Africa fondly as a second home.*

'My first two marriages did not really have a chance to survive,' Compton reflected later. 'Test cricketers have the hardest job of all to hold their marriages together because of all the touring.' Compton was also an incredibly glamorous figure, a dazzling cricketer and handsome man who received many approaches. 'The temptations were always there,' he added. 'I remember once sitting having my dinner on board ship on the way to Australia when a beautiful blonde lady came from her table and asked me to autograph her menu. As she thanked me, she pushed her table napkin furtively into my hands. Written in lipstick on the napkin was the number of her cabin . . . I think it is fair to say that I was always one of the boys.'

George Mann himself met his future wife – a South African, Margaret Marshall Clark – on the voyage home from the 1948–49 tour; they were married a few months later. Mike Brearley met his wife Mana while touring India as vice-captain to Tony Greig.

Modern tours are far more compact than they used to be, with fewer days of leisure and fewer low-key 'side matches', and perhaps this has resulted in fewer cricketers meeting their future wives on their travels. Those women who met a cricketer while he was on tour at least had an inkling of the type of itinerant life he led, but that did not necessarily make it any easier to cope when they were subsequently left alone for months on end. Bill Edrich, Denis Compton's 'twin' on the field for Middlesex and England, got through five marriages of his own and, as Geoffrey Howard's anecdote about Edrich throwing a photograph of his wife out of a ship's porthole suggested, touring was doubtless a contributory factor in the breakdown of some of those relationships.

---

* Richard Compton's son Nick Compton played 16 Tests for England, touring India, New Zealand and South Africa.

Ian Wooldridge, who covered the 1962–63 Australia tour, described the impact the constant round of social events provided by British High Commissions, state premiers and local cricket associations had on the players. 'These [functions] were invariably attended by many attractive wives and daughters of our generous hosts. To my knowledge, three English marriages collapsed during that tour, but there may have been more. There were certainly several narrow escapes.' The surprise was not how many marriages collapsed as a result of touring, but how many survived.

If couples were to survive, they needed to be stable to endure the separation and hardship. Phil Tufnell's relationship with Jane McEvoy was far from steady when he went to India and Sri Lanka in 1992–93, and his fragile mental state was only compounded by some erratic performances in the build-up to the first Test. Tufnell badly lost his temper during a warm-up match at Visakhapatnam, angered by some adverse umpiring decisions and a missed stumping of Sachin Tendulkar, and he continued to rage throughout a disciplinary meeting with the management at which he was fined £500. He only calmed down later after putting away a couple of drinks while sitting on the edge of a rooftop balcony which his room-mate Robin Smith estimated to be 50 metres above the ground. Smith found Tufnell there in a distressed state and summoned help from the Reverend Andrew Wingfield-Digby, who was acting as a spiritual adviser to the team. Smith wrote later that he feared Tufnell might take his own life. Tufnell recovered sufficiently to bowl well later on the tour, but Jane left him after he returned from a West Indies tour the following year.

It was at the time of that same India tour that Gooch's own marriage to Brenda, which he had gone to such lengths to protect in the 1980s, finally broke down. The relationship had been in difficulties during his many absences on tour, with Gooch's profile and commitments growing exponentially with his promotion to the England captaincy, but news of the impending split only broke on the eve of departure. Gooch had told his wife two weeks before Christmas that he would not be returning home once the tour was over. In an interview, Brenda recounted how when he went away on tour the children kept asking when he was coming home: 'Is it today, Mummy?'

The irony was that while Gooch might have regarded Tufnell as a potential liability on tour, it was Gooch who had on a number of occasions opted to stay at home in the winter. In fact, Gooch had one of the biggest discrepancies between home and away Test appearances of all England cricketers (74 Tests at home, 44 away), whereas Tufnell played for England far more overseas (12 home, 30 away).

International cricketers have always been away from home an inordinate amount of time, but in recent years the game's administrators, albeit under pressure from players' agents and union representatives, have striven to provide them with as much holistic support as they can. No England player would now be expected to put the team before their own family. Unfortunately there will still be occasions when they are in the wrong place at the wrong time, but these are far fewer than in the past.

CHAPTER 17

Christmas and New Year

Packed houses, parties and plum pudding

An integral part of many of the bigger tours is the showpiece Tests over Christmas and New Year. Commercially these are among the most prized in the calendar. The general public is on holiday and able to turn out in large numbers, and provided the fixture is an attractive one and the weather good, they will generally do so. If the host city is also a tourist-friendly one, England's travelling support will be strong.

Generally, England tours of Australia and South Africa satisfy these criteria best, with the modern pattern in Australia being for Melbourne to host the Boxing Day Test and Sydney the one around New Year; in South Africa the location of the Boxing Day match varies – with Durban a recent favourite – while Cape Town has staged a Test at New Year on every England tour since 1922–23. Partly because of these well-established schedules, an agreement between players and the ECB was reached around the turn of the century whereby England tours to other countries would not be held at this time in order to allow the cricketers to be at home for at least two out of every four Christmases. On a number of occasions since they have arrived back from the subcontinent on 22, 23, or 24 December, but the deal has been stuck to.

Overall, around one in four of all England's Tests in Australia have been played during this holiday period and one in three of their Tests in South Africa.* Apart from the bumper gate receipts, such scheduling tends to greatly enhance broadcast revenues as well.

The practice of squeezing two Tests into this 'golden fortnight' was started by the South Africans, who by the inter-war period were engineering fast turnarounds between Christmas Tests in Johannesburg and New Year ones in Cape Town. This continued through to the last of England's visits before the anti-apartheid boycott began. On George Mann's tour of 1948–49, the players of both sides were given just one day to get themselves from Johannesburg (where a record crowd of 33,000 watched on 27 December) to Cape Town in order to start a fixture on 1 January. Two-day gaps between Tests featured in South Africa long before they became the norm elsewhere, and even after ICC insisted on a minimum three days between Tests, Cricket South Africa successfully lobbied the world governing body to allow only two days between the Christmas and New Year Tests on the 2015–16 tour. The Cape Town Test of 1956–57 was played without a rest day – an unusual practice for that era – in order to maximise holiday crowds.

The pattern in Australia was less frantic. England would often play a Test in Sydney in the lead-up to Christmas in the expectation that it would finish before Christmas, although as Tests there were played to a conclusion before the Second World War there were no guarantees as to how many days a match might last. On Arthur Gilligan's tour, a Test in Sydney starting on Friday, 19 December required two rest days to take account

---

* Matches played during the Christmas and New Year period are defined here as those games starting on dates between 20 December and 5 January. As England venture overseas every winter, they tend to be away from home over this period more often than any other country. By way of comparison, Australia have only six times played Tests outside their own country at this time, and not at all since 1969–70.

of a Sunday and Christmas Day, and did not conclude until Saturday, 27 December, and therefore spanned nine days from start to finish. The aggregate gate was a very healthy 165,706, higher than anything achieved in any of the Tests on the previous tour of 1920–21.*

For many years, the cricketing focal point of the festive period in Australia was a Test around New Year assigned to Melbourne, always the largest and most lucrative venue in the country. The match fitted seamlessly into the social calendar, as Margaret Hughes noted in 1954–55: 'Over 65,000 cricket enthusiasts flocked to the cricket ground on the first day, Friday, New Year's Eve, most of whom were going to sit through the day's cricket, go on to three or four parties during the night, not go to bed at all but get to the ground early again for Saturday's play.' Some of the highest officially recorded attendances for any cricket matches anywhere in the world were achieved when England played in Melbourne at this time. The 1936–37 Test starting on New Year's Day with the Ashes in the balance was watched by 350,534 (including an unprecedented 87,798 on Monday, 4 January), the one in 1946–47 also starting on the first day of the year drew 343,675, and the 1950–51 Test beginning on New Year's Eve aggregated 300,270.

It was not until the mid-1970s that the Australian Cricket Board first put on Tests in Melbourne starting on Boxing Day, followed by one in Sydney at New Year, and this formula was not repeated until the early 1990s. Before then, the usual practice was to allow the touring cricketers to head out of the big cities and spend Christmas in a more relaxed environment,

---

* Two England Tests overseas have involved successive rest days because a Sunday fell next to Christmas Day at a time when both days were regarded as off-limits in playing terms: at Johannesburg in 1922–23 and Melbourne 1950–51. On the first occasion, 18 wickets fell on an indented pitch on the first day, but after two days without play the pitch changed character and South Africa scored 420 in their second innings to set up a win. On the second in Melbourne, with the match in the balance at the point of the two-day hiatus, some of the England players stayed up until 4 a.m. on Christmas Eve and drank 20 bottles of champagne on Christmas Day. They lost the match.

even if they might still be required to play a number of low-key fixtures in places such as Bendigo, Ballarat or Geelong, usually involving play on Christmas Eve or Boxing Day, before heading to Melbourne. But back-to-back Boxing Day–New Year Tests proved a financial winner with both public and the TV companies, and attending the start of the Boxing Day Test became a firm tradition among Melbournians. Since 1990–91, every England tour of Australia (like those to South Africa) has featured back-to-back 'holiday' Tests.

The sheer size of the Melbourne Cricket Ground, which was redesigned to host the Olympic Games in 1956 and underwent further redevelopments which took its capacity to around 100,000, made it the most imposing of cricket's traditional venues. Even in the 1930s, Neville Cardus described the MCG as a 'great amphitheatre' that 'dwarfed the sense of personal identity', the crowd letting out great roars when Don Bradman went out to bat or when they sensed English blood. 'Who would not be anxious going in to bat in the vast amphitheater of the Melbourne Cricket Ground?' asked Christopher Martin-Jenkins in the 1970s. 'To the players themselves the seething holiday crowd of 77,165 must have seemed like all the Romans in the Empire screaming for the blood of innocent Christians.'

More recent modifications to the players' facilities were made primarily to suit Australian Football, the other sport the MCG seasonally hosted; as a consequence the changing rooms were down in a dungeon, leaving a 50-metre walk simply to get onto the field. Matt Prior called the MCG 'as close to a colosseum as you're going to get'. Jonathan Trott said: 'Before you get to the field . . . you feel the heat and hear the noise.' It was Andrew Strauss who described Boxing Day simply as 'Pom-bashing day'.

The commercial potential of the Christmas–New Year period was evident from the earliest times. The very first match played by an English team in Australia started on 1 January 1862, and across the four days that Heathfield Stephenson's team took on Eighteen of Victoria at the Paddock in Yarra Park, Melbourne, around 45,000 people, including Sir Henry Barkly, the Governor of Victoria, were estimated to have attended. It helped that a public holiday was declared and the weather was glorious, even if the intense heat blistered the skin of the visiting cricketers. With the money taken at the gates supplemented by revenue generated from advertising hoardings, scorecards and pitches sold to refreshment stalls, the tour organisers Spiers and Pond took a stupendous £7,000, guaranteeing the financial success of the tour in one hit.

The opening fixture of the third English tour of Australia under W. G. Grace in 1873–74 began on Boxing Day and was watched by more than 40,000. 'The promoters of the trip looked very smiling as they saw the piles of half-crowns on the desks,' James Southerton's dispatch noted. One thing these pioneering tours established was that the cricketers could strike it rich if they were prepared to play when everyone else was on holiday, or not at work.

One of the advantages of air travel was that it allowed teams heading to the West Indies to start their tours later and thereby enjoy Christmas at home rather than on a boat fighting the Atlantic swell. This did not spare Len Hutton's team in 1953–54, when they became the first England touring team to travel out by plane, only for a ten-day stopover in Bermuda to be thrown in en route to Jamaica. Originally it was proposed that they should play a match there on Christmas Day, but this idea was scrapped, and instead the players were hosted either at Government House or by local families. They thought it a pretty cheerless experience.

Until the 1980s, most tours of the subcontinent spanned Christmas and New Year and it was in Delhi in 1972 that England for the only time played Test cricket on Christmas Day. It was the fifth and final day of the game, and England, having been left 207 to win, started on 106 for three need- ing another 101 for victory. They quickly lost one of their overnight batsmen, Barry Wood, but were then seen to their target by Tony Lewis, captaining England for the first time, with an unbeaten 70 and Tony Greig on 40 not out. There followed a glass of champagne and congratulatory telegrams, and then some of the team rode back to the hotel on the roof of their bus to salute the crowds. 'There were no paper hats in the dressing room,' Lewis wrote in his autobiography. 'It was just like any day of Test cricket except that in the lift of the hotel they had Bing Crosby singing, "Chestnuts roasting on an open fire".' The players then headed off to the British High Commission to drink beer and play darts.* Next day they flew to Calcutta.

Eden Gardens, Calcutta was a regular venue for a New Year Test match, and the game there starting on 1 January 1982 was watched by what was almost certainly the largest crowd to see a cricket match; the overall attendance was put at 394,000, but was probably even more, due to officials selling on around about 2,000 extra tickets per day. Indian gate figures were generally only loosely calculated.

It was in an attempt to take advantage of a captive holiday market that it was agreed to abandon the New Year Test at Melbourne in 1970–71 on the third day after rain prevented a start and instead stage a limited-overs match – what is now regarded as the first ever one-day international. More than 46,000 people turned up, generating healthy receipts of £17,000. Inevitably, when England next toured the administrators tried to have it both ways, arranging Tests in Melbourne on Boxing Day and Sydney on 4 January, with an ODI at the MCG on New Year's Day. It did not really work, only 20,000 turning up for the one-dayer, probably because the Melbourne Test went the full five days and ended in a thrilling draw, sating local

---

* England have played ten Tests in which Christmas Day formed a rest day. They started on 19 December (Sydney 1924–25); 22 December (Melbourne 1950–51); 23 December (Johannesburg 1922–23 and 1964–65; Delhi 1981–82); and 24 December (Johannesburg 1927–28, 1930–31, 1938–39 and 1956–57; Melbourne 1994–95).

appetites. The Australian board continued to juggle Tests and ODIs over the holiday period until it concluded from 1994–95 onwards that back-to-back Tests alone was the way to go.

England teams have spent more than 80 Christmases on tour. It could be a difficult time to be away, although it was made easier once families were allowed to come out during this period. To make matters worse, England teams rarely arrived at Christmas holding a lead in the Test series. This has happened only four times since the First World War in series in which one Test had been played by Christmas, and only four times at all when two or more Tests had been completed by then. The only England teams since 1978 to reach Christmas with a lead were Mike Gatting's side in Australia in 1986–87, when they were 1–0 up after three, and Michael Vaughan's in South Africa in 2004–05 on the back of a seven-wicket win in Port Elizabeth four days earlier. Of course, it was not always necessary to be ahead in the series for Christmas to be a memorable occasion: Len Hutton's side enjoyed a riotous Christmas party having just levelled things up at 1–1 with a thrilling 38-run win in Sydney.

In any case, a lead guaranteed nothing. Neville Cardus described Christmas Eve in Sydney in 1936, with England a scarcely believable 2–0 up, thus: 'We all gave presents to [Gubby] Allen and congratulated him "in advance", though there was always the thought of Bradman in our minds. The jubilation in England, telegraphed to us, rather damped our high spirits; it was the optimism which breeds trouble. The team was never really good enough to beat Australia in Australia; as one or two of the English players said: "We are getting away with it".' Sure enough, Australia recovered and emerged 3–2 victors.

Denis Compton eloquently described his feelings of melancholy at spending Christmas away from his wife Doris and young son Brian on the first Test tour undertaken by England after the war. Compton had served three years in India and after demobilisation had been home only six months before he left for Australia on 31 August 1946. He had married his wartime sweetheart and now found himself on the other side of the world for more than seven months. To an extent, Compton and his teammates had little time to dwell on their absence from loved ones, because they had a string of holiday fixtures to fulfil: a two-day game in Newcastle ending on 23 December, another two-dayer in Canberra on 27 and 28 December, before they moved on to Bendigo for a match on 30 December. There was then just time to take the train to Melbourne for the New Year Test. Christmas itself was spent in Sydney.

'How strange it all seemed. Christmas in the sun; cricket on the eve of the Festive Day; loved ones 11,000 miles away,' Compton wrote in *Testing Time for England*, published the following year.

> I can assure you the parting from my wife, Doris, and small son, Brian, hit me very hard at this time. To some extent I felt very homesick, and when Koala Bears for Brian came in from fans, and one, without giving his name, sent a toy dog to which was attached a card on which was printed: 'For Your Son', I felt like taking the first boat home! ... Long partings, now I have settled down, are never welcome.

A Christmas dinner was put on by Walter Hammond, the captain, and manager Rupert Howard and 'every man encouraged to act as if he were at home with his folks'. Paper hats were worn, everyone had to give a speech and Dick Pollard entertained the group at the piano. Compton's day was spoiled by a phone call he had booked home not coming through; by the time it did, on Boxing Day, he was on the morning train to Canberra. 'Naturally I was upset.'

Paul Gibb, another member of the party, found Christmas in Sydney every bit as challenging as Compton. On arrival from Newcastle on Christmas Eve, Gibb received a batch of mail but deliberately held off until the next morning from opening his letters. Later on Christmas Day he wrote in his diary: 'The thought of the kids safely wrapped up for the night and the biggest thrill of their little lives in the morning. Cannot claim team's Christmas dinner was huge success. One or two raised a sparkle after a few drinks, but obviously all wished they were at home. Skipper Walter did his best to get liquor into me: I turned down all offers. Dick played a few songs on [the] piano before we put on paper caps and ate our dinner.'

The mood would not have been helped by England's heavy defeats in the first and second Tests, and this may have explained senior fast bowler Bill Voce's speech at the dinner 'pledging all support for his captain'. Gibb kept wicket in the first Test but thereafter played only a minor role on the tour, which surely made his ordeal harder. Not required for the Canberra match, he was among those seconded to attend a garden party at the British high commissioner's house where there was little food or drink ('not a great advertisement for the United Kingdom'). They also met the Duke of Gloucester. Those not involved in the Canberra match shared grumbles about the way the tour was being run.

Things ran more smoothly on and off the field in South Africa two winters later. The South African Cricket Association arranged phone calls home for Len Hutton and Johnny Wardle, while the South African Broadcasting Corporation helped each member of George Mann's party to send Christmas Day messages to their families. With the team having sneaked to a two-wicket win in the first Test in Durban, spirits were high once the players got through a two-day fixture against a Natal Country Districts XI at Ladysmith and arrived in Johannesburg. There on Christmas Eve they went to see *Oklahoma!* and had supper at the Carlton Hotel, where they were treated to a lavish display of fresh meat at a time when most British people were only used to the tinned variety. Mike Green, the manager, called it 'quite a sensation'.

On the earliest tours of Australia, the Christmas period was often treated as one for recreation and relaxation, and if cricket was played it was very much of the social variety. It was just such an occasion, a casual afternoon game on the paddock at the Rupertswood estate at Sunbury, north of Melbourne, that sealed the legend of the Ashes on Christmas Eve 1882. After Ivo Bligh's team completed the formality of victory over the local side, the hostess Lady Janet Clarke – as previously alluded to – presented the English captain with a small urn containing some ashes, a reference to a story already in popular circulation since the *Sporting Times*'s mock obituary of English cricket following the defeat at the Oval four months earlier.

Bligh's team were on a mission to reclaim the ashes that the obituary stated had been taken to Australia – Bligh's own early speeches on the tour confirmed as much – and now the quest had a physical manifestation.* Bligh actually spent ten days at Rupertswood over the holiday period, and the other amateurs in the team a week there, Bligh having formed a strong attachment to Florence Morphy, a governess at the house. The amateur members of the team all spent Christmas Day at the house before heading next morning to Ballarat for a noon start in a three-day match against a local XVIII. Life was less glamorous for the four professionals left behind in Melbourne; part of their Christmas Day involved taking the train to Ballarat.

Such journeys were not unusual. George Lohmann, the great Surrey bowler, once took the train from Melbourne to Ballarat huddled in the baggage van of a crowded train in order to be there in time for a Boxing Day match. He enjoyed a happier Christmas in South Africa as a member of Lord Hawke's 1898–99 side: his lordship and the other amateurs in the party were

---

* Bligh's team were duly judged successful in their quest, not by winning a Sunday afternoon game at Rupertswood, but by prevailing in two of three Test matches against Australia, the first of which started on 30 December, six days after Lady Janet's presentation. An additional Test was played later on the tour (and was won by Australia) but did not form part of the original three-match series.

treated to a picnic at a government farm at High Constantia, but in the evening amateurs and professionals dined together at the Royal Hotel, where they had plum pudding, strawberries and cream. Lord Hawke, always mindful of the needs of his professionals at Yorkshire, distributed presents to all his players.

Bert Relf, one of the professionals on the first MCC-organised tour of Australia, also found some of his Christmas Day taken up with preparations for a match against an XVIII in Bendigo, although there was also time for 'singing and dancing'. Relf's diary entries for Christmas Eve and Christmas Day 1903 included the following: '24 December, Melbourne: Went to theatre to see *The Great Millionaire*, before Mr Christie took us round Chinese quarters in Little Bourke Street – interesting to see opium smoking and gambling dens but would not go again. 25 December: Very hot. Packing. Stroll around having drink or two to old folks at home. After dinner, drawing-room, some singing and dancing. Left for Bendigo game by 4.50 train.' The fixture at the goldfield city of Bendigo became something of a Boxing Day staple in the years before the First World War.

On one of Andrew Stoddart's tours, the entire party, amateurs and professionals, were given a week's holiday over Christmas at Gippsland Lakes, where they were able to hunt, shoot and fish. On Christmas Eve, a group went to Lake Tyers where, according to J. T. Hearne's diary, they 'finished up a good day's sport by getting about 40 brace of snipe, one hare (very large), one blue crane and two very fine specimens of blue snake and all of us soaking wet through up to the knees'. Tom Richardson shot dead a snake measuring 5 or 6 feet, and Stoddart dispatched a stag.

Hearne recorded that they spent Christmas Day travelling by train back to Melbourne, but the caterer aboard 'gave us real Christmas dinner', adding: 'One might have fancied they were at home except for the beautiful green peas we had – not so at home.' They otherwise played poker most of the way. Boxing Day was spent at leisure, though Hearne noted that 'the chaps that have not been from home at Christmas [before] seem a bit down, Ted Wainwright especially. He remarked very feelingly at the breakfast table, "I wish I was in the little cot [cottage] turning the meat."' Two days later the team reached Bendigo, where they took on a local XVIII in temperatures touching 119 degrees (48°C). On Stoddart's previous tour the players were in Sydney for Christmas and spent Boxing Day at Randwick races.

Such days of relaxation were to be treasured. One Christmas, Charles Fry scaled Table Mountain only to come down to earth, literally, with two single-figure scores in an unexpected defeat to a Western Province XV. On Christmas Day of the Bodyline tour, Bill Bowes and Hedley Verity climbed Mount Wellington overlooking Hobart while their captain Douglas Jardine fished up-country with friends. The following winter in India, during a two-week hiatus in play, Jardine left most of his team to be entertained by the Mayor of Calcutta while he went off in pursuit of his first tiger kill; he failed but Charles Marriott, his hunting companion and the team's leg-spinner, did not.

As we have seen with Tony Lewis's team, India tour schedules made little accommodation for Christmas Day. The first side to go there after the war spent the day at the Calcutta Cricket Club, where everyone in the party took part in a social match in which those going out to bat walked past a lit-up Christmas tree. Ted Dexter's side completed a match in Cuttack on 24 December before travelling on to Calcutta, where their Christmas Day entertainment involved lunch at the Great Eastern Hotel and, for a few, a visit to the exclusive Tollygunge club, before starting another three-day game on Boxing Day. 'Some were more homesick than others,' Dexter recalled matter-of-factly.

The Calcutta club was also the focal point of Christmas for Tony Greig's team, whose drinking got a little out of hand, resulting in Keith Fletcher cracking a bone in his ankle falling down some stairs. 'We managed to get him back to the Grand Hotel [where] the stricken batsman was left outside [physio Bernard] Thomas's room, lying on a room-service trolley, with a tablecloth covering him,' Fletcher's room-mate Mike Selvey wrote. 'We knocked and ran away.' Fletcher's foot ended up in plaster and he missed the next two Tests. While the rest of the tour party were farmed out to local expat families, Fletcher and Selvey stayed behind and ate mutton curry garnished with a sprig of plastic holly in the hotel coffee shop. The team spent much of Boxing Day at the airport waiting to fly north to Guwahati.

The next full Test tour of India under Fletcher's captaincy saw the team preparing for a Test match starting on 23 December with an eight-hour journey down the Grand Trunk Road straight after completing an ODI in Jullundur. They arrived in Delhi at 2 a.m. on the eve of the game. Remarkably, England managed to bat for all of the first two days (before the Christmas Day rest day), losing only four wickets in the process.

The camaraderie among players on tour grew as the social barriers between amateurs and professionals came down, and the sheer familiarity of travelling together bred something close to content. The more regular the tours, the more entrenched became the habits. Christmas became something of a compulsory party, an opportunity for enforced jollity to keep flagging spirits alive. A fancy-dress party became a routine feature of Christmases in Australia especially, and was generally considered a successful way of helping everyone through a difficult day when most wives or families were not around.

Until the mid-1990s, first-time tourists were often required to perform a sketch. The fancy-dress party probably had its origins in the days when teams travelled out by boat, such parties being common entertainments with all passengers during long sea voyages. Godfrey Evans as Carmen Miranda was a staple feature. Bob Wyatt's team heading to the Caribbean in 1934–35 was actually aboard ship on Christmas Day. There was a service to start with – Errol Holmes, Wyatt's vice-captain, noting how strange it was 'to be singing well-known hymns and carols at sea and in broiling heat' – but the evening was given over to a fancy-dress party at which Maurice Leyland and Walter Hammond dressed up as convicts.*

The following winter Holmes led a non-Test tour of Australia and New Zealand which saw the team involved in a first-class game against Canterbury on Christmas Day, but play did not start until the afternoon in order to allow the players to attend morning service. Before English visits to New Zealand got tacked onto the end of Australia tours, it was something of a tradition for the MCC–Canterbury fixture to take place on Christmas Day; this happened on the 1922–23 tour which was led by the ageing Archie MacLaren and on the first England tour that involved Tests under Harold Gilligan in 1929–30. On the first of these occasions, an earthquake briefly interrupted play during the afternoon, shaking the timbers of the grandstand at Lancaster Park.†

Church going was strong among touring parties for many years. Cricket in England was not played on Sundays until the 1960s, but when England teams went abroad there were times when they were expected to play on the Sabbath. This was especially the case in India, where a number of England's early Tests involved Sunday play: England's first Test there in Bombay in 1933 drew an estimated crowd of 45,000 on a Sunday. This led to difficulties on Arthur Gilligan's tour in 1926–27 shortly before India's promotion to Test status, with Jack Parsons refusing to turn out in games with Sunday play until Gilligan threatened to send him home at his own cost unless he did so. In the end a compromise was reached whereby Parsons was allowed to leave a game early in order to attend evening services. Parsons was subsequently ordained into the church in 1929.

---

* This was one of two Christmases England teams have spent travelling on their outward journeys at the start of tours, the other being on a boat to the West Indies in 1947–48. The team that flew to India on 31 December 1963 was the only one in international transit when the year changed.

† Lancaster Park would be totally destroyed by an earthquake in February 2011.

Andrew Sandham and Patsy Hendren routinely attended Mass on tour in Australia in the 1920s, and wherever he was the young Colin Cowdrey read the lesson every Sunday during his first Ashes tour. David Sheppard, ordained into the church several years earlier, preached to full houses across Australia and New Zealand during the 1962–63 tour, although his evangelising irritated some of his teammates. The gradual move towards Sunday play in Test cricket across the world from the 1970s onwards led to a breakdown in church going. Cowdrey himself took part in several Test matches in Australia featuring Sunday play before he retired.

Geoff Boycott described Christmas away from home as a sombre experience which you had to learn to live with – and to liven up. He also considered it important that the whole tour party stuck together over this period, because otherwise older tourists who had made friends locally on previous tours might go elsewhere, leaving the new boys alone – hence, in part, the fancy-dress parties. It also became a Christmas Day tradition for the players to share a drink with the press, once the press pack had reached sufficient size, and on David Gower's tour of India the press laid on for the players a champagne breakfast and sketch of their own. 'Christmas away from home is as painful for them [the press] as it is for us,' Mike Gatting once noted. This fraternisation would be ended abruptly following a vote among the players during the Zimbabwe tour of 1996–97.

It was unfortunate that around the time the players started to be able to afford to bring out partners and families, the Boxing Day–New Year Test double-bill became a standard fixture in the calendar. This meant the players had less free time to be with wives and children, and the management was more likely to view the families as a potential distraction. The first tour on which wives and children came out in significant numbers was over Christmas on Mike Denness's tour of Australia, Frank Keating of the *Guardian* noting the horrified reaction of Keith Miller, the former Australia all-rounder and in Keating's words a 'man's man', at the door of the breakfast room at the Windsor Hotel, Melbourne. 'At least it gave him on a plate his front-page column for the next day's *Daily Express*: "The dining-room is littered with high chairs, with England's so-called heroes popping Cornflakes into their youngsters' mouths. Test cricketers? These men are weak-kneed imposters. Wives and children must never again tour with players."' Of course, not every tour was considered a viable proposition for families. When for the only time an England Test team spent Christmas in Pakistan – in 1977–78 – families remained at home, and the players relied on the assistance of the BBC to send messages back to loved ones from Lahore.*

Even if families came out, some managers would try to keep them at arm's length by permitting them only to join the pre-Christmas lunch drinks, before dispatching them to an adjoining room to tend to their children and have their own Christmas meal. This absurd convention was still in place during Bob Willis's tour of Australia but was torn up soon after; thereafter players and families were allowed to co-mingle throughout the day. By the time of the next tour of Australia in 1986–87, Mike Gatting and his players were appearing live on the Noel Edmonds Christmas TV show, which linked them up with relatives in studios around England. Given the time difference, there was a fair bit of hanging around until they were on air late in the evening in Melbourne, but Mike Gatting described it as the best Christmas he experienced with England overseas, an opinion possibly coloured by England winning the Boxing Day Test to retain the Ashes.

Things came to a head on the tour of South Africa in

---

* Geoff Boycott, having not been required for an ODI in Sahiwal on 23 December, arranged matches for and against Lahore Gymkhana on the two days before Christmas, scoring hundreds in each. He then sought another game on Christmas Day itself, only for rain to wash it out. Boycott probably gave himself his best Christmas present when four years later in Delhi on 24 December 1981 he broke Garry Sobers' Test runs record of 8,032.

1995–96, when Ray Illingworth, head coach, manager and old-school cricketer, recoiled at the sight of 50 additional family members joining the tour just as the Test series, level-pegged at 0–0, headed into the decisive contests in Durban, Port Elizabeth and Cape Town. Illingworth feared that this influx would change the dynamics of the team. 'I'll never get them [the players] back, not now this lot are here,' he was reported as saying. England drew the third and fourth Tests but badly lost the final match, and with it the series.

As a result, and as already alluded to, wives and girlfriends were barred altogether from Zimbabwe and New Zealand the following winter. It proved a serious error of judgment, leaving some of the regular players aggrieved that for the third winter in a row the team were away over Christmas. Graham Thorpe called it one of the worst decisions the England management ever made. It proved a watershed. No England tour since then, outside Australia and South Africa, has involved cricket over Christmas or New Year.

Boxing Day Tests effectively turned Christmas Day into simply another day of training and planning, and this was something that not even one or two players or coaches wearing Father Christmas hats in deference to the occasion could change. Apart from anything else, team selection would happen that day, with profound consequences for some. When Steven Finn was dropped in Australia in 2010–11 and reacted by locking himself in the toilet, it was Christmas Day when he was given the news. Tests over New Year lacked such emotional freight, but the England team were on one occasion most unhappy when in Sydney a decision was taken to give the entire ground staff New Year's Day off, with the result that the pitch was saturated by rain because it had been left inadequately covered. The toss, which was won by Australia, proved decisive. England batsman Geoff Boycott called it 'a scandalous neglect of duty'.

*

Local crowds turned up to watch the big holiday matches to savour the occasion, enjoy the weather and the company of friends, but ideally to see England beaten. The general tenor of these matches was usually benign, inasmuch as there was more of a family vibe than at some other games, especially floodlit one-dayers, but there was often also a minority who turned up for the drinking and male boisterousness, and to verbally dish it out to the visitors.

It was mainly innocuous stuff, but there were times when a line was overstepped and some rowdier elements had to be ejected from the ground, assuming they could be identified. The partisan nature of many crowds meant they acted like a twelfth man for their side, but over the years a degree of equilibrium was restored with the growth in travelling support for England to levels unmatched by any other team. Now, whenever England win a Test overseas, the players routinely credit the die-hard supporters who made the journey across the world to cheer them on, sing them on, chant them on. These supporters could turn places such as Cape Town, Barbados and Antigua into virtual home fixtures. The biggest turnouts would be over Christmas, New Year and Easter.

England were not often on tour over Easter weekends, and they have played only nine Tests at this time, seven of them in New Zealand and West Indies, whose domestic seasons tend to run latest during English winters. They also once played an ODI in Trinidad on an Easter Monday watched by 25,000. Easter had a significant impact on the scheduling of the West Indies tour of 1990; to avoid play on Good Friday, which was taken as a rest day, the Antigua Test started only two days after the Barbados Test ended, the teams travelling between islands on the solitary day's break between games. England lost heavily.*

---

* Another modern instance of a rest day being taken after one day of play in an England Test match, rather than after the customary three, occurred at Bombay in February 1980, when a solar eclipse was due to take place on what would normally have been the second day. The Indian board did not want some 50,000 spectators damaging their eyes by looking into the sun. There was also an eclipse of the sun on the first day of England's Test at Port Elizabeth on the 1895–96 tour.

This was the first time England played Test cricket on Easter Sunday. The players thought it crazy to play such a big game so soon after the previous one, but one of them, Jack Russell, said other factors were at play: 'The crowded itinerary had to take into account the thousands of British holidaymakers who wanted to see two Tests, and the fact that we had to report back soon to our counties.' On Easter Sunday 2004, Brian Lara took his score from 86 to 313, en route to a world record 400 not out against England, also at Antigua's Recreation Ground.

Certain destinations had long provided elements of English support. Servicemen on duty at British garrisons around the Caribbean, or sailors on leave from ships that happened to be in dock at port cities, would often turn up and lend their support to countrymen engaged in another kind of representative duty overseas. Ivo Bligh's team playing in Tasmania in 1882 found themselves being urged on by sailors ashore from HMS *Nelson*. England supporters' tours also dated back a long way. In its issue of 12 September 1939, *The Cricketer* ran an in-house advert for a package trip to follow a forthcoming Test tour of India, advising its readers that 'at a time of the year when the weather can be at its worst in England [this was] an excellent plan for a winter holiday'. Sadly, by the time the magazine appeared the tour had already been cancelled owing to the outbreak of war in Europe.

Hospitality groups, almost exclusively made up of men over the age of 60, started accompanying England teams abroad in the 1960s, and by the 1970s tours to West Indies and Australia routinely attracted supporters' groups arranged and managed by companies such as Gullivers Sports Travel and John Snow Travel, a company set up and owned by the former England fast bowler. Initially they ventured to some of the less obviously alluring places such as Jamaica, Bangalore and Hyderabad, but Perth, as the most convenient point of entry into Australia, and Barbados quickly became established favourites.

Geoff Boycott noted appreciatively the sight of Union Jack flags at the WACA on the 1978–79 tour. It was estimated that the influx of England supporters to Barbados and Antigua on the 1980–81 tour was worth over £1 million to the local economies. One English reporter described them as 'Britain's monstrous regiment of cricketing tourists, handkerchiefs knotted on their heads and their beach robes trailing behind them'. The Barbados Test on the next tour of West Indies in 1985–86 reportedly attracted 5,000 supporters from the UK. It was the start of a mass-travel phenomenon that still thrives.

England's Christmas and New Year Tests

England have played 89 Test matches during the Christmas and New Year period, defined here as matches starting on dates between 20 December and 5 January. Of these, 48 took place in Australia, 30 in South Africa, nine in India, one in Pakistan and one in Zimbabwe. England played Christmas *and* New Year Tests on 14 tours of South Africa (starting in 1913–14) and 11 tours of Australia (1950–51 and 1974–75 being the only cases before 1990–91). The only time they have won both was in South Africa in 1913–14, 1927–28 and 1956–57; and in Australia in 2010–11. They lost both in Australia in 2006–07 and 2013–14. The commonest starting dates were 26 December and 1 January (19 times each), 2 January (11 times) and 30 and 31 December (seven times each).

Venue	First staged	Christmas (matches starting Dec 20–27 onwards)				New Year (matches starting Dec 29–Jan 5 onwards)			
		P	W	L	D	P	W	L	D
Melbourne (Aus)	1878–79					22+	8	11	3
	1950–51	13	4	7	2				
Johannesburg	1905–06					3	1	2	0
(SA)*	1913–14	8	3	2	3				
Cape Town (SA)	1922–23					13	4	3	6
Calcutta (Ind)	1933–34					7	1	2	4

Venue	First staged	Christmas (matches starting Dec 20–27 onwards)				New Year (matches starting Dec 29–Jan 5 onwards)			
Delhi (Ind)	1972–73	2	1	0	1				
Sydney (Aus)	1950–51					13	2	7	4
Hyderabad (Pak)	1977–78					1	0	0	1
Port Elizabeth (SA)	1995–96	1	0	0	1				
Harare (Zim)	1996–97	1	0	0	1				
Durban (SA)	1999–2000	4	2	0	2				
Centurion (SA)	2019–20	1	0	1	0				
Total		30	10	10	10	59	16	25	18

+ In addition, a New Year Test at Melbourne, scheduled for 31 December 1970–5 January 1971 was completely washed out.
*All of these matches were at the Old Wanderers ground except for two Christmas Tests at the New Wanderers (won in 1956–57, drawn in 1964–65).

England played 16 ODIs on dates between 20 December and 5 January, although none of these games took place later than 2005–06. One took place on 26 December and four on 1 January. Nine were in Australia, three in Pakistan, two in India and two in Zimbabwe. Another scheduled ODI in Australia on 26 December 1978 was washed out. England have played only two T20s during this period, in India on 20 and 22 December 2012.

CHAPTER 18

Crimes and Misdemeanours
Car crashes, curfews and cover-ups

On Tuesday, 17 February 1925, while England were making Australia follow on at the Melbourne Cricket Ground and pushing for what would be their first victory in an Ashes Test for 13 years, the team's vice-captain Johnny Douglas was sitting in a coroner's court providing evidence to an inquest into the death of a man killed in a car crash while driving Douglas back to the Windsor Hotel. The touring party had been guests of William Watt, the speaker of the House of Representatives and chairman of the MCG's trustees, at a dinner at the West Brighton club the previous weekend. Ebenezer Baker, 52, the manager of the Melbourne Sports Depot, died when the car he was driving collided with a horse and cart on the streets of a Melbourne suburb. Douglas was in the passenger seat beside him.

There were conflicting reports about the accident, which occurred in heavy rain in the early hours of a Sunday morning. Sun Kee, the driver of the cart, was a Chinese gardener and, given his ethnicity and Australia's policy towards non-white communities, he may not have been received entirely sympathetically. There were suggestions, for instance, that his cart was on the wrong side of the road, but he denied this and said his horse had been frightened by the car lights. He also told police that at one point three cars drove alongside each other on the road. Baker's Buick smashed into the wagon, one of whose shafts crashed through the windscreen, piercing Baker's chest. When the shaft then broke, the car was pushed sideways, and carried on moving until Douglas managed to turn off the engine, bringing the car to a halt on a pavement. Douglas told the court that thanks to Baker falling to his left as he was struck, he himself was spared serious injury. Douglas sustained severe bruising to his arm which prevented him from taking any further part in MCC's ongoing match with Victoria. Another passenger, Dr Devereux Gwynne-Hughes, was also unhurt.

In his statement, Douglas said that Baker and he were 'quite sober', but a police constable reported that Douglas and Gwynne-Hughes 'were slightly under the influence of liquor but Dr Hughes more so'. One of the Melbourne newspapers put it more bluntly: '[Douglas] denies being drunk but constable says he was.' Police also concluded that lights were burning on the wagon even though Douglas and Gwynne-Hughes claimed they were not. Douglas denied hearing a shouted warning from the wagon driver. The coroner found death by 'accidental collision'.

Douglas had led England to victory in the field in Australia in 1911–12, but he was now 42 years of age and his bowling had lost much of the zip which had characterised his early playing days, when he was regarded as one the best exponents of 'swerve' in the game. He had featured only in the second Test of this tour, and even before the accident it was unlikely he would have played in the fourth or fifth Tests. As it was, he did not play on the tour again.

The accident and inquest were dealt with extensively in the Australian press, but more selectively by English newspapers. *The Guardian* carried a detailed report of the accident sent by Exchange Telegraph, and the *Evening Standard* ran a

one-paragraph report from Reuters, but *The Times*, the mouthpiece of the establishment, carried only the Reuters bulletin
shorn of any reference to the car crash, meaning that it reported
Douglas injuring his arm, without explaining how. A natural
assumption might have been that he had done it on the field of
play. The inquest was ignored. Probably as a result, few English
publications, and no subsequent biographies of Douglas, have
ever made mention of the incident.

There have been many cases of players – and indeed some
coaches and managers – getting into scrapes on tour. Most were
nothing like as tragic as the one involving Johnny Douglas, but
they often involved drink. Drinking has long been a part of the
culture of English cricket, and part of the cricketing cultures of
many countries England visited. Teams tended to drink whether
in victory or defeat, but it was best to be careful where you
publicly drank in defeat; people were liable to think you did not
care about being beaten if it seemed you were having too good
a time. Generally, drinking on tour was a beneficial thing. It
bonded players and helped pass the time. But there were times
when it had a detrimental impact on performances on the field,
and brought unwanted trouble.

Anyone who behaved in an errant or ill-disciplined fashion
risked straining their relationships with teammates and management, and jeopardising the team's chances of success, so such
conduct was always liable to attract some kind of punishment.
In the worst cases this normally took the shape of fines, or the
withholding of good-conduct bonuses, but there was also the
last resort of sending someone home. These sanctions were principally designed as deterrents and a means of maintaining the
smooth running of a tour; there was not much desire to activate
them and then go public with the reasons why, as this would
simply bring further unwanted attention, and potentially create
more instability. So even if a player was found guilty of misconduct, the full details may have been hidden. This explains
why the course of sending someone home, though frequently

threatened, was so rarely applied, because it could hardly be done without explanation.*

The introduction of an ICC code of conduct in the 1990s to deal with on-field indiscipline took much of the pressure off captains and tour managers to deal with miscreants themselves, while also bringing some consistency to the punishments. Previously, these were a matter of individual judgment. Fred Titmus, for example, was threatened by his tour manager Donald Carr with being sent home for verbally abusing South Africa's Eddie Barlow during a Test in Cape Town in the 1960s. While verbal abuse was much less common then than it later became, in that instance relations between the teams had already deteriorated, with neither sets of players any longer prepared to walk, largely because they no longer trusted the umpiring; moreover, when Titmus gave Barlow a verbal volley for standing his ground after what appeared a perfectly good catch to slip, Barlow gave as good as he got. In the end, Titmus was simply told to apologise to Barlow, which he did, rather grudgingly.†

Les Ames, as manager of a tour of Pakistan, considered sending home John Snow after Snow, as we saw earlier, bowled a barrage of bouncers at Tom Graveney, the team's vice-captain, in the nets. Graveney had been instrumental in Snow's omission from the first Test of the series after Snow had refused to bowl off his long run-up in practice. 'He talked about sending Snow

---

* Sending players home from tours less high-profile than full England ones was less complex precisely because the fallout was more manageable; in playing terms the stakes were lower and there was less external scrutiny. Ben Stokes and Matt Coles were sent home from an England Lions tour of Australia in 2012–13 after two acts of late-night drinking.

† Carr's hardline approach may have owed something to his own experiences as captain of an England A tour to Pakistan in 1955–56 when his players played a prank on local umpire Idris Begh, who was reputed to be Pakistan's best umpire but gave a number of decisions against Carr's side. After an evening of drinking, a few of the players 'kidnapped' Begh and doused him in water. The joke was not received in the way intended, and it took an apology from MCC president Lord Alexander of Tunis to prevent the tour being abandoned. Carr was severely reprimanded.

home on the spot,' Graveney recalled. 'I convinced him this might be counterproductive.'

Another available course of action in dealing with difficult players was to rule them out of consideration for future tours. This was effectively what happened to Basil D'Oliveira ahead of his notorious omission from the original party for South Africa in 1968–69. It may also have been politically expedient to leave out D'Oliveira because as a Cape Coloured his inclusion was always likely to trigger objections from John Vorster's apartheid government and thereby jeopardise the tour – but his drinking and socialising on the previous winter's tour of West Indies had in the eyes of many disqualified him from touring again.

One teammate, Pat Pocock, recounted D'Oliveira being the worse for wear on several occasions and, in drink, manhandling a Jamaican taxi driver he suspected of over-charging. The management knew: Les Ames had to take him aside at one point and remind him of his responsibilities, while Colin Cowdrey wrote back to Lord's that he was not pleased with the hours D'Oliveira was keeping. D'Oliveira himself admitted he got it wrong: 'The hospitality was out of this world . . . I was gullible and just accepted it all. I had too much to drink, I lived too well.'

He was aware he had jeopardised his future in Test cricket and, sure enough, when it came to picking the team for South Africa, Cowdrey and Ames were disinclined to back him. At the time, little was publicly known of this side of D'Oliveira's personality, though some hinted at it. E. M. Wellings wrote on the eve of the decisive selection meeting: 'Few who were in the West Indies last winter would contemplate another tour for D'Oliveira.'*

Some types of errant behaviour could not be swept under the

---

* In the end, D'Oliveira was added to the tour party after Tom Cartwright withdrew. Sure enough, the South African government raised objections to his presence and England cancelled the tour rather than be dictated to over who could be in their side. D'Oliveira went on two subsequent Test tours, to Pakistan as the replacement trip in 1968–69 and Australia and New Zealand in 1970–71 – and carried on drinking.

carpet. When Ted Pooley landed himself in jail over a betting dispute in New Zealand ahead of England's first overseas Tests in Melbourne in 1876–77, his absence could hardly go unnoticed. He was eventually acquitted of breaking into and trashing the hotel room of a local man, Ralph Donkin, with whom he had fallen out, but not in time to take part in the Tests across the Tasman Sea. As the touring party consisted of only 12 players, the absence of the first-choice wicketkeeper was problematic, and it was left to Harry Jupp to fill in. It was fortunate that Jupp had recovered in health; for much of the tour he was incapacitated with sciatica and impaired vision in one eye, and at one stage went three months without playing a match. Partly as a result of the Pooley incident, it quickly became the norm for memorandums of agreement (or tour contracts) to be drawn up between organisers and players containing clauses stipulating that a portion of any fee would be deducted in the case of 'impropriety or misconduct'.

Even so, heavy drinking – or what Alfred Shaw called 'feasting and merrymaking' – was commonplace in the early years. When England appeared to be heading for defeat in the first Test of the 1894–95 series, some of the players spent the night carousing, only for overnight rain to turn the pitch in Sydney into a quagmire, making Australia's run-chase much less of a formality than it had appeared. They were to resume on 113 for two, needing 64 more. The services of Bobby Peel, the Yorkshire left-arm spinner, were suddenly crucial, but both Peel and Bill Lockwood arrived late, with Peel scarcely in a fit state to play. While Peel was put under a shower, Jim Blackham, the Australia captain, generously agreed to a slightly delayed start, and when play eventually got underway Peel captured five of the remaining wickets to bowl England to victory by 10 runs.

Allegations of further drinking surrounded England's defeat in the Adelaide Test, with an Australian paper reporting: 'The insobriety of one of the Englishmen is said to have called forth Capt. [Andrew] Stoddart's threat to oust the offender from the team, under the behaviour clause in their agreement, unless he steadies himself.' Any doubt that Peel was the man in question can probably be put to bed by a subsequent item in an English paper after the tour concluded which dubbed Peel 'the champion grogster'. It suggested he had been fined so often for 'unfitness for play' that it had wiped out his entire tour fee of £300.

England captains of the amateur era could be among the worst offenders. Percy Chapman led one of the most successful tours of Australia, but even by this relatively early stage of his career – he was only in his late twenties – drink was already starting to take what would be a devastating toll on his body. Chapman could be an elusive figure, and during the third Test he had to be retrieved from the ladies' stand by Jack Hobbs. The next match at Adelaide was the only time Bill Ferguson, the team's scorer and baggage man, said he saw Chapman annoyed when there was not a drink waiting for him when he came off at lunch (this was a time when it was not uncommon for players to drink alcohol in the intervals).

Chapman then did not play the final Test, for reasons that were never fully explained. He was reported to have suffered from flu in the lead-up, but actually fielded as substitute for most if not all of Australia's fourth-innings long run chase. Christopher Martin-Jenkins described his withdrawal through illness as a 'partial pretext'. It was arguable as to whether by this stage of the series he was still worth a place in the side (and England were 4–0 up).* By the time Chapman led England in South Africa two years later, his ballooning weight had had an

---

* Chapman was also reported to have been upset by an incident that occurred in a match against Victoria at the MCG six days before the final Test there, when a crowd of 12,000 barracked his fastest bowler Harold Larwood for returning to the attack when last man Bert Ironmonger, a hopeless batsman, arrived at the crease. In response to the noisy 'counting out' by the spectators, Larwood pulled up in his delivery stride four times, so Chapman and Bill Woodfull went over to the spectators in the Wardill Stand in a vain attempt to urge calm. Jack Ryder eventually ended the impasse by declaring the Victoria innings closed. It was claimed that Chapman was jostled and insulted in the members' enclosure.

even more detrimental effect on his cricket. He was dropped for the final Test at home against Australia in 1930 as captain and player, and in South Africa scored only 75 runs in seven innings. He never played Test cricket again.

The precise nature of Walter Robins's misconduct as Gubby Allen's vice-captain in Australia is unclear; rather than drink it may have been simply a matter of not taking his duties seriously enough and setting a bad example to those under him. Allen wrote to his father between the third and fourth Tests: 'He [Robins] is very difficult on occasions when he should be setting a good example and is now ... saying he hates cricket, and is no good at it, and wants to go home ... He will never go on another tour, I know, and on the whole I think it is a good thing ... He has done some unwise things and the pros don't respect him anymore. He thinks it is clever to defy authority and refuses to see that it is a hopeless view to take, especially on a tour.'*

Godfrey Evans's crime on the South Africa tour of 1948–49 very much related to drink. Unhappy at being singled out to pay for a round after a poor performance in Cape Town, he poured a pint of beer over the head of the manager Mike Green. George Mann, the captain, waited until the team arrived in Johannesburg several weeks later for the next Test before writing Evans a note informing him that he had been dropped. Evans conceded his behaviour was 'not the best career move', but he regained his place the following summer and, despite further trouble in the West Indies in 1953–54, remained England's first-choice wicketkeeper for the next ten years.

Freddie Brown put himself out of the last two days of a six-day Test in Adelaide after crashing into a tramway pole while

---

* Robins got his wish to leave the tour early. Having been dropped for the fifth Test, he was allowed to depart midway through the match and skip the fixtures in New Zealand. It had been agreed in advance with MCC that he could miss New Zealand if his business commitments required. Robins captained England at home the following summer but, as Allen predicted, never toured again.

driving back late at night to the team hotel in Glenelg from a dinner at Government House. Brown had Mike Green with him in the car at the time. Both men were thrown against the windscreen and Green was admitted to hospital in a semi-conscious state, suffering from various injuries including a fractured nose. Brown needed stitches to gashes to his left knee, shin and forehead. Brown told police that he had swerved to avoid a vehicle that pulled out in front of him on North Terrace. His absence from the rest of the game meant that Denis Compton temporarily took over the captaincy, a significant moment as he was the first professional (albeit a stand-in) to lead England in an overseas Test since the 1880s, but Australia were already in a strong position and Brown's absence merely compounded a hopeless situation for his team. It was suggested Brown might have batted had the cause not been lost, but the game was over by midway through the final afternoon.

Jack Nash, joint manager alongside Green, later refuted claims that a driving ban had been placed on the players. In fact, a general ban might have made good sense. Major Booth and Andrew Sandham had previously missed Tests in South Africa following car crashes, and on a later tour of Australia in 1958–59 Peter Loader and Brian Statham were both ruled out of the final Test after receiving minor injuries in a driving accident.

One of the most vexed incidents occurred at the Marine Hotel on the Saturday night of the Barbados Test in 1953–54, when the wife of an MCC member alleged to Len Hutton and Charles Palmer that two of their players in an inebriated state had pushed a food trolley up and down a corridor before getting in a lift and jostling and insulting her. The players were identified as Tony Lock and Fred Trueman, two of the youngest members of the party, and they were duly summoned to a meeting with Hutton, Palmer and the lady in question, whose theme, according to Jim Swanton, 'was what was expected of English teams abroad in the way of behaviour and example'.

Afterwards, Hutton told Trueman that he thought he had

taken the dressing-down well, to which Trueman replied: 'So do I, since it weren't us.' The identity of the real culprits was never satisfactorily established, but a few days later, with the Test going badly for England, Ross Hall of the *Mirror* provided some alternative suspects. Hall wrote that Hutton was being let down by some of his senior players who were jaded from late-night partying, and suggested that Denis Compton and Godfrey Evans 'do not always act as if the sole reason for their being out here is to win for England'.

This was a difficult situation for Hutton. As England's first modern professional captain, he could not afford to appear incapable of maintaining law and order among his men, and for this reason urged his players not to socialise too much. He had also been preferred for the captaincy ahead of Compton despite Compton being vice-captain to Brown in Australia three years earlier. Hutton knew Compton loved to live life to the full off the field, and his private view – expressed more openly in later years – was that Compton and Bill Edrich should have been sent home from the first post-war tour of Australia for their off-field excesses. Nonetheless, Compton and Evans were senior players whom Hutton needed by his side as he attempted to win, or at least not lose, his first overseas assignment as captain. Realpolitik probably prevailed. Hutton responded to Hall's charges by giving an interview to Crawford White in the *News Chronicle* in which he rejected wild rumours of 'drunkards and playboys'.

Trueman was less fortunate. As a naïve, aggressive and unpredictable youngster, he gave Hutton several problems the captain could have done without. Most profoundly, Hutton's tour report unequivocally held Trueman responsible for verbally abusing umpire Cecil Kippins during a match in British Guiana, and although he also protested his innocence over this incident as well, Trueman did not tour again for five years. Umpiring decisions were a constant cause of friction during the 1953–54 series, and there was no escaping the reluctance of the English players to take their setbacks with good grace, so Hutton could not protect his position without taking the Kippins incident seriously.

Various attempts were made to forcibly keep players on the straight and narrow, with mixed results. Too strict a line invited rebellion, which is probably why curfews were rarely well received. Most tours operated best when players were encouraged to act responsibly and make their own decisions about what constituted sensible behaviour and sensible hours. When Freddie Brown moved from captaining tours to managing them, and attempted to impose a midnight curfew on New Year's Eve ahead of the Cape Town Test starting on 1 January 1957, his strictures were breezily ignored by Compton and Evans, as well as Trevor Bailey, all of whom stayed up until 4 a.m. at the Kelvin Grove Club ball. Fortunately, the late night did not seem to affect their performance: Bailey opened the batting and scored 34 while Compton, batting three, made 58. The next day Evans chipped in with 62.

Geoff Boycott perhaps provided the one case of someone being sent home from a tour on disciplinary grounds – although he would have argued that this was not the case. Officially, he left India in 1981–82 after the fourth of six Tests because, in the words of tour manager Raman Subba Row, 'physical health problems had affected his [Boycott's] perspective.' In truth, Boycott's selfishness had fractured beyond repair relations with teammates, who insisted he be kicked off the tour.

Having already batted twice, Boycott had fallen ill over the rest day and penultimate day of the Calcutta Test with diarrhoea and a temperature and retired to his bed. Feeling slightly better on the final day, he went to the ground to collect his kit, with India smoothly batting their way to a draw. Seemingly uninterested in fielding or lending support to his colleagues with his presence, Boycott suggested a game of golf at the nearby Tollygunge club with two non-playing members of the side, Paul Allott and Geoff Cook. When they declined, he went anyway and played 14 holes alone.

He returned to the hotel to an interrogation from Keith Fletcher and Bob Willis, the captain and vice-captain, Bernard Thomas, the physio, and Subba Row. The unanimous feeling was that by playing golf without permission during a Test match in which he was involved Boycott had committed the cardinal sin of betraying team solidarity. An apology was demanded and eventually received – Boycott pinning a written note to a table in the team room at the hotel – but Boycott countered by saying that unless he could consult a British Consulate doctor in Delhi he would quit the tour.

This offer of resignation was accepted by the management the next morning even as Boycott, perhaps realising the magnitude of what he was suggesting, had second thoughts. 'Boycott's apparent reluctance to contribute anything made it very clear to me that he should never tour with England again,' Fletcher said. But the management was anxious that it should not appear as though Boycott had been sent home in disgrace, and that the full details should be kept under wraps as best as possible. Subba Row did not inform the travelling press of his departure until Boycott was airborne.

There was a drive to impose curfews on tours in the 1980s, no doubt in response to the nocturnal habits of several high-profile players, but it was largely unsuccessful. Probably on instruction from Lord's, Doug Insole as manager in Australia in 1982–83 issued an edict that players were not to be seen drinking in public after midnight, with draconian fines of £1,000 for those who breached the rule. But the players were vehemently opposed, and it seemed that it was rare for anyone to be fined. In hindsight this was a mistake.

Ian Botham, in particular, had been given too long a lead. The following winter involved a tour of New Zealand and Pakistan, and with Pakistan known to offer little in terms of Western-style nightlife, the team made the most of New Zealand. 'Every night seems like Saturday night,' one cricket correspondent noted. Once a New Zealand newspaper levelled the first allegation of drug-taking (almost certainly inaccurate in its details, as it turned out), Fleet Street's news desks went into overdrive. The team had moved on to Pakistan by the time the *Mail on Sunday* published a story that Botham had smoked pot on the tour. He initially denied this but, after a lengthy legal battle, conceded that he had indeed smoked pot at various times, sometimes, he said, 'simply in order to relax – to get off the sometimes fearful treadmill of being an international celebrity'.

In the summer of 1986 he was banned from all cricket for two months. Subsequently, several members of the tour party admitted dope had been smoked. Allan Lamb admitted to dabbling 'here and there' with pot, 'but only socially', while David Gower wrote of the New Zealand tour in his autobiography: 'There probably was some sex and possibly some drugs. There was some partying, for sure . . . There was a bit of wacky baccy on that tour.' Gower added of Willis, the captain: 'He was part of some of the fun . . . but he kept himself at arm's length from the rest of it.'

Botham made himself unavailable for three of the next five winter tours, but when he did tour life was far from easy, as the tabloids tracked his every move. In the West Indies in 1985–86, the *News of the World* ran a story in which Lindy Field, a former Miss Barbados, claimed to have had sex with Botham, and shared cocaine with him, at the team hotel (with a bed being broken in the process). There were suspicions that Botham had been set up: the cocaine story did not ring true, and Lindy Field was reportedly paid £25,000 to tell her tale. The idea of a curfew was floated on the next winter's tour of Australia, but was again rejected by senior players such as Botham, Lamb and Gower. Botham, in fact, spent much of that tour holed up in his hotel room, or Bat Cave as it became known, to stay out of sight of reporters. Touring had become more trouble than it was worth for him.

The idea that English cricket dealt too softly with its biggest stars was reinforced by events in Pakistan in 1987–88 on a tour marred by umpiring disputes. Chris Broad's reluctance to leave the field after being given out lbw in Lahore, a row between England captain Mike Gatting and umpire Shakoor Rana which led to the loss of a day's play in Faisalabad before peace was brokered, and several lengthy delays in batsmen walking off in Karachi, all might have triggered sanctions in the past, but in this instance cricket manager Micky Stewart and tour manager Peter Lush shared the grievances of the players at what they viewed as 'one-eyed' officiating. Indeed, towards the end of the tour, Subba Row, by this point chairman of the TCCB, unilaterally informed the players that they would be receiving a hardship bonus of £1,000 each, but greater thought was subsequently given to what constituted acceptable conduct and what punishments could be meted out when necessary. A more considered framework was drawn up in relation to fines and the processes by which a player could be removed from a tour.

When David Gower and John Morris took their impromptu flight in a Tiger Moth at Carrara Oval on Queensland's Gold Coast and twice buzzed the ground, the management was initially minded to send home both players. Graham Gooch and Micky Stewart as captain and team manager were intent on instilling a more disciplined team ethic and were under particular pressure as England were 2–0 down in the Test series, so were in no mood for leniency. Gooch had had particular difficulties with Gower, his predecessor, including a heated dressing-room exchange in the most recent Test about the team's approach. Not unreasonably, Gooch and Stewart felt Gower was not setting the best example to younger players, of whom Morris was one. However, under the terms of the players' tour contracts, an individual fine of £1,000 was the maximum available punishment for a first offence. Sending someone home could only occur after a second breach.

This issue arose again on the next tour of Australia. Phil Tufnell, after his problems with an earlier relationship in India in 1992–93, had recently re-married, but within days of his arrival in Perth he and his partner were experiencing difficulties. The distress this caused led to Tufnell suffering some sort of breakdown. He confessed his turmoil to David Roberts, the team's physio, and was later visited in his room by two of his closest teammates, Phil DeFreitas and Graham Thorpe, but this only made things worse. 'It all came out in a rush,' Tufnell recalled in his autobiography. 'I started sobbing, huge gutting sobs that I felt welling up inside my stomach. I was rocking and running into things, completely out of control. Lampshades, cricket coffins, anything I could see was booted or punched or thrown.'

Eventually, Roberts and M. J. K. Smith, the manager, took him in a taxi to a psychiatric unit for assessment, but as he was being questioned by a doctor, Tufnell came to his senses and swiftly discharged himself. Back at the hotel, he found Mike Atherton, the captain, and apologised: 'I've let everything get a bit on top of me. It won't happen again.' The next day, he went to the ground, bowling in the nets and helping out with twelfth-man duties during the match against Western Australia; however, the management were sufficiently concerned about his mental state to want the option of sending him home if necessary. They therefore summoned him to a meeting at which he was told 'We cannot have conduct like that on a cricket tour', and handed a £1,000 fine. In fact, Tufnell did not step out of line again and was selected for four of the five Tests. Just as remarkably, the team kept a lid on the story for the entire tour.*

The fear of adverse publicity from sending a player home played its part in keeping Dominic Cork on a tour of New Zealand in 1996–97. Cork had missed the preceding leg of the tour in Zimbabwe (thereby managing to spend Christmas and

---

* This was at least the third time Tufnell was fined on an England tour. During a one-day series in Australia in 1990–91 he was relieved of £500 for turning up late for duty in Adelaide after staying out all night. In India in 1992–93, he was fined £500 for 'ungentlemanly conduct towards an umpire' during a warm-up match in Visakhapatnam (the incident described on page 205).

New Year at home), but even when he joined the tour he was obstreperous with teammates and boorish towards opponents. After watching the Wellington Test, Ian MacLaurin, the new ECB chairman, proposed sending Cork home because, in the words of head coach David Lloyd, 'his conduct on the field did not fit his [MacLaurin's] image of what an England cricketer should be.'

Michael Atherton, as captain, resisted, as did Lloyd, who wrote: 'I agreed with the sentiment but not the cure . . . If we had sent him home then, the tour would have been finished. The press would have focused on that to the exclusion of all else.' In the end, Cork stayed and played a winning role in the final Test in Christchurch, vindicating the stance taken by Atherton and Lloyd. But it did not spare Cork a critical tour report – or a visit to his home from MacLaurin.

The most serious misconduct on a recent England tour probably involved Andrew Flintoff, whose drinking culminated in him being stripped of the vice-captaincy at the World Cup in West Indies in 2007. Flintoff had found the strain of leading an injury-stricken England side in Australia particularly hard. England held the Ashes but were whitewashed 5–0 and Flintoff, captaining the side in the absence of the injured Michael Vaughan, struggled to switch off from his responsibilities. 'I was drinking too much,' he recalled. 'And not just heavy drinking, but the wrong kind of heavy drinking . . . I'd retreat to my room and hit the minibar.'

This behaviour continued into a triangular one-day series that followed the Ashes, and on one occasion he turned up to a training session in Sydney badly hung over. Flintoff was not alone; several other members of the team were drinking more than usual, and when they won that one-day series it only emboldened them to keep going at the World Cup. There, in the wake of an opening defeat to New Zealand in St Lucia, Flintoff and several players and backroom staff embarked on a late-night drinking session which culminated – according to a report in the *News of the World* – in Flintoff being rescued from a pedalo in the early hours. Head coach Duncan Fletcher fined six players who were out after midnight, while Flintoff was dropped from the next game against Canada and stripped of the vice-captaincy. Fletcher decided against imposing a curfew, telling the players they should know the right thing to do, but warned that if they were caught out late again 'you will be on the first plane home.'

When two years later Flintoff and Steve Harmison joined a 'booze cruise' hours after England were bowled out for 51 in Jamaica, it marked the beginning of the end of their international careers. They had been given permission to go on the cruise by Andrew Strauss, the Test captain, but their decision to spend a night on the boat before disembarking at Ocho Rios on the other side of the island and being helicoptered back to the team hotel, was out of kilter with the fresh start Strauss and Andy Flower, the new coach, were intent on making. They were looking for committed, hungry players – not thirsty ones. At a crisis meeting in which Flower mapped out the way forward, he told the players: 'I've got a problem with the way you practise, the amount you're drinking, some of the shots you play under pressure.' Six months later Flintoff and Harmison played their final Tests.

In 2017 a permanent midnight curfew was imposed on England teams home and abroad. This time it was largely accepted by the players. It came as a consequence of two incidents. The first involved a night of late drinking following a late-season ODI in Bristol which culminated in Ben Stokes facing assault charges (of which he was subsequently cleared); the second occurred in a bar in Perth where Jonny Bairstow allegedly head-butted an opposing player, Cameron Bancroft. The Bairstow incident was largely a set-up among Australian players and media but Strauss, by now director of England cricket, felt that, coming so soon after the Stokes case, it was time to take a firm grip on off-field behaviour.

There were no more cases like these, but the curfew remained until 2022, which was as much as anything a reflection of the risks inherent in sportsmen visiting bars where other patrons armed with camera phones could cause them embarrassment. There was a reminder of this at the end of the final Ashes Test in Hobart in January 2022 when phone footage shared on social media confirmed a 6 a.m. visit at the team hotel by police to break up a gathering among players and coaches of both camps.*

Some acts that might have been considered ill-disciplined proved to be their own punishment. No further action was necessary. William Barnes, the great all-rounder of the Victorian era, had just bowled England to victory in a feisty and close-fought match in Sydney when in the aftermath he threw a punch at the Australia captain Percy McDonnell, missed and damaged his hand on a wall, and was unavailable for the next Test as a consequence. England were sufficiently short of players that they had to summon Reginald Wood from Melbourne club cricket to fill the gap. Charles Fry went riding in South Africa and broke his ankle jumping off a horse that had bolted from a stable yard; the injury put him out of the final Test in Cape Town. Johnny Wardle slipped a cartilage playing snooker in Port Elizabeth, required manipulative surgery and was ruled out of a crucial final Test which England lost, with the upshot that the series was drawn 2–2.

Fred Titmus, England's vice-captain, lost four left toes to a propeller on the side of a boat while swimming off Barbados; he did not play again on the tour, but made a swift recovery and was playing county cricket for Middlesex a little more than two months later (he also won four more Test caps, in Australia). On

---

* Some of the heaviest drinking has been done by those charged with running tours. As manager in India and Pakistan in 1961–62, Tom Pearce's response to the team visiting a 'dry' state was to arrange functions across the border after a day's play. 'Fifty miles there in this bleeding old bus, and fifty miles back, and we couldn't start the journey back till the manager had been carried onto the bus!' recalled Ken Barrington.

a later Caribbean tour, Ashley Giles pulled a groin muscle while
clinging to a two-man inflatable pulled along behind a speed-
boat piloted by Ian Botham, by now working as a television
pundit, off Grenada. Publicly, Giles's absence from three ODIs
was put down to an injury niggle picked up in the nets. Jonny
Bairstow missed two ODIs and a Test match after twisting his
ankle playing football with teammates during warm-ups ahead
of a game in Sri Lanka. Rory Burns sustained a similar injury
attempting a shot on goal under pressure from his captain Joe
Root during a friendly game of football among the players on
the eve of a match at Newlands, and missed the last three Tests
of the series.

Captains and coaches did all they could to keep their players
together. What they feared most was mishaps to front-line
performers that could tear up plans and change team dynamics.
Injuries or illness were a constant threat, and few tours escaped
unscathed. Breakdowns in mid-match were a particular concern
and multiple injuries the stuff of nightmares. On one occasion
while batting in Sydney, Trevor Bailey broke a thumb and Doug
Wright strained a groin muscle, preventing either from bowling
for the remainder of the game; it meant the three remaining
members of the attack had to shoulder 123 overs between them.
Another time, also in Sydney, Ian Botham stepped up heroically
in intense heat during an afternoon session when Bob Willis
fell ill and Mike Hendrick went off the field suffering from
dehydration. When John Murray injured his shoulder diving to
take an early catch in Australia, Peter Parfitt took over behind
the stumps for the majority of an innings lasting more than 100
overs. 'I had never kept in my life,' Parfitt later recalled.

It was no less challenging when such problems arose just
before a match, making it difficult to muster an able-bodied XI.
Frank Mann's party in South Africa was reduced to 11 fit men
for the opening Test in Johannesburg, which meant they had no
one to do twelfth-man duties; they drafted in Bill Hitch, who

was coaching in Bloemfontein and had come to the Wanderers to watch the game. As he did not have any kit with him, Hitch was provided with trousers and shirt from Vallance Jupp, socks from Percy Fender, boots from Greville Stevens, cap from Jack Russell and blazer from George Macaulay.

In Trinidad in 1947–48, England were obliged to open the batting with the uncapped Billy Griffith, the reserve keeper, who did not have a first-class century to his name. In the event, he rose to the task magnificently and scored 140 (only to be dropped for the next match when more players were available). A combination of ailments reduced the playing strength to just 11 in Bombay in 1963–64 – and one of the 11, Micky Stewart, was barely well enough to take the field – and as a result England named a side containing six bowlers and two wicketkeepers. They still came away with a draw.

In Faisalabad in 1983–84, there were nominally 12 players to choose from, but not all were fully fit: Graham Dilley, 'sunken-eyed and deathly pale', was struggling so badly that he started the match with a 12-ball over. England scored 546 and drew. The tour of Australia led by Mike Atherton in 1994–95 was so severely hit by injuries that by the fourth Test in Adelaide the selectors were picking from just 12; as a result wicketkeeper Steve Rhodes batted No 6, followed by five bowlers. That England went on to win by 106 runs defied both form book and logic.

In the 48 hours before the Test in Rawalpindi in December 2022, England's first in Pakistan for 17 years, a viral infection laid low around half the 16-man playing squad, raising the possibility that the match might have to be put back a day in order to give the touring team a chance of putting out an XI. At 7.30 a.m. on the morning of the game, England announced they could field a team, and first-choice wicketkeeper Ben Foakes was the only player ruled too unwell to play. Uncapped Surrey all-rounder Will Jacks was told he was playing less than an hour before the start. Again, England won.

For a badly injured player, the speed with which they were removed from a tour they had spent months striving to get on could be painfully abrupt. 'You go for a scan because you're sore and two days later you're on a plane,' Joe Root once said of his bowlers. 'You're no longer part of that tour and that must be very difficult ... you're already so far away physically from everything you've just held so dear and worked so hard to get to.' Perhaps this explained why some who were invalided home would do all they possibly could to return. On Jim Parks's first tour he was hit on the head in practice, developed eye trouble and was sent home; he later attempted to return, only to collapse at Heathrow airport suffering from pneumonia. Mike Gatting did manage to rejoin a tour of the West Indies after having his nose broken by a ball from Malcolm Marshall, but had his thumb fractured in his first game back.

Once it became logistically feasible to fly in additional players, touring parties could change dramatically. The Atherton-led tour of Australia saw six extra players drafted in: even one of the original replacements, Neil Fairbrother, became incapacitated, while Dave Roberts, the team's physiotherapist, broke a finger during fielding drills. Four additional players were needed in Australia in 2002–03, and there have been several instances of touring parties on lengthy tours of Australia and South Africa being bolstered by three extra men. In such crises, the quality of the back-ups can be vital.

Some emergency replacements were readily to hand, playing or coaching in the vicinity; by such means Harry Lee and Ken Palmer (both in South Africa) and Tony Pigott (New Zealand) all won their only Test caps for England. In Pigott's case, he postponed his wedding to play in Christchurch, where England, in one of their most miserable Test performances, were dismissed for 82 and 93 and lost in three days.

Others had to be brought in from farther afield, and some undertook remarkable journeys to respond to the call. Len Hutton was originally given the winter off, but when injuries depleted an already weak team in the Caribbean in 1947–48 and an SOS went out, Yorkshire consented to Hutton's release to join the tour; he was the first player to fly out as an emergency replacement on an England Test tour and arrived 13 days after the original cable was sent. On the next tour of Australia in 1950–51, Brian Statham and Roy Tattersall, both of Lancashire, were sent out as reinforcements; the outward journey was tortuously long and took in seven flights.

The youthful Ted Dexter was in Paris when he was requested to get himself to Sydney as fast as possible to reinforce the 1958–59 tour. Pea-soup fog meant it took him two days to get back to London, before further fog delayed his departure for Australia. During the delay, he secured his engagement to Susan Longfield, 'to deter predators'. Engine trouble in Bahrain set him back further. Unsurprisingly, Dexter struggled to make an impact, scoring only 18 runs in four innings against Australia, but his trip was made worthwhile by a maiden Test hundred in Christchurch two weeks later.

It was striking how creditably many players performed after completing vast trans-continental journeys. Colin Milburn once took two days to get from Australia, where he was playing state cricket, to Pakistan, where after a couple of hits in the nets he scored 139 in the Karachi Test. Alastair Cook, then uncapped, was called away from an England Lions tour of the West Indies to join the main team in India; the journey took three days, but when he got there Cook nonetheless occupied the crease for nine and a half hours, scoring 60 and 104 not out.

A few years later, Ravi Bopara was pulled off a Lions tour of New Zealand to reinforce England in the Caribbean; he was in transit for 41 hours but shook off jetlag effectively enough to score a century in a warm-up match and then another in the Barbados Test. At the age of 41 Colin Cowdrey was called from home in southern England to Perth and, despite a 24-hour delay in Bombay leaving him short of preparation, he managed to bat for more than two hours in each innings against Jeff Thomson and Dennis Lillee at their most uncompromising. (Thomson was less than impressed at Cowdrey arriving at the crease to greet him with: 'I don't think we've met – I'm Colin.' 'That's not going to help you,' Thomson replied. 'Now piss off.') Less happily, later on the same tour, Barry Wood took 63 hours to get from Barbados to Auckland, where he was then out for a first-ball duck.

One of the most unorthodox journeys was undertaken by Sam Billings, after injuries to Jos Buttler and Jonny Bairstow left England without a specialist keeper going into the final Test of the 2021–22 Ashes series. Billings, who had only played white-ball cricket for his country to this point, was asked to abandon plans to fly home from Queensland's Gold Coast at the end of his stint playing Big Bash with Sydney Thunder and make his way to Sydney to meet up with the team before they moved on to Hobart. Owing to Covid-19 restrictions, he was told he must drive rather than fly – a road trip of almost 600 miles. During a stop, he tweeted: 'Just an observation . . . Australia is a reallyyyyy big place!' He made it in time, played in the Test and scored 30 as well as taking five second-innings catches.

Touring teams can be tested in many unexpected ways, whether by errant behaviour among members of the squad, or a spate of injuries and illnesses necessitating emergency reinforcements. It is crucial that team managements respond to these setbacks in proportionate fashion if they are not to destabilise things more than is already the case.

CHAPTER 19

The Great Comebacks
The value of crisis meetings

England habitually made a poor start to overseas series, and on only a few occasions did they begin badly and manage to turn things round. Of the 50 times they lost the first Test, in only nine instances did they recover to win the series; in two further cases, both in the Caribbean, they were able to salvage a draw. On Len Hutton's tour of the West Indies they drew 2–2 despite starting with defeats in Jamaica and Barbados; arguably this still stands as England's greatest comeback operation. The following winter, Hutton's side turned a 1–0 deficit into a 3–1 triumph to become the first English side to win a series in Australia for more than 20 years. It is one of only two times they have won a five-match series in Australia from 1–0 down. No other England captain has two such notable fightbacks on foreign soil to their name, and it stands as testimony to Hutton's extraordinary resilience as leader and man.

All the teams that turned things round were clearly good sides – winning away from home is never easy – but there were generally things that needed fixing. There may have been elements of misfortune in them falling behind in the first place, but in the main results changed for the better because of adjustments to personnel or tactics, or both. The challenge was identifying the problems, and doing so quickly enough to put things right in time. In all nine cases of sides winning the series after going 1–0 down, they immediately bounced back and won the second Test.

These teams tended to share common features: strong team spirit, firm leadership and good decision-making.* As ever, the stakes were highest for the captains. One of the most unlikely escapes – simply because the captain was not reckoned to be particularly strong, or particularly well regarded by his senior players – was Mike Denness's side coming away with a 1–1 draw in West Indies in 1973–74. They were beaten decisively in the first Test in Trinidad, but thanks to a string of exceptional individual performances managed to escape likely defeat in Jamaica and Barbados, then force a win in the last match back at the Queen's Park Oval.

The fightback began with Dennis Amiss holding out for nine and a half hours for an unbeaten 262 at Sabina Park – what Christopher Martin-Jenkins called 'one of the great pieces of individual heroism' – and ended in a low-scoring final Test with Geoff Boycott scoring 99 and 112, and Tony Greig taking 13 wickets with off-breaks rather than his usual medium-pacers to take advantage of the typical, slow-spinning Trinidadian conditions. Ironically, Boycott and Greig would have been among the leading candidates to replace Denness had the series been lost.

There were times when various members of the team lost

---

* Another factor could be good luck. When Frank Mann's team won in South Africa in 1922–23 after losing the first Test they were fortunate in the next match at Cape Town to have an Englishman (and a former England Test cricketer) umpiring in the shape of George Thompson, the Northamptonshire all-rounder. Thompson had never stood in a first-class match before. With the scores level, England's last man George Macaulay walked in front of his stumps to his first ball from Alf Hall, but after a delay Thompson gave him not out. Two balls later Macaulay struck the single that gave his side a series-levelling victory by one wicket. 'The match was remarkable for the number of unsuccessful appeals, and I would prefer not to say which side appealed to the umpires the most,' wrote E. W. Ballantine, a veteran *Natal Mercury* journalist. England went on to take the series 2–1.

faith in the captain but, buoyed by everyone's refusal to give up, Denness's leadership changed for the better; he became less dour, more approachable and tactically sharper. It was still something of a mystery why West Indies were unable to drive home their advantage. In Boycott's estimation, West Indies 'had a pretty low opinion of us and reckoned it was going to be easy . . . they paid the price for complacency and over-confidence.' The final chapter of Martin-Jenkins' tour account was titled, 'Analysis of a Daylight Robbery'.

It is only natural for captains in trouble to question themselves. When England trailed 1–0 in Sri Lanka in 2000–01, Nasser Hussain doubted whether he should remain in charge; he had scored one half-century in his last 12 Tests and feared he no longer commanded the respect of his players. 'I was very close to going,' he wrote in his autobiography. In the end, after some sleepless nights, he was encouraged by senior players, notably Mike Atherton, to carry on. Similarly Michael Vaughan in New Zealand in 2007–08 had no doubt that if the opening defeat in Hamilton was followed by another in Wellington 'I would have to resign.' Things may have worked out in the end, but these tours were characterised by some dark hours for both men at the helm.

The course taken by Vaughan and head coach Peter Moores to remedy the situation in New Zealand was among the more drastic. They dropped Matthew Hoggard and Steve Harmison, both of whom had more than 200 Test wickets to their names, after performing sluggishly in Hamilton, in favour of a pair of energetic tyros in Stuart Broad and James Anderson. Harmison was struggling for confidence while Hoggard was short of pace, as well as going through some personal difficulties, but this was not such an obvious swap at the time as it later seemed. The double change worked, though. Broad and Anderson helped England win the next two games and went on to become two of the greatest champions English cricket has produced, while Hoggard never played Test cricket again and Harmison appeared only six more times. Vaughan and Moores were in agreement on what to do on that occasion, but generally their management styles clashed – Vaughan found Moores's relentless enthusiasm for challenging the players in training grating and felt, at the age of 33, that Moores was looking to push him out – and within a few months Vaughan had succumbed to injury and fatigue and was gone as captain and player.

The comeback in South Africa under Joe Root in 2019–20 also owed much to an injection of fresh blood. Partly out of necessity and partly design, England brought in three young players following a defeat in the Boxing Day Test in Centurion: Zak Crawley aged 21 and Dom Bess and Ollie Pope, both 22. They were not the stars in a hard-fought, series-levelling win in Cape Town achieved with 50 balls to spare, but they all contributed in small but important ways. With Sam Curran also in the team, it was the first time England had ever fielded four players under the age of 23 in a Test XI. In the victory that followed in Port Elizabeth, Pope scored 135 not out and Crawley 44, while Bess took five for 51 in the first innings.

The most precious commodity in a crisis can be time. On modern tours, there are usually only a few days to regroup after each Test, and when a team has just been beaten that makes it hard to formulate new plans and take remedial action in the nets. Earlier touring teams did not face these problems. When Ivo Bligh's team lost the first Test of their tour in 1882–83 – the original mission to regain the Ashes – they had two weeks to prepare for the second Test, and spent much of it on a trip to Tasmania where they played and won two games against local XVIIIs. On returning to Melbourne, Bligh declined an invitation two days out from the Test to join a picnic attended by the Australian players, and instead opted for an additional training session with his team. England duly won the second and third Tests and took the series 2–1.* Hutton's team in Australia also

---

* The additional Test match 18 days later not, as we have seen, being regarded as part of the original three-match series.

had the considerable advantage over later generations of a 16-day break between first and second Tests, during which Frank Tyson made some crucial refinements to his run-up. Tyson's 25 wickets in the next three Tests effectively decided the series in England's favour.

When a tour is in difficulty it sometimes helps that the players have little choice but to be together and search for solutions among themselves. This can go one of two ways but, depending on the people involved and the circumstances at hand, they might hammer out a means of retrieving a seemingly hopeless position. Were the same situation to arise during a home series things could well play out differently: a losing XI might be bolstered with players who had previously not been involved, while those who were struggling would be sent away. The group would disperse to their county teams or homes before the next match, and though they might return fresher there might be less of a feeling of collective enterprise among a radically altered team.

On tour, the players who got themselves into a hole are essentially the only ones who can get them out of it, and this can be advantageous. Matthew Hoggard, though he was jettisoned from the team in just such a situation during Vaughan's tour of New Zealand, was personally involved in seven England teams that went 1–0 down in the first Test of an overseas series, and noted: 'The greatest feeling of togetherness comes when you've just lost a game but still have the chance to play your way back into the series ... for some reason those situations seem to bring a touring squad together.'

Perhaps the times when this comradeship in adversity worked to best effect were in Australia in 1911–12, when Johnny Douglas began shakily as Pelham Warner's stand-in, and the two tours under Hutton, when it became clear that he could not cope with the strain of leadership alone and the players under him came to his rescue.

Douglas was deputed to take over once Warner fell ill with ulcer trouble in the early days of his tour. Prior to departure, Warner had not nominated a vice-captain and, given that convention dictated that the role should be filled by an amateur, the choice when it came to it could only rest between Douglas and Frank Foster, as they were the only other non-professional members of the party. Foster had just led Warwickshire to a county championship title in his first season as captain, and Douglas had only been in charge for one year at Essex, but Douglas was 29 to Foster's 22 and was the much more experienced cricketer.

Douglas duly took over, and led the touring team during a lengthy build-up to the first Test. However, Warner's view, gathered from conversations with others players, was that Douglas had failed to get matters in hand by the time of the first Test. Douglas, he wrote, did not have 'any fixed idea as to who were his best batsmen and bowlers, nor were the fielders always in the places to which they are accustomed. The side was somewhat "ragged" to look at, and this should not have been so, for between my falling ill and the first Test match he had command of the side in the field for five matches.' In the first Test itself, Douglas erred in giving himself the new ball with Foster rather than the brilliant but obstreperous Sydney Barnes, who was incensed at being overlooked. Australia scored 477 and England's batsmen struggled with the mystery spin of H. V. Hordern, whose 12 wickets sealed an overwhelming win for the home side.

What followed was one of the more dramatic crises on an England tour. Probably fortunately, because the first Test lasted six days, a fixture with Combined Universities was scrapped, meaning that in the eight days before the second Test the only cricket scheduled was a two-day Boxing Day fixture at Bendigo. This left time for reflection, although the first of two key meetings actually took place even before the journey from Sydney to Melbourne, which some in the party made by train, others by sea. It involved Warner receiving some of the senior players at his bedside at a nursing home in Sydney. There was some discussion about whether a change in captain should be made, which could only mean Foster taking over, but Jack Hobbs, who was the same age as Douglas and on his second tour of Australia, spoke up in support of the acting leader, partly out of loyalty to a man he admired but also because he probably feared – quite rightly – that a change of captain risked causing friction and unpleasantness.

Douglas, meanwhile, independently asked for the views of Hobbs and two other senior professionals, Wilfred Rhodes and Herbert Strudwick, about where things had gone wrong. Douglas may not have been a master tactician – it was once said that 'of his captaincy no good idea emerged' – but he was resourceful enough to seek feedback from his best professionals, with whom he had a far closer affinity than most amateurs, including Warner. 'He was one of us, more of a professional amateur than an amateur of the old school,' Tiger Smith said. Douglas heeded the advice that in future Barnes must open the bowling and he also acted on Foster's recommendation that Smith, who kept wicket to Foster's distinctive left-arm in-swing bowling at Warwickshire, would be a better choice behind the stumps than Strudwick. Smith learned of his promotion on Christmas Day, so within four days of the defeat in Sydney. 'Johnny took our criticism very good naturedly,' Rhodes said.

Keeping Douglas as captain, and giving Barnes and Foster the new ball, went a long way towards turning things round, along with Hobbs breaking Hordern's hold over the English batsmen with an attacking innings of 126 not out that sealed victory in the next Test. On the first morning of that game, Barnes – now armed with the new ball – produced a spell of 9-6-3-4 that ranks among the greatest ever produced in a Test match for England, an effort all the more remarkable considering he was unwell for two days before the game. The crowd also riled Barnes so much that at one point he threw the ball to the ground and refused to go on until they ceased heckling him.

England won the third, fourth and fifth Tests as well, and across the series as a whole Barnes claimed 34 wickets and Foster 32, and Hobbs racked up 662 runs. Douglas readily acknowledged that he regularly sought Warner's advice and acted upon it – Warner had after all captained a winning side in Australia eight years earlier – but again credit must go to Douglas for not being too stubborn to try and go it alone. Warner's view, in an autobiography published in 1951, was that the 1911–12 team was on a par with Percy Chapman's side of 1928–29 and Douglas Jardine's in 1932–33. 'I would be prepared to back them against any team of my experience,' he wrote.

Clear-the-air talks between captain and senior players were also at the heart of the turnaround in fortunes of Hutton's team in the Caribbean, the only time an England team have avoided defeat after losing the first two matches of a series.* In this instance it took longer for the crisis point to be reached, perhaps because Hutton was on his first tour as the first professional formally appointed to the England captaincy. For him to admit to those under him that he had got things wrong, or for others to openly challenge his approach, would have been an unusually delicate matter.

But even before the end of the second Test it was evident that Hutton's touring party was not a happy one. Not only had England been soundly beaten twice, but the captain's handling of the tour was also causing serious difficulties. Off the field he was sternly disapproving of players drinking and socialising in the evenings – again, probably out of anxiety to demonstrate his authority – while on it his insistence on attritional, risk-free batting dismayed several batsmen to whom this style of play was anathema. It may have suited Hutton himself, but it did not suit them. Even Alex Bannister, the *Daily Mail* journalist,

---

* England have been 2–0 down after two in an away series of four or more Tests on 19 occasions: 13 times in Australia, four times in the West Indies and twice in South Africa. Of these, they have lost 18 and drawn one.

and an ally of Hutton's, concluded that he was 'wedded to a false strategy'. 'Never was his hold on the reins of leadership so insecure,' Bannister wrote; 'never was he the target for such harsh and adverse criticism. Nearly everything that could have gone wrong for Hutton had done so.'

Halfway through the six days of the second Test, Compton led a deputation to Hutton's hotel room after England had just spent a whole day grinding out 128 runs from 114 overs. Probably by now even Hutton was starting to realise the folly of his ways. 'It was time, I pointed out, to throw away our chains and to allow the stroke-players to play the game their own way,' Compton recalled. 'Len said then that he wouldn't interfere with such a policy, and so a new plan went into operation. We were to attack, and attack we did.' England's second innings was a much better effort, with four batsmen making half-centuries and Alf Valentine not being allowed to dictate terms with the ball in quite the same way. The game was lost but the turn-around had started.

A 12-day break ahead of the third Test, during which a game against British Guiana was won by an innings but marred by ugly exchanges between the English players and the umpires, brought the team further together. With less scope for partying in Georgetown, there was more time for the players to further plot their fightback. Without Hutton's knowledge, Trevor Bailey, the vice-captain, arranged a dinner for senior players. At it, Bailey supported Compton's call for a more positive approach with the bat, but also asked for more support for both the captain and the younger members of the team who might be disheartened by the quandary they were in.

The decision to lend Hutton and the younger players more support was probably partly motivated by a desire to make amends for the ill-feeling and embarrassment created by the high jinks on the first night of the Barbados Test, which had led to Tony Lock and Fred Trueman carrying the can. This was not a time to be giving Hutton any further reason to worry. 'Several little pep talks were held during the course of the next few days, and I think they had material effect in producing the will-to-win spirit which swept through the side,' Bannister wrote. In his 2021 book on the tour, David Woodhouse wrote: 'Several players remembered British Guiana as the place where the better team spirit that had been hammered out after "Black Tuesday" [the slow batting day in Barbados] became fully forged.' Hutton agreed to lighten his attitude to off-field relaxation, and before the third Test began the captain publicly made reference to 'a far more united side, maybe drawn together by the constant criticism'.

England duly bounced back in Georgetown, perhaps helped by West Indian complacency. Hutton played a magnificent innings of 169, but there was also a great collective effort from the bowlers after West Indies were made to follow on. A high-scoring draw ensued on the mat in Trinidad before England won the fifth Test back in Jamaica, where Bailey moved the ball around in deadly fashion to take seven wickets on the first day and Hutton produced one of the greatest innings by any England batsman overseas – let alone by a captain – as he batted nine hours for 205.

In Australia the following winter, there was less need for a change of strategy after the first Test defeat. This time it was more a case of keeping faith with a plan that was in danger of unravelling. The huge defeat at the Gabba had been down to a combination of things, including an unfortunate injury to Denis Compton and the illness of Godfrey Evans. Hutton's decision to bowl first was a mistake, but at least it was consistent with his selection of an all-pace attack, and it might not have turned out quite so badly but for a string of missed catches.

Hutton's despair after the game has been much dwelt upon since, but he pulled himself together sufficiently swiftly that after the game he summoned to his hotel room Brian Statham and Frank Tyson, his principal strike bowlers, along with first lieutenant Bill Edrich, for a glass of champagne. 'He was far from disheartened,' Tyson recalled. 'Less [sic] injuries and better catching and we should extend and beat Australia. Even at this stage Len Hutton had confidence in his fast bowlers and, as Brian and I listened, we realised that the series was far from over.' The previous winter's experience of recovering from 2–0 down perhaps also helped keep matters in perspective; the series was retrievable as long as England held their nerve.

Suitably inspired, Tyson put behind him figures of one for 160 in Brisbane and used the two-week gap before the second Test to work on his fitness and modify his approach to the wicket. During a four-day match against Victoria, he reverted to a lengthier run-up involving ten long strides after a series of short steps. 'It is not too long – about 20 yards including the shorter steps, and it should enable me to retain my forward impetus in the delivery stride and follow-through,' Tyson noted in his diary. 'Hopefully, I should retain my speed and increase my accuracy.' It worked a treat: bowling at high pace, Tyson took a career-best six for 68 against Victoria, five of his wickets bowled.

When Statham and Tyson then swept England to victory in the second Test at the SCG, Hutton faced a major selection issue ahead of the third match in Melbourne: should he keep faith with the bowlers who had just delivered a win or find room for Alec Bedser, who was fit for selection and would normally command a place in the side without question? Things had changed, though. Statham and Tyson had just demonstrated their value twice over: not only was their pace incisive but they also took so long to bowl their overs that they allowed Hutton to control the tempo of the game. Bob Appleyard and Johnny Wardle, two other members of the bowling attack, had also contributed with bat as well as ball.

Hutton found the task of telling such a great bowler as Bedser that he was no longer needed so difficult that by the morning of the Melbourne Test he had still not informed Bedser of his impending omission. So emotionally stricken was he that he was incapable of rising from his bed. It required a visit from a doctor and several senior players, including Compton, Evans and Edrich, to convince him that there was nothing fundamentally the matter with him and he must get himself to the ground. 'He was depressed,' said Geoffrey Howard, the manager. 'Len didn't look overjoyed at the doctor's opinion ... but he did as he was told.' Hutton eventually dealt with the Bedser problem by pinning a team-sheet to the dressing-room door 30 minutes before the start of play. It was a poor way of communicating bad news to a valued player, but it was the right call. Statham and Tyson delivered another win to put England 2–1 up, and this was followed by a third victory in Adelaide to secure the Ashes.

Visiting sides have found it notoriously difficult to win in Asia – all the more so in recent years in India when there has been a willingness to produce drastically under-prepared pitches to suit the home team's strength in spin – so it is notable that England have three times come from behind to win there. This reinforces the impression that it may be possible to adjust techniques to slow, turning surfaces perhaps more easily than to fast bouncy ones. There was also the undeniable fact that long Asian tours tended to bring touring parties together rather in the way that happened with Hutton's players in Georgetown, with so many fewer social distractions available. If everyone was obliged to spend more time with each other in hotels, there was less excuse for not building up a good corporate spirit. If a tour began badly, they were well placed to get their heads together and turn things round.

David Gower's team that won in India could hardly have had a more turbulent start, with the assassinations of Prime Minister Indira Gandhi and the Deputy High Commissioner Percy Norris throwing the tour into doubt and forcing the team to retreat to Sri Lanka until the political situation calmed down. Even after the first Test was lost, the schedule hardly helped as, during the eight days between that game and the second Test, the team had to travel by bus three and a half hours each way from Bombay to Pune for a one-day international ('I can't imagine many international sportsmen putting up with it,' Graeme Fowler's diary noted) before playing a three-day fixture against North Zone. But the tour party was a young one and only four of them had been to India before, so perhaps they were less cynical and less complaining than they would have been had they been more seasoned. 'The serious turn of events beyond the cricket bound together the players and the press corps,' Vic Marks, one of players, remembered. 'With so much uncertainty around we all felt that we were in this together.'

Gower's overall Test record as captain was unimpressive, and the following winter he would preside over a 5–0 whitewash at the hands of the West Indies, but he handled the turbulence of this tour adroitly. He made a forceful complaint in his captain's report about the umpiring of Swaroop Kishen in the first Test, which meant that Kishen did not stand again and there were no controversies about the officiating in the last three Tests. He also galvanised his players into believing the second Test could still be won with a forceful address during the lunch interval on the final day; they responded by taking India's last six wickets for 28 and knocking off the 125 needed to win with time to spare. The pitches did not turn much, which put a premium on the control provided by Phil Edmonds and Pat Pocock, while the surface in Madras had enough life in it for Neil Foster to take 11 wickets and help drive home the advantage given them by double-hundreds from Fowler and Mike Gatting.

When Nasser Hussain's side lost the first Test in Sri Lanka in 2000–01 only weeks after they had pulled off a stunning series win in Pakistan, it would have been easy to become despondent. They had the worst of some atrocious umpiring in the game – the quality of the decision-making would remain poor throughout the series – but there were some positive aspects to their performance. They fought hard in the field, made good use of cutters on an unresponsive pitch, and Marcus Trescothick had showed how to bat against Muttiah Muralitharan by making regular use of the sweep shot. Importantly, during the eight-day gap before the second Test in Kandy, head coach Duncan Fletcher demanded a revision to the itinerary, insisting that a three-day fixture in remote Kurunegala was cut to one day to reduce time spent travelling and playing in sweltering heat.

Hussain highlighted the camaraderie in the group. 'We had great team spirit. We found humour in our predicament. It was like, "We're not heroes any more" and, "We could lose 3–0 out here."' There was also a pivotal moment at tea on the first day of the second Test when Fletcher – at Hussain's request – gave the players a dressing-down because they were flat in the field and Sri Lanka, on 216 for four, were in danger of taking the game and series out of England's reach. 'You look like raggy-arsed rangers, now tidy it up,' Fletcher told them. With Darren Gough leading the charge, Sri Lanka were dismissed for 297 and with Hussain, emboldened by his decision not to quit as captain, scoring a hundred, England went on to win a nerve-jangling game by three wickets. Moving on to Colombo full of confidence, they played an even better game and, thanks particularly to Graham Thorpe's brilliant batting, won again.

The circumstances behind the win in India under Alastair Cook in 2012–13 were not dissimilar. England had put in a lot of work batting against spin after being been badly beaten by Pakistan in the United Arab Emirates the previous winter. Some of the groundwork was laid with the centuries Jonathan Trott and Kevin Pietersen scored in contrasting styles during a two-match series in Sri Lanka shortly after the Pakistan tour. Now in India, England were well beaten in the first Test in Ahmedabad, but even though defeat was almost inevitable they showed clear signs they were starting to adapt to conditions by mustering 406 in their second innings.

Cook himself batted more than nine hours for 176. 'I felt, as captain, I had to lead by example … sweeping consistently and choosing my moments to use my feet,' he wrote in his autobiography. 'Batting in India is a mental challenge. The first 20 or 30 balls are very hard work. Everyone is around you, chatting away ... You must learn to manipulate the field, to milk runs carefully but decisively. It is a case of low risk, high reward. Once I demonstrated what was possible, my words carried additional authority ... My message at the end of the game was disarmingly simple: we had to learn how to defend, and when to attack on our own terms.'

England won the second and third Tests – and ultimately the series – because they followed Cook's advice and batted well for totals of more than 400 in Mumbai, 500 in Kolkata and 300 in both innings in Nagpur. Cook himself scored two more hundreds and Pietersen played brilliantly for 186 in the second Test. India also made a tactical error in reacting to England's improved showing in the second innings in Ahmedabad by preparing a turning pitch in Mumbai. This simply served to bring Graeme Swann and Monty Panesar more into the game, and they finished with 19 wickets between them there and then took another eight in Kolkata, where James Anderson's command of reverse swing was also influential.

The nature of the win under Tony Greig in 1976–77, when the side led from the front and never let up until they held an unassailable advantage, has never been matched, but given the nature of the difficult start and the challenge presented by the pitch used in Mumbai, this probably stands as England's finest series win in India.

England Bouncing Back

England have won nine overseas series after losing the first Test.

Series	Captain	Results sequence	Days and matches between losing first Test and start of second Test		Series outcome
Australia 1882–83*	Ivo Bligh	LWW	16	2	England won 2–1
Australia 1911–12	Johnny Douglas	LWWWW	8	1	England won 4–1
South Africa 1922–23	Frank Mann	LWDDW	3	0	England won 2–1
Australia 1954–55	Len Hutton	LWWWD	15	3	England won 3–1
India 1984–85	David Gower	LWDWD	8	2	England won 2–1
Sri Lanka 2000–01	Nasser Hussain	LWW	8	1	England won 2–1
N Zealand 2007–08	Michael Vaughan	LWW	3	0	England won 2–1
India 2012–13	Alastair Cook	LWWD	3	0	England won 2–1
South Africa 2019–20	Joe Root	LWWW	4	0	England won 3–1

*After this original series of three Tests against the Australian side that toured England in 1882, another Test was staged against a team involving additional Australian players; it was won by Australia but regarded as separate from the earlier games.

England have on two occasions drawn an overseas series of four or more matches after losing the first Test.

Series	Captain	Results sequence	Days and matches between last defeat and next Test		Series outcome
West Indies 1953–54	Len Hutton	LLWDW	11	1	England and West Indies drew 2–2

Series	Captain	Results sequence	Days and matches between last defeat and next Test		Series outcome
West Indies 1973–74	Mike Denness	LDDDW	8	1	England and West Indies drew 1–1

In the following away series of two or three matches, England came back from losing the first Test to draw 1–1: v Australia in 1876–77 (two matches); v New Zealand 1977–78 (three matches); and v Sri Lanka 2011–12 (two matches).

CHAPTER 20

The Wheels Come Off
The 2021–22 Ashes and other debacles

The Ashes tour of 2021–22 was a classic of its type, a study in how badly and how thoroughly an overseas mission can unravel. There were various reasons why England might not have beaten Australia in any case, but so many strategic and tactical errors were made that whatever hope the players began with quickly disappeared. At almost no stage across the five Tests did England hold the initiative. The team appeared to lack any sense of drive or purpose; apart from a few passages of play in Sydney, the batsmen were almost entirely passive, barely throwing a punch in six weeks. As always, the players took their lead from those in charge, but that did not necessarily mean the players agreed with their coaches, their captain, or indeed one another; far from it, in fact. The players fell out, and so too did the coaches. Some of the biggest decisions, such as the extraordinary course of action in leaving out Stuart Broad and James Anderson from the first Test, caused big bust-ups.

With Australia winning two Tests in three days and another in four, the series was done and dusted in 20 playing days, the shortest five-match Ashes series in Australia since the very first in 1884–85. England failed to score 300 in any innings in a series of five or six matches away from home for the first time in 63 years. No England batting side playing a series of such length in Australia had ever averaged fewer than this one did (20.21).

What was striking was how much – and from how far out – head coach Chris Silverwood and captain Joe Root staked on the tour. Silverwood, previously the fast-bowling coach, had been brought in as coach in October 2019 with instructions to revive England's Test team after they had spent years playing second fiddle to the one-day side's drive to win a World Cup, but he needed no encouragement to make regaining the Ashes in Australia his principal aim. He did not moderate this talk even when the pandemic disrupted planning. Six months before the tour he said: 'We want to travel to Australia, fitter, faster, leaner, more ready than ever before. They [our players] get off the plane and it is, "Right, we're here, we mean business and we're full of confidence," and that will take us through [to the end of the tour].'

Root had been on two previously losing Ashes tours, the second as captain, and he expressed his intention to put that right. He said shortly before the start: 'I'm absolutely determined to put the record straight. Look at the two previous [Australia] tours. Performances weren't good enough. If we go and approach things in the exact same manner then we're likely to get similar results. It's really important we are brave and take the game to them.'

As discussed in Chapter 12, it is not uncommon for England touring teams to lose the plot tactically by the time of the first Test, and this was certainly the case here. Overly concerned with trying to manage their bowling resources across five Tests in six weeks, Silverwood and Root held back from their first Test XI Anderson and Broad and included left-arm spinner Jack Leach, who had not played a Test in nine months. Root conceded that as a player you could never really ready yourself for the uncompromising nature of an away Ashes series, but

England nonetheless started the series with seven players who had not appeared in a Test in Australia before. (Apart from Broad and Anderson, they also left out Jonny Bairstow, who had scored a century in Perth four years earlier). To compound matters, Root won the toss and chose to bat in conditions ideal for bowling, as though he was desperate to live up to his call for bravery. The batting duly failed, with Rory Burns out to the first ball of the match, and Root himself was also out without scoring. Leach was given attacking fields and conceded 100 runs in 12.1 overs.

Surprisingly, given Root's insistence on not repeating past mistakes, England went into the next Test in Adelaide, a day-night game, with a seam attack including Anderson, Broad and Chris Woakes, all of whom had played in the corresponding fixture four years earlier, but not Mark Wood, the one bowler of genuine pace. After the game was lost, Root publicly criticised their inability to bowl a full length, but was himself challenged for not demanding during the game itself that this happen. 'If you can't influence your bowlers on what lengths to bowl, what are you doing on the field?' asked Ricky Ponting, the former Australia captain. Probably as a consequence of this performance, Broad was left out of the third Test in Melbourne, a must-win game on a surface that would probably have suited him.

Across the five Tests, England made 12 changes, a turnover that smacked more of panic than any coherent plan to keep everyone fit. In any case, the original aim was not met; by the final Test, Ben Stokes had strained a side and Ollie Robinson was afflicted by back spasms. The impact of such successful senior players as Broad and Anderson being left out is hard to quantify, but history suggests it creates a climate in which people start playing for themselves. Ahead of the fourth Test, Root appealed for unity: 'It would be easy to get fractious and point fingers at who could be better. We need to stick tight and stay together.' But a few days later, Broad went ahead and pointed a finger at the batsmen anyway. 'You live by first-innings runs and we haven't delivered,' he said. 'It doesn't matter what bowlers you play if you're being bowled out for 140. It might be brutal but that's the truth in Test cricket.'

There were mitigating circumstances. A World T20 had been put back 12 months because of the pandemic and was staged directly before the tour began; several members of the squad and Silverwood arrived in Australia nine days later than the main body of players and under local Covid regulations had to be kept apart until quarantine was complete. 'Ideally you'd want more space between the World Cup and the Ashes,' conceded the performance director Mo Bobat. 'We mustn't underestimate how much energy that is going to take out of the guys.' Obviously, Australia also had some of their Ashes players involved in the T20 World Cup, but those that were not were able to prepare in their domestic Sheffield Shield tournament, leaving them far better placed than any of the touring party.

To make matters worse, rain washed out all but a few hours of two intra-squad warm-up matches on the Gold Coast, meaning almost all the England players went into the first Test having had little or no red-ball cricket for three months. A Covid outbreak in the camp over Christmas delayed the second day's play in the Melbourne Test by 30 minutes and forced several coaches and family members into isolation; Silverwood missed the fourth Test in Sydney as a consequence. Although the players themselves escaped infection, anxiety levels mounted as they feared being taken out of action.

The handling of the tour by Cricket Australia and the local government authorities left a lot to be desired, and even after the series began the venue for the final Test was switched from a day-time game in Perth to a day-nighter in Hobart. After England went 3–0 down after 12 days of play, director of cricket Ashley Giles admitted: 'Performance has almost been the last thing we've had to think about. How much time have we had to think strategically? Not a lot.'

The most robust defence was delivered by assistant coach Paul Collingwood, a playing veteran of two previous Ashes tours.

If you had given us the best England cricketers from the last 100 years and put them in the same environment that those boys have lived in over the past two years with the preparation that we had going into this Ashes, even they wouldn't have had a chance ... Australia is the hardest place to go to when you've got your best team in form and everyone's playing consistently, never mind during a period of mental fatigue ... The fact we actually turned up and agreed a five-match Ashes series, the guys should be given medals for that. Australia were not bothered that they were going to receive an England team who were mentally fatigued, they just wanted to get the product out there. They just wanted the Ashes. We were sitting ducks.*

In the previous 18 months under pandemic conditions, England had played 18 Tests, Australia four.

Australia's uncompromising attitude was best summed up two months before the series began by Tim Paine, the then Australia captain, who told the England players, who were still considering whether to agree to the proposed quarantine restrictions: 'The Ashes are going ahead ... whether Joe [Root] is here or not.'† But ultimately nothing could excuse England's tactical blunders, or their timid cricket.

---

* Collingwood's argument that Australia's over-riding concern was simply that the English side turned up has historical precedent. Directly after the First and Second World Wars, England agreed to tour Australia with understandably weakened teams – and with understandable results. Australia would have actually had both teams come earlier if they could, but MCC held out for an extra year in each instance; had they not done so, England in 1919–20 would have left home after a season of purely two-day cricket and in 1945–46 after a summer of no meaningful cricket whatsoever.

† As it turned out, Paine was forced to resign as Australia captain over a sexting scandal 19 days before the series began. The Ashes did indeed go ahead, but without him, not Root.

There have been a number of tours where things disintegrated in this way. If there was one feature they had in common it was that when things began to fall apart it proved almost impossible to make the process stop. 'To be captain of a struggling touring side must be one of the worst jobs in the world,' Christopher Martin-Jenkins wrote in respect of Mike Denness's tour of Australia. 'Mistakes tend to be hounded down by the press and used in evidence against the victim.' Frances Edmonds noted the sense of fatalism that took hold of the Caribbean tour of 1985–86 when England lost 5–0: 'When the demon of defeatism takes a team by the throat . . . it requires a very special spirit, or a very special character, to tear him off.'

A few England tours began well before tailing off badly and ending in disappointment, unpicked by injuries and fatigue, and possibly having flattered to deceive in the first place. The side that went to South Africa in 1927–28 under Ronnie Stanyforth won the first two Tests before wilting through a combination of draining humidity in Durban, where the third and fifth Tests were played, and an elbow injury to their best bowler on matting, George Geary. This series was a particular test of stamina as all five Tests were played inside seven weeks, which was very compact for the era – the shortest five-Test series England played before the jet age. The final Test was lost in just three days of play.

Peter May's side also surrendered a 2–0 lead in South Africa. In that instance, Alan Ross put the reason down to an overly long build-up phase contributing to 'tiredness, staleness [and] the accumulation of injuries'. The most bitterly disappointing collapse, though, because it came so close to achieving a singular triumph against an Australia team led by Don Bradman (who never lost a series as captain), was Gubby Allen's team going 2–0 up in 1936–37 only to lose the next three Tests – by margins of 365 runs, 148 runs and an innings and 200 runs. The sheer weight of runs from Bradman's own bat was a major factor, as was the physical demand of five Tests played to a finish in harsh conditions. But Allen's men were found wanting in a more fundamental way: 'The failure, as Australians realistically perceived and as they frankly stated – though in different words, was, at the pinch, a failure as much of character as of technique,' Neville Cardus wrote in *Australian Summer*. Allen's personal failings are dealt with more fully on pages 458–60.

In any search for explanations as to why a particular tour goes badly, breakdowns in relationships usually come high on the list, with the involvement of the captain often to the fore. W. G. Grace as captain in Australia in the early 1890s was as unpopular with his own team as he was with the opposition and the local press, which delighted in mocking the British class system and the evident hypocrisies in a player such as Grace earning more from the game than the professionals. Grace's remuneration from the tour's sponsor Lord Sheffield was staggering, especially as he was 43 and nothing like the player he had once been.

Towards the end, *The Bulletin* reported a contretemps between Grace and one of his star professionals, George Lohmann: 'When the team was bidding Sydney adieu, he [Lohmann] told Grace straight: "Not for £1,000 per week would I again join a team captained by you."' Then, just after the team left for England, *The Bulletin* had fresh Grace-related gossip to impart, again involving Lohmann as well as Andrew Stoddart, the team's other star amateur bat: 'It is reported that English cricketers Grace and Lohmann had a little serious mill in Adelaide a couple of weeks ago. Later on Grace insulted Stoddart and was promptly "plugged". An exchange of blows again took place between the two on the morning of the embarkation per *Valleta* for London. It is known that one of the Englishmen was served with a writ for assault in a row at the bottom of which was a barmaid. Lord Sheffield squared the writ for £90.' Morale among the touring party was doubtless not helped by them losing the first and second Tests despite taking first-innings leads in each. England lost the series 2–1.

No one came under greater pressure when things were going

badly than the captain. With England losing the first two Tests of the 1920–21 series by huge margins, and his own form poor, Johnny Douglas found his position in the side under question as discussions turned to how Percy Fender, a leg-spinning all-rounder, might be fitted into the team. According to Fender, it was the manager Frederick Toone who put forward the idea of Douglas stepping down, and it was one that apparently had the support of Jack Hobbs and Frank Woolley, but Douglas refused to countenance the suggestion and, as it turned out, it proved possible to find room in the side for Fender anyway as Jack Hearne remained hospitalised with suspected malaria and would take no further part in the series.

Douglas's grasp of tactics caused disquiet among some of the players (as it had initially in Australia nine years earlier before England overturned a deficit to win 4–1), and his decision to bring his family on the tour left him further isolated from Fender and Rockley Wilson, the two other amateur players, as well as Toone. This prompted Sidney Rogerson, biographer of Wilfred Rhodes, to note: 'Though there was no outward clash of personalities it would be an exaggeration to say that all was harmony and good fellowship, especially among the amateur element.' Douglas's own form improved markedly but the score-line did not: England went down 5–0.

Just as Douglas was leading a makeshift side directly after a world war, so Wally Hammond found himself doing the same a generation later, and suffered a not dissimilar fate. Hammond's players considered him out of touch – he was ten years older than most of them – and the Australians thought him a sore loser when he brooded on Don Bradman's early reprieve in the Brisbane Test and asked for replacement umpires later in the series. Denis Compton described him as a disappointment, aloof in manner and tactically defensive, and Paul Gibb's heavy-hearted diary recounted frequent grumbles among the players about lackadaisical organisation.

In Gibb's opinion there was a 'complete lack of interest on

the part of captain and manager [Major Rupert Howard] in the welfare of their team'. When Gibb had to undergo surgery for an ulcer on his head, 'neither Hammond nor Howard showed any interest ... Not that I care a button, but if I was captain I'd show more interest in the players under me.' There were reports of Hammond sharing car journeys with his players and barely uttering a word for hours on end, although he had some reason to be distracted as his divorce to Dorothy, his wife of 17 years, was finalised while the tour was going on, and the details would not escape the attentions of the press. In the end he pulled out of the final Test on the grounds of ill health.

Mike Denness in Australia in 1974–75 was unfortunate to fall ill on the outward flight and take three weeks to shake off a kidney infection, but what added most to his problems was his own technical difficulties batting against fast bowling. These had been apparent during the West Indies tour the previous winter, but the pitches there were more benign and to an extent he had got away with it. In Australia, Dennis Lillee and Jeff Thomson laid bare frailties in the English batsmen that were barely known to exist before they left home; nor did Denness and his players have any inkling of the test in store: Lillee was coming back from major back surgery and Thomson had previously made only one unsuccessful appearance in Test cricket.

It soon became clear they were bowling on lively pitches with a skill and speed few could withstand. Within two Tests, Denness was under pressure for his place in the side, and although he saved himself with runs in a state match – Keith Fletcher was dropped for the first time in eight series instead – he later bowed to pressure and left himself out for the fourth Test after scoring 65 runs in six innings. He soon returned, but tactically had a poor game in Adelaide where he failed to use Fred Titmus in tandem with Derek Underwood at the right time. To confirm the impression that he was a strong player against moderate bowling, Denness scored 188 in the final Test when Lillee and Thomson were missing. 'Was there ever a more controversial, more talked-about captain of England?' asked Christopher Martin-Jenkins. 'By the fifth Test at Adelaide, Denness was having to combat backbiting from his own team as well as his own poor form as a batsman ... On the whole his players on this tour could be said to have followed him faithfully in the field, but not to have respected him fully off it.'

Within three years, England *did* have a more controversial, more talked-about captain than Denness, when Geoff Boycott took charge of a tour of Pakistan and New Zealand after Mike Brearley had his arm broken while batting in a minor one-day match ahead of the final Test of the Pakistan leg. England did not lose either Test series, but in Wellington were beaten by New Zealand for the first time in a Test anywhere. The circumstances behind their efforts to level things up in Christchurch led to one of the most blatant revolts against an England touring captain. Boycott's natural aversion to risk saw him bat slowly when England went in a second time on the fourth afternoon with a lead of 183. His painstaking start with Brian Rose exasperated the dressing room and, after Rose and Derek Randall were dismissed, Ian Botham was promoted by vice-captain Bob Willis to no. 4 in an attempt to inject urgency into proceedings.

In an incident that subsequently aroused much debate about Botham's actions, about 20 minutes into the partnership Boycott was run out. John Lever, who was a non-playing member of the team, recalled: 'Beefy was fairly stirred up, as we all were. We wanted to declare and bowl at them that night, but knew Boycott was happy to bat through to the next day ... I think it [the run-out] just happened, and nobody was too upset because it gave us the opportunity to win the game ... Boycs came in [to the dressing room] and sat in the corner with a towel over his head muttering something like, "He's run me out, he's run me out" ... and nobody was taking any notice.' Even then, it was not until shortly before the re-start the next morning that Boycott, under pressure from colleagues, declared the innings closed, leaving New Zealand 280 to win. With Willis and Botham spearheading the bowling effort, England won at a canter. An excruciatingly dull draw on a turgid pitch in Auckland then ensured the series ended 1–1.

Boycott never captained England again, and sometimes cut a difficult figure on subsequent tours. In Australia two winters later, he attempted to declare himself unfit with a stiff neck ahead of a Test in Sydney on what looked like being a particularly juicy pitch, but Brearley was having none of it. 'Heated words were exchanged, and I was practically forced to play,' Boycott wrote in his tour book, in which he elsewhere had a sly dig at Brearley's captaincy as so casual that it encouraged 'a bad lack of discipline'. As we have seen, Boycott also fell out so badly with the team in India in 1981–82 that he was effectively sent home. If the definition of a good tourist is someone who puts personal wishes behind those of the team, then perhaps Boycott tested that requirement more often than any other regular England cricketer. Even so, he spent 11 winters on major tours, so presumably was not that difficult to handle.

There were some tours that England were probably never going to win, and the team David Gower took to the Caribbean in 1985–86 would certainly come into this category. The West Indies side of that era were one of the strongest in history and had already won all five Tests in England in 1984; a repeat on their own territory was always a strong possibility. That Gower's team lost was one thing; the manner in which they capitulated was another. Gower's light-touch leadership style had worked well in India 12 months earlier, freeing them up to produce their best cricket, but now it was blamed for the tour going into free-fall. At one point, Ian Botham, the star all-rounder, came within a whisker of being dropped for the first time in eight years.

Frances Edmonds, wife of Phil Edmonds, chronicled the dark mood in rather more detail than the tour management would have thanked her for. Her husband had been staggered, she said, to attend a meeting at which Bob Willis, a regular tourist for 14 years and now assistant manager, had complained that it was the worst tour he had ever been on in terms of team spirit, and claimed that the team was 'riddled with cliques'. She also recorded how exasperated her husband had been at what he perceived to be 'a lack of determination and leadership' and 'defeatist fucking tactics'. She observed: 'It is certainly difficult to avoid the impression that the team was weakened from the very beginning: by players who made no secret of the fact that they wanted to go home from the outset.'*

John Thicknesse asserted in his report for *Wisden* that the team badly missed Mike Gatting, Gower's vice-captain, during the three weeks Gatting spent off the tour after breaking his nose during a one-day international in Jamaica. Without him there was no one else to pump ginger into them. 'The side was like a ship without a rudder,' Thicknesse wrote.

The losing tours that hurt the most were those that began with high expectations. Any assignment to Australia that ended in defeat when England had left home as holders of the Ashes was especially bitter, and this largely explained the notoriety that attached to the tours under Peter May in 1958–59, Andrew Flintoff in 2006–07 and Alastair Cook in 2013–14 – as well as the Denness tour of the 1970s.

In some instances, it was not simply that England possessed the Ashes. By the time of the Peter May tour, England were unbeaten in 14 series home and away over eight years. By autumn 2013, Cook's team had not been beaten in 13 Tests, while Australia were without a win in nine; the form of the sides appeared to point to only one outcome. Yet all these tours resulted in not only failure, but also some of the heaviest defeats England have suffered, as the teams collapsed under the weight

---

* This remains the only overseas series of more than three Tests in which no England batsman scored a hundred. The highest individual innings across the five matches was Gower's 90 in the final Test in Antigua.

of expectation and the gradual realisation that the old chemistry was no longer there.

The lengthier the tour, the greater the scope for implosion, and, given that Australia tours are typically the longest England undertake, these are the ones that can become most dysfunctional. The May, Flintoff and Cook tours – like the Root one of 2021–22 – all saw relations between players and management break down. All, too, saw the fight go out of the side by the time of the final Test, which in each instance was lost with at least five sessions remaining.

As with Root's tour, there were mitigating circumstances in respect of May's mission. Injuries took a heavy toll. Two left-handers, Raman Subba Row and Willie Watson, were earmarked to bat at the top of the order to counter Australia's left-armers Alan Davidson and Ian Meckiff, but both sustained injuries; Subba Row did not play any of the Tests and Watson appeared in two. In all, England had to call on 17 players in the series, more than they had used in any away series to that point.*

As so often in Australia before third-country officials became the norm, some important umpiring decisions also went against England, unsettling their confidence. More profoundly still, Australia deployed in Meckiff and Gordon Rorke, two of the worst offenders when it came to 'chucking', a phenomenon that was blighting the game around this time; Meckiff's 14 wickets were instrumental in Australia winning the first and second Tests. Such was their malign impact on the series that it accelerated steps towards a game-wide review of bowling actions and to the eventual weeding out of the worst throwers.

England were not exempt themselves: the actions of Peter Loader and Tony Lock also aroused suspicion. After coming across Meckiff in an early state game against Victoria, some of

---

* The only overseas series in which England have used more personnel than this was in Australia in 2013–14, when they called on 18 players in five Tests.

the senior players wanted tour manager Freddie Brown to lodge a formal protest, but Brown and May ducked the issue, and once the Tests got under way and England began losing it was too late. 'The desire not to antagonise the host country let sleeping throwers lie,' Frank Tyson wrote.

The throwing controversy masked deep-seated problems within the touring party; Trevor Bailey called it 'a convenient alibi'. Before departure, Johnny Wardle was pulled off the tour as a consequence of his row with Yorkshire, while May's relationship with Jim Laker, his senior spinner, broke down. A peace was brokered but held only loosely. When Laker pulled out of the fourth Test on the morning of the game citing a sore spinning finger, May was upset but incapable of finding a satisfactory solution. Bill Edrich, covering the tour as a journalist, noted: 'A stronger captain than May might well have ordered the Surrey off-spinner to play.' Instead, May contented himself with writing in his tour report: 'He [Laker] can never be an ideal tourist.'

As a consequence of the injuries, Bailey was pushed up the order to provide ballast, but was condemned for crawling to the slowest half-century ever recorded in first-class cricket, leaving outsiders baffled as to England's tactics. The *Daily Mirror*'s verdict ran under the headline 'Spineless England'. The real problem was that the team was ageing and stale, while May was too detached a character to revive things. Tyson referred to 'a clash of personalities and conflicting interests'. 'We were never a team,' said Tom Graveney. Bailey felt the players were too arrogant and ready to complain. Rather than watch play in the opening Test at the Gabba and learn what they could, some of the non-playing members of the side preferred to head off on an excursion to the Barrier Reef. Bailey, Laker, Tyson and Watson got home and never played Test cricket again.

The 2006–07 tour had similarities with 2021–22 in so far as events beforehand made success a long shot. In this case, injuries ruled out England's established captain Michael Vaughan, who was tactically shrewd on the field and a calming influence off it, and had guided the side to an historic Ashes win in 2005. Also missing was fast bowler Simon Jones, who was England's best exponent of reverse-swing and would have found conditions to his liking. Ashley Giles, the senior spinner, had not played a first-class match for a year because of a hip problem. Then, in the early days of the tour, Marcus Trescothick, the senior opening batsmen, returned home because of his stress-related illness.

It was almost inconceivable that England might overcome these losses, and their only hope was to start strongly. In fact, they could hardly have begun worse. Steve Harmison's first-ball wide was one indication of a lack of mental toughness; another was that only Paul Collingwood and Kevin Pietersen showed any aggression towards the Australian players, who thrived off any signs of weakness among opponents. 'Nobody else was interested, even the captain,' Fletcher stated. Flintoff had been narrowly chosen ahead of Andrew Strauss as Vaughan's replacement, on the basis that after his heroics in the 2005 series he was a figure around whom the other players could rally. In the event, Flintoff showed himself a reluctant leader in the dressing room, and on the pitch less gung-ho than his public persona suggested. He coveted the captaincy, but did not know how to use it to the benefit of the team. As we have seen, as the series unravelled and the pressure mounted, Flintoff sought refuge in drink.

The turning point was a second Test defeat in Adelaide that ranks among the most brutal England have ever experienced. After scoring 551 for six batting first, they appeared to have made themselves immune from defeat – had never previously lost from such a position – but when Australia replied with a score only just short of their own, they lost their way on the final morning when a draw was there for the taking. Sensing their hesitation, Shane Warne piled on the pressure and England subsided from 69 for one to 129 all out, Australia running out winners with something to spare. What might have been 1–1 became 2–0 down, and the series was effectively over.

'People don't realise how much it affects you, how much it drains you and the team,' Collingwood said of that defeat. 'That took the guts out of us. We were absolutely demoralised after that. The feeling was, "This could get really bad."' It did, England losing 5–0 in Australia for the first time in 86 years. 'Mentally it was the toughest tour I've ever been on,' Collingwood added. To their credit, several of that England side rallied to win the Ashes at home in 2009 and triumph in Australia in 2010–11.

The Cook team of 2013–14 had lost its youth. The average age of the team that took the field in the first Test was 31, three years older than the Flintoff side, and they were struggling for motivation after several years at or near the top of the international game. Andy Flower was jaded after five years as head coach. When Jonathan Trott went home after the trauma of the first Test the collapse came, in Cook's own words, 'with bewildering speed'. Another 5–0 whitewash ensued. 'Individually, several players were past their best,' Cook would reflect. 'Collectively, we lacked the cohesion that defined the team that climbed to no. 1 in the world . . . A team that once had a unique form of resilience was falling apart.'

Relationships fractured. Some of these breakdowns involved Kevin Pietersen, who had a stand-up row with batting coach Graham Gooch on the balcony at the WACA after Pietersen holed out on the boundary hitting into the Fremantle breeze. When Matt Prior was dropped after the third Test, Pietersen objected to Prior's continued input at team meetings. Pietersen also delivered a withering assessment of Flower at a players-only gathering in Melbourne, and made his feelings known when a training session ahead of the Sydney Test was less than full-on. Realising that Flower had come to the end, Cook, who was still relatively new to the captaincy, accepted that he needed to take a more prominent role, and advocated terminating Pietersen's England career. It proved an incendiary decision that led to months of back-biting. Pietersen and Graeme Swann never played Test cricket again, and Trott and Prior – whose body, like Swann's, had had enough – featured only fleetingly.

That team deserved a measure of sympathy. Jonathan Trott and Graeme Swann were coming to the end, and Kevin Pietersen was struggling with a long-standing knee problem. The administrators, though, had arranged back-to-back Ashes series, and only five weeks separated the home series from the tour of Australia. 'It was extremely difficult,' Ian Bell told me.

> You'd just won the Ashes and given absolutely everything. At the end of an Ashes series, you all know the reason why there's a couple of years' break – it takes a lot out of you. To then jump on that plane again . . . If we're brutally honest, we had a few guys on that tour that weren't at the top of their games, and a few guys who weren't 100 per cent wanting to be there. Australia exploited that. It's not the environment you can go to unless guys are absolutely committed to the kind of contest you're going to get, on and off the field. We went into our shells a lot. You've got to throw a few punches. That's the way to win Ashes cricket over there. We didn't do that.

England's Heaviest Overseas Defeats

England have played 60 overseas Test series of five or six matches, not counting one in West Indies in 2008–09 when a scheduled four-match series was supplemented by an additional fixture after an early abandonment in Antigua. In 16 of these 60 series, or just over one in four, they lost four or more times: 13 times in Australia and once each in India, South Africa and West Indies. In eight series they were beaten by a margin of four or five matches.

Series	Captain	Results sequence	Total days played	Series outcome
Australia 1920–21	Johnny Douglas	LLLLL	24*	Australia won 5–0
Australia 1958–59	Peter May	LLDLL	27*	Australia won 4–0
West Indies 1985–86	David Gower	LLLLL	20	West Indies won 5–0
Australia 2006–07	Andrew Flintoff	LLLLL	22	Australia won 5–0
Australia 2013–14	Alastair Cook	LLLLL	21	Australia won 5–0
India 2016–17	Alastair Cook	DLLLL	24	India won 4–0
Australia 2017–18	Joe Root	LLLDL	25	Australia won 4–0
Australia 2021–22	Joe Root	LLLDL	20	Australia won 4–0

*Tests in 1920–21 were played to a finish, and in 1958–59 were spread over six days; all subsequent series listed here involved matches played across a maximum of five days.

Overseas Series in Which England Surrendered Leads

England have four times overseas surrendered a lead and lost the series, and on another two occasions led 2-0 before being pegged back to a 2–2 draw.

Series	Captain	Results sequence	Series outcome
South Africa 1927–28	Ronald Stanyforth	WWDLL	England and South Africa drew 2–2
West Indies 1934–35	Bob Wyatt	WLDL	West Indies won 2–1
Australia 1936–37	Gubby Allen	WWLLL	Australia won 3–2

Series	Captain	Results sequence	Series outcome
South Africa 1956–57	Peter May	WWDLL	England and South Africa drew 2–2
India 1972–73	Tony Lewis	WLLDD	India won 2–1
West Indies 1989–90	Graham Gooch	WDLL	West Indies won 2–1

England went 1–0 up but were ultimately held to 1–1 draws in the following series: v West Indies 1929–30 (four matches), India 1951–52 (five matches), Australia 1962–63 (five matches), Australia 1965–66 (five matches), New Zealand 2001–02 (three matches), West Indies 2015–16 (three matches), Bangladesh 2016–17 (two matches) and New Zealand 2022–23 (two matches).

CHAPTER 21

The Final Test, the Final Reckoning

How and why England (sometimes) win

England teams have rarely won Test matches abroad through playing flamboyant cricket. It is not the style of much Test cricket anyway, and it is certainly not the instinctive style of the English game, historically based on the no-frills principles of hard work and tenacity. Their own conditions encourage batsmen whose instincts are watchful and bowlers who seam and swing the ball, and are frugal in outlook. On the longer tours to the stronger territories, England's approach has even more tended towards perspiration rather than inspiration. Successful English teams typically first and foremost make themselves hard to beat, and then strive to take their chances when they present themselves. They are not natural front-runners.

The style of cricket developed under Ben Stokes at home in the summer of 2022 was unusually aggressive for an English side, but it was noticeable that they achieved most of their wins after fighting back pugnaciously from disadvantageous positions. How well such an approach would translate to overseas conditions remained to be seen, only to be gloriously vindicated with some exhilaratingly attacking cricket in Pakistan a few months later, which delivered three wins in three matches, and suggested it was possible even for England teams to successfully apply a one-day or T20 mindset to the Test arena.

The side that Andrew Strauss led to no. 1 in the world ground out big totals but also strove for containment in the field. In the three Tests they won in Australia in 2010–11, they set up each game first with the ball. 'By concentrating on starving the opposition of runs, they [the bowlers] would be able, as a unit, to create enough pressure to induce a batsman into making a mistake,' Strauss wrote. 'Guys who didn't like to be dominated tended to be the most susceptible ... We had found what the England cricket team's unique strength was.' Other winning captains operated along similar lines: Douglas Jardine curbed Australia's run-scoring with leg theory and Len Hutton did so with fast, accurate bowling and a suffocating over-rate. Ray Illingworth gave opponents no respite. England's best captains were not often risk-takers.

There was no shame in this. Bitter experience showed that such hard-headed practicality was necessary, especially on tours where so much was stacked against the visitors. Of course, for many years such an outlook ran counter to the romantic notions harboured by the administrators at Lord's, suited up and sitting at their desks, cup of tea at one hand and a telephone that rarely rang at the other, holding dear the amateur ideals of attacking cricket they been brought up to respect, but which meant little to English players thousands of miles away in hot, uncomfort-able up-country hotels, dusting themselves off after a 36-hour journey by train.

The calls for enterprising play were usually quietly ignored by the men on the ground whose task it was to actually win games rather than talk about it. The rise of professionalism was one factor behind this increasingly pragmatic approach; another was the gritty, loveless nature of touring, which pushed most into emotional bunkers. Writing of England's players in the 1950s, Jim Swanton, the lord protector of the amateur ethos, dolefully reflected: 'The conviction grew among them that this Test cricket was a desperately tough, grim affair in which, if you wanted to win, the opposition had to be kept well at arm's length. The team tended to withdraw into their own tight circle.'

The attritional mindset went back further than that. Wally Hammond was widely admired for his cover drives, but he played those shots only selectively in Test cricket, and in Australia on Percy Chapman's tour he accumulated a record 905 runs, the most in any series for England home or away, at a painstakingly slow strike-rate of 36 per 100 balls. Illingworth's victory in Australia in 1970–71 was in part built on the heavy run-scoring at the top of the order of Geoff Boycott and John Edrich, both of whom made survival their first priority; each had a strike-rate of less than 38. The pivotal innings when Mike Brearley's team retained the Ashes in 1978–79 was Derek Randall taking almost ten hours to score 150 in the fourth Test in Sydney; it turned on its head a game Australia had been winning. The only bigger innings for England away from home made at a slower rate than that was one of Hammond's hundreds on the 1928–29 tour. Randall staved off loneliness during his long vigil by talking to the Australian fieldsmen, advising them as to how they might best set their fields. They did not like that.

Attrition was often England's watchword and often brought results. During the 1960s, when draws were far more common in Test cricket, England won a number of overseas series by narrow margins. Peter May's side came away with a 1–0 result in the West Indies that saw them win the second Test match in Trinidad, a game scarred by riots, and then protect that lead for three games. Walter Robins, the team manager and a disciple of the old school, would have preferred it if Colin Cowdrey, acting captain in May's absence, had made a game of the final Test, but even Cowdrey, despite his Tonbridge, Oxford and Kent background, would have nothing to do with the idea. Robins got short shrift from the players when he attempted to give Cowdrey a dressing-down on the matter.

Cowdrey returned to the Caribbean eight years later as official captain and used go-slow tactics to frustrate Garry Sobers, his opposite number. This worked so well that Sobers made an impulsive declaration in the fourth Test at Port of Spain (after England ground out 404 in 175.4 overs in their first innings) in an attempt to force a result. By this stage Cowdrey was so fixed in his defensiveness (and in any case was always inclined towards caution) that he needed persuading by teammates to go for a target of 215 in 165 minutes. The win was secured with three minutes to spare.

This left England needing a draw in Guyana to take the series, but it took one of their finest rearguards to see them safe. At 41 for five with two sessions left, defeat looked inevitable, but a young Alan Knott, who was not even part of the team at the start of the series, batted for more than four hours, first in a long partnership with Cowdrey himself, and then with the tail. It was an innings that made his reputation. The final act of heroism belonged to Jeff Jones, the no. 11, who amid unbearable tension played out the final over from Lance Gibbs. Such was the local anger at the result that a crowd threw stones from a road behind the pavilion as the English players ran to their vehicles. Tony Lock was hit on the head and Cowdrey had a long wait in the pavilion before police judged it safe for him to leave.

It was ironic that Cowdrey resorted to such tactics, given that Brian Close had been sacked as England captain before the tour for time-wasting in a county championship match. Ray Robinson, the Australian writer, thought it was because Cowdrey had effectively been third in line for the captaincy – M. J. K. Smith was invited to lead the side before him, but was unavailable – that 'iron entered his soul'. Cowdrey even banned his players from golf and fishing on the rest day in Jamaica; he was absolutely determined not to lose.

Even if Smith had agreed to take the side, it is unlikely he would have been any more enterprising. That was evident from the way he had previously captained series in India, South Africa and Australia; 12 of the 15 Tests were drawn and England beaten only once. Under Smith, England won 1–0 in South Africa thanks to an emphatic victory in the opening Test at Kingsmead, followed by four draws in which they were only once briefly in any real danger of defeat. Smith's ultra-defensive approach was criticised in the tour report of manager Donald Carr, whose views were predictably endorsed by Gubby Allen, but by this stage the powers that be were struggling to find credible captaincy candidates who still shared their enterprising views, even though falling attendances showed that interest in Test cricket was dying.

Illingworth's win in Australia was cut from the same cloth. In fact, Illingworth was shrewder and more ruthless than any of his recent predecessors, and he withstood numerous provocations that would have got the better of lesser men. The umpiring of Lou Rowan and Max O'Connell in particular left a lot to be desired and served only to make Illingworth's task harder.* The administrators foisted on the teams at short notice an additional Test to save the Australian board's finances following the washed-out third Test, and the inability of the umpires and the ground authorities to control unruly crowds, who conducted several pitch invasions and threw bottles and cans at England players during the deciding Test in Sydney, was scandalous.

When, against procedure, Rowan gave Snow an official warning for intimidation after bowling one short ball at Terry Jenner (which Jenner ducked into, leading him to retire hurt), Illingworth quite reasonably took issue with him, but at the end of the over the crowd littered the outfield with drinks containers. Illingworth and his players gathered in the middle and sat down until the trouble subsided. When the game re-started and Snow took up a position on the boundary's edge, his shirt

---

* England were not awarded one lbw decision during the six Tests of this series. They also secured only four lbws in the previous series in Australia in 1965–66, and two of those were decisions against tailenders. In mitigation, the lbw law at the time required the ball to be pitching in line with the stumps (rather than in line with the stumps or outside off stump) in order to be given out.

was grabbed by a spectator, so Illingworth took his players off until the situation calmed. He initially refused to be cowed by threats from the umpires and Australian officials that if he did not resume the game he was liable to forfeit it. 'A lot was made out of very little by everyone,' Keith Fletcher recalled. 'One or two police could have sorted it out by pushing back a few spectators who'd had too much to drink.'

To his great credit, Illingworth had one of his finest games in this fraught, low-scoring contest, scoring 71 runs and taking three wickets to bowl England to victory despite Snow being incapacitated by a hand injury. The England captain was criticised in some quarters for not accepting the challenge of scoring 271 in four hours in Melbourne and not enforcing the follow-on in Adelaide, but England were already 1–0 up and had two batsmen carrying injuries in the first game and bowlers whose energies needed conserving in the second. 'Illingworth's side in 1970–71 were mentally the toughest English side I played against,' Greg Chappell said. 'He subjected us to mental intimidation by aggressive field-placings, and physical intimidation by constant use of his pace attack, ably led by one of the best fast bowlers of my experience, John Snow.'*

England's attempts at grim efficiency did not always bear fruit. India in 1981–82 were widely criticised for producing sterile pitches after taking an early lead in Mumbai, but Keith Fletcher's side were just as culpable for the negative cricket that followed, making it virtually impossible for them to achieve the win they needed to get back on level terms.†

---

* The manner of Illingworth's victory was not enough for some. Jim Swanton criticised Snow's 'hot-tempered words' to Rowan after his warning, and suggested Snow was asking to be jostled by spectators by standing so close to the boundary, but meanwhile failed to condemn the pitch invasions by Australians fans, which he passed off as 'high-spirited demonstrations'.

† After the final Test in Kanpur, an Indian spectator was so disgusted with the nature of the cricket that he filed a writ in a local court demanding the passports of the England players be impounded. Unfortunately for him, but fortunately for the England players, the date set for the hearing was after Fletcher's team had left the country.

The tactics deployed by Graham Gooch's team in the West Indies in 1989–90 anticipated those used by Strauss 20 years later: Gooch did not pick a spinner in any of the four Tests (a fifth game in Guyana was washed out), and the fast and fast-medium bowlers he deployed were under instruction to deny the West Indies batsmen boundaries. England won the first Test in Jamaica, their first win against West Indies home or away since 1974, and probably would have won the second had not rain interfered. England's best batsmen, Allan Lamb and Robin Smith, well supported by Jack Russell, then expended so much energy in a failed bid to save the Test in Barbados that when it came to the decider in Antigua they had nothing left. In front of what *Wisden* described as one of the noisiest crowds in the world at the steamily compact Recreation Ground, the visitors were dispatched in four days.

England similarly held their own in South Africa for four matches against a strong side in 1995–96 thanks to a heroic rearguard at the Wanderers, where Mike Atherton held out for almost 11 hours for 185, with Russell again providing able support, only to be beaten in three days in the last Test in Cape Town. Disciplined for so much of the series, they lost the plot during an unexpected last-wicket stand between David Richardson and Paul Adams.

This pattern was repeated in the Caribbean in early 2022, when Joe Root's side had the better of two grinding draws in Antigua and Barbados and went into the third day in the decider in Grenada on even terms, only to fold under pressure as the series reached crunch time. Here again, the inability to extract lower-order batsmen proved decisive, the last two West Indies wickets adding 120 in a low-scoring game.

Those series may have ended in defeat, but these sorts of tight, backs-to-the-wall situations often resonated with the English character and produced unusually strong responses. It was bloody-minded determination that underpinned the win in Pakistan under Nasser Hussain in 2000–01, when for most of the time England were simply holding on as best they could. Pakistan's batting showed few signs of fragility until the final afternoon of the final Test in Karachi, a ground where Pakistan had never lost. Then, in Hussain's words, 'a clatter of wickets suddenly gave us a sniff of what we had been hanging on in there for over the last 14 days.' Pakistan collapsed to 158 all out, leaving England to chase 176 in 44 overs, which, thanks to firm umpiring from Steve Bucknor, a 'neutral' third-country official, they were given the opportunity to do in fading light. It was a classic heist.

Perhaps the closest comparison to Karachi was the chase undertaken by George Mann's team at Port Elizabeth in 1948–49, when they took on the task of scoring 172 in what transpired to be the equivalent of 32 six-ball overs, and won by three wickets with one ball to spare. Mann, educated at Eton and Cambridge, and Middlesex captain, was widely praised for the verve shown on this occasion, but the situation was largely created by South Africa's declaration in search of a series-levelling win. Much of the cricket earlier in the series, following on from a narrow England win in the first Test, was no less cagey than usual.

The draw in Georgetown in 1968 was one of two occasions when England's last-wicket pair have held out in the final Test of a series. The Georgetown game resulted in Cowdrey's team winning the series, whereas the other instance in Auckland in 2012–13 guaranteed them a 0-0 draw with New Zealand in what must rank as one of England's greatest feats of escapology. Striving to bat out the game, they began the fifth day already four wickets down, but lost only one wicket in the morning session, two in the afternoon, and two more after tea. Ian Bell batted six hours and Matt Prior four and a half, while Stuart Broad spent 102 minutes at the crease before scoring his first run, a world record. Prior and last man Monty Panesar saw out the final 19 balls, though not without alarm; Panesar once drifted out of his crease, inexplicably looking to get back on strike, only to be sent scrambling back to safety.*

It is striking that in overseas Tests decided by margins of one, two or three wickets, or by fewer than 30 runs, England have won more than they lost by a margin of 17 to 13 (understandably they are further ahead in home Tests, 15 to eight). By comparison, Australia away from home have lost more narrow games than they have won, by 12 to 19.

There had been times before Stokes when England adopted a more enterprising manner and it worked well for them, but these were very much the exceptions that proved the rule. When Andrew Stoddart's first team to Australia won the deciding Test in Melbourne, the defining innings was played by the sturdy Yorkshireman Jack Brown, who went in at 28 for two with England chasing 297 and attacked from the start. He played a number of risky aerial shots and was dropped twice, but raced to his fifty in 28 minutes and his hundred in 95 minutes before falling for 140.

Root's side won 3–0 in Sri Lanka in 2018–19 playing an ultra-attacking game against Sri Lanka's spinners, sweeping and reverse-sweeping to an extent no England Test side had done before, or has done since. They had the important advantage of having got the measure of some Sri Lankan bowlers in a one-day series that preceded the Tests, and this gave them greater confidence in taking the approach they did.† There was a price for that tactical triumph, however, because it convinced England they could play that way elsewhere, only to come unstuck in the West Indies and at home to Australia, when they opened

---

* There have been four instances of England drawing overseas Tests at earlier stages of the series with their last pair at the crease: at Galle in 2002–03 (first Test); at Centurion and Cape Town in 2009–10 (first and third Tests); and Sydney 2021–22 (fourth Test). Graham Onions played out the last six balls in both Centurion and Cape Town.

† England's run-rate in the Sri Lanka Tests in 2018–19 was at 3.66 per over their second fastest in any overseas series of three or more matches, behind only New Zealand in 2001–02 (3.77) – until the spectacular events under Ben Stokes in Pakistan in late 2022 when the rate hit 5.50, and 4.73 in New Zealand in early 2023.

the batting with Jason Roy, essentially a white-ball specialist. Root subsequently conceded this was a mistake.

England series wins away from home are all the sweeter for their rarity. Those secured in the final Test, when celebrations can proceed in the knowledge that no more serious work lies ahead, are especially sweet. When Douglas Jardine's team won the Ashes in 1932–33 with a match to spare, there was champagne in the dressing room and a celebratory dinner-dance afterwards, but they had a train to catch the next day so there was a limit to how much they could indulge.

Len Hutton's team also won the Ashes in the fourth game of five, but with a full month before the series concluded in Sydney there were fewer constraints. More than 100 bottles of champagne were signed off by the tour manager on the night of victory in Adelaide. The party started in the dressing room before continuing back at the Pier Hotel in Glenelg, where Bill Edrich shinned 20ft up one of the marble pillars in the lounge and Frank Tyson fell asleep under a grand piano. Edrich eventually disappeared for two days of carousing with an old RAF friend, and was found poleaxed in his hotel bed when the bus was ready to leave for the airport.

The Sydney Cricket Ground, which has staged the final Test of more England series than any other foreign ground, did at least provide the finales for Illingworth, who was chaired from the field there by his players, and for Strauss's team, who were able to sit on the outfield and savour the completion of their triumph early on the final morning. When Hussain's team won in Karachi, the players danced to the theme tune from *The Great Escape* as their buses took them back to the hotel.*

*

---

* England wins in the final Tests of five- or six-match series overseas are uncommon. Since 1979 they have won just three out of 23 such games: at Centurion in 1999–2000 (when South Africa's captain Hansie Cronje nefariously contrived a finish in return for a leather jacket from gambler Marlon Aronstam), and Sydney in 2002–03 and 2010–11.

As has been pointed out frequently, the mental toll of many aspects of touring is heaviest on the captains. Few of those who have regularly led England sides abroad have been able to sustain their form, or even reproduce the form expected of them at home. Most England captains are batsmen, yet only seven have scored more than 450 runs in any series away from home; four of those instances occurred in West Indies, where pitches have at times been very good for batting, with only one case each in Australia, India and South Africa – a remarkable statistic in the case of Australia given that England have toured there for four or more Tests 34 times.*

Australian teams have made no secret of their determination to target the opposition captain, believing it is one of the most effective ways to undermine the visitors' camp, and in this endeavour they have been very successful: of the six Ashes tours of the twenty-first century, only one hundred has been scored by an England captain – Andrew Strauss at the Gabba in 2010–11. Strauss's observation that touring captains have to be involved in many more meetings than rank-and-file players, and that as a result they get fewer free days, probably explains why they all too soon end up exhausted.

This in part also explains why the likes of Percy Chapman and Mike Denness left themselves out of Tests on tour. Such are the demands and the strains of leading a tour that the desire to withdraw from the fray is sometimes overwhelming. Even Douglas Jardine proposed leaving himself out during the Bodyline series: ahead of the third and fourth Tests, he put forward this idea to his fellow selectors on the grounds that he was out of form and that the team would endure less animosity from the crowd without him (they swiftly rejected his proposals).

---

* The full list comprises: in Australia, Ted Dexter (481 in 1962–63); in India, Alastair Cook (562 in 2012–13); in South Africa, Wally Hammond (609 in 1938–39); in the West Indies, Len Hutton (677 in 1953–54), Colin Cowdrey (534 in 1967–68), Mike Atherton (510 in 1993–94) and Andrew Strauss (541 in 2008–09). There have been 13 cases of England captains scoring 450 runs in a home series.

Wally Hammond, the oldest man to lead England in Australia since W. G. Grace, pulled out of the final Test of his last tour citing fibrositis, while privately informing the MCC committee of his intention to retire from international cricket at the end of the tour 'because of pressure from business' (not to mention his domestic situation). Ian Botham did not drop himself on his one tour as captain to the West Indies, but during the team's visit to Montserrat, with England 2–0 down with two Tests to play, Frank Keating noticed that he already looked broken from his ordeal. 'His eyes have lost the challenging, defiant sparkle they had when we first arrived in Antigua all those aeons ago. His once-mighty shoulders honestly seem to have hunched visibly.'

Andrew Stoddart was feted on his first tour of Australia as captain, but three years later found the experience altogether more traumatic, and not only because of the devastating news of his mother's death. He was further upset by his team being outplayed and the sustained hostility of the Australian public, and particularly upset by the behaviour of those on the terraces at Sydney during the final Test. During Australia's fourth-innings run-chase they 'howled' and 'hooted' when Tom Richardson bowled a full toss over the head of Joe Darling, 'to such an extent that . . . he had lost his head and lost his bowling'. Stoddart said Richardson had come to him 'almost with tears in his eyes'.

As a partnership developed between Darling and Jack Worrall which would decide the game, the public screamed insults at the English fielders, and Tom Hayward dropping a catch off Darling was attributed to this distracting cacophony. In his speech following the game, and in an interview he gave shortly afterwards with the *Sydney Referee*, Stoddart made plain his distress. He said he would probably not tour Australia again, and called on those in authority to stamp out a 'system of barracking' that the English players had encountered 'on all the grounds, and in all our big matches'. It was a sour end to the international career of one of Test cricket's early champions. Barracking remained a feature of international cricket in Australia.

Few England captains in Australia have struggled as painfully as Gubby Allen. In terms of results, he and his side did well to take a 2–0 lead against an Australian team led by the indomitable Don Bradman, and there was no shame in ultimately losing 3–2, but for England captains a tour Down Under has always been about more than results. 'He [an England captain in Australia] becomes one of the lions of society out there and cannot avoid, without discourtesy, numerous social obligations,' the *Evening Standard* correspondent Bruce Harris noted. 'He is a social ambassador as well as a cricket opponent.' But as another newspaperman, L. V. Manning of the *Daily Mail*, anticipated before the tour began, Allen was 'hyper-sensitive to criticism and is certain to make hard labour of his responsibilities'. Sure enough, Allen's many letters home to family and friends expressed constant grumbles about the number of social functions he was expected to attend, and speeches he was required to make.* Things need not have been so bad, though. Allen himself was partly responsible for this state of affairs, as from the outset he was reluctant to appoint a vice-captain – Walter Robins eventually filled this role – or delegate to his manager, Captain Rupert Howard.

Allen also over-bowled himself in the build-up to the first Test, and towards the end of the series was so exhausted that he was forced to take a break between the fourth and fifth Tests, when the series stood level at 2–2, and it would have been better if he could have got himself attuned for the

---

* Allen appeared to find the full-time demands of touring onerous, as did many amateurs, who were used to picking and choosing their fixtures at home. He rarely played many first-class matches in an English season; the 16 he played in 1936 was his most since 1926, and of those all but four took place in London, at Lord's or the Oval. 'I have had to give up almost all private parties just before or during big matches,' he wrote during the 1936–37 tour. Douglas Jardine's refusal to give him more time off in Australia in 1932–33 was the real cause of their falling-out then rather than Allen's supposed opposition to Jardine's Bodyline tactics.

decider. 'These Test matches simply knock hell out of me, I get so worked up and excited,' he confessed during the first Test. Not only did his contributions with bat and ball tail away, but tactically he also made some costly errors, notably in the pivotal third Test when he delayed his declaration on a rain-affected pitch that could have provided England's bowlers with rich pickings. 'I was terrified that Gubby Allen would declare and send us in for an hour or so on that pig of a pitch,' Bradman stated. 'I was afraid to look towards the pavilion, lest I saw him waving a hand to call us in. But he waited.' William Pollock of the *Daily Express* said of Allen: 'You cannot honestly rank him among the great captains.' In a letter written during the voyage home, Allen admitted: 'I reckon I was nearer to a mental storm when I came on board this boat than I have ever been.'

Mike Green managed tours of South Africa and Australia shortly after the war, and wrote in an autobiography published in 1956: 'There are few captains who can go through an Australian tour without having to go away for a couple of weeks' rest. The strain is largely mental and, since the cricket writers have become so numerous and active, the pressure is very much greater.' Green referred to how Len Hutton had struggled on the 1954–55 tour, when he had remained with the team throughout 'and his play showed signs of deterioration', adding: 'Had he rested, he might well have come back fresh.' Green said that fatigue was not just confined to captains: 'I noticed that the keenness and energy of the players decreased as the tour was reaching its end. Inevitably they became tired and in some cases stale, and the desire to be back with wives, children and sweethearts increased as the date for the return to England approached.' In South Africa, Green even sought the advice of a doctor, who prescribed vitamin pills, which Green thought seemed to produce the desired effect of 'renewed energy and keenness'.

Hutton was partly exhausted by the strain of his status as professional captain – the scrutiny it brought to every decision he made, and the hostility he knew existed towards him among the 'inner circle' at Lord's and many of the broadsheet correspondents. There was also the self-imposed pressure of wanting to win, or at least not lose, as well as the toll of handling the fastest bowling as an opening batsman. He needed at various times cajoling and reassuring. He said the particular strains of the West Indies tour, on which he struggled for sleep even after resorting to medication, took two years off his career. It was originally intended that he would continue as England captain in the summer of 1955, but he ruled himself out through ill health and never played Test cricket again.

Peter May, who took over from Hutton and captained in 41 Tests, also felt acutely the strain of the job, and that combined with ill health forced him to miss ten Tests in 1959 and 1960, expediting his retirement at the early age of 32. Frank Tyson, who made all his Test tours under Hutton and May, listed among the issues tour managers had to deal with, 'illnesses which spring from worry'.

Green's suggestion that captains should take a break during long tours was feasible during the era of up-country fixtures, but once these were stripped out of itineraries the scope for anyone leaving a tour for several days greatly diminished. Among the last to enjoy such luxury were Mike Brearley, who once stayed behind in Sydney while the team spent six days in Tasmania between Tests, and David Gower, who between the second and third Tests in India missed a three-day game against East Zone in Gauhati and went off tiger hunting in Rajasthan with his opening batsman Tim Robinson.

Bob Willis carried a particularly heavy burden as a fast-bowling captain. He said he usually took two or three weeks to adjust his body clock in Australia, but when he led the side there on his fifth visit he found it hard to sleep throughout the tour as he fretted over the team's poor performances, the impossibility of balancing the team when his star all-rounder Ian Botham was not bowling well, and his own mistake in putting Australia into bat in Adelaide (a decision that, according to one of Willis's players, Vic Marks, 'almost destroyed him as captain'). Those were the issues, Willis told his diary, 'which have helped to keep me awake for weeks'.

Most England captains found that doing the job for three or four winters was more than enough for them, and that the winters aged them more than the summers. Mike Atherton wanted to resign as captain ahead of the West Indies tour of 1997–98, by which time he had been in charge for four years, but was persuaded against his better judgment to carry on. Towards the end of the Ashes series the previous home summer, he was struggling to switch off, had become completely self-absorbed, and needed sleeping pills at night. 'I don't think that I was in any fit mental state to be captaining England,' he wrote in his autobiography – though he somehow managed to lead them to a consolatory victory at the Oval.

The Caribbean trip did not go well, England missing opportunities to win a series that they eventually lost 3–1, and after it was over Atherton announced he was quitting. This time no one tried to dissuade him. His sleep patterns had not been improved by two nerve-racking games in Trinidad, and he wondered whether the result might not have been different had someone else led the side. 'A different captain may well have had a fresh outlook, and have been able to drag a little extra out of the players . . . He may have had that vital spark, or energy, that I felt on my fifth tour as captain was lacking.' As we have seen, Nasser Hussain went through a crisis of confidence during his second winter in charge, but rallied and eventually got through four before quitting the one-day captaincy after England's early exit from the World Cup in South Africa. He relinquished the Test job at home a few months later.

Michael Vaughan, like Atherton, got through five winters, although his involvement in the fourth of these was greatly restricted by injury, and by the end was similarly struggling mentally to keep things on an even keel, despite giving up one-day cricket the previous year (a standard ploy for those wanting to extend their time in charge of the Test side). Vaughan's diary entries during his last winter in Sri Lanka and New Zealand chronicled his feelings of stress and anxiety, and his uneasy relationship with Peter Moores, the new head coach. When he wrote after a gruelling day in the field, 'I'm beginning to question whether I am really the right man to captain. My head is constantly aching,' he could have been writing for many an England captain on many an England tour. When a home Test series against South Africa was lost the following summer, Vaughan did not need to question whether he was the right man any longer; he knew and within hours had resigned. As we have also seen, when Andrew Flintoff stood in for the injured Vaughan in Australia, he found the task overwhelmingly difficult and was never the same player again. 'That tour really drained him mentally,' Paul Collingwood said.

More recent Test captains such as Andrew Strauss, Alastair Cook and Joe Root, and white-ball captain Eoin Morgan, appeared to cope with the demands better than many of their predecessors. There were obvious reasons for this. The most significant was an increasing division of labour: Cook stopped playing international white-ball cricket altogether around halfway through his four years as Test captain, and Root only ever led England in Test matches. Morgan, in turn, was able to focus all his energies on leading England's ODI and T20 teams without the distraction of trying to sustain a Test match career. This worked to everyone's benefit.

Central contracts also meant players were expending virtually all their energies in the cause of the national team rather than their counties. There was also better support for the players medically, psychologically and holistically. Mark Saxby was a confidant of many senior players for many years before his duties were formally expanded from masseur to player support coach in 2019. (When Vaughan first toyed with quitting the Test captaincy, he first ran the idea past Saxby and was talked out of it.)

'He has a high level of emotional intelligence and empathy [and] a really strong level of trust with the players,' Ashley Giles said of Saxby. 'They are prepared to open up to him and share things they might not with others.' It should be no surprise therefore that the reigns of four of the five England captains to lead the side in 50 or more Tests, and of four of the six to lead the side in 19 or more Tests overseas, date from 2003.

Even so, the job got to them all in the end. Despite a number of setbacks, Root seemed to wear his crown lightly for more than five years before resigning shortly after returning from a tour of West Indies in early 2022. He kept his real feelings in check until he had scored a century against New Zealand at Lord's in his first Test back in the ranks, when he confessed: 'It had become a very unhealthy relationship, the captaincy and me. It started to take a really bad toll on my personal health. I couldn't leave it at the ground any more, it was coming home. It wasn't fair on my family, on people close to me, and it wasn't fair on myself either. I had thrown everything at it, but it got to the stage where it was time for someone else to lead.'

England's Biggest Wins Overseas

Overseas series in which England won by a margin of three or more matches

Series	Captain	Results sequence	Series outcome
Australia 1978–79	Mike Brearley	WWLWWW	England won 5–1
South Africa 1913–14	Johnny Douglas	WWWDW	England won 4–0
Australia 1911–12	Johnny Douglas*	LWWWW	England won 4–1
Australia 1928–29	Percy Chapman	WWWWL	England won 4–1
Australia 1932–33	Douglas Jardine	WLWWW	England won 4–1
South Africa 1895–96	Lord Hawke**	WWW	England won 3–0

Series	Captain	Results sequence	Series outcome
New Zealand 1962–63	Ted Dexter	WWW	England won 3–0
West Indies 2003–04	Michael Vaughan	WWWD	England won 3–0
Sri Lanka 2018–19	Joe Root	WWW	England won 3–0
Pakistan 2022–23	Ben Stokes	WWW	England won 3–0

*Douglas led England in all five Tests; Pelham Warner was the officially appointed captain at the start of the tour but fell ill after the first state match.
**Lord Hawke missed the first Test, when the side was led by Timothy O'Brien.

England's Overseas World Cups 1987–2015

An overseas World Cup was a sufficiently large event, spanning anything from six to eight weeks including the build-up, that it was virtually equivalent to a Test tour. Often, too, England would attach bilateral series directly before or after the tournament. When a World Cup followed straight on from a major Test tour, the demands could be extreme. Some players were away for 92 days in 1991–92 (New Zealand tour, then World Cup), 140 days in 2002–03 (Ashes tour, World Cup) and 151 days in 2010–11 (Ashes tour, World Cup).

It was as a result of a dispute between players and the ECB about the team not being allowed to return home for a few days between the end of the Australia tour and the start of the World Cup in 2002–03 that the board eventually moved to de-couple a World Cup winter from an Ashes tour; this led to a tour of Australia taking place in 2013–14 rather than 2014–15.

Hosts	Dates	Days*	England placed	Other elements of tour (if any)
India/Pakistan	30 Sep–9 Nov 1987	41	Runners-up	Before ODIs/Tests in Pakistan
Australia/New Zealand	16 Feb–27 Mar 1992	40	Runners-up	After ODIs/Tests in New Zealand

Hosts	Dates	Days*	England placed	Other elements of tour (if any)
Pakistan/India/ Sri Lanka	3 Feb– 12 Mar 1996	39	Quarter-final	None
South Africa/ Zimbabwe/Kenya	28 Jan– 6 Mar 2003	38	Group	After Tests/ODIs in Australia
West Indies	2 Mar– 22 Apr 2007	52	Super Eights	None
India/Sri Lanka	7 Feb– 28 Mar 2011	50	Quarter-final	After Tests/T20s/ ODIs in Australia
Australia/ New Zealand	2 Feb– 15 Mar 2015	42	Group	After ODIs in Australia

*How long England were at the tournament, including preparation time and, where applicable, inward and outward journeys from the UK.

England also competed in five overseas Champions Trophy tournaments between 1998 and 2009 (initially simply known as the Wills International Cup and ICC Knockout). The first of these overlapped with the start of the 1998–99 Ashes tour, so England were permitted to send a second-string squad. The five tournaments were staged in Bangladesh 1998 (England played one match), Kenya 2000 (two matches), Sri Lanka 2002 (two matches), India 2006 (three matches) and South Africa 2009 (four matches; England for the only time abroad reached the semi-finals, where they were beaten by Australia).

England's Overseas T20 World Cups 2007–2022

England won their first global limited-overs tournament when they lifted the T20 World Cup in the West Indies in May 2010. They made a late change to their plans following a warm-up match against an England Lions side two months earlier, in which Michael Lumb and Craig Kieswetter opened the batting for the Lions and looked better suited to the role than England's incumbent pair of Jonathan

Trott and Joe Denly. Lumb and Kieswetter were then members of an XI led by Paul Collingwood that barely changed throughout the seven-match campaign (Kevin Pietersen missed one match through paternity leave and was replaced by Ravi Bopara). Five bowlers – Ryan Sidebottom, Tim Bresnan, Stuart Broad, Graeme Swann and Michael Yardy – bowled all but two of England's overs.

England lost the final of the 2016 tournament to West Indies in Kolkata when, with 19 needed at the start of the final over, Ben Stokes had his first four balls hit for six by Carlos Brathwaite. Redemption arrived in 2022 when Stokes was instrumental in them lifting the T20 World Cup for a second time with a match-winning innings against Pakistan in the final in front of 80,000 people at Melbourne. An unexpected defeat to Ireland in a rain-affected game and a washout against Australia, both in the group stage, meant England, under Jos Buttler, had to win every game thereafter, which they did – beating New Zealand, Sri Lanka, India (raucously by ten wickets in the semi-final) and Pakistan.

Hosts	Dates	Days*	England placed	Other elements of tour
South Africa	9–20 Sep 2007	12	Group	Before ODIs in Sri Lanka
West Indies	25 Apr–16 May 2010	23	Winners	None
Sri Lanka	13 Sep–3 Oct 2012	21	Group	None
Bangladesh	15–31 Mar 2014	17	Group	After ODIs/T20s in West Indies
India	8 Mar–5 Apr 2016	29	Finalist	None
UAE	4 Oct–11 Nov 2021	39	Semi-finalist	Before Tests in Australia
Australia	15 Oct–15 Nov 2022	32	Winners	After T20s in Pakistan/ Australia and before ODIs in Australia

*How long England were at the tournament, including preparation time and where applicable inward and outward journeys to the UK.

CHAPTER 22

The Homecoming
Revels, reviews and recriminations

Long before the end of a big tour, thoughts would turn towards home. For a team that was winning, or a player who was in golden touch, the days might not weigh quite so heavily at this late stage, but for others the end probably could not come soon enough. There was only so much one could tolerate of cricket grounds and net sessions, of hotel lobbies and airport lounges. Not everyone might have gone quite so far as Geoff Miller on a four-month tour of the subcontinent by ritually counting off each day on an umpire's ball-counter, but calculations about how much time was left were common.

Frank Keating described the last two weeks of Ian Botham's ill-starred venture to the Caribbean as 'like the approaching end of term at a ramshackle prep school, the pent-up excitement being progressively released by the boys as the days were ticked off ... Are they always as homesick and deflated in defeat as this?' Keating possibly answered his own question by judging the tour 'one of the most calamitous trips (morally, spiritually and statistically) for over a century'. Emotions were generally mixed, though. However tired one became of touring, it was not easy to walk away from Sydney or Cape Town, Barbados or Grenada, and not feel some ache of remorse. 'Touring is a strange business,' Bob Willis once wrote. 'No matter how many headaches and heartaches are endured during the long period away from home, there are always regrets when it is time to leave.'

Generally, the bigger the tour, the less tidily they ended. The case for keeping a group of players together throughout an entire trip was powerful; it allowed team spirit to develop and be sustained. But as the final days approached, the collective spirit tended to dissipate as mental and physical fatigue took over. There were sometimes also sound practical reasons for breaking up the squad. When England teams used to go on to New Zealand for a few Tests at the end of an Australian tour – Tests in which their batsmen often filled their boots – the size of the party might be trimmed because it was no longer necessary to keep, say, 17 players prepared when 14 would do; in those circumstances, those who were carrying an injury niggle or were judged excess to requirements might be allowed an early boat or plane home.

On Wally Hammond's tour of Australia, only 13 players took the flying boat on to New Zealand, with four others staying behind in Sydney before sailing home. One of the four, Paul Gibb, felt conflicted as he saw them go. He had spent much of the tour as a non-playing reserve. 'I feel a new man with a sense of greater freedom,' he wrote. 'Free from what, I don't exactly know. Free, perhaps, from an ever-present awareness of my erstwhile skipper's presence ... I wouldn't trust Wally Hammond any further than I can see him ... [but] perhaps the blame, if blame it can be called, lies more within myself. I have no longer to put up any pretence of mixing with and enjoying the company of my fellow players. I liked them all, yet always wanted to be left alone.'

Modern tours became fragmented for different reasons. Nowadays, itineraries are divided into red-ball and white-ball blocks, and players who specialise in one or other sphere will come and go from tours at different times. Only the multi-format players – of whom there might be perhaps up to five or six – would be present throughout. Such divisions of labour became standard practice after a humiliating failure at the 1996 World Cup finally persuaded the authorities that it was necessary to cultivate one-day specialists rather than simply hope the best Test match cricketers would be able to adapt to a fast-changing short-form game.

Once split squads were established, the pattern of interspersing Tests with ODIs on tour stopped; instead, a series of ODIs was played either before or after the Tests – usually the latter. Of 38 bilateral tours involving Tests and white-ball matches since 1997, 24 saw England play the ODIs (and sometimes T20s) at the end.* It is necessary to go back to West Indies in 1993–94 for the last time a group of England players returning home from Tests and one-dayers was overwhelmingly made up of the same personnel who had originally set off.

Odd though it now seems, when the pace of touring life was more leisurely it was not unusual for further fixtures to be played against local state or zonal teams after the conclusion of the Test series. This was essentially a consequence of teams needing to head back to port at, say, Adelaide, Cape Town or Bombay, and awaiting their appointed sailing. If there was time, they might play a farewell game before departure.

It was as one tour of South Africa wound down in this way in the 1920s that, en route for Cape Town, the team stopped at Grahamstown for a two-day fixture against a combined schools side; with the English batsmen going well, Ian Peebles, their leg-spinner, no doubt embracing the end-of-term mood, took himself off to bathe in a nearby river. As he recounted: 'The time passed more quickly than we had calculated, and when I

---

* Since January 1997, the only England tour that saw ODIs staged in the midst of a Test series was in Australia in 2002–03, when they played four ODIs between the third and fourth Tests. They still used separately tailored squads.

got back, we were in the field and I was soundly and properly berated by Ronnie [Stanyforth, the captain]. However, no one was more amused than he when next day the *Cape Times* in their score of the match had a line: "Peebles absent bathing 0", an entry surely unique in the scorebooks of the world.'*

The practice of fixtures taking place after the final Test effectively ended with the move to air travel: the last non-international fixture of note to round off a tour was M. J. K. Smith's team playing a three-dayer against North Zone at Amritsar in 1963–64, which was the first winter in which England travelled both ways by plane. In 1981–82, Keith Fletcher's team flew to Trivandrum after completing a Test in Sri Lanka specifically to play a benefit match for Govind Bawji, who had for many years served as England's baggage-manager in India, which raised £3,000.

Waiting around for a ship to sail was one thing, but things could get tricky if matches were arranged too close to departure dates. England had to abandon as draws two final Test matches that had been intended to be played to a finish – one in Kingston, Jamaica in April 1930 and the other in Durban in March 1939 – after the games went on so long that the English players were in danger of missing their voyages home. The Jamaica Test spanned ten days (including one Sunday off and two wash-outs) and the Durban Test 12 days (including two Sundays and one wash-out). At the end in Durban, England were 654 for five in pursuit of an improbable target of 696, so one more session would have been enough for a conclusion. Time, though, had sadly run out on this most famous of 'timeless Tests': the touring party needed to take a train to Cape Town to catch their boat.

Sometimes players were allowed to leave before the rest of the team. One of the most extraordinary instances occurred when

* Peebles probably achieved another first when he alighted from his train at Waterloo armed with a Portuguese-speaking parrot purchased at Madeira during the return voyage.

Douglas Jardine sought permission from both teams to depart the game should the final Test of the 1928–29 series in Australia, where matches were played to a finish, extend beyond a fifth day. He needed to leave Melbourne for Perth (a train journey of more than 2,000 miles) in time to board the *Maloja* bound for India, as he had arranged to visit the country of his birth on the way back to England. As it happened, it took almost five full days of play in Melbourne for both sides to complete their first innings, compromising Jardine's ability to make a worthwhile contribution when England batted again.

Opening the batting alongside Jack Hobbs (as he had in the first innings, as Herbert Sutcliffe had been rested for this game), Jardine was out for a first-ball duck during a short passage of play before stumps on the fifth evening. This left him free to head off as planned by the next afternoon's train for the long journey to the west coast. Jardine seemingly had alternative arrangements in place should he have needed to bat on the sixth day; it was reported that he would have chartered a plane if necessary. Percy Chapman fielded substitute in Jardine's absence but agreed not to take up any of his specialist positions – though this did not stop the Australian press accusing the English of chicanery. In the event, Australia won by five wickets.*

The early tours were such great enterprises that the English cricketers were rarely allowed to leave without a proper send-off. This might have entailed grand banquets, the exchanging of gifts, and of course more speeches, and were generally amicable occasions, with any disputes or rancour that might have marred earlier stages of the tour diplomatically forgotten. Not so W. G. Grace's tour of Australia in 1873–74, the professional members of the English team boycotting the farewell dinner in protest at being 'shabbily and snobbishly treated'.

---

* Greville Stevens was allowed to leave the 1922–23 tour of South Africa several weeks early because he was in his final year of studies at Oxford University; he had played in the first Test of the series but was unlikely to feature again.

Winners or losers, when they boarded their ship, large crowds would gather at the quayside to send them on their way with good wishes. Of the departure from Cape Town in 1949, one member of the party wrote: 'Literally hundreds were throwing streamers to the boat. They sang, shouted and waved their fare-wells till even Table Mountain seemed small as it sank into the blue, calm sea.' These days, England's cricketers leave foreign countries seamlessly, with little fanfare or fuss. They leave their luggage outside their hotel room doors on their last night and are often able to go through off-airport check-in at the hotel before leaving the lobby. The closest they come to a celebratory dinner might be a few beers with the opposition after the final match.

A small number of English cricketers did not return home with their teams but chose to stay on to pursue business oppor-tunities. William Caffyn and Charles Lawrence remained in Australia after early tours to coach. During the days of the gold rush, Aubrey Smith and Monty Bowden, members of the inaugural side of 1888–89, remained in South Africa to set up a stockbroking firm; the venture failed and Bowden never saw England again, dying in miserable circumstances three years later. Frank Hearne, another member of the same 1888–89 side, did return home but headed back to the Cape the following year to settle, and ended up playing for South Africa against the next English team to visit. Frank Milligan stayed in South Africa after the 1898–99 tour and died during the siege of Mafeking 12 months later.

When George Parr's team sailed from Quebec in October 1859, the ship's captain instructed a large board to be brought onto the deck of the *North Briton* as it passed the *Nova Scotian*, the vessel which had carried out the cricketers two months earlier. On the board was chalked the message, 'Won all matches'. The news was greeted with deafening cheers from all aboard the other vessel, while the senior officers on the bridge waved their caps in salute. 'We responded, by giving them such hearty cheers as only can proceed from English throats,' Fred Lillywhite wrote. 'Thus we parted.'

It was a rare moment of pleasure on the two-week voyage to Liverpool. A few days in, the *North Briton* encountered severe storms, during which one of the anchors was lifted by a wave and crushed the legs of a member of the crew, John Evans, aged 63. He never regained consciousness and died as the ship reached port. The cricketers were among those who raised £30 for the sailor's widow. 'Although the whole of the cricketers have abundant reason to be satisfied with their trip ... it is a very great question whether some of their number could be persuaded again to undergo the suffering and inconvenience consequent upon such a voyage,' Lillywhite added. But persuaded some of them were, and so too many others.

Better ships smoothed future voyages, and calmer routes home were found. Before the jet age, a popular way of returning from New Zealand, where many Australasian tours ended, was across the Pacific — and across the International Date Line — to Vancouver, San Francisco or Los Angeles, from where the team might travel across North America by train before embarking on the Atlantic crossing from Montreal or New York. It was a round-the-world trip known as the Red Route, as everywhere visited — bar Hawaii — was on the red- or pink-coloured part of the map denoting British Empire territory.

Jardine's Ashes-winning side left Auckland for Fiji, where they would have played a match had it not rained, before stopping off in Hawaii, where they were entertained by the British Consul. They docked at Vancouver, where after a short stay they boarded the Canadian Pacific train for a four-day journey broken by a stop to visit Niagara Falls. At one 20-minute station visit, Maurice Tate was sent off to find liquor as the train was 'dry'; he duly came back with the goods, just in time. That Atlantic crossing turned out to be one of the worst as the *Duchess of Atholl* battled to dodge icebergs. She was eventually re-routed from Liverpool to Greenock.

Four years later, Gubby Allen's side followed a similar route. They went surfing during a stopover in Honolulu, and upon arrival in Los Angeles headed for the Hollywood studios, where they met numerous silver-screen stars including David Niven and Boris Karloff. Allen had friends there including Aubrey Smith, who having failed as a stockbroker in Johannesburg had now developed a successful film career, while also managing Hollywood Cricket Club. Allen harboured dreams – never realised – of following in Smith's footsteps and stayed on for a holiday, while his players travelled home. Occasionally, teams returned via the Panama Canal, as was the case with the first England team to play Tests in New Zealand led by Harold Gilligan.

One of the toughest journeys must have been undertaken by Johnny Douglas's side shortly after the First World War when, with an immediate return series arranged for the English season, they were obliged to sail on the same boat as Warwick Armstrong's Australians.

On an individual level, few returns can have been as traumatic as Bob Wyatt's from the Caribbean in 1934–35. The England captain's jaw had been broken by the Bajan fast bowler Manny Martindale during the final Test – Eric Hollies, sitting in the dressing room behind closed windows, said it sounded like a revolver shot – but with the boat home due to sail from Port Antonio four days later, Wyatt was desperate to be on board. He discharged himself from hospital and with the help of the manager Carlton Levick headed for the dock.

'It was a voyage I would be glad to forget,' he later recalled. 'They had not wired my jaw, I was still suffering from shock, and as I could eat nothing solid I existed on a diet of Ovaltine, Horlicks and Guinness, followed later by a little spinach. I very nearly died.' At one point during the voyage, the ship's doctor judged that sepsis was setting in and his jaw was drained for several hours, but Wyatt was one of the toughest – as well as one of the most injury-prone – cricketers

England produced, and he survived. He got home, had the jaw rebuilt with a bone graft and three months later was back captaining a Test match against South Africa at Trent Bridge. He scored 149.

A similar escape was accomplished by wicketkeeper Herbert Strudwick at the end of a pre-First World War tour of South Africa. Strudwick contracted malaria, played the final Test purely as a batsman, and was thereafter confined to bed in Cape Town but, determined to make the voyage back to Southampton with his teammates, he managed to remove the thermometer from his mouth while the doctor was distracted by Colin Blythe. Given the all-clear, he headed for the docks — and home.

Even once flying became an option, not everyone was keen to sign up, partly out of anxiety about this new-fangled method of travel and partly because intercontinental air travel was far from straightforward, although also a huge adventure for those with the stomach for flying boats. Those members of the 1946–47 team who went on to New Zealand and then flew home from Auckland spent eight days reaching Poole Harbour. Their journey included stops at Darwin, Singapore, Rangoon, Calcutta, Karachi, Bahrain, Basra, Cairo and Palermo. When they reached Cairo, the flying boat touched down on the Nile and the players headed off in black tie for a night of festivities before leaving again at dawn. 'We'd fly in the day and stop at hotels at night,' Alec Bedser recalled. Once jet travel shortened journeys further, the concerns over the impact of long-haul flights on the body meant that English teams were initially subjected to layovers, and the opportunity was taken to use these stops to play further flag-flying fixtures in places such as Hong Kong. The practice was soon abandoned.*

---

* England teams played matches in the following countries on the way home from international tours: United States 1878–79 (one match), Honduras 1959–60 (two matches), Hong Kong 1965–66 (two matches), Bermuda 1973–74 (two matches) and Hong Kong 1974–75 (two matches).

The pace of life was slower by sea but not without its advantages. Alan Ross closed his account of *Australia '55* with a view from the ship's bar: 'The ice clinks in cocktail-shakers; shapely, and some less shapely, bodies splash in and out of the swimming pool ... It is also time for Raffaele to concoct that delicious and decorative Singapore cocktail, of which I have, for some minutes now, been dreaming.'

And so, in various stages of readiness and by various means of transport, they make landfall. Until relatively recently, when live TV coverage of overseas matches brought viewers closer to the action, and social media allowed the public to communicate more readily their feelings about their team's performances, it was not easy for the cricketers to gain a proper sense of the impact they had made on people back home. Inklings of the mood might be gained from a letter or a precious phone call, and there might even be a cable from Lord's, although these were usually reserved for crises. A losing team heading for home might hope for sympathy or even indifference, but on the worst occasions they would know that what awaited them was anger, hostility and quite possibly a Lord's-led Grand Inquisition. Winners had much less need to fret, although in the days when pay levels were lower, they might have wondered whether their achievements merited a public subscription.

When Len Hutton arrived home victorious from Australia by boat – a nervous flyer, he had opted against returning by air – he did not even have chance to disembark from the *Oronsay* before Ronnie Aird, the MCC secretary, came and found him to award him his MCC tie. This was a much-prized possession which Hutton would have been grateful to receive, but the irony would not have escaped him of MCC claiming him as one of its own, now he had brought home the Ashes, when for so long the club had done so much to block the path of the professional cricketer.

Typically, reporters strove to be aboard the train from Tilbury docks to central London to buttonhole the England captain for some fresh quotes; the really enterprising ones might even have joined the boat at Plymouth for the final leg up to Tilbury. Andrew Stoddart, returning in triumph in the 1890s, did not lack for the company of newspapermen on this final part of his journey, but he lost several of his professionals at Plymouth as they hurried off for trains to take them to various county matches starting the next day. Stoddart himself was soon treated to a dinner at the Café Monico hosted by the Hampstead club he played for. Attendees included W. G. Grace and J. M. Barrie.

Those in charge of the heavy luggage had to clear customs, which was not always straightforward. When former England wicketkeeper George Duckworth returned from Australia as baggage-manager in 1958–59, customs happened to search his cases and found them stuffed with cigarettes and alcohol. His career as baggage-man on three England Test tours and three Commonwealth tours of India was over.

Losing captains became adept at avoiding press interrogations. Johnny Douglas, having endured the voyage with Armstrong's crowing Australians back through the Suez Canal and the Mediterranean, chose not to disembark with his players at Toulon for the overland journey by train, but stayed on board ship and thereby evaded the general clamour when the teams reached England. Douglas was also absent when a lunch was arranged to welcome the Australians to London some days later.

On the way back from the incendiary Bodyline tour, Pelham Warner, the assistant manager, who had found the whole furore distressing, took care to arrange a holiday in New York that ensured he got back home a week later than the team, by which time the mood was less feverish. This return was a sorry contrast to the one Warner had savoured after leading his team in glory in 1903–04, when he was feted at a lavish dinner held by MCC five days after arriving back.* Warner devoted a whole chapter of his tour book to a description of the evening and the speeches delivered, his own containing the memorable sentence: 'I tried to convert that strip of 22 yards into a battlefield.' Reaching home again in 1933, he might have reflected that now he really knew what cricket as war looked like.

There were no such antics from Jardine, who met his fate head-on. When the *Duchess of Atholl* reached Greenock, the players were welcomed by pipes and drums, after which Jardine headed down by train to Euston, where he was met by a party of MCC top brass including Viscount Lewisham, the president, Kynaston Studd and Lord Hawke. The Bodyline debriefings began and, gradually, Jardine was excommunicated.

Air travel offered no more escape from media scrutiny. Bob Willis came back from Australia into Heathrow where he was whisked away to a press room to be interviewed by, among others, BBC's new *Breakfast Time* show. He chafed at his team being labelled as 'abject failures', based largely on their one-day performances rather than their improvement towards the end of the Test series, which was sadly now a fast-receding memory. David Gower went through the same sort of grilling on returning from a 5–0 drubbing in the Caribbean, when the headlines were being made as much by off-field scandals as ineptitude on the pitch. Not that the cricketing shortcomings went unnoticed; Peter May, the chairman of selectors, had already dropped hints about 'heads rolling'. Gower survived one Test into the summer before the axe fell.

---

* After both this tour and the one in 1911–12, Warner captained an MCC Touring Team XI against the Rest of England in a fixture that for many years was a common feature of the domestic season following a major England tour. Tellingly, the 1911–12 team was led in the game at Lord's by Warner rather than Douglas, even though Douglas had captained the Tests in Australia owing to Warner's illness. Warner further reasserted his authority by scoring 136. From 1903–04 to 1936–37, every side that went to Australia bar the 1920–21 one fulfilled such fixtures, as did a number of South Africa and West Indies touring sides. In July 1963 Ted Dexter's Australian touring team played the Rest at Lord's as a substitute for the recently disbanded Gentlemen–Players match, but the experiment was not repeated.

Regrets were long expressed about touring teams not returning home as one body; Bruce Harris at the end of 1950–51
wrote: 'Let the team be chosen as one, travel as one and return
as one. Have the MCC no sense of showmanship?' But once it
was possible to travel by plane as well as boat, not everyone was
willing to return by the same means at the same time. Come
the era of red-ball and white-ball specialists, and multi-format
cricketers, such aspirations had lost all meaning. This was a pity
in the case of Andrew Strauss's victorious team in Australia;
rather than return to a fanfare, as they should have done, many
of the same players including Strauss headed straight into some
one-day matches before moving on to the subcontinent for a
World Cup. Having scaled the summit of English cricket at
Sydney on 7 January, many of them did not get back to England
until 28 March, 80 days later. As with Willis's side, by then the
mood had become contaminated by one-day failure.

Luckier was Percy Chapman, who, despite taking a lengthy
holiday in New Zealand and Canada at the end of England's
great victory in Australia in 1928–29, was still feted on his
return. A special dinner at Mansion House for him and his
players was held back until mid-July and staged during the
Gentlemen–Players match at Lord's. Hutton's team similarly
was treated to a gala dinner at the Dorchester Hotel, and Ray
Illingworth's side to both a dinner at Mansion House and a visit
to Downing Street. The MCC bigwigs and their apologists took
Hutton's win with a better grace than they did Illingworth's,
cavilling at the shows of dissent towards officials rather than the
numerous provocations the team had endured. Few people took
much notice; for the old guard, the game was very nearly up.
A rare case of a losing team being afforded a welcome-home
dinner was provided by Ted Dexter, chairman of the England
committee, after Graham Gooch's team lost the World Cup
final to Pakistan in 1992.

Some of the most touching celebrations involved the professional players returning to their local communities. Jack

Brown, Stoddart's match-winner in 1894–95, was honoured with a celebratory fixture in his home town of Driffield; he was also presented by the Earl of Londesborough with a silver tea and coffee service paid for by local subscription. Bobby Peel was celebrated in Morley and Herbert Sutcliffe in Pudsey, where 15,000 turned out. Harold Larwood and Bill Voce went back to Nottingham after Jardine's tour and were presented with handsome testimonial cheques. Alec Bedser was granted a civic reception in Woking and a waxwork model of himself in Madame Tussauds after his heroic bowling in Australia in 1950–51.

Eventually, whether a winner or a loser, the touring cricketer would return to his home to be greeted by his family, and perhaps by small children who had been without their father too long and would shout in delight: 'Daddy's home!' And then: 'Is he staying the night?'

Grand inquisitions, inquests, bloodlettings . . . call them what you will, there have been a number of messy fallouts to failed tours. It was a routine requirement of those at managerial level on tour to submit reports to the authorities in which they were expected to dispense the unvarnished truth as to what had gone on; sometimes they even did so. After the reports came the meetings at Lord's at which fates would be determined – good-conduct bonuses awarded or withheld, captains or coaches sacked, black marks put against names which would never appear on touring lists in future.

In terms of results on the field, the Bodyline tour was of course an unqualified success, but such was the ill feeling it created in Australia that it took MCC years to extricate itself from the embarrassment. It did so largely through guarantees that Jardine and Larwood would not take the field in Ashes matches again, and an unspoken promise that any fast bowler selected for England in these contests would bowl neither particularly fast nor particularly short. Australia went unbeaten for the next 20 years. Hutton's tour of West Indies was also not a failure, except diplomatically. The main conclusion from that post-mortem was that no one should ever again be cast in the role of player-manager, as Charles Palmer had been.

Like major wars, a disastrous tour could trigger change. The bravest administrators made sure they did not waste a crisis. The 5–0 defeat in the West Indies in 1985–86 led directly to the creation of the role of cricket manager, later re-cast as head coach. This position had long been mooted, but it was the ill-disciplined nature of that tour under David Gower as captain and Tony Brown and Bob Willis as managers that finally prompted a change in how England teams operated overseas. Micky Stewart immediately made a success of the role the following winter.

Much less successful were the recommendations arising out of the report into the defeat in Australia in 2006–07 produced by Ken Schofield, a former executive director of the European golf tour for almost 30 years. Some of his suggestions were sound enough, but others proved impractical. The volume of county cricket only grew rather than being cut back, as he had suggested, and the idea of a selector always being on tour as a counterweight to the head coach and captain was unrealistic and largely unnecessary. Michael Vaughan, the England Test captain at the time, damned the Schofield Report as 'formulated by a golf administrator [and] largely a public relations ploy that grew arms and legs, a knee-jerk reaction from the ECB to what was obviously a disappointing tour'. Schofield did however recommend creating the role of managing director of England cricket, a post that has so far survived the test of time.

While it was quite common for cricket managers and head coaches to step down or be sacked after a tour, captains more often survived, perhaps because the coaches were held more directly responsible for the environment in which a team operated, and such environments were easier to judge on tour than at home. Keith Fletcher, however, did not remain as captain after the India tour of 1981–82. The sterility of England's cricket was one thing, but Fletcher's own petulance in knocking off the bails after being given out in Bangalore, and a sit-down protest in Calcutta when the umpires took the players off for bad light, would have also counted against him. It was not until a month into the county season that he was given the news via a phone call from Peter May, the chairman of selectors.

Another captain who lost his job in the aftermath of a tour was Kevin Pietersen, in his case within two weeks of returning from India in 2008–09. This was primarily down to a break-down in his relationship with head coach Peter Moores, but there were other factors at play, notably the divisions among the players caused by the Mumbai terrorist attacks, and discussions as to whether the tour should carry on or be abandoned. 'The group had been fractured ... by the magnitude of events and the misplaced force of personality,' Alastair Cook wrote in his 2019 autobiography. 'Dressing-rooms inevitably breed alpha males, and friction had become wearing. KP's relationship with Freddie Flintoff was extremely difficult.' Cook suggested that Flintoff's decision to call a team meeting from which Pietersen was excluded was a seminal moment. Ultimately, Pietersen's wish to complete the tour overrode Flintoff's call to scrap it, but eventually Pietersen was sacked because he demanded the removal of Moores as head coach, while Moores lost his job because too many players were unhappy with his methods. One of the unwritten rules of England captaincy thereafter (if it had not been already) was that it was inadvisable to speak out against the coach, whatever the private reservations.

Remarkably, Cook himself remained in post as captain after Australia in 2013–14 despite losing the Tests 5–0 and an ODI series 4–1. Instead, the initial heat was taken by the resigning head coach Andy Flower and Pietersen, who was sacked as a player. Cook endured months of abuse on social media for his part in Pietersen's removal, but he and his players eventu-ally turned things round during a home series against India the following summer and went on to regain the Ashes in England in 2015.

Even that turbulent period was overshadowed by the fallout from the failures in Australia and West Indies in the winter of 2021–22. Rarely had the bloodletting been so extreme. After the team returned from the Ashes tour, Chris Silverwood was removed as head coach and, the following day, Ashley Giles as managing director of cricket. A makeshift selection panel, headed by Andrew Strauss as interim managing director, dropped eight players for the Test tour of West Indies which began five weeks later.

When that series also resulted in defeat, Joe Root voluntarily stepped down after five years as Test captain less than 48 hours before Rob Key, a former England batsman who was now a Sky Sports TV commentator, was confirmed as the new permanent director. A few weeks earlier Key had criticised Root's captaincy on Sky. 'I [originally] thought if you get in someone [as head coach] who is so cricket-savvy that they can help Joe Root then that would allow him to continue as captain,' he said, 'but I just don't think that's right . . . There are not loads of options [to replace Root] but Ben Stokes would be the man for me.' Following Root's resignation, Key duly appointed Stokes captain and brought in Brendon McCullum as head coach of the Test side – and a renaissance started almost before an ECB-led high-performance review into how the England teams were run had begun, let alone finished.

Departing After Winter Tours

England Test captains

For many years, captains were effectively appointed on a tour-by-tour basis; by the 1970s more stability had been brought to the role. Since the early 1980s, six England Test captains have either resigned or been sacked after a tour and before the team next played.

In addition to the six cases below, Nasser Hussain (2002–03), Michael Vaughan (2006–07) and Andrew Strauss (2010–11) all resigned as ODI captain at the end of overseas World Cups. Alastair Cook was as sacked as ODI captain following a bilateral series in Sri Lanka in December 2014, less than three weeks before the team departed for the build-up to a World Cup in Australia and New Zealand.

Test captain	Period in post	Last assignment	Departure	Days since last match
Keith Fletcher	1981–82	India/Sri Lanka 1981–82	Sacked 21 May 1982	87
Bob Willis	1982–84	New Zealand/ Pakistan 1983–84	Sacked 22 May 1984	74
Mike Atherton	1993–98	West Indies 1997–98	Resigned 24 Mar 1998	0*
Kevin Pietersen	2008–09	West Indies/India 2008–09	Sacked 6 Jan 2009	14
Alastair Cook	2012–17	Bangladesh/India 2016–17	Resigned 5 Feb 2017	47
Joe Root	2017–22	West Indies 2021–22	Resigned 15 Apr 2022	19

*Atherton resigned on the final day of the final Test of the series in West Indies, ahead of a five-match ODI series with which the tour concluded (the ODI team was led by Adam Hollioake instead).

England head coaches

Eight of the 11 completed reigns of England cricket managers or head coaches ended directly after a winter tour. The only exceptions were Micky Stewart (1986–92), David Lloyd (1996–99) and Trevor Bayliss (2015–19), who left during or at the end of a home season. Andy Flower (Test team) and Ashley Giles (ODI and T20 teams) shared the coaching responsibilities between 2012 and 2014.

Coach/ manager	Period in post	Last assignment	Departure	Days since final match
Keith Fletcher	1992–95	Australia 1994–95	Sacked 8 Mar 1995	29
Ray Illingworth	1995–96	World Cup 1996	Resigned 25 Mar 1996	16
Duncan Fletcher	1999–2007	World Cup 2007	Resigned 19 Apr 2007	0*
Peter Moores	2007–09	India 2008–09	Sacked 6 Jan 2009	14
Andy Flower	2009–14	Australia 2013–14	Resigned 31 Jan 2014	26
Ashley Giles	2012–14	T20 World Cup 2014	Sacked 19 Apr 2014 +	19
Peter Moores	2014–15	West Indies 2015	Sacked 9 May 2015	1**
Chris Silverwood	2019–22	Australia 2021–22	Sacked 3 Feb 2022	18

*Duncan Fletcher gave notice of his resignation two days before his last match in charge, in Barbados; he is the only one whose departure was confirmed while still on tour.

+ Ashley Giles, while still in nominal charge of the white-ball teams, was a candidate for the job of overall head coach after Andy Flower stepped down from running the Test side. He lost out to Peter Moores on 19 April 2014, when Moores was put in overall charge of all England teams.

** Moores was sacked in 2015 the day after coaching England in an ODI against Ireland in Dublin and six days after the final Test of a tour of West Indies.

AFTERWORD

The bilateral international cricket tour stands at a crossroads. The old-style tours, first of all involving up-country games, games against local state or provincial sides, and Test matches, and later a mix of Tests and one-day internationals and many fewer 'side' matches, had a particular rhythm of their own. There were periods of frantic activity around the big Test matches for sure, but there would be longueurs too, chances to take stock, recharge the body and mind, and take in some of the sights of a foreign country. Touring was, above all, an adventure. This kind of touring has gone, and it is hard to imagine it ever returning.

Nowadays, a tour is pared to the bone – a day or so to shake off the effects of a long flight, a few training days, and then into the serious action. The advent of a world Test championship, in which a minimum of two matches constitutes a series, has encouraged further fragmentation. Under this arrangement, a team can fulfil several series every year. An away series of such brevity is effectively a business trip. In and out, get the job done, go home. The ICC's decision to stage regular global white-ball tournaments has taken further time out of the calendar.

Also, with the move towards players specialising in different formats – Test cricket, ODI cricket and T20s – there is little to be gained by a tour taking in two or three of these elements.

For the cost of a return flight, each format can stand a tour on its own. So, even more short tours, even more in–and–out business trips.

To an extent, England have been spared the worst of this atomisation. They are available to tour from October to March when many other countries want to host them, and financially they remain a highly attractive option. The ICC's Future Tours Programme for 2023–27 sees England touring both India and Australia for five Test matches apiece. They will not be flying visits; far from it. Of the four other Test series they will play away from home during this period, three of them were scheduled to consist of three matches and only one of two. That represents a far greater commitment to Test cricket than most countries will manage. In the main, England Test tours remain pretty substantial.

Twenty-five years ago, international cricket had very little to do with tournaments, aside from a 50-overs World Cup held every four years. But the rise of domestic T20 leagues, with their compact narrative spanning a few weeks culminating in deciding knockout games, has left the rest of the sport looking flat-footed by comparison. A sprawling Test championship staged over two years does not really cut it with modern audiences.

This revolution has happened so fast that it is hard to predict how things will look once the dust settles. In the space of 15 years five domestic leagues of apparent significance have been established in India (where the Indian Premier League is the runaway leader in the field), Australia, England, Pakistan and West Indies. In 2023, three more came on line, in South Africa, the United Arab Emirates and the United States.

Those who run these leagues have little sense of irony or proportion; most care only about chasing dollars – and chasing a pretty thin field of genuine T20 stars. There are perhaps 50–75 really top T20 cricketers in the world, and that is nothing like enough to go round. The inflated names of franchise teams betray their lack of history, and their desperation to be taken seriously – they are Gladiators, Warriors and Giants; Kings and Royals; Lions, Tigers and Vipers. Perhaps one day the Lions, Tigers and Vipers will eat one another.

As most of the world's best players will tell you, Test cricket remains the pinnacle. They may be able to earn a million dollars faster and with less effort bowling leg-breaks and smashing sixes in the IPL, but if they want to be tested to the full, they know there is only one format that will give them that opportunity. And a Test tour spanning several weeks, played in alien conditions, will show them what they are really made of.

The stories of heroes past have been passed down the generations among watchers as well as players – Len Hutton's, Ray Illingworth's and Andrew Strauss's teams winning in Australia, and the great fast bowling feats of Harold Larwood, Frank Tyson and John Snow on the hard pitches Down Under, are part of English cricketing folklore. So, too, Derek Randall's audacious, impish century in the Centenary Test of 1977. Alastair Cook's many hundreds around Asia and Ben Stokes's extraordinary batting and bowling in Cape Town – and the intrepid batting of his England team in Pakistan – are exploits that people will remember and cherish long after an evening of T20 mayhem has been forgotten. There are no better sights in the cricketing world than sun-soaked full houses at Newlands, Adelaide or Bridgetown.

Stokes himself could have made several millions as a T20 specialist, but in 2022 he chose to devote himself to reviving England's Test fortunes. 'Test cricket will never die,' he said. One hopes he is right.

STATISTICAL APPENDIX

List of England tours

England teams have undertaken 145 overseas tours on which they played Tests, one-day internationals or T20s, plus a tour of Sri Lanka in 2020–21 which was abandoned six days before a two-Test series was due to begin because of the Covid-19 pandemic. This does not include visits for one-off games to Ireland (2006–19, six matches) and Scotland (2008–18, four matches). In the table below, ODI or T20 competitions involving three or four teams are described as tri-series or quadrangulars; bigger events are given their full titles. In some cases, the whole tour party did not depart or return on the same day; in those instances the dates given, and the number of days a tour is calculated to have lasted, is taken from when it is believed most players left or arrived back in the UK.

Prior to the first of these trips in 1876–77, English cricketers made four major pioneering tours to North America and Australasia that lay ground for later expeditions.

Principal pioneering tours

Dates	Days	Venue	Official Captain	Matches
7 Sep–11 Nov 1859	66	Canada and United States	George Parr	5
20 Oct 1861–12 May 1862	205	Australia	Heathfield Stephenson	12
15 Oct 1863–13 Jun 1864	243	Australia and New Zealand	George Parr	17
23 Oct 1873–17 May 1874	207	Australia	W. G. Grace	15

England's international tours

Dates	Days	Venue (tournament)	Official Captain	Test	ODI	T20
21 Sep 1876–22 Jun 1877	254	Australia/New Zealand	James Lillywhite	1–1		
17 Oct 1878–19 May 1879	214	Australia/New Zealand (1)	Lord Harris	0–1		
17 Sep 1881–4 May 1882	230	Australia/New Zealand (2)	Alfred Shaw	0–2		
14 Sep 1882–25 Apr 1883	223	Australia (3)	Ivo Bligh	2–2		
19 Sep 1884–16 May 1885	239	Australia (4)	Arthur Shrewsbury	3–2		
18 Sep 1886–8 May 1887	232	Australia	Shrewsbury	2–0		
15 Sep 1887–28 Apr 1888*	227	Australia	Martin Hawke**	1–0		
15 Sep 1887–12 May 1888*	241	Australia/New Zealand	Aubrey Smith**			
21 Nov 1888–15 Apr 1889	145	South Africa	Smith	2–0		
2 Oct 1891–8 May 1892*	219	Australia (5)	W. G. Grace	1–2		
21 Nov 1891–8 Apr 1892*	139	South Africa	Walter Read	1–0		
21 Sep 1894–8 May 1895	229	Australia (3)	Andrew Stoddart	3–2		
30 Nov 1895–12 Apr 1896	134	South Africa	Hawke	3–0		
17 Sep 1897–23 Apr 1898	218	Australia	Stoddart	1–4		
3 Dec 1898–21 Apr 1899	139	South Africa	Hawke	2–0		
27 Sep 1901–27 Apr 1902	212	Australia	Archie MacLaren	1–4		
25 Sep 1903–17 Apr 1904	205	Australia	Pelham Warner	3–2		

Dates	Days	Venue (tournament)	Official Captain	Test	ODI	T20
11 Nov 1905–21 Apr 1906	161	South Africa	Warner	1–4		
20 Sep 1907–14 Apr 1908	206	Australia	Arthur Jones	1–4		
6 Nov 1909–2 Apr 1910	147	South Africa	Henry Leveson Gower	2–3		
29 Sep 1911–7 Apr 1912	191	Australia (3)	*Warner***	4–1		
18 Oct 1913–31 Mar 1914	164	South Africa	Johnny Douglas	4–0		
18 Sep 1920–17 Apr 1921	211	Australia (3)	Douglas	0–5		
20 Oct 1922–26 Mar 1923	156	South Africa	Frank Mann	2–1		
18 Sep 1924–16 Apr 1925	210	Australia (3)	Arthur Gilligan	1–4		
21 Oct 1927–12 Mar 1928	143	South Africa	Ronnie Stanyforth	2–2		
18 Sep 1928–21 Apr 1929	215	Australia (3)	Percy Chapman	4–1		
28 Sep 1929–2 Apr 1930*	186	*Australia*/New Zealand	Harold Gilligan	1–0		
14 Dec 1929–26 Apr 1930*	134	West Indies	Freddie Calthorpe	1–1		
17 Oct 1930–30 Mar 1931	164	South Africa	Chapman	0–1		
17 Sep 1932–6 May 1933	231	Australia/ New Zealand (3)	Douglas Jardine	4–1 0–0		
22 Sep 1933–28 Mar 1934	187	India	Jardine	2–0		
15 Dec 1934–4 Apr 1935	111	West Indies	Bob Wyatt	1–2		
12 Sep 1936–26 Apr 1937	226	Australia/*New Zealand* (3)	Gubby Allen	2–3		

Dates	Days	Venue (tournament)	Official Captain	Test	ODI	T20
21 Oct 1938–31 Mar 1939	161	South Africa	Walter Hammond	1–0		
31 Aug 1946–9 Apr 1947	221	Australia/ New Zealand	Hammond	0–3 0–0		
23 Dec 1947–27 Apr 1948	127	West Indies	Allen	0–2		
7 Oct 1948–1 Apr 1949	177	South Africa	George Mann	2–0		
14 Sep 1950–3 Apr 1951	201	Australia/ New Zealand (3)	Freddie Brown	1–4 1–0		
18 Sep 1951–22 Mar 1952	187	India/Pakistan/Ceylon	Nigel Howard	1–1		
14 Dec 1953–20 Apr 1954	128	West Indies (6)	Len Hutton	2–2		
15 Sep 1954–5 Apr 1955	203	Australia/ New Zealand (3)	Hutton	3–1 2–0		
4 Oct 1956–29 Mar 1957	177	South Africa	Peter May	2–2		
21 Sep 1958–23 Mar 1959	184	Australia/ New Zealand (3)	May	0–4 1–0		
8 Dec 1959–6 Apr 1960	121	West Indies (7)	May	1–0		
8 Oct 1961–20 Feb 1962	136	Pakistan/ India/Ceylon	Ted Dexter	1–0 0–2		
27 Sep 1962–23 Mar 1963	177	Australia/ New Zealand (3)	Dexter	1–1 3–0		
31 Dec 1963–28 Feb 1964	60	India	M. J. K. Smith	0–0		

Dates	Days	Venue (tournament)	Official Captain	Test	ODI	T20
15 Oct 1964–19 Feb 1965	128	South Africa	Smith	1–0		
16 Oct 1965–21 Mar 1966	157	Australia/ New Zealand (8)	Smith	1–1 / 0–0		
27 Dec 1967–5 Apr 1968	101	West Indies	Colin Cowdrey	1–0		
21 Jan 1968–9 Mar 1969***	48	*Ceylon*/Pakistan	Cowdrey	0–0		
18 Oct 1970–11 Mar 1971	143	Australia/ New Zealand	Ray Illingworth	2–0 / 1–0	0–1	
29 Nov 1972–30 Mar 1973	121	India/*Sri Lanka*/ Pakistan	Tony Lewis	1–2 / 0–0		
11 Jan 1973–11 Apr 1974	91	West Indies (9)	Mike Denness	1–1		
21 Oct 1974–16 Mar 1975	147	Australia/ New Zealand (10)	Denness	1–4 / 1–0	1–0 / 0–0	
23 Nov 1976–19 Mar 1977	116	India/*Sri Lanka*/ Australia	Tony Greig	3–1 / 0–1		
24 Nov 1977– 12 Mar 1978	109	Pakistan/ New Zealand	Mike Brearley / Geoff Boycott	0–0 / 1–1	2–1	
24 Oct 1978– 18 Feb 1979	118	Australia	Brearley	5–1	1–2	
4 Nov 1979–21 Feb 1980	110	Australia (tri-series)/ India	Brearley	0–3 / 1–0	5–4	

Dates	Days	Venue (tournament)	Official Captain	Test	ODI	T20
15 Jan–Apr 1981	93	West Indies	Ian Botham	0–2	0–2	
5 Nov 1981–24 Feb 1982	112	India/	Keith Fletcher	0–1	1–2	
		Sri Lanka		1–0	1–1	
12 Oct 1982–29 Feb 1983	140	Australia/	Bob Willis	1–2		
		Australia (tri-series)/			4–6	
		New Zealand			0–3	
29 Dec 1983–28 Mar 1984	91	New Zealand/	Willis	0–1	2–1	
		Pakistan (11)		0–1	1–1	
30 Oct 1984–6 Mar 1985	128	India/*Sri Lanka*/	David Gower	2–1	4–1	
		Australia (World Championship)			0–3	
20–29 Mar 1985	10	Sharjah (quadrangular)	Norman Gifford		0–2	
25 Jan–18 Apr 1986	84	West Indies	Gower	0–5	1–3	
9 Oct 1986–16 Feb 1987	131	Australia/	Mike Gatting	2–1	4–0	
		Australia (Perth Challenge)/			6–4	
		Australia (tri-series)			2–1	
28 Mar–10 Apr 1987	14	Sharjah (quadrangular)	John Emburey ·			

Dates	Days	Venue (tournament)	Official Captain	Test	ODI	T20
30 Sep–23 Dec 1987	85	Pakistan/India (World Cup)/	Gatting	0–1	5–3	
		Pakistan			3–0	
11 Jan–22 Mar 1988	72	Australia/	Gatting	0–0	0–1	
		New Zealand		0–0	2–2	
7 Oct–1 Nov 1989	26	India (Nehru Cup)	Graham Gooch		3–3	
25 Jan–18 Apr 1990	84	West Indies	Gooch	1–2	0–4	
18 Oct 1990–18 Feb 1991	124	Australia/	Gooch	0–3	2–6	
		Australia (tri-series)/			1–2	
		New Zealand				
27 Dec 1991–27 Mar 1992	92	New Zealand/	Gooch	2–0	3–0	
		Australia/New Zealand (World Cup)			6–3	
28 Dec 1992–22 Mar 1993	85	India/	Gooch	0–3	3–3	
		Sri Lanka		0–1	0–2	
14 Jan–22 Apr 1994	99	West Indies	Mike Atherton	1–3	2–3	
18 Oct 1994–19 Feb 1995	115	Australia/	Atherton	1–3	2–2	
		Australia (quadrangular)				

Dates	Days	Venue (tournament)	Official Captain	Test	ODI	T20
18 Oct 1995–23 Jan 1996	98	South Africa	Atherton	0–1	1–6	
3 Feb–12 Mar 1996	39	Pakistan/India (World Cup)	Atherton		2–4	
25 Nov 1996–5 Mar 1997	101	Zimbabwe/	Atherton	0–0	0–3	
		New Zealand		2–0	2–2	
1–21 Dec 1997	21	Pakistan/Sharjah (quadrangular)	Adam Hollioake		4–0	
3 Jan–10 Apr 1998	99	West Indies	Atherton	1–3	1–4	
			Hollioake			
17–27 Oct 1998*	11	Bangladesh (ICC Knockout)	Hollioake		0–1	
22 Oct 1998–15 Feb 1999*	119	Australia/	Alec Stewart	1–3		
		Australia (tri-series)	Stewart		5–7	
28 Mar–12 Apr 1999	16	Pakistan/Sharjah (tri-series)			1–3	
26 Oct 1999–25 Feb 2000	123	South Africa/	Nasser Hussain	1–2	2–4	
		South Africa (tri-series)/			3–0	
		Zimbabwe				
28 Sep–12 Dec 2000	76	Kenya (ICC Knockout)/	Hussain		1–1	
		Pakistan	Hussain	1–0	1–2	
30 Jan–28 Mar 2001	58	Sri Lanka	Hussain	2–1		
			Graham Thorpe		0–3	

Dates	Days	Venue (tournament)	Official Captain	Test	ODI	T20
26 Sep–15 Oct 2001	20	Zimbabwe	Hussain		5–0	
12 Nov–24 Dec 2001	43	India	Hussain	0–1	3–3	
13 Jan–4 Apr 2002	82	India/ New Zealand	Hussain	1–1	2–3	
12–22 Sep 2002	11	Sri Lanka (Champions Trophy)	Hussain		1–1	
17 Oct 2002–6 Mar 2003	140	Australia/ Australia (tri-series)/ South Africa (World Cup)	Hussain	1–4	3–7 / 3–2	
6 Oct–22 Dec 2003	78	Bangladesh/ Sri Lanka	Michael Vaughan	2–0 / 0–1	3–0 / 0–1	
25 Feb–6 May 2004	72	West Indies	Vaughan	3–0	2–2	
16 Nov 2004–14 Feb 2005	90	Namibia/ Zimbabwe/ South Africa	Vaughan	2–1	4–0 / 1–4	
25 Oct–22 Dec 2005	59	Pakistan	Vaughan / Marcus Trescothick / *Vaughan***	0–2	2–3	
12 Feb–16 Apr 2006	64	India	Andrew Flintoff	1–1	1–5	

Dates	Days	Venue (tournament)	Official Captain	Test	ODI	T20
6–30 Oct 2006	25	India (Champions Trophy)	Flintoff		1–2	
3 Nov 2006–13 Feb 2007	102	Australia/	Flintoff	0–5	5–5	
		Australia/	Vaughan		5–4	
		Australia (tri-series)	Vaughan			0–1
2 Mar–22 Apr 2007	52	West Indies (World Cup)	Vaughan			
9 Sep–14 Oct 2007	36	South Africa (World T20)/	Paul Collingwood		3–2	1–4
		Sri Lanka				
15 Nov–23 Dec 2007	39	Sri Lanka	Vaughan	0–1		
26 Jan–28 Mar 2008	63	New Zealand	Collingwood		1–3	
			Vaughan	2–1		2–0
21 Oct–24 Dec 2008****	65	West Indies/	Kevin Pietersen	0–1	0–5	
		India				
21 Jan–5 Apr 2009	75	West Indies	Andrew Strauss	0–1	3–2	0–1
21 Sep–4 Oct 2009	14	South Africa (Champions Trophy)	Strauss		2–2	
1 Nov 2009–18 Jan 2010	79	South Africa	Strauss	1–1	2–1	1–1
14 Feb–25 Mar 2010	40	UAE (v Pakistan)/	Collingwood		3–0	1–1
		Bangladesh	Alastair Cook	2–0		
25 Apr–16 May 2010	23	West Indies (World T20)	Collingwood			5–1
29 Oct 2010–28 Mar 2011	151	Australia/	Strauss	3–1	1–6	
			Collingwood			1–1
		India/Sri Lanka (World Cup)	Strauss		3–3	

Dates	Days	Venue (tournament)	Official Captain	Test	ODI	T20
3–30 Oct 2011	28	India	Cook		0–5	
			Graeme Swann			1–0
2 Jan–28 Feb 2012	58	UAE (v Pakistan)	Strauss	0–3		
			Cook		4–0	
			Stuart Broad			2–1
9 Mar–8 Apr 2012	31	Sri Lanka	Strauss	1–1		
13 Sep–3 Oct 2012	21	Sri Lanka (World T20)	Broad			2–3
25 Oct–23 Dec 2012	60	Dubai/India	Cook	2–1	2–3	
			Eoin Morgan			1–1
2 Jan–28 Mar 2013	86	India/ New Zealand	Cook	0–0	2–1	
			Broad			2–1
24 Oct 2013–4 Feb 2014	104	Australia	Cook	0–5	1–4	
			Broad			0–3
28 Feb–31 Mar 2014	32	West Indies/ Bangladesh (World T20)	Broad		2–1	1–2
						1–3
6 Nov–17 Dec 2014	32	Sri Lanka	Cook		2–5	
6 Jan–15 Mar 2015	69	Australia (tri-series)/ Australia/New Zealand (World Cup)	Morgan		2–3	
					2–4	
2 Apr–6 May 2015	35	West Indies	Cook	1–1		

Dates	Days	Venue (tournament)	Official Captain	Test	ODI	T20
30 Sep–1 Dec 2015	63	UAE (v Pakistan)	Cook	0–2		
			Morgan		3–1	2–0
10 Dec 2015–22 Feb 2016	75	South Africa	Cook	2–1		
			Morgan		2–3	0–2
8 Mar–5 Apr 2016	29	India (World T20)	Morgan			4–2
29 Sep–23 Dec 2016	86	Bangladesh/	Cook	1–1		
			Jos Buttler		2–1	1–2
		India	Cook	0–4		
5 Jan–1 Feb 2017	29	India	Morgan		1–2	
22 Feb–10 Mar 2017	17	West Indies	Morgan		3–0	
28 Oct 2017–5 Apr 2018	160	Australia/	Joe Root	0–4		
			Morgan		4–1	
		Australia/New Zealand (tri-series)/	Morgan			1–3
		New Zealand	Root	0–1		
			Morgan		3–2	
1 Oct–27 Nov 2018	58	Sri Lanka	Morgan		3–1	
			Root	3–0		1–0
11 Jan–11 Mar 2019	60	West Indies	Root	1–2		
			Morgan		2–2	3–0

Dates	Days	Venue (tournament)	Official Captain	Test	ODI	T20
21 Oct–3 Dec 2019	44	New Zealand	Morgan / Root	0–1		2–2
13 Dec 2019–18 Feb 2020	68	South Africa	Root / Morgan	**3–1**	1–1	**2–1**
2–15 Mar 2020***	14	Sri Lanka	Root	Cancelled		
16 Nov–10 Dec 2020***	25	South Africa	Morgan		Cancelled	**3–0**
2 Jan–29 Mar 2021	87	Sri Lanka/India	Root / Morgan	2–0 / 1–3	1–2	2–3
4 Oct 2021–20 Jan 2022*	109	UAE (World T20)/Australia (12)	Morgan / Root	0–4		4–2
15 Jan–1 Feb 2022*	18	West Indies	Morgan			2–3
24 Feb–30 Mar 2022	35	West Indies	Root	0–1		
14–23 Jun 2022	10	Netherlands	Morgan		3–0	
14 Sep–24 Nov 2022*	72	Pakistan/Australia/Australia (World T20)	Buttler		0–3	4–3 / 2–0 / **5–1**
18 Nov–23 Dec 2022*	36	Pakistan (13)	Ben Stokes	3–0		
19 Jan–2 Feb 2023*	15	South Africa	Buttler		1–2	
27 Jan–2 Mar 2023*	35	New Zealand	Stokes	1–1		
23 Feb–15 Mar 2023*	21	Bangladesh	Buttler		**2–1**	0–3

Scorelines that appear in bold represent series or tournaments won by England

*Tours or tournaments ran concurrently or partly overlapped in the winter seasons of 1887–88, 1891–92, 1929–30, 1998–99, 2021–22 and 2022–23. The only instance of England Test tours taking place at the same time occurred in Australia and South Africa in 1891–92 and New Zealand and West Indies in 1929–30 (the South Africa tour in 1891–92 and the West Indies tour of 1929–30 were only retrospectively judged of Test status).

**The officially appointed captains did not play in international matches on these tours. The two English sides that went to Australia in 1887–88 combined forces to play the only Test match under a different captain, Walter Read. Pelham Warner in 1911–12 and Michael Vaughan in 2005–06 started the tour as captain but were unable to take part in the Tests owing to illness or injury, and were replaced respectively by Johnny Douglas and Andrew Flintoff.

***These tours were abandoned – in Pakistan in 1968–69 owing to rioting at the stadium in Karachi on the third day of the final Test match; and in Sri Lanka in 2019–20 and South Africa in 2020–21 ahead of respectively a two-match Test series and a three-match ODI series, both owing to Covid-19 concerns.

****The team in India in 2008–09 returned to England for several days, and then went on to the United Arab Emirates, awaiting security clearance to resume the tour following terrorist attacks in Mumbai.

NOTES IN TABLE

(1) Played in the United States on the return journey.
(2) Played in the United States on the outward journey.
(3) Played in Ceylon on the outward journey.
(4) Played in Egypt on the outward journey.
(5) Played in Malta and Ceylon on the outward journey.
(6) Played in Bermuda on the outward journey.
(7) Played in Honduras on the return journey.
(8) Played in Ceylon on the outward journey and Hong Kong on the return journey.
(9) Played in Bermuda on the return journey.
(10) Played in Hong Kong on the return journey.
(11) Played in Fiji on the outward journey.
(12) Training camp in Oman at the start.
(13) Training camp in Abu Dhabi at the start.

When England tour

The overwhelming majority of England's overseas Tests have been played between November and April. Seven Tests have started in October (all against Pakistan or Bangladesh, the earliest beginning on 13 October 2015 against Pakistan in Abu Dhabi) and 15 in April or May (13 on Caribbean islands, one in South Africa and one in Sri

Lanka; the latest beginning on 1 May 2015 against West Indies in Barbados). The following summary is based on the scheduled start dates of England's international matches overseas.

Format	Sep	Oct	Nov	Dec	Jan	Feb	Mar	Apr	May	Jun
Tests		7	45	121	128	109	95	14	1	
ODIs	5	45	29	39	107	106	77	24	3	3
T20s	15	12	19	3	12	21	24	1	7	
Total	20	64	93	163	247	236	196	39	11	3

Joe Root is the only England batsman in any format to score a century on St George's Day, commemorating the patron saint of England: he scored 118 not out v West Indies in the second Test match in Grenada on 23 April 2015; he eventually finished unbeaten on 182.

Summary of bilateral visit

This excludes the 24 stand-alone ODI and T20 tournaments held overseas in which England teams participated, which include seven World Cups, five Champions Trophies and six World T20s.

Country	Visits	Tests only	Tests and ODIs	Tests and T20s	Tests, ODIs and T20s	ODIs only	T20s only	ODIs and T20s
First instance		1876 –77	1970 –71	2012 –13	2006 –07	1982 –83	2009 –10	2011 –12
Australia	42*	26*	12		4			
South Africa	22	14	3		3	1	1	
New Zealand	22	11	5		4	2		
West Indies	20	9	6		2	1	1	1
India	20	9	5	1	1	2		2

Country	Visits	Tests only	Tests and ODIs	Tests and T20s	Tests, ODIs and T20s	ODIs only	T20s only	ODIs and T20s
Pakistan *(in Pakistan)*	9	4	5					
Pakistan *(in UAE)*	3				2		1	
Sri Lanka	9	2	5		1	1		
Zimbabwe	4		1			3		
Bangladesh	4		3					1
Netherlands	1					1		

*These tallies count the two English tours of 1887–88, which saw both visiting teams combine to play a Test match against Australia, as one Test tour.

Postponements/cancellations

It has not been uncommon for the scheduled dates of tours to be revised, or in a few cases for an entire tour to be postponed by a year or more, often due to circumstances beyond the control of the cricket authorities. The changes are generally made by mutual consent.

In a few instances, England tours have been cancelled at particularly short notice. These include India in 1939–40 (cancelled on 4 September due to the outbreak of war in Europe), South Africa in 1968–69 (24 September, due to South African government objections to the selection of Basil D'Oliveira) and India 1988–89 (7 October, because of Indian government objections to the South African links of several England players). One of the latest deferments came when the ECB announced it would not be going ahead with a short visit to Pakistan for two T20s in mid-October 2021 because of scheduling difficulties; the decision came on 22 September. It was eventually rearranged as a seven-match series in September–October 2022.

Major centres to stage England matches

England have played Test cricket at 67 overseas grounds, and Tests, ODIs and T20s at 112 overseas venues. Several cities have had a number of international grounds, and the table below groups them under one entry. Long-standing centrally located venues in Dhaka, Georgetown and Kandy have all been replaced in recent years by new stadiums built around 10km out of town; these are regarded as belonging to the original centres. The following 36 centres have staged three or more England Tests. The tally of ODIs/T20s includes internationals against teams other than the host country. The most internationals England have played in one centre not listed below is Sharjah (18), St Lucia (11), Harare and Abu Dhabi (both nine). The most matches staged without any of them being a Test is seven in Dambulla and Pune.

City	First match	Grounds	Tests	Won	Lost	Drawn	ODIs/ T20s	Total matches
Melbourne (A)	1877	1	57	20	29	8	37	94
Sydney (A)	1882	2	57	22	27	8	37	94
Adelaide (A)	1884	1	33	9	19	5	20	53
Port Elizabeth (SA)	1889	1	10	6	1	3	6	16
Cape Town (SA)	1889	1	21	10	5	6	14	35
Johannesburg (SA)	1896	3	29	10	10	9	9	38
Durban (SA)	1910	2	19	7	2	10	7	26
Brisbane (A)	1928	2	23	5	13	5	18	41
Christchurch (NZ)	1930	2	16	8	1	7	12	28
Bridgetown (WI)	1930	1	17	3	6	8	25	42
Wellington (NZ)	1930	2	12	4	2	6	14	26
Port of Spain (WI)	1930	1	19	6	7	6	9	28
Auckland (NZ)	1930	1	17	4	2	11	13	30
Georgetown/ Providence (WI)	1930	2	9	1	4	4	8	17

City	First match	Grounds	Tests	Won	Lost	Drawn	ODIs/ T20s	Total matches
Kingston (WI)	1930	1	15	3	6	6	3	18
Mumbai (I)	1933	3	13	4	4	5	6	19
Kolkata (I)	1934	1	10	2	3	5	6	16
Chennai (I)	1934	2	13	4	7	2	3	16
Delhi (I)	1951	1	7	3	0	4	7	14
Kanpur (I)	1952	1	6	1	0	5	4	10
Dunedin (NZ)	1955	2	3	1	0	2	5	8
Lahore (P)	1961	1	8	1	2	5	9	17
Dhaka/Mirpur (P/B)	1962	2	5	2	1	2	11	16
Karachi (P)	1962	1	8	2	1	5	10	18
Perth (A)	1970	2	14	1	10	3	18	32
Bangalore (I)	1977	1	3	0	1	2	6	9
Antigua (WI)	1981	2	11	0	4	7	7	18
Ahmedabad (I)	1981	2	4	0	3	1	8	12
Colombo (SL)	1982	3	7	4	2	1	18	25
Faisalabad (P)	1984	1	4	0	0	4	1	5
Chandigarh/ Mohali (I)	1985	2	4	0	3	1	4	8
Centurion (SA)	1995	1	6	1	2	3	8	14
Galle (SL)	2001	1	7	3	2	2	0	7
Kandy/Pallekelle (SL)	2001	2	4	2	1	1	7	11
Chattogram (B)	2003	2	3	3	0	0	10	13
Dubai (UAE)	2010	1	3	0	3	0	11	14
Other grounds		55	23	6	8	9	160	183
Totals		**112**	**520**	**158**	**191**	**172**	**551**	**1071**

England in Test matches overseas

Opposition/hosts	Dates	P	W	L	D	Series won/lost
Australia	1877–2022	185	57	99	29	14–25
South Africa	1889–2020	85	34	20	31	12–5
West Indies	1930–2022	74	15	28	31	3–10
New Zealand	1930–2023	53	19	7	27	10–3
India	1933–2021	64	14	22	28	5–8
Pakistan*	1961–2022	33	5	9	19	3–5
Sri Lanka	1982–2021	18	9	5	4	4–3
Zimbabwe	1996	2	0	0	2	0–0
Bangladesh	2003–16	6	5	1	0	2–0
Total		**520**	**158**	**191**	**171**	

*England played six Tests against Pakistan in the United Arab Emirates in 2011–12 and 2015–16 (won 0, lost 5, drawn 1).

England in one-day internationals overseas

The results summarised below include matches played each side both in their own countries and on neutral territory overseas in tri-series, quadrangulars or other larger tournaments, including World Cups and Champions Trophies. Of the 437 one-day internationals England have played outside Great Britain, 117 were held at neutral venues; of these, they won 67, lost 49 and there was one no result, a much superior record to that in overseas bilateral ODI series.

Opposition	Dates	P	W	L	Tie	NR	Neutral venue matches	Bilateral series won/lost
Australia	1971–2022	82	27	54	0	1	8	2–6
New Zealand	1975–2018	59	24	31	2	2	16	4–4
Pakistan	1977–2015	40	23	16	0	1	21	4–2
West Indies	1979–2019	61	29	29	0	3	18	3–6

Opposition	Dates	P	W	L	Tie	NR	Neutral venue matches	Bilateral series won/lost
India	1981–2021	61	21	39	1	0	10	1–7
Sri Lanka	1982–2018	43	20	22	0	1	17	2–4
South Africa	1992–2023	40	13	24	1	2	7	1–4
Zimbabwe	1992–2004	21	15	6	0	0	6	2–1
Bangladesh	2000–23	16	12	4	0	0	3	4–0
Ireland+	2007–11	2	1	1	0	0	–	2
Scotland+	2015	1	1	0	0	0	1	1–0
Netherlands	2022	6	6	0	0	0	3	1–0
*Others+	1996–15	5	5	0	0	0	5	
Total		437	197	226	4	10		

*Afghanistan, Canada, Kenya, Namibia and United Arab Emirates.
+All at World Cups.

England in international T20s overseas

2007–23: Played 114, Won 59, Lost 51, Tied 2, No Result 2

Leading Test tour captains

Twelve England captains have led the side in four or more Test series overseas, and their records are listed below. The only other captain to have been in charge for more than 12 overseas Tests is J. W. H. T. Douglas, who oversaw 15 matches (won 8, lost 6, drawn 1) across three series; in the case of the 1911–12 series in Australia he was a late stand-in after Pelham Warner was taken ill. Douglas Jardine is the only other England captain to win six overseas Tests (played 9, won 6, lost 1, drawn 2). Both Douglas and Jardine won two series. Of those who captained England in ten Tests both home and away, only three had a better win–loss record away than they did at home: Ted Dexter (+2 away, 0 at home), Mike Gatting (0 away, —3 at home) and David Gower (—4 away, —9 at home).

Captain	Period	Tours	Series	Played	Won	Lost	Drawn	Series won/ lost
Peter May	1956–60	3	4	15	4	6	5	2–1
Ted Dexter	1961–63	2	4	16	5	3	8	2–1
M. J. K. Smith	1964–66	3	4	18	2	1	15	1–0
Mike Brearley	1977–80	3	4	12	6	4	2	2–1
Mike Gatting	1986–88	3	4	12	2	2	8	1–1
Graham Gooch	1990–93	4	5	11	3	4	4	1–4
Mike Atherton	1993–98	5	6	26	5	10	11	1–4
Nasser Hussain	1999–2003	6	6	22	6	9	7	2–3
Michael Vaughan	2003–08	7*	7	22	9	5	8	4–3
Andrew Strauss	2009–12	5	5	19	5	7	7	1–2
Alastair Cook	2010–16	8	9	31	8	15	8	3–3
Joe Root	2017–22	9*	10	33	10	17	6	3–7

*Vaughan started a tour of India in 2005–06 as captain but did not play any Tests due to injury; Joe Root was captain of a tour of Sri Lanka in 2019–20 that was abandoned before the Test series due to Covid-19.

Most overseas Test tours

These tallies include some tours which players joined after the start after being called up as reinforcements, or those they left early for injury or other reasons. The totals for Stuart Broad, Joe Root and Ben Stokes do not count the tour of Sri Lanka in 2020–21, which was abandoned during the warm-up phase because of the Covid-19 pandemic.

1877–1947	1938–84	1977–2005	1999–2023
8 W. R. Hammond (1927–47; 41 Tests)	11 M. C. Cowdrey (1954–75; 59 Tests)	14 A. J. Stewart (1989–2003; 59 Tests)	27 J. M. Anderson (2003–23; 78 Tests)
7 J. Briggs (1884–98; 23)	10 G. Boycott (1964–82; 51)	13 N. Hussain (1989–2004; 49)	24 S. C. J. Broad (2007–23; 69)
7 W. Rhodes (1903–30; 34)	10 R. G. D. Willis (1970–84; 49)	13 G. P. Thorpe (1993–2005; 51)	19 I. R. Bell (2001–16; 53)**
7 J. B. Hobbs (1907–29; 34)	8 T. G. Evans (1946–59; 37)	11 M. W. Gatting (1977–95; 40)	19 A. N. Cook (2005–18; 72)
7 F. E. Woolley (1909–30; 34)	8 J. B. Statham (1950–63; 33)	11 G. A. Gooch (1978–95; 44)	17 J. E. Root (2012–23; 63)
6 G. Ulyett (1876–89; 15)	8 D. L. Underwood (1968–82; 44)	11 M. A. Atherton (1990–2001; 48)	15 K. P. Pietersen (2005–14; 51)
6 H. Strudwick (1903–25; 20)*	7 L. Hutton (1938–55; 35)	10 D. I. Gower (1978–91; 52)	15 B. A. Stokes (2013–23; 52)
6 E. H. Hendren (1920–35; 28)	7 K. F. Barrington (1959–68; 36)	10 I. T. Botham (1977–92; 43)	13 J. M. Bairstow (2012–22; 39)
6 R. E. S. Wyatt (1927–37; 25)	7 T. W. Graveney (1951–69; 31)		12 A. Flintoff (1999–2009; 38)*
6 L. E. G. Ames (1928–39; 25)*	7 A. P. E. Knott (1967–77; 39)		12 P. D. Collingwood (2003–11; 36)*
	7 C. M. Old (1972–81; 22)		12 M. S. Panesar (2005–14; 28)*
	7 K. W. R. Fletcher (1968–82; 39)		

*Includes one tour on which the player did not appear in Tests.
**Includes two tours on which the player did not appear in Tests.

Leading Test batsmen

(2,750 runs, top 12 averages)

Batsman	Span	Innings	Runs	HS	Average	100
Ken Barrington	1960–68	58	3,459	172	69.18	14
Wally Hammond	1927–47	72	4,245	336*	66.32	13
Jack Hobbs	1908–29	62	3,475	187	59.91	10
Len Hutton	1938–55	61	3,041	205	55.29	6
Joe Root	2012–23	120	5,324	228	47.11	12
Geoff Boycott	1964–82	93	3,758	142*	46.97	8
Alastair Cook	2006–18	136	5,904	263	46.48	18
David Gower	1978–91	91	3,777	173*	46.06	8
Colin Cowdrey	1954–75	100	4,087	151	44.91	13
Graham Thorpe	1994–2005	94	3,401	200*	44.16	9
Andrew Strauss	2004–12	73	2,992	177	42.74	11
Kevin Pietersen	2005–14	92	3,644	227	41.88	8

Leading Test batsmen in major regions

(1,150 runs, average 40 in Australia; 1,000 runs, average 40 elsewhere)

Batsman/Region	Span	Innings	Runs	HS	Average	100
Australia						
Herbert Sutcliffe	1924–33	25	1,529	194	63.70	6
Wally Hammond	1928–47	35	1,981	251	61.90	7
Jack Hobbs	1908–29	45	2,493	187	57.97	9
John Edrich	1965–75	26	1,283	130	55.78	4
Len Hutton	1946–55	28	1,170	156*	50.86	2
Alastair Cook	2006–18	36	1,664	244*	48.94	5
Geoff Boycott	1965–80	37	1,396	142*	45.03	2

Batsman/Region	Span	Innings	Runs	HS	Average	100
David Gower	1978–91	45	1,824	136	44.48	5
South Africa						
Wally Hammond	1927–39	26	1,447	181	62.91	4
West Indies						
Colin Cowdrey	1960–68	18	1,025	148	60.29	4
Geoff Boycott	1968–81	25	1,179	116	51.26	3
Alec Stewart	1990–98	28	1,099	143	42.26	2
Asia						
David Gower	1980–85	24	1,138	173*	56.90	2
Alastair Cook	2006–16	55	2,710	263	53.13	9
Joe Root	2012–22	45	2,117	228	49.23	5
Marcus Trescothick	2000–05	34	1,306	193	40.81	3
Kevin Pietersen	2005–12	42	1,573	186	40.33	4

Leading Test bowlers

(100 wickets)

Bowler	Span	Tests	Wickets	Best	Average	5wi
James Anderson	2003–23	78	256	6–40	29.68	8
Stuart Broad	2007–23	69	206	6–17	31.06	6
Ian Botham	1978–92	43	157	7–48	29.63	10
Derek Underwood	1969–82	44	152	7–113	27.36	7
Bob Willis	1971–84	49	149	6–53	27.20	6
Graeme Swann	2008–13	28	135	6–82	30.88	10
Sydney Barnes	1901–14	17	126	9–103	17.96	15
Matthew Hoggard	2001–08	34	126	7–61	30.26	5
Andrew Flintoff	1999–2009	38	110	5–58	30.60	1
Andrew Caddick	1994–2003	29	106	7–46	29.70	7
Darren Gough	1994–2001	26	105	6–49	26.90	4

Bowler	Span	Tests	Wickets	Best	Average	5wi
Brian Statham	1951–63	33	104	7–57	27.79	2

Leading Test bowlers in major regions

(50 wickets, average under 30 in Australia and in Asia; 40 wickets in South Africa and West Indies)

Bowlers/Region	Span	Tests	Wickets	Best	Average	5wi
Australia						
Billy Bates	1881–87	15	50	7–28	16.42	4
Bobby Peel	1884–95	14	63	6–67	21.55	3
Sydney Barnes	1901–12	13	77	7–60	22.42	8
Harold Larwood	1928–33	10	51	6–32	26.82	3
Ian Botham	1978–87	18	69	6–78	28.44	3
Maurice Tate	1924–29	10	55	6–99	28.69	5
Bob Willis	1971–83	24	72	5–44	29.80	3
South Africa						
Sydney Barnes	1913–14	4	49	9–103	10.93	7
Stuart Broad	2009–20	12	45	6–17	23.95	1
West Indies						
Angus Fraser	1990–98	12	54	8–53	20.29	4
Asia						
Graeme Swann	2008–12	13	73	6–82	25.97	5
Derek Underwood	1969–82	22	73	5–28	26.65	3
James Anderson	2003–22	28	82	6–40	26.78	2
Matthew Hoggard	2001–07	14	50	6–57	28.22	1

Leading white-ball tour captains

Best win percentages, minimum of 28 matches; ODIs and T20s played outside Great Britain (i.e. excluding matches played in England, Wales, Ireland and Scotland).

Official Captain	Period	Played	Won	Lost	Tie/ NR	Series Won/ lost	Tournament wins	Win %
+Mike Gatting	1987–88	30	20	10	0/0	1–1	2	66.7
Eoin Morgan	2014–22	98	54	39	2/3	12–8	0	55.1
Paul Collingwood	2007–11	29	15	12	1/1	2–1	1	51.7
Michael Vaughan	2003–07	31	16	12	1/2	2–3	1	51.6
Jos Buttler	2015–23	30	15	14	0/1	3–3	1	50.0
+Nasser Hussain	1997–2003	46	23	23	0/0	2–2	0	50.0
Alastair Cook	2010–14	32	14	18	0/0	3–4	0	43.8
+Graham Gooch	1989–93	35	15	17	0/3	0–1	0	42.9
Andrew Strauss	2006–11	28	12	15	1/0	2–1	0	42.9

+ ODIs only

Leading ODI batsmen

(2,000 runs, best strike-rates)

Batsman	Span	Innings	Runs	HS	Average	Rate	100
Jos Buttler	2012–23	74	2,501	162*	41.00	119.03	6
Eoin Morgan	2009–22	90	2,632	121	32.90	88.44	6
Kevin Pietersen	2004–13	77	3,204	130	47.82	87.30	8
Joe Root	2013–20	64	2,854	125	53.84	83.67	8

Batsman	Span	Innings	Runs	HS	Average	Rate	100
Paul Collingwood	2001–11	112	3,196	120*	36.73	76.80	4
Ian Bell	2004–15	86	2,732	141	33.72	75.05	2
Allan Lamb	1983–92	77	2,577	108*	38.46	74.50	1
Graeme Hick	1992–2001	84	2,667	126*	35.56	73.49	5

Leading ODI bowlers

(60 wickets, best strike-rates)

Bowler	Span	Matches	Wickets	Best	Average	SR	Econ
Steven Finn	2011–17	37	64	5–33	26.18	31.4	4.99
Adil Rashid	2009–23	51	80	5–85	30.13	31.5	5.73
Stuart Broad	2007–16	56	86	4–15	29.81	32.7	5.46
Chris Woakes	2011–23	65	94	6–45	31.37	33.5	5.62
Darren Gough	1994–2005	82	126	5–44	25.46	35.0	4.36
Andrew Flintoff	1999–2009	81	94	5–19	25.88	35.6	4.35
Ian Botham	1977–92	69	89	4–31	26.01	38.5	4.05
James Anderson	2002–15	103	134	5–23	32.11	38.5	5.00

The figures in the two tables above exclude ODIs in England, Wales, Ireland and Scotland.

All figures correct up to 29 August 2023.

SOURCES IN THE TEXT

1. The Fragile Machine

'It's going to take two years and six times around the world . . .' Andy Flower, *The Edge*, directed by Barney Douglas, 2019

'Almost hot enough to set your clothes on fire' James Southerton, *The Cricket Tour of Australia and New Zealand by Lillywhite's Twelve in 1876-1877*, p. 17

'It was a terrible day for a fast bowler . . .' Bob Wyatt, *R. E. S. Wyatt: Fighting Cricketer*, p. 107

'Anyone who has fielded out for a day in Melbourne . . .' Douglas Jardine, *In Quest of the Ashes*, p. 59

'The grounds are hard, the ball is hard, the men are hard,' Len Hutton, quoted in *Ambassadors of Goodwill: MCC Tours 1946-47–1970/71*, p. 98

'It's very nearly too hot here for Europeans . . .' Keith Fletcher, *Wisden 1994*, p. 982

'The protracted physical and mental effort . . .' John Woodcock, *The Times*, 4 January 1971

'Touring teams should be treated as guests . . .' ICC annual board meeting resolutions, 2 July 2018

'I think the chances are even . . .' Len Hutton, quoted in *The Long Hop*, p. 37

'It may be that his [Malan's] game . . .' Ed Smith, quoted in *The Times*, 6 August 2018

'The big solution would be county cricket played on much flatter pitches . . .' Ed Smith, interview with author

'Look at some of the young batters . . .' Joe Root, press conference, Hobart, 16 January 2022

'When you are looking at selecting teams . . .' Andrew Strauss, press conference, Lord's, 9 February 2022

'Why do these things have to happen to touring cricket teams?' *At the heart of English cricket: The Life and Memories of Geoffrey Howard*, p. 24

'Somewhere very hot and very far away . . .' Miles Kington, quoted in *Another Bloody Day in Paradise!*, p. 147

'To win a rubber in Australia . . .' *Australian Summer: The Test Matches of 1936–7*, pp. 15–16

'Playing in Australia, everyone's just looking . . .' Matt Prior, *The Edge*

'I'd been there four years previously . . .' Steve Harmison, *Speed Demons*, p. 287

'Cricket is a unique sport in how much time you spend together . . .' Ben Stokes, press conference, The Oval, 7 September 2022

'You have these short periods of action . . .' *At the heart of English cricket: The Life and Memories of Geoffrey Howard*, p. 150

'You cannot consider yourself a seasoned captain . . .' Michael Vaughan, *Time to Declare*, p. 173

'On cricket tours, it is essential . . .' Arthur Gilligan, 'The Spirit of Fascism and Cricket Tours', *The Bulletin*, May 1925

'A public relations officer, agricultural consultant . . .' Doug Insole, cited in the *Sunday Telegraph*, 22 August 2004

'My past certainly influenced me as a coach . . .' Andy Flower, *The Edge*

'At the height of our touring . . .' ibid

'Lord Hawke... might have taken the same view . . .' John Woodcock, *The Times*, 29 January 1975

'What would you do if you were in the army?' Tim Lamb, quoted in *Dazzler: The Autobiography*, p. 181

2. Staying Sane

'We all get homesick sooner or later . . .' Tony Lock, quoted in *Who Only Cricket Know: Hutton's Men in the West Indies 1953/54*, p. 188

'How lonely touring life can become' Graeme Fowler, *The Captain's Diary: England in Fiji, New Zealand and Pakistan 1983–84*, p. 153

'It is a long time away from home . . .' Fowler, *Fox on the Run*, p. 3

'On tour everything is heightened . . .' ibid, p. 28

'I try to keep my feelings repressed . . .' ibid, p. 35

'Touring is a peculiar life . . .' ibid, p. 38

'You talk to some of the experienced pros . . .' Phil Edmonds, *A Singular Man*, p. 93

'International cricket, above all, is a mental challenge . . .' Mike Atherton, *The Times*, 15 January 2020

'The first few tours you go on . . .' Andrew Strauss, interview with author

'The only thing that kept me going . . .' Steve Harmison, interview with author

'Utterly miserable throughout . . .' Marcus Trescothick on Harmison, *Coming Back to Me*, p. 136

'Rarely did you leave the hotel . . .' Harmison, interview with author

'Turn on your telly at home . . .' Ashley Giles, interview with author

'In the subcontinent, it is about dealing with the heat . . .' *Sunday Times*, 22 November 2020

'I wanted to put the reader into the England dressing-room . . .' Nathan Leamon, *Oborne & Heller On Cricket* podcast, 8 May 2020

'I am coming towards the end of my twenty-fifth consecutive summer . . .' *The Test*, p. 67

'To a greater and lesser degree all sportsmen die in hotels' *Sydney Morning Herald*, 20 March 2007

'Touring is an important characteristic . . .' Thomas McCabe, Nicholas Peirce, Paul Gorcynski and Neil Heron, 'Narrative review of mental illness in cricket with recommendations for mental health support', BMJ Open Sport & Exercise Medicine, January 2021

'Environment and timings of training and matches . . .' ibid

'Creation of a psychologically aware . . .' ibid

'Looking back, I almost cannot believe . . .' Trescothick, *Coming Back to Me*, p. 185

'You've had six years of constant playing . . .' ibid, p. 251

'Surely he could have helped me . . .' ibid, p. 327

'Homesickness was a recurring problem . . .' Jonathan Trott, *Unguarded: My Autobiography*, p. 18

'His departure put the jitters up the side . . .' Andy Flower, ibid, p. 71

'Creeping into the lifeboat on the *Titanic* with the women and children' *Daily Telegraph*, 15 August 2020

'Given my time again, [I] would have asked him . . .' Alastair Cook, *The Autobiography*, pp. 173–74

'It felt different because the stresses, strains and intensity . . .' Trescothick, quoted in *Daily Telegraph*, 2 March 2021

'Work with the person as much as the player' Flower, *The Edge*

'I felt I had to [stay] after leaving the Ashes tour' Trott, *Unguarded: My Autobiography*, p. 3

'That was my "Marcus Trescothick moment"' Harmison, interview with author

'I felt he was not only on my side . . .' ibid

'Test cricket is 90 per cent mental . . .' Stuart Broad, *The Edge*

'Trescothick's book was brilliant . . .' Jos Buttler quoted in 'How lockdown gave Buttler the space to light up the summer', *Daily Telegraph*, 2 October 2020

'When you're on a tour . . .' Strauss, interview with author

'If you play poorly for a certain period of time . . .' ibid

'A mental ghost train' Strauss, *Driving Ambition*, p. 160

'Vaughany, I think I'm going cuckoo . . .' Matthew Hoggard, *Hoggy: Welcome to My World*, p. 299

'My wife said, "Now that you've been dropped . . ."' Hoggard, interview with author

'Sarah said that I'd done things . . .' Hoggard, *Hoggy: Welcome to My World*, p. 302

'Nowadays it has ramped up to another level' Ashley Giles, interview with author

'I just remember locking myself in the toilet . . .' Steven Finn, *The Edge*

'If you're consumed by the game of cricket . . .' ibid

'I probably didn't realise just how much of an issue . . .' Ben Stokes, 'I was in a dark place but now I am buzzing for the Ashes!', *Daily Mirror*, 26 October 2021

'Massive panic attack' Sam Mendes, *Ben Stokes: Phoenix from The Ashes*

'We have to understand . . .' Tom Harrison, speaking on *Test Match Special*, 10 September 2021

'Leaving at this stage of the World Cup campaign . . .' Michael Yardy statement, quoted in the *Guardian*, 24 March 2011

'Touring as captain is tough . . .' Strauss, interview with author

3. Why Tours Are Arranged

'The decision, albeit taken under strong pressure from Australia . . .' *Wilfred Rhodes*, p. 129

'The Australian cricket authorities were extremely upset . . .' Jardine, *In Quest of the Ashes*, p. 60

'Oh, it doesn't matter about New Zealand . . .' *At the heart of English cricket: The Life and Memories of Geoffrey Howard*, p. 159

'There was disappointment on the part of the less rich nations . . .' Tim
    Lamb, interview with author

'This was potentially disastrous . . .' ibid

'And took the risks of the gates failing . . .' Lord Harris, quoted in *The
    Times*, 16 September 1924

'Small turn of 7–8 per cent interest' *Swallows and Hawke: English Cricket
    Tours, the MCC and the Making of South Africa 1888–1968*, p. 95

'A nice sum to come 14,000 miles for' *The Cricket Tour of Australia and
    New Zealand by Lillywhite's Twelve in 1876–1877*, p. 86

'If you bring a strong eleven . . .' John Conway, quoted in *'Give Me
    Arthur': A Biography of Arthur Shrewsbury*, p. 29

'It is terribly hard on these small communities . . .' *In Quest of the Ashes
    1950–51*, p. 151

'A great dearth of leisure facilities . . .' *'Ave A Go, Yer Mug! Australian
    Cricket Crowds from Larrikin to Ocker*, p. 25

'For the sake of a few pounds' W. G. Grace, *Cricketing Reminiscences*, p. 99

'Covered with small stones' ibid, p. 99

4. How MCC Ran Tours

'Did not see why our players should go out . . .' Lord Hawke, quoted in
    Cricket: A Weekly Record of the Game, 19 September 1901

'The success of a tour depends, to a very large extent . . .' Sir Frederick
    Toone, 'Australian Tours and their Management', *Wisden 1930*,
    p. 270

'At present they, a private club . . .' *No Ashes for England*, p. 14

'If we are to compete we must . . .' ibid, p. 20

'The spectre of Bodyline still haunted the corridors of power' Len
    Hutton, quoted in *Who Only Cricket Know: Hutton's Men in the West
    Indies 1953/54*, pp. 95–6

'A weariness of the flesh' *How We Recovered the Ashes: An Account of the
    1903–04 MCC Tour of Australia*, p. 167

'Utterly meaningless' and 'To their only glimpse of the touring side . . .'
    Yorkshire and Back: The Autobiography of Ray Illingworth, p. 90

'As regards the loss sustained . . .' *How We Recovered the Ashes: An Account
    of the 1903–04 MCC Tour of Australia*, pp. 317–18

'Under the terms at present offered . . .' *England v Australia: The Record of a
    Memorable Tour*, pp. 218–19

'We had three or four journeys on Sundays . . .' *In Quest of the Ashes
    1950–51*, p. 82

'To meet people, form relationships . . .' MCC president Robin Marlar, quoted by Christopher Martin-Jenkins in *The Times*, 21 March 2006

'I don't think MCC knew till I got back . . .' *At the heart of English cricket: The Life and Memories of Geoffrey Howard*, p. 19

'Touring teams economized . . .' *In the Eye of the Typhoon: Recollections of the Marylebone Cricket Club tour of Australia 1954–55*, p. xiii

'Books had to be kept and gate receipts checked . . .' Alec Bedser, *Twin Ambitions*, p. 85

'He had no track record or qualifications . . .' *As it Was: The Memoirs of Fred Trueman*, p. 274

'He was hopeless . . .' *Bob Barber: The Professional Amateur*, p. 128

'He was incompetent and wasn't fit to be a manager' ibid, p. 125

'I fear some of the professionals started talking . . .' *Sporting Campaigner*, p. 69

'The West Indies Board of Control . . .' *Cricket Cauldron: With Hutton in the Caribbean*, p. 197

'Surely, then, the MCC should take a firmer line . . .' ibid, p. 198

'While the British public contribute freely . . .' Norman Preston, 'Notes by the Editor', *Wisden 1955*, p. 85

'Pertinent, though often critical, observations' *Trevor Bailey: A Life in Cricket*, p. 91

'The duration of the longer MCC tours must be curtailed' MCC statement, reported in *The Times*, 26 September 1958

'The smallest bonanza ever to come out of a series . . .' *Opening Up*, p. 115

'To Swanton, this exchange was symptomatic . . .' Mark Peel, *Ambassadors of Goodwill: MCC Tours 1946-47–1970/71*, p. 258

'We were down for ten one-day games . . .' *The Captain's Diary: England in Australia and New Zealand 1982–83*, p. 13

'Physiotherapist Laurie Brown is fast becoming . . .' *Triumph in Australia*, p. 163

'The Australian board would cut off the tour expenses . . .' ibid, p. 166

'We will be touring 22 out of 26 weeks,' Mike Gatting, quoted in *The Times*, 29 September 1987

'Met the man from the local bank . . .' *The Captain's Diary: England in Fiji, New Zealand and Pakistan 1983-84*, p. 106

5. Picking the Right Man

'He regarded the behavior of individuals on tour . . .' Gubby Allen, quoted in *Who Only Cricket Know: Hutton's Men in the West Indies 1953/54*, p. 308

'Most of them realized what was expected of them . . .' Mike Green, *Sporting Campaigner*, p. 55

'I wouldn't sit them down before each tour . . .' Ashley Giles, interview with author

'The jobs of England captain at home and abroad . . .' Jim Swanton, quoted in *Who Only Cricket Know: Hutton's Men in the West Indies 1953/54*, pp. 332–333

'Must be men of good character, high principle . . .' Sir Frederick Toone, 'Australian Tours and their Management', *Wisden 1930*, p. 270

'We have talked about him leading and winning in Australia . . .' Ashley Giles, BBC Radio interview, 16 November 2019

'I'm not quite sure what anyone is expecting . . .' Giles, press conference, 26 November 2019

'The most abused man of the day' *Plum Warner*, p. 34

'An unprecedented shadow to fall on an England touring leader . . .' *Another Bloody Day in Paradise!*, p. 3

'Jackson seemed ill at ease . . .' *R. E. S. Wyatt: Fighting Cricketer*, p. 36

'It was on that tour . . .' *Three Straight Sticks*, p. 48

'The captain of a team going to Australia . . .' *Percy Chapman: A Biography*, p. 76

'It should be the time and place . . .' Frank Mann, *Frank and George Mann: Brewing, Batting and Captaincy*, p. 89

'Of the very highest order' Ian Peebles, *Talking of Cricket*, p. 63

'Would not tolerate anything shady or underhand' Errol Holmes obituary, *Wisden 1961*, p. 948

'We were to make active efforts to induce Australia . . .' *Flannelled Foolishness: A Cricketing Chronicle*, p. 109

'[I] learnt something of the social aspect of a touring team . . .' ibid, p. 89

'Not to stand down under any circumstances' *At the heart of English cricket: The Life and Memories of Geoffrey Howard*, p. 121

'He'd had things too easy in his life' ibid, p. 114

'A kind, efficient, delightful man but no disciplinarian . . .' Denis Compton, *Cricket and All That*, p. 87

'I became a sort of aide-de-camp, adviser, secretary . . .' Bill Edrich, *Cricket and All That*, p. 102

'As soon as I was inside the pavilion ...' *Ted Dexter: 85 Not Out*, p. 113

'I'd found the tension created by Robins' selection process ...' ibid, p. 115

'[They] believed there would be a most unfavourable public reaction ...' MCC minutes, cited in *England: The Biography*, p. 329

'Denness suffers by comparison with his predecessor ...' *Assault on the Ashes: MCC in Australia and New Zealand 1974–75*, p. 165

'His handling not only of the crowds ...' *MCC in India 1976–77*, p. 139

'There's more than a touch of who you are ...' *Opening Up*, p. 167

'Exposure does involve risk, especially to captains ...' Mike Brearley, *The Art of Captaincy*, p. 229

'I realised pretty soon that I needed to be briefed ...' *Sunday Times*, 28 May 2022

'Like a schoolboy who ran third in an egg-and-spoon race ...' *The Wildest Tests*, p. 84

'Between games, one of my most important tasks ...' Bob Willis, *Diary of a Cricket Season*, p. 146

'It took him three weeks to accept the offer ...' *The Toughest Tour: The Ashes Away Series Since the War*, p. 78

'Certainly did not act as the strong, tactful disciplinarian ...' *No Ashes for England*, p. 16

'In six major tours overseas ...' Denis Compton, *Cricket and All That*, p. 69

6. Picking the Tour Party

'They had to be flung straight into the battle ...' *No Ashes for England*, p. 13

'We picked the worst squad that had ever been selected' *The Toughest Tour: The Ashes Away Series Since the War*, p. 18

'The weakest conglomeration of cricketers ...' *Cricket All The Year*, p. 119

'Mostly ex-England captains and players ...' *Sporting Campaigner*, p. 186

'The team should not, in my opinion, be chosen in four lots ...' *Gubby Allen: Man of Cricket*, p. 205

'The ideal team upon paper is not so easily transferred to a liner' *The MCC in South Africa*, Preface, p. 1

'I am inclined to think that a side representing England in Australia ...' *In Quest of the Ashes*, p. 32

'I made a great mistake ...' Lord Harris, cited by John Woodcock, *The Times*, 5 January 1971

'We are being pragmatic . . .' Ed Smith, press conference, 21 January 2021

'I was sorry not to have been one of the party . . .' *On and Off the Field*, p. 165

'The tour simply involved too much travelling . . .' *Opening Up*, p. 169

'Those who consistently fail to make the Test team . . .' *Diary of a Cricket Season*, pp. 146–47

'I can understand how cricketers are more likely . . .' *Original Spin: Misadventures in Cricket*, p. 129

'Did you have a good tour, lad?' Peter Loader obituary, *Wisden 2012*, p. 207

'I was thinking about the Ashes . . .' quoted in the *Guardian*, 27 September 2021

'He now knows the swimming-pools of Australia . . .' *Assault on the Ashes: MCC in Australia and New Zealand* 1974–75, p. 169

'Not once did he show it or let up . . .' *Another Bloody Day in Paradise!*, p. 150

'I'll have a lot of speeches to make . . .' David Allen, *Wisden 2015*, p. 173

'Yet another instance of "old school tie" officiousness . . .' *Cricket All The Year*, p. 120

'His general behaviour on the field . . .' Johnny Wardle obituary, *Wisden 1986*, p. 1220

'Not many people on tour have got on well with Johnny . . .' Godfrey Evans, *Who Only Cricket Know: Hutton's Men in the West Indies 1953/54*, p. 188

'Snowy said, "What am I doing here . . . ?" Dennis Amiss, interview with author

'I'm not sure that Graham was ever entirely happy . . .' *Unleashed,* p. 113

'Playing home Test matches . . .' Mark Ramprakash, interview with author

'Yes, there can be less scrutiny, less pressure . . .' Nathan Leamon, interview with author

'To get to the point where we're not debuting anybody . . .' Chris Silverwood, quoted in the *Daily Telegraph*, 19 May 2021

'I did a bit of work on winning in Australia and India . . .' Leamon, interview with author

'I have been instructed to invite you . . .' *Jack Hobbs: England's Greatest Cricketer*, p. 75

'[It] was surprising news to all three' Simon Hughes, *A Lot of Hard Yakka*, p. 92

7. Final Days, Final Minutes

'Departure day seemed to arrive so fast' *The Captain's Diary: England in Australia and New Zealand 1982–83*, p. 21

'We had guys who didn't want to be there' Ian Bell interview, 'Mitchell Johnson was unbelievable – he was a one-man hit', *Sunday Times*, 19 November 2017

'I went there on the back of being in some of my best form ...' Moeen Ali, quoted in *The Times*, 19 November 2020

'The best-prepared England party ever' *Unleashed*, p. 103

'We just weren't fit enough' ibid, p. 111

'Are you trying to hurt me, Harold?' *Bodyline Autopsy*, p. 48

'Jardine asked me if I thought I could bowl on the leg stump ...' *The Larwood Story*, p. 78

'For now I merely ask you ...' *MCC: Autobiography of a Cricketer*, p. 176

'Even before we got into the aeroplane ...' Tom Graveney, *Ambassadors of Goodwill*, p. 216

'See which of the guys coped best with the pressure' Graham Gooch, *Captaincy*, p. 15

'To ensure the players were aware ...' *Behind the Shades: The Autobiography*, p. 321

'We brought the players in much earlier ...' Andrew Strauss, interview with author

'I built a model of playing Test matches in Australia ...' Leamon, interview with author

'One was leaving really well ...' ibid

'The genesis of the trip was our Ashes planning ...' Strauss, interview with author

'Shared hardship brings people together ...' Andy Flower, *The Edge*

'[We were] absolutely exhausted ...' Andrew Strauss, *The Edge*

'The food was awful ...' *Alastair Cook: The Autobiography*, p. 170

'One of the most dangerous things you ever do ...' interview with author

'We ended up playing a different series ...' Leamon, interview with author

'There were no such modern luxuries ...' *Wilfred Rhodes,* p. 57

'"Get fit" and "see your dentist"' *Original Spin: Misadventures in Cricket*, p. 124

'I have some personal matters ...' Dominic Cork statement, quoted in the *Guardian*, 23 November 1996

'I'm going to Australia. I'll be back in April' George Duckworth, *At the heart of English cricket: The Life and Memories of Geoffrey Howard*, p. 46

'Addressed us as though we were just off to Agincourt ...' *MCC: Autobiography of a Cricketer*, p. 55

'I want you all to go out there ...' *At the heart of English cricket: The Life and Memories of Geoffrey Howard*, p. 24

'Some of us in the touring party ...' *In the Eye of the Typhoon: Recollections of the Marylebone Cricket Club tour of Australia 1954–55*, p. 6

'From end to end the platform ...' and 'in a charming speech ...' *England v Australia: The Record of a Memorable Tour*, p. 16

'Quite the most exciting event of our lives' and 'What excitement as the players arrived!' *Percy Chapman: A Biography*, p. 74

'Well, good luck, old boy ...' *At the heart of English cricket: The Life and Memories of Geoffrey Howard*, p. 110

'I jumped into a carriage doorway ...' *The Long Hop*, p. 22

'Assisted by shy glances at the marginal notes ...' *My Dear Victorious Stod: a Biography of A. E. Stoddart*, p. 145

'A multitude of rainbow-hued umbilical cords' and 'The shore crew retract ...' *In the Eye of the Typhoon: Recollections of the Marylebone Cricket Club tour of Australia 1954–55*, p. 15

'When you get to Ceylon, Cowdrey ...' *Ambassadors*, p. 98

'An elaborate prelude of conferences ...' *MCC The Autobiography of a Cricketer*, p. 55

'Sponsors' Girl Fridays ...' *Another Bloody Day in Paradise!*, pp. 1–2

'Somebody from this placid party ...' ibid, p. 13

'There will be no logic then ...' *In the Fast Lane: The West Indies Tour 1981*, p. 1

8. The Outward Journey

'New-fangled sail-and-steam ship ...' Robin Marlar introduction in *The English Cricketers' Trip to Canada and the United States in 1859*

'It is apparent that both passenger comfort and fatigue requirements ...' *Diamonds in the Sky: A Social History of Air Travel*, p. 147

'It pitched and rolled for most of the ten-day voyage ...' *Ted Dexter: 85 Not Out*, p. 83

'Our acclimatising and flag-waving stop-over' *The Captain's Diary: England in Fiji, New Zealand and Pakistan 1983–84*, p. 21

'Coral beads, mandolins, fruit and vegetables ...' and, 'Many cases of Vermouth ...' Rockley Wilson, *The Times*, 23 January 1921

'Gunn talked of leaving the ship at Naples ...' *'Give Me Arthur': A Biography of Arthur Shrewsbury*, p. 56

'The waves swept right over the boat ...' *The MCC in South Africa*, p. 1

'The brilliant rays of the sun ...' W. G. Grace, *Cricketing Reminiscences*, p. 66

'The colour of the sky is most wonderful ...' *Just a Few Lines ... The Unseen Letters and Memorabilia of Brian Close*, p. 118

'Which has been highly charged ...' James Southerton, quoted in *Summers in Winter: Four England Tours of Australia*, p. 18

'This day will be long remembered ...' Fred Lillywhite, *The English Cricketers' Trip to Canada and the United States in 1859*, p. 13

'For three weeks, all but a few hours ...' *Australia 55: A Journal*, p. 20

'A long voyage is always a test of human nature ...' *How We Recovered the Ashes: An Account of the 1903–04 MCC Tour of Australia*, p. 1

'The snobbishness on an ocean-going liner ...' *Australian Summer: The Test Matches of 1936–7*, p. 17

'The sun liquefies the conscience ...' and, 'Cutting cleanly through the middle seas ...' *Australia 55: A Journal*, p. 11

'Shipboard life has a romantic antique ritual ...' ibid, p. 12

'There is, of course, consistently too much drinking ...' ibid, p. 12

'All bar records for the line have been broken ...' and, 'so formally stabilised ...' *Cape Summer*, p. 130

'We have plenty of good singing ...' and, 'Aboard ship life is not very pleasant ...' *'Give Me Arthur': A Biography of Arthur Shrewsbury*, p. 57

'Have led an idle life on board ...' James Southerton, quoted in *Summers in Winter: Four England Tours of Australia*, p. 22

'It's nothing to have four eggs or more ...' *Just a Few Lines ... The Unseen Letters and Memorabilia of Brian Close*, p. 116

'The first lunch I ate on board ...' *In the Eye of the Typhoon: Recollections of the Marylebone Cricket Club tour of Australia 1954–55*, p. xiii

'Several of us quickly acquired the reputations ...' ibid, p. 12

'Verity read *Seven Pillars of Wisdom* ...' *Australian Summer: The Test Matches of 1936–7*, p. 23

'Wasted little time in getting to know ...' *Flannelled Foolishness: A Cricketing Chronicle*, p. 113

'I have become very attached to a good-looking Sydney girl ...' *In the Eye of the Typhoon: Recollections of the Marylebone Cricket Club tour of Australia 1954–55*, p. 38

'I was in his cabin one day ...' *At the heart of English cricket: The Life and Memories of Geoffrey Howard*, p. 27

'I had the distinct impression that Keith and I ...' *In the Eye of the Typhoon: Recollections of the Marylebone Cricket Club tour of Australia 1954–55*, p. 142

'Where lovely hothouse flowers ...' *The MCC in South Africa*, p. 1

'Mauve peaks swathed in turbans of cloud ...' *Cape Summer*, p. 129

'The Arabs rowed half the distance ...' *The Complete History of Cricket Tours at Home & Abroad*, p. 26

'We have not the slightest illness on board ...' *'Give Me Arthur': A Biography of Arthur Shrewsbury*, p. 56

'They are not allowed to handle the coin ...' ibid, p. 57

'They escorted Denis and I round the town ...' *Just a Few Lines ... The Unseen Letters and Memorabilia of Brian Close*, p. 121

'The most filthy, wretched, and disgusting place ...' *The Cricket Tour of Australia and New Zealand by Lillywhite's Twelve in 1876–1877*, p. 6

'In our cabin the heat registered 96 degrees ...' *'Give Me Arthur': A Biography of Arthur Shrewsbury*, p. 57

'There is scarcely a soul on board ...' *Australian Summer: The Test Matches of 1936–7*, p. 18

'One could sense that violence was only just around the corner ...' *In the Eye of the Typhoon: Recollections of the Marylebone Cricket Club tour of Australia 1954–55*, p. 34

'We thought we were playing in an open-air sauna-bath ...' ibid, p. 33

'All in a moment there loomed out of the darkness ...' *Cricket's Burning Passion: Ivo Bligh and the Story of the Ashes*, p. 48

'I don't know what is the matter with me ...' Fred Morley, quoted in *Talks with Old English Cricketers*, p. 291

'In a towering sea two little boats ...' *Australian Summer: The Test Matches of 1936–7*, p. 24

'As the ground became resonant with the cheering ...' ibid, p. 24

'A door of bleak utility' ibid, p. 25

'A shabby ghost town' *In the Eye of the Typhoon: Recollections of the Marylebone Cricket Club tour of Australia 1954–55*, p. 39

'We had to get up early, and there was nothing to keep us up late ...' Percy Fender, *Defending the Ashes*, quoted in *Daily Telegraph*, 4 May 2020

'Good luck, Chapman!' *Percy Chapman: A Biography*, p. 76

'As soon as we landed in Australia ...' *In Quest of the Ashes*, p. 59

'May I express the hope and belief ...' *Douglas Jardine: Spartan Cricketer*, p. 172

'It took my hosts less than the time ...' Denis Compton, *Cricket and All That*, p. 74

9. Board and Lodging

'As a side, I feel confident we shall work well together ...' *How We Recovered the Ashes: An Account of the 1903–04 MCC Tour of Australia*, p. 40

'This was quite a departure from precedent ...' ibid, p. 43

'We were driven off at a rattling pace to Melbourne ...' James Southerton's dispatch to *The Sporting Life*, 18 February 1874

'As all were paid for coming out ...' ibid

'I was glad when the trip was over ...' Arthur Carr quoted in *Mann's Men: The MCC team in South Africa 1922–23*, p. 127

'Sometimes I feel I should like to kill him' *Gubby Allen: Bad Boy of Bodyline?*, p. 21

'Tea immediately follows ...' *The English Cricketers' Trip to Canada and the United States in 1859*, p. 18

'The selection of the hotels at which the team will stay ...' Sir Frederick Toone, 'Australian Tours and their Management', *Wisden 1930*, p. 271

'Like furnaces' *Jack Hobbs: England's Greatest Cricketer*, p. 124

'Then we would be taken to our hosts' home ...' *A History of Indian Cricket*, p. 82

'It was hit or miss as far as we were concerned ...' *At the heart of English cricket: The Life and Memories of Geoffrey Howard*, p. 113

'We had quite a decent sleep ...' ibid, p. 118

'You could fall out of bed ...' ibid, p. 121

'We were slightly arrogant and distinctly intolerant ...' *Trevor Bailey: A Life in Cricket*, p. 80

'The segregation of a touring side into amateur and professional ...' *A Typhoon called Tyson*, p. 190

'Halfway between uneasy and poisonous' *Round the Wicket*, p. 133

'Not knowing whether ...' Fred Trueman, *The Toughest Tour: The Ashes Away Series Since the War*, p. 52

'Filthy insult' Trueman, *Fred Trueman: The Authorised Biography*, p. 169

'None of the professionals were ever invited to dinner ...' Ray Illingworth, *The Toughest Tour: The Ashes Away Series Since the War*, p. 49

'It was one of the reasons I didn't perform for England ...' Illingworth, ibid, p. 57

'On arrival at our hotel we found goats in the bedrooms ...' Dennis Amiss, *Not Out at Close of Play: A Life in Cricket*

'It could have been a thoroughly miserable experience ...' Ibid

'It seemed to me they enjoyed the tour ...' John Woodcock, *The Cricketer*, May 1973

'Travelling together in a strange land' *MCC in India 1976–77*, p. 138

'They were well fed beneath a colourful tent of red ...' ibid, p. 75

'He had been stabbed to death and the cook had been arrested' *The Best Job in the World*, p. 48

'I got to this villa I was sharing with Jack Richards ...' John Emburey, interview with author

'The England party stayed in one of those hotels ...' *Cricket Wallah: With England in India 1981–2*, p. 86

'Pakistan is the sort of place every man should send his mother-in-law ...' quoted in *The Times*, 20 March 1984

'Scarcely a day passed without our being entertained to champagne breakfasts ...' *The Trailblazers: The First English Cricket Tour of Australia: 1861–62*, p. 130

'If we were not actually killed by kindness ...' *MCC The Autobiography of a Cricketer*, p. 112

'This needs to be done immediately ...' Huw Bevan, interview with author

'We compare it to a car petrol tank ...' Emma Gardner, interview with author

'It shocked me when I started ...' ibid

'Some "new boys" had appeared a little overawed ...' *Triumph in Australia*, p. 19

'At 35 years of age I am too old for the dormitory ethic' *A Singular Man*, p. 85

'Some of these are eccentrics ...' Mike Brearley, 'Life in a bubble', *The Cricketer*, December 2020

'This world was a godsend to me ...' ibid

'Tension between narcissism and "groupishness"' Mike Brearley, 'Is Cricket the loneliest game?', *The Cricketer*, June 2021

'Clad in vest, pyjamas and under all the blankets ...' *Fox on the Run*, p. 10

'We are too high-spirited for each other ...' ibid, p. 68

'Ever since I have been in the game ...' *The Captain's Diary: England in Fiji, New Zealand and Pakistan 1983–84*, p. 155

'He didn't drink so it didn't affect his performance ...' *The Judge: More Than Just a Game*, p. 174

'His fastidious routine would begin at around 10 p.m. ...' Dennis Amiss, *Not Out at Close of Play: A Life in Cricket*

'He is making all these flies and catches nothing . . .' Alan Mullally, 'I
    put a shark in Atherton's bed on my first tour', *Daily Telegraph*, 14
    December 2017
'Two players apiece to each pokey room . . .' Ian MacLaurin, *Tiger by the
    Tail: A Life in Business from Tesco to Test Cricket* (Macmillan, 1999),
    p. 181
'Mark has been unbelievable . . .' Dawid Malan, interview with author
'Sometimes with security being so high . . .' Ian Bell, interview with author

10. The Political Dimension

'Equality and fraternity between England and her Colonies . . .' *Alfred
    Shaw Cricketer: His Career and Reminiscences*, p. 61
'This sporting imperialism wasn't just an adjunct of economics . . .' *A War
    to the Knife: England v West Indies in the 1930s*, p. 98
'Cricket has been used as a tool through history . . .' Ebony Rainford-
    Brent, quoted in the *Independent*, 28 May 2021
'Harsh on Australians generally' J. T. Hearne diary extract, *The Cricketer*,
    January 1983
'Our 16 trainee ambassadors' *Another Bloody Day in Paradise!*, p. 13
'Derived strength from diversity . . .' Eoin Morgan, 'My Pride at leading
    these multi-cultural winners', *Daily Mail*, 2 April 2020
'A dirty little town, with old, rusty derelict barges . . .' *Just a Few
    Lines . . . The Unseen Letters and Memorabilia of Brian Close*, p. 139
'A vast prison camp with barbed wire and armed guards' *Swallows and
    Hawke: English Cricket Tours, the MCC and the Making of South Africa
    1888–1968*, p. 256
'We were passing through a land full of tragedy . . .' *The MCC in South
    Africa*, p. 42
'The ideological, political and economic partnership . . .' *Swallows and
    Hawke: English Cricket Tours, the MCC and the Making of South Africa
    1888–1968*, p. 13
'Anybody in the street after that hour was arrested . . .' *Jack Hobbs:
    England's Greatest Cricketer*, p. 145
'A remarkable political act by a sports team' and 'We were regarded as
    ambassadors from the old country' *Caught Behind: Race and Politics
    in Springbok Cricket*, p. 9
'It is one of the tragedies of South African cricket . . .' *Swallows and
    Hawke: English Cricket Tours, the MCC and the Making of South Africa
    1888–1968*, p. 28

'Sport, and more especially cricket ...' *Caught Behind: Race and Politics in Springbok Cricket*, p. 13

'Not for nothing did the club ...' Andre Odendaal, 'Cricket and representations of beauty: Newlands Cricket Ground and the roots of apartheid in South African cricket', *The Cambridge Companion to Cricket*, p. 219

'The Newlands-based cricket establishment ...' ibid, p. 219

'It is far easier, in this easy country ...' *Cape Summer*, p. 162

'On the eve of the selection ...' *Dexter v Benaud: MCC Tour Australia 1962–3*, p. 5

'We were well briefed before we left ...' John Murray, *MCC in South Africa 1964-5*, p. 15

'At a time when the new Labour Government in England ...' ibid, p. 19

'Entrenched system of racialist prejudice' Gordon K. Lewis, *The Growth of the Modern West Indies* (Ian Randle Publishers, 2004) p. 234

'The worst place in the world' *Who Only Cricket Know: Hutton's Men in the West Indies 1953/54*, p. 217

'Strict segregation scarcely exists any more ...' *Through the Caribbean*, p. 67

'That the captain of England should be subjected ...' *Cricket Cauldron: With Hutton in the Caribbean*, p. 31

'Sullen resentment and dissatisfaction ...' Richard Hart, *Labour Rebellions of the 1930s in the British Caribbean Region Colonies* (Socialist History Society, 2002)

'I doubt whether the real reason ...' *Cricket Cauldron: With Hutton in the Caribbean*, p. 92

'I know of a letter sent from a British Guiana official ...' ibid, p. 189

'Some two or three score of English residents ...' ibid, p. 98

'There is evidence to show that the team had given the impression ...' quoted in *A Social History of English Cricket*, p. 286

'Uphold the so-called racial supremacy' Trevor Bailey, *Who Only Cricket Know: Hutton's Men in the West Indies 1953/54*, p. 148

'We wanted to win, but not for them' Charles Palmer, *Who Only Cricket Know: Hutton's Men in the West Indies 1953/54*, p. 17

'Shocked at the intensity of anti-British feeling here' ibid, p. 253

'On the 1953–54 tour, the imperial mindset and the amateur ethos ...' ibid, p. 18

'The constant on-and-off-the-field complaints ...' *Through the Caribbean*, p. 25

'Cricket was once more the means by which ...' *A Corner of a Foreign Field: The Indian History of a British Sport*, p. 209

'Transcended the barriers of caste, class, gender and religion . . .' ibid, p. 175

'Every sixer hit by CK against the visitors' slow bowlers . . .' ibid, p. 205

'[We were] told we would be deported . . .' Matthew Engel, *Financial Times*, 8 December 2017

'Our preferences counted for nothing' *Wounded Tiger: A History of Cricket in Pakistan*, p. 200

'The MCC party were let down over Dacca . . .' ibid, p. 200

'Tony Brown was a bit harsh . . .' *Fox on the Run*, p. 5

'When the news sank in . . .' ibid, p. 26

'No one seems too concerned with what the players think . . .' ibid, p. 26

11. The Build-Up

'Was decidedly uncomfortable when he played this type of bowling . . .' *Three Straight Sticks*, p. 88

'All we need to do is to play forward – we'll never get out' and 'The atmosphere is probably "rarer"' *Flannelled Foolishness: A Cricketing Chronicle*, p. 70

'It is always difficult to play well in the first match . . .' *Put to the Test: England in Australia 1978–79*, p. 16

'Our mental state was badly affected by the lack of organisation . . .' *In the Fast Lane: The West Indies Tour 1981*, p. 35

'All the spare nets have gone fishing' *Another Bloody Day in Paradise!*, p. 36

'The events of the first month of a long cricket tour . . .' *Assault on the Ashes: MCC in Australia and New Zealand 1974–75*, p. 28

'I'd managed more stitches than runs' Mark Butcher, 'Black eye, borrowed bat – but I hit a century', *Sunday Times*, 22 October 2017

'I decided to borrow a bat off Alec' ibid

'At home you were left to your own devices in terms of preparation' Mark Butcher, interview with author

'Leaving him out was more a protective move . . .' *Triumph in Australia*, p. 34

'The bird brought Peter nothing but bad luck' Compton, *Cricket and All That*, p. 89

'Playing the one-day series first . . .' Paul Farbrace, quoted in the *Sunday Times*, 8 March 2020

'The number of warm-up matches is important . . .' Leamon, interview with author

'Warm-up games in recent years . . .' Mo Bobat, press conference, 14
     October 2021

'Boys' nights out, playing golf . . .' Alastair Cook, quoted in the *Sunday
     Times*, 8 August 2021

'It is all too easy to get carried away in the bar . . .' *The Captain's Diary:
     England in Australia and New Zealand 1982–83*, p. 25

'We had a great time for the first few weeks . . .' Phil DeFreitas, quoted in
     The Cricketer, December 2020, p. 16

'What each one thought he was afraid to admit . . .' *The Cricket Tour of
     Australia and New Zealand by Lillywhite's Twelve in 1876–1877*, p. 90

'I could swim, and I had to swim . . .' George Ulyett, *Talks with Old
     English Cricketers*, p. 303

'Not one of us was fit to play cricket . . .' *Alfred Shaw Cricketer: His Career
     and Reminiscences*, p. 59

'People at home do not know or do not think . . .' *The Cricket Tour of
     Australia and New Zealand by Lillywhite's Twelve in 1876–1877*, p. 103

'Thousands of miles . . . in ancient, lumbering trains' *Ted Dexter: 85 Not
     Out*, p. 108

'After the brief settling-in period in Bombay . . .' *MCC in India 1976–77*,
     p. 41

'Whenever the train did stop, a sea of faces . . .' *Cricket Wallah: With
     England in India 1981–2*, p. 67

'Partly with a view to keeping up practice . . .' *Gilligan's Men: A Critical
     Review of the MCC tour of Australia 1924–25*, p. 199

'The true Australians . . .' *The Toughest Tour: The Ashes Away Series Since
     the War*, p. 7

'How are your dozen or so young men . . .' Phillip Sheridan, *Sydney
     Evening News*, 16 July 1907

'We once more had high jinks at Sydney' *The Trailblazers: The First
     English Cricket Tour of Australia: 1861–62*, p. 130

'Here and there were small patches of grass . . .' *Cricketing Reminiscences*,
     p. 77

'One-day games of no consequence' E. M. Wellings, 'MCC in Australia
     and New Zealand 1970–71', *Wisden 1972*, p. 895

'It is a very important PR exercise to take cricket into the districts . . .'
     Put to the Test: England in Australia 1978–79, p. 32

'I am convinced that a captain of an MCC touring team . . .' *Gubby Allen:
     Man of Cricket*, p. 206

'They have to be officially welcomed in each city . . .' *The Long Hop*,
     p. 160

'The heat, travelling and constant social functions ...' *Wisden 1935*,
    p. 642

12. The Shock of the First Test

'For everyone the nerves are always worse on the first day of a new
    series ...' Bob Willis, *The Captain's Diary: England in Australia and
    New Zealand 1982–83*, p. 41
'There is no pretending that the first Test match of an Australian tour ...'
    Douglas Jardine, *In Quest of the Ashes*, p. 87
'The pre-match publicity would have had us believe ...' *Opening Up*,
    p. 146
'I insisted we should start the series by having one at least ...' *Triumph in
    Australia*, p. 46
'I have sat through these dinners dozens of times ...' *In the Fast Lane: The
    West Indies Tour 1981*, p. 45
'I do not think we especially helped ourselves with our team meeting ...'
    Time to Declare, p. 103
'Everyone builds towards this moment ...' *The Captain's Diary: England
    in Australia and New Zealand 1982–83*, pp. 40–41
'The side suffered considerably through the blunder ...' *Cricket*, 30
    January 1908
'A surprise and a disappointment to me ...' *Opening Up*, p. 166
'[The toss] is a very public occasion over here ...' *Triumph in Australia*,
    p. 47
'I found the unusual ritual of playing the national anthems ...' *Time to
    Declare*, p. 104
'Private contraptions complete with sofas ...' *Through the Caribbean*, p. 30
'An hour before the start on the first day ...' *Cricket in Three Moods*, p. 39
'When Bedser prepared to bowl the first ball of the series ...' *Australia
    55: A Journal*, p. 91
'There was a part of me which said, "I'll do it, I'll just turn up"'
    Harmison, *Speed Demons*, p. 286
'McCormick's first ball, which he bowled like a hurricane ...' *Australian
    Summer: The Test Matches of 1936–7*, pp. 37–38
'The press box is the dirtiest I have been in ...' *The Long Hop*, p. 65
'We were all pretty tense ...' Ashley Giles, quoted in the *Guardian*, 24
    November 2006
'We were on a big coach with blacked-out windows ...' Ian Bell,
    interview with author

'I knew it was going to be brutal . . .' Joe Root, *The Ultimate Test*, episode two

'Steaming, hideous, shanty suburb of a capital' *Through the Caribbean*, p. 129

'Kingston does not have a happy atmosphere . . .' *Cricket in Three Moods*, p. 62

'Shorn of grass, it shone like the polished floor . . .' *Cricket Cauldron: With Hutton in the Caribbean*, p. 44

'I have never felt it more likely that we should see someone killed' John Woodcock, *The Times*, 24 February 1986

'I saw some very scared faces . . .' Desmond Haynes, quoted in Rob Steen, *Desmond Haynes: Lion of Barbados* (H. F. & G. Witherby, 1993), p. 142

'MCC touring teams rarely give much attention to fielding . . .' *MCC in South Africa 1964–5*, p. 25

'Never mind, lads, there are still four Tests to go . . .' *In the Fast Lane: The West Indies Tour 1981*, p. 78

'In this colossal funfair . . .' *Cricket My World*, p. 124

13. The Role of Crowds

'Bronzed men from country parts' Tom Horan, quoted in *England v Australia: The Record of a Memorable Tour*, p. 150

'You felt you were part of something that mattered . . .' Michael Atherton, *The Times*, 13 March 2022

'West Indians crowding to Tests bring with them . . .' *Beyond a Boundary*, p. 233

'A certain amount of tension was created before a ball had been bowled . . .' Reg Hayter, 'The MCC Team in West Indies 1953–54', *Wisden 1955*, p. 762

'The actual terms of the abuse did not concern me . . .' *Opening Up*, p. 78

'All day the game has been played in a hubbub . . .' *MCC in India 1976/77*, p. 44

'There was usually a double purpose behind his performances . . .' ibid, p. 139

'These firecrackers made the stadium an artillery range' *Cricket Wallah: With England in India 1981–2*, p. 66

'I've heard stories of Olympic teams . . .' *The Zen of Cricket*, p. 146

'The attitude of the entire Australian side was very aggressive . . .' ibid, p. 68

'There is a more or less continuous flow . . .' Philip Trevor, *With the MCC in Australia 1907–08*, p. 229

'I defy any seasoned player to do himself justice . . .' Jack Hobbs, quoted in *The Glen Innes Examiner*, 12 February 1912

'A symbol which gives them an opportunity . . .' Jardine, *Quest for the Ashes*, p. 211

'The overpowering impulse which comes from the crowded stands . . .' *Swallows and Hawke: English Cricket Tours, the MCC and the Making of South Africa 1888–1968*, p. 268

'I was seen by the man in the Sydney street . . .' Mike Brearley, *The Art of Captaincy*, p. 226

'The Aussies we met in the grounds were the ugly ones . . .' interview with author

'People in England can have no conception . . .' *How We Recovered the Ashes: An Account of the 1903–04 MCC Tour of Australia*, p. 126

'Terribly pleased' *Cricket Wallah: With England in India 1981–2*, p. 54

'A visiting side has to be half as good again to win in India . . .' ibid, p. 54

'Today's incident involving Chris Broad was a culmination . . .' *A Cricket Odyssey: England on Tour 1987–88*, p. 116

'The pitch was so wet and the light so bad . . .' *Behind the Shades: The Autobiography*, p. 104

'We shouldn't have started in bad light . . .' *White Lightning: Allan Donald, The Autobiography*, p. 318

'As I took my guard, I could feel water . . .' *Playing with Fire: The Autobiography*, p. 262

14. Players as Reporters

'To have left no record . . .' Fred Lillywhite, preface to *The English Cricketers' Trip to Canada and the United States in 1859*

'Exceeded the fair limits of criticism upon cricketers . . .' ibid

'The constant attacks of seasickness . . .' W. G. Grace, *Cricketing Reminiscences*, p. 86

'Enabled us to dispense with the tedious coach drives . . .' ibid, p. 220

'The ship rolled awfully' *Stoddy's Mission: The First Great Test Series: 1894–1895*, p. 186

'Once outside Port Philip, the *Loongana* began to jump . . .' and 'Members of the MCC 1903–04 team remember . . .' *England v Australia: The Record of a Memorable Tour*, p. 110

'Will not allow the fascinations of journalism and book-writing ...' W. A. Bettesworth, *Cricket*, 13 August 1903

'Wilson was naturally amazed that the pavilion people should have done such a thing ...' *Jack Hobbs: England's Greatest Cricketer*, p. 197

'Only a very little while ago Lord Hawke ...' Philip Trevor, *Daily Telegraph*, 2 March 1921

'The members of the MCC England team have no desire ...' *Bodyline Autopsy*, p. 214

'Put him beyond the pale of being selected for England' Sydney Southerton, 'Notes by the Editor', *Wisden 1935*, p. 331

'I knew some of the professionals in the team ...' *Sporting Campaigner*, p. 69

'I fail to see what useful purpose can be served ...' Jardine, *Quest for the Ashes*, p. 107

'I am quite sure that the MCC committee ...' Ronnie Aird, quoted in *Who Only Cricket Know: Hutton's Men in the West Indies 1953/54*, p. 319

'Don't bother us, we're trying to win a Test' Duke of Norfolk, *Ted Dexter: 85 Not Out*, p. 124

'We wanted to go there as a team ...' *Triumph in Australia*, p. 19

15. The rise of the Press and TV

'With the keenest possible interest' W. G. Grace, *Cricketing Reminiscences*, p. 105

'Is there not too much of this so-called Test match cricket?' *The Times*, 19 March 1935

'He never let us down once ...' Percy Chapman, quoted in *Wisden 1936*, p. 29

'I don't want to see you, Mr Warner ...' *Bodyline Autopsy*, p. 185

'Neville Cardus on the Tests should be *good!*' *At the heart of English cricket: The Life and Memories of Geoffrey Howard*, p. 158

'Most of the press use typewriters for their reports ...' *The Long Hop*, p. 48

'Large headlines saying that Brown was becoming a second Jardine ...' *Sporting Campaigner*, p. 60

'A regrettable aloofness between Brown and most of the journalists ...' *In Quest of the Ashes 1950–51*, p. 17

'And they were not the type who wanted sensation and scandal ...' *Sporting Campaigner*, p. 71

'The press provides one of the biggest problems ...' ibid, p. 56

'They all hate him of course ...' *At the heart of English cricket: The Life and Memories of Geoffrey Howard*, p. 20

'Your business is to criticise decisions ...' ibid, p. 50

'They rake up all the mud they can find ... *'Cricket Cauldron: With Hutton in the Caribbean*, p. 183

'It was a reporter from one of the papers ...' W. G. Grace, *Cricketing Reminiscences*, p. 80

'The usual method is to give a visiting side a good welcome ...' *Sporting Campaigner*, p. 181

'[I] received a lecture on the illegality of myself ...' ibid, p. 132

'My days there resolved themselves into a delicious pattern ...' *Through the Caribbean*, p. 129

'He had very little to do with the players ...' quoted in *Ambassadors of Goodwill: MCC Tours 1946-47–1970/71*, p. 144

'A press censor' *Dexter v Benaud: MCC Tour Australia 1962–3*, p. 8

'By the presence of a sycophantic following ...' quoted in *Ambassadors of Goodwill: MCC Tours 1946-47–1970/71*, p. 163

'Greig is well aware of his responsibilities ...' *MCC in India 1976/77*, pp. 139–40

'If we lose, a few heads will roll' *In the Fast Lane*, p. 65

'There was ... a potential front-page story ...' Don Mosey, *The Best Job in the World*, p. 140

'On tour, the cricket correspondent travels ...' ibid, p. 140

'I remember the kerfuffle the incident caused ...' Pat Gibson, quoted in *Ian Botham: The Power and the Glory*, p. 99

'Captains the side like a great big baby' Henry Blofeld, ibid, pp. 161–2

'So that I could write his story while he waited' *The Captain's Diary: England in Fiji, New Zealand and Pakistan 1983–84*, p. 76

'We are by no means the first sporting side overseas ...' ibid, p. 123

'One of the first things that hit me ...' and 'In the build-up to the first Test ...' *Time to Declare*, p. 101

'You'd go out for dinner ...' Paul Collingwood, quoted in the *Sunday Times*, 5 November 2017

'It does make a difference ...' Stuart Broad, press conference, 16 October 2021

'It's a complete shot in the dark ...' 'Broad: criticism was unfair and made me angry', *The Times*, 2 June 2018

'Reminding them of the millions at home ...' *The Captain's Diary: England in Australia and New Zealand 1982–83*, p. 42

'It was not disconnected with the idea of telex ...' Patrick Eagar, interview with author

'It really was the only picture that existed ...' Graham Morris, interview with author

'I think they wanted you to see ...' ibid

'Scurrilous and disgusting article' and 'I warned Compton ...' and 'wearing pyjamas, in bed, unshaven ...' *Sporting Campaigner*, p. 164

'Although the smile playing at the side of his lips ...' *Denis Compton: The Untold Stories of the Greatest Sporting Hero of the Century*, p. 139

'Ragging with Evans' *Sporting Campaigner*, p. 163

'Unwittingly knocked against a lamp post ...' *The Truth*, 31 December 1950

'With its batteries of press cameras ...' *Cricket My World*, p. 121

'Right into the hospital' *At the heart of English cricket: The Life and Memories of Geoffrey Howard*, p. 52

16. Births, Marriages and Deaths

'You have to be open to that ...' Jos Buttler, 'My family have already sacrificed so much – I may reject Ashes call', *Sunday Times*, 22 August 2021

'Quite simply, if they can't ...' Michael Vaughan, Twitter, June 2021

'Families are the most important part of a player's make-up' Kevin Pietersen, Twitter, June 2021

'We're very grateful to get the opportunity ...' Joe Root press conference, 2 November 2021

'Touring before you've got kids ...' Graeme Swann, *The Edge*

'Normally the MCC, like other cricketing bodies ...' *Cricket Cauldron: With Hutton in the Caribbean*, p. 147

'Much heartburning and loneliness would be saved' ibid, p. 148

'If wives want to join their husbands ...' *The Long Hop*, p. 160

'From the moment they arrived, their husbands ...' *At the heart of English cricket: The Life and Memories of Geoffrey Howard*, p. 157

'There's no doubt the whole business ...' *The Toughest Tour: The Ashes Away Series Since the War*, p. 41

'Few professional cricketers could have afforded it' *Ted Dexter: 85 Not Out*, p. 87

'Have caused mass suicide (by apoplexy) ...' *Another Bloody Day in Paradise!*, p. 99

'When you're married to a famous person ...' *Fred Trueman: The Authorised Biography*, p. 176–77

'The house hasn't been empty all day' *At the heart of English cricket: The Life and Memories of Geoffrey Howard*, p. 94

'They were regarded with huge suspicion . . .' and 'Throughout my Test career . . .' Dennis Amiss, *Not Out at Close of Play: A Life in Cricket*

'I have played my best cricket . . .' Alan Knott's testimony in Greig v Insole case, 1978, cited in *The Australian*, 7 August 2021

'It is difficult to conceive of any company . . .' *Another Bloody Tour: England in the West Indies 1986*, p. 13

'Tended to create a more cohesive and convivial collective' ibid, p. 110

'My argument was that it would reduce stress . . .' *The Judge: More Than Just a Game*, p. 212

'I asked him what other sportsmen . . .' *Dazzler: The Autobiography*, p. 127

'It was disrespectful to the women . . .' and 'There are sacrifices . . .' Andrew Strauss quoted in *Sunday Times*, 8 August 2021

'It was heartbreaking when I finally told her . . .' and 'big baby', *The Judge: More Than Just a Game*, p. 131

'I couldn't play cricket while a child . . .' *Playing with Fire: The Autobiography*, p. 372

'I printed it off and stared into her eyes' Harmison, *Speed Demons,* p. 114

'Him coming home from Pakistan . . .' Phil Neale, interview with author

'Alice gave birth at 10.30 p.m. . . .' Alastair Cook quoted in *Sunday Times*, 8 August 2021

'I knew then that it had taken him a long time . . .' *MCC: Autobiography of a Cricketer*, p. 57

'No, they said, because nobody could put a time on how long . . .' *Another Bloody Day in Paradise!*, pp. 99–100

'It was a terrible shock . . .' *An Endangered Species*, p. 142

'If any additional incentive had been required . . .' *The English Cricketers' Trip to Canada and the United States in 1859*, p. 40

'Owing to one of our lot fancying some other person's bed . . .' *The Cricket Tour of Australia and New Zealand by Lillywhite's Twelve in 1876–1877*, p. 87

'On tours cricketers come in for a great deal of hero worship . . .' Arthur Carr, quoted in *Mann's Men: The MCC team in South Africa 1922–23,* p. 126

'Dancing girls? Oh yes, they were at our behest . . .' *A History of Indian Cricket*, p. 83

'A philanderer on the grand scale' *Wally Hammond: The Reasons Why*, p. 196

'A glorious place . . .' *Cricket My World*, p. 55

'All the girls who wanted to come ...' *Just a Few Lines ... The Unseen Letters and Memorabilia of Brian Close*, p. 140

'All the beautiful young girls of Melbourne' *The Long Hop*, p. 50

'The same knots of awed local girls ...' *Observer*, 14 December 1958

'It is pointless to pretend that three- and four-month tours ...' *Another Bloody Tour: England in the West Indies 1986*, p. 82

'He used to say, "some players on that tour" ...' Bob Platt, quoted in *Who Only Cricket Know: Hutton's Men in the West Indies 1953/54*, p. 308

'It took just one tour to convince me ...' Lindsay Lamb in Allan Lamb, *My Autobiography*, p. 123

'If you don't keep your husband's bed warm ...' ibid, p. 127

'The church was crammed to suffocation ...' *The Argus*, 18 March 1898

'That is just what he did *not* do!" and 'He was our only "casualty",' *Flannelled Foolishness: A Cricketing Chronicle*, p. 113

'Attractive, smart and charming girls' Mike Green, *Sporting Campaigner*, p. 81

'My first two marriages did not really have a chance ...' Compton, *Denis Compton: The Untold Stories of the Greatest Sporting Hero of the Century*, p. 167

'The temptations were always there ...' ibid, p. 165

'These were invariably attended by ...' Ian Woolridge, *The Toughest Tour: The Ashes Away Series Since the War*, p. 53

'Is it today, Mummy?' *Daily Mail*, 30 December 1992

17. Christmas and New Year

'Over 65,000 cricket enthusiasts ...' *The Long Hop*, p. 102

'Great amphitheatre' that 'dwarfed the sense of personal identity' *Australian Summer: The Test Matches of 1936–7*, p. 88

'Who would not be anxious going in to bat ...' *Assault on the Ashes: MCC in Australia and New Zealand 1974–75*, p. 92

'As close to a colosseum as you're going to get' Matt Prior, *The Edge*

'Before you get to the field ...' Jonathan Trott, ibid

'Pom-bashing day' Andrew Strauss, ibid

'The promoters of the trip looked very smiling ...' James Southerton's dispatch to *The Sporting Life*, 18 February 1874

'We all gave presents to Allen ...' *Australian Summer: The Test Matches of 1936–7*, p. 85

'How strange it all seemed ...' and 'Every man encouraged to act ...' and 'Naturally I was upset' *Testing Time for England*, pp. 90–91

'The thought of the kids safely wrapped up . . .' and 'pledging all support
   for his captain' and 'not a great advertisement . . .' Paul Gibb,
   extract from his tour diary, *Wisden Cricket Monthly*, December 1979
'Quite a sensation' *Sporting Campaigner*, p. 104
'24 December, Melbourne: Went to theatre . . .' quoted in *The Spectator*,
   16 December 2006
'Finished up a good day's sport . . .' and 'Gave us real Christmas dinner'
   and 'One might have fancied . . .' and 'the chaps that have not been
   from home . . .' and 'I wish I was in the little cot . . .' J. T. Hearne's
   diary, *The Cricketer*, January 1983
'Some were more homesick than others' *Ted Dexter: 85 Not Out*, p. 105
'We managed to get him back to the Grand hotel . . .' Mike Selvey, 'On
   tours of old, the odd broken bone was our idea of a Christmas
   cracker to remember', the *Guardian*, 23 December 2009
'To be singing well-known hymns . . .' *Flannelled Foolishness: A Cricketing
   Chronicle*, p. 69
'Christmas away from home . . .' *Triumph in Australia*, p. 101
'At least it gave him on a plate his front-page column . . .' Frank Keating,
   The Spectator, 16 December 2006
'I'll never get them back, not now . . .' Ray Illingworth, quoted in the
   Guardian, 23 December 2009
'A scandalous neglect of duty' *Opening Up*, p. 149
'The crowded itinerary had to take into account . . .' *Unleashed*, p. 110
'Britain's monstrous regiment of cricketing tourists . . .' *Another Bloody
   Day in Paradise!*, p. 86

18. Crimes and Misdemeanors

'Quite sober', 'slightly under the influence of liquor' and 'denies being
   drunk' *The Argus*, Melbourne, 18 February 1925
'He talked about sending Snow home . . .' Tom Graveney quoted in
   Ambassadors of Goodwill: MCC Tours 1946/47–1970/71, p. 249
'The hospitality was out of this world . . .' *Basil D'Oliveira: Cricket and
   Conspiracy: The Untold Story*, p. 133
'Few who were in the West Indies last winter . . .' E. M. Wellings in *The
   D'Oliveira Affair*, p. 106
'Feasting and merrymaking' *Alfred Shaw Cricketer: His Career and
   Reminiscences*, p. 120
'The insobriety of one of the Englishmen . . .' *Stoddy's Mission: The First
   Great Test Series: 1894–1895*, p. 141

'The champion grogster' ibid, p. 198

'Partial pretext' *Assault on the Ashes: MCC in Australia and New Zealand 1974–75*, p. 112

'He is very difficult on occasions . . .' Gubby Allen, *Gubby Under Pressure*, p. 54

'Not the best career move' Godfrey Evans, quoted in *Frank and George Mann: Brewing, Batting and Captaincy*, p. 94

'Was what was expected of English teams abroad . . .' Jim Swanton, *Who Only Cricket Know: Hutton's Men in the West Indies 1953/54*, p. 199

'So do I, since it weren't us' Fred Trueman, ibid, p. 200

'Do not always act as if the sole reason . . .' Ross Hall, ibid, p. 206

'Drunkards and playboys' ibid, p. 206

'Physical health problems had affected his perspective' *Boycs: The True Story*, p. 230

'Boycott's apparent reluctance to contribute . . .' ibid, p. 230

'Every night seems like Saturday night' Michael Carey, cited in *Ian Botham: The Power and the Glory*, p. 235

'Simply in order to relax . . .' ibid, p. 273

'Here and there' and 'but only socially' Allan Lamb, *My Autobiography*, p. 120

'There probably was some sex and possibly some drugs . . .' and 'He was part of some of the fun . . .' *An Endangered Species*, p. 130

'It all came out in a rush' and 'I've let everything get a bit on top of me . . .' and 'We cannot have conduct like that' *Phil Tufnell: The Autobiography*, pp. 217–20

'His conduct on the field did not fit his image' David Lloyd, *The Autobiography: Anything But Murder*, p. 189

'I agreed with the sentiment but not the cure . . .' ibid, p. 189

'I was drinking too much . . .' Andrew Flintoff, *Second Innings*, p. 131

'You will be on the first plane home' *Behind the Shades: The Autobiography*, p. 353

'I've got a problem with the way you practice . . .' Andy Flower, *The Edge*

'Fifty miles there in this bleeding old bus . . .' *Another Bloody Day in Paradise!*, p. 103

'I had never kept in my life' Peter Parfitt, *The Cricketer*, June 2020

'Sunken-eyed and deathly pale' *Wisden 1985*, p. 907

'You go for a scan because you're sore . . .' Joe Root, *The Ultimate Test*, episode two

19. The Great Comebacks

'One of the great pieces of individual heroism' *Testing Time: MCC in the West Indies 1974*, p. 145

'The match was remarkable for the number of unsuccessful appeals ...' E. W. Ballantine, quoted in *Mann's Men: The MCC team in South Africa 1922–23*, p. 62

'Had a pretty low opinion of us ...' *In the Fast Lane: The West Indies Tour 1981*, p. 11

'I was very close to going' *Playing with Fire: The Autobiography*, p. 308

'I would have to resign' *Time to Declare*, p. 350

'The greatest feeling of togetherness comes ...' Hoggard, *Hoggy: Welcome to My World*, p. 102

'He was one of us, more of a professional amateur ...' *'Tiger' Smith of Warwickshire and England*, p. 31

'Johnny took our criticism very good naturedly' *Wilfred Rhodes*, p. 106

'Wedded to a false strategy' *Cricket Cauldron: With Hutton in the Caribbean*, p. 59

'Never was his hold on the reins of leadership ...' ibid, p. 59

'It was time, I pointed out, to throw away our chains ...' Compton, *Who Only Cricket Know: Hutton's Men in the West Indies 1953/54*, p. 209

'Several little pep talks were held ...' *Cricket Cauldron: With Hutton in the Caribbean*, p. 92

'Several players remembered British Guiana ...' *Who Only Cricket Know: Hutton's Men in the West Indies 1953/54*, p. 220

'A far more united side ...' ibid, p. 221

'He was far from disheartened ...' *At the heart of English cricket: The Life and Memories of Geoffrey Howard*, p. 25

'It is not too long – about 20 yards ...' *In the Eye of the Typhoon: Recollections of the Marylebone Cricket Club tour of Australia 1954–55*, p. 117

'He was depressed ...' *At the heart of English cricket: The Life and Memories of Geoffrey Howard*, p. 87

'I can't imagine many international sportsmen ...' *Fox on the Run*, pp. 33–34

'The serious turn of events beyond the cricket ...' *Original Spin: Misadventures in Cricket*, p. 157

'We had great spirit ...' *Playing with Fire: The Autobiography*, p. 306

'You look like raggy-arsed rangers ...' *Behind the Shades: The Autobiography*, p. 161

'I felt, as captain, I had to lead by example ...' Alastair Cook, *The Autobiography*, pp. 155–56

20. The Wheels Come Off

'We want to travel to Australia, fitter, faster, leaner ...' Chris Silverwood, quoted in the *Guardian*, 19 May 2021

'I'm absolutely determined to put the record straight ...' Joe Root, quoted in the *Guardian*, 7 December 2021

'If you can't influence your bowlers ...' Ricky Ponting, speaking on post-match TV coverage, Adelaide, 20 December 2021

'It would be easy to get fractious and point fingers ...' Joe Root, quoted in *The Times*, 3 January 2022

'You live by first-innings runs and we haven't delivered ...' Stuart Broad, quoted in *The Times*, 7 January 2022

'Ideally you'd want more space between the World Cup and the Ashes ...' Mo Bobat, press conference, 14 October 2021

'Performance has almost been the last thing we've had to think about ...' Ashley Giles, quoted in *The Times*, 4 January 2022

'If you had given us the best England cricketers from the last 100 years ...' Paul Collingwood, quoted in the *Guardian*, 26 January 2022

'The Ashes are going ahead ... whether Joe is here or not' Tim Paine on SEN Radio, quoted in *The Age*, 2 October 2021

'To be captain of a struggling touring side ...' *Assault on the Ashes: MCC in Australia and New Zealand 1974–75*, p. 142

'When the demon of defeatism takes a team by the throat ...' *Another Bloody Tour: England in the West Indies 1986*, p. 158

'Tiredness, staleness [and] the accumulation of injuries' *Cape Summer*, p. 243

'The failure, as Australians realistically perceived ...' *Australian Summer*, p. 187

'When the team was bidding Sydney adieu ...' *Bulletin*, 12 March 1892, quoted in *George Lohmann, Pioneer Professional*, p. 120

'It is reported that English cricketers Grace and Lohmann ...' ibid, p. 120

'Though there was no outward clash of personalities ...' *Wilfred Rhodes*, p. 131

'Complete lack of interest on the part of captain and manager ...' Paul Gibb, extract from tour diary, *Wisden Cricket Monthly*, January 1980

'Neither Hammond nor Howard showed any interest ...' ibid, May 1980

'Was there ever a more controversial, more talked-about captain of England?' *Assault on the Ashes: MCC in Australia and New Zealand 1974–75*, p. 163

'Beefy was fairly stirred up, as we all were . . .' John Lever, interview with author; quoted in *Ian Botham: The Power and the Glory*, p. 104

'Heated words were exchanged . . .' *Opening Up*, p. 150

'A bad lack of discipline' ibid, p. 168

'Riddled with cliques' *Another Bloody Tour: England in the West Indies 1986*, p. 86

'A lack of determination and leadership' ibid, p. 95

'Defeatist fucking tactics' ibid, p. 125

'It is certainly difficult to avoid the impression . . .' ibid, p. 95

'The side was like a ship without a rudder' John Thicknesse, 'England in the West Indies 1985–86', *Wisden 1987*, p. 904

'The desire not to antagonise the host country . . .' *A Typhoon Called Tyson*, pp. 195–96

'A convenient alibi' *Trevor Bailey: A Life in Cricket*, p. 133

'A stronger captain than May . . .' *Cricket and All That*, p. 108

'He can never be an ideal tourist' Peter May's tour report, quoted in *Ambassadors of Goodwill: MCC Tours 1946/47–1970/71*, p. 132

'A clash of personalities and conflicting interests' *A Typhoon Called Tyson*, p. 184

'We were never a team' *The Toughest Tour: The Ashes Away Series Since the War*, p. 41

'Nobody else was interested, even the captain' *Behind the Shades: The Autobiography*, p. 330

'People don't realise how much it affects you . . .' Paul Collingwood, quoted in the *Sunday Times*, 5 November 2017

'With bewildering speed' *Alastair Cook: The Autobiography*, p. 172

'Individually, several players were past their best . . .' ibid, p. 170

'It was extremely difficult . . .' Ian Bell interview, *Sunday Times*, 19 November 2017

21. The Final Test, The Final Reckoning

'By concentrating on starving the opposition of runs . . .' *Driving Ambition: My Autobiography*, p. 289

'Iron entered his soul' *The Wildest Tests*, p. 84

'A lot was made out of very little by everyone' *The Toughest Tour: The Ashes Away Series Since the War*, p. 75

'Illingworth's side in 1970–71 were mentally the toughest . . .' ibid, p. 83

'Hot-tempered words' *Swanton in Australia with MCC 1946–1975*, p. 160

'High-spirited demonstrations' ibid, p. 154

'A clatter of wickets suddenly gave us a sniff . . .' *Playing with Fire: The Autobiography*, p. 301

'Because of pressure from business' *The Times*, 10 March 1947

'His eyes have lost the challenging, defiant sparkle . . .' *Another Bloody Day in Paradise!*, p. 122

'To such an extent that . . . he had lost his head and lost his bowling' and 'almost with tears in his eyes' *'Ave A Go, Yer Mug! Australian Cricket Crowds from Larrikin to Ocker*, p. 49

'System of barracking' and 'on all the grounds, and in all our big matches' *My Dear Victorious Stod: a Biography of A. E. Stoddart*, pp. 160–61

'He becomes one of the lions of society . . .' Bruce Harris, quoted in *Gubby Under Pressure*, p. 23

'Hyper-sensitive to criticism . . .' L. V. Manning, ibid, p. 8

'These Test matches simply knock hell out of me . . .' Gubby Allen, ibid, p. 26

'I have had to give up almost all private parties . . .' Allen, ibid, p. 29

'I was terrified that Gubby Allen would declare . . .' Don Bradman, ibid, p. 51

'You cannot honestly rank him among the great captains' William Pollock, ibid, p. 68

'I reckon I was nearer to a mental storm . . .' Allen, ibid, p. 96

'There are few captains who can go through an Australian tour . . .'; 'And his play showed signs of deterioration'; and 'Had he rested, he might well have come back fresh' *Sporting Campaigner*, p. 50

'I noticed that the keenness and energy of the players decreased . . .' ibid, p. 58

'Renewed energy and keenness' ibid, p. 59

'Illnesses which spring from worry' Frank Tyson, *A Typhoon Called Tyson*, p. 194

'Almost destroyed him as captain' *Original Spin: Misadventures in Cricket*, p. 132

'Which have helped to keep me awake for weeks' *The Captain's Diary: England in Australia and New Zealand 1982–83*, p. 132

'I don't think that I was in any fit mental state . . .' *Opening Up: My Autobiography*, p. 207

'A different captain may well have had a fresh outlook . . .' ibid, p. 215

'I'm beginning to question whether I am really the right man . . .' *Time to Declare*, p. 339

'That tour really drained him mentally' Paul Collingwood, interview with author

'He has a high level of emotional intelligence . . .' Ashley Giles, 'Mark Saxby – The Man who Kept England Sane in the Bubble', *Daily Telegraph*, 19 October 2020

'It had become a very unhealthy relationship, the captaincy and me . . .' Joe Root, press conference, Lord's, 5 June 2022

22. The Homecoming

'Like the approaching end of term at a ramshackle prep school . . .' *Another Bloody Day in Paradise!*, p. 147

'One of the most calamitous trips . . .' ibid, p. 147

'Touring is a strange business . . .' *The Captain's Diary: England in Australia and New Zealand 1982–83*, p. 174

'I feel a new man with a sense of greater freedom . . .' Paul Gibb, extract from tour diary, *Wisden Cricket Monthly*, June 1980

'Shabbily and snobbishly treated' James Southerton's dispatch to *The Sporting Life*, 13 May 1874

'Literally hundreds were throwing streamers to the boat . . .' Mike Green, *Sporting Campaigner*, p. 120

'We responded, by giving them such hearty cheers . . .' *The English Cricketers' Trip to Canada and the United States in 1859*, p. 56

'Although the whole of the cricketers have abundant reason . . .' ibid, p. 58

'It was a voyage I would be glad to forget . . .' *R. E. S. Wyatt: Fighting Cricketer*, p. 147

'We'd fly in the day and stop at hotels at night' *The Toughest Tour: The Ashes Away Series Since the War*, p. 11

'The ice clinks in cocktail-shakers . . .' *Australia 55: A Journal*, p. 243

'I tried to convert that strip of 22 yards into a battlefield' *How We Recovered the Ashes: An Account of the 1903–04 MCC Tour of Australia*, p. 322

'Abject failures' *The Captain's Diary: England in Australia and New Zealand 1982–83*, p. 176

'Let the team be chosen as one . . .' *In Quest of the Ashes 1950–51*, p. 168

'Formulated by a golf administrator [and] largely a public relations ploy . . .' Michael Vaugha

BIBLIOGRAPHY

Allen, David Rayvern, *Cricket on the Air* (BBC Books, 1985)

Allen, David Rayvern, *Jim: The Life of E. W. Swanton* (Aurum, 2004)

Amiss, Dennis, *In Search of Runs: An Autobiography* (Hutchinson, 1976)

Amiss, Dennis, with Graham-Brown, James, *Not Out at Close of Play: A Life in Cricket* (History Press, 2020)

Anderson, James, *Jimmy: My Story* (Simon & Schuster, 2012)

Arlott, John, *Basingstoke Boy* (Collins Willow, 1990)

Atherton, Michael, *Opening Up: My Autobiography* (Hodder & Stoughton, 2002)

Bailey, Jack, *Conflicts in Cricket* (Kingswood Press, 1989)

Bailey, Jack, *Trevor Bailey: A Life in Cricket* (Metheun, 1993)

Bannister, Alex, *Cricket Cauldron: With Hutton in the Caribbean* (Stanley Paul, 1954)

Barker, Ralph, and Irving Rosenwater, *England v Australia: A Compendium of Test Cricket Between the Countries 1877–1968* (Batsford, 1969)

Barnes, Simon, *Phil Edmonds: A Singular Man* (Kingswood Press, 1986)

Barrington, Ken, *Playing It Straight* (Stanley Paul, 1968)

Bassano, Brian, *MCC in South Africa 1938–39* (J. W. McKenzie, 1997)

Bassano, Brian, *Mann's Men: The MCC team in South Africa 1922–23* (J. W. McKenzie, 2004)

Bateman, Anthony, and Jeffrey Hill (editors), *The Cambridge Companion to Cricket* (Cambridge University Press, 2011)

Baxter, Peter, *Test Match Special* (Queen Anne Press, 1981)

Beckles, Hilary McD., *The Development of West Indies Cricket* (Vols 1 and 2; Pluto Press, 1998)

Bedser, Alec, *Twin Ambitions* (Stanley Paul, 1986)

Bentley, Richard, *A War to the Knife: England v West Indies in the 1930s* (Matador, 2019)

Berry, Scyld, *Cricket Wallah: With England in India 1981–2* (Hodder & Stoughton, 1982)

Berry, Scyld, *A Cricket Odyssey: England on Tour 1987–88* (Pavilion Books, 1988)

Berry, Scyld, and Rupert Peploe, *Cricket's Burning Passion: Ivo Bligh and the Story of the Ashes* (Methuen, 2006)

Birley, Derek, *The Willow Wand* (Queen Anne Press, 1979)

Birley, Derek, *A Social History of English Cricket* (Aurum, 1999)

Blofeld, Henry, *Cricket in Three Moods* (Hodder & Stoughton, 1970)

Blofeld, Henry, *The Packer Affair* (Collins, 1979)

Booth, Keith, *George Lohmann, Pioneer Professional* (SportsBooks, 2007)

Booth, Keith, *A Class Act: Walter Read, Surrey Champion, ACS Lives in Cricket* (Association of Cricket Statisticians and Historians, 2011)

Booth, Keith, *Tom Richardson: A Bowler Pure and Simple, ACS Lives in Cricket* (Association of Cricket Statisticians and Historians, 2012)

Bose, Mihir, *A History of Indian Cricket* (André Deutsch, 1990)

Bowes, Bill, *Express Deliveries* (Stanley Paul, 1949)

Boycott, Geoffrey, and Brindle, Terry, *Put to the Test: England in Australia 1978–79* (Arthur Barker, 1979)

Boycott, Geoffrey, and Brindle, Terry, *Opening Up* (Arthur Barker, 1980)

Boycott, Geoffrey, and Brindle, Terry, *In the Fast Lane: The West Indies Tour 1981* (Arthur Barker, 1981)

Brearley, Mike, *The Art of Captaincy* (Hodder & Stoughton, 1985; 1987 edition)

Brodribb, Gerald, *The Croucher: A Biography of Gilbert Jessop* (London Magazine Editions, 1974)

Burns, Michael, *A Flick of the Fingers: The Chequered Life and Career of Jack Crawford* (Pitch Publishing, 2015)

Cardus, Neville, *Australian Summer: The Test Matches of 1936–7* (Rupert Hart-Davis, 1937)

Cardus, Neville, *Cricket All the Year* (Collins, 1952)

Cardus, Neville, *Cardus on Cricket* (Souvenir Press, 1977)

Carter, Andy, *Beyond the Pale: Early Black and Asian Cricketers in Britain 1868–1945* (Troubador, 2020)

Cashman, Richard, *Players, Patrons and the Crowd* (Orient Longman, 1980)

Cashman, Richard, *Australian Cricket Crowds: The Attendance Cycle. Daily Figures, 1877–1984* (Kensington, 1984)

Cashman, Richard, *'Ave A Go, Yer Mug! Australian Cricket Crowds from Larrikin to Ocker* (Collins, 1984)

Chalke, Stephen, *At the Heart of English Cricket: The Life and Memories of Geoffrey Howard* (Fairfield Books, 2001)

Chalke, Stephen, and Derek Hodgson, *No Coward Soul: The Remarkable Story of Bob Appleyard* (Fairfield Books, 2003)

Chalke, Stephen, *Micky Stewart and the Changing Face of Cricket* (Fairfield Books, 2012)

Clarke, John, *With England in Australia: the MCC Tour 1965–66* (Stanley Paul, 1966)

Coldham, James D., *Lord Harris* (Allen & Unwin, 1983)

Coldham, James D., *Lord Hawke: A Cricketing Legend* (Crowood Press, 1990)

Compton, Denis, *Testing Time for England* (Stanley Paul, 1948)

Compton, Denis, *End of an Innings* (Oldbourne Press, 1958)

Compton, Denis, and Bill Edrich, *Cricket and All That* (Pelham Books, 1978)

Cook, Alastair, *Starting Out: My Story So Far* (Hodder & Stoughton, 2008)

Cook, Alastair, *The Autobiography* (Michael Joseph, 2019)

Cowdrey, Colin, *MCC: The Autobiography of a Cricketer* (Hodder & Stoughton, 1976)

Dexter, Ted, *Ted Dexter Declares: An Autobiography* (Stanley Paul, 1966)

Dexter, Ted, *Ted Dexter: 85 Not Out* (Quiller, 2020)

D'Oliveira, Basil, *The D'Oliveira Affair* (Collins, 1969)

Donald, Allan, *White Lightning: Allan Donald, the Autobiography* (Collins Willow, 2000)

Douglas, Christopher, *Douglas Jardine: Spartan Cricketer* (Allen & Unwin, 1984)

Duckworth, Leslie, *S. F. Barnes: Master Bowler* (Hutchinson, 1967)

Duckworth, Leslie, *Holmes and Sutcliffe: The Run Stealers* (Hutchinson, 1970)

Edmonds, Frances, *Another Bloody Tour: England in the West Indies 1986* (Kingswood Press, 1986)

Edrich, Bill, *Round the Wicket* (Muller, 1959)

Edwards, Alan, *Lionel Tennyson: Regency Buck* (Robson Books, 2001)

Evans, Godfrey, *The Gloves Are Off* (Hodder & Stoughton, 1960)

Fay, Stephen, and David Kynaston, *Arlott, Swanton and the Soul of English Cricket* (Bloomsbury, 2018)

Fender, Percy, *Defending the Ashes* (Chapman & Hall, 1921)

Ferguson, Bill, *Mr Cricket* (Nicholas Kaye, 1957)

Fletcher, Duncan, *Behind the Shades: The Autobiography* (Simon & Schuster, 2007)

Fletcher, Keith, *Captain's Innings: An Autobiography* (Hutchinson, 1983)

Fletcher, Keith, *Ashes to Ashes: The Rise, Fall and Rise of English Cricket* (Headline, 2005)

Flintoff, Andrew, *Second Innings* (Hodder & Stoughton, 2015)

Foot, David, *Wally Hammond: The Reasons Why* (Robson Books, 1998)

Fortune, Charles, *MCC in South Africa 1964–5* (Hale, 1965)

Fowler, Graeme, with Peter Ball, *Fox on the Run* (Viking, 1988)

Francis, Tony, *The Zen of Cricket* (Stanley Paul, 1992)

Frith, David, *My Dear Victorious Stod: a Biography of A. E. Stoddart* (Lutterworth Press, 1977)

Frith, David, *Stoddy's Mission: The First Great Test Series: 1894–1895* (Queen Anne Press, 1994)

Frith, David, *The Trailblazers: The First English Cricket Tour of Australia: 1861–62* (Boundary Books, 1999)

Frith, David, *Bodyline Autopsy* (Aurum, 2002)

Fry, C. B., *Life Worth Living* (Eyre & Spottiswoode, 1939)

Gatting, Mike, *Triumph in Australia: Mike Gatting's 1986–87 Cricket Diary* (Queen Anne Press, 1987)

Gibson, Alan, *The Cricket Captains of England* (Cassell, 1977)

Giller, Norman, *Denis Compton: The Untold Stories of the Greatest Sporting Hero of the Century* (André Deutsch, 1997)

Gooch, Graham, with Patrick Murphy, *Captaincy* (Hutchinson, 1992)

Gough, Darren, *Dazzler: The Autobiography* (Michael Joseph, 2001)

Gower, David, *An Endangered Species: The Autobiography* (Simon & Schuster, 2013)

Grace, W. G., *Cricketing Reminiscences* (James Bowden, 1899)

Green, Brigadier M. A., *Sporting Campaigner* (Stanley Paul, 1956)

Guha, Ramachandra, *A Corner of a Foreign Field: The Indian History of a British Sport* (Picador, 2002)

Hamilton, Duncan, *Harold Larwood: The Authorised Biography of the World's Fastest Bowler* (Quercus, 2009)

Hamilton, Duncan, *The Great Romantic: Cricket and the Golden Age of Neville Cardus* (Hodder & Stoughton, 2019)

Hammond, Walter, *Cricket My Destiny* (Stanley Paul, 1946)

Hammond, Walter, *Cricket My World* (Stanley Paul, 1948)

Hammond, Walter, *Cricket's Secret History* (Stanley Paul, 1952)

Harmison, Steve, *Speed Demons* (Trinity Mirror Sport, 2017)

Harris, Bruce, *In Quest of the Ashes 1950–51* (Hutchinson, 1951)

Heald, Tim, *Jardine's Last Tour: India 1933–34* (Methuen, 2011)

Hill, Alan, *Herbert Sutcliffe: Cricket Maestro* (Simon & Schuster, 1991)

Hill, Alan, *Peter May: A Biography* (André Deutsch, 1996)

Hill, Alan, *Brian Close: Cricket's Lionheart* (Methuen, 2002)

Hoggard, Matthew, *Hoggy: Welcome to My World*
        (HarperCollins, 2009)

Holmes, E. R. T., *Flannelled Foolishness: A Cricketing Chronicle* (Hollis
        & Carter, 1957)

Holt, Richard, *Sport and the British: A Modern History* (Clarendon
        Press, 1989)

Howat, Gerald, *Walter Hammond* (HarperCollins, 1984)

Howat, Gerald, *Plum Warner* (HarperCollins, 1987)

Hudson, Kenneth, and Pettifer, Julian, *Diamonds in the Sky: A Social
        History of Air Travel* (Bodley Head, 1979)

Hughes, Margaret, *The Long Hop* (Stanley Paul, 1955)

Hughes, Simon, *A Lot of Hard Yakka* (Headline, 1997)

Hussain, Nasser, *Playing with Fire: The Autobiography* (Michael
        Joseph, 2004)

Illingworth, Ray, *Yorkshire and Back: The Autobiography of Ray
        Illingworth* (Queen Anne Press, 1980)

Illingworth, Ray, with Jack Bannister, *One-Man Committee: The
        Complete Story of his Controversial Reign* (Headline, 1996)

Insole, Douglas, *Cricket from the Middle* (Heinemann, 1961)

James, C. L. R., *Beyond a Boundary* (Hutchinson, 1963)

James, Steve, *The Plan: How Fletcher and Flower Transformed English
        Cricket* (Transworld, 2012)

Jardine, Douglas, *In Quest of the Ashes* (Hutchinson, 1933)

Jones, Simon, *The Test: My Life, and the Inside Story of the Greatest
        Ashes Series* (Yellow Jersey, 2015)

Keating, Frank, *Another Bloody Day in Paradise!* (André Deutsch, 1981)

Kilburn, J. M., *Sweet Summers: The Classic Cricket Writing of J. M. Kilburn*
        (edited by Duncan Hamilton; Great Northern Books, 2008)

Kynaston, David, *Bobby Abel: Professional Batsman* (Secker &
        Warburg, 1982)

Laker, Jim, *Over to Me* (Frederick Muller, 1960)

Lamb, Allan, *My Autobiography* (Collins Willow, 1996)

Larwood, Harold, *Body-Line? An Account of the Test Matches between England and Australia 1932–33* (Elkin Mathews & Marrot, 1933)

Larwood, Harold, *The Larwood Story* (W. H. Allen and Co, 1965)

Lazenby, John, *Test of Time: Travels in Search of a Cricketing Legend* (John Murray, 2005)

Lazenby, John, *The Strangers Who Came Home* (Wisden, 2015)

Lazenby, John, *Edging Towards Darkness: The Story of the Last Timeless Test* (Wisden, 2017)

Leamon, Nathan, *The Test* (Constable, 2018)

Lee, Alan, *Lord Ted: The Dexter Enigma* (Gollancz, 1995)

Lemmon, David, *Johnny Won't Hit Today: A Cricketing Biography of J. W. H. T. Douglas* (Allen & Unwin, 1983)

Lemmon, David, *Percy Chapman: A Biography* (Queen Anne Press, 1985)

Leveson Gower, H. D. G., *Off and On the Field* (Stanley Paul, 1953)

Lewis, Tony, *Taking Fresh Guard: A Memoir* (Headline, 2003)

Lillywhite, Frederick, *The English Cricketers' Trip to Canada and the United States in 1859* (World's Work, 1980; with an introduction by Robin Marlar)

Lloyd, David, *The Autobiography: Anything But Murder* (Collins Willow, 2000)

Lock, Tony, *For Surrey and England* (Hodder & Stoughton, 1957)

Lyttelton, R. H. (with C. B. Fry, George Giffen and W. J. Ford) *Giants of the Game* (1899)

McKinstry, Leo, *Boycs: The True Story* (Partridge Press, 2000)

McKinstry, Leo, *Jack Hobbs: England's Greatest Cricketer* (Yellow Jersey, 2011)

Marks, Vic, *Original Spin: Misadventures in Cricket* (Allen & Unwin, 2019)

Marqusee, Mike, *Anyone But England: Cricket, Race and Class* (Verso Books, 1994)

Martin-Jenkins, Christopher, *Testing Time: MCC in the West Indies 1974* (Macdonald and Jane's, 1974)

Martin-Jenkins, Christopher, *Assault on the Ashes: MCC in Australia and New Zealand 1974–75* (Macdonald and Jane's, 1975)

Martin-Jenkins, Christopher, *MCC in India 1976–77* (Macdonald and Jane's, 1977)

Martin-Jenkins, Christopher, *Ball by Ball: The Story of Cricket Broadcasting* (Grafton, 1990)

May, Peter, *A Game Enjoyed* (Stanley Paul, 1985)

Meredith, Anthony, *Summers in Winter: Four England Tours of Australia* (Kingswood Press, 1990)

Miller, Douglas, *M. J. K. Smith: No Ordinary Man, ACS Lives in Cricket* (Association of Cricket Statisticians and Historians, 2013)

Miller, Douglas, *Raman Subba Row: Cricket Visionary* (Charlcombe Books, 2017)

Miller, Keith, and R. S. Whitington, *Catch! An Account of Two Cricket Tours* (Latimer House, 1951)

Moore, Andrew, *The 'Fascist' Cricket tour of 1924–25, Australian Society for Sports History Publications* (May 1991)

Mosey, Don, *The Best Job in the World* (Pelham Books, 1985)

Murray, Bruce, and Christopher Merrett, *Caught Behind: Race and Politics in Springbok Cricket* (University of Kwazulu Natal Press, 2004)

Noble, M. A., *Gilligan's Men: A Critirial Review of the MCC Tour of Australia 1924–25* (Sportsman's Book Club, 1955)

Noble, M. A., *The Fight for the Ashes 1928–29* (Harrap, 1929)

Oborne, Peter, *Basil D'Oliveira: Cricket and Conspiracy: The Untold Story* (Little, Brown, 2004)

Oborne, Peter, *Wounded Tiger: A History of Cricket in Pakistan* (Simon & Schuster, 2014)

Parry, Richard, and Odendaal, André, *Swallows and Hawkes: English Cricket Tours, the MCC and the Making of South Africa 1888–1968* (Pitch Publishing, 2022)

Pawle, Gerald, *R. E. S. Wyatt: Fighting Cricketer* (Allen & Unwin, 1985)

Peebles, Ian, *Talking of Cricket* (Museum Press, 1953)

Peebles, Ian, *Batter's Castle* (Souvenir Press, 1958)

Peebles, Ian, *Patsy Hendren* (Macmillan, 1969)

Peel, Mark, *Ambassadors of Goodwill: MCC Tours 1946–47–1970/71* (Pitch Publishing, 2018)

Pietersen, Kevin, *KP: The Autobiography* (Little, Brown, 2014)

Pollock, William, *So This is Australia* (Barker, 1937)

Pringle, Derek, *Pushing the Boundaries: Cricket in the Eighties* (Hodder & Stoughton, 2018)

Pullin, A. W., *Talks with Old English Cricketers* (William Blackwood, 1900)

Rae, Simon, *W. G. Grace* (Faber & Faber, 1998)

Rae, Simon, *It's Not Cricket: A History of Skulduggery, Sharp Practice and Downright Cheating in the Noble Game* (Faber & Faber, 2001)

Ranjitsinhji, Kumar Shri, *With Stoddart's Team in Australia* (Bowden, 1898)

Rendell, Brian, *Gubby Allen: Bad Boy of Bodyline?* (Cricket Lore, 2004)

Rendell, Brian, *Gubby Under Pressure: Letters from Australia, New Zealand and Hollywood 1936/37* (ACS Publications, 2007)

Rendell, Brian, *Walter Robins: Achievements, Affections and Affronts, ACS Lives in Cricket* (Association of Cricket Statisticians and Historians, 2013)

Rendell, Brian, *Frank and George Mann: Brewing, Batting and Captaincy* (ACS Publications, 2015)

Robinson, Ray, *The Wildest Tests* (Pelham Books, 1973)

Rogerson, Sidney, *Wilfred Rhodes* (Hollis & Carter, 1960)

Ross, Alan, *Australia 55: A Journal* (Constable, 1985)

Ross, Alan, *Cape Summer and the Australians in England* (Constable, 1986)

Ross, Alan, *Through the Caribbean: England in the West Indies, 1960* (Pavilion Cricket Library, 1986)

Russell, Jack, *Unleashed* (Collins Willow, 1997)

Schindler, Colin, *Bob Barber: The Professional Amateur* (Max Books, 2015)

Scoble, Christopher, *Colin Blythe: Lament for a Legend* (Sportsbooks, 2005)

Shaw, Alfred, *Alfred Shaw Cricketer: His Career and Reminiscences* (Cassell and Co, 1902)

Sissons, Ric, *The Players: A Social History of the Professional Cricketer* (Kingswood Press, 1988)

Smith, E. J., as told to Pat Murphy, *'Tiger' Smith of Warwickshire and England* (Lutterworth Press, 1981)

Smith, Robin, with Smyth, Rob, *The Judge: More Than Just a Game* (Yellow Jersey Press, 2019)

Snow, John, *Cricket Rebel: An Autobiography* (Hamlyn, 1976)

Southerton, James, annotated by Gault, Adrian, *The Cricket Tour of Australia and New Zealand by Lillywhite's Twelve in 1876–1877* (Mitcham Cricket Club, 2021)

Statham, Brian, *Cricket Merry-Go-Round* (Stanley Paul, 1956)

Stewart, Alec, *Playing for Keeps* (BBC Books, 2003)

Strauss, Andrew, *Winning the Ashes Down Under: The Captain's Story* (Hodder & Stoughton, 2011)

Strauss, Andrew, *Driving Ambition: My Autobiography* (Hodder & Stoughton, 2013)

Streeton, Richard, *p. G. H. Fender* (Faber & Faber, 1981)

Swanton, E. W., *Swanton in Australia with MCC 1946–1975* (Collins, 1975)

Swanton, E. W., *Gubby Allen: Man of Cricket* (Hutchinson, 1985)

Tennant, Ivo, *Graham Gooch: The Biography* (H. F. & G. Witherby, 1993)

Tomlinson, Richard, *Amazing Grace: The Man who was W. G.* (Little, Brown, 2015)

Trescothick, Marcus, *Coming Back to Me* (HarperCollins, 2008)

Trevor, Major Philip, *With the MCC in Australia 1907–08* (A. Rivers, 1908)

Trott, Jonathan, *Unguarded: My Autobiography* (Sphere, 2016)

Trueman, Fred, *As It Was: The Memoirs of Fred Trueman* (Macmillan, 2004)

Tufnell, Phil, *Phil Tufnell: The Autobiography* (Collins Willow, 2000)

Turbervill, Huw, *The Toughest Tour: The Ashes Away Series Since the War* (Aurum, 2010)

Turnbull, Maurice, and Allom, Maurice, *The Book of the Two Maurices* (E. Allom, 1930)

Turnbull, Maurice, and Allom, Maurice, *The Two Maurices Again* (E. Allom, 1931)

Tyson, Frank, *A Typhoon Called Tyson* (Heinemann, 1961)

Tyson, Frank, *In the Eye of the Typhoon: Recollections of the Marylebone Cricket Club tour of Australia 1954–55* (Parrs Wood Press, 2004)

Vaughan, Michael, *Time to Declare* (Hodder & Stoughton, 2009)

Warner, David, *Just a Few Lines . . . The Unseen Letters and Memorabilia of Brian Close* (Great Northern Books, 2020)

Warner, Pelham, *Cricket in Many Climes* (Heinemann, 1900)

Warner, Pelham, *How We Recovered the Ashes: An Account of the 1903–04 MCC Tour of Australia* (1904; Methuen 2003 edition)

Warner, p. F., *The MCC in South Africa* (Chapman & Hall, 1906)

Warner, p. F., *England v Australia: The Record of a Memorable Tour* (Mills & Boon, 1912)

Warner, Pelham, *Cricket Between the Wars* (Chatto & Windus, 1942)

Warner, Pelham, *Long Innings: The Autobiography* (Harrap, 1951)

Waters, Chris, *Fred Trueman: The Authorised Biography* (Aurum, 2011)

Wellings, E. M., *No Ashes for England* (Evans Bros, 1951)

Wellings, E. M., *Dexter v Benaud: MCC Tour of Australia 1962–3* (Bailey Brothers & Swinfen, 1963)

Westcott, Chris, *Class of '59 From Bailey to Wooller: The Golden Age of County Cricket* (Mainstream, 2000)

Wilde, Simon, *England: The Biography* (Simon & Schuster, 2019)

Wilde, Simon, *Ian Botham: The Power and the Glory* (Simon & Schuster, 2011)

Williams, Charles, *Gentlemen & Players: The Death of Amateurism in Cricket* (Weidenfeld & Nicolson, 2012)

Williams, Jack, *Cricket and Broadcasting* (Manchester University Press, 2011)

Williams, Marcus (and others), *Test Match Grounds of the World* (Collins Willow, 1990)

Willis, Bob, *Diary of a Cricket Season* (Pelham Books, 1979)

Willis, Bob, *The Captain's Diary: England in Australia and New Zealand 1982–83* (Collins Willow, 1983)

Willis, Bob, *The Captain's Diary: England in Fiji, New Zealand and Pakistan 1983–84* (Collins Willow, 1984)

Willis, Bob, *Lasting the Pace* (Collins Willow, 1985)

Wilton, Iain, *C. B. Fry: An English Hero* (Richard Cohen Books, 1999)

Woodhouse, David, *Who Only Cricket Know: Hutton's Men in the West Indies 1953/54* (Fairfield Books, 2021)

Wyatt, Bob, *Three Straight Sticks* (Stanley Paul, 1951)

Wynne-Thomas, Peter, *'Give Me Arthur': A Biography of Arthur Shrewsbury* (Arthur Barker, 1985)

Wynne-Thomas, Peter, *The Complete History of Cricket Tours at Home & Abroad* (Hamlyn, 1989)

Wynne-Thomas, Peter, *The History of Cricket* (Stationery Office, 1997)

Yardley, Norman, *Cricket Campaigns* (Stanley Paul, 1950)

ACKNOWLEDGEMENTS

I am indebted to various England players, administrators, journalists and broadcasters for allowing me to interview them for the purposes of this book, in some cases more than once. It was particularly helpful to receive the thoughts of Ashley Giles and Andrew Strauss, as two former England players and later managing directors of England cricket. Among others were Dennis Amiss, Peter Baxter, Ian Bell, Philip Brown, Mark Butcher, Giles Clarke, Gareth Copley, Barney Douglas, Patrick Eagar, John Emburey, Emma Gardner, Steve Harmison, Matthew Hoggard, Tim Lamb, Nathan Leamon, John Lever, Dawid Malan, Graham Morris, Phil Neale, Mark Ramprakash, Ed Smith and Graham Thorpe.

Apart from books and publications, a number of films and documentaries proved particularly useful; they included *The Edge* (2019) directed by Barney Douglas, and *Ben Stokes: Phoenix from The Ashes* (2022) directed by Sam Mendes and released on Amazon Prime Video. Also helpful was *The Ultimate Test* series on the ECB website released in the build-up to the Ashes series of 2021–22.

My particular thanks to Ian Marshall, who originally commissioned the book; my agent David Luxton for encouraging the idea of a sister volume to *England: The Biography 1877–2019*; Graham Coster for his knowledge and editing skills; Frances

Jessop and Sophia Akhtar at Simon & Schuster for so smoothly taking over the project; and to Scyld Berry for reading parts of the manuscript. As always, too, my gratitude to my wife Gayle and children Freddie, Lily and Eve for tolerating my absences on tour and my absences at home on adventures like this one.

INDEX